BARRON'S

TOEIC®

TEST OF ENGLISH FOR INTERNATIONAL COMMUNICATION

5TH EDITION

Lin Lougheed

Ed.D., Teachers College
Columbia University

Always Innovative & Informative

NHÀ XUẤT BẢN TỔNG HỢP TP. HỒ CHÍ MINH

TOEIC, 5ᵀᴴ EDITION
by **Lin Lougheed**
Copyright © 2010, 2007, 2003, 1999, 1995 by Barron's Educational Series Inc.
All rights reserved.

Published by arrangement with Barron's Educational Series, Inc.
Hauppauge, NY 11788, USA.

TOEIC, 5ᵀᴴ EDITION
Vietnamese edition © 2012 by First News – Tri Viet Co., Ltd.

Công ty First News – Trí Việt giữ bản quyền xuất bản và phát hành ấn
bản tiếng Việt theo hợp đồng chuyển giao bản quyền với Barron's
Educational Series, Inc., Hoa Kỳ.

Bất cứ sự sao chép nào không được sự đồng ý của First News và Barron's
đều là bất hợp pháp và vi phạm Luật Xuất bản Việt Nam, Luật Bản
quyền Quốc tế và Công ước Bảo hộ Bản quyền Sở hữu Trí tuệ Berne.

CÔNG TY VĂN HÓA SÁNG TẠO TRÍ VIỆT – FIRST NEWS

11H Nguyễn Thị Minh Khai, Quận 1, TP. HCM

Tel: (84.8) 38227979 – 38227980 – 38233859 – 38233860

Fax: (84.8) 38224560; Email: triviet@firstnews.com.vn

Website: **www.firstnews.com.vn**

Contents

IMPORTANT NOTE

This TOEIC preparation book is available with or without audio CD components. If you have purchased the book without audio CD components, please refer to the audioscripts starting on page 575 when prompted to listen to an audio passage. To purchase the audio CDs separately, please call Barron's Customer Service department at 1-800-645-3476 or visit *www.baronseduc.com*.

Overview of the TOEIC

There are two sections on the TOEIC: Listening Comprehension and Reading. Specific information about each section is given in detail in this book. The kinds of questions asked and the strategies you'll need to master in order to perform well are provided in the respective chapters. The timing for the TOEIC is as follows:

The TOEIC

Total Time: 2 hours

Section 1 (45 minutes)	Listening Comprehension Part 1: Photographs Part 2: Question-Response Part 3: Conversations Part 4: Talks	10 Questions 30 Questions 30 Questions 30 Questions

Section 2
(75 minutes)
	Reading
	Part 5: Incomplete Sentences
	Part 6: Text Completion
	Part 7: Reading Comprehension
	   • Single passages
	   • Double passages
		40 Questions
		12 Questions
		
		28 Questions
		20 Questions

To the Teacher

Rationale for a TOEIC Preparation Course

Barron's TOEIC ® preparation book may be used as either a self-study course or a class course. In a class situation, this text will provide an excellent structure for helping the students improve their English language skills and prepare for the TOEIC.

Adult learners of English are very goal-oriented. For many adults who are required to take the TOEIC, their goal is, obviously enough, a high score. Having a goal that can be easily measured will be very motivating for your students.

Many teachers do not like to "teach to the test." They feel that developing a general knowledge of English will be more useful to the students than reviewing test items. But students want to "study the test." They don't want to "waste their time" learning something that might not be tested.

Both arguments ignore what actually happens during a TOEIC preparation course. General English is used to discuss how the exam is structured, what strategies should be used, and what skills should be developed. General English is used to explain problems and to expand into other areas. By helping students prepare for an exam, you can't help but improve their general knowledge of English.

A TOEIC preparation course gives the students what they want: a streamlined approach to learning what they think they need to know for the exam. The course gives the teachers what they want: a scheme to help them improve the English language ability of their students.

Organization of a TOEIC Preparation Course

TIMETABLE

Every test-preparation course faces the same dilemma: how to squeeze a total review of English into a class timetable. Some of you may have an afternoon TOEIC orientation; others may have a one-week intensive class; some may have a ten-week session. However long your class time, one thing is true: no class is ever long enough to cover everything you want to cover.

As a guideline, you might want to follow this plan and expand it as your time allows.

- First period: Study Chapter 1, Introduction.
  Have students sign the TOEIC Contract.
- Next period: Take a Model Test.
  Evaluate answers; determine the weak areas of the class.
- Subsequent periods: Review Listening Comprehension.
  Take the Mini-Test.
  Review Reading.
  Take the Mini-Test.
  Take additional Model Tests.
- Last Period: Take a final Model Test and note the improvement in scores.

After students have completed the exercises, the Mini-Tests, or the Model Tests, they can check the Answer Key for quick access to the correct answer or read the Explanatory Answers for reasons why the correct answer is right and the incorrect answers are wrong.

These abbreviations are used in the exercises and Explanatory Answers.

adjective	(adj)	noun	(n)
adverb	(adv)	preposition	(prep)
article	(art)	pronoun	(pron)
auxiliary	(aux)	subject of a sentence	(sub)
conjunction	(conj)	verb	(v)
interjection	(interj)		

The symbol $\not=$ is also used, to mean "is not the same as," "is different from," and "does not equal."

Teaching Listening Comprehension

The more students hear English, the better their listening comprehension will be. Encourage a lot of discussion about the various strategies mentioned in the Listening Comprehension activities. Have the students work in pairs or small groups to increase the amount of time they will spend listening and speaking.

First News
Always Innovative & Informative

All tests require the students to choose a correct answer. This means the students must eliminate the incorrect answers. There are common distractors (traps) on an exam that a student can be trained to listen for. And coincidentally, while they are learning to listen for these traps, they are improving their listening comprehension.

The Listening Comprehension activities in this text are a gold mine. You can use them for the stated purpose, which is to help students learn how to analyze photos, answer choices, question types, and language functions. In addition, you can use them for a variety of communicative activities.

PHOTOGRAPH EXERCISES

The photographs can be used to help students develop their vocabulary. There are over 140 photographs in this text. Have the students pick a photograph and, in pairs or small groups, name everything they can see in the picture.

Then, in the same small groups (or individually) have them use those words in a sentence. They can write a short description of the photograph or, even better, they can write a short narrative. The narratives can be extremely imaginative—the more imaginative the better. Have the students describe what happened before the photograph was taken and what might happen afterwards.

Once students have the vocabulary under control, they can make an oral presentation. The other students or groups will then have to retell the narrative. This will help them evaluate their own listening comprehension.

QUESTION-RESPONSE EXERCISES

In this section, there is one short question, followed by an equally short answer. There is sometimes just a statement followed by a short response. This is not the way people communicate. Have the students establish a context for the short question or statement. Where are the speakers? Who are they? What are they talking about? What were they doing before? What will they do next? What did they say before? What will they say next?

Have them create a short skit that a pair of students can act out. Then have others in the class try to summarize the dialogue. Again, you are helping them evaluate their own listening comprehension.

CONVERSATION EXERCISES

The same technique can work here. Actually, it will be easier, because there is more dialogue for the students to use as a basis. This time have the students listen to the skit created by their colleagues and ask "wh" questions. Have them learn to anticipate *who, what, when, where, why,* and *how.*

TALKS EXERCISES

There are a variety of short talks: some are about the weather; others are public service announcements; some are advertisements. Have the students take one of the small talks and rewrite it. If it is a weather announcement, have them take a rainy day and make it sunny; have them change an advertisement for a television into an advertisement for a car.

Then, as with the other activities, have the other students create the "wh" questions. See if they can stump their colleagues. Have them make these talks challenging.

Teaching Reading

Again, the best way for students to improve their reading is to read, read, read. On the TOEIC, even the grammar activities focus on reading. They demand that students understand the whole context of the statement, not just an isolated part. That is why the structure tests are in the Reading section.

As in the Listening Comprehension section, it is as important to know why an answer is wrong as it is to know why an answer is right. Training your students to use the strategies mentioned in these sections will make them more efficient readers.

VOCABULARY EXERCISES

All students want to know words and more words. Remind them that it is important to know how to use them. They will learn more by reading and learning words in context than they will from memorizing word lists.

They can and should create their own personal word lists. Every time they encounter an unfamiliar word, they should write it down in a notebook. They should try to use it in a sentence, or even better, in a dialogue. Have the students create their own skits using the words in their own personal word lists.

If the students insist on lists, show them all the charts of words in the various sections of both the Listening and Reading sections. Have the students use these words to learn how to use words in context.

GRAMMAR EXERCISES

The grammar reviewed in this text covers those areas that are most likely to be found on the TOEIC and that most likely will give students the most problems. You can help students focus their attention by having them analyze their mistakes in the Model Tests.

READING EXERCISES

The strategies emphasized in the Reading review are not only for reading on the TOEIC. They can be, and should be, applied to all reading a student might have to do. Use outside reading materials such as English news magazines and newspapers. Have the students read not only the articles but also the ads, announcements, subscription forms, and Table of Contents. In fact, have them scan and read the entire magazine. Everything found in a news magazine, including charts and graphs, is found on the TOEIC.

As the students did in the Listening Comprehension review, have them create "wh" questions for the articles, graphs, tables, etc., they find. Let them try to stump their colleagues. To make the lesson even more communicative, have the students give an oral presentation of what they have read. Let the "wh" questions be oral, too.

Use a Model Test as a diagnostic

If the students have several errors on questions testing prepositions, you would suggest they concentrate on the problems dealing with prepositions. Lists in the front of Chapter 2 and Chapter 3 provide an easy way for you to find the specific exercises your students need. (See pages 19 and 137.) By focusing on problem areas, they will be able to study more efficiently and effectively.

First News

Always Innovative & Informative

TEACHING IS A GROUP EFFORT

This text was the result of the ideas and suggestions of teachers and TOEIC administrators who have used my materials in Japan, Korea, Taiwan, Vietnam, Thailand, Malaysia, France, Switzerland, Canada, and the United States. As the TOEIC widens its footprint, I would like to hear from other teachers in other countries. The more help I have from you, the more the subsequent editions will contain just what you need for your own teaching situation. You may contact me by e-mail or in care of Barron's at the address below. I look forward to hearing from you. Good luck and enjoy your class.

Lin Lougheed (E-mail: *books@lougheed.com*)
TOEIC Editorial
c/o Barron's Educational Series, Inc.
250 Wireless Blvd.
Hauppauge, NY 11788
USA
www.barronseduc.com

CHAPTER 1

Introduction

> **WHAT TO LOOK FOR IN THIS CHAPTER**
>
> - Questions and Answers Concerning the TOEIC
> - Study Plan for the TOEIC
> - Self-Study Activities
> - On Test Day

Questions and Answers Concerning the TOEIC

Online Resources

You can also learn more at the TOEIC website <http://www.toeic.com> or at my website <http://www.lougheed.com>.

More than 4,500,000 people take the TOEIC each year, and this number is growing. The TOEIC is administered in Europe, Asia, North America, South America, and Central America. Since the test is relatively new (compared to the TOEFL, which was first given in 1963), many test-takers are unfamiliar with the TOEIC. The following are some commonly asked questions about the TOEIC.

What Is the Purpose of the TOEIC?

Since 1979, the TOEIC (the Test of English for International Communication) has been used internationally as a standard assessment of English-language proficiency. The TOEIC has been developed by linguists, language experts, and staff at The Chauncey Group International Ltd. to evaluate the English language skills of non-native speakers of English in the field of business.

What Skills Are Tested on the TOEIC?

The TOEIC consists of two sections: Listening Comprehension (100 multiple-choice questions) and Reading (100 multiple-choice questions). Audio is used to test Listening Comprehension.

The content of the TOEIC is not specialized; the vocabulary and content are familiar to those individuals who use English in daily activities.

Who Uses the TOEIC?

Government agencies, multinational corporations, and international organizations use the TOEIC to ascertain the English-language capabilities of employees and prospective employees. The scores are used as an independent measure of proficiency and can be helpful in identifying personnel capable of handling language-specific

responsibilities, in placing personnel in language-training programs, and in promoting personnel to positions where reliable linguistic standards are met.

Language-training programs use the TOEIC to establish language-training goals and to assess students' progress in overall English ability.

Who Takes the TOEIC?

In addition to the staffs of the companies and organizations previously mentioned, individuals take the TOEIC to document their abilities for personal and professional reasons.

What Is the Format of the TOEIC?

The TOEIC consists of two sections:

Listening Comprehension	
Part 1: Photographs	10 questions
Part 2: Question-Response	30 questions
Part 3: Conversations	30 questions
Part 4: Talks	30 questions
Reading	
Part 5: Incomplete Sentences	40 questions
Part 6: Text Completion	12 questions
Part 7: Reading Comprehension	
• Single passages	28 questions
• Double passages	20 questions

There are a total of 200 items; total time allowed for the test (including administrative tasks) is approximately 2½ hours. The Listening Comprehension section takes 45 minutes; the Reading section takes 75 minutes.

Why Are TOEIC Questions so Tricky?

TOEIC questions are carefully designed to test your knowledge of English. The questions must be difficult in order to discriminate between test-takers of varying abilities. That is, the difficult questions separate those who are more proficient in English from those who are less proficient. A test question and the answer options may use one or more of these tricks to test your language competence:

- Use words with similar sounds.
- Use homonyms.
- Use related words.
- Omit a necessary word.
- Include unnecessary words.
- Alter the correct word order.

How Is the TOEIC Score Determined?

Separate scores are given for Listening Comprehension (5 to 495) and Reading (5 to 495). These two sub-scores are added to arrive at the total score. The TOEIC score is represented on a scale of 10 to 990 and is based on the total number of correct answers.

What Do TOEIC Scores Mean?

There is no established minimum passing score; each institution, through experience, sets up its own acceptable score.

How Are TOEIC Scores Obtained?

TOEIC test-takers who are sponsored by companies, institutions, or organizations receive their scores from their sponsors. Those examinees who register individually to take the TOEIC receive their scores directly.

When and Where Can I Take the TOEIC?

The TOEIC is offered worldwide and is generally available upon demand. The dates, times, and locations of the test sites are determined by the local TOEIC representatives. For test fees, test dates, and locations, contact the TOEIC office in your country or contact ETS in the USA. The TOEIC representative offices are listed on ETS website, *www.ets.org*.

How Long Are TOEIC Scores Kept?

TOEIC representatives keep individual test scores for two years.

How Can I Prepare for the TOEIC?

If you plan to take the TOEIC, make a concerted effort to use English as much as possible, and in many different situations.

The best preparation is using a book/audio combination such as this—a program designed to help you specifically with the TOEIC. Following through with this book will:

- make you aware of certain test-taking skills;
- make you familiar with the format of the test; and
- improve your total score.

Additional suggestions are found in the next section, entitled "Study Plan for the TOEIC."

How Can I Get a Better Score on the TOEIC?

Assuming you have prepared well for the TOEIC, you can maximize your score on the test day by following these suggestions:

- Read the directions carefully.
- Work quickly.
- Do not make notes in the test booklet.
- Guess if you're not sure.
- Mark only one answer.

Additional suggestions are found in the next section, "Study Plan for the TOEIC."

Study Plan for the TOEIC

There is an English expression: "You can lead a horse to water, but you can't make him drink." Similarly, this book can lead you through the TOEIC, but it can't make you think. Learning is a self-motivated activity. Only you can prepare yourself for the TOEIC.

TOEIC Contract

It takes a lot of discipline to learn a foreign language. You need to formalize your commitment by signing a contract with yourself. This contract will obligate you to spend a certain number of hours each week learning English for a certain period of time. You will promise (1) to study *Barron's TOEIC* book and other Barron's TOEIC preparation materials, and (2) to study on your own. Sign the contract below to make your commitment.

- Print your name on line 1.

- Write the time you will spend each week studying English on lines 4–8. Think about how much time you have to study every day and every week and make your schedule realistic.

- Sign your name and date the contract on the last line.

- At the end of each week, add up your hours. Did you meet the requirements of your contract? Did you study both the *Barron's TOEIC* and the self-study activities?

TOEIC STUDY CONTRACT

I, _____, promise to study for the TOEIC. I will begin my study with *Barron's TOEIC* and I will also study English on my own.

I understand that to improve my English I need to spend time on English.

I promise to study English _____ hours per week.

I will spend _____ hours per week listening to English.

I will spend _____ hours per week writing English.

I will spend _____ hours per week speaking English.

I will spend _____ hours per week reading English.

This is a contract with myself. I promise to fulfill the terms of this contract.

_____   _____
Signed   Date

Good TOEIC Preparation Tips

1. **Study regularly.** Pick the same time of day to practice. If you don't develop a routine, you won't develop good study habits. Tell yourself that you can't watch television at 7:30 because that is your TOEIC time. If you do miss your scheduled time one day, don't worry. Try to make it up later that day. But don't study at a different time every day. You will never get any studying done.

2. **Do a little at a time.** Tell yourself that you will study for ten minutes on the train every morning or ten minutes just before you go to bed. It is better to learn one thing very well in a short period of time than to spend long periods trying to study everything.

3. **Budget your time.** The TOEIC is a timed test, so time your study sessions. Give yourself ten minutes to study and then stop. You must use your time effectively. Learn how to take advantage of short periods of time.

4. **Write out a study schedule.** If you put something in writing, you are more likely to do it.

5. **Know your goal.** Why are you taking the TOEIC? If it's to qualify for a better position in your company, picture yourself in that job. What kind of score will you need? Work for that score (or a higher one).

6. **Develop a positive attitude.** Before Olympic athletes compete, many shut their eyes and imagine themselves skiing down the mountain, running around the track, or swimming the fastest and passing the finish line first. They imagine themselves performing perfectly, scoring the best, and winning. This is the power of positive thinking. It is not just for athletes. You can use it, too.

   You must have a positive attitude when you take the TOEIC. Every night just before you fall asleep (when the right side of the brain is most receptive) repeat the following sentence ten times. "I understand English very well, and I will score very high on the TOEIC." The subconscious mind is very powerful. If you convince yourself that you can succeed, you are more likely to succeed.

7. **Relax.** Don't become anxious about the exam. Get a good night's rest the night before the exam. Don't study that night. Relax and have a good time. Your mind will be more receptive if you are calm. Relax before, during, and especially after the exam.

Using *Barron's TOEIC*®

1. **Become familiar with the TOEIC questions and directions.** Read the sections on the TOEIC and the introductions to the Listening Comprehension and Reading chapters carefully. They contain information and advice that will help you raise your score.

2. **Take a Model Test.** Use the Explanatory Answers as a guide to help you determine your weaknesses. If you miss more questions about prepositions than

about adverbs of frequency, then you should spend your time studying prepositions. Use the lists of problems found on pages 19 and 137–138 to easily find the exercises you need most.

3. **Study efficiently.** When time is limited, concentrate on what you really need to study. Don't try to do everything if you don't have enough time.

4. **Study and use the strategies.** This book lists many strategies that will help you score well on the exam. A strategy is a technique to use to help you approach a problem. In this case, a strategy will help you comprehend spoken and written English.

5. **Study all the potential problems.** Know what to look for in the Listening Comprehension and Reading sections. You should learn how to recognize an incorrect answer.

6. **Do the exercises, Review Exercises, and Mini-Tests.** All of the exercises are designed like those on the TOEIC. You will develop both your English ability and your test-taking skills by studying these exercises.

7. **Review the Explanatory Answers.** All of the answers for the review exercises, Mini-Tests, and the Model Tests are explained thoroughly at the end of the chapter in which they appear. Studying these explanations will sharpen your ability to analyze a test question. Knowing why you made an error will help you avoid the error the next time.

   Answer Keys are provided. You can use these keys to quickly find out which questions you did not answer correctly. Then, go to the Explanatory Answers to learn where you went wrong. This will help you to focus your studies on the areas in which you need the most practice.

8. **Use other Barron's TOEIC preparation materials.** Improve your TOEIC vocabulary with *Barron's 600 Essential Words for the TOEIC*. Get more test practice with *Barron's TOEIC Practice Exams*. You can order both of these books online at *www.barronseduc.com*

Do a Little Every Day

It is worth repeating this advice. Following a consistent study routine will help you prepare for the TOEIC. You may not have to study everything in this book. Study the types of questions for which you need additional practice. But do it every day!

Self-Study Activities

1. **Listen to as much English as you can.** The best way to improve your listening comprehension is by listening. As you listen, ask yourself these questions:

Who is talking?
Who are they talking to?
What are they talking about?
Where are they talking?
Why are they talking?

As you answer these questions, you will improve your ability to understand English through context.

2. **Read as much English as you can.** It should be no surprise that the best and easiest way to improve your reading comprehension is by reading. Concentrate

First News — Always Innovative & Informative

on weekly news magazines. Look at the tables of contents, the advertisements, the announcements, and the articles. Read anything in English you can find: want ads, train schedules, hotel registration forms, etc. Again, always ask yourself questions as you read.

Use the PSRA reading strategy technique discussed on pages 285–288. That will help you on the TOEIC and every time you read anything—even reading material in your own language!

3. **Write and speak as much English as you can.** Every time you listen and ask yourself who, what, when, where, why, give your answers out loud and then write them down.

4. **Keep a vocabulary notebook.** Be on the lookout for new vocabulary. Be aggressive about it. Get on the Internet and start reading websites. Any English website will be useful, but you can get both reading and listening practice on many of them such as CNN and BBC. Many newspapers, magazines, zines, and blogs are on the Internet. Do a search on an area of interest to you. You may be surprised how many sites are available.

Here are some ways you can practice your listening, reading, speaking, and writing skills in English. You will find many opportunities to practice English in books and magazines as well as on the Internet. Check the ones you plan to try and add some ideas of your own on the blank lines provided.

TIP

Don't bother learning long lists of words. That will not help you as much as learning words in context. Look at the suggestions in the "Analyzing Vocabulary" section on page 141.

If you like lists, there are lists in Chapter 2, *Listening Comprehension*, and in Chapter 3, *Reading*. Study the lists and the examples given in context.

Listening

___ Listen to podcasts on the Internet
___ Listen to news websites: CNN, BCC, NBC, ABC, CBS
___ Watch movies and television in English
___ Find YouTube videos that interest you
___ Listen to CNN and BBC on the radio or on the Internet
___ Listen to Pandora or other Internet radio applications
___ Listen to music in English
___ _____
___ _____

Speaking

___ Describe what you see and what you do out loud
___ Practice having a conversation with a buddy
___ Use Skype to talk to English speakers
___ _____
___ _____

Writing

___ Write a daily journal
___ Write a letter to an English speaker

First News

A l w a y s   I n n o v a t i v e   &   I n f o r m a t i v e

___ Make lists of the things that you see everyday
___ Write descriptions of your family and friends
___ Write e-mails to website contacts
___ Write a blog
___ Leave comments on blogs and YouTube
___ Post messages in a chat room
___ Use Facebook and MySpace
___ _____
___ _____

Reading

___ Read newspapers and magazines in English
___ Read books in English
___ Read graphic novels in English
___ Read news and magazine articles online
___ Do web research on topics that interest you
___ Follow blogs that interest you
___ _____
___ _____

Examples of Self-Study Activities

Whether you read an article in a newspaper or on a website, you can use that article in a variety of ways to practice reading, writing, speaking, and listening in English.

- Read about it
- Paraphrase and write about it
- Give a talk or presentation about it
- Record or make a video of your presentation
- Listen to or watch what you recorded
- Write down your presentation
- Correct your mistakes
- Do it all again

Here are some specific examples you can do to study on your own.

PLAN A TRIP Go to *www.concierge.com*
Choose a city and a hotel, go to that hotel's website and choose a room, then choose some sites to visit (*reading*). Write a report about the city. Tell why you want to go there. Describe the hotel and the room you will reserve. Tell what sites you plan to visit and when. Where will you eat? How will you get around?

Now write a letter to someone recommending this place (*writing*). Pretend you have to give a lecture on your planned trip (*speaking*). Make a video of yourself

talking about this place, and then watch the video and write down what you said. Correct any mistakes you made and record the presentation again. Then choose another city and do this again.

SHOP FOR AN ELECTRONIC PRODUCT Go to *www.cnet.com*
Choose an electronic product and read about it (*reading*). Write a report about the product. Tell why you want to buy the product. Describe its features.

Now write a letter to someone recommending this product (*writing*). Pretend you have to give a talk about this product (*speaking*). Make a video of yourself talking about this product, and then watch the video and write down what you said. Correct any mistakes you made and record the presentation again. Then choose another product and do this again.

DISCUSS A BOOK OR A CD Go to *www.amazon.com*
Choose a book, CD, or any product. Read the product's description and reviews (*reading*). Write a report about the product. Tell why you want to buy the product or why it is interesting to you. Describe its features.

Now write a letter to someone recommending this product (*writing*). Pretend you have to give a talk about this product (*speaking*). Make a video of yourself talking about this product, and then watch the video and write down what you said. Correct any mistakes you made and record the presentation again. Then choose another product and do this again.

DISCUSS ANY SUBJECT Go to *http://simple.wikipedia.org/wiki/Main_Page*
This website is written in simple English. Pick any subject and read the entry (*reading*).

Write a short essay about the topic (*writing*). Give a presentation on the topic (*speaking*). Record the presentation, and then watch the video and write down what you said. Correct any mistakes you made and record the presentation again. Choose another topic and do this again.

DISCUSS ANY EVENT Go to *http://news.google.com*
Google News has a variety of links. Pick one event and read the articles (*reading*).

Write a short essay about the event (*writing*). Give a presentation about the event (*speaking*). Record the presentation, and then watch the video and write down what you said. Correct any mistakes you made and record the presentation again. Then choose another event and do this again.

REPORT THE NEWS Listen to an English-language news report on the radio or watch a news program on television (*listening*). Take notes as you listen. Write a summary of what you heard (*writing*).

Pretend you are a news reporter. Use the information from your notes to report the news (*speaking*). Record the presentation, and then watch the video and write down what you said. Correct any mistakes you made and record the presentation again. Then listen to another news program and do this again.

First News
Always Innovative & Informative

EXPRESS AN OPINION Read a letter to the editor in the newspaper (*reading*). Write a letter in response in which you say whether or not you agree with the opinion expressed in the first letter. Explain why (*writing*).

Pretend you have to give a talk explaining your opinion (*speaking*). Record yourself giving the talk, and then watch the video and write down what you said. Correct any mistakes you made and record the presentation again. Then read another letter to the editor and do this again.

REVIEW A BOOK OR MOVIE Read a book (*reading*). Think about your opinion of the book. What did you like about it? What didn't you like about it? Who would you recommend it to and why? Pretend you are a book reviewer for a newspaper. Write a review of the book stating your opinion and recommendations (*writing*).

Give an oral presentation about the book. Explain what the book is about and state your opinion (*speaking*). Record yourself giving the presentation, and then watch the video and write down what you said. Correct any mistakes you made and record the presentation again. Then read another book and do this again.

You can do this same activity after watching a movie (*listening*).

SUMMARIZE A TELEVISION SHOW Watch a television show in English (*listening*). Take notes as you listen. After watching, write a summary of the show (*writing*).

Use your notes to give an oral summary of the show. Explain the characters, setting, and plot (*speaking*). Record yourself speaking, and then watch the video and write down what you said. Correct any mistakes you made and record the presentation again. Then watch another television show and do this again.

On Test Day

You are well prepared. You studied this book and other Barron's preparation material, and now it is test day. Here are some suggestions that will help you on the day of the test.

1. **Be early.** You should avoid rushing on the test day. Leave yourself plenty of time to get to the testing center.

2. **Be comfortable.** If you can, choose your own seat; pick one that is away from distractions. You don't want to be near an open door where you can watch people pass outside. On the other hand, you might want to be near a window to get good light. Try, if you can, to sit near the audio player. If you can't hear well, be sure to tell the test administrator.

3. **Bring what you need.** Your test site may provide pencils with erasers, but to be safe you should bring three or four No. 2 pencils with erasers. You may find a watch useful, too.

4. **Listen to the directions.** Even though you will know the format after using this book, you should listen to the directions carefully. Listening to the familiar directions will help you relax.

First News
Always Innovative & Informative

5. **Answer all questions.** Even if you do not know an answer, you should mark your best answer. But try to make it an educated guess. When time is running out, just blacken any letter for the questions you have not answered—even if you didn't have time to read the question. You may be right.

6. **Match the numbers.** Make sure that the number on your answer sheet matches the number in your test book.

7. **Mark only one answer per question on the answer sheet.** Only one black mark will be counted. If you make a mistake and erase, do it completely. Do not make any other marks on the answer sheet.

8. **Answer the easy questions first.** In the Reading section, you can pace yourself. If you do not immediately know an answer to a question, skip that question and go to one you can answer. At the end of the section, come back and do the more difficult questions. This will give you an opportunity to answer as many questions as you can.

9. **Pace yourself.** The audio player will keep you moving in the Listening Comprehension section. But in the Reading section you will be able to adjust your own pace. You will have less than 45 seconds for each question in the Reading section.

10. **Leave time at the end.** If you can, try to leave a minute at the end to go over your answer sheet and make sure you have filled in every question.

11. **Celebrate after the exam.** Go ahead. Have a good time. You deserve it. Congratulations on a job well done.

IMPORTANT NOTE

This TOEIC preparation book is available with or without audio CD components. If you have purchased the book without audio CD components, please refer to the audioscripts starting on page 575 when prompted to listen to an audio passage. To purchase the audio CDs separately, please call Barron's Customer Service department at 1-800-645-3476 or visit *www.barronseduc.com*.

CHAPTER 2

Listening Comprehension

WHAT TO LOOK FOR IN THIS CHAPTER

- Overview
  - Directions for the Listening Comprehension section, Parts 1, 2, 3, and 4
  - Examples of TOEIC Listening Comprehension questions
- Listening Comprehension Targets
  - Analyzing pictures
  - Analyzing answer choices
  - Analyzing question types
  - Analyzing language functions
- Strategies to Improve Your Listening Comprehension Score
- Mini-Test for Listening Comprehension Parts 1, 2, 3, and 4
  - Answer Keys for Targets 1–33 and Mini-Test for Listening Comprehension Parts 1, 2, 3, and 4
  - Explanatory Answers for Targets 1–33 and Mini-Test for Listening Comprehension Parts 1, 2, 3, and 4

Overview—Parts 1, 2, 3, and 4

There are four parts to the Listening Comprehension section of the TOEIC. You will have approximately 45 minutes to complete this section.

Part 1:	Photographs	10 Questions
Part 2:	Question-Response	30 Questions
Part 3:	Conversations	30 Questions
Part 4:	Talks	30 Questions

This overview will show you the kind of questions you will have to answer on Parts 1–4. You should familiarize yourself with the actual directions used on the TOEIC before you take the exam. You can find these directions online at *www.toeic.org*.

SECTION I: LISTENING COMPREHENSION

Part 1: Photographs

Directions: You will see a photograph. You will hear four statements about the photograph. Choose the statement that most closely matches the photograph and fill in the corresponding oval on your answer sheet. The statements will not be printed and will be spoken only once.

Sample Questions

Question 1

You will hear: Look at the photo marked number 1 in your test book.

<table>
<tr><td>(A) They're waiting at the bus stop.</td><td></td></tr>
<tr><td>(B) They're leaving the building.</td><td></td></tr>
<tr><td>(C) They're selling tickets.</td><td></td></tr>
<tr><td>(D) They're getting off the bus.</td><td></td></tr>
</table>

Statement (D), "They're getting off the bus," best describes what you see in the photo. Therefore, you should choose answer (D).

Question 2

You will hear: Look at the photo marked number 2 in your test book.

(A) He's carrying a suitcase.
(B) He's wearing a new suit.
(C) He's boarding the plane.
(D) He's packing his bag.

Statement (A), "He's carrying a suitcase," best describes what you see in the photo.
Therefore, you should choose answer (A).

Part 2: Question-Response

Directions: You will hear a question and three possible responses. Choose the
response that most closely answers the question and fill in the corresponding
oval on your answer sheet. The statements will not be printed and will be spoken only once.

There are three types of questions in Part 2

- Question
- Tag question
- Statement

Sample Questions

Question 1

You will hear: 1. How can I get to the airport from here?

       (A) Take a taxi. It's just a short ride.
       (B) No, I don't.
       (C) You can get on easily.

The best response to the question "How can I get to the airport from here?" is choice (A), "Take a taxi. It's just a short ride." Therefore, you should choose answer (A).

Question 2

You will hear: 2. You've tried Indian food before, haven't you?

       (A) Yes, I tied it.
       (B) Only once.
       (C) No, the food isn't Indian.

The best response to the question "You've tried Indian food before, haven't you?" is choice (B), "Only once." Therefore, you should choose answer (B).

Question 3

You will hear: 3. It's hot in here.

       (A) He's looked there already.
       (B) I'm not here.
       (C) Open a window.

The best response for the statement "It's hot in here" is choice (C), "Open a window." Therefore, you should choose answer (C).

Part 3: Conversations

Directions: You will hear a short conversation between two people. You will see three questions on each conversation and four possible answers. Choose the best answer to each question and fill in the corresponding oval on your answer sheet. The conversations will not be printed and will be spoken only once.

Sample Questions

You will hear: Man: We'll need your medical history so take this form and fill it out, please.

               Woman: Will there be a long wait for my appointment?

               Man: No, the doctor is seeing patients on schedule.

               Woman: That's good news. The last time I was here, I waited almost an hour.

               Man: I'd say you won't have to be in the waiting room longer than a few minutes. Certainly not a half an hour. Not even twenty minutes.

Question 1

You will read: Where are the speakers?

        (A) At a sidewalk cafe   Ⓐ Ⓑ Ⓒ ●
        (B) In a history class
        (C) At an airport check-in counter
        (D) In a physician's office

The best response to the question "Where are the speakers?" is choice (D), "In a physician's office." Therefore, you should choose answer (D).

Question 2

You will read: Who is likely talking?

        (A) A doctor and a nurse   Ⓐ Ⓑ ● Ⓓ
        (B) A clerk and a shopper
        (C) A receptionist and a patient
        (D) A pilot and a passenger

The best response to the question "Who is likely talking?" is Choice (C), "A receptionist and a patient." Therefore, you should choose answer (C).

Question 3

You will read: How long will the woman have to wait?

        (A) A little bit   ● Ⓑ Ⓒ Ⓓ
        (B) Twenty minutes
        (C) Thirty minutes
        (D) Over an hour

The best response to the question "How long will the woman have to wait?" is Choice (A), "A little bit." Therefore, you should choose answer (A).

Part 4: Talks

Directions: You will hear a short talk given by a single speaker. You will see three questions on each talk, each with four possible answers. Choose the best answer to each question and fill in the corresponding oval on your answer sheet. The talks will not be printed and will be spoken only once.

Sample Questions

You will hear: In five minutes, for one hour only, women's coats and hats go on sale in our fifth-floor Better Fashions department. All merchandise is reduced by twenty-five to forty percent. Not all styles in all sizes, but an outstanding selection nonetheless. You should hurry to the fifth floor now. Last week, we sold out completely in a matter of minutes. We don't want any of you to be disappointed.

Question 1

You will read: 1. When does the sale begin?

        (A) In five minutes   ● Ⓑ Ⓒ Ⓓ
        (B) In one hour
        (C) At 2:45
        (D) Tomorrow

The best response to the question "When does the sale begin?" is Choice (A), "In five minutes." Therefore, you should choose answer (A).

Question 2

You will read: 2. What is going on sale?

        (A) Men's coats   Ⓐ ● Ⓒ Ⓓ
        (B) Women's hats
        (C) Cosmetics
        (D) Old merchandise

The best response to the question "What is going on sale?" is Choice (B), "Women's hats." Therefore, you should choose answer (B).

Question 3

You will read: 3. How long will the sale last?

        (A) Five minutes   Ⓐ Ⓑ ● Ⓓ
        (B) Fifteen minutes
        (C) Sixty minutes
        (D) One week

The best response to the question "How long will the sale last?" is choice (C), "Sixty minutes." Therefore, you should choose answer (C).

Listening Comprehension Targets Parts 1–4

To prepare for the four parts of the Listening Comprehension section, you must develop certain analytical skills:

Skills Needed	Part 1	Part 2	Part 3	Part 4
Analyzing photographs	3			
Analyzing answer choices	3	3	3	3
Analyzing question types		3	3	3
Analyzing language functions		3	3	3

For Part 1, you will need skills in analyzing both pictures and answer choices. For Parts 2, 3, and 4, you will need to develop skills in analyzing answer choices, questions types, and language functions. Improving your skills in these areas will improve your TOEIC score.

TARGETS LIST

Analyzing Photographs Target
1. Assumptions, p. 20
2. People, p. 22
3. Things, p. 24
4. Actions, p. 26
5. General Locations, p. 28
6. Specific Locations, p. 30

Analyzing Answer Choices Target
7. Similar Sounds, p. 32
8. Related Words, p. 34
9. Homonyms, p. 38
10. Same Sound and Same Spelling but Different Meaning, p. 40
11. Time, p. 42
12. Negation, p. 45
13. Word Order, p. 48
14. Comparisons, p. 50
15. Modals, p. 54
16. Used to, p. 58

Analyzing Question Types Target
17. People, p. 60
18. Occupations, p. 62
19. Speakers' Relationship, p. 64
20. Location, p. 66
21. Time, p. 68
22. Activities, p. 70
23. Events or Facts, p. 72
24. Emotions, p. 74
25. Reasons, p. 76
26. Measurements, p. 78
27. Opinions, p. 82
28. Main Topics, p. 84

Analyzing Language Functions Target
29. Conditionals, p. 86
30. Suggestions, p. 88
31. Offers, p. 90
32. Requests, p. 92
33. Restatements, p. 94

Answer Keys and Explanatory Answers for Targets 1–33 can be found beginning on page 112.

First News
A l w a y s   I n n o v a t i v e   &   I n f o r m a t i v e

Analyzing Photographs

TARGET

Assumptions

You may have to *make assumptions* when you listen to the TOEIC. These assumptions will be based on what you can infer in the photograph. You will have to determine which of the four statements you hear is true or might be true. One statement (answer choice) will be true or will most likely be true. That choice will be the correct answer.

Problem	The answer choices may all seem true.
Solution	Listen carefully to the whole sentence and determine which one choice best matches the photo.

Example

These statements are true.

This is a laboratory.

The people are wearing protective clothing.

There are bottles on the shelves.

There are at least four people in the lab.

There is equipment on the counter.

Wires run from the equipment.

These statements are probably true, but you can't tell for sure.

The people are lab technicians.

They look like technicians, but they could be pharmacists.

The people are students with a teacher.

A teacher may be working with a class, or they may all be employees.

The technicians are doing experiments.

They might be doing experiments, or they might be producing some chemical compound.

CD 1 Track 2

Exercise

Part 1: Photographs

Choose the statement that best describes what you see in the photo on page 20.

Note

If you do not have access to an audio CD player, please refer to the audio-scripts beginning on page 575 when prompted to listen to an audio passage.

For more practice, look at the other photos in this book and try to make assumptions about what you see.

TARGET 2 People

You may have to *identify the people* in a photograph. You may identify them by number, gender, location, description, activity, or occupation.

Problem	The people may be incorrectly identified.
Solution	Determine the number, gender, location, description, activity, and occupation of the people as best you can.

Example

Number:	There are four people in the photo.
Gender:	There are two men and two women in the photo.
Location:	On the left, there are two men.
	On the right, there are two women.
Description:	One of the men is wearing glasses.
	The woman on the right is shorter than the other woman.
Activity:	The group is looking at a map.
	One woman is pointing to the map.
	All four people are leaning on the table.
Occupation:	Their profession is unknown. They are looking at and discussing a map. We can assume they are planners of some sort.

You may not be able to answer all questions. You may not know their occupation, for example. However, the more assumptions you can make, the easier it will be to answer the questions.

Exercise

Part 1: Photographs

Choose the statement that best describes what you see in the photo on page 22.

TARGET
3   Things

You may have to *identify things* in a photo. When you look at a photo, try to name everything you see. On the TOEIC, you will NOT have to know words, expressions, or idioms that are specific to one particular occupation. For example, in the photo below, you should know the general word "piano." You do not have to know the specific term "upright piano."

Problem	You may not know the words needed to identify the things in the photo.
Solution	Use the context of the photo to help you identify the things.

Example

Find the following items in the photo. Keep in mind the context of the photo: It is a family scene, at home, in a living room or family room.

Words to Find

mother	woman	painting	wall
father	parents	plant	door
son	curtains	sweater	door knob
daughter	television	toys	skirt
boy	video recorder (VCR)	hair	pants
girl	piano	eyes	TV stand
man	sheet music	carpet	chair

Exercise

Part 1: Photograph

Choose the statement that best describes what you see in the photo on page 24.

For more vocabulary practice, look at the other photos in this book and try to name as many things as you can.

TARGET

4   Actions

You may have to *identify the actions* in a photo. When you look at a photo, analyze the time sequence of the actions. This will help you understand what is happening *now*.

Problem	You may not understand what is happening in the photo.
Solution	Use the context of the photo to help you make assumptions about what happened before, during, and after the action.

Example

Past: The workers removed the earth.
Present: They are laying a pipe.
Future: They will cover the pipe with earth.

You know only what you see—the workers are laying a piece of pipe in a trench. Of course, they must have dug the trench, but you didn't see it. You can only assume it. They will probably cover the pipe with earth, but you won't see it. You can only assume it.

The more assumptions you can make, the easier it will be for you to answer the questions.

Exercise

Part 1: Photographs

Choose the statement that best describes what you see in the photo on page 26.

Ⓐ Ⓑ Ⓒ Ⓓ

For more practice, look at the other photos in this book and identify past, present, and future actions.

Always Innovative & Informative

TARGET

General Locations

You may have to *identify the general location* of a photograph. When you look at a picture, analyze the clues to determine a location. If you see a car, a mechanic, some tools, and a customer in a photo, you can assume the location is an automobile repair shop. If you see men and women working at desks with computers, you can assume the location is an office. A photo is full of clues to help you identify the general location.

Problem	You may not understand where the action is taking place.
Solution	Use the context of the photograph to help you make assumptions about the general location.

Example

The following is a list of context clues in the photo. You may hear these words or variations of these words in Part I. Pay attention—the words may differ on the actual test.

For more practice, look at the other photos in this book and find the clues that will help you identify the general location.

Context Clues

Security checkpoint
Departure information
Gate sign
People with baggage
Porter with luggage cart
Security personnel

Security officers
Man with mobile phone
Airline names
Names of destinations
Sign about X-ray
Uniformed personnel

Exercise

Part 1: Photographs

Choose the statement that best describes what you see in the photo on page 28.

STRATEGY

Use context clues to determine where the action is taking place.

TARGET 6 Specific Locations

You may have to *identify the specific location* of people and things in a photograph. When you look at a photo, analyze the relationship of the people and things.

Problem	The wrong preposition may be used to identify a location.
Solution	Listen for the correct preposition.

Examples

Prepositions and Phrases of Location

above	beneath	far from	near	over
across	beside	in	next to	to the left of
around	between	in back of	on	to the right of
at	by	in front of	on top of	under
below	close to	inside	outside	underneath

Exercise

Part 1: Photographs

Choose the statement that best describes what you see in the photo on page 30.

For more practice, look at the other photos in this book and identify the specific location of each person or thing. You should also study the section on Prepositions in Chapter 3, p. 185.

STRATEGY SUMMARY

Strategies for Analyzing Photographs

- When you look at a photograph, analyze the people. Determine their number, gender, location, and occupation.
- Look for context clues in the photo.
- Listen for the meaning of the *whole sentence* to determine which choice best matches the photo.

Analyzing Answer Choices

7   Similar Sounds

On the TOEIC, you may have to distinguish between words with *similar sounds*. When you hear the answer choices, pay attention to the meaning. There will be context clues that help you understand the meaning. Do not be confused by words with similar sounds.

Problem	The answer choices contain words with similar sounds.
Solution	Listen carefully to the *meaning* of the statement or question and determine which answer choice really answers the question.

Examples

Here are examples of similar sounds:

Different Vowel Sounds			
bass base	car core	deep dip	gun gone
boots boats	cart court	fall full	grass grease
bus boss	drug drag	fun phone	letter later

Different Initial Consonant Sounds			
back pack rack	core tore sore	race case place	hair fair tear

Different Final Consonant Sounds			
cab cap	little litter	nab nap	think thing

Two or More Words That Sound Like One Word			
mark it market	sent her center	letter let her	in tents intense

Words That Have Sounds That Are Part of a Longer Word			
nation imagination	mind remind	give forgive	intention unintentional

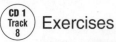

Exercises

Part 1: Photographs

Choose the statement that best describes what you see in the photograph.

Ⓐ Ⓑ Ⓒ Ⓓ

Part 2: Question-Response

Choose the best response to the question.

Ⓐ Ⓑ Ⓒ

Part 3: Conversations

Choose the best answer to the question.

1. What does the woman enjoy?

   (A) Wearing her new boots
   (B) Talking on the phone
   (C) Selling a new house
   (D) Sailing her boat

   Ⓐ Ⓑ Ⓒ Ⓓ

2. When does the man want to get together with the woman?

   (A) Today
   (B) In two days
   (C) On Sunday
   (D) On Tuesday

   Ⓐ Ⓑ Ⓒ Ⓓ

3. How is the weather today?

   (A) Rainy
   (B) Sunny
   (C) Cold
   (D) Clear

   Ⓐ Ⓑ Ⓒ Ⓓ

First News
Always Innovative & Informative

Part 4: Talks

Choose the best answer to the question.

1. What does the woman want people to do?

   (A) Mark all answers
   (B) Change clothes
   (C) Leave the store
   (D) Buy some plant seed

   Ⓐ Ⓑ Ⓒ Ⓓ

2. When does the woman want people to do this?

   (A) In fifteen minutes
   (B) In sixteen minutes
   (C) In fifty minutes
   (D) In sixty minutes

   Ⓐ Ⓑ Ⓒ Ⓓ

3. What will happen tomorrow?

   (A) The store will be open.
   (B) Clothes will go on sale.
   (C) There will be a holiday.
   (D) Money will be collected.

   Ⓐ Ⓑ Ⓒ Ⓓ

TARGET

Related Words

On the TOEIC, you may have to distinguish between *related words*. When you hear the answer choices, pay attention to the meaning. Be careful of words from the same word family or words with associated meanings.

Sometimes these related words may not be written down or spoken. They may be suggested by the picture. For example, a photo of someone putting on snow skis may make you think of the related word *mountain*, even if a mountain is not in the picture.

Problem	The answer choices may contain words that are related to the context.
Solution	Listen and look for the choice that completely answers the question or exactly matches the picture.

Examples

These are some related words:

Airline				
ticket seatbelt	pilot flight attendant	reservation ticket counter	baggage claim crew	check-in turbulence

Plants				
bud root	seed leaf	stem blossom	flower bush	branch tree

Nature				
river stream	rural farm	mountain brook	country hill	field lake

Weather				
sunny cold freezing snow chilly	cool sleet warm humid humidity	rain rainstorm hot smoggy fog	drizzle mist cloudy thunder lightning	wind breeze blizzard tornado hurricane

Energy				
oil coal	electricity gas	solar power windmill	atomic energy oil well	hydroelectric power nuclear energy

SUMMARY

The photo provides the context for the meaning of a word. Make sure the meaning of the word in the photo matches the meaning of the word in the statement, question, and answer choices. Answer options that contain related words are generally incorrect. Do not be confused by related words.

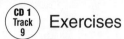

Exercises

Part 1: Photographs

Choose the statement that best describes what you see in the photo.

Ⓐ Ⓑ Ⓒ Ⓓ

Part 2: Question-Response

Choose the best response to the question.

Ⓐ Ⓑ Ⓒ

Part 3: Conversations

Choose the best answer to the question.

1. Where are the speakers?

   (A) In a car
   (B) In a plane
   (C) At sea
   (D) On a bus

2. What does the man want the woman to do?

   (A) Sit down
   (B) Stand up
   (C) Show her ticket
   (D) Get some air

3. What is the woman worried about?

   (A) Not being able to breathe
   (B) Losing her seat
   (C) Falling down
   (D) Landing too fast

   ⓐ ⓑ ⓒ ⓓ

Part 4: Talks

Choose the best answer to the question.

1. What does this announcement concern?

   (A) Sporting events
   (B) Auto repair garages
   (C) Garden center hours
   (D) The weekend weather

   ⓐ ⓑ ⓒ ⓓ

2. What should people do this weekend?

   (A) Use their umbrellas
   (B) Watch golf on TV
   (C) Buy flowers
   (D) Enjoy the outdoors

   ⓐ ⓑ ⓒ ⓓ

3. What will happen on Monday?

   (A) It will rain.
   (B) People will have a day off work.
   (C) Traffic lights will be repaired.
   (D) There will be a golf tournament.

   For more practice,
   with related words,
   study Target 3,
   Word Families,
   page 150.

TARGET

9 Homonyms

On the TOEIC, you may have to determine whether the answer choices contain a word that is a *homonym*. Homonyms are words that are pronounced the same, but have different meanings and different spellings.

Problem	A homonym may be used.
Solution	Listen and look for the meaning of the word in the context of the picture, sentence, or conversation.

Examples

Homonyms

week	for	male	seen	sowing
weak	four	mail	scene	sewing
wait	bear	sail	morning	steak
weight	bare	sale	mourning	stake
flour	steel	fare	threw	bough
flower	steal	fair	through	bow
plane	tale	rite	flew	due
plain	tail	right	flu	dew
too	feet	light	pale	sight
two	feat	lite	pail	site
to				

Exercises

Part 1: Photographs

Choose the statement that best describes what you see in the photo.

Ⓐ Ⓑ Ⓒ Ⓓ

Part 2: Question-Response

Choose the best response to the question.   Ⓐ Ⓑ Ⓒ

Part 3: Conversations

Choose the best answer to the question.

1. Why can't the man help?

   (A) The field is too wet to sow.   Ⓐ Ⓑ Ⓒ Ⓓ
   (B) He's out of thyme.
   (C) He's too busy.
   (D) There are only four buttons.

2. What is the matter with the woman's jacket?

   (A) The whole sleeve is torn.   Ⓐ Ⓑ Ⓒ Ⓓ
   (B) It's too small.
   (C) It has a hole.
   (D) She doesn't know where it is.

3. When can the man help her?

   (A) After he loses weight.   Ⓐ Ⓑ Ⓒ Ⓓ
   (B) After he gets home tomorrow.
   (C) After he works out tonight.
   (D) After he goes running.

Part 4: Talks

Choose the best answer to the question.

1. What is the man talking about?

   (A) Whether to buy two storm windows   Ⓐ Ⓑ Ⓒ Ⓓ
   (B) The weather
   (C) His son
   (D) The reign of the king

2. What will happen tomorrow?

   (A) The man will go into mourning.   Ⓐ Ⓑ Ⓒ Ⓓ
   (B) Bus fares will go up.
   (C) Flour will go on sale.
   (D) It might snow.

3. When will the speaker make the next announcement?

   (A) 1:00   Ⓐ Ⓑ Ⓒ Ⓓ
   (B) 2:00
   (C) 4:00
   (D) 8:00

TARGET

10 Same Sound and Same Spelling But Different Meaning

On the TOEIC, you may have to distinguish between *words that have the same sound and same spelling but have a different meaning.* When you hear the answer choices, pay attention to the meaning. Be careful of words with the same sounds and same spellings, but with different meanings.

Problem	A word that sounds like the correct word may be used.
Solution	Listen and look at the context for the word that answers the question.

Examples

Different Meanings for the Same Word

Call:	Animal or bird noise		*File:*	Folder
	Shout			Row
	Telephone call			Tool
Class:	Social position		*Hard:*	Difficult
	Group of students			Tough
	Level of quality			Firm
Court:	Tennis court		*Note:*	Musical note
	Court of law			Short letter
	Royal court			Currency
Date:	Type of fruit		*Seat:*	A chair
	Meeting with someone			Location of power
	Particular day			Membership in a club

Exercises

Part 1: Photographs

Choose the statement that best describes what you see in the photo.

Ⓐ Ⓑ Ⓒ Ⓓ

Part 2: Question-Response

Choose the best response to the question.   Ⓐ Ⓑ Ⓒ

Part 3: Conversations

Choose the best answer to the question.

1. What will the man do?

   (A) Call the woman on the phone   Ⓐ Ⓑ Ⓒ Ⓓ
   (B) Give her an engagement ring
   (C) Take a summer vacation
   (D) Call the woman names

2. Why does the man want to talk to the woman?

   (A) To ask her the date   Ⓐ Ⓑ Ⓒ Ⓓ
   (B) To invite her to dinner
   (C) To ask for help with a hard job
   (D) To tell her about the rest of his summer

3. Why doesn't the woman want the man to call next week?

   (A) She fell and hurt her neck   Ⓐ Ⓑ Ⓒ Ⓓ
   (B) Her phone isn't working
   (C) She will be busy
   (D) She feels weak

Part 4: Talks

Choose the best answer to the question.

1. What does the speaker suggest people do?

   (A) Get married at Valley Springs   Ⓐ Ⓑ Ⓒ Ⓓ
   (B) See a tennis game
   (C) Go to a nightclub
   (D) Not use the last match

2. What will happen in the evening?

   (A) There will be a tennis class.   Ⓐ Ⓑ Ⓒ Ⓓ
   (B) Court will be in session.
   (C) There will be an awards ceremony.
   (D) Watches will go on sale.

3. When will the next tournament take place?

   (A) Next Sunday   Ⓐ Ⓑ Ⓒ Ⓓ
   (B) Next month
   (C) Next May
   (D) Next spring

TARGET
11 Time

On the TOEIC, you may have to determine the sequence of time. When you hear the answer choices, pay attention to the meaning. Listen for time markers. A time marker is any word that indicates a time when something happened, happens, or will happen. Time markers will help you determine the order of events.

Problem	You may not hear or see a time marker.
Solution	Listen and look for the time marker.

Examples

The following chart shows sequence time markers. The sentences below the chart illustrate sequences of events.

Happened before	Happened close to the same time	Happened after
before	when	after
prior to	while	once
until	during	then
preceding	as soon as	afterwards
no later than	as	following
already		and

The manager <u>cleared his desk</u> before he left.

1st	2nd
What happened first?	He cleared his desk.
What happened next?	He left.
What happened before he left?	He cleared his desk.

The <u>mail was sorted</u> as soon as it arrived.

2nd	1st
What happened first?	The mail arrived.
What happened next?	It was sorted.
What happened as the mail arrived?	It was sorted.

First News
Always Innovative & Informative

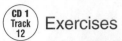

Exercises

Part 1: Photographs

Choose the statement that best describes what you see in the photo.

Ⓐ Ⓑ Ⓒ Ⓓ

Part 2: Question-Response

Choose the best response to the question.

Ⓐ Ⓑ Ⓒ

Part 3: Conversations

Choose the best answer to the question.

1. What will the speakers do first with the proposal?

   (A) Copy it
   (B) Show it to Mr. Kim
   (C) Submit it to the director
   (D) Proofread it

   Ⓐ Ⓑ Ⓒ Ⓓ

2. When does the woman want to eat lunch?

   (A) Before they proofread the proposal
   (B) After they proofread the proposal
   (C) Before they write the directions
   (D) After they write the directions

   Ⓐ Ⓑ Ⓒ Ⓓ

First News
A l w a y s I n n o v a t i v e & I n f o r m a t i v e

3. What will the speakers do last?

    (A) Edit the proposal   
    (B) Go to the golf course
    (C) Give the proposal to the director
    (D) Invite Mr. Kim to lunch

Part 4: Talks

Choose the best answer to the question.

1. How long has Mr. Saleh been Chairman?

    (A) Until next quarter   
    (B) About twenty years
    (C) For five years
    (D) Since his retirement

2. What will Mr. Saleh do first?

    (A) Attend a party
    (B) Take a vacation
    (C) Open a business
    (D) Get a job at Rotel International

3. Which of the following did Mr. Saleh do first?

    (A) Become Chairman
    (B) Start working at Mercury Corporation
    (C) Plan to open a small business
    (D) Retire

TARGET

12 Negation

On the TOEIC, you may have to determine whether a statement is *positive* or *negative*. When you hear the answer choices, pay attention to the meaning. Listen for "negative markers," which will help you determine if the sense of the statement is positive or negative. Look for negative markers in the answer choices.

Remember that a negative prefix contradicts the word it joins. This usually results in a negative meaning. For example, *unfriendly* contradicts *friendly* and has the negative meaning *not friendly*. But when a negative prefix is added to a negative word, the resulting meaning can be positive. For example, *unselfish* contradicts *selfish* and has the positive meaning *not selfish*.

Problem	You cannot tell whether a statement is positive or negative.
Solution	Listen and look for a negative marker.

Examples

The following is a list of common negative markers.

Before verbs/ clauses	Before nouns/ phrases	Negative prefixes	Positive meaning from negative prefixes
not	no	un- undone	unlimited
isn't/can't/ doesn't/won't	nowhere	im- impossible	unparalleled
shouldn't/couldn't/hasn't	nothing	il- illegal	invaluable
mustn't		in- indefinite	nonrestrictive
	at no time	non- nonsense	nonviolent
rarely/only rarely	not at this time		
hardly	in no case		
scarcely	by no means		
seldom			
never			
barely			
not since			
not until			
and neither . . .			

TIP

Having two negative expressions in a sentence makes the sentence positive. For example, *This is <u>not illegal</u>* means *This is legal.*

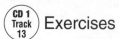 Exercises

Part 1: Photographs

Choose the statement that best describes what you see in the photo.

Ⓐ Ⓑ Ⓒ Ⓓ

Part 2: Question-Response

Choose the best response to the question.

Ⓐ Ⓑ Ⓒ

Part 3: Conversations

Choose the best answer to the question.

1. What does the man advise the woman?

   (A) Take more than she needs
   (B) Take less than she needs
   (C) Buy what she needs later
   (D) Take only what she needs

   Ⓐ Ⓑ Ⓒ Ⓓ

2. What does the woman think of the man's advice?

   (A) She agrees with him.
   (B) She disagrees with him.
   (C) She can't say what she thinks.
   (D) She thinks everyone will disagree with him.

   Ⓐ Ⓑ Ⓒ Ⓓ

First News
A l w a y s   I n n o v a t i v e   &   I n f o r m a t i v e

3. How many suitcases does the woman usually travel with?

    (A) No more than two   Ⓐ Ⓑ Ⓒ Ⓓ
    (B) Fewer than three
    (C) At least three
    (D) Seven

Part 4: Talks

Choose the best answer to the question.

1. What word or phrase describes this report?

    (A) Extremely positive   Ⓐ Ⓑ Ⓒ Ⓓ
    (B) Extremely negative
    (C) Unenthusiastic
    (D) Mediocre

2. What describes the employees mentioned in this report?

    (A) Selfish   Ⓐ Ⓑ Ⓒ Ⓓ
    (B) Dedicated
    (C) Unsuccessful
    (D) Unimaginative

3. What does the speaker say about the banquet?

    (A) She's very happy about it.   Ⓐ Ⓑ Ⓒ Ⓓ
    (B) She thinks it shouldn't be done.
    (C) She hopes no one will attend.
    (D) She thinks the employees don't deserve it.

TARGET

13 **Word Order**

On the TOEIC, you may need to pay attention to the *word order* to determine whether a sentence is a question or a statement, or is positive or negative. When you hear the answer choices, pay attention to the word order. Note the placement of the subject and the auxiliary verb.

Problem	You may not be able to tell whether the sentence is a question or a statement or is positive or negative.
Solution	Listen and look for the word order.

Examples

What a big boy you are!	means	*You are a very big boy.*
Never has this room been so crowded.	means	*This room has never been so crowded.* and *There are a lot of people in this room.*

CD 1
Track
14

Exercises

Part 1: Photographs

Choose the statement that best describes what you see in the photo.

Ⓐ Ⓑ Ⓒ Ⓓ

Part 2: Question-Response

Choose the best response to the question.

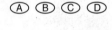

Part 3: Conversations

Choose the best answer to the question.

1. What does the woman think about the trip?

    (A) It will be long.
    (B) It will be exciting.
    (C) She doesn't envy the man.
    (D) It will not be as great as he thinks.

    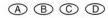

2. What does the woman say about Europe?

    (A) It takes a long time to get there.
    (B) There isn't much to see there.
    (C) It's beautiful at this time of year.
    (D) The weather is too hot there.

3. What does the woman want to know?

    (A) Who will travel with the man.
    (B) How much time the man will spend there.
    (C) How the man will get there.
    (D) When the man will leave on his trip.

Part 4: Talks

Choose the best answer to the question.

1. What is the weather this morning?

    (A) Unchanged
    (B) Hot
    (C) Still
    (D) Very windy

2. When did it rain?

    (A) Yesterday morning
    (B) Yesterday at noon
    (C) Yesterday afternoon
    (D) Last night

3. What does the speaker think of the weather?

    (A) She's seen stranger weather.
    (B) She's enjoying it.
    (C) It's confusing.
    (D) It's beautiful.

First News

A l w a y s I n n o v a t i v e & I n f o r m a t i v e

TARGET

14 **Comparisons**

On the TOEIC, you may need to determine whether words are being *compared*. It is important to know the relationship between two things or actions.

Problem	You cannot determine the relationship between things being compared.
Solution	Look for "comparison markers."

Examples

The following table shows three types of comparison markers.

Comparison Markers

Three degrees of comparison			Examples
Positive	tall	expensive	This brand of fax paper is expensive.
Comparative	taller	more expensive	The fax paper is more expensive.
Superlative	tallest	most expensive	This third brand is the most expensive.
Comparisons of equals			
as ... as			Your office is as large as mine.
not as ... as			This window is not as dirty as that one.
not as many ... as ...			There are not as many seats as we need.
not as much ... as ...			
Double comparative			
The + (comparative) ... the + (comparative)			The less you work, the less you will earn.
			The more you travel, the less time you will have at home.

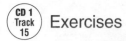

Exercises

Part 1: Photographs

Choose the statement that best describes what you see in the photo.

Part 2: Question-Response

Choose the best response to the question.   Ⓐ Ⓑ Ⓒ

Part 3: Conversations

Choose the best answer to the question.

1. What do they think about the meeting?

   (A) It's not long enough.   Ⓐ Ⓑ Ⓒ Ⓓ
   (B) It will begin soon.
   (C) It's not very interesting.
   (D) It will end soon.

2. What is true about yesterday's meeting?

   (A) It was longer than this one.   Ⓐ Ⓑ Ⓒ Ⓓ
   (B) It was shorter than this one.
   (C) It was more boring than this one.
   (D) It was just as boring as this one.

3. Why is the woman tired?

   (A) She attends too many meetings.   Ⓐ Ⓑ Ⓒ Ⓓ
   (B) She woke up early this morning.
   (C) The meeting is too long.
   (D) The meeting is over.

Part 4: Talks

Choose the best answer to the question.

1. What is said about roads and cars?

   (A) Fewer people drive nowadays.   Ⓐ Ⓑ Ⓒ Ⓓ
   (B) The number of cars will increase as roads improve.
   (C) There will be less cars on the roads in the future.
   (D) There are fewer good roads today.

2. Why will more people start driving smaller cars?

   (A) The price of gasoline is going up.   Ⓐ Ⓑ Ⓒ Ⓓ
   (B) The roads are getting crowded.
   (C) The roads are getting smaller.
   (D) The price of bigger cars is too high.

3. According to the speaker, what is the advantage
   of a plane over a car?

   (A) It is cheaper.   Ⓐ Ⓑ Ⓒ Ⓓ
   (B) It is bigger.
   (C) It is faster.
   (D) It is less crowded.

TARGET
15 Modals

On the TOEIC, you may need to determine how *modals* affect the meaning of the statement, conversation, or talk.

Problem	You may not hear the modal.
Solution	Listen carefully for the modal.

Examples

The following tables show modals, their meanings, and specific sentences using them.

Modal	Meaning	Examples
can	present ability permission (informal) possibility	She can use the new phone system. They can leave when they want. The machine can be on.
could	past ability permission (polite) possibility	They could not send a fax until they were trained. Could you come in, please? The train could be late.
may/might	permission possibility	May I interrupt, please? They may/might sign the contract.
should	advisability logical conclusion	He should work harder. It should be cooler in the refrigerated room.
must	necessity probability authority/requirement	Everyone must register at the door. Here's a reply to my fax; she must have sent it immediately.
have to/ have got to	necessity	We have to pick up the files before the meeting.
ought to	obligation (spoken English) generally	They ought to be more positive in their response.
will	future polite request polite refusal	I will deliver this for you tonight. Will you reserve a table for two at 8:00? I will not be able to accept your invitation.
would	past habit polite request polite refusal	She would park in the same location every day. Would you be available for a meeting at 2:00? They would not agree to our terms.
had better	advisability	Your presentation is in ten minutes. You had better get ready.
had rather	preference	He'd rather memorize his speech than use notes.

Past Form of Modal	Meaning	Examples
may/might have + (past participle)	past possibility (action may not have occurred)	She may have sent the package by regular mail. We aren't sure.
should have + (past participle)	advisable action (action did not occur)	He should have signed for the shipment.
ought to have + (past participle)	advisable action (action did not occur)	We ought to have made a reservation.
must have + (past participle)	probability	We cannot wait any longer; he must have missed the train.
would have + (past participle)	past intention (unfulfilled)	They would have ordered more supplies.
could have + (past participle)	past possibility (action may or may not have occurred)	The designer could have used color photographs in the annual report, but it would have cost more.

CD 1
Track
16

Exercises

Part 1: Photographs

Choose the statement that best describes what you see in the photo.

Ⓐ Ⓑ Ⓒ Ⓓ

First News
Always Innovative & Informative

Part 2: Question-Response

Choose the best response to the question.   Ⓐ Ⓑ Ⓒ

Part 3: Conversations

Choose the best answer to the question.

1. Did the woman go to the reception?

    (A) She didn't go because she was busy.   Ⓐ Ⓑ Ⓒ Ⓓ
    (B) She went because she had nothing else to do.
    (C) She went because there was no charge.
    (D) She didn't go because there was an admission fee.

2. Did the man go to the reception?

    (A) No, he had to be somewhere else.   Ⓐ Ⓑ Ⓒ Ⓓ
    (B) Yes, and it was very interesting.
    (C) No, he went to a more interesting place.
    (D) Yes, but he didn't have a good time.

3. Will the woman go to the party tomorrow?

    (A) Yes, she definitely plans to go.   Ⓐ Ⓑ Ⓒ Ⓓ
    (B) No, she has too much work to do.
    (C) Maybe, if she can finish her work.
    (D) Yes, because she has to write a report about it.

Part 4: Talks

Choose the best answer to the question.

1. How does this critique describe the presentation?

   (A) Interesting   Ⓐ Ⓑ Ⓒ Ⓓ
   (B) Confusing
   (C) Visually exciting
   (D) Colorful

2. What does the speaker say about the presenter?

   (A) He should speak louder.   Ⓐ Ⓑ Ⓒ Ⓓ
   (B) He was easy to hear.
   (C) He should speak more clearly.
   (D) He was easy to follow.

3. What advice does the speaker give for the presenter?

   (A) Practice speaking with an aide.   Ⓐ Ⓑ Ⓒ Ⓓ
   (B) Don't give the presentation again.
   (C) Make some visual aids.
   (D) Use a microphone.

TARGET

 16 *Used to*

On the TOEIC, you may have to determine from the context which meaning of *used to* is correct. One form means habitual action and the other means to be accustomed to something.

Problem	You don't know which meaning of *used to* is correct.
Solution	Listen for a form of the verb *be*. If a form of *be* appears, the meaning is *accustomed to*.

Examples

Modal Form	Meaning	Examples
used to	habitual action	We used to have a staff meeting every Friday.
be used to	be accustomed to	They are used to long flights.
be used to ... -ing	be accustomed to	She is used to working without lunch.

 CD 1 Track 17

Exercises

Part 1: Photographs

Choose the statement that best describes what you see in the photo.

Ⓐ Ⓑ Ⓒ Ⓓ

Part 2: Question-Response

Choose the best response to the question.

Ⓐ Ⓑ Ⓒ

Part 3: Conversations

Choose the best answer to the question.

1. What does the man say about himself?

   (A) He recently started giving more speeches.
   (B) He often gave presentations at conferences.
   (C) He never speaks in public.
   (D) He can't think of anything people want to hear.

   (A) (B) (C) (D)

2. What can the man talk about?

   (A) Only certain kinds of things
   (B) Different kinds of names
   (C) Working with the press
   (D) Many different subjects

   (A) (B) (C) (D)

3. What does the woman say about herself?

   (A) She used to speak in public.
   (B) She doesn't like to speak in public.
   (C) She isn't impressed by public speaking.
   (D) She is used to hearing the man speak.

   (A) (B) (C) (D)

Part 4: Short Talks

Choose the best answer to the question.

1. What changes did the photocopier bring about?

   (A) People no longer use carbon paper.
   (B) People don't write as much.
   (C) People don't type as well.
   (D) People are not yet used to making many copies.

   (A) (B) (C) (D)

2. What are people used to doing now?

   (A) Making more copies than necessary
   (B) Typing one letter multiple times
   (C) Making just one copy at a time
   (D) Writing more correspondence than they used to

   (A) (B) (C) (D)

3. What is a problem now?

   (A) It takes time and effort to use a photocopier.
   (B) People receive too much correspondence.
   (C) A lot of trash is generated.
   (D) Photocopier paper weighs too much.

   (A) (B) (C) (D)

STRATEGY SUMMARY
Strategies for Analyzing Answer Choices

- Find context clues.
- Listen and look for the *meaning* of the statement, question, and answer choices. Do not be confused by similar sounds, homonyms, related words, etc.
- Listen and look for sequence time markers. Attend to negative markers and comparison markers.
- Watch the word order.
- Determine how the modal affects the meaning.

Analyzing Question Types

TARGET
17 People

Most questions about people begin with *who* or *what*. These questions are generally answered by a person's title, occupation, or relationship to another person.

In Parts III and IV, the speakers are identified most frequently by their occupational titles or their relationship to one another. This will be discussed more completely in the following sections.

Problem	The question asks about people.
Solution	Look for names or group terms (*class, family, tourists*) in the answer choices BEFORE you hear the audio.

Examples

If you see or hear these question types, look or listen for answers about people.

Common Questions

Questions with **What**	Questions with **Who**
What is your name?	Who is taking part in this conversation?
What is her title?	Who is the man?
	Who is the woman?
	Who are the speakers?

If you see or hear these answers, the question may be about people.

Common Answers

Proper names	Identification by activity or role	Identification by group
Mr. Tanza	A tourist	Business people
Mrs. Green	A passenger	Family members
Ms. Hu	A driver	College students
Dr. Shapiro	A jogger	

CD 1 Track 18

Exercises

Part 2: Question-Response

Choose the best response to the question.

Ⓐ Ⓑ Ⓒ

Part 3: Conversations

Choose the best answer to the question.

1. Who are the speakers?

    (A) Lifeguards at the beach
    (B) Painters
    (C) Salespeople selling coats
    (D) Bartenders

    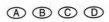

2. Who will prepare the wall?

    (A) The man
    (B) The woman
    (C) The boss
    (D) The helper

    Ⓐ Ⓑ Ⓒ Ⓓ

3. Who owns the house?

    (A) The man's father
    (B) The man's mother
    (C) The man's brother
    (D) The man's friend

    Ⓐ Ⓑ Ⓒ Ⓓ

Part 4: Talks

Choose the best answer to the question.

1. Who is listening to this announcement?

    (A) Migrant workers
    (B) Airline passengers
    (C) Gas station attendants
    (D) Customs officers

2. Who will pass out the forms?

    (A) Customs officers
    (B) Attendants
    (C) Passengers
    (D) Immigration officials

    Ⓐ Ⓑ Ⓒ Ⓓ

3. Who should follow the blue signs?

    (A) Foreign visitors
    (B) Senior citizens
    (C) Citizens of this country
    (D) People with small children

    Ⓐ Ⓑ Ⓒ Ⓓ

TARGET

18 Occupations

Questions about a person's occupation are commonly asked on the TOEIC. You should first look at the answer choices to see what four occupations are given. Then you should try to think of words related to those occupations. These words will be clues.

It is important to listen for occupational clues in the conversations and short talks. If a person is an auto mechanic, you might hear references to engines, cars, oil, brakes, gas stations, etc. If you hear those words, it is likely that the correct answer is *auto mechanic*.

Problem	The question asks about a speaker's occupation.
Solution	Look for types of occupations in the answer choices BEFORE you hear the audio. Make assumptions about those occupations and listen for the clues.

Examples

If you see or hear these question types, look or listen for answers about someone's occupation.

Common Questions

What kind of job does the man have?
What type of work does the woman do?
What is the man's job?
What is the woman's occupation?

What is the man's profession?
What does this woman do?

What is Mr. Smith's present position?
How does this man earn a living?
What kind of job is available?
Who can benefit from seeing this memo?
Who was interviewed?
Who would most likely use the conference hall?

The answers to those questions are usually job titles. If you see or hear answers like these, look or listen for questions about someone's occupation.

Common Answers

Architect	Pilot	Flight attendant
Housekeeper	Psychologist	Telephone installer
Secretary	Operator	Receptionist
Political advisor	Travel agent	Teacher
Chemist	Information clerk	Office manager
Driving instructor	Railroad conductor	Reporter
Theater employee	Manager	Accountant
Police officer	Personnel director	Chairman of the Board
Sign painter	Sales representative	Branch manager
Reporter	Technician	Professor of Mathematics
Novelist	Hotel clerk	Senior Vice-President

CD 1 Track 19 Exercises

Part 2: Question-Response

Choose the best response to the question. Ⓐ Ⓑ Ⓒ

Part 3: Conversations

Choose the best answer to the question.

1. What is the woman's occupation?

   (A) Running coach
   (B) Baseball player
   (C) Telephone operator
   (D) Telephone installer

   Ⓐ Ⓑ Ⓒ Ⓓ

2. What is the man's job?

   (A) Mailman
   (B) Website designer
   (C) Employment counselor
   (D) Mail order company owner

   Ⓐ Ⓑ Ⓒ Ⓓ

3. Who is responsible for answering the phone?

   (A) The man only
   (B) The woman only
   (C) Everyone at the company
   (D) Some of the customers

   Ⓐ Ⓑ Ⓒ Ⓓ

Part 4: Talks

Choose the best answer to the question.

1. Who is listening to this talk?

   (A) Students
   (B) Patients
   (C) Professors
   (D) Museum visitors

2. Who will speak today?

   (A) A doctor
   (B) A student
   (C) A hotel manager
   (D) A museum director

3. Who is Mary Little?

   (A) A museum guide
   (B) A teacher
   (C) A student
   (D) A historian

   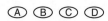

TARGET
19 Speakers' Relationship

Questions about the speakers' relationship are also commonly asked on the TOEIC. You should first look at the answer choices to see what four relationships are given. Then you should try to think of words related to those relationships. These words will be clues.

It is important to listen for relationship clues in the conversations and short talks. If a person is a family member, you might hear references to *mother, father, aunt*, etc. If you hear those words, it is likely that the correct answer is *family member*.

Problem	The question asks about the speakers' relationship.
Solution	Look for types of relationships in the answer choices BEFORE you hear the audio. Make assumptions about those relationships and listen for the clues.

Examples

If you see or hear these question types, look or listen for answers about the speakers' relationship.

Common Questions

What is the relationship between the speakers?
What is the relationship between the man and the woman?
What is the relationship of the man to the woman?
What is the relationship of the woman to the man?

The answers to those questions usually indicate a professional or personal relationship. If you see or hear answers like these, look or listen for questions about the speakers' relationship.

Common Answers

Professional relationship	*Personal relationship*
Employer and employee	Brother
Professor and pupil	Uncle
Doctor and patient	Father
Lawyer and client	Cousin
Waiter and customer	Sister
Bank manager and customer	Aunt
Librarian and patron	Mother
Teacher and student	Husband
Salesperson and customer	Wife
Colleagues	Friend

CD 1
Track
20

Exercises

Part 2: Question-Response

Choose the best response to the question.

Ⓐ Ⓑ Ⓒ

Part 3: Conversations

Choose the best answer to the question.

1. What is the relationship of the speakers?

   (A) Banker and client
   (B) Accountant and cashier
   (C) Waiter and customer
   (D) Coffee grower and bean picker

   Ⓐ Ⓑ Ⓒ Ⓓ

2. Who is the woman with?

   (A) Her mom
   (B) Her son
   (C) Her friend
   (D) Her daughter

   Ⓐ Ⓑ Ⓒ Ⓓ

3. Who had coffee?

   (A) The man
   (B) The woman
   (C) The cashier
   (D) The doorman

   Ⓐ Ⓑ Ⓒ Ⓓ

Part 4: Talks

Choose the best answer to the question.

1. What two people might pay attention to this message?

   (A) Librarian and patron
   (B) Author and publisher
   (C) Police officer and speeder
   (D) Bookseller and customer

   Ⓐ Ⓑ Ⓒ Ⓓ

2. Who is responsible for children's behavior?

   (A) The other patrons
   (B) The children themselves
   (C) The parents
   (D) The director

   Ⓐ Ⓑ Ⓒ Ⓓ

3. Who should show a driver's license?

   (A) People who want to use a meeting room
   (B) People who live in other areas
   (C) People who want to attend special events
   (D) People who plan to travel to other areas

   Ⓐ Ⓑ Ⓒ Ⓓ

TARGET
20 Location

Most questions about location begin with *where*. These questions are generally answered by locations preceded by *in, on,* or *at.*

Problem	The question asks about location.
Solution	Look for prepositions of location (such as *in, on,* or *at*) among the answer choices BEFORE you hear the audio. Listen carefully for those prepositions in the audio.

Examples

If you see or hear these question types, look or listen for answers about the speakers' location. Note the questions will begin with *where.*

Common Questions

Where did the conversation probably take place?
Where did the conversation likely occur?

Where is the man?
Where is the woman?
Where is the speaker?

Where are the man and woman?
Where are the speakers?

Where has the man/woman been?
Where does the man/woman want to go?
Where did the man/woman come from?

Where are they going?

Where did the man think the woman was?

Where should he call?

The answers to those questions usually indicate a location. The location can be identified either with or without a preposition. If you see or hear answers like these, look or listen for questions about the speakers' location.

Common Answers

Without prepositions	*With prepositions*	
The train station.	On the bus.	On a tennis court.
The store.	At the movies.	In an architect's office.
The office.	In Union Station.	In a banker's office.
The house.	In a city office building.	In a lawyer's office.

Exercises

Part 2: Question-Response

Choose the best response to the question.   

Part 3: Conversations

Choose the best answer to the question.

1. Where did he put the letter?

    (A) On the shelf   
    (B) Under the books
    (C) On top of the books on the desk
    (D) In the drawer

2. Where is the shelf?

    (A) By the door   
    (B) By the computer
    (C) By the desk
    (D) By the letterbox

3. Where does the woman want the man to
   put the letter?

    (A) Next to the printer   
    (B) In a box
    (C) In a folder
    (D) On top of her computer

Part 4: Talks

Choose the best answer to the question.

1. Where should you put your initials?

    (A) At the bottom of the communication   
    (B) Next to your name
    (C) Under your name
    (D) On every list

2. Where should people put their outgoing letters?

    (A) In the mailroom   
    (B) On the floor
    (C) In the outbox
    (D) Under the door

3. Where is incoming mail placed?

    (A) In the inbox   
    (B) On the recipient's desk
    (C) In the individual's mailbox
    (D) At the head of the stairs

TARGET
21 Time

Most questions about time begin with *when* or *how long*. These questions are generally answered by time of day, days of the week, seasons, and dates. The answers give a specific time or a duration. Some answers are in adverbial clauses:

When can I have breakfast?
You can have breakfast { whenever you want.
when you get up.
as soon as the coffee is ready.

Problem	The question asks about time.
Solution	Look for clues on time in the answer choices BEFORE you hear the audio. Listen carefully for those clues in the audio.

Examples

If you see or hear these question types, look or listen for answers about time. Note the questions begin with *when* and *how*.

Common Questions

Questions with **When**	Questions with **How**
When did the conversation take place?	How long will the manager live in Tokyo?
When is the man's birthday?	How long will it take to arrive?
When is the woman's vacation date?	How often is the magazine published?
When is the restaurant open?	
When was the meeting?	How many weeks were most people away each year?
When will the increase go into effect?	
When did he join the firm?	

STRATEGY

Listen for time questions. They generally begin with *when, how often, how many days,* or *how long*. Make sure that the correct response addresses the question that was asked. For example, the response to a question asking *when* answers *when*, not *how long*.

The answers to those questions usually indicate a time. The time can be identified either with or without a preposition. It can be a specific moment or a duration. It can be a time, a day, a date, a season, a year. If you see or hear answers like these, look or listen for questions about time.

Common Answers

11:00 A.M.	In January.	1946.	This week.
Noon.	In February.	1964.	This month.
3:00 P.M.	January 3.	1914.	Next week.
Midnight.	February 14.	1916.	Next month.
At 6:00.	January 3 of this year.	In the summer.	On weekday evenings.
Before 5:30.	January 30 of next year.	In the fall.	Any evening from 6:30 to 8:30.
After 8:00.		In the spring.	
Sunday.	On January 3rd.	Tomorrow.	
Monday.	On February 14th.	Yesterday.	
Tuesday.			

CD 1 Track 22

Exercises

Part 2: Question-Response

Choose the best response to the question.   Ⓐ Ⓑ Ⓒ

Part 3: Conversations

Choose the best answer to the question.

TIP

Note that the times are listed in ascending order, with the smallest number first. This will help you find the number you are looking for faster.

1. How much longer will the man stay?

    (A) 10 minutes   Ⓐ Ⓑ Ⓒ Ⓓ
    (B) 15 minutes
    (C) 30 minutes
    (D) 60 minutes

2. When is the man's appointment?

    (A) 8:00   Ⓐ Ⓑ Ⓒ Ⓓ
    (B) 8:30
    (C) 9:00
    (D) 9:30

3. How long will it take the man to get home?

    (A) twenty minutes   Ⓐ Ⓑ Ⓒ Ⓓ
    (B) twenty-five minutes
    (C) forty minutes
    (D) forty-five minutes

Part 4: Talks

Choose the best answer to the question.

1. How often has it snowed?

    (A) Every hour   Ⓐ Ⓑ Ⓒ Ⓓ
    (B) Daily
    (C) Only once last week
    (D) Twice a month

2. When was the last time the region had this much snow?

    (A) Seven years ago   Ⓐ Ⓑ Ⓒ Ⓓ
    (B) Eleven years ago
    (C) Sixty years ago
    (D) Seventy years ago

3. When will winter end?

    (A) Today   Ⓐ Ⓑ Ⓒ Ⓓ
    (B) In one week
    (C) In one month
    (D) In two months

TARGET
22   Activities

Most questions about activities begin with *what*. Some questions can begin with *how*. These questions are generally answered by short phrases or complete sentences. You should first look at the answer choices to see what four activities are given. Then you should try to think of words related to those activities. These words will be activity clues.

It is important to listen for activity clues in the conversations and short talks. For example, the activity playing golf might have words such as *golf club, bag, course, fairway, hole,* and *green* in the audio.

Problem	The question asks about activities.
Solution	Look for types of activities in the answer choices BEFORE you hear the audio. Make assumptions about those activities and listen for the clues.

Examples

If you see or hear these question types, look or listen for answers about an activity. Note the questions begin with *what* and *how*.

Common Questions

*Questions with **to Do***
What will the man do?
What did the woman do?
What has the customer
   decided to do?
What are they planning to do?
What does the woman have to do?
What is the man going to do?
What is Mrs. Park supposed to do?
What are they doing?

Questions about an event or occurrence
What happened?
What occurred?
What took place?
What happened to the woman?
What will happen next?

*Questions with **How***
How can the package be sent?
How will the room be changed?

The answers to those questions usually indicate an activity. The activity can be identified either in a phrase or a complete sentence. It can be a specific event or represent a method. If you see or hear answers like these, look or listen for questions about an activity.

Common Answers

Activities in phrases
See a movie.
Go out for lunch.
Take a Spanish course.
Play golf.
Attend tonight's lecture.
Finish the proposal.
Take the day off.
Read the fax.

Activities in complete sentences
They will go out for dinner.
He will send a fax.
She should call her office.

Events or occurrences
The car stopped.
The conference let out early.
The chemical tanker arrived on schedule.
She was late for the meeting.
The phone lines were out of service.

Method or manner
By overnight mail.
By express mail.
By messenger.
By courier.
By moving the desk.

By painting the walls.
By covering the windows.
By adding more light.

Exercises

Part 2: Question-Response

Choose the best response to the question. Ⓐ Ⓑ Ⓒ

Part 3: Conversations

Choose the best answer to the question.

1. What are they doing? Ⓐ Ⓑ Ⓒ Ⓓ

   (A) Taking a walk
   (B) Taking a nap
   (C) Buying a map
   (D) Driving a car

2. What did they do earlier? Ⓐ Ⓑ Ⓒ Ⓓ

   (A) Rested
   (B) Played in the snow
   (C) Had dinner
   (D) Rented a movie

3. What will they do next? Ⓐ Ⓑ Ⓒ Ⓓ

   (A) Read
   (B) Go to bed
   (C) See a play
   (D) Go to the movies

Part 4: Talks

Choose the best answer to the question.

1. What will happen if it rains?

   (A) The picnic will be rescheduled. Ⓐ Ⓑ Ⓒ Ⓓ
   (B) The office cafeteria will be closed.
   (C) The mail will not be delivered.
   (D) The picnic will be held inside.

2. What will happen on Friday? Ⓐ Ⓑ Ⓒ Ⓓ

   (A) The picnic will take place.
   (B) Shirley will buy dishes.
   (C) The food will be ordered.
   (D) Everyone will go home early.

3. How should people communicate with Shirley about the picnic? Ⓐ Ⓑ Ⓒ Ⓓ

   (A) By phone
   (B) By e-mail
   (C) By letter
   (D) In person

TARGET

23 Events or Facts

Most questions about events begin with *what*. These questions are generally answered by phrases or complete sentences. The strategy for these questions is similar to the strategies for the previous questions. Read the answer choices, make some assumptions about the events listed, and listen for the relevant clues.

Problem	The question asks about events.
Solution	Look for clues on events or facts in the answer choices BEFORE you hear the audio. Listen carefully for those clues in the audio.

Examples

If you see or hear these question types, look or listen for answers about an event or fact. Note that the questions begin with *what*.

Common Questions

What is the conversation about?   What happens if they don't like the movie?

What are they talking about?   What is unusual about this event?

What are they discussing?   What was the outcome of the meeting?

The answers to those questions are usually events or facts. They can be in phrases or short sentences. If you see or hear answers like these, look or listen for questions about an event or fact.

Common Answers

Phrases   *Sentences*

Cost of insurance.   It's free.

Shipping fees.   They can leave.

Overdue accounts.   The companies decided not to merge.

Methods of delivery.

CD 1
Track
24
Exercises

Part 2: Question-Response

Choose the best response to the question. ⒜ ⒝ ⒞

Part 3: Conversations

Choose the best answer to the question.

1. What will happen if the goods don't clear customs?

   (A) Production will be postponed. ⒜ ⒝ ⒞ ⒟
   (B) The advertisers will complain.
   (C) More customs duty will be paid.
   (D) They will wait until Friday.

2. What will happen on Monday?

   (A) There will be a meeting. ⒜ ⒝ ⒞ ⒟
   (B) The shipment will be released.
   (C) Production will begin.
   (D) A new shipment will arrive.

3. What does the woman say about the delay?

   (A) It's strange. ⒜ ⒝ ⒞ ⒟
   (B) It's the first time this has happened.
   (C) It has happened before.
   (D) It happens every day.

Part 4: Talks

Choose the best answer to the question.

1. What is unusual about this past week?

   (A) The earthquakes in all regions ⒜ ⒝ ⒞ ⒟
   (B) The absence of disasters
   (C) The large number of disasters
   (D) The blizzard in the South

2. What will happen if a new disaster happens soon?

   (A) The president will send aid to the victims. ⒜ ⒝ ⒞ ⒟
   (B) Victims will be sent to other areas of the country.
   (C) There may not be enough people or money to
       help victims.
   (D) Emergency personnel will flood the area.

3. What will the president do on Sunday?

   (A) Address some letters ⒜ ⒝ ⒞ ⒟
   (B) Visit the Midwest
   (C) Make a speech
   (D) Move to a new address

First News
Always Innovative & Informative

TARGET

24 Emotions

Most questions about an emotion begin with *what* or *how*. These questions are generally answered by single words or phrases.

Problem	The question asks about emotions.
Solution	Look for clues on emotions in the answer choices BEFORE you hear the audio. Listen carefully for those clues.

Examples

If you see or hear these question types, look or listen for answers about an emotion. Note that the questions begin with *what* or *how*.

Common Questions
What is the man's mood?
What is the woman angry about?
How does the speaker feel?

STRATEGY

Read the answer choice and look for words that imply emotions, then make an assumption about that emotion. For example, if the word "nervous" is an answer choice, imagine what might cause someone to be nervous. When you listen to the questions and answers, pay attention to the emphasis that speakers place on words. Their tone and emphasis can indicate emotions.

The answers to those questions are usually emotions or feelings. Usually single words answer the questions about moods and feelings, and short phrases answer the questions about the cause of the emotion. If you see or hear answers like these, look or listen for questions about an emotion.

Common Answers

Emotion or feeling
Afraid.
Angry.
Annoyed.
Ashamed.
Bored.
Cold.
Confused.
Disappointed.
Disgusted.
Ecstatic.
Embarrassed.
Exhausted.

Frustrated.
Full.
Happy.
Hot.
Hungry.
Ill.
Jealous.
Mad.
Miserable.
Nervous.
Pleased.
Proud.
Sad.

Shocked.
Sick.
Sleepy.
Surprised.
Thirsty.
Unhappy.
Upset.
Worried.

Cause of emotion or feeling
His job.
Leaving home.
Being alone.

CD 2 Track 1 Exercises

Part 2: Question-Response

Choose the best response to the question.   Ⓐ Ⓑ Ⓒ

Part 3: Conversations

Choose the best answer to the question.

1. How do the speakers feel?   Ⓐ Ⓑ Ⓒ Ⓓ

   (A) Hungry   (C) Angry
   (B) Worried   (D) Lost

2. How does the man feel about their ability to get
   what they need?   Ⓐ Ⓑ Ⓒ Ⓓ

   (A) Relaxed   (C) Happy
   (B) Good   (D) Doubtful

3. How does the woman feel about their ability
   to get what they need?   Ⓐ Ⓑ Ⓒ Ⓓ

   (A) Confident   (C) Bad
   (B) Unsure   (D) Afraid

Part 4: Talks

Choose the best answer to the question.

1. Why are the neighbors upset?

   (A) There is no parking for them.   Ⓐ Ⓑ Ⓒ Ⓓ
   (B) Cars are parked on their property.
   (C) Employees leave early.
   (D) No one waters the lawns.

2. How do employees feel about the shortage
   of parking?

   (A) Patient   Ⓐ Ⓑ Ⓒ Ⓓ
   (B) Happy
   (C) Sad
   (D) Frustrated

3. How does the speaker feel about the contractor?

   (A) Bad   Ⓐ Ⓑ Ⓒ Ⓓ
   (B) Worried
   (C) Pleased
   (D) Displeased

Always Innovative & Informative

25 Reasons

Most questions about reasons begin with *why*. Sometimes the question can begin with *what*. These questions are generally answered by complete sentences, but sometimes by short phrases. Use the same strategies that you have been using for the other question types.

Problem	The question asks about a reason.
Solution	Look for clues on reasons in the answer choices BEFORE you hear the audio. Listen carefully for those clues.

Examples

If you see or hear these question types, look or listen for answers about a reason. Note that most of the questions begin with *why*.

Common Questions

Why did the man come?   Why is she going by taxi?
Why did the woman come?   Why is he going by train?
Why did the man leave?   Why is she going by car?
Why did the woman leave?

                                                          What does the man say about the delay?
Why does he need a typewriter?
Why does she need a map?   What did she request?

The answers to these questions are usually in complete sentences, but are sometimes in short phrases. If you see or hear answers like these, look or listen for questions about a reason.

Common Answers

He wanted to take a tour.   A taxi is faster than the train.
She wanted to pick up the package.   The train goes directly to New York.

He didn't have a reservation.   It will be only ten more minutes.

He needs to write a letter.   More justification for expenses.
She needs directions to the
    conference.

Exercises

Part 2: Question-Response

Choose the best response to the question.   Ⓐ Ⓑ Ⓒ

Part 3: Conversations

Choose the best answer to the question.

1. Why don't they travel by car?

   (A) It's being repaired.   Ⓐ Ⓑ Ⓒ Ⓓ
   (B) They like to read while traveling.
   (C) The train is cheaper.
   (D) They need to get to work faster.

2. Why does the woman like the train?

   (A) It's comfortable.   Ⓐ Ⓑ Ⓒ Ⓓ
   (B) It's convenient.
   (C) It's never delayed.
   (D) It's fun.

3. Why is the woman traveling today?

   (A) Business   Ⓐ Ⓑ Ⓒ Ⓓ
   (B) A visit to her mother
   (C) Vacation
   (D) A visit to her brother

Part 4: Talks

Choose the best answer to the question.

1. Why is there a delay?

   (A) Workers are staging a work action.   Ⓐ Ⓑ Ⓒ Ⓓ
   (B) The weather is bad.
   (C) There are flight control problems.
   (D) Passengers are boarding slowly.

2. Why should passengers get something to eat now?

   (A) The restaurants will close at midnight.   Ⓐ Ⓑ Ⓒ Ⓓ
   (B) The restaurants won't be open tomorrow.
   (C) There will be no food served on the flight.
   (D) There are some restaurants close to the gate.

3. Why should passengers pay attention
   to the announcements?

   (A) To find out which gate their flight will leave from   Ⓐ Ⓑ Ⓒ Ⓓ
   (B) To hear which restaurants are open
   (C) To keep from getting bored
   (D) To know when it is time to board the flight

TARGET

Measurements

The way things are measured in American English may be different than the way things are measured in British, Canadian, or Australian English. Since the TOEIC is an international test, it is important to understand the different measurement systems that might be encountered on the TOEIC.

Problem	More than one number is given.
Solution	Listen carefully for numbers and words that indicate a mathematical calculation.

You will not have to do mathematical calculations on the TOEIC, but you will be expected to know that *sixty minutes* is *one hour*, a *dozen eggs* means *twelve eggs*, or *two weeks* is *fourteen days*.

Problem	There are numbers in the question.
Solution	Be prepared to give an equivalent measurement.

Examples

Look at these words that express measurements and their equivalents. The first part of the list should be part of your *active* vocabulary: memorize and use these terms and concepts. The second part is *passive*—you need only be familiar with these terms.

Common Measurements—Active

Quantity	
1 dozen	12 units
1 half dozen	6 units

Money	
penny	1 cent
nickel	5 cents
dime	10 cents
quarter	25 cents
half dollar	50 cents
dollar	100 cents

Time

60 seconds	minute
60 minutes	1 hour
24 hours	1 day
noon	12:00 midday
midnight	24:00 in the night

Morning: 6 A.M. to noon

Afternoon: Noon to 6 P.M.

Evening: 6 P.M. to 10 P.M.

Night: 10 P.M. to 6 A.M.

Common Measurements—Passive

Temperature

Fahrenheit	Centigrade
32 degrees	0 degrees
212 degrees (water boils)	100 degrees (water boils)

Distance

foot	meter
1 inch	2.54 centimeters
1 yard	0.9144 meter
1 mile	1.609 kilometers
12 inches	1 foot
3 feet	1 yard

Quantity

1 ounce	28.350 grams
1 pound	453.59237 grams
1 US ton = 2000 pounds	0.907 metric ton of 907 kilograms
1 British ton = 2240 pounds	0.1016 metric ton or 1016 kilograms
1 cup	8 ounces
2 cups	1 pint
4 cups	1 quart
8 cups	1/2 gallon
16 cups	1 gallon

(continued)

Fluid measurement	
1 ounce	29.573 milliliters
1 pint	0.473 liter
1 quart	0.946 liter
1 gallon	3.785 liters
1 imperial gallon	4.55 liters
Dry measurement	
pint	0.551 liter
quart	8.810 liter
Average seasonal weather in the United States	
Spring	March 21 to June 20 (temperate)
Summer	June 21 to September 20 (hot)
Autumn (fall)	September 21 to December 20 (cool)
Winter	December 21 to March 20 (cold)

Look at these words that indicate a mathematical calculation.

Common Mathematical Calculations

twice	100 becomes 200
three times	100 becomes 300
half as much	100 becomes 50
twice as much	100 becomes 200
half as much again	100 becomes 150
half off	100 becomes 50
third off	100 becomes 66.66
10% off	100 becomes 90
per hour	$100 for 6 hours becomes $600
per day	$100 for 3 days becomes $300

 STRATEGY

Although you are not tested on your mathematical ability, you may have to perform simple math calculations. Listen carefully for words that indicate division, multiplication, addition, or subtraction.

You hear: Bob bought a half-dozen eggs.
Question: How many eggs did he buy?
Answer: 6

You hear: The door is 30 inches wide and the window is twice as wide as the door.
Question: How wide is the window?
Answer: 60 inches wide (5 feet wide)

These two examples test your understanding of the words *half*, *dozen*, and *twice*.

Exercises

Part 2: Question-Response

Choose the best response to the question.   Ⓐ Ⓑ Ⓒ

Part 3: Conversations

Choose the best answer to the question.

1. What do they think about the weather?

   (A) It's cool.   Ⓐ Ⓑ Ⓒ Ⓓ
   (B) It's warm.
   (C) It's really cold.
   (D) It's hot.

2. What was the temperature last week?

   (A) Ten degrees   Ⓐ Ⓑ Ⓒ Ⓓ
   (B) Thirteen degrees
   (C) Thirty degrees
   (D) Forty degrees

3. How much snow fell last month?

   (A) Six inches   Ⓐ Ⓑ Ⓒ Ⓓ
   (B) Eight inches
   (C) Twelve inches
   (D) Twenty-four inches

Part 4: Talks

Choose the best answer to the question.

1. What is the potential discount on an order of $200?   Ⓐ Ⓑ Ⓒ Ⓓ

   (A) $10   (C) $20
   (B) $15   (D) $25

2. During a seasonal sale, what would be the price
   of an item that normally costs $200?   Ⓐ Ⓑ Ⓒ Ⓓ

   (A) $25   (C) $160
   (B) $150   (D) $175

3. How much sales tax is charged for a $200 purchase?   Ⓐ Ⓑ Ⓒ Ⓓ

   (A) $5   (C) $25
   (B) $10   (D) $50

TARGET

27 Opinions

Most questions about opinions begin with *what*. These questions are generally answered by complete sentences that begin with *it* or clauses that begin with *that*. Some opinion questions begin with an auxiliary verb like *is/are/was/were, do/does/did, will, can,* etc. Questions that begin with an auxiliary verb are *yes/no* questions, because they are answered with either *yes* or *no*. Use the same strategies here that you used for the other question types.

Problem	The question asks about opinions.
Solution	Look for clues on opinions in the answers BEFORE you hear the audio. Listen carefully for those clues.

Examples

If you see or hear these question types, look or listen for answers about an opinion.

Common Questions

What *questions*

What did the man think about the play?
What did the speaker think about the talk?
What did the woman say about the presentation?
What was the matter with the conference?
What do you think about the new manager?

Yes/No questions

Did you like the movie?
Does she like her new job?

The answers to those questions are usually opinions. If you see or hear answers like these, look or listen for questions that ask about an opinion.

Common Answers

*To **What** questions*

It was too long.
It was boring.
That she is qualified.

*To **Yes/No** questions*

Yes, I did.
Yes, she does.

CD 2
Track
4

Exercises

Part 2: Question-Response

Choose the best response to the question.   Ⓐ Ⓑ Ⓒ

Part 3: Conversations

Choose the best answer to the question.

1. What did they like about the speaker?

    (A) His short presentation
    (B) His humor
    (C) His clothes
    (D) His folks

2. What is the man's opinion of the hotel?

    (A) The décor is nice.
    (B) The food is great.
    (C) The seats are too hard.
    (D) The room is too big.

    Ⓐ Ⓑ Ⓒ Ⓓ

3. What does the woman think of the hotel?

    (A) It's very expensive.
    (B) It's cheaper than she expected.
    (C) The tables are nice.
    (D) It's uncomfortable.

    Ⓐ Ⓑ Ⓒ Ⓓ

Part 4: Talks

Choose the best answer to the question.

1. What kind of a movie is it?

    (A) A short one
    (B) One with four stars
    (C) One without credits
    (D) A sad one

2. What does the speaker say about the movie theater?

    (A) It's too hot.
    (B) It's not very big.
    (C) It's very comfortable.
    (D) The cost is too high.

    Ⓐ Ⓑ Ⓒ Ⓓ

3. What does the speaker say about the theater's
    location?

    (A) It's too far from the subway.
    (B) It's out of town.
    (C) It's very convenient.
    (D) It's not close to restaurants.

    Ⓐ Ⓑ Ⓒ Ⓓ

TARGET
28   Main Topics

Answers to questions are often found among details, but sometimes they are about larger ideas. Questions about the main topic require you to understand the general purpose of the conversation or small talk.

Problem	No specific purpose is evident.
Solution	Look for ideas that indicate the general purpose.

Examples

If you see or hear these question types, look or listen for answers about the main topic. When you see or hear these types of questions, you should look in the answer choices for the overall subject of what you heard. Sometimes the question might ask for the purpose or the speaker of the passage: it might be a safety warning from a firefighter or instructions from the boss.

Common Questions

Who is listening to this information?   What is the subject of the discussion?

Where does this conversation take place?   What problem must be solved?

The answers to those questions are usually about topic, purpose, and speaker. When you see or hear these types of answers, you should look for the overall subject in the answer choices. The answer will not be one that asks for a specific detail.

Common Answers

General categories	Specific examples
A role, job title, or group	A client.
	A ticket clerk.
	The woman's colleagues.
	Airline passengers.
A kind of place or a situation	In an office.
	At a convention.
	During a banquet.
	At an airport.
Any subject	The new machinery.
	Politics.
	Environmental responsibility.
	An advertising campaign.
A summary or implication	The supervisor doesn't agree with the idea.
	They need more time to finish the project.
	A change in the regulations.
	Consumers' confidence in the product.

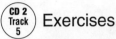

Exercises

Part 2: Question-Response

Choose the best response to the question.　　　Ⓐ Ⓑ Ⓒ

Part 3: Conversations

Choose the best answer to the question.

1. What does the man mean?

   (A) He is a generous person.　　　Ⓐ Ⓑ Ⓒ Ⓓ
   (B) The woman has no shame.
   (C) He needs a loan.
   (D) The woman's clothes are too small.

2. What describes the woman?

   (A) She is careful with money.　　　Ⓐ Ⓑ Ⓒ Ⓓ
   (B) She is generous.
   (C) She is ashamed.
   (D) She is usually helpful.

3. What does the woman think of the man?

   (A) She thinks he has a bad personality.　　　Ⓐ Ⓑ Ⓒ Ⓓ
   (B) She believes he is just.
   (C) She considers him a fake.
   (D) She likes him.

Part 4: Talks

Choose the best answer to the question.

1. What changes are taking place in the company?

   (A) The Board of Directors resigned.　　　Ⓐ Ⓑ Ⓒ Ⓓ
   (B) The Managing Director was fired.
   (C) The workers went on strike.
   (D) All letters will be sent by computer.

2. Who is the speaker addressing?

   (A) Some clients　　　Ⓐ Ⓑ Ⓒ Ⓓ
   (B) His coworkers
   (C) A server
   (D) The director

3. What does the speaker plan to do soon?

   (A) Become a clothes salesman　　　Ⓐ Ⓑ Ⓒ Ⓓ
   (B) Start a business
   (C) Go to college
   (D) Work as a restaurant manager

STRATEGY

Strategy for Analyzing Question Types

Read the answer choices before you hear the audio. Make reasonable assumptions about the choices listed and listen for relevant clues.

Analyzing Language Functions

TARGET

29 Conditionals

You may need to pay attention to *conditional* clauses. There are two kinds of conditional clauses: real conditions and unreal conditions. Real conditions express what is possible. Unreal conditions express something that is not true or not possible. They both contain the marker *if*. Unreal conditions contain the marker *would* in the independent clause.

Problem	You may not be able to tell if the statement is actually true or conditionally true.
Solution	Listen and look for the word *if* and modals such as *will*, *should*, and *would*.

Examples

Real Conditions
If we start by ten, we finish by noon.
If we start by ten, we will finish by noon.
If we start by ten, we will be finished by noon.

Unreal Conditions (Present)
If we started by ten, we would finish by noon.
(but we can't start by ten)

Unreal Conditions (Past)
If we had started by ten, we would have finished by noon.

Exercises

Part 2: Question-Response

Choose the best response to the question. Ⓐ Ⓑ Ⓒ

Part 3: Conversations

Choose the best answer to the question.

1. What should the speakers have done?

   (A) Submitted a budget   Ⓐ Ⓑ Ⓒ Ⓓ
   (B) Asked for more money
   (C) Asked for less money
   (D) Completed the project anyway

2. What does the man want to do now?

   (A) Write another budget   Ⓐ Ⓑ Ⓒ Ⓓ
   (B) Not complete the project
   (C) Wait until next year
   (D) Ask for more time

3. When do they need the money?

   (A) By September   Ⓐ Ⓑ Ⓒ Ⓓ
   (B) By December
   (C) By the first of next year
   (D) By the end of next year

Part 4: Talks

Choose the best answer to the question.

1. What will investors do if stock prices decrease?

   (A) Decrease their holdings   Ⓐ Ⓑ Ⓒ Ⓓ
   (B) Wait until fall
   (C) Change brokers
   (D) Buy at the lowest point

   TIP

   Learn to recognize conditional clauses. Look for *if*.

2. What do inexperienced investors tend to do?

   (A) Wait for prices to hit rock bottom   Ⓐ Ⓑ Ⓒ Ⓓ
   (B) Avoid the stock market
   (C) Read about the market
   (D) Buy high-priced stock

3. How can an investor avoid losing money?

   (A) Pay top dollar for stock   Ⓐ Ⓑ Ⓒ Ⓓ
   (B) Invest during the fall
   (C) Hire a stockbroker
   (D) Share his plans with other investors

For more practice with conditional statements, study the section entitled "Conditional Sentences" on page 238.

First News

Always Innovative & Informative

TARGET

30 Suggestions

On the TOEIC, we usually find answers in the statements. But sometimes the key to the answer is in the question.

Problem	The answer is not in the statements.
Solution	Look for an answer in the suggestion question itself.

Examples

If you see or hear these question types, look or listen for answers about suggestions.

Common Suggestions

Shall we
Why don't we
Perhaps we should
You could always
Let's
Why not
You may/might want to
Maybe we should
What if you
Shouldn't you
You should
If I were you, I'd
If I were in your shoes, I'd
} leave?

How about
What about
Have you ever thought of
Try
} leaving?

The answers to those questions are usually responses to a suggestion. The responses can be positive (*let's go*) or negative (*let's not*). If you see or hear answers like these, look or listen for questions that are suggestions.

Common Answers

Yes, let's.
That's a good idea.
Why not?
Suits me.

What a brilliant idea!
No, I haven't yet.
OK.
Good idea.

 Exercises

Part 2: Question-Response

Choose the best response to the question.   Ⓐ Ⓑ Ⓒ

Part 3: Conversations

Choose the best answer to the question.

1. What does the man suggest the woman do?

   (A) Go last
   (B) Go first
   (C) Have something to drink
   (D) Save money

   Ⓐ Ⓑ Ⓒ Ⓓ

2. Why does he want the woman to do this?

   (A) She needs to use the projector.
   (B) She has a meeting later.
   (C) She's speaking on an important topic.
   (D) She needs to rest.

   Ⓐ Ⓑ Ⓒ Ⓓ

3. What does the woman suggest the man do?

   (A) Allow late arrivals
   (B) Ask people to arrive on time
   (C) Start at 8:00
   (D) Interpret the meeting for her

   Ⓐ Ⓑ Ⓒ Ⓓ

Part 4: Talks

Choose the best answer to the question.

1. What does the man suggest?

   (A) We get a new job.
   (B) We move homes.
   (C) We help the needy.
   (D) We consider four doses.

   Ⓐ Ⓑ Ⓒ Ⓓ

2. How does the speaker suggest listeners get information to do this?

   (A) Call the radio station
   (B) Ask certain individuals
   (C) Visit a website
   (D) Call a charitable organization

   Ⓐ Ⓑ Ⓒ Ⓓ

3. When should listeners do this?

   (A) All year
   (B) On holidays
   (C) Only during warm weather
   (D) Only during cold weather

   Ⓐ Ⓑ Ⓒ Ⓓ

TARGET

31   Offers

When the answer is not in a statement, sometimes it is in an offer. Learn to recognize the words, phrases, and sentences that indicate an offer.

Problem	The answer is not in the statement.
Solution	Look for an offer marker in the question.

Examples

If you see or hear these question types, which begin with these common offer markers, look or listen to see what is being offered.

Common Offers

Let me
Allow me to
Can I
Shall I
Do you want me to
Would you like me to
} carry your books.

The answers to those questions are usually polite responses that accept or decline an offer. If you see or hear answers like these, look or listen for questions that make an offer.

Common Answers
Thank you.
That's very kind of you.
I'd appreciate that.
You're too kind.
No, thanks. I can manage.

 ## Exercises

Part 2: Question-Response

Choose the best response to the question.   Ⓐ Ⓑ Ⓒ

Part 3: Conversations

Choose the best answer to the question.

1. How will they get warm?

    (A) Have some hot coffee   Ⓐ Ⓑ Ⓒ Ⓓ
    (B) Get on the train
    (C) Go back home
    (D) Walk on the platform

2. What does the woman offer the man?

   (A) To fill out a form   Ⓐ Ⓑ Ⓒ Ⓓ
   (B) To change places with him
   (C) To give him some money
   (D) To go inside

3. What does the man offer to get for the woman?

   (A) A newspaper   Ⓐ Ⓑ Ⓒ Ⓓ
   (B) Salt and pepper
   (C) Writing paper
   (D) A new sweater

Part 4: Talks

Choose the best answer to the question.

1. What is being offered?

   (A) First class upgrades   Ⓐ Ⓑ Ⓒ Ⓓ
   (B) Frequent Flyer cards
   (C) Early boarding
   (D) Infant travel seats

2. What will be offered during the flight?

   (A) Three snacks   Ⓐ Ⓑ Ⓒ Ⓓ
   (B) Free refreshments
   (C) New seats
   (D) Playing cards

3. What is offered especially for children?

   (A) A flying class   Ⓐ Ⓑ Ⓒ Ⓓ
   (B) A talk with the flight attendants
   (C) A children's meal
   (D) A visit with the pilot

TARGET

32 Requests

A request is a polite way of asking someone to do something. Learn to recognize requests and the information in them.

Problem	The answer is not in the statements.
Solution	Look for a request marker in the question.

Examples

If you see or hear these question types, which begin with these common request markers, look or listen to see what is being requested.

Common Requests

Can you
May I
Would you
Could you   speak louder?
Do you think you could
How about
Would you mind   speaking louder?

The answers to those questions are usually polite responses that acknowledge a request. If you see or hear answers like these, look or listen for questions that make a request.

Common Answers

Of course.   I'm sorry. I can't.
Is this OK?   Regretfully, no.
No problem.   Not at all. I'd be glad to.

Exercises

Part 2: Question-Response

Choose the best response to the question.   Ⓐ Ⓑ Ⓒ

Part 3: Conversations

Choose the best answer to the question.

1. What did the man ask the woman to do?

   (A) Mail a letter   Ⓐ Ⓑ Ⓒ Ⓓ
   (B) Go to the bank
   (C) Stay home
   (D) Finish a novel

2. What did the woman ask the man to do?

    (A) Cook a meal   Ⓐ Ⓑ Ⓒ Ⓓ
    (B) Sweep the floor
    (C) Close the door
    (D) Sleep on the floor

3. When did she want him to do this?

    (A) Now   Ⓐ Ⓑ Ⓒ Ⓓ
    (B) Today
    (C) Tonight
    (D) On Tuesday

Part 4: Talks

Choose the best answer to the question.

1. What does the speaker request the audience do?

    (A) Stop smoking   Ⓐ Ⓑ Ⓒ Ⓓ
    (B) Stop talking
    (C) Applaud enthusiastically
    (D) Be seated

2. Where is smoking allowed?

    (A) In the seats   Ⓐ Ⓑ Ⓒ Ⓓ
    (B) In the manager's office
    (C) In the reception area
    (D) In the lobby

3. What is the audience requested to do before entering the auditorium?

    (A) Turn the pages   Ⓐ Ⓑ Ⓒ Ⓓ
    (B) Walk slowly
    (C) Turn off cell phones
    (D) Call home

TARGET
33 Restatements

The answer to a question is often a restatement of what you hear in a conversation. Usually the answer restates what you heard in the second or third line of the short conversation in Part III. You will not hear restatements in Part 1 or Part 2.

Problem	The question asks for a restatement.
Solution	Pay attention to synonyms and similar phrases that restate the meaning of a statement.

Examples

Most questions that ask for restatement ask you for an interpretation: *What does the man mean? What does the woman mean? What is the purpose of the letter?*

When you hear these questions, look for a restatement.

Look at these restatements.

Statement: She would rather live in a warm, dry climate.
Restatement: She prefers arid conditions.

Statement: Unlike me, most people don't like to commute by car.
Restatement: I like to drive to work.

Statement: This is the oldest building in the neighborhood and it was built just 2 years ago.
Restatement: The community is relatively new.

Exercises

Part 2: Question-Response

Choose the best response to the question.   Ⓐ Ⓑ Ⓒ

Part 3: Conversations

Choose the best response to the question.

1. What does the woman imply?

    (A) She'll leave if he is not punctual.   Ⓐ Ⓑ Ⓒ Ⓓ
    (B) She'd been waiting a long time.
    (C) She never gets angry.
    (D) She doesn't believe his excuses.

2. What does the man imply?

    (A) He won't be late again.   Ⓐ Ⓑ Ⓒ Ⓓ
    (B) He won't wait for the woman next time.
    (C) He'll get there in five minutes.
    (D) He's bored.

3. What does the woman want the man to do?

    (A) Buy her a wallet   Ⓐ Ⓑ Ⓒ Ⓓ
    (B) Go home
    (C) Pay for her ticket
    (D) Speak to the waiter

Part 4: Talks

Choose the best answer to the question.

1. What is the purpose of the form?

    (A) To make a complaint   Ⓐ Ⓑ Ⓒ Ⓓ
    (B) To borrow money
    (C) To apply for a job
    (D) To get a license

2. How will copies of the form be made?

    (A) Carbon paper   Ⓐ Ⓑ Ⓒ Ⓓ
    (B) Photocopier
    (C) Computer
    (D) Fax machine

3. When will the listener be contacted?

    (A) In two days   Ⓐ Ⓑ Ⓒ Ⓓ
    (B) In four days
    (C) In ten days
    (D) In fourteen days

STRATEGY

Strategy for Analyzing Language Functions

Remember that when the answer is not in the statement, it may be in the question.

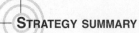

STRATEGY SUMMARY

Strategies to Improve Your Listening Comprehension Score

The following strategies are a review of those presented in this Listening Comprehension Review. Using these strategies will improve your score on the TOEIC.

Problems Analyzing Photographs

- When you look at the photo, analyze the people. Determine their number, gender, location, occupation, etc.
- Look for context clues in the photo.
- Listen for the meaning of the *whole sentence* to determine which choice best matches the photo.
- Try to analyze every detail in the photograph.
- Try to describe these details in English to yourself.
- Listen to all answers until you hear the obviously correct one. Once you are sure, don't listen to the rest of the answer options. Start analyzing the next photograph.
- If you aren't sure, keep your pencil on the most likely correct answer. If you listen to all options and have no other choice, mark that answer and move on quickly.

Problems Analyzing Answer Choices

- Listen and look for context clues.
- Listen and look for the *meaning* of the statement, question, and answer choices. Do not be confused by words with similar sounds, homonyms, and related words.
- Listen and look for sequence time markers, negative markers, and comparison markers.
- Pay attention to word order.
- Listen and look for modals and determine how the modal affects the meaning.
- Rephrase the question you hear. This will help you find the unique answer.
- Listen carefully to the entire question and ALL the answer choices before making a final decision.

Problems Analyzing Question Types

- Learn to recognize types of questions. Study the common questions and common answers presented in this chapter. Remember that questions about people generally begin with *who* or *what*, questions about location generally begin with *where*, questions about time generally begin with *when* or *how long*, etc.
- Read the answer choices, make assumptions about the items listed, and listen for relevant clues.

Problems Analyzing Language Functions

- Learn to recognize conditional clauses. Look for *if* and a modal.
- Look for suggestions, offer markers, and request markers in the question. Remember that when the answer is not in the statement, it may be in the question.

Strategies for Conversations and Talks

- Focus on the question. Read the three questions before you hear the talk. Don't read the answer choices. Try to listen carefully for the answer.
- As the conversations and talks start, write your potential answer choices in the exam book.
- Focusing on the details of the talk will also help you with inference and main idea questions.

Many thanks to my readers, especially Jean-Pierre Saint-Aimé, who have provided valuable tips on test-taking strategies.

Mini-Test
Answer Sheet

Mini-Test for Listening Comprehension

PART 1: PHOTOGRAPHS

1. Ⓐ Ⓑ Ⓒ Ⓓ   4. Ⓐ Ⓑ Ⓒ Ⓓ   7. Ⓐ Ⓑ Ⓒ Ⓓ   10. Ⓐ Ⓑ Ⓒ Ⓓ
2. Ⓐ Ⓑ Ⓒ Ⓓ   5. Ⓐ Ⓑ Ⓒ Ⓓ   8. Ⓐ Ⓑ Ⓒ Ⓓ
3. Ⓐ Ⓑ Ⓒ Ⓓ   6. Ⓐ Ⓑ Ⓒ Ⓓ   9. Ⓐ Ⓑ Ⓒ Ⓓ

PART 2: QUESTION-RESPONSE

11. Ⓐ Ⓑ Ⓒ   15. Ⓐ Ⓑ Ⓒ   19. Ⓐ Ⓑ Ⓒ   23. Ⓐ Ⓑ Ⓒ
12. Ⓐ Ⓑ Ⓒ   16. Ⓐ Ⓑ Ⓒ   20. Ⓐ Ⓑ Ⓒ   24. Ⓐ Ⓑ Ⓒ
13. Ⓐ Ⓑ Ⓒ   17. Ⓐ Ⓑ Ⓒ   21. Ⓐ Ⓑ Ⓒ   25. Ⓐ Ⓑ Ⓒ
14. Ⓐ Ⓑ Ⓒ   18. Ⓐ Ⓑ Ⓒ   22. Ⓐ Ⓑ Ⓒ

PART 3: CONVERSATIONS

26. Ⓐ Ⓑ Ⓒ Ⓓ   30. Ⓐ Ⓑ Ⓒ Ⓓ   34. Ⓐ Ⓑ Ⓒ Ⓓ   38. Ⓐ Ⓑ Ⓒ Ⓓ
27. Ⓐ Ⓑ Ⓒ Ⓓ   31. Ⓐ Ⓑ Ⓒ Ⓓ   35. Ⓐ Ⓑ Ⓒ Ⓓ   39. Ⓐ Ⓑ Ⓒ Ⓓ
28. Ⓐ Ⓑ Ⓒ Ⓓ   32. Ⓐ Ⓑ Ⓒ Ⓓ   36. Ⓐ Ⓑ Ⓒ Ⓓ   40. Ⓐ Ⓑ Ⓒ Ⓓ
29. Ⓐ Ⓑ Ⓒ Ⓓ   33. Ⓐ Ⓑ Ⓒ Ⓓ   37. Ⓐ Ⓑ Ⓒ Ⓓ

PART 4: TALKS

41. Ⓐ Ⓑ Ⓒ Ⓓ   44. Ⓐ Ⓑ Ⓒ Ⓓ   47. Ⓐ Ⓑ Ⓒ Ⓓ   50. Ⓐ Ⓑ Ⓒ Ⓓ
42. Ⓐ Ⓑ Ⓒ Ⓓ   45. Ⓐ Ⓑ Ⓒ Ⓓ   48. Ⓐ Ⓑ Ⓒ Ⓓ   51. Ⓐ Ⓑ Ⓒ Ⓓ
43. Ⓐ Ⓑ Ⓒ Ⓓ   46. Ⓐ Ⓑ Ⓒ Ⓓ   49. Ⓐ Ⓑ Ⓒ Ⓓ   52. Ⓐ Ⓑ Ⓒ Ⓓ

Mini-Test for Listening Comprehension Parts 1, 2, 3, and 4

Part 1: Photographs

Directions: You will see a photograph. You will hear four statements about the photograph. Choose the statement that most closely matches the photograph and fill in the corresponding oval on your answer sheet.

See page 111 for the Answer Key and page 127 for the Explanatory Answers for this Mini-Test.

1.

2.

3.

4.

5.

6.

7.

8.

9.

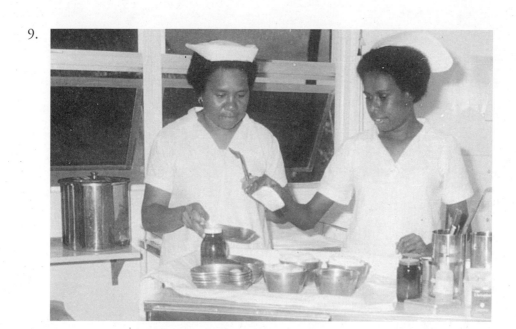

10.

Part 2: Question-Response

Directions: You will hear a question and three possible responses. Choose the response that most closely answers the question and fill in the corresponding oval on your answer sheet.

11. Mark your answer on your answer sheet.

12. Mark your answer on your answer sheet.

13. Mark your answer on your answer sheet.

14. Mark your answer on your answer sheet.

15. Mark your answer on your answer sheet.

16. Mark your answer on your answer sheet.

17. Mark your answer on your answer sheet.

18. Mark your answer on your answer sheet.

19. Mark your answer on your answer sheet.

20. Mark your answer on your answer sheet.

21. Mark your answer on your answer sheet.

22. Mark your answer on your answer sheet.

23. Mark your answer on your answer sheet.

24. Mark your answer on your answer sheet.

25. Mark your answer on your answer sheet.

Part 3: Conversations

Directions: You will hear a conversation between two people. You will see three questions on each conversation and four possible answers. Choose the best answer to each question and fill in the corresponding oval on your answer sheet.

26. What are the speakers going to do?

    (A) View some art
    (B) Play tennis
    (C) Go to the theater
    (D) See a movie

27. What time do they have to be there?

    (A) 2:00
    (B) 5:00
    (C) 6:00
    (D) 7:00

28. What is the weather?

    (A) Sunny
    (B) Icy
    (C) Rainy
    (D) Snowing

29. What does the woman want to discuss at the meeting?

    (A) Planes
    (B) Lunch plans
    (C) A conference
    (D) Ordering office supplies

30. When will the speakers meet?

    (A) Sunday
    (B) Monday
    (C) Tuesday
    (D) Friday

31. Where will the speakers meet?

    (A) At the woman's office
    (B) At the man's office
    (C) At a restaurant
    (D) At a café

32. Why is the man exchanging the shirt?

    (A) It's the wrong size.
    (B) It's the wrong color.
    (C) It has a hole.
    (D) Its sleeves are too long.

33. What size shirt does the man want?

    (A) 8
    (B) 15
    (C) 16
    (D) 18

34. What color shirt does he want?

    (A) White
    (B) Black
    (C) Green
    (D) Blue

35. When does the man have his vacation?

    (A) Spring
    (B) Summer
    (C) Fall
    (D) Winter

36. Where does the woman suggest he go?

    (A) New York
    (B) Paris
    (C) Florida
    (D) Hawaii

37. How many weeks is the man's vacation?

    (A) One
    (B) Two
    (C) Three
    (D) Four

38. Where was the man this morning?

(A) At his desk
(B) At the store
(C) In a meeting
(D) In the supply closet

39. How many messages did he get?

(A) Four
(B) Seven
(C) Eleven
(D) Forty-two

40. What does he want the woman to do?

(A) Answer the messages
(B) Buy something
(C) Order some supplies
(D) Bring him a form

Part 4: Talks

CD 2 Track 14

Directions: You will hear a talk given by a single speaker. You will see three questions on each talk, each with four possible answers. Choose the best answer to each question and fill in the corresponding oval on your answer sheet.

41. What is the current temperature?

    (A) 3 degrees
    (B) 15 degrees
    (C) 50 degrees
    (D) 53 degrees

42. What should people take to work in the morning?

    (A) Snow boots
    (B) Luggage
    (C) Sunscreen
    (D) Umbrellas

43. When will the weather clear up?

    (A) By 6:00 A.M
    (B) By noon
    (C) By late afternoon
    (D) By early evening

44. Why is power being turned off?

    (A) To reduce total demand
    (B) To save money
    (C) To make it cooler
    (D) To make the city pay its bill

45. How long will power be off?

    (A) Longer than two hours
    (B) Less than two hours
    (C) For one day
    (D) Until the weather changes

46. How can a customer get more information?

    (A) Go online
    (B) Call the company
    (C) Visit the company
    (D) Listen to the radio

47. Where does this announcement take place?

    (A) On a tour bus
    (B) At the shore
    (C) In a cocktail lounge
    (D) On a ship

48. What is required for the first excursion?

    (A) A hearty breakfast
    (B) Some beautiful clothes
    (C) A ticket
    (D) A health report

49. What time will the first excursion begin?

    (A) 4:00
    (B) 7:30
    (C) 9:00
    (D) 9:30

50. What is being offered?

    (A) A television
    (B) A radio
    (C) A video recorder
    (D) A remote control device

51. How can a consumer learn more?

    (A) Have a salesperson call at home
    (B) Visit their office
    (C) Call a toll-free number
    (D) Read an electronic magazine

52. When can a consumer get a free magazine subscription?

    (A) Today only
    (B) Tuesday only
    (C) Anytime this month
    (D) After the end of this month

First News
Always Innovative & Informative

Answer Key for Listening Comprehension— Targets 1–33

Explanatory Answers can be found beginning on page 112.

ANALYZING PHOTOGRAPHS

Target	Part 1
Target 1 Assumptions	(B)
Target 2 People	(A)
Target 3 Things	(A)
Target 4 Actions	(D)
Target 5 General Locations	(B)
Target 6 Specific Locations	(A)

ANALYZING ANSWER CHOICES

Target	Part 1	Part 2	Part 3	Part 4
Target 7 Similar Sounds				
1.	(D)	(A)	(D)	(C)
2.			(D)	(A)
3.			(A)	(C)
Target 8 Related Words				
1.	(B)	(A)	(B)	(D)
2.			(A)	(D)
3.			(C)	(A)
Target 9 Homonyms				
1.	(A)	(A)	(C)	(B)
2.			(C)	(D)
3.			(B)	(A)
Target 10 Same Sound and Same Spelling But Different Meaning				
1.	(B)	(B)	(A)	(B)
2.			(B)	(C)
3.			(C)	(B)
Target 11 Time				
1.	(A)	(A)	(D)	(C)
2.			(A)	(A)
3.			(C)	(C)
Target 12 Negation				
1.	(C)	(A)	(A)	(A)
2.			(A)	(B)
3.			(C)	(A)
Target 13 Word Order				
1.	(C)	(C)	(B)	(D)
2.			(C)	(D)
3.			(D)	(C)

Target	Part 1	Part 2	Part 3	Part 4
Target 14 Comparisons				
1.	(A)	(A)	(C)	(B)
2.			(B)	(A)
3.			(C)	(C)
Target 15 Modals				
1.	(D)	(A)	(A)	(B)
2.			(D)	(A)
3.			(C)	(C)
Target 16 *Used to*				
1.	(A)	(A)	(B)	(A)
2.			(D)	(A)
3.			(B)	(C)

ANALYZING QUESTION TYPES

Target	Part 2	Part 3	Part 4
Target 17 People			
1.	(A)	(B)	(B)
2.		(B)	(B)
3.		(A)	(C)
Target 18 Occupations			
1.	(A)	(D)	(A)
2.		(D)	(D)
3.		(C)	(C)
Target 19 Speakers' Relationship			
1.	(B)	(C)	(A)
2.		(B)	(C)
3.		(B)	(A)
Target 20 Location			
1.	(A)	(C)	(B)
2.		(A)	(C)
3.		(D)	(B)
Target 21 Time			
1.	(A)	(C)	(B)
2.		(B)	(A)
3.		(D)	(B)
Target 22 Activities			
1.	(B)	(D)	(D)
2.		(C)	(C)
3.		(D)	(B)

Target	Part 2	Part 3	Part 4
Target 23 Events or Facts			
1.	**(A)**	**(A)**	**(C)**
2.		**(A)**	**(C)**
3.		**(C)**	**(C)**
Target 24 Emotions			
1.	**(A)**	**(A)**	**(B)**
2.		**(D)**	**(D)**
3.		**(A)**	**(C)**
Target 25 Reasons			
1.	**(B)**	**(B)**	**(A)**
2.		**(B)**	**(A)**
3.		**(C)**	**(D)**
Target 26 Measurements			
1.	**(A)**	**(C)**	**(C)**
2.		**(D)**	**(B)**
3.		**(A)**	**(B)**
Target 27 Opinions			
1.	**(A)**	**(B)**	**(D)**
2.		**(B)**	**(C)**
3.		**(A)**	**(C)**
Target 28 Main Topics			
1.	**(B)**	**(C)**	**(B)**
2.		**(A)**	**(B)**
3.		**(D)**	**(B)**

ANALYZING LANGUAGE FUNCTIONS

Target	Part 2	Part 3	Part 4
Target 29 Conditionals			
1.	**(A)**	**(C)**	**(D)**
2.		**(A)**	**(D)**
3.		**(A)**	**(C)**
Target 30 Suggestions			
1.	**(C)**	**(B)**	**(C)**
2.		**(C)**	**(C)**
3.		**(B)**	**(A)**
Target 31 Offers			
1.	**(C)**	**(A)**	**(C)**
2.		**(C)**	**(B)**
3.		**(A)**	**(D)**
Target 32 Requests			
1.	**(A)**	**(A)**	**(D)**
2.		**(B)**	**(D)**
3.		**(B)**	**(C)**
Target 33 Restatements			
1.	**(A)**	**(A)**	**(B)**
2.		**(A)**	**(A)**
3.		**(C)**	**(D)**

Answer Key for Mini-Test for Listening Comprehension Parts 1, 2, 3, and 4

Explanatory Answers are on page 127.

PART 1: PHOTOGRAPHS

1. **(C)**	3. **(C)**	5. **(A)**	7. **(A)**	9. **(D)**
2. **(D)**	4. **(A)**	6. **(D)**	8. **(B)**	10. **(A)**

PART 2: QUESTION-RESPONSE

11. **(B)**	14. **(B)**	17. **(A)**	20. **(C)**	23. **(A)**
12. **(A)**	15. **(A)**	18. **(C)**	21. **(A)**	24. **(B)**
13. **(C)**	16. **(B)**	19. **(A)**	22. **(C)**	25. **(C)**

PART 3: CONVERSATIONS

26. **(C)**	29. **(C)**	32. **(A)**	35. **(C)**	38. **(C)**
27. **(D)**	30. **(C)**	33. **(D)**	36. **(D)**	39. **(B)**
28. **(C)**	31. **(B)**	34. **(D)**	37. **(A)**	40. **(D)**

PART 4: TALKS

41. **(D)**	44. **(A)**	47. **(D)**	50. **(D)**
42. **(D)**	45. **(B)**	48. **(C)**	51. **(C)**
43. **(B)**	46. **(A)**	49. **(C)**	52. **(C)**

Explanatory Answers for Listening Comprehension—Targets 1–33

ANALYZING PHOTOGRAPHS

Target 1 Assumptions

(B) In Choice (B) you can assume from the context that the people in white laboratory coats are technicians and that they could be doing experiments. Choice (A) is incorrect because the photo shows several people who could be pharmacists but none who could be customers. Choice (C) is incorrect because there are no laboratory animals pictured. Choice (D) is incorrect because the shelves contain bottles, jars and supplies.

Target 2 People

(A) Choice (A) correctly identifies the number and activity of the people. Choice (B) is incorrect because the men are in shirt sleeves. Choice (C) is incorrect because one woman is not as tall as the men. Choice (D) is incorrect because one of the women is pointing to the map.

Target 3 Things

(A) Choice (A) correctly identifies the location of the people (the floor), who they are (the children), and their activity (playing). Choice (B) is incorrect because the television is on. Choice (C) is incorrect because the mother is playing the piano. Choice (D) is incorrect because the curtains are shut.

Target 4 Actions

(D) Choice (D) correctly describes what the people (workers) are doing (laying pipeline). Choice (A) is incorrect because the men are *laying pipe,* not *smoking pipes.* Choice (B) identifies an incorrect action. Choice (C) identifies a *previous* action.

Target 5 General Locations

(B) Choice (B) assumes that the people are passengers and are passing through a security checkpoint. Choice (A) incorrectly identifies the scene as a store. Choice (C) incorrectly identifies the scene as a bank. Choice (D) takes place on the plane, not at airport security.

Target 6 Specific Locations

(A) Choice (A) correctly identifies the specific location of the waiters. Choice (B) incorrectly identifies the location of the man; he is *across* from the woman. Choice (C) incorrectly identifies the location of the bottle; it's *on* the table. Choice (D) incorrectly identifies the location of the other table; it's *behind* the first table, so the people are also *behind* the first table.

ANALYZING ANSWER CHOICES

Target 7 Similar Sounds

PART 1: PHOTOGRAPHS

(D) Choice (D) is correct because the other choices do not match the picture. Choice (A) has similar sounds: *fair/air* and *night/flight.* Choice (B) has similar sounds: *plane/train.* Choice (C) has similar sounds: *car door/cargo.* Listen for the meaning of the whole sentence; note the context clues in the picture.

PART 2: QUESTION-RESPONSE

(A) Choice (A) answers the *yes/no* question with *Yes.* Choice (B) has related words: *delivery/truck* and similar sounds: *letter/ladder, delivered/delivery.* Choice (C) has similar sounds: *today/Tuesday; Was the/was he.* Listen for the whole meaning; note the grammar clue such as a *yes/no* question that begins with the auxiliary *was.*

PART 3: CONVERSATIONS

1. **(D)** *Sailing her boat* in Choice (D) matches the second line of the conversation: The woman is really having fun sailing her boat. Choice (A) has similar sounds: *boat/boots.* Choice (B) has similar sounds: *fun/phone.*

Choice (C) has similar sounds: *selling/sailing.* Listen for the meaning of the whole conversation; note the context clues such as *boat* and *sailing.*

2. **(D)** The man suggests getting together on Tuesday for a boat ride. Choices (A) and (B) sound similar to the correct answer. Choice (C) has similar sounds: *Sunday/someday.*

3. **(A)** The woman says that it is rainy today. Choice (B) has similar sounds: *sun/fun.* Choice (C) has similar sounds: *cold/old.* Choice (D) repeats the word *clear.*

PART 4: TALKS

1. **(C)** Before shoppers leave the store, they must pass through the check-out counters to pay for their purchases. Choice (A) has similar sounds: *market/mark all.* Choice (B) has similar sounds: *closing/clothes.* Choice (D) has similar sounds: *proceed/plant seed.* Listen for the meaning of the whole talk; note the context clues such as *shoppers, market, check-out.*

2. **(A)** The announcer says that the market will close in 15 minutes, so shoppers should leave the store by then. Choices (B), (C), and (D) sound similar to the correct answer.

3. **(C)** The announcer says *...the store will be closed tomorrow because of the holiday.* Choice (A) has similar sounds: *be open* and *reopen.* Choice (B) has similar sounds: *clothes* and *close.* Choice (D) has similar sounds: *money* and *Monday.*

Target 8 Related Words

PART 1: PHOTOGRAPHS

(B) The context clues in the picture indicate the people are engaged in skiing on a mountain. Choice (A) has the related words: *shoveling snow/snow.* Choice (C) has the related words: *iceberg/ice, cold.* Choice (D) has similar sounds: *skiers' poles/polls.* Listen for the meaning of the whole sentence; note the context clues in the picture.

PART 2: QUESTION-RESPONSE

(A) Listen for the whole meaning; note the grammar clue: *How long* and the verb *married* suggests

a length of time. Choice (A) gives the appropriate answer (ten years) to *how long.* Choice (B) has the related words: *long/five feet,* but the question refers to time, not distance. Choice (C) has the related words: *married/bride.*

PART 3: CONVERSATIONS

1. **(B)** Listen for the meaning of the whole conversation; note the context clues such as *seatbelt, to land,* and *in the air.* These words suggest air travel. Choice (A), a car, also has *seat belts,* but it does not agree with the context. Choice (C) has similar sounds: *seat* and *sea* and related words: *land* (v)/ *land* (n). Choice (D) has the related word *bus* but does not fit the context.

2. **(A)** The man says *return to your seat.* Choice (B) is related to *seat,* but is the opposite of what the man asks the woman to do. Choice (C) is also related to *seat.* Choice (D) repeats the word *air* out of context.

3. **(C)** The woman says that she doesn't want to *fall down in the aisle.* Choice (A) is related to *air.* Choice (B) is related to *return to your seat.* Choice (D) repeats the word *land.*

PART 4: TALKS

1. **(D)** The correct answer is given in the first few words of the talk. Note the context clues such as *weather, weekend,* and *temperature.* Choice (A) has the related word *sporting,* but only *golf* is mentioned briefly. Choice (B) has related words: *chores/repairs.* Choice (C) has related words: *gardening/garden center.*

2. **(D)** The announcer suggests outdoor activities such as playing golf and gardening because the weather will be nice. Choice (A) is related to *rain,* which is the predicted weather for Monday. Choice (B) is related to *golf.* Choice (C) is related to *gardening.*

3. **(A)** The announcer says that it will rain. Choice (B) relates *work* to *commute.* Choice (C) relates *traffic lights* to *traffic.* Choice (D) relates *golf tournament* to *golf.*

Target 9 Homonyms

PART 1: PHOTOGRAPHS

(A) The location of the people and their movement suggests they are commuters, people who travel from home to work. We can assume they're in a hurry and rushing. Choice (B) has similar sounds: *train/trained*. Choice (C) has homonyms: *boarding* windows/*boarding* train. Choice (D) has homonyms: *stare/stairs*. Listen for the meaning of the whole sentence; note the context clues in the picture.

PART 2: QUESTION-RESPONSE

(A) The tag question *doesn't he?* requires a *yes/no* answer. Choice (A) answers the question and tells when he will leave. Choice (B) has homonyms: *week/weak*. Choice (C) has homonyms: *leaves* (v)/ *leaves* (n).

PART 3: CONVERSATIONS

1. **(C)** Listen for the meaning of the whole conversation; note the context clues such as *sew, button,* and *don't have time*. Choice (C) means the same as the man's excuse: *I don't have time now*. Choice (A) has homonyms: *sew/sow* and similar sounds: *to wait/too wet*. Choice (B) has homonyms: *time/thyme*. Choice (D) has homonyms: *for/four*.

2. **(C)** The woman complains that there is a hole on the sleeve of her jacket. Choice (A) confuses the homonyms *whole* and *hole*. Choice (B) repeats the word *small*; it is the hole, not the jacket, that is small. Choice (D) confuses the homonyms *where* and *wear*.

3. **(B)** The man says he will help her after *I get home from work tomorrow*. Choice (A) confuses the homonyms *weight* and *wait*. Choice (B) confuses *work* and *work out*. Choice (D) confuses the meaning of run as a form of exercise with *run* (operate) a machine.

PART 4: TALKS

1. **(B)** Listen for the meaning of the whole talk; note the context clues such as *sun, rain,* and *spring weather*. These clues indicate the weather. Choice (A) has homonyms: *weather/whether; by/buy; too/two* and similar sounds: *winds, too/windows*. Choice (C) has homonyms: *sun/son*. Choice (D) has homonyms: *rain/reign* and similar sounds: *spring/king*.

2. **(D)** The speaker says that it will get cold tonight so there may be snow tomorrow morning. Choice (A) has the homonyms: *mourning/morning*. Choice (B) has homonyms: *fare/fair*. Choice (C) has homonyms: *flour/flower*.

3. **(A)** The speaker says *Tune in at 1:00 for the next update*. Choice (B) has homonyms: *two/to*. Choice (C) has homonyms: *four/for*. Choice (D) has similar sounds: *eight* and *update*.

Target 10 Same Sound and Same Spelling But Different Meaning

PART 1: PHOTOGRAPHS

(B) The correct answer is (B), which describes a first-class airline cabin. In Choice (A) *class* means *instructional period*. In Choice (C) *class* means *socioeconomic level*. In Choice (D) *classified* means *restricted*.

PART 2: QUESTION-RESPONSE

(B) The phrase in (B) *Not for me* is a *no* answer to the *yes/no* question. It means, *No, the bed is not too hard for me. A hard* bed is a *firm* bed. Choice (A) incorrectly interprets *hard* to mean *difficult*. In Choice (C) *bed* means *a place for flowers*.

PART 3: CONVERSATIONS

1. **(A)** The correct answer is (A). *To ring* someone is *to call* them on the phone. In Choice (B) *ring* means *jewelry*. The related word here, *engagement*, comes from the incorrect assumption that a *bachelor* may be getting engaged or married. Choice (C) has related words: *summer vacation*. Choice (D) repeats the word *call*, but does not fit the context of the conversation.

2. **(B)** The man says he wants to ring the woman to talk about going on a dinner date.

Choice (A) uses the word *date* with the meaning of *particular day*. Choice (C) incorrectly interprets *hard* to mean *difficult* and repeats the word *job*. Choice (D) uses the word *rest* to mean *remainder*, instead of *relax*.

3. **(C)** The woman says that she will be busy next week. Choice (A) uses the word *fall(fell)* to mean *go down*, rather than a season of the year. Choice (B) uses *working* to mean *operating* rather than *do a job*. Choice (D) confuses *weak* with its homonym *week*.

PART 4: TALKS

1. **(B)** The word *tennis* is the first word in the talk. There are other context clues such as *final match* and *championship match*. Choice (A) interprets *match* to mean *marriage*. Choice (C) confuses *night club* with *tennis club*. Choice (D) interprets *match* to mean *a light for a cigarette*.

2. **(C)** The announcer says that *prizes will be awarded* in the evening. Choice (A) interprets *class* to mean *a place to learn*. Choice (B) interprets *court* to mean *a place for trials*. Choice (D) interprets *watch* to mean *timepiece*.

3. **(B)** The announcer says that the next tournament will begin *next month*. Choice (A) is when the final match of the current tournament will take place. Choice (C) interprets *may* to mean the *name of a month*. Choice (D) interprets *spring* to mean a *season of the year*.

Target 11 Time

PART 1: PHOTOGRAPHS

(A) Only Choice (A) matches the tense of the question. The question is in the past tense. Choice (B) indicates future action. Choice (C) indicates action happening at the same time.

PART 2: QUESTION-RESPONSE

(A) Only (A) answers the statement about time. Choice (B) refers to cost. Choice (C) uses the associated word *timed* and repeats the word *already*.

PART 3: CONVERSATIONS

1. **(D)** The speakers will proofread the proposal first. Choice (A) is not mentioned. Choice (B) is the second thing they will do. Choice (C) is the third thing they will do.

2. **(A)** The woman wants to eat lunch before proofreading because she is hungry and tired. Choice (B) is the man's suggestion. Choices (C) and (D) confuse *directions* with *director*.

3. **(C)** The last thing they will do is submit the proposal to the director. Choice (A) confuses *edit* with the similar-sounding word *submit*. Choice (B) confuses *golf course* with *of course*. Choice (A) repeats *Mr. Kim* and *lunch*.

PART 4: TALKS

1. **(C)** The company merged with Rotel five years ago. At that time, Mr. Saleh became Chairman. Choice (A) confuses *retiring at the end of next quarter* with *duration of office* and does not use an appropriate time marker. Choice (B) indicates time with the company, not time as Chairman. Choice (D) indicates future action (happening at the same time as a future retirement).

2. **(A)** Before Mr. Saleh leaves the company, he will attend his retirement party. Choices (B) and (C) are things he will do after he retires. Choice (D) is confused with the merger between his company and Rotel International, which happened several years ago.

3. **(C)** Mr. Saleh planned to open a small business before he started working at Mercury Corporation. Choice (A) happened after he had worked at Mercury Corporation for several years. Choice (B) happened after he made his plan to open a business. Choice (D) happened after all the other choices.

Target 12 Negation

PART 1: PHOTOGRAPHS

(C) Only Choice (C) matches the picture. The negative expressions in the other choices make the statements false. Choice (A) is incorrect because the seats *are* occupied. Choice (B) is incorrect

because the men *are* sitting down. Choice (D) is incorrect because one person is wearing glasses.

PART 2: QUESTION-RESPONSE

(A) A law-abiding citizen does not do anything illegal. Everything they do is legal because they obey the law. Choice (B) has negative/positive related words: *illegal/legal.* Choice (C) has negative terms with similar sounds: *illegal/illegible.*

PART 3: CONVERSATIONS

1. **(A)** In Choice (A), *You can never take too much* means *you should take a lot.* Choices (B) and (D) are contradicted by *I even have what I don't need.* Choice (C) is incorrect because she is *taking* what she needs, not *buying* it.

2. **(A)** The woman says *I can't say that I disagree with you,* meaning that she agrees with him. Choices (B) and (D) repeat the word *disagree.* Choice (C) repeats the phrase *can't say.*

3. **(C)** The woman says *I seldom travel with fewer than three suitcases,* meaning she usually travels with three or more. Choice (A) confuses *two* with *too.* Choice (B) repeats the phrase *fewer than three.* Choice (D) confuses *seven* with the similar-sounding word *even.*

PART 4: TALKS

1. **(A)** All of the adjectives in the report are very positive. Choice (B) is incorrect because the adjectives in the report are positive, not negative. Choice (C) is incorrect because the report is *enthusiastic,* not *unenthusiastic.* Choice (D) is incorrect because the report is *positive,* not *mediocre.*

2. **(B)** The report attributes the success of the company to *the selfless dedication of our employees.* Choice (A) confuses *selfish* with *selfless.* Choice (C) confuses *unsuccessful* with *success.* Choice (D) confuses *unimaginative* with *unimaginable.*

3. **(A)** The speaker says *I can't tell you how pleased I am about this.* Choice (B) is confused with *...we will do what has never been done before,* meaning that this is the first ban-

quet. Choice (C) is confused with *... I hope no one will be unable to attend,* meaning he hopes everyone will attend. Choice (D) is confused with *I can't think of anyone who deserves this honor more...,* meaning these employees deserve it more than anyone else.

Target 13 Word Order

PART 1: PHOTOGRAPHS

(C) Only Choice (C) matches the picture. Choice (A) reverses the subject and the verb, but there are no brochures in the picture. Choice (B) does not describe the picture. Choice (D) is contradicted by the picture.

PART 2: QUESTION-RESPONSE

(C) *Nobody does as much as you* means *You do more than anybody else.* Choice (A) is almost a paraphrase, not a response. Choice (B) is not an appropriate response to a compliment.

PART 3: CONVERSATIONS

1. **(B)** *Isn't that great* means *that is really GREAT!* Choice (A) is incorrect because the speakers don't mention the length of the trip. Choice (C) is contradicted by *How I envy you!* Choice (D) is contradicted by *Isn't that great!*

2. **(C)** The woman exclaims *How beautiful Europe is this time of year!* Choice (A) uses *time* to mean length of time instead of *season of the year.* Choice (B) is the opposite of what the woman says. Choice (D) confuses *hot* with the similar-sounding word *not.*

3. **(D)** The woman asks *Are you leaving soon?* Choices (A), (B), and (C) use *who* and *how* as question words rather than as parts of exclamations.

PART 4: TALKS

1. **(D)** *It has never been so windy* means *it is very windy.* Choice (A) is contradicted by *How the weather changes!* Choice (B) is contradicted by *The temperature has fallen.* Choice (C) is contradicted by *It has never been so windy.*

2. **(D)** The speaker says *Never has it rained as hard as it did last night!* Choice (A) is when the weather was hot and sunny. Choice (B) is when the temperature began to fall. Choice (C) confuses *afternoon* with the similar-sounding word *noon*.

3. **(C)** The woman says *What a confusing week!* Choice (A) is the opposite meaning of what the woman says: *Never have I seen stranger weather.* Choice (B) is how people usually feel about the weather this time of year. Choice (D) is what the speaker says the weather usually is.

Target 14 Comparisons

PART 1: PHOTOGRAPHS

(A) The man on the right is trying on clothes to wear in extremely cold weather. Choice (B) is incorrect because only one man is wearing glasses. Choice (C) is incorrect because both have beards. Choice (D) is incorrect because one pair of pants is a dark shade and the other is a light shade.

PART 2: QUESTION-RESPONSE

(A) Choice (A) repeats the superlative *fastest* and provides an answer: *a train*. Choice (B) has related words: *fastest/plane* and similar sounds: *home/Rome*, but does not answer the question. Choice (C) has similar sounds: *fastest/farther*, but does not answer the question.

PART 3: CONVERSATIONS

1. **(C)** The meeting was *the longest* and *the most boring*. Choice (A) is contradicted by *will never end, is longer than yesterday's*, and for being *the longest*. Choice (B) is incorrect because *the lecture has begun*. Choice (D) is contradicted by *will never end*.

2. **(B)** The woman says about today's meeting *It's even longer than yesterday's*; therefore yesterday's meeting was shorter. Choice (A) is incorrect because today's meeting is longer. Choices (C) and (D) are incorrect because today's meeting, according to the man, is the most boring.

3. **(C)** The woman says *the longer the meeting, the more tired I get*. Choice (A) is confused with the fact that they mention more than one meeting. Choice (B) repeats *wake up*. Choice (D) repeats the phrase *the meeting is over*.

PART 4: TALKS

1. **(B)** The better the roads, the more drivers there are. More drivers means more cars. Choice (A) is contradicted by *there never used to be as many cars* and *more people want to drive*. Choice (C) is contradicted by *the more cars there will be*. Choice (D) is contradicted by *as we improve the roads*.

2. **(A)** The speaker says *The higher the price of gasoline, the smaller cars get*. Choice (B) is a true statement but is not the reason given for smaller cars. Choice (C) repeats the word *smaller*, but it is cars, not roads, that will get smaller. Choice (D) is confused with the price of gasoline getting high.

3. **(C)** The speaker says *If you want to get somewhere quickly, you still have to go by plane*. Choice (A) is incorrect because the price of a plane ticket is cheaper than it used to be, not cheaper than a car trip. Choice (B) repeats the word *bigger*, but it is cars, not planes, that are bigger. Choice (D) repeats the word *crowded*, but it is roads, not planes or cars, that are crowded.

Target 15 Modals

PART 1: PHOTOGRAPHS

(D) We can assume that the people standing in line are waiting to check in. They *will* check in; they have not already checked in. Choice (A) is possible but it is not <u>directly</u> related to the picture and is not as accurate as (D). Choice (B) has the related phrase *check bags* but incorrectly places the action in the past. Choice (C) has the related word *plane* but we cannot determine from the picture whether the plane is on time or not.

PART 2: QUESTION-RESPONSE

(A) *I'd rather go* is a contraction for *I would rather go*. Therefore the answer *I would too* is correct.

Choice (B) has similar sounds: *first class/first time,* but does not answer the question. Choice (C) has similar sounds: *economy/money,* but is not logical.

PART 3: CONVERSATIONS

1. **(A)** She was busy; she was NOT free (*if I had been free*). The reasons given in Choices (B), (C), and (D) are incorrect because the woman had other plans and was not free to attend the reception. Choice (C) has related words: *free/charge.* Choice (D) has similar sounds: *free/fee.*

2. **(D)** The man went but he wishes he *had been somewhere else more interesting.* Choice (A) repeats *somewhere else.* Choices (B) and (C) repeat *interesting.*

3. **(C)** The woman says *I might not be able to,* and explains that she has to finish a report. Choice (A) repeats *plans (planning).* Choice (B) is related to the report she has to finish, but is incorrect because she *might* go if she finishes it. Choice (D) repeats *report,* but the report she is writing is not about the party.

PART 4: TALKS

1. **(B)** The listeners felt *lost* during the presentation; they felt confused. Choice (A) is contradicted by *could have been more interesting.* Choice (C) is contradicted by *if the speakers had used some visuals.* Choice (D) is contradicted by *Colorful visuals...would have made it easier.*

2. **(A)** The speaker says *The presenter should also speak more loudly.* Choice (B) is incorrect because the speaker says that people *...could not hear him very well.* Choice (C) repeats the word *clearly.* Choice (D) is incorrect because the speaker says that people *...were not able to follow his main points.*

3. **(C)** The speaker says *...this presenter should develop some visual aids.* Choice (A) confuses *aide* (a person) with *aid* (a thing). Choice (B) is confused with *Before giving this presentation again....* Choice (D) is associated with *... speak more loudly,* but is not mentioned.

Target 16 *Used to*

PART 1: PHOTOGRAPHS

(A) We can assume that a professional kitchen is hot. People who work in such kitchens are chefs; they must be accustomed to the heat. Choice (B) has a related word, *cook,* but does not describe the picture. Choice (C) has related words, *pans* and *mix,* but they refer to paint, not food. Choice (D) has the related word *food,* but does not describe the picture.

PART 2: QUESTION-RESPONSE

(A) Since the person works at night, we assume he is accustomed to not sleeping much in the evening. Choice (B) suggests the speaker said *I used to work at night.* Choice (C) has the related words: *used to/used* and *night/days* but does not answer the question.

PART 3: CONVERSATIONS

1. **(B)** A *frequent speaker* is one who often gives presentations at conferences. Choices (A) and (C) are contradicted by *used to be a frequent speaker at conferences.* Choice (D) is contradicted by *anything people wanted to hear.*

2. **(D)** The man says *I got used to speaking about all kinds of things.* Choice (A) is the opposite of the correct answer. Choice (B) uses the word *name* out of context. Choice (C) has similar sounds: *press* and *impress.*

3. **(B)** The woman says *I don't think I could ever get used to speaking in public.* Choice (A) confuses the meaning of *used to* in the woman's statement. Choice (C) repeats the word *impress.* Choice (D) repeats the phrase *used to.*

PART 4: TALKS

1. **(A)** People used carbon paper to make copies before the photocopier was invented. In Choice (B), *as much* suggests frequency of writing, which is not mentioned. In Choice (C), *as well* suggests quality of typing, which is not mentioned. Choice (D) is contradicted by *We are now used to making many copies.*

2. **(A)** The speaker says ...*people have gotten used to making more copies than they may really need*. Choice (B) repeats the word *multiple*. Choice (C) repeats the phrase *just one* and is the opposite of the correct answer. Choice (D) repeats the word *correspondence*, but no mention is made of writing more now than in the past.

3. **(C)** People make unnecessary copies and, according to the speaker, this *generates a great deal of waste*. Choice (A) is contradicted by *It costs little time or effort....* Choice (B) repeats the word *correspondence*, but no mention is made of receiving more now than in the past. Choice (D) associates *weighs too much* with *tons of office paper*.

ANALYZING QUESTION TYPES

Target 17 People

PART 2: QUESTION-RESPONSE

(A) Marketing Director is her title. Choice (B) incorrectly answers how long has she worked here. Choice (C) has similar words: *say/talk* and confuses *title* and *book*.

PART 3: CONVERSATIONS

1. **(B)** Listen for the context clues such as *sand, wall, first coat of paint*, and *mix the color*. Choice (A) suggests a related word for lifeguard: *sand* at the beach as opposed to the verb to *sand* a wall. Choice (C) has a word with the same sound but a different meaning: *coat of paint* (layer) and *coat* (clothing). Choice (D) has a related expression *to mix paints* (painters) and *to mix drinks* (bartenders).

2. **(B)** The man tells the woman to *sand* the wall. Choice (A) is incorrect because the man tells the woman to do the job. Choice (C) has similar sounds: *boss* and *gloss*. Choice (D) confuses *helper* with *I'll help you*.

3. **(A)** The speakers talk about the kind of paint the father prefers and say they hope he will like his house when it's painted, so the house belongs to the father. Choices (B) and (C) confuse *mother* and *brother* with the similar-sounding word *other*. Choice (D) has similar sounds: *friend* and *end*.

PART 4: TALKS

1. **(B)** The general category that includes everyone is *airline passengers*. Look for the context clues: *flight attendants*, *cabin*, and *before we land*. Choices (A), (C), and (D) name people who might listen to the announcement, but *only if* they were passengers on the plane.

2. **(B)** The announcer says that flight attendants will pass out immigration forms. Choice (A) repeats the word *customs*. Choice (C) are the people who will receive the forms. Choice (D) repeats the word *immigration*.

3. **(C)** The announcer says *Citizens of this country should follow the blue signs*. Choice (A) is the people who should follow the red signs. Choices (B) and (D) are people who can request help from an attendant.

Target 18 Occupations

PART 2: QUESTION-RESPONSE

(A) A housekeeper is usually responsible for towels and linens in a room. The occupations listed in (B) and (C) would not concern themselves with towels and linens.

PART 3: CONVERSATIONS

1. **(D)** Look for the context clues such as *put one in each room, wires along the baseboard*, and *phone rings*. Choice (A) confuses the meanings of *run wires/running* as in jogging. Choice (B) has similar sounds: *baseboard/baseball*. Choice (C) has related words: *phone rings/telephone operator*.

2. **(D)** The woman says the man needs a lot of phones because he has a mail order company. Choice (A) has related words *mailman* and *mail*. Choice (B) repeats the word *website*. Choice (C) has related words *employment* and *employee*.

3. **(C)** The man says *We're all responsible for answering the phone here*. Choices (A), (B), and (D) are contradicted by the correct answer.

PART 4: TALKS

1. **(A)** The speaker addresses the listeners as *class* and reminds them of their *mid term*

exam, assignments, and *grades,* so the speaker is a professor speaking to students. Choice (B) has related words *patients* and *exams.* Choice (C) is the person who is speaking. Choice (D) has related words *museum visitors* and *museum director.*

2. **(D)** The speaker is getting ready to introduce the special guest speaker, who is director of the City Art Museum. Choice (A) has similar sounds: *doctor* and *director.* Choice (B) is the audience for this talk. Choice (C) has related words: *hotel manager* and *guest.*

3. **(C)** Mary Little will be the first student to give a presentation following the exam. Choice (A) has related words: *museum guide* and *museum director.* Choice (B) is the person who is speaking. Choice (D) has related words: *historian* and *history.*

Target 19 Speakers' Relationship

PART 2: QUESTION-RESPONSE

(B) Browsing is the only possible option. The context clues of *Son* and *Father* suggest the speaker may be a woman and perhaps the boy's mother. Choice (A) does not answer the question. There is the similar sound of *do son* and *innocent.* Choice (C) does not match the tense of the question.

PART 3: CONVERSATIONS

1. **(C)** Look for the context clues: the polite *Would you like...; the check; pay at the cashier.* Choice (A) is suggested by related words like the banking terms *check* and *cashier,* but coffee is not served at a bank. Choice (B) also confuses related words such as *check* and *cashier.* Choice (D) uses related words for coffee production, but the conversation takes place in a restaurant, not a coffee plantation.

2. **(B)** The woman says that her little boy would like more water, so she is with her son. Choice (A) has similar sounds: *mom* and *ma'am.* Choice (C) has similar sounds: *friend* and *end.* Choice (D) has similar sounds: *daughter* and *water.*

3. **(B)** The man offers the woman more coffee. Choice (A) is the person who serves the coffee. Choice (C) repeats the word *cashier.* Choice (D) has related words: *doorman* and *door.*

PART 4: TALKS

1. **(A)** Notice the context clues: *library's representative, fine, borrowed book, borrowers, library.* Choice (B) uses the related word *book,* but the context of the talk is not publishing. Choice (C) suggests the related words *to collect a fine,* but the context of the talk is not a traffic violation. Choice (D) uses the related word *book,* but the context of the talk concerns lending and borrowing books, not selling and buying them.

2. **(C)** The speaker says *Parents are expected to make sure that their children follow the rules and behave appropriately.* Choice (A) is the people who might be disturbed by children. Choice (B) is contradicted by the correct answer. Choice (D) has similar words: *director* and *directed.*

3. **(A)** To reserve a meeting room, people should show proof of residency, such as a driver's license. Choice (B) is the people who need special permission to reserve a meeting room. Choice (C) repeats the phrase *special events.* Choice (D) repeats the phrase *other areas* and has related words: *travel* and *driver's license.*

Target 20 Location

PART 2: QUESTION-RESPONSE

(A) Listen for the context clue *where.* When you hear a *where* question, scan all the answer choices and listen for the correct location when you hear the dialogue. Choices (B) and (C) use prepositions of location, but a person could not conveniently wait *in an envelope* or *under a cushion.*

PART 3: CONVERSATIONS

1. **(C)** Listen for the context clue: *I left the letter....* Choice (A) is contradicted by *the stack on the desk.* Choices (B) and (D) are contradicted by *on top of these books.*

2. **(A)** The woman mentions *the shelf by the door*. Choices (B), (C), and (D) have repeated words *computer, desk,* and *box*.

3. **(D)** The woman tells the man to put the letter on top of her computer next time. Choices (A), (B), and (C) have repeated words *printer, box,* and *folder*.

PART 4: TALKS

1. **(B)** Listen for the context clue: *Please initial the routing.... Next to* is similar to *by*. Choices (A), (C), and (D) are contradicted by *initial the routing next to your name*.

2. **(C)** People are asked to place their outgoing letters *in the outbox located next to each office door*. Choice (A) is confused with the mention of *mailroom staff*. Choice (B) is the place to put large packages. Choice (D) repeats the word *door*.

3. **(B)** According to the talk, *Mail addressed to a specific individual is placed on that individual's desk*. Choice (A) is confused with *outbox*; an *inbox* is not mentioned. Choice (C) repeats the word *individual*. Choice (D) repeats the word *head*, from *department head*.

Target 21 Time

PART 2: QUESTION-RESPONSE

(A) A file that takes *too long* to download needs either a faster Internet connection and/or a faster computer. Choice (B) uses the similar-sounding word *strong* for *long*. Choice (C) repeats the word *down*.

PART 3: CONVERSATIONS

1. **(C)** A half-hour is equal to 30 minutes. You may sometimes have to change hours to minutes: for example, one and a half hours is 90 minutes. Choice (A) indicates when the man had planned to leave. Choice (B) is not mentioned. Choice (D) indicates how long the woman asked him to stay.

2. **(B)** The woman says that the man's appointment is at 8:30. Choice (A) sounds similar to the correct answer. Choices (C) and (D) have similar sounds: *nine* and *time*.

3. **(D)** The woman says that the man can get to his house in 45 minutes. Choices (A) and (B) have similar sounds: *twenty* and *plenty*. Choice (C) sounds similar to the correct answer.

PART 4: TALKS

1. **(B)** *Every day* means *daily*. Choice (A) confuses *sixty inches/sixty minutes (one hour)*. Choice (C) is contradicted by *every day now for the last week*. Choice (D) confuses *two months/twice a month*.

2. **(A)** The speaker says that the bad winter of seven years ago was the last time the region had this much snow. Choice (B) sounds similar to the correct answer. Choice (C) is confused with 60 inches, the total amount of snow expected. Choice (D) is confused with 70 inches, the amount of snow that fell seven years ago.

3. **(B)** There is only one week of winter left. Choice (A) repeats the word *today*. Choice (C) repeats the word *month*. Choice (D) is confused with the phrase *in the last two months*.

Target 22 Activities

PART 2: QUESTION-RESPONSE

(B) Look for the context clue *what are you doing?* The subject and the tense of the verb match the question. Choice (A) has similar sounds: *report/ sports*. Choice (C) answers *what are you doing* but not the intended meaning, *why do you have the report?*

PART 3: CONVERSATIONS

1. **(D)** Look for the context clues *turn left, one-way street,* and *map*. Choice (A) is contradicted by *one-way street*. Choice (B) has similar sounds: *map/nap*. Choice (C) is contradicted by *should have bought a map*.

2. **(C)** The man mentions a restaurant, the woman mentions *dinner*. Choice (A) has similar sounds: *rested/restaurant*. Choice (B) has similar sounds: *snow/show*. Choice (D) has similar sounds: *rent/spent* and repeats the word *movie*.

3. **(D)** They are looking for a movie theater. Choice (A) has similar sounds: *read/need*. Choice (B) has similar sounds: *bed/ahead*. Choice (C) associates *play* with *theater*.

PART 4: TALKS

1. **(D)** Look for the context clues: *event of rain, not be postponed, held as scheduled*, and *take place in the cafeteria*. Choice (A) has similar sounds: *scheduled/rescheduled* and is contradicted by *the picnic will not be postponed*. Choice (B) is contradicted by *will take place in the office cafeteria*. Choice (C) confuses the related word *post* with *postponed/mail*.

2. **(C)** The speaker says that the food will be ordered early Friday afternoon. Choice (A) is incorrect because it is never mentioned exactly when the picnic will take place. Choice (B) repeats the word *dish*. Choice (D) repeats the words *home* and *early*.

3. **(B)** Listeners are asked to send Shirley an e-mail before Friday. Choice (A) has similar sounds: *phone/home*. Choice (C) has similar sounds: *letter/let her*. Choice (D) has similar sounds: *person/personnel*.

Target 23 Events or Facts

PART 2: QUESTION-RESPONSE

(A) Look for the context clue: *What happened to you?* Only Choice (A) has an event. Choice (B) has similar sounds: *last night/last Friday*. Choice (C) gives a time, not an event.

PART 3: CONVERSATIONS

1. **(A)** Look at the second line of the conversation. *Production will be delayed if the shipment is not released from customs.* Choices (B), (C), and (D) might be further results of delayed production but are not mentioned.

2. **(A)** The man says that there is a meeting scheduled for Monday. Choices (B) and (C) are incorrect because the speakers don't know when these things will happen. Choice (D) repeats the word *shipment*, but no mention is made of a new shipment arriving.

3. **(C)** The woman says *This isn't the first time our shipment has been delayed in this way.* Choice (A) repeats the word *strange*, but the woman says that the situation is not strange. Choice (B) repeats the phrase *the first time*, but the woman says it is not the first time. Choice (D) has similar sounds: *everyday/way*.

PART 4: TALKS

1. **(C)** Be careful of the negative inversion: *Never have so many disasters happened at one time* means *There have been a lot of disasters*. Choice (A) is incorrect because only the West has had earthquakes. Choice (B) is contradicted by the list of disasters given. Choice (D) is incorrect because the blizzard was in the Northeast.

2. **(C)** The speaker says *...there may not be enough personnel or resources to provide the necessary aid.* Choice (A) repeats the words *president* and *aid*. Choice (B) is confused with the president's visiting different areas of the country. Choice (D) repeats the phrase *emergency personnel* and uses the word *flood* out of context.

3. **(C)** The president will *address the nation* on Sunday. Choices (A) and (D) use the word *address* out of context. Choice (B) is what the president will do next week.

Target 24 Emotions

PART 2: QUESTION-RESPONSE

(A) Only Choice (A) answers the question. Choice (B) answers *who*. Choice (C) answers *where*.

PART 3: CONVERSATIONS

1. **(A)** Look for the context clues: *starving, stomach growling, haven't eaten, Let's eat.* Choice (B) is not mentioned. Choice (C) has related words: *growl/angry*. Choice (D) has related words: *find/lost*.

2. **(D)** The speakers are looking for a place to eat because they are hungry. The man says *I'm afraid there's no place...* and *I've never seen anything that looks good*, so he doubts that they can find a restaurant. Choice (A) is confused with the woman telling the man to

relax. Choice (B) repeats the word *good.* Choice (C) repeats the word *happy.*

3. **(A)** The woman says *I'm sure there are plenty of places.* Choice (B) confuses *unsure* with *sure.* Choice (C) repeats the word *bad.* Choice (D) repeats the word *afraid.*

PART 4: TALKS

1. **(B)** The neighbors are not pleased; they are upset because cars are being parked on their lawns. Choice (A) has the repeated word *parking.* Choice (C) is incorrect because the employees' quitting time is not mentioned. Choice (D) is incorrect because nothing is said about neighbors watering their lawns. The word *lawn* is repeated here.

2. **(D)** The speaker says *We understand that many of you are frustrated…* Choice (A) is how the speaker wants the employees to feel. Choice (B) is how the speaker feels about the plans for the parking lot. Choice (C) has similar sounds: *sad/bad.*

3. **(C)** The speaker is pleased to announce the signing of the agreement with the contractor. Choice (A) describes the current parking situation. Choice (B) has similar sounds: *worried/hurry.* Choice (D) is the opposite of the correct answer.

Target 25 Reasons

PART 2: QUESTION-RESPONSE

(B) Black coffee is coffee without cream or milk. The speaker prefers coffee without cream or milk. Choice (A) has similar sounds: *coffee/cough.* Choice (C) has related words: *coffee/tea.*

PART 3: CONVERSATIONS

1. **(B)** Neither speaker can read in the car. But they can read on a train or plane. The reasons in Choices (A), (C), and (D) are not mentioned in the conversation.

2. **(B)** The woman says that the train is convenient. Choice (A) is what the man says about planes. Choice (C) has similar sounds: *delay/way.* Choice (D) has similar sounds: *fun/done.*

3. **(C)** The woman says she is going to the beach for a vacation. Choice (A) is the man's guess. Choices (B) and (D) confuse *mother* and *brother* with the similar sound *other.*

PART 4: TALKS

1. **(A)** A work slowdown is a work action. A slowdown is like a strike except workers show up, but do not work at their normal speed. They work more slowly. Choices (B), (C), and (D) do not give the reason *why.*

2. **(A)** The announcer suggests that people should eat now because the restaurants will close at midnight. Choice (B) is confused with …*won't reopen until tomorrow.* Choice (C) repeats the word *flight,* but no mention is made of whether or not there will be food on the flight. Choice (D) confuses *close (near)* with *close (opposite of open).*

3. **(D)** The announcer suggests listening to the announcements to hear when flights are ready for boarding. Choice (A) repeats the word *gate.* Choice (B) repeats the word *restaurants.* Choice (C) has similar sounds: *bored/board.*

Target 26 Measurements

PART 2: QUESTION-RESPONSE

(A) A half hour is thirty minutes (10 × 3). Choice (B) confuses the amount of work done and the amount of time it took. Choice (C) is contradicted by Tom having more time to finish.

PART 3: CONVERSATIONS

1. **(C)** A record low temperature means it's really cold. Choices (A), (B), and (D) are contradicted by *record low.*

2. **(D)** It's thirty degrees today, and last week it was ten degrees warmer. Choice (A) is the difference between today's temperature and last week's. Choice (B) has similar sounds *thirteen/thirty.* Choice (C) is today's temperature.

3. **(A)** Since the twelve inches of snow predicted for this weekend is twice the amount that fell last month, six inches fell last month. Choice (B) has similar sounds:

eight/wait. Choice (C) is the amount of snow predicted for this weekend. Choice (D) is twice twelve.

PART 4: TALKS

1. **(C)** If you purchase more than $100 worth of pencils, the supplier will give you a 10 percent discount. Ten percent of $200 is $20 (200 – 10%).

2. **(B)** Seasonal sales often have a 25% discount; 25% of 200 is 50. Choice (A) confuses the dollar amount of the discount with the percentage. Choice (C) is the price with a 20% discount. Choice (D) is the price with a 25 dollar, not percent, discount.

3. **(B)** Sales tax is 5%; and 5% of 200 is 10. Choice (A) confuses the dollar amount of the tax with the percentage. Choice (C) is the sales discount, not the tax. Choice (D) confuses 5 with 50.

Target 27 Opinions

PART 2: QUESTION-RESPONSE

(A) Choice (A) is the only reason given. Choice (B) answers how the speaker got the book. Choice (C) refers to habitual action.

PART 3: CONVERSATIONS

1. **(B)** The context clues all refer to humor: *funny, laughed, jokes.* Be careful: *I never laughed so hard* means *I laughed harder than ever before.* Choice (A) has the related words: *speaker/presentation.* Choice (C) is not mentioned. Choice (D) confuses similar sounds: *jokes/folks.*

2. **(B)** The man says that the food is great. Choice (A) is the woman's opinion. Choice (C) has similar sounds, *seats/eat,* and confuses the meaning of *hard.* Choice (D) is incorrect because it is the portions of food that are big, not the room.

3. **(A)** The woman says …*it's quite a bit on the expensive side.* Choice (B) is confused with *I'd expected it to be cheaper.* Choice (C) has similar sounds, *tables/uncomfortable,* and

nice/price. Choice (D) is how the woman feels about the price, not the hotel.

PART 4: TALKS

1. **(D)** Look for the context clues: *handkerchiefs, four-hanky movie,* and *crying.* Choice (A) confuses *short/within ten minutes.* Choice (B) is incorrect because the actors are not mentioned. Choice (C) is contradicted by *opening credits.*

2. **(C)** The speaker describes the seats as comfortable. Choice (A) is how the popcorn is described. Choice (B) repeats the word *big.* Choice (D) is incorrect because the speaker says the theater is worth the high cost.

3. **(C)** The speaker describes the theater's location as convenient. Choice (A) is the opposite of what the speaker says. Choice (B) confuses *out of town* with *downtown.* Choice (D) is the opposite of what the speaker says.

Target 28 Main Topics

PART 2: QUESTION-RESPONSE

(B) The other choices are not about a particular subject and do not answer the question. Choice (A) does not answer a question about talking. Choice (C) refers to the length of the program, not a topic of conversation.

PART 3: CONVERSATIONS

1. **(C)** The man is looking for a generous person, but the woman declares that she is not at all generous. The man's comment *I won't ask for your help,* then suggests he would have asked her for help (money) if she had been generous. Choice (A) may be true, but this does not answer the question. Choice (B) repeats the word *shame.* Choice (D) confuses the words *tight* and *small.*

2. **(A)** The woman says *I'm very tight with money.* Choice (B) is what the man asks. Choice (C) has similar sounds: *ashamed/shame.* Choice (D) confuses *helpful* with *help.*

3. **(D)** The woman says that she likes the man. Choice (A) has similar sounds *personality/*

personally. Choice (B) confuses the meaning *just (fair)* with *just (only)*. Choice (C) has similar sounds: *fake/take.*

PART 4: TALKS

1. **(B)** The phrases *asked me to submit my letter of resignation* and *told me to leave by the close of business today* both indicate that the Managing Director was *fired.* Choice (A) repeats the words *Board of Directors* and *resignation.* Choice (C) is not mentioned. Choice (D) repeats the word *letter.*

2. **(B)** The speaker says *I will no longer work as your managing director,* so he is speaking to his staff. Choice (A) has related words *clients/ business.* Choice (C) confuses the meaning of *serve.* Choice (D) is the speaker's position.

3. **(B)** The speaker says that he hopes to open up a consulting business. Choice (A) has homonyms: *clothes/close.* Choice (C) has similar sounds: *college/colleague.* Choice (D) has similar sounds: *restaurant/rest* and related words: *manager/managing.*

ANALYZING LANGUAGE FUNCTIONS

Target 29 Conditionals

PART 2: QUESTION-RESPONSE

(A) Only Choice (A) matches the tense of the suggestion. Choice (B) is the past tense. Choice (C) repeats the word *if* and does not answer the question.

PART 3: CONVERSATIONS

1. **(C)** Look for the context clue following the conditional clause: *If we had asked for less money....* Choice (A) is incorrect because they DID submit a budget. Choice (B) is incorrect because they asked for too much money and the budget was not approved. Choice (D) is incorrect because they cannot complete the project without money.

2. **(A)** The man suggests rewriting the budget. Choice (B) repeats the phrase *complete the project.* Choice (C) repeats the phrase *next year.* Choice (D) repeats the word *time.*

3. **(A)** The woman says that they'll be able to complete the project if they get money by September. Choice (B) has similar sounds: *September/December.* Choice (C) is when they may be able to complete the project. Choice (D) repeats the phrase *next year.*

PART 4: TALKS

1. **(D)** Prices *continue to fall* means prices *decrease.* Choice (A) uses vocabulary typical of investment advice—*decrease* and *holdings.* Choice (B) repeats *fall* and *wait* from the talk. Choice (C) has a related word *broker* but this statement is not mentioned.

2. **(D)** Inexperienced investors lose money by buying high-priced stock. Choice (A) is what wise investors do. Choice (B) repeats the word *avoid.* Choice (C) is what inexperienced investors are advised to do.

3. **(C)** Inexperienced investors are advised to work with a stockbroker. Choice (A) is what they are advised not to do. Choice (B) confuses the meaning of the word *fall.* Choice (D) confuses the meaning of the word *share.*

Target 30 Suggestions

PART 2: QUESTION-RESPONSE

(C) Choice (C) answers the *yes/no* suggestion with *Yes* and suggests a time to leave. Choice (A) has similar sounding and related word phrases: *leave more time/left my watch.* Choice (B) confuses similar sounds: *more/anymore.*

PART 3: CONVERSATIONS

1. **(B)** Look for the context clue with the suggestion marker *should: should start with your report.* Choice (A) is the woman's suggestion, not the man's. Choice (C) confuses *first* with *drink (thirst).* Choice (D) confuses *save mine/save money.*

2. **(C)** The man says that the woman's report is important for the rest of the meeting. Choice (A) has similar sounds: *projector/projections.* Choice (B) repeats the word *meeting.* Choice (D) confuses the meaning of the word *rest.*

3. **(B)** The woman wants the man to tell everyone not to arrive late. Choice (A) repeats the words *late arrivals,* which is what the woman says she doesn't want. Choice (C) has similar sounds: *eight/late.* Choice (D) has similar sounds: *interpret/interrupt.*

PART 4: TALKS

1. **(C)** Look for the context clue with the suggestion marker *should: shouldn't we all try to help the needy.* Choice (A) has related words: *job/unemployment.* Choice (B) has related words: *homeless/home.* Choice (D) repeats words (*consider*) and sounds (*four, fortunate*) from the talk.
2. **(C)** The speaker says that listeners should help the needy by giving to a charitable organization and that there is information about these organizations on the radio station's website. Choice (A) is confused with the web address that belongs to a radio station. Choice (B) repeats the word *individual.* Choice (D) repeats the words *charitable organization,* but nothing is mentioned about calling them.
3. **(A)** The speaker says that needy people need to help all year round. Choices (B) and (D) are the times when people tend to think about those in need. Choice (C) is when people tend not to think about those in need.

Target 31 Offers

PART 2: QUESTION-RESPONSE

(C) The other choices do not respond to the offer to accompany them out for coffee. Choice (A) uses words associated with *coffee* like *milk* and *sugar.* Choice (B) uses the location for having coffee, *a café.*

PART 3: CONVERSATIONS

1. **(A)** The man offered to get the woman some coffee. Choice (B) is incorrect because the train is late so they can't get on it. Choice (C) has similar sounds: *hot/home.* Choice (D) has similar sounds: *warm/platform* and related words: *train/platform.*

2. **(C)** The woman offers to pay for the coffee. Choice (A) has similar sounds: *form/platform.* Choice (B) confuses the meanings of *change* and *place.* Choice (D) is what the man will do in order to get the coffee.
3. **(A)** The man offers to get a newspaper at the same time as he gets the coffee. Choices (B), (C), and (D) all sound similar to the correct answer.

PART 4: TALKS

1. **(C)** The speaker offered the opportunity to board the aircraft early to several types of passengers. Choices (A) and (B) describe related items passengers can have to board early. Choice (D) confuses similar sounds: *infants/infant seats* and uses the related word *travel.*
2. **(B)** Free snacks and drinks will be offered once the flight is in the air. Choice (A) has similar sounds: *three/free.* Choice (C) repeats the word *seat.* Choice (D) confuses the meaning of the word *card.*
3. **(D)** Children are invited to visit the cockpit and talk with the pilot and copilot. Choice (A) confuses the meaning of the word *class.* Choice (B) is confused with talking to the flight attendants to let them know of your interest in this offer. Choice (C) repeats the word *meal.*

Target 32 Requests

PART 2: QUESTION-RESPONSE

(A) The other choices do not respond to the request. Choice (B) has related words: *window/ door.* Choice (C) has related words: *window/ curtains.*

PART 3: CONVERSATIONS

1. **(A)** The other activities were mentioned, but they were not part of the request to mail a letter. Choice (B) describes one thing the woman will do herself. Choices (C) and (D) describe what the man himself wants to do.

2. **(B)** The woman said *Would you mind sweeping the floor?* Choice (A) has similar sounds: *cook/book* and *meal/mail.* Choice (C) has similar sounds: *door/floor.* Choice (D) has similar sounds: *sleep/sweep.*

3. **(B)** The woman said that it needs to be done today. Choice (A) is when the man will do it. Choice (C) has similar sounds: *tonight/ right.* Choice (D) has similar sounds: *Tuesday/today.*

PART 4: TALKS

1. **(D)** The answer is part of the request for the audience to return to their seats. Choices (A) and (B) are appropriate in the lobby; people are not asked to stop. Choice (C) is an expression of thanks, not a request.

2. **(D)** The speaker thanks the listeners for using the lobby for smoking. Choice (A) repeats the word *seats.* Choice (B) has related words *manager/management.* Choice (C) confuses the meaning of the word *reception.*

3. **(C)** The speaker asks the audience to turn off their cell phones and pagers. Choice (A) confuses the meaning of the word *turn* and has similar sounds: *pages/pagers.* Choice (B) has similar sounds: *walk/talk.* Choice (D) has similar sounds: *home/phone.*

Target 33 Restatements

PART 2: QUESTION-RESPONSE

(A) The first speaker doesn't want to eat at home, and the response restates this by asking if he wants to go to a restaurant. Choice (B) repeats the word *mood.* Choice (C) repeats the words *dinner* and *home.*

PART 3: CONVERSATIONS

1. **(A)** The woman says this is the last time she'll wait, meaning that in the future she will leave if he's not on time. Choice (B) is incorrect because she's only been waiting for five minutes. Choice (C) is contradicted by the man asking her not to be mad. Choice (D) is not mentioned.

2. **(A)** The man says that the woman will never have to wait for him again, implying that he won't be late. Choice (B) is incorrect because it's the woman who has had to wait for the man. Choice (C) repeats the phrase *five minutes.* Choice (D) repeats the word *bored.*

3. **(C)** When the woman says *I hope you brought your wallet,* she means that she wants the man to pay for her. Choice (A) repeats the word *wallet.* Choice (B) repeats the word *home.* Choice (D) has similar sounds: *waiter/wait.*

PART 4: TALKS

1. **(B)** The talk says the form is to track your loan application. Choices (A), (C), and (D) are not mentioned.

2. **(A)** The listener is instructed to *press firmly* when filling out the form; that is a necessity when making multiple carbon copies. Choices (B), (C), and (D) are all possible ways of making copies but are not implied in the talk.

3. **(D)** The speaker says that the listener will be contacted within *two weeks,* which is the same as fourteen days. Choice (A) repeats the word *two.* Choice (B) is the number of copies that will be made. Choice (C) has similar sounds: *ten/then.*

Explanatory Answers for Mini-Test for Listening Comprehension Parts 1, 2, 3, and 4

Part 1: Photographs

1. **(C)** Choice (C) identifies people (*men*) and a location (*the buffet*). Choice (B) shows negation: there are not guests in the photo. Choice (C) refers to an *officer,* whose uniform might resemble that of the waiters. Choice (D) confuses similar sounds: *bus* with *busboy.*

2. **(D)** Choice (D) identifies action: *boat leaving harbor*. Choice (A) confuses similar sounds: *sheep* with *ship*. Choice (B) confuses a related word: *water*. Choice (C) confuses similar sounds: *votes* with *boats*.

3. **(C)** Choice (C) identifies location: *large hall*. Choice (A) incorrectly identifies the location as a bank. Choice (B) confuses similar sounding *floor* with *flower*. Choice (D) is incorrect because the passengers are *at the ticket counters*, not *on the plane*.

4. **(A)** Choice (A) describes the studio as *cluttered*. Choice (B) is incorrect because there is no panel in the photo. Choice (C) is incorrect because the man is wearing, not holding, a headset. Choice (D) is incorrect because the flipchart is blank.

5. **(A)** Choice (A) identifies the occupation, *operator*, and the action, *pushing a button*. Choice (B) describes an incorrect action. Choice (C) confuses different meanings for *button* (in clothing) and *button* (on machinery). Choice (D) has the related phrase *going up*, but concerning stocks, not elevators.

6. **(D)** The men, probably construction architects, engineers, or workers, are holding building plans. Choice (A) uses the similar-sounding word *plane* for *crane*. Choice (B) uses the associated word *building* but they are building a building not entering one. Choice (C) uses the associated word *watching*. They are observing the construction, not a parade.

7. **(A)** Choice (A) identifies a thing: *electrical wires*. Choice (B) confuses the related word *poles*. Choice (C) confuses the related phrase *light fixture*. Choice (D) confuses homonyms (*polls* with *poles*) and similar sounds (*election* with *electricity*).

8. **(B)** Choice (B) identifies the action: *works with her hands*. Choice (A) cannot be assumed from the photo. Choice (C) incorrectly identifies the occupation of the woman and her action. Choice (D) is incorrect because the woman is not holding a saw.

9. **(D)** Choice (D) identifies the location: *in front of a window*. Choice (A) describes an incorrect action. Choice (B) confuses similar

sounds: *purse* with *nurse*, and incorrectly describes the location. Choice (C) confuses *pharmacists* with *nurses*.

10. **(A)** The flight attendant is distributing newspapers to the passengers. Choice (B) uses the similar-sounding word *paper* for *newspaper* and the associated word for *paper*, which is *writing*. Choice (C) misidentifies the action. Choice (D) uses the associated word for *offering*, which is *serving*, and the similar-sounding word *wafer* for *paper*.

Part 2: Question-Response

11. **(B)** Choice (B) is a logical response to a question about *location*. Choice (A) confuses similar sounds: *live* with *five*. Choice (C) confuses similar sounds: *live* with *leave* and is not a logical response to a question about *location*.

12. **(A)** Choice (A) is a logical response to a question about *time*. Choice (B) confuses similar sounds: *late* with *ate*. Choice (C) confuses similar sounds: *late* with *later*.

13. **(C)** Choice (C) is a logical response to a question about *who*. Choice (A) confuses similar sounds: *wait* with *weight*. Choice (B) confuses similar sounds: *wait* and *way*.

14. **(B)** After hearing that it will rain later, the second speaker decides to wear a raincoat. Choice (A) confuses *letter* with the similar-sounding word *later*. Choice (C) confuses *train* with the similar-sounding word *rain*.

15. **(A)** Choice (A) is a logical response to a question about *possession*. Choice (B) confuses similar sounds: *chair* with *cheer*. Choice (C) confuses similar sounds: *chair* with *fair*.

16. **(B)** Choice (B) is a logical response to a question about *time*. Choice (A) has the related word *train* but answers *how*, not *when*. Choice (C) has related the word *mail* but is not a logical answer; people don't arrive by mail.

17. **(A)** Choice (A) is a logical response to a question about *duration*. Choice (B) has the related word *work* but answers *which day* not *how long*. Choice (C) confuses similar sounds: *here* with *hear*; *long* with *along*.

18. **(C)** Choice (C) is a logical response to a question about *location*. Choice (A) confuses

similar sounds: *park* with *dark*. Choice (B) confuses different meanings: *park* (leave your car) and *park* (recreational area).

19. **(A)** Choice (A) is a logical response to a question about *activity*. Choice (B) confuses similar sounds: *should* with *wood*. In Choice (C), *were* (past tense) does not answer *should do now* (present tense).

20. **(C)** Choice (C) is a logical response to a question about *time*. Choice (A) confuses similar sounds: *meet* with *meat*. Choice (B) confuses related words: *start* (begin) with *start* (turn on, engine turn-over).

21. **(A)** Since the first speaker doesn't like the color of the walls, the second speaker suggests repainting them. Choice (B) confuses *ball* with the similar-sounding word *walls*. Choice (C) confuses *calls* with the similar-sounding word *walls*.

22. **(C)** Choice (C) is a logical response to a question about *size*. Choice (A) confuses similar sounds: *large* with *inches*. Choice (B) confuses similar sounds: *com(pany)* with *penny*.

23. **(A)** Choice (A) is a logical response to a question about *where*. Choice (B) confuses similar sounds: *eat* with *heat*. Choice (C) confuses similar sounds: *eat* with *eight*.

24. **(B)** Choice (B) is a logical response to a question about *no electricity*. Choice (A) has the related word *gas* but does not answer the question. Choice (C) confuses similar sounds: *electricity* with *elections*.

25. **(C)** The first speaker is going to the bank, so the second speaker asks to have a check cashed. Choice (A) associates *hungry* with *lunch*. Choice (B) confuses *thank* with the similar-sounding word *bank*.

Part 3: Conversations

26. **(C)** The speakers say that they are going to see a play. Choice (A) confuses *view* with the similar-sounding word *review*. Choice (B) uses the word *play* out of context. Choice (D) associates *movie* with *review*.

27. **(D)** The woman says that the play starts at 7:00. Choice (A) confuses *two* with the similar-sounding word *too*. Choice (B) con-

fuses *five* with the similar-sounding word *drive*. Choice (C) is the time right now.

28. **(C)** The woman mentions the rain. Choice (A) confuses *sun* with the similar-sounding word *fun*. Choice (B) confuses *ice* with the similar-sounding word *nice*. Choice (D) confuses *snow* with the similar-sounding word *slow*.

29. **(C)** The woman says she wants to discuss conference plans. Choice (A) confuses *planes* with the similar-sounding word *plans*. Choice (B) repeats the words *lunch* and *plans*. Choice (D) repeats the words *order* and *office*.

30. **(C)** The speakers finally agree to meet on Tuesday. Choices (A) and (B) are confused with the similar-sounding phrase *one day*. Choice (D) is the man's suggestion.

31. **(B)** The man says he wants to meet at his office. Choice (A) sounds similar to the correct answer. Choice (C) confuses *restaurant* with the similar-sounding word *rest*. Choice (D) is the woman's suggestion.

32. **(A)** The man says that the shirt is too small. Choice (B) is incorrect because the man asks for the same color shirt. Choice (C) confuses *hole* with the similar-sounding word *though*. Choice (D) is confused with the description of the shirt as long-sleeved.

33. **(D)** The woman suggests size eighteen, and the man agrees. Choice (A) sounds similar to the correct answer. Choice (B) sounds similar to the size of the shirt he is returning. Choice (C) is the size of the shirt he is returning.

34. **(D)** The woman says she can give him blue, the same color as the old shirt. Choice (A) confuses *white* with the similar-sounding word *right*. Choice (B) confuses *black* with the similar-sounding word *that*. Choice (C) confuses *green* with the similar-sounding words *sixteen* and *eighteen*.

35. **(C)** The woman asks the man where he will go this fall. Choice (A) confuses *spring* with the similar-sounding word *think*. Choice (B) confuses *summer* with the similar-sounding word *some*. Choice (D) repeats the word *winter*.

36. **(D)** The woman suggests going to Hawaii because it is always warm there. Choices (A) and (B) are the places the woman asks about. Choice (C) is the man's idea.

37. **(A)** The man says he has only one week to go somewhere. Choice (B) confuses *two* with the similar-sounding word *to*. Choice (C) is the length of the woman's vacation. Choice (D) confuses *four* with the similar-sounding word *for*.

38. **(C)** The man says he was in a meeting. Choice (A) is where the woman put the phone messages. Choice (B) associates *store* with *purchase*. Choice (D) is where the purchase order forms are kept.

39. **(B)** The woman says he got seven messages. Choice (A) confuses *four* with the similar-sounding word *for*. Choice (C) sounds similar to the correct answer. Choice (D) confuses *forty-two* with the similar-sounding phrase *for you*.

40. **(D)** The man asks the woman to bring him a purchase order form. Choice (A) is incorrect because the man says he will take care of the messages. Choice (B) associates *buy* with *purchase*. Choice (C) repeats the words *purchase* and *supply*.

Part 4: Talks

41. **(D)** The announcer says that the temperature is fifty-three degrees. Choices (A), (B), and (C) sound similar to the correct answer.

42. **(D)** If there is *rain early in the morning* they should take *umbrellas*. Choice (A) is incorrect because snow is not predicted; the day will be *seasonably mild*. Choice (B), *luggage*, may be associated with *National Airport*. Choice (C), *sunscreen*, may be associated with *clear skies*, but today will be *mild*.

43. **(B)** It says skies *clearing by noon*. Choice (A) is incorrect because *rain early in the morning* suggests rain at *6:00 A.M.* Choices (C) and (D) are contradicted by *clearing by noon* and *winds developing in the evening*.

44. **(A)** It is being turned off to *reduce total demand*. Choice (B) is incorrect because it will save *power*, not *money*. Choice (C) confuses *make cooler* with *hot weather*. Choice (D) is not mentioned.

45. **(B)** *Power will not be out longer than two hours* means it will be out *less than two hours*. Choices (A), (C), and (D) are contradicted by *not longer than two hours*.

46. **(A)** Listeners are asked to visit the company's Web site. Choice (B) confuses *call* with the similar-sounding word *all*. Choice (C) repeats the word *visit*. Choice (D) associates *radio* with *turn off*.

47. **(D)** *Cruise, at sea, ashore,* and *Main Deck* indicate the announcement is *on a ship*. Choice (A) is incorrect because tour buses are not found at sea. Choice (B) confuses *at the shore* with *ashore, shore excursion*. Choice (C) confuses *report to the lounge* (room with comfortable chairs) and *cocktail lounge*.

48. **(C)** People are requested to *report for a ticket*. Choice (A) is incorrect because *enjoy your breakfast* does not mean that breakfast is required. Choices (B) and (D) are incorrect because *clothing* and *health* are not mentioned.

49. **(C)** The announcer says that the excursion will depart at 9:00 A.M. Choice (A) confuses *four* with the similar-sounding word *shore*. Choice (B) is the time the announcement is being made. Choice (D) sounds similar to the correct answer.

50. **(D)** They advertise a *new remote control*. Choices (A), (B), and (C) are devices you can operate with the remote control.

51. **(C)** Choice (C)—Consumers can *call our toll-free number for more information*. Choice (A) is contradicted by no *sales personnel will call*. Choices (B) and (D) are not mentioned.

52. **(C)** The offer is good until the end of the month. Choice (A) repeats the word *today*, when the listener is asked to call. Choice (B) confuses *Tuesday* with the similar-sounding word *today*. Choice (D) confuses *after the end of the month* with *until the end of the month*.

CHAPTER 3

Reading

WHAT TO LOOK FOR IN THIS CHAPTER

- Overview
  - Directions for the Reading Section, Parts 5, 6, and 7
  - Examples of TOEIC Reading Questions
- Reading Targets Parts 5 and 6
  - Analyzing vocabulary
  - Analyzing grammar
  - Strategies to improve your reading score
- Mini-Test for Reading Parts 5 and 6
- Reading Comprehension Targets
- Reading Comprehension Passages
- Strategies to Improve Your Reading Comprehension
- Mini-Test for Reading Comprehension Part 7
  - Answer Keys for Targets 1–60 and Mini-Tests for Reading Parts 5–7
  - Explanatory Answers for Targets 1–60 and Mini-Tests for Reading Parts 5–7

Overview—Parts 5–7

There are three parts to the Reading section of the TOEIC. You will have approximately 75 minutes to complete this section.

Part 5:	Incomplete Sentences	40 questions
Part 6:	Text Completion	12 questions
Part 7:	Reading Comprehension	
	• Single passages	28 questions
	• Double passages	20 questions

This overview will show you the kind of questions you will have to answer on Parts 5–7. You should familiarize yourself with the actual directions used on the TOEIC before you take the exam. You can find these directions in the Model TOEIC and the TOEIC Bulletin. You can download these publications from *www.toeic.org.*

SECTION II—READING

Part 5: Incomplete Sentences

Directions: You will see a sentence with a missing word. Four possible answers follow the sentence. Choose the best answer to the question and fill in the corresponding oval on your answer sheet.

Sample Questions

Question 1

You will read:

1. They have decided _____ business class.

    (A) fly
    (B) to fly
    (C) flying
    (D) flew

The best way to complete the sentence "They have decided _____ business class" is Choice (B), "to fly." Therefore you should choose answer (B).

Question 2

You will read:

2. Her inexperience was _____ from the types of mistakes she made.

    (A) apparition
    (B) applicable
    (C) application
    (D) apparent

The best way to complete the sentence "Her inexperience was _____ from the types of mistakes she made" is Choice (D), "apparent." Therefore, you should choose answer (D).

Part 6: Text Completion

Directions: You will see short passages, each with three blanks. Under each blank are four answer options. Choose the word or phrase that best completes the sentence.

There are three types of questions most common in Part 6.

- Vocabulary questions
- Grammar questions
- Context questions

Sometimes you will have to read just the sentence with the blank to answer the question. Usually, you will have to understand the complete passage to be able to complete the sentence.

The following targets will help you prepare for these questions.

Question Type	Target
Vocabulary	1, 2, 3, 4
Grammar	5 through 41
Context	3, 4, 12, 14, 18

Sample Questions

You will read this passage:

Dear Mr. Sanders,

I enjoyed _____ you at the conference last week. I am enclosing the brochures that
    1. (A) met
        (B) meet
        (C) to meet
        (D) meeting

you requested. I hope _____ are useful to you. If I can be of further assistance,
        2. (A) it
            (B) they
            (C) we
            (D) its

please let me _____.
      3. (A) know
         (B) understand
         (C) realize
         (D) learn

Sincerely,
Bertha Smith

Question 1 (Grammar)

1. (A) met
    (B) meet
    (C) to meet
    (D) meeting

The best way to complete the sentence "I enjoyed _____ you at the conference last week" is Choice (D) "meeting." The participle *meeting* follows the verb *enjoyed.* Therefore, you should choose answer (D).

Question 2 (Context)

2. (A) it
    (B) they
    (C) we
    (D) its

The best way to complete the sentence "I hope _____ are useful to you" is Choice (B) "they." You must read beyond this sentence to answer the question. Sometimes you have to look back; sometimes forward. In this case, you look back. The pronoun *they* refers back to the plural noun *brochures.* Therefore, you should choose answer (B).

Question 3 (Vocabulary)

3. (A) know
    (B) understand
    (C) realize
    (D) learn

The best way to complete the sentence "If I can be of further assistance, please let me _____" is Choice (A) "know." This is an example of a context question. All of the words have a similar meaning, but only *know* fits the context. Therefore, you should choose answer (A).

Part 7: Reading Comprehension

Directions: You will see a variety of reading passages followed by several questions. Some will be single passages; each passage will have between two and five questions. There will also be four sets of double passages; each set will have five questions. Each question has four answer choices. You will choose the best answer to the question and fill in the corresponding oval on your answer sheet.

Sample Questions

You will read:

Questions 1 and 2 refer to the following web page and e-mail.

National Business Delivery Courier: Package Tracking

Tracking Number: XD2M22390
Signed for by: Not received
Ship date: June 1, 20—
Delivery date: Not received

To: Commercial Address
Weight: Under 5 pounds
Courier service: Express overnight*

*Guaranteed delivery within 24 hours. Not applicable for international shipments.
Current status: In transit /Customs delay

Date/Time	Activity
June 1, 20— 10: 17 A.M.	Picked up, 152 Hudson St. New York, NY, USA
June 1, 20— 11: 00 A.M.	Depart on NBDC vehicle from New York
June 1, 20— 10:00 P.M.	Arrived at Toronto sorting facility
June 2, 20— 8:00 A.M.	Customs Processing

Estimated time of arrival: June 3, 9:00 A.M.

Call 222-NBDC to request further information related to this delivery.

> **To:** <customerservice@nbdc.com>
> **From:** <candywright@canadamail.ca>
> **Subject:** Delivery Status
>
> On June 1, I sent a package from the U.S. to Canada. Your firm promises overnight delivery but the package sent on June 1 in the morning has still not arrived.
>
> Our trade fair takes place tomorrow morning at 9:00 A.M. My colleagues are setting up our booth this afternoon, and they need the package that contains our brochures and pricing information.
>
> Can you please investigate and get us our package on time (within 24-hours) as your advertisements promise?
>
> Thank you,
> Candy Wright

Question 1

1. Why does Wright require the brochures today?

   (A) Because the career fair has already started.
   (B) Her colleagues are leaving at 8:00 A.M. tomorrow.
   (C) She needs to fly to Toronto.
   (D) She wants to prepare for tomorrow's event.

The best response to the question "Why does Wright require the brochures today?" is Choice (D), "She wants to prepare for tomorrow's event." Therefore, you should choose answer (D).

Question 2

2. How might NBDC respond to the problem?

   (A) The package was sent to the wrong city.
   (B) International delivery is not guaranteed.
   (C) She shipped too late on June 1.
   (D) The Customs Office was closed.

The best response to the question "How might NBDC respond to the problem?" is Choice (B), "International delivery is not guaranteed." Therefore, you should choose answer (B).

Reading Targets Parts 5 and 6

The targets below frequently appear on Parts 5 and 6 of the Reading section of the TOEIC. If you study these targets carefully and review the strategies at the end of this chapter, you will improve your score on the TOEIC.

> Please read *Grammar and Vocabulary Terms* on page 139. This will introduce the terms and abbreviations used in this section.

TIP

The Answer Key and Explanatory Answers for all Targets in this Chapter can be found beginning on page 328.

TARGETS LIST

Analyzing Vocabulary
Grammar and Vocabulary Terms, p. 139
Target
1. Prefixes, p. 142
2. Suffixes, p. 146
3. Word Families, p. 150
4. Similar Words, p. 152

Targets 1–4 Review, p. 154

Analyzing Grammar
Count and Non-count Nouns, p. 157
Target
5. Non-count Nouns and Plural Verbs, p. 158
6. Differences in Meaning Between Count and Non-count Nouns, p. 160

Targets 5–6 Review, p. 162

Articles, p. 164
Target
7. Specified Noun with Incorrect Article, p. 166
8. Unspecified Count Noun without *the*, p. 167
9. Wrong Article with Generic Count Noun, p. 169
10. Article with Generic Non-count Noun, p. 171
11. Wrong Form of *a* or *an*, p. 173

Targets 7–11 Review, p. 175

Subject-Verb Agreement, p. 177
Target
12. Subject and Verb May Not Agree, p. 178
13. *You* as Subject, p. 180
14. Nouns and Pronouns: Singular or Plural, p. 182

Targets 12–14 Review, p. 184

Prepositions, p. 185
Target
15. Incorrect Preposition, p. 186
16. Prepositional Phrase and Verb Agreement, p. 188

Targets 15–16 Review, p. 190

Coordinating Conjunctions, p. 191
Target
17. Wrong Coordinating Conjunctions, p. 192
18. Joined Forms Not Parallel, p. 194

Targets 17–18 Review, p. 196

Subordinating Conjunctions, p. 198
Target
19. Misplaced Subordinating Conjunctions, p. 198
20. Incorrect Subordinating Conjunctions, p. 200

Targets 19–20 Review, p. 202

First News
Always Innovative & Informative

First News
A l w a y s I n n o v a t i v e & I n f o r m a t i v e

GRAMMAR AND VOCABULARY TERMS
Parts of Speech

In the "Analyzing Vocabulary" and "Analyzing Grammar" sections that follow, words such as *noun, adjective, verb,* and *adverb* are used. These words are called parts of speech, and each one has a different use. If you understand how a word is used in a sentence, you will be able to understand when it is used incorrectly. Studying the parts of speech and their functions will help you analyze a sentence.

These are the eight parts of speech and their abbreviations:

Part of Speech (Abbreviations)	Definition	Example
noun (n)	a person, animal, place, or thing	*man, dog, hotel, car*
pronoun (pron)	a word that replaces a noun	*I, you, it,* etc. / *someone, anyone*
adjective (adj)	a word that describes a noun	an *honest* man
verb (v)	a word that is a state of being or an action	He *became* tired. I *made* a cake.
adverb (adv)	a word that describes a verb	She drives *carefully.*
preposition (prep)	a word that shows a relationship between two things	the book *on* my desk
conjunction (conj)	a word that connects two phrases or clauses	Come here *and* bring a pen.
interjection (interj)	a word that represents some sort of exclamation	*Wow!* That's an amazing story.

Look at the following analysis of the parts of speech in these statements.

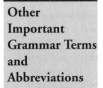

Other Important Grammar Terms and Abbreviations

article (art)
auxiliary (aux)
coordinate (coord)
gerund (ger)
infinitive (inf)
object (obj)
subordinate (sub)
subject (subj)

Examples

We   usually   have   coffee   in   the   morning,
pron   adv   v   n   prep   art   n

but   we   cannot   find   any   clean   cups.
conj   pron   aux + adv   v   adv   adj   n

Hey!   Where   are   the   cups?
interj   adv   v   art   n

Parts of speech can make up phrases.

Examples

n phrase	**prep phrase**	**v phrase**
any clean cups	in the morning,	cannot find
adv adj n	prep art n	aux + adv v

Parts of a Sentence

The parts of a sentence can also be classified. A sentence is usually made up of an independent clause: a subject and verb that can stand on its own and make sense. An independent clause is also referred to as a *main clause*.

Example

We all have coffee in the morning.
         main clause

Another main clause can be added and joined to the first with a coordinate conjunction:

I bring the pastries,   and   we all have coffee in the morning.
   main clause   coord conj   main clause

A clause that cannot stand alone and is joined to a main clause is called a *subordinate clause* (or a *dependent clause*). A subordinate clause is preceded by a subordinate conjunction. A subordinate clause can come before or after the main clause.

Before we start working, we usually have coffee.
   sub clause   main clause

Subordinate clauses can also be referred to by their function:

adverbial clause: a clause that contains an adverbial word that modifies a verb phrase.

Before we start working, we usually have coffee.
   adverbial clause   main clause

TIP

Again, note that in some grammar books, a main clause is called an independent clause and a subordinate clause is called a dependent clause.
   These terms will help you as you study the "Analyzing Vocabulary" and the "Analyzing Grammar" sections.

noun clause: a clause that usually begins with the word *that* and can be substituted completely by words like *it*, *this*, or *that*.

Everyone knows that we usually have coffee in the morning.
   main clause   noun clause

adjective clause: a clause that describes a noun.

We like coffee that is very strong.
   main clause   adj clause

Analyzing Vocabulary

It is difficult to learn vocabulary by studying long lists of words. Studies have shown that it is important to learn new words in context, that is, to learn what words mean in a sentence, what the sentence means in a paragraph, and what the paragraph means to the whole reading passage.

In the "Study Plan" section on page 4, you were advised to start your own vocabulary notebook. In this notebook, you should write down the new words you learn. You should also write down the sentences in which you found them. If you also create your own sentence using the word, you will increase your chances of remembering the word. The more often you use a word and the more ways you use it, the more likely you will not forget its meaning.

In this section, you will study about word families. When you learn a new word, look it up in the dictionary and find other members of the same word family. Write these words in your vocabulary notebook, too.

In a dictionary, you may also find the synonyms and antonyms of a word. Write these words down, too. But be careful. Not all synonyms can be interchanged. Study Target 4, "Similar Words," on page 152.

TARGET

Prefixes

A prefix is a syllable added to the beginning of the root of a word. The prefix can change the meaning of the root word.

The most commonly used prefixes are negative prefixes. They all mean *not*.

Negative Prefixes

Prefix	Word	Meaning
dis-	disloyal	not loyal
in-	incapable	not capable
im-	impatient	not patient
ir-	irregular	not regular
mis-	misplace	not placed correctly
non-	nonresident	not a resident
un-	unable	not able

Other Common Prefixes

Prefix	Meaning	Word	Actual Meaning
a-	without	apolitical	without an interest in politics
ante-	before	anteroom	waiting room
anti-	against	anti-war	pacifist
bi-	two, twice	bicoastal	on the East Coast and the West Coast of the United States
bio-	life	biography	an account of a person's life
circum-	around	circumscribe	to limit
co-	together	cochair	shared chairmanship
contra-	opposing	contradict	assert opposite information or opinion
counter-	opposing	counterattack	an attack designed to reply to another attack
de-	removal of something	debug	get the mistakes out (usually a computer program)
e-	from	emit	to give off
en-	cause to be	encourage	to give emotional support to
em-	cause to be	empower	give authority to
ex-	from	expedite	to speed up a process
ex	former	ex-president	no longer president
fore-	before	foremost	first in rank or knowledge
in-	not	invaluable	priceless; cannot have a monetary value placed on it
in-	in	inbound	headed toward a city, port, etc.

Other Common Prefixes

Prefix	Meaning	Word	Actual Meaning
im-	not	impartial	unbiased; fair
im-	in	impress	to affect or influence
ir-	not	irregular	without symmetry or pattern
inter-	between	interview	a meeting in which one person asks questions of another
intra-	within	intramural	consisting of students from the same school
macro-	big	macroeconomy	general aspects of an economy
mal-	wrong	malfunction	failure to function correctly
mega-	big	megacorporation	a large company formed by acquisition of smaller ones
micro-	small	microeconomy	particular aspects of an economy
mid-	middle	midstream	halfway across a stream
mis-	wrong	misgivings	doubts or apprehension
mono-	one	monotonous	lacking variety
multi-	many	multimedia	use of several media in combination
non-	not	nonprofessional	not trained in a particular profession; an amateur
over-	more than	overpass	a bridge or elevated walkway
para-	beside	parameter	within specified limits
poly-	many	polyphasic	doing several things at the same time
post-	after	postpone	to defer or delay
pre-	before	prevent	to keep from happening
pre-	already	prearranged	arranged in advance
pre-	preliminary	preschool	classes before elementary grades
pro-	supportive	pro-business	biased towards business
pseudo-	false	pseudonym	pen name; alternative name used by a writer
re-	again	recite	to quote a literary passage
re-	restore	replace	put back
re-	backward	retract	withdraw
semi-	half, part	semiannual	twice a year
sub-	under	subclass	a division of a class
super-	over	supersede	to replace in authority
sur-	over	surpass	to exceed
trans-	across	transfer	to change from one person or place to another
ultra-	extremely	ultraclean	germ-free
un-	not	unfocused	lacking direction or purpose

Problem	The prefix or root does not match the context.
Solution	Choose the appropriate prefix or root.

Examples

Incorrect: Gina *refers* using a computer to a typewriter.
Correct: Gina *prefers* using a computer to a typewriter.

Gina prefers using a computer to a typewriter.
  n   v   ger   n phrase   prep phrase

Explanation: *Refer* (back–to carry: to carry back) means to direct someone to someone or something. *I referred John to you because I thought you could help him. Prefer* (before–carry; to carry in front) means to choose someone or something more than something else. Gina would rather use a computer than a typewriter.

Incorrect: The audience left early because they were *immobile*.
Correct: The audience left early because they were *impatient*.

The audience left early because they were impatient.
  n phrase   v   adv   conj   pron   v   adj

Explanation: The prefix *im-* means not. *Immobile* means not mobile. If the audience was immobile, they could not move and, therefore, could not leave early. They left early because they had exhausted their patience.

Exercises

Part 5: Incomplete Sentences

Choose the one word or phrase that best completes the sentence.

Even though he usually tells the truth, this story was _____.

    (A) unbelievable
    (B) unavailable
    (C) uncomfortable
    (D) unsuccessful

    Ⓐ   Ⓑ   Ⓒ   Ⓓ

Part 6: Text Completion

Read the letter and choose the one word or phrase that best completes each sentence.

Hi Martha,

It's that time of year again when everything gets hectic around here. With my busy schedule there will be a number of odd jobs around the office that I will be _____ over to you.

    1. (A) controlling
          (B) decreasing
          (C) handling
          (D) transferring

Here are a few priorities for this week:

Our old printer is broken, and it's time to _____ it. It will be

              2. (A) replay
                  (B) replace
                  (C) display
                  (D) displace

cheaper to buy a new one than to fix the old one. We need to do this soon. We have to print copies of the annual report in time for our yearly board meeting.

In addition, I need you to write up a welcome newsletter for the new board members. Include any _____ information about the company such

              3. (A) extraordinary
                  (B) introductory
                  (C) contrary
                  (D) precautionary

as business hours, contact names and numbers, and rules and regulations. Think of it as a mini version of our company manual.

Bill

TARGET

2 Suffixes

A suffix is a letter, syllable, or group of syllables added to the end of the root of a word. The suffix can change the grammatical structure of the root word.

Look at these suffixes and their meanings:

Suffix	Added to	Form	Meaning	Example
-ability	adj	n	state of the adjective	capability
-able	v	adj	describe effect	lovable
-age	n, v, adj	n	state	marriage
-al	n	adj	relationship	national
-al	v	n	action	burial
-ance	v	n	action	attendance
-ant	v	n	occupation	accountant
-ant	v	n	effect	pollutant
-arian	n	n	association	vegetarian
-ary	n, v	adj	describe characteristics	momentary
-ary	n	n	occupation	notary
-cy	adj, n	n	describe quality	consistency
-cy	n	n	occupation	consultancy
-ee	v	n	occupation	trainee
-en	n, adj	v	process	darken
-en	n	adj	describe characteristic	wooden
-ence	v	n	action	existence
-ence	adj	n	quality	confidence
-ent	v	adj, n	person, process	student
-er	v	n	person	walker
-er	v	n	thing	computer
-ery	v	n	action	robbery
-ery	adj, n	n	behavior	bravery
-ery	v, n	n	place	bakery
-ess	n	n	person	waitress
-ful	n	n	amount	handful
-ful	n	adj	characteristic	beautiful

Suffix	Added to	Form	Meaning	Example
-hood	n	n	states	childhood
-ian	n, adj	n	job	physician
-ibility	adj	n	state	feasibility
-ible	v	adj	characteristic	accessible
-ic	n	adj	characteristic	idiotic
-fy	(root)	v	process	amplify
-ion	v	n	state	decision
-ish	adj	adj	small characteristic	largish
-ish	n	adj	characteristic	childish
-ism	n, adj	adj	concepts	consumerism
-ist	n, adj	n	person	capitalist
-ist	n	n	field	scientist
-ity	adj	n	condition	equality
-ize	n	v	action	criticize
-ize	n, adj	v	process	colonize
-less	n	adj	without	flawless
-less	n, v	adj	cannot be measured	countless
-let	n	n	smaller example	booklet
-ly	adj	adv	manner	clearly
-ly	n, adj	adj	characteristic	costly
-ly	n	adj	frequency	monthly
-ment	v	n	result of process	assignment
-ness	adj	n	quality	illness
-or	v	n	person	editor
-ous	(root)	adj	quality	curious
-some	n, v	adj	characteristic	lonesome
-ular	n	adj	characteristic	angular
-ure	v	n	action	enclosure
-y	n	adj	characteristic	dirty

Familiarity with suffixes can help you understand the meaning of words. However, it is best for you to learn words in context. Knowing the suffixes will help you determine a word's part of speech in a sentence. See the related information in Target 3, "Word Families," on page 150.

Problem	The suffix does not match the required part of speech or the meaning of the root does not match the context.
Solution	Choose the appropriate suffix and root.

Examples

Incorrect: Check the schedule to see how *frequency* the trains run.
Correct: Check the schedule to see how *frequently* the trains run.

(You)	check	the schedule	to see	how	frequently	the trains	run.
understood subj	v	n phrase	inf	conj	adv	n phrase	v

Explanation: *Frequency* is a noun formed by adding *-cy* to the adjective *frequent*. The sentence requires an adverb. Adding *-ly* to the adjective *frequent* gives us the adverb *frequently*.

Incorrect: The accountant was terminated because of her *effectiveness*.
Correct: The accountant was terminated because of her *carelessness*.

The accountant	was terminated	because of	her carelessness.
n phrase	passive v	prep	n phrase

Explanation: An accountant would not be fired because she was too effective. *Effectiveness* does not match the context.

Exercises

Part 5: Incomplete Sentences

Choose the one word or phrase that best completes the sentence.

The _____ for the job filled out the wrong form.

(A) defendant
(B) applicant
(C) occupant
(D) assistant

Ⓐ Ⓑ Ⓒ Ⓓ

Part 6: Text Completion

Read the announcement and choose the one word or phrase that best completes each sentence.

March Is Food Awareness Month

_____ research studies have shown that it is better for your

1. (A) Count
   (B) Countless
   (C) Countable
   (D) Undercounted

health to eat less meat. The evidence is overwhelming. It is clear that vegetarians are healthier people than meat eaters. Doctors today suggest aiming for a _____ meal.

2. (A) larger
   (B) more colorful
   (C) strictly vegetarian
   (D) balanced

Parents have the added responsibility of making sure that their children eat healthy foods. In the past, dietitians recommended a balance of the major food groups. Today, we know that meat does not provide the same _____ as green, red, and yellow fruits and vegetables. However,

3. (A) nourished
   (B) nourishment
   (C) nutritious
   (D) nutritional

some meat or other form of protein is still required.

TARGET

3 Word Families

Word families are created by adding endings to a word. These endings will change the word into a noun, verb, adjective, or adverb.

Common Word Endings

noun	verb	adjective	adverb
-ance	-en	-able	-ly
-ancy	-ify	-ible	-ward
-ence	-ize	-al	-wise
-ation		-ful	
-ian		-ish	
-ism		-ive	
-ist		-ous	
-ment			
-ness			
-ship			
-or			
-er			

Common Word Families

| noun | | verb | adjective | adverb |
thing	person			
application	applicant	apply	applicable	
competition	competitor	compete	competitive	competitively
criticism	critic	criticize	critical	critically
decision		decide	decisive	decisively
economy	economist	economize	economical	economically
finale	finalist	finalize	final	finally
interpretation	interpreter	interpret	interpretive	
maintenance	maintainer	maintain	maintainable	
management	manager	manage	managerial	
mechanism	mechanic	mechanize	mechanical	mechanically
nation	nationalist	nationalize	national	nationally
negotiation	negotiator	negotiate	negotiable	
politics	politician	politicize	political	politically
production	producer	produce	productive	productively
prosperity		prosper	prosperous	prosperously
repetition	repeater	repeat	repetitious	repetitively
simplification		simplify	simple	simply
theory	theoretician	theorize	theoretical	theoretically

| **Problem** | The word may be the wrong part of speech. |
| **Solution** | Check the ending of the word to determine the part of speech. |

Examples

Incorrect: The manager read the report *careful.*

Correct: The manager read the report *carefully.*

Explanation: *Careful* is an adjective. Adverbs modify verbs. *How* did the manager read the report? Change the adjective *careful* to the adverb *carefully* to modify the verb *read.*

The manager   read   the report   carefully.
   n phrase   v   n phrase   adv

Incorrect: That process is not *economize* in the factory.

Correct: That process is not *economical* in the factory.

Explanation: *Economize* is a verb. The sentence requires an adjective to modify *process.* Change the verb *economize* to the adjective *economical* to modify *process.*

That process   is not   economical   in the factory.
   n phrase   v   adj   prep phrase

Exercises

Part 5: Incomplete Sentences

Choose the one word or phrase that best completes the sentence.

The director of purchasing can _____ the best price.

  (A) negotiable
  (B) negotiate
  (C) negotiator
  (D) negotiation

Ⓐ Ⓑ Ⓒ Ⓓ

Part 6: Text Completion

Read the newspaper article and choose the one word or phrase that best completes each sentence.

Springfield News—Wednesday Edition   F1-FINANCIAL NEWS

Workers at the Springfield Furniture Factory went on strike yesterday. All _____ at the factory has stopped.

  1. (A) produce
       (B) producer
       (C) production
       (D) productive

Employees promise that they will not return to work until they _____ a new contract with the factory owners.

  2. (A) negotiate
       (B) negotiator
       (C) negotiable
       (D) negotiation

The Springfield economy has been strong since last February when three new factories opened. Unemployment is at an all-time low. Due to an increase in job _____, workers can now demand higher pay.

  3. (A) training
       (B) requirements
       (C) availability
       (D) loss

TARGET
4   Similar Words

It is easy to confuse words that have similar meanings, similar spellings, or similar sounds. However, these words CANNOT be interchanged.

Common Similar Words

accept	except	accede	expect
advise	advice	advisory	advisable
affect	effect	affection	effective
borrow	lend	loan	lease
develop	expand	elaborate	enhance
lose	loose	loss	lost
money	cash	currency	coin
obtain	earn	win	achieve
raise	rise	elevate	ascend
say	tell	speak	talk
travel	commute	go	journey

Problem	The meaning or usage of a word may be incorrect for the sentence.
Solution	First try to understand the meaning of the sentence. Then determine the correct word, in meaning, usage, and spelling, for that sentence.

Examples

Incorrect: Mr. Chang *said* his secretary to schedule a meeting.
Correct: Mr. Chang *told* his secretary to schedule a meeting.

Explanation: *Say* is followed by a direct object. *Tell* is followed by an indirect object. Use *say* when you just say something. (Mr. Chang *said* to schedule a meeting.) Use *tell* when you say something *to someone else.* (Mr. Chang *told his secretary* to schedule a meeting.)

Mr. Chang   said   to schedule a meeting.
  n phrase   v   direct obj

Mr. Chang   told   his secretary   to schedule a meeting.
  n phrase   v   n phrase: direct obj
                          indirect obj

Incorrect: The vice-president will *commute* to Tahiti on her vacation.
Correct: The vice-president will *travel* to Tahiti on her vacation.

Explanation: *Commute* means to travel to and from work every day. It cannot be used for other trips. Change *commute* to *travel,* which can be used for vacations and other trips.

The vice-president   will travel   to Tahiti   on her vacation.
   n phrase   v   prep phrase   prep phrase

First News

Always Innovative & Informative

Incorrect: My typewriter ribbon is *lose*.
Correct: My typewriter ribbon is *loose*.

Explanation: The spelling of a word can change it into a different word. To *lose* something means that you cannot find it. Check the spelling; *lose* should probably be *loose*, which means not tight.

My typewriter ribbon is loose.
     n phrase   v   adj

Exercises

Part 5: Incomplete Sentences

Choose the one word or phrase that best completes the sentence.

New employees _____ only a small salary during the first six months.

   (A) win   Ⓐ Ⓑ Ⓒ Ⓓ
   (B) gain
   (C) reach
   (D) earn

Part 6: Text Completion

Read the e-mail and choose the one word or phrase that best completes each sentence.

To: sam@home.com
From: sarah@garrisonsprings.com
Subject: Shopping

Sam,

I _____ extra money this month because I worked overtime. I'm going to the bank today to cash my

   1. (A) added
       (B) gained
       (C) earned
       (D) won

check. Then I'm _____. Would you like to come?

    2. (A) getting my hair cut
        (B) going shopping
        (C) going back to work
        (D) looking for a new job

I know that you hate going to the mall when you don't have any money. I'd be happy to _____ you some money. You could pay me back as soon as you get paid.

    3. (A) lend
        (B) borrow
        (C) lease
        (D) rent

Call me and tell me what you think. I need some new clothes, and you know I hate shopping alone!

Sarah

TARGETS 1–4 REVIEW
Prefixes, Suffixes, Word Families, and Similar Words

Part 5: Incomplete Sentences

Directions: In sentences 1–5, decide which part of speech is necessary in the sentence. Then, choose the one word or phrase that best completes the sentence. In sentences 6–10, choose the one word or phrase that best completes the sentence.

Sentences 1–5

1. The manager should _____ the procedure to reduce errors.

   (A) noun   (E) simple   Ⓐ Ⓑ Ⓒ Ⓓ
   (B) verb   (F) simplify   Ⓔ Ⓕ Ⓖ Ⓗ
   (C) adjective   (G) simplicity
   (D) adverb   (H) simplification

2. Arguing over the use of the copy machine is very _____ .

   (A) noun   (E) fool   Ⓐ Ⓑ Ⓒ Ⓓ
   (B) verb   (F) fooled   Ⓔ Ⓕ Ⓖ Ⓗ
   (C) adjective   (G) foolish
   (D) adverb   (H) foolishly

3. We could print newspaper ads to _____ our new restaurant.

   (A) noun   (E) publicity   Ⓐ Ⓑ Ⓒ Ⓓ
   (B) verb   (F) publicize   Ⓔ Ⓕ Ⓖ Ⓗ
   (C) adjective   (G) public
   (D) adverb   (H) publication

4. The _____ will be announced on Friday.

   (A) noun   (E) decision   Ⓐ Ⓑ Ⓒ Ⓓ
   (B) verb   (F) decide   Ⓔ Ⓕ Ⓖ Ⓗ
   (C) adjective   (G) decisive
   (D) adverb   (H) decisively

5. Our research facility is better _____ to manage this project.

   (A) noun   (E) qualify   Ⓐ Ⓑ Ⓒ Ⓓ
   (B) verb   (F) qualification   Ⓔ Ⓕ Ⓖ Ⓗ
   (C) adjective   (G) quality
   (D) adverb   (H) qualified

Sentences 6–10

6. The project was separated into _____ parts.

   (A) equal   Ⓐ Ⓑ Ⓒ Ⓓ
   (B) same
   (C) match
   (D) likable

7. He was _____ pleased by the results of the team effort.

   (A) specialist   Ⓐ Ⓑ Ⓒ Ⓓ
   (B) especially
   (C) specialty
   (D) special

8. Everyone left the building _____ the security guard.

   (A) except   Ⓐ Ⓑ Ⓒ Ⓓ
   (B) excess
   (C) access
   (D) accept

9. Airline ticket prices _____ when the cost of fuel increases.

   (A) raise   Ⓐ Ⓑ Ⓒ Ⓓ
   (B) grow
   (C) rise
   (D) elevate

10. Mr. Arnold can _____ a pen from Ms. Lee.

    (A) lend   Ⓐ Ⓑ Ⓒ Ⓓ
    (B) give
    (C) offer
    (D) borrow

Part 6: Text Completion

Directions: Read the e-mail and choose the one word or phrase that best completes each sentence.

To: gloriacummings@bargainboy.com
From: hankrichards@bargainboy.com
Subject: Offices

Gloria,

I need a favor. My office is being painted, and I was hoping I could use your office this afternoon while you are at your client's reviewing their account. I need to _____ several people

    1. (A) review
        (B) preview
        (C) interview
        (D) overview

for the job opening in our department. Sorry this is such a last-minute request. I just found out myself about the painters coming in.

I thought of you because I overheard you telling George that you would be out of the office for some meetings late this afternoon. There are four _____, and I have appointments with all of them after lunch.

    2. (A) applications
        (B) applicants
        (C) applicable
        (D) appliance

I don't know if you were even planning on coming back to the office after your _____.

    3. (A) meetings
        (B) accounting class
        (C) luncheon
        (D) interview

If not, then you won't even notice that I'm there. Either way, it won't take long. I can easily finish before 3:30. Then you can have your office back.

Before you leave for the afternoon can you make sure to clear any confidential papers from your workspace? Thank you in advance.

Hank

Analyzing Grammar

COUNT AND NON-COUNT NOUNS

Count nouns are nouns that can be counted. Count nouns can be either singular or plural, and they can use either singular or plural verbs.

Singular	The client	has	his	invitation.
	count n	v	pron	count n
Plural	The clients	have	their	invitations.
	count n	v	pron	count n

Non-count nouns are nouns that cannot be counted. Non-count nouns do not have plural forms and therefore cannot use plural verbs.

Singular	Quality	is	our	goal.
	non-count n	v	pron	count n
Plural	*No plural*			

Non-count nouns are often (1) nouns that are "whole" and made up of smaller parts (*cash, furniture*); (2) nouns about food (*coffee, fruit*); (3) some nouns about weather (*wind, rain*); and (4) abstract nouns (*efficiency, progress*).

Common Count and Non-count Nouns

Whole (non-count)	Parts (count)
cash	dimes, nickels, pennies, dollar bills
furniture	chairs, tables, desks, lamps
Weather (non-count)	**Weather (count)**
(some) weather	one storm, two storms...
(some) rain	one shower, two showers...
(some) sunshine	one ray of sunshine, two rays of sunshine...
Food (non-count)	**Foods (count)**
(some) fruit	one apple, two apples...
(some) coffee	one cup, two cups...
Abstract (non-count)	
(some) efficiency	
(some) progress	

(continued)

Common Count and Non-count Nouns (continued)

	Irregular plural (count)
	one fish, two fish...
	one child, two children...
	one foot, two feet...

TARGET

5   Non-count Nouns and Plural Verbs

Non-count nouns use singular verbs.

Problem	A non-count noun has a plural verb.
Solution	Use a singular verb with the non-count noun, or add a countable quantity.

Examples

Incorrect: *Confidence are* reassuring to clients.
Correct: *Confidence is* reassuring to clients.

Explanation: *Confidence* is a non-count noun. It never has a plural form, and always uses a singular verb. Change the verb to *is*.

Non-count   Confidence is reassuring to clients.
             n   v   adj   prep phrase

Incorrect: The new *furnitures look* good in the lobby.
Correct: The new *furniture looks* good in the lobby.
Correct: The new *pieces of furniture look* good in the lobby.

Explanation: *Furniture* is a non-count noun. It never has a plural form, and always uses a singular verb. Change the verb to *looks*.

Use a countable quantity with a non-count noun. You cannot count *furniture,* but you can count *pieces.* Because *pieces* is plural, use a plural verb.

Non-count   The new furniture looks good in the lobby.
        n phrase   v   adv   prep phrase

Count   The new pieces of furniture look good in the lobby.
         n phrase   v   adv   prep phrase

Exercises

Part 5: Incomplete Sentences

Choose the one word or phrase that best completes the sentence.

The employees collected several _____ to give to the poor.

(A) clothes
(B) some clothes
(C) bags of clothes
(D) bag of clothes

Ⓐ Ⓑ Ⓒ Ⓓ

Part 6: Text Completion

Read the advertisement and choose the one word or phrase that best completes each sentence.

SHOP FOR A GOOD CAUSE
WEEKEND SALE

Don't miss the big holiday sale at Murray's Department Store. This week-end only, all living room _____ is on sale for 30% off the regular

1. (A) paint
   (B) lighting
   (C) furniture
   (D) art

price. This includes sofas, coffee tables, and entertainment stands. You can't beat a bargain like that.

Murray's is a proud member of the Food for Families community program. Last month ten boxes of food _____ collected thanks to kind

2. (A) is
   (B) are
   (C) was
   (D) were

shoppers like you. Buy a new _____ furniture and Murray's will

3. (A) pieces
   (B) piece
   (C) piece of
   (D) a piece

donate five dollars worth of food to this charity.

TARGET

Differences in Meaning Between Count and Non-count Nouns

> **Problem**   Some nouns have different count and non-count meanings.
>
> **Solution**   Pay attention to the meanings of the noun.

Examples

Incorrect: *Fish* is swimming in the office pond.
Correct: Ten *fish* are swimming in the office pond. *(count)*
Correct: *Fish* makes a healthy dinner. *(non-count)*

Explanation: *Ten fish* is countable because it means ten individual living things. *Fish* for dinner is a non-count noun like *food*. Nouns, such as *light* or *hair*, change meanings depending on whether they are count or non-count nouns. For example:

Non-count: There's not enough light to read.
Count: The street lights go on at dusk.

Non-count	Fish	makes	a healthy dinner.
	n phrase	v	n phrase

Count	Ten fish	are swimming	in the office pond.
	n phrase	v	prep phrase

Incorrect: The shop sells many different *wool*.
Correct: The shop sells many different *wools*. *(count)*
Correct: The shop sells many different kinds of *wool*. *(non-count)*

Explanation: The non-count noun *wool* can be a plural count noun when it refers to different varieties of *wool*. The non-count noun *wool* can be used with a countable quantity *kinds of*.

Non-count	The shop	sells	many	different	kinds	of	wool.
	n phrase	v	adv	adj	n	prep	n

Count	The shop	sells	many	different	wools.
	n phrase	v	adv	adj	n

Exercises

Part 5: Incomplete Sentences

Choose the one word or phrase that best completes the sentence.

We need more _____ on this shelf.

(A) room
(B) rooms
(C) places of room
(D) places of rooms

Ⓐ Ⓑ Ⓒ Ⓓ

Part 6: Text Completion

Read the review and choose the one word or phrase that best completes each sentence.

SATURDAY SPECIAL
Restaurants in Review

Restaurant: White Cottage Restaurant
Rating: ***

The new White Cottage Restaurant was a unique dining experience. Unfortunately, it was not very clean. The napkins were dirty and there were spots on our water and wine glasses. However the food was delicious. We really enjoyed the fried chicken, and it was served promptly.

The _____ wasn't great. It was too dark and we couldn't see what

1. (A) music
   (B) atmosphere
   (C) meal
   (D) service

we were eating. We had to ask the server to open the curtains and let some _____ into the room. Luckily, the _____ was

2. (A) light
   (B) lighting
   (C) lights
   (D) lighten

3. (A) music
   (B) songs
   (C) singers
   (D) musician

tolerable. There was a local jazz band playing while we were dining.

TARGETS 5–6 REVIEW
Count and Non-count Nouns

Part 5: Incomplete Sentences

Directions: Choose the one word or phrase that best completes the sentence. (Note: There are only two answer options in this practice section, unlike the actual TOEIC, which has four.)

1. The movie theater has a sign that reads, "Maximum capacity: 650 _____."

   (A) peoples
   (B) persons
        Ⓐ Ⓑ

2. Most Americans eat three different _____ for dinner: a protein, a starch, and a vegetable.

   (A) foods
   (B) food
        Ⓐ Ⓑ

3. Of all the so-called "white" kinds of meat, _____ the most popular.

   (A) chicken is
   (B) chickens are
        Ⓐ Ⓑ

4. The roads are dangerous for driving because a lot of _____ fell last night.

   (A) snows
   (B) snow
        Ⓐ Ⓑ

5. In order to do a good job on that report, we'll need a lot more _____.

   (A) informations
   (B) information
        Ⓐ Ⓑ

Part 6: Text Completion

Directions: Read the e-mail and choose the one word or phrase that best completes each sentence.

To: georgemiller@johnsonco.com
From: margmason@johnsonco.com
Subject: Dinner

George,
Don't forget we are going to Rita's house for dinner tonight. I want to give her something special, so I thought I would get her a basket of _____.

    1. (A) gift
        (B) fruit
        (C) flowers
        (D) cookies

Do you think that's a good idea? You know Rita better than I do. In fact, I've only met her a few times. She might prefer candy or something else.

I also want to bring something for the dinner. I plan to stop at Brown's Grocery on my way home from work. The _____ there are delicious.

    2. (A) food
        (B) desserts
        (C) beverages
        (D) sandwiches

Strawberry pie is my favorite, so I hope everyone likes that flavor. I'll get some ice cream, too. The wine costs very little there, so I might get some of that, too. Even if we don't drink any, Rita will have it for another time.

Should we offer Mary and Mike a ride? I'm sure we have enough _____

    3. (A) room
        (B) rooms
        (C) seat
        (D) chair

in the car for them since Eric isn't coming. Let me know what you think. I can call both of them this afternoon on my coffee break.

See you tonight,
Margaret

ARTICLES

Nouns are usually preceded by the articles *a*, *an*, or *the*. Articles indicate whether a noun is specified (you are identifying which one you are talking about), unspecified (you are not identifying which one you are talking about), or generic (you are talking about something in general).

Common Use of Articles

N	Specified	Unspecified	Generic
Singular (count)	the	a (an)	a (an)
Plural (count)	the	some (many, etc.)	— —
Non-count	the	some (a lot of, etc.)	— —

TIP

Remember: If you identify (specify) the noun, use *the*. Unspecified nouns can become specified nouns.

Specified Nouns

Use *the* when you are specifying a noun (you are identifying which thing you are talking about). *The* is used with all nouns (singular and plural count nouns and non-count nouns).

Count (singular)	*The book* is on the table.
Count (plural)	*The books* are on the table.
Non-count	*The stuff* is on the table.

Unspecified Nouns

Use *a* or *an* when you are talking about a singular noun that is unspecified (you are not identifying which one you are talking about). Using *a* or *an* is a way of saying *one*. Consequently, neither *a* nor *an* can be used with plural nouns or non-count nouns. You can use a quantity word (e.g., *some* or *lots*) for plural and non-count nouns.

Count (singular)	I read *a book* that was very good.
Count (plural)	I read *some books* that were very good.
Non-count	I read *some literature* that was very good.

Count (singular)	I read *a book* that was very good. The title of *the book* was...
Count (plural)	I read *some books* that were very good. The author of *the books* was...
Non-count	I read *some literature* that was very good. The theme of *the literature* was...

Consonant Sounds	Vowel Sounds
a book	an easy chair
a job	an office
a hobby*	an honor*
a university**	an untruth**

*Notice that in the word *hobby*, the *h*, which is a consonant sound, is pronounced, so we say *a hobby*. But even though the word *honor* begins with an *h*, it is not pronounced. Therefore, the first sound is a vowel sound, so we say *an honor*.

**Notice that in the word *university*, the *u*, which is a vowel letter, is pronounced with the glide "y," which we consider a semiconsonant in English. That's why we say *a university*, because the first sound is like a consonant, not a vowel. But in the word *untruth*, the first sound is the schwa /ə/, which is a vowel sound, so we say *an untruth*.

Generic Nouns

Sometimes you talk about something in general and do not need to identify which particular "thing." Therefore, you do not need to use an article.

You do not need to use an article with most generic plural nouns and non-count nouns. But generic singular nouns must always use the article *a* or *an*.

Count (singular)	I always take *a book* on vacation.
Count (plural)	I always take *books* on vacation.
Non-count	I always take *stuff* to read on vacation.

TARGET

7   Specified Noun with Incorrect Article

If a noun is specified, it can be preceded by *the*. A or *an* is not used with specified nouns.

Problem	A specified noun may be used without *the*.
Solution	Replace the article used with *the*.

Examples

Incorrect: The name of *a company* is Swiss Marketing Associates.
Correct: The name of *the company* is Swiss Marketing Associates.

Explanation: You know which company you are talking about. Use *the*.

Specified   The name of the company is Swiss Marketing Associates.
                       n phrase   prep phrase   v   n phrase

Incorrect: Please answer *questions* on this form.
Correct: Please answer *the questions* on this form.

Explanation: You know which questions you are talking about. Use *the*.

Specified   Please answer the questions on this form.
                       v phrase   art   n   prep phrase

Exercises

Part 5: Incomplete Sentences

Choose the one word or phrase that best completes the sentence.

_____ of the entire department made the project a success.

    (A) An effort
    (B) A effort
    (C) Effort
    (D) The effort

Ⓐ Ⓑ Ⓒ Ⓓ

First News
Always Innovative & Informative

Part 6: Text Completion

Read the notice and choose the one word or phrase that best completes each sentence.

NOTICE

To: All employees
Re: Staff meeting

There will be a staff meeting next Friday at 11:00 a.m. All employees are required to attend _____ and to arrive on time. _____ of

    1. (A) meeting   2. (A) Topic
        (B) a meeting   (B) Topics
        (C) the meeting   (C) A topic
        (D) some meeting   (D) The topic

the meeting is *Improving Employee Morale.*

Though it has been a long cold winter, we need to stay positive at work. As usual we have invited a guest speaker to join us. _____ at this

                          3. (A) A speaker
                                (B) Guest speakers
                                (C) The speaker
                                (D) Speakers

month's meeting will be talking about methods of positive thinking.

Thank you

TARGET

8   Unspecified Count Noun Without *the*

If a count noun is not specified, it can be preceded by *a* or *an*. *The* is not used with unspecified count nouns.

Problem	*The* may be used with an unspecified singular count noun.
Solution	Replace *the* with *a* or *an*.

Examples

Incorrect: Mr. Jackson needs to hire *the* new secretary.
Correct: Mr. Jackson needs to hire *a* new secretary.

Explanation: *Secretary* is unspecified. Mr. Jackson needs to hire one new secretary. Use *a*.

  Unspecified   Mr. Jackson needs to hire a   new secretary.
                       n phrase   v phrase   art unspecified n phrase

First News
Always Innovative & Informative

Exercises

Part 5: Incomplete Sentences

Choose the one word or phrase that best completes the sentence.

_____ always interrupts your work during the day.

(A) Long meeting
(B) The long meeting
(C) A long meeting
(D) The meeting

Ⓐ Ⓑ Ⓒ Ⓓ

Part 6: Text Completion

Read the memorandum and choose the one word or phrase that best completes each sentence.

MEMO

Subject: Good-bye

Hey Mark,
It's been great having you here. We hope you enjoyed your stay.

Don't forget to stop at the Airport Bookstore before you get on the plane
to buy _____. It's always a good idea to have something to read

    1. (A) a ticket
       (B) a book
       (C) newspaper
       (D) food

when you are taking _____. However, don't buy snacks there

        2. (A) trip
          (B) long trip
          (C) a long trip
          (D) the long trip

because they are expensive and you'll get a meal on the plane.

Have a safe flight home. Don't forget to give us _____ when you

            3. (A) phone calls
              (B) a call
              (C) the call
              (D) a phone

get back to Florida to let us know that you arrived safely. We hope you'll
be back at Christmas.

Fondly,
Janice and Fred

TARGET

9 Wrong Article with General Count Noun

An article should precede a count noun in the general sense unless the noun is plural.

Problem	The wrong article, or no article, may be used with a count noun in the general sense.
Solution	Remove the article if the noun is plural. Change the article to *a* or *an* if the noun is a singular count noun.

Examples

Incorrect:	*Computer* processes information quickly.
Correct:	*A computer* processes information quickly.
Correct:	*Computers* process information quickly.

Explanation:	*Computer* is a count noun used in a generic sense. Use *a* with the singular form (*a computer*) or no article with the plural form (*computers*).

Generic   Computers process information quickly.
              count n   v   n   adv

Incorrect:	*The pictures* add color to an office.
Correct:	*Pictures* add color to an office.

Explanation:	*Picture* is a count noun used here in a generic sense. Use no article with the plural form (*pictures*).

Generic   Pictures add color to an office.
              count n   v   n   prep phrase

Exercises

Part 5: Incomplete Sentences

Choose the one word or phrase that best completes the sentence.

_____ keeps an office running smoothly.

(A) The schedule   Ⓐ Ⓑ Ⓒ Ⓓ
(B) Schedule
(C) A schedule
(D) Schedules

Part 6: Text Completion

Read the notice and choose the one word or phrase that best completes each sentence.

COMPUTER INNOVATION INC.

_____ to frequently asked questions are available on our

1. (A) Answer
   (B) Answers
   (C) An answer
   (D) The answer

company's website. Or call our customer service line at 800-873-0984. A staff member is always ready to help you.

Remember, just like human brains, _____ are all different. The

2. (A) computer
   (B) computers
   (C) the computers
   (D) a computer

computer you had last year may function differently from the one you own today. To understand your computer better, read through _____

3. (A) the manual
   (B) manuals
   (C) a manual
   (D) manually

that came with your system carefully.

TARGET
10
Article with Generic Non-count Noun

An article should NOT precede a non-count noun in the generic sense.

Problem	An article may be used with a generic non-count noun.
Solution	Remove the article if the noun is non-count.

Examples

Incorrect: *A software* processes information in many ways.
Correct: *Software* processes information in many ways.

Explanation: *Software* is a non-count noun used in a generic sense. Do not use an article.

Generic   Software processes information in many ways.
      non-count n   v   n   prep phrase

Incorrect: Fast copiers increase *the efficiency*.
Correct: Fast copiers increase *efficiency*.

Explanation: *Efficiency* is a non-count noun used in a generic sense. Do not use an article.

Generic   Fast copiers increase efficiency.
      n phrase   v   non-count n

Exercises

Part 5: Incomplete Sentences

Choose the one word or phrase that best completes the sentence.

Employees with high production rates will receive _____ at the banquet.

(A) recognition
(B) a recognition
(C) the recognition
(D) several recognition

Ⓐ Ⓑ Ⓒ Ⓓ

Part 6: Text Completion

Read the announcement and choose the one word or phrase that best completes each sentence.

BUSINESS TIP FOR MONDAY MARCH 1st

A number of studies have shown that music increases worker productivity. Slow music helps workers focus, while fast music increases _____ at work.

1. (A) efficiency
   (B) a efficiency
   (C) an efficiency
   (D) a few efficiency

Before you turn on any music in your office, ask your supervisor for _____. Some work environments are not suitable for music.

2. (A) the permission
   (B) permits
   (C) permission
   (D) a permission

If other staff members prefer _____ and quiet, consider using

3. (A) peace
   (B) a peace
   (C) the peace
   (D) to peace

headphones.

TARGET
11 Wrong Form of *a* or *an*

The use of *a* or *an* depends on the initial sound of the next word. If the word begins with a vowel sound, *an* is used. If the word begins with a consonant sound, *a* is used. This is not often tested on the TOEIC.

Problem	The wrong form of *a* or *an* may be used.
Solution	Pay attention to the beginning sound of the word after *a* or *an*.

Examples

Incorrect: Ms. Rolf received *a* interesting job offer.
Correct: Ms. Rolf received *an* interesting job offer.

Explanation: The word *interesting* begins with a vowel sound. Use *an*.

Vowel sound   Ms. Rolf received an interesting job offer.
                    n phrase   v   art   n phrase

No vowel sound   Ms. Rolf received a   job offer.
                    n phrase   v   art n phrase

Incorrect: The power company sends us *an* utility bill every month.
Correct: The power company sends us *a* utility bill every month.

Explanation: The word *utility* begins with the consonant sound *y* (although it starts with *u*). Use *a*.

Vowel sound   The power company charges us an increase every year.
                      n phrase   v phrase   art   n phrase

No vowel sound   The power company sends us a utility bill every month.
                      n phrase   v phrase art   n phrase

Exercises

Part 5: Incomplete Sentences

Choose the one word or phrase that best completes the sentence.

Mr. Sohasky was eager to make _____ announcement about the new project.

(A) an
(B) a
(C) those
(D) these

Ⓐ Ⓑ Ⓒ Ⓓ

Part 6: Text Completion

Read the notice and choose the one word or phrase that best completes each sentence.

NOTICE

To: All Employees
Effective date: February 1, 20—
Re: Staff uniforms

Each employee is required to wear _____ during work hours.

    1. (A) uniform
        (B) a uniform
        (C) an uniform
        (D) those uniform

This will make it _____ easy task to distinguish staff members

    2. (A) a
        (B) an
        (C) the
        (D) some

from customers.

Women should wear a colorful blouse with black pants or a knee-length skirt. Men should wear black pants with _____ or red T-shirt. No

    3. (A) an ordinary
        (B) a plain
        (C) a white
        (D) an orange

white, beige, or neutral-colored tops, please.

Posted by Management

TARGETS 7–11 REVIEW
Articles

Part 5: Incomplete Sentences

Directions: Choose the one word or phrase that best completes the sentence.

1. _____ are expected to attend the seminar.

   (A) Manager   Ⓐ Ⓑ Ⓒ Ⓓ
   (B) A manager
   (C) Managers
   (D) The manager

2. _____ is sending the goods through customs.

   (A) The shipper   Ⓐ Ⓑ Ⓒ Ⓓ
   (B) The shippers
   (C) Shipper
   (D) Shippers

3. _____ of human resources is interviewing applicants.

   (A) Director   Ⓐ Ⓑ Ⓒ Ⓓ
   (B) The directors
   (C) The director
   (D) Directors

4. The new computer has improved _____ in the office.

   (A) efficiency   Ⓐ Ⓑ Ⓒ Ⓓ
   (B) the efficiency
   (C) an efficiency
   (D) efficiencies

5. If we do not see _____ soon, we will cancel the project.

   (A) one progress   Ⓐ Ⓑ Ⓒ Ⓓ
   (B) a progress
   (C) the progress
   (D) some progress

Part 6: Text Completion

Directions: Read the e-mail and choose the one word or phrase that best completes each sentence.

To: headoffice@homeappliancecenter.com
From: vicepresident@homeappliancecenter.com
Subject: FW: Tonight's Awards

Tonight we were pleased to give _____ to Samantha Jones for

    1. (A) award
          (B) a award
          (C) an award
          (D) these award

exceptional service to the company. The award for exceptional service is one that has been given out only three times before. It is given to a staff member who goes beyond the call of duty on a daily basis. _____

    2. (A) Effort
          (B) Efforts
          (C) The effort
          (D) The efforts

she has put forth from the day she started with this company is exemplary.

Though this is an honor that few of our employees get, Ms. Jones certainly deserves it. She has shown us that _____ always brings results

    3. (A) work
          (B) a work
          (C) the work
          (D) the works

and that hard work brings great results. Everyone, including supervisors and management, can learn a lot from Ms. Jones. Please join me in congratulating her when you see her at the office this week.

SUBJECT-VERB AGREEMENT

The subject and the verb of a sentence must match in person (*I, we, he, they,* etc.) and in number (singular or plural forms of the verb *be* [am/are/is/was/were] and base form or 3rd person singular form with *-s* or *-es* on all other verbs).

Singular The *service desk is* always busy.
Plural The *service desks are* always busy.

Phrases and clauses that come between the subject and the verb do not affect subject-verb agreement. For example, a clause or phrase that comes between the subject and the verb does not affect the verb. In the example below, *specialists* is plural, but *team* is singular. The verb must agree with *team,* which is the real subject of the sentence.

A team of specialists is coming to our clinic.
n phrase   phrase   v   prep phrase

Some nouns appear plural, but are really singular and the verb must reflect this. Other nouns have irregular plurals that look singular, but the verb must agree with these, too.

Singular Nouns
the United States
measles
ham and eggs
National Autos

Plural Nouns
people
the police
phenomena
cattle

Some nouns are in a state of transition. They come from Latin and have kept their Latin singular and plural endings. This has created confusion for English speakers, who think the Latin plural ending is singular. Here are three nouns in question. Both the singular and plural verb forms are acceptable to many native speakers.

datum (singular), **data** (plural, but now considered singular by many English speakers)

The *data is/are* ready to be analyzed now.

medium (singular), **media** (plural, but now considered singular by many English speakers)

The *media has/have* covered that story in detail.

bacterium (singular), **bacteria** (plural, but now considered singular by many English speakers)

Bacteria *exists/exist* everywhere on our planet.

TARGET

12   Subject and Verb May Not Agree

Problem	The verb may not match the subject.
Solution	Change the verb to match the subject.

Examples

Incorrect: The *suppliers* in the Southeast Asian region *is* very prompt.
Correct: The *suppliers* in the Southeast Asian region *are* very prompt.

Explanation: The subject of the sentence is *suppliers*. It requires a plural verb (*are*).

The suppliers in the Southeast Asian region are very prompt.
plural n as subj   prep phrase   v   adj phrase

Incorrect: The *schedule* for the June meetings *have changed*.
Correct: The *schedule* for the June meetings *has changed*.

Explanation: The subject of the sentence is *schedule*. It requires a singular verb (*has changed*).

The schedule for the June meetings has changed.
singular n as subj   prep phrase   v

Incorrect: This *group* of business leaders *are* held in high esteem.
Correct: This *group* of business leaders *is* held in high esteem.

Explanation: The subject of the sentence is *this group*. It requires the 3rd person singular of the verb (*is*).

This group   of business leaders is held in high esteem.
singular n   appositive genitive   v   prep phrase
as subj   phrase

Exercises

Part 5: Incomplete Sentences

Choose the one word or phrase that best completes the sentence.

The officers of the company _____ today at 1:00.

(A)   is meeting
(B)   meets
(C)   has met
(D)   are meeting

Ⓐ Ⓑ Ⓒ Ⓓ

Part 6: Text Completion

Read the message and choose the one word or phrase that best completes each sentence.

Silverwood Secondary School Newsletter   Edition 3—page 6

Message from the Principal:

Note to parents: Many students at our school _____ their schedule

     1. (A) does not choose
           (B) is not choosing
           (C) has not chosen
           (D) do not choose

wisely. Some students choose classes just to be with their friends. Other students try to take too many classes in one semester. Students who take work home feel overworked and unfocused because they don't have a spare period. Before students _____ which classes to take this

     2. (A) decide
           (B) decides
           (C) deciding
           (D) to decide

semester, they should think about their options. Help them to discover their interests.

Note to students: Take classes that interest you. We recommend taking only four classes per semester. Allow one spare period for studying and catching up. More importantly, think about how much time you have to study. Remember, your teachers and parents can _____ you.

     3. (A) help
           (B) helping
           (C) helps
           (D) helped

Principal McDonald

STRATEGY

Ask Yourself...

What is the subject of this sentence?
What is the number of the subject?
How do I change this verb to match the subject?
Are there phrases between the subject and the verb?

First News
Always Innovative & Informative

TARGET

13 *You* as Subject

Problem	*You* may be used with a singular verb.
Solution	Use a plural verb.

Examples

Incorrect:	You *is* offered the position of purchasing clerk.
Correct:	You *are* offered the position of purchasing clerk.

Explanation: Even though *you* refers to one person in this sentence, use a plural verb (*are*).

Singular You are offered the position of purchasing clerk.
subj   v phrase   n phrase   prep phrase

Plural You are offered the positions of purchasing clerks.
subj   v phrase   n phrase   prep phrase

Incorrect:	*You has* a message on your machine.
Correct:	*You have* a message on your machine.

Explanation: Even though *you* refers to one person in this sentence, use a plural verb (*have*).

Singular You have a message on your machine.
subj   v   n phrase   prep phrase

Plural You have messages on your machine.
subj   v   n phrase.   prep phrase

Exercises

Part 5: Incomplete Sentences

Choose the one word or phrase that best completes the sentence.

You _____ the only person who can do this job.

(A) is
(B) are
(C) was
(D) has

Ⓐ Ⓑ Ⓒ Ⓓ

First News
A l w a y s   I n n o v a t i v e & I n f o r m a t i v e

Part 6: Text Completion

Read the memorandum and choose the one word or phrase that best completes each sentence.

MEMO

From the Desk of: Cheryl Roberts, Manager
To: Timothy Higgins, Clerk

Timothy,

Are you feeling OK today? You _____ behind in your work. This

      1. (A) be
          (B) is
          (C) are
          (D) was

is not like you. Usually you are on time with all of your submissions. You
_____ your trip report yet. This was due yesterday.

2. (A) haven't turned in
    (B) hasn't turned in
    (C) doesn't turn in
    (D) aren't turning in

I know you _____ to be going to a meeting at 2:00. Please cancel

    3. (A) be supposed
        (B) are supposed
        (C) is supposed
        (D) was supposed

this meeting. You need to have the report on my desk by the end of the day. Please come and talk to me if you aren't feeling well.

Thanks,
Cheryl

TARGET

14 Nouns and Pronouns: Singular or Plural

Problem	The verb may not match the subject.
Solution	Know whether the subject is considered singular or plural.

Examples

Incorrect: Thirty dollars *are* not too much to pay for that shirt.
Correct: Thirty dollars *is* not too much to pay for that shirt.

Explanation: *Thirty dollars* is <u>one</u> sum of money and is treated as a singular (= it). Use 3rd person singular.

Plural   All the employees like comfortable desk chairs.
              subj   v   n phrase

Singular   Everybody in the company likes comfortable desk chairs.
              subj   v   n phrase

Incorrect: *National Autos own* this factory.
Correct: *National Autos owns* this factory.

Explanation: Even though the name *National Autos* ends in a plural word (*Autos*), it is one company. It is singular. Use a singular verb (*owns*).

Plural   Mr. Ho and his partner own this factory.
              subj   v   n phrase

Singular   National Autos owns this factory.
              subj   v   n phrase

Exercises

Part 5: Incomplete Sentences

Choose the one word or phrase that best completes the sentence.

The police _____ very conscientious about parking violations.

(A) is
(B) are
(C) was
(D) has

Part 6: Text Completion

Read the advertisement and choose the one word or phrase that best completes each sentence.

Axel Exterminators

Do you have a problem with mice in your house? Mice _____ dirt

1. (A) bring
   (B) brings
   (C) is bringing
   (D) has brought

inside and can cause a lot of damage. Worry no more! Axel Exterminators _____ the most experienced company around.

2. (A) be
   (B) is
   (C) are
   (D) were

Many people _____ to solve their pest problems themselves. By

3. (A) tries
   (B) tried
   (C) try
   (D) to try

setting up homemade traps you are more likely to make the matter worse.

Remember: Poison is dangerous to small children. Very small children may think the pellets are food. Toxic fumes from sprays can get into their lungs. Use Axel Exterminators instead. We will rid your house safely of mice in 24 hours, guaranteed. Call today: 333-PEST

TARGETS 12–14 REVIEW
Subject-Verb Agreement

Part 5: Incomplete Sentences

Directions: Choose the one word or phrase that best completes the sentence.

1. The manager from headquarters _____ us this afternoon.

   (A) are visiting   Ⓐ Ⓑ Ⓒ Ⓓ
   (B) is visiting
   (C) to visit
   (D) visiting

2. Everyone in these departments _____ assigned to the programming team.

   (A) be   Ⓐ Ⓑ Ⓒ Ⓓ
   (B) are
   (C) is
   (D) will

3. The police _____ when the alarm goes off.

   (A) arrive quickly   Ⓐ Ⓑ Ⓒ Ⓓ
   (B) is arriving
   (C) arrives quickly
   (D) has arrived

4. International Communications _____ merging with ERI.

   (A) is   Ⓐ Ⓑ Ⓒ Ⓓ
   (B) are
   (C) are being
   (D) have

5. Every employee _____ his own desk.

   (A) get   Ⓐ Ⓑ Ⓒ Ⓓ
   (B) gotten
   (C) getting
   (D) gets

Part 6: Text Completion

Directions: Read the notice and choose the one word or phrase that best completes each sentence.

NOTICE

To: All Staff
Re: Business Travel
Change Effective: Immediately

Business Travel Policy

Employees returning from a business trip on behalf of the company _____

    1.   (A) is
            (B) be
            (C) are
            (D) has

required to submit their expense report within one week of returning. All employees must use a valid company credit card when traveling on business. Employees must also present all receipts. If you _____ your report on time, you may have to wait another

    2.   (A) don't submit
            (B) doesn't submit
            (C) isn't submitting
            (D) hasn't submitted

month for reimbursement.

When planning business travel, remember that Johnson and Associates is the travel agency we use. As long-term clients, we receive a twenty percent discount through this agency. Please do not approach your supervisor with other travel deals from the newspaper or elsewhere. We have just signed a contract with Johnson and Associates and they will be keeping all of our travel records. The people in that office _____ to get

    3.   (A) are promising
            (B) promise
            (C) is promising
            (D) has promised

you the best and most comfortable accommodations available.

Posted by Management

PREPOSITIONS

Prepositions show the relationships between nouns or pronouns and other words. A prepositional phrase begins with a preposition and ends with a noun.

Common Prepositions

about	as	between	in	out	toward(s)
above	at	beyond	inside	outside	under
across	before	by	into	over	until
after	behind	down	like	past	up
against	below	during	near	since	upon
along	beneath	except	of	through	with
among	beside	for	off	till	within
around	besides	from	on	to	without

TARGET
15   Incorrect Preposition

Problem	The wrong preposition may be used.
Solution	Pay attention to the meaning and use of the preposition.

Examples

Incorrect: The meeting is *on* 3:00.
Correct: The meeting is *at* 3:00.

Explanation: *On* is used with days of the week. (*The meeting is on Wednesday.*) *At* is used with specific times.

Days of week   The meeting   is on   Monday.
                    n phrase   v prep obj of prep

Specific time   The meeting   is at   3:00.
                     n phrase   v prep obj of prep

Incorrect: Edit the report *by* a pencil.
Correct: Edit the report *with* a pencil.

Explanation: *By* is used for deadlines (*by 3:00*) and for how something was transmitted (*by fax; by telephone*). *With* indicates the instrument used (*wrote with a pen; cut with a knife*).

Edit the report with a pencil.
 v   n phrase   prep obj of prep

Exercises

Part 5: Incomplete Sentences

Choose the one word or phrase that best completes the sentence.

Just leave the report _____ my desk before you go to lunch.

(A) into
(B) on   Ⓐ Ⓑ Ⓒ Ⓓ
(C) along
(D) for

Part 6: Text Completion

Read the telephone message and choose the one word or phrase that best completes each sentence.

TELEPHONE MESSAGE

For: *Marcia Stevens*
From: *Bob Evans*
Call back: *No*
Urgent: *No*

Message:
Mr. Evans called this morning. He is catching a flight _____

                          1. (A) at
                              (B) to
                              (C) over
                              (D) with

New York early tomorrow. He needs you to run some errands while he is away. He left a list for you _____ *your desk drawer. The list is*

                2. (A) of
                   (B) on
                   (C) in
                   (D) next

in order of priority. Most important: You need to mail the monthly newsletter to all board members. If you have any problems reading his writing, call him _____ *his cell phone. Mr. Evans said he*

             3. (A) at
                  (B) on
                  (C) in
                  (D) to

thinks you have the number stored on your computer. If not, call his wife at home. She will give it to you.

Message received by: *Erica Myers*

TARGET
16 Prepositional Phrase and Verb Agreement

A prepositional phrase between the subject and the verb does not change the subject of the sentence or the need for subject-verb agreement.

Problem	The verb may match the prepositional phrase instead of the subject.
Solution	Pay attention to the number of the subject.

Examples

Incorrect: The *order* for office supplies *were* on my desk.
Correct: The *order* for office supplies *was* on my desk.

Explanation: The subject of the sentence is *order*. It requires a singular verb (*was*).

Singular subject The order for office supplies was on my desk.
noun phrase   prep phrase   v   prep phrase

Plural subject Duplicate orders for office supplies were on my desk.
noun phrase   prep phrase   v   prep phrase

Exercises

Part 5: Incomplete Sentences

Choose the one word or phrase that best completes the sentence.

The award for the best office manager _____ to Ms. Ajai.

   (A) is
   (B) go
   (C) goes
   (D) are

Ⓐ Ⓑ Ⓒ Ⓓ

Part 6: Text Completion

Read the memorandum and choose the one word or phrase that best completes each sentence.

Memo

To: All Trainees
Cc: Training Supervisors
From: Elliot
Re: Vacations

A number of you have e-mailed me recently about our vacation policies. I apologize that the rules related to holiday time _____ in the

        1. (A) needs to print
               (B) are not printed
               (C) isn't printed
               (D) not printing

training manual. We realize that many updates for the training manual _____. A new manual should be available next spring.

2. (A) requires
    (B) is required
    (C) are required
    (D) requiring

The forms for requesting vacation leave _____ available from the

        3. (A) is
             (B) be
             (C) are
             (D) was

office manager. Your number of allowed vacation days depends on your length of service with this company. Please see Judy, the Benefits Manager, for more details. Judy can e-mail you the information you need.

STRATEGY

Learn the meaning and usage of common prepositions.

TARGETS 15–16 REVIEW
Prepositions

Part 5: Incomplete Sentences

Directions: Choose the one word or phrase that best completes the sentence.

1. The messenger left the package _____ the receptionist's desk.

   (A) on   Ⓐ Ⓑ Ⓒ Ⓓ
   (B) to
   (C) until
   (D) through

2. The convention will be held _____ Stuttgart.

   (A) at   Ⓐ Ⓑ Ⓒ Ⓓ
   (B) from
   (C) for
   (D) in

3. There is a meeting _____ Friday.

   (A) by   Ⓐ Ⓑ Ⓒ Ⓓ
   (B) on
   (C) in
   (D) at

4. The banquet starts _____ 7:00 P.M. in the Terrengauv Room.

   (A) on   Ⓐ Ⓑ Ⓒ Ⓓ
   (B) at
   (C) in
   (D) for

5. Mr. Kim will not know the results of the negotiations _____ tomorrow.

   (A) on   Ⓐ Ⓑ Ⓒ Ⓓ
   (B) from
   (C) until
   (D) at

Part 6: Text Completion

Directions: Read the advertisement and choose the one word or phrase that best completes each sentence.

Busby's Sporting Goods

Visit Busby's for all your sporting goods needs.
Located _____ 125 Lincoln Avenue in the heart of the downtown

1. (A) on
   (B) in
   (C) of
   (D) at

shopping district. Open seven days a week, _____ 7:30 A.M. to 7:30 P.M.

2. (A) to
   (B) at
   (C) from
   (D) until

Sale! This week only, all equipment for water sports is on sale for 25% off.
Become a Busby's member and receive special benefits and discounts.
Applications for membership _____ available from any Busby's cashier.

3. (A) being
   (B) are
   (C) is
   (D) be

Sale does not include clothing.
Sorry, we do not provide lessons.

COORDINATING CONJUNCTIONS

Coordinating conjunctions are used to join words, phrases, and clauses of equal importance and whose functions are grammatically similar. For example, a coordinating conjunction may join two adjectives, two prepositional phrases, or two independent clauses.

Coordinating Conj			**Paired Coordinating Conj**	
and	nor	so	either...or	not only...but also
but	for		neither...nor	both...and
or	yet			

Conjunction Joining Two Adjectives

The conference was long, but interesting.
 n phrase   v   adj   conj   adj

Conjunction Joining Two Prepositional Phrases

The keys are on the desk or in a drawer.
 n phrase   v   prep phrase conj   prep phrase

Conjunction Joining Two Clauses

She attached the file and she sent the e-mail.
 independent clause   conj   independent clause

TARGET

17   Wrong Coordinating Conjunctions

Problem	The wrong coordinating conjunction may be used.
Solution	Pay attention to the meaning of the conjunction.

Examples

Incorrect: The meeting was interesting *or* productive.
Correct: The meeting was interesting *and* productive.

Explanation: *Or* indicates a choice. *The meeting was interesting* or *The meeting was productive* but not both. *And* indicates both: *The meeting was interesting; it was also productive.*

Positive
The meeting was both interesting and productive.
n phrase   v   conj   adj   conj   adj

Positive option
The meeting was interesting and productive.
n phrase   v   adj   conj   adj

Negative
The meeting was neither interesting nor productive.
n phrase   v   conj   adj   conj   adj

Negative option
The meeting was not interesting or productive.
n phrase   v   adj   conj   adj

Incorrect: Would you like a window seat *and* an aisle seat?
Correct: Would you like a window seat *or* an aisle seat?

Choice
Would you like a window seat or an aisle seat?
subj   v   n phrase   conj   n phrase

Exercises

Part 5: Incomplete Sentences

Choose the one word or phrase that best completes the sentence.

Ms. Sam's work is both creative _____ accurate.

(A) but
(B) or
(C) and
(D) nor

Ⓐ Ⓑ Ⓒ Ⓓ

Part 6: Text Completion

Read the telephone message and choose the one word or phrase that best completes each sentence.

TELEPHONE MESSAGE

To: *Jenny Ng*
From: *Colleen Christopher*
Re: *Travel Arrangements*
Callback Requested: *No*

Message: *Mrs. Christopher from New York called about your upcoming business trip. She wanted to talk to you about the train schedules. She said you can take either a local train at 7:00* _____ *an express*

1. (A) nor
   (B) or
   (C) but
   (D) and

train at 8:00. Expect the later train to be much busier because it is designed for people going to work. Both the local train and the commuter train leave from Platform 10. She would prefer it if you arrive in the office by 9 a.m. at the latest. Neither the local train _____ *the express train take more than half an hour from*

2. (A) and
   (B) nor
   (C) or
   (D) also

your hotel. Either way, before you go in on Monday, give her a call. She might be able to pick you up. That way you won't have to take the train at all. However, if you have never taken the train in New York, I think you should do it for the experience. Trains in New York are _____ *exciting and modern compared to ours.*

3. (A) both
   (B) neither
   (C) or
   (D) and

TARGET

18 Joined Forms not Parallel

The two words, phrases, or clauses joined by a coordinating conjunction must be alike: two noun forms, two verb forms, two gerunds, etc.

Problem	The joined items may not be alike.
Solution	Make them alike.

Examples

Incorrect: The boss likes *to type* and *proofreading* her own letters.
Correct: The boss likes *to type* and *to proofread* her own letters.
    The boss likes *to type* and *proofread* her own letters.
    The boss likes *typing* and *proofreading* her own letters.

Explanation: *To type* is an infinitive; *proofreading* is a gerund. You cannot use a coordinating conjunction to join two different forms. Make them both infinitives (*to type* and *to proofread)* or both gerunds (*typing* and *proofreading).* Note that when using two infinitives, it is not necessary to repeat the second infinitive marker (*to).*

Infinitive   The boss likes to type and to proofread her own letters.
        n phrase   v   verbal   conj   verbal   n phrase

Gerund   The boss likes typing and proofreading her own letters.
        n phrase   v   verbal   conj   verbal   n phrase

Incorrect: *The manager* or *assisting her* made the request.
Correct: *The manager* or *her assistant* made the request.

Explanation: *The manager* is a noun phrase; *assisting her* is a verb phrase. Because *the manager* is the subject of the sentence, make both of the joined items noun phrases (*the manager* or *her assistant).*

The manager or her assistant made the request.
    n phrase   conj   n phrase   v   n phrase

Incorrect: *The president issued the memo* but *written by her secretary.*
Correct: *The president issued the memo* but *her secretary wrote it.*
    The president issued the memo, but *it was written by her secretary.*

Explanation: *The president issued the memo* is a sentence; *written by her secretary* is a sentence fragment. Add a subject and verb to the fragment to make it a complete active voice sentence (*her secretary wrote it),* or add a subject and auxiliary to the past participle to make it a complete passive voice sentence (*it was written by her secretary).*

sentence	**conj**	**sentence**

The president issued the memo, but her secretary wrote it.
    n phrase   v   n phrase   conj   n phrase   v   pron

sentence	**conj**	**sentence**

The president issued the memo, but it was written by her secretary.
    n phrase   v   n phrase   conj   pron   passive v   prep phrase

| Incorrect: | Mr. Lee types *quickly* and is *accurate.* |
| Correct: | Mr. Lee types *quickly* and *accurately.* |

| Explanation: | *Quickly* is an adverb; *accurate* is an adjective. Make them both adverbs (*quickly* and *accurately*) to modify the verb types. |

Mr. Lee types quickly and accurately.
n phrase   v   adv   conj   adv

| Incorrect: | This report is *long* and it *bores* me. |
| Correct: | This report is *long* and *boring.* |

| Explanation: | *Long* is an adjective; *bores* is a verb. Make them both adjectives (*long* and *boring*) to modify the noun *report.* |

This report is long and boring.
n phrase   v   adj   conj   adj

STRATEGY

Recognize the correct grammatical form: Learn to distinguish gerunds from infinitives, noun phrases from verb phrases, adjectives from adverbs, etc.

Exercises

Part 5: Incomplete Sentences

Choose the one word or phrase that best completes the sentence.

Mr. Medeiros likes to arrive early or _____ to get his work done.

(A) is staying late
(B) stays late
(C) stay late
(D) staying late

Ⓐ Ⓑ Ⓒ Ⓓ

Part 6: Text Completion

Read the announcement and choose the one word or phrase that best completes each sentence.

CUSTOMER COMMENT CARD

Our company is dedicated to product quality and customer _____. Therefore,

1. (A) satisfy
   (B) satisfied
   (C) satisfying
   (D) satisfaction

_____ and friendly customer service is a priority. According to our motto, the

2. (A) prompt
   (B) promptly
   (C) prompted
   (D) promptness

customer is always right. However, we also recognize that nobody is perfect. If our service providers have acted in any way that seems unfair or _____ we want to know

3. (A) unprofessionally
   (B) they were unprofessional
   (C) have acted unprofessional
   (D) unprofessional

about it. Please flip over this card and provide your feedback. Tell us what we did right or what we did wrong.

*Please make comments anonymously. Do not include any personal information.

Thank you for taking the time to help us improve.

TARGETS 17–18 REVIEW
Coordinating Conjunctions

Part 5: Incomplete Sentences

Directions: Choose the one word or phrase that best completes the sentence.

1. Would you like a room overlooking the park _____ the river?

    (A) but   Ⓐ Ⓑ Ⓒ Ⓓ
    (B) so
    (C) or
    (D) that

2. My letters _____ my phone calls have not been answered.

    (A) or   Ⓐ Ⓑ Ⓒ Ⓓ
    (B) and
    (C) but
    (D) so

3. Mr. Dairova will work the morning shift, _____ he prefers to work in the evenings.

    (A) but   Ⓐ Ⓑ Ⓒ Ⓓ
    (B) or
    (C) when
    (D) and

4. Our hotel is located between the business district _____ the historical district.

    (A) or   Ⓐ Ⓑ Ⓒ Ⓓ
    (B) if
    (C) but
    (D) and

5. Dr. Corso can see you at 10:00 _____ at 10:30.

    (A) or   Ⓐ Ⓑ Ⓒ Ⓓ
    (B) and
    (C) but
    (D) though

Part 6: Text Completion

Directions: Read the letter and choose the one word or phrase that best completes each sentence.

Greene and Associates
21 Dundas St.
Whitby, Ontario
L1N 9BY

Mr. J. Kang
14 Harborfront St.
Toronto, Ont.
M58 2B3

Dear Mr. Kang,   May 3, 20—

I enjoyed meeting you at last week's conference and discussing business prospects in your city. We are very interested in opening a firm in Toronto and have been researching it further since the conference. I would be happy to meet with you at your office sometime this month, _____ the date you suggested is not convenient for me. I could

1. (A) so
   (B) but
   (C) and
   (D) nor

visit either on May 16 _____ May 18. I hope one of these dates

2. (A) neither
   (B) either
   (C) or
   (D) and

suits you.

My assistant will call you this week to arrange an appointment and _____ directions to your office. If you have any locations in

3. (A) get
   (B) gets
   (C) getting
   (D) will get

mind for us, please forward them to me ahead of time so that I can drive by and view the areas before we meet. I look forward to seeing you.

Sincerely,
Edna Greene
Edna Greene

SUBORDINATING CONJUNCTIONS

Subordinating conjunctions are used to join clauses (not words or phrases) that have grammatically different functions. A subordinating conjunction together with its following clause acts like a part of the main clause.

Common Subordinating Conjunctions

after	before	that	when
although	if	though	where
as	once	until	while
because	since		

The subordinating conjunction must be the first word in the subordinate clause for the sentence to make sense. The subordinate clause can be before or after the main clause.

TARGET

19   Misplaced Subordinating Conjunctions

> **Problem**   The subordinating conjunction may be in the wrong clause.
>
> **Solution**   Put the subordinating conjunction at the beginning of the subordinate clause.

Examples

Incorrect: The mail arrived *after* the clerk sorted it.
Correct: *After* the mail arrived, the clerk sorted it.
Incorrect: *After* the clerk sorted it, the mail arrived.
Correct: The clerk sorted the mail *after* it arrived.

Explanation: *The clerk sorted the mail* is the main clause; subordinate conjunctions cannot start main clauses. Move *after* to the subordinate clause (*after the mail arrived*).

main clause			subordinate clause		
The clerk	sorted	the mail	after	it	arrived.
n phrase	first v	n phrase	conj	pron	second v

Incorrect: *While* the copier broke, we were typing the report.
Correct: The copier broke *while* we were typing the report.
Incorrect: We were typing the report *while* the copier broke.
Correct: *While* we were typing the report, the copier broke.

Explanation: *The copier broke* is the main clause; subordinate conjunctions cannot start main clauses. Move *while* to the subordinate clause (*while we were typing the report*).

main clause		subordinate clause			
The copier	broke	while	we	were typing	the report.
n phrase	first v	conj	pron	second v	n phrase

Exercises

Part 5: Incomplete Sentences

Choose the one word or phrase that best completes the sentence.

The project has moved faster _____.

    (A) the computers arrived since
    (B) the computers since arrived
    (C) since arrived the computers
    (D) since the computers arrived

Ⓐ Ⓑ Ⓒ Ⓓ

Part 6: Text Completion

Read the notice and choose the one word or phrase that best completes each sentence.

Store Refund and Exchange Policy

_____ an item to the store within 30 days of the purchase

  1. (A) You return
      (B) If you return
      (C) You return if
      (D) If return you

date, you will receive a full refund. Items returned after this date may be exchanged for up to ninety days. Please remember to have the receipt with you _____ the item back to the store. A receipt is necessary for a

  2. (A) bring
      (B) when bring
      (C) when you bring
      (D) when bring you

refund or an exchange.

_____ honor this policy, an exchange or refund will not be granted

  3. (A) Generally we although
      (B) Although we generally
      (C) We generally although
      (D) We although generally

for items that are damaged or used. The store manager has the right to refuse to give you a refund even if you return the item within 30 days.

TARGET

20 Incorrect Subordinating Conjunctions

Problem	The wrong subordinating conjunction may be used.
Solution	Pay attention to the relationship between the two clauses.

Examples

Incorrect: *Because* Ms. Do worked very hard, she did not receive a promotion.
Correct: *Although* Ms. Do worked very hard, she did not receive a promotion.

Explanation: *Because* indicates cause and effect. It is not likely that working hard would cause someone to lose a promotion. Therefore, *because* has the wrong meaning for the sentence. *Although* indicates that one thing happens in spite of another (*she did not receive a promotion in spite of her hard work*). This makes sense, so *although* can be used in this sentence.

Although	Mrs. Do	worked hard,	she	did not receive	a promotion.
conj	n phrase	v phrase	pron	v phrase	n phrase

Because	Mrs. Do	worked hard,	she	received	a promotion.
conj	n phrase	v phrase	pron	v	n phrase

Incorrect: The secretary will mail the letter *though* his manager signs it.
Correct: The secretary will mail the letter *when* his manager signs it.

Explanation: *Though* indicates unexpected actions. This sentence reflects the expected actions (the manager will sign the letter; the secretary will mail the letter). Therefore, *though* has the wrong meaning for the sentence. *When* indicates a logical time relationship between the events, so it can be used in this sentence.

The secretary	will mail	the letter	when	his manager	signs it.
n phrase	v phrase	n phrase	conj	n phrase	v phrase

Exercises

Part 5: Incomplete Sentences

Choose the one word or phrase that best completes the sentence.

The usher allowed Ms. Sello into the concert hall _____ she was late.

(A) because
(B) yet
(C) even though
(D) before

Ⓐ Ⓑ Ⓒ Ⓓ

Part 6: Text Completion

Read the e-mail and choose the one word or phrase that best completes each sentence.

To: All Staff
From: mariomanendez@realtorbros.com
Subject: Retreat

Hi everyone,

I hope you are all working hard this week. Yolanda and I have been thinking of you and wondering how you are doing. _____ the

1. (A) Although
    (B) Because
    (C) However
    (D) Since

weather was rainy, the weekend work retreat went very well. We worked inside most of the day. _____ the skies cleared in the late

2. (A) Before
    (B) While
    (C) Until
    (D) After

afternoon, we enjoyed some relaxing outdoor activities.

We will be coming home on Wednesday, but won't be back in the office until Friday. We will need a day of rest after this retreat. You may not believe this, but we have been putting in some very long hours. We are actually looking forward to coming back to a relaxing work environment, _____ this has been a great learning experience.

3. (A) if
    (B) even though
    (C) that
    (D) because

Yours,
Mario

TARGETS 19–20 REVIEW
Subordinating Conjunctions

Part 5: Incomplete Sentences

Directions: Choose the one word or phrase that best completes the sentence.

1. _____ the team worked very hard, their proposal was not accepted.

   (A) Because   Ⓐ Ⓑ Ⓒ Ⓓ
   (B) Although
   (C) Before
   (D) Where

2. Mr. Atari started his company in the town _____ he grew up.

   (A) although   Ⓐ Ⓑ Ⓒ Ⓓ
   (B) that
   (C) where
   (D) if

3. _____ Mr. Lafer joined our company, he had worked for our competitor.

   (A) After   Ⓐ Ⓑ Ⓒ Ⓓ
   (B) During
   (C) Before
   (D) While

4. Please sign for the package _____ it arrives.

   (A) because   Ⓐ Ⓑ Ⓒ Ⓓ
   (B) until
   (C) although
   (D) when

5. _____ Ms. Belazi missed her connection, she had to take a later flight.

   (A) Although   Ⓐ Ⓑ Ⓒ Ⓓ
   (B) Because
   (C) If
   (D) Where

Part 6: Text Completion

Directions: Read the memorandum and choose the one word or phrase that best completes each sentence.

To: Sales Manager
From: Head Office
Re: Ms. P. Kwan

Dear Mrs. Chan,

I received your recommendation this week regarding Ms. P. Kwan's position. _____ Ms. Kwan has put in a lot of extra effort over the past

1. (A) Because
   (B) Although
   (C) Since
   (D) Once

few months, I don't feel that it is appropriate at this time to give her a promotion. I looked through her employee file and was rather unimpressed. _____ working at this company last year, her work was carelessly

2. (A) She began
   (B) When she began
   (C) She began when
   (D) When began she

done and she often arrived at the office late. As far as I can tell, she didn't improve her efforts until she decided to ask for a promotion a few months ago.

I believe Ms. Kwan's currently salary and position are fair, and she needs more time to prove herself. I don't think she deserves to become a supervisor just _____ she worked more than usual for a couple of months.

3. (A) once
   (B) while
   (C) until
   (D) because

There are other people in your department who I may consider. Let me know if you have anyone in mind.

Sincerely,

Mr. J. Lee

COMPARISONS WITH ADJECTIVES AND ADVERBS

Adjectives and adverbs can be used to show the similarities and differences among people, places, things, and actions. There are three degrees of comparison: (1) positive; (2) comparative (*-er* and *more* forms); and (3) superlative (*-est* and *most* forms).

One-syllable adjectives and two-syllable adjectives that end in *-y* have the *-er* and *-est* forms. Certain other two-syllable adjectives also have these forms. All three-syllable adjectives use *more* and *most*. Adverbs follow a similar pattern.

Adjectives and adverbs that have the *-er/-est* forms:

Adjectives

Positive	Comparative	Superlative
pretty	prettier	the prettiest
thick	thicker	the thickest
narrow	narrower	the narrowest

Adverbs

Positive	Comparative	Superlative
far	farther	the farthest
soon	sooner	the soonest
lively	livelier	the liveliest

Adjectives and adverbs that have the *more/most* forms:

Adjectives

Positive	Comparative	Superlative
beautiful	more beautiful	the most beautiful
popular	more popular	the most popular
competent	more competent	the most competent

Adverbs

Positive	Comparative	Superlative
politely	more politely	the most politely
efficiently	more efficiently	the most efficiently
quickly	more quickly	the most quickly

Some adjectives and adverbs are irregular. They do not form their comparative and superlative degrees by using *-er/more* or *-est/most*.

Adjectives

Positive	Comparative	Superlative
good	better	the best
bad	worse	the worst

Adverbs

Positive	Comparative	Superlative
well	better	the best
little	less	the least

There are two kinds of comparisons: (1) equal comparisons and (2) unequal comparisons.

Use the positive form with *as—as* to make an equal comparison.

Equal comparison between two things:

Adverb   My computer retrieves information *as quickly as* yours does.
Adjective   My chair is *as comfortable as* yours.

Unequal comparison between two things:
Use the comparative form to make an unequal comparison between two things. Use *than.*

Adverb   My computer processes information *faster than* yours.
Adjective   My chair is *more comfortable than* your chair.

Unequal comparison between three or more things:
Use the superlative form to make an unequal comparison among three or more things. Use *the.*

Adverb   My computer runs *the fastest.*
Adjective   My chair is *the most comfortable* chair in the office.

TARGET
21   Use of *as—as*

An equal comparison can be made using the positive form of an adjective or adverb with *as—as*.

Problem	*As* may be used only once.
Solution	Make sure you use *as* on both sides of the adjective or adverb.

Examples

Incorrect: Her work is *accurate as* his.
Incorrect: Her work is *as accurate* his.
Correct: Her work is *as accurate as* his.

Explanation: *As* must be used twice before the comparison is complete.

Comparison

Her work	is	as	accurate	as	his.
n phrase	v		adj		pron

Incorrect: That printer operates *quietly as* the computer.
Incorrect: That printer operates *as quietly* the computer.
Correct: That printer operates *as quietly as* the computer.

Explanation: *As* must be used twice before the comparison is complete.

Comparison

That printer	operates	as	quietly	as	the computer.
n phrase	v		adv		n phrase

Exercises

Part 5: Incomplete Sentences

Choose the one word or phrase that best completes the sentence.

The new employee would like to be _____ his predecessor.

(A) popular as
(B) as popular as
(C) as popular
(D) popular than

Ⓐ Ⓑ Ⓒ Ⓓ

Part 6: Text Completion

Read the memorandum and choose the one word or phrase that best completes each sentence.

From the Desk of: Sarah Whitney
To: Luis Danza
Response required: Yes___ No <u>X</u>

Luis,

I don't think we should buy the photocopier that Marta recommended. I went to the computer shop last night to test it out. It doesn't copy _____ as our old Samuri L1 copier. It also costs almost

   1. (A) quick
        (B) quickly
        (C) as quickly
        (D) as quickly as

_____ other copiers that have many more features. The thing

   2. (A) more
        (B) much
        (C) much as
        (D) as much as

I loved about our old copier was the small size.

The product that I was most impressed with was Samuri's new L2 model. It's just as _____ as our old one. It will take up only as much room

       3. (A) compact
           (B) slow
           (C) expensive
           (D) modern

as our old copier, if not less. And, it's a good price. Let me know if you want me to order one.

Sara

TARGET
22   *More/-er* or *Than* Omitted

An unequal comparison between two things uses the positive form with *more* and *than* or *-er* and *than*.

Problem	*More/-er* or *than* may be left out.
Solution	Make sure you use a *more/-er* form of the adjective or adverb. Use *than* after the adjective or adverb.

Examples

Incorrect: Her work is *more accurate* his.
Incorrect: Her work is *accurate than* his.
Correct: Her work is *more accurate than* his.

Explanation: *More/-er* and *than* must be used before the comparison is complete.

Comparison

Her work	is	more accurate	than	his.
n phrase	v	adj	conj	pron

Incorrect: His work is *neater* hers.
Incorrect: His work is *neat than* hers.
Correct: His work is *neater than* hers.

Explanation: *More/-er* and *than* must be used before the comparison is complete.

Comparison

His work	is	neater	than	hers.
n phrase	v	adj	conj	pron

Incorrect: He drives *faster* his father.
Incorrect: He drives *fast than* his father.
Correct: He drives *faster than* his father.

Explanation: *More/-er* and *than* must be used before the comparison is complete.

Comparison

He	drives	faster	than	his father.
pron	v	adv	conj	n phrase

Incorrect: That printer operates *more quietly* the computer.
Incorrect: That printer operates *quietly than* the computer.
Correct: That printer operates *more quietly than* the computer.

Explanation: *More/-er* and *than* must be used before the comparison is complete.

Comparison

That printer	operates	more quietly	than	the computer.
n phrase	v	adv	conj	n phrase

Exercises

Part 5: Incomplete Sentences

Choose the one word or phrase that best completes the sentence.

The view from your office is _____ from mine.

(A) better than
(B) better
(C) the better
(D) the better of

Ⓐ Ⓑ Ⓒ Ⓓ

Part 6: Text Completion

Read the e-mail and choose the one word or phrase that best completes each sentence.

To: jbendetti@tritowers.org
From: groberts@tritowers.org
Subject: My office

Dear Mr. Bendetti,

I am very grateful for my promotion. However, I am very unhappy with my new office. Because it is close to the elevator, it is _____ my old

1. (A) noisy
   (B) noise
   (C) noisier
   (D) noisier than

office. As you know, none of the offices on the third floor have doors on them. Also, this office has only one small window, so it is _____

2. (A) dark
   (B) darker
   (C) dark than
   (D) darker than

the office I am used to. It is hard for me to work here. Could you please look into seeing if there is a _____ one available? If not, would it be

3. (A) more quiet
   (B) quieter
   (C) quieter than
   (D) more quieter

possible to get a door put on my office? It's very distracting when people walk through the hall, and I'm worried that I am not being as productive as I could be.

Ginger Roberts

TARGET

23 *The* or *Most/-est* Omitted

An unequal comparison among three or more things can be made using the positive form with: (1) *the* and *most* or (2) *the* and *-est*.

Problem	*The* or *most/-est* may be left out.
Solution	Make sure you use *the* and the superlative form of the adjective or adverb.

Examples

Incorrect: She works *hardest* of anyone in the office.
Incorrect: She works *the hard* of anyone in the office.
Correct: She works *the hardest* of anyone in the office.

Explanation: *The* and *most/-est* must be used before the comparison is complete.

Comparison

She	works	the	hardest	of anyone in the office.
pron	v	art	adv	prep phrases

Incorrect: Her work is *the neat* of all.
Incorrect: Her work is *neatest* of all.
Correct: Her work is *the neatest* of all.

Explanation: *The* and *most/-est* must be used before the comparison is complete.

Comparison

Her work	is	the	neatest	of all.
n phrase	v	art	adj	prep phrase

Incorrect: He commutes *farthest* of anyone in the office.
Incorrect: He commutes *the far* of anyone in the office.
Correct: He commutes *the farthest* of anyone in the office.

Explanation: *The* and *most/-est* must be used before the comparison is complete.

Comparison

He	commutes	the	farthest	of anyone in the office.
pron	v	art	adv	prep phrase

Incorrect: That printer operates *most quietly* of all the equipment.
Incorrect: That printer operates *the quietly* of all the equipment.
Correct: That printer operates *the most quietly* of all the equipment.

Explanation: *The* and *most/-est* must be used before the comparison is complete.

Comparison

That printer	operates	the	most quietly	of all the equipment.
n phrase	v	art	adv	prep phrase

Exercises

Part 5: Incomplete Sentences

Choose the one word or phrase that best completes the sentence.

Johnson's Delivery is _____ messenger service in town.

(A) the faster than   Ⓐ Ⓑ Ⓒ Ⓓ
(B) faster
(C) fastest
(D) the fastest

Part 6: Text Completion

Read the e-mail and choose the one word or phrase that best completes each sentence.

To: pchang@casanova.net
From: suntours@travel.com
Subject: Hotels

Dear Ms. Chang,

As you have requested, I have booked you a room at _____

1. (A) cheap
   (B) the cheap
   (C) the cheaper
   (D) the cheapest

hotel in the downtown area. It is a nice, clean hotel with a view of the city and costs about fifty dollars less than most of the other local hotels per night. However, it is also _____ distance from the convention

2. (A) the far
   (B) farthest
   (C) the farthest
   (D) the farther

center. You will have to take a taxi because it is too far to walk.

If you are willing to pay an extra twenty-five dollars, I can get you a _____ hotel. It won't be the best hotel, but it will be closer

3. (A) nicer
   (B) more convenient
   (C) more closer
   (D) cleaner

to where you need to be. It doesn't have a view, however, and I've heard that the rooms aren't always cleaned properly. Please let me know what you prefer. I have to cancel the booking today in order to get the deposit back.

Amanda Peters
Sun Tours Travel Agency

TARGETS 21–23 REVIEW
Comparisons with Adjectives and Adverbs

Part 5: Incomplete Sentences

Directions: Choose the one word or phrase that best completes the sentence.

1. The comptroller has _____ office on this floor.

   (A) the most spacious   Ⓐ Ⓑ Ⓒ Ⓓ
   (B) more spacious
   (C) spacious
   (D) space

2. Ms. Voss types _____ than Mr. Prince.

   (A) accurately   Ⓐ Ⓑ Ⓒ Ⓓ
   (B) most accurately
   (C) more accurately
   (D) the accurately

3. Their prices have always been _____ than ours.

   (A) highest   Ⓐ Ⓑ Ⓒ Ⓓ
   (B) the higher
   (C) the highest
   (D) higher

4. This idea is _____ the previous one.

   (A) good as   Ⓐ Ⓑ Ⓒ Ⓓ
   (B) as good as
   (C) better as
   (D) best as

5. It is _____ to call than to write.

   (A) quickest   Ⓐ Ⓑ Ⓒ Ⓓ
   (B) quickly as
   (C) quicker
   (D) quicker than

Part 6: Text Completion

Directions: Read the advertisement and choose the one word or phrase that best completes each sentence.

Techno Business Academy

Hone your office skills at Techno Business Academy. We guarantee to train you _____ any other business school. We guarantee the

1. (A) faster than
   (B) more professionally than
   (C) longer than
   (D) more costly than

lowest prices in town. We guarantee that _____ you finish our

2. (A) as soon as
   (B) soon as
   (C) sooner
   (D) soon

three-month course, you will be in demand at all the best offices in town. That's three guarantees. Our recent graduates earn _____

3. (A) high
   (B) higher
   (C) highest
   (D) the highest

salaries than other office professionals with years of experience. All other Business Academies require at least six months of training. Our professors are professionals, just like theirs.

Why study longer?
Why go anywhere else?

ADVERBS OF FREQUENCY

Adverbs of frequency tell *when* or *how often* something happens.

Common Adverbs of Frequency

always	seldom
usually	hardly ever
often	rarely
sometimes	never occasionally

ADVERBS OF FREQUENCY NORMALLY OCCUR

- after the verb *be*:

  They **are <u>rarely</u>** late for work.
  She **is <u>hardly ever</u>** sick.

- before the main verb:

  They **<u>usually</u> start** work at eight.
  We **<u>sometimes</u> misinterpret** the data.

- between the 1st auxiliary and verb:

  They **can <u>always</u> work** overtime.
  I **will <u>often</u> have** lunch at 1 o'clock.

- between the 1st and 2nd auxiliary:

  They **have <u>often</u> been** docked for being late.
  You **should <u>never</u> have** said that to the boss.

We also have adverbial time words or phrases.

Common Adverbs of Definite Frequency

every day, daily	every year, yearly
twice a week	every other week
once a month	from time to time
on occasion	once in a while

Adverbial time words or phrases normally occur at the beginning or the end of a sentence.

Adverbial Time Phrase

I   study   for the TOEIC   every day.
pron   v   prep phrase   adv of definite
                                   frequency

Every day   I   study   for the TOEIC.
                pron   v   prep phrase

Common Adverbs of Indefinite Frequency

always	seldom	often
rarely	usually	occasionally
never	sometimes	

Adverbs of indefinite frequency occur in the middle of the sentence. They occur:

1. after the auxiliary verb;
2. before any main verb except *be*; or
3. after *be* if it is the main verb.

After the auxiliary	They	can	always work	until six.
	pron	aux	adv and v	prep
Before main verb	They		usually start	at eight.
	pron		adv and v	prep
After *be* (main verb)	They		are never	on time.
	pron		adv and v	prep

TARGET

24 Misplaced Adverbial Time Words and Phrases

> **Problem** An adverbial time word or phrase may be in the middle of a sentence.
>
> **Solution** Move the adverbial time word or phrase to the beginning or end.

Examples

Incorrect: The manager *twice a week* arrives early.
Correct: The manager arrives early *twice a week*.
Correct: *Twice a week*, the manager arrives early.

Explanation: *Twice a week* cannot occur in the middle of a sentence. Move it to the beginning or the end of the sentence.

The manager	arrives early	twice a week.
n phrase	v phrase	adv of definite frequency

Twice a week,	the manager	arrives early.
adverbial time phrase	n phrase	v phrase

Incorrect: The editor *every day* eats lunch in the park.
Correct: The editor eats lunch in the park *every day*.
Correct: *Every day*, the editor eats lunch in the park.

Explanation: *Every day* cannot occur in the middle of a sentence. Move it to the beginning or the end of the sentence.

The editor	eats lunch in the park	every day.
n phrase	v phrase	adv of definite frequency

Every day,	the editor	eats lunch in the park.
adverbial time phrase	n phrase	v phrase

Exercises

Part 5: Incomplete Sentences

Choose the one word or phrase that best completes the sentence.

_____ with each of his employees.

(A) The manager once a month talks
(B) The manager once talks a month
(C) Once a month the manager talks
(D) Once the manager talks a month

Ⓐ Ⓑ Ⓒ Ⓓ

Part 6: Text Completion

Read the notice and choose the one word or phrase that best completes each sentence.

NOTICE

To: All Sales Teams
Re: Meetings
Effective Date: January 1, 20—
Posted by: Sales Managers

As you all know our department meets four times a year to discuss our progress on various projects. This has been the policy for the past three years. Before then _____, but we decided that such frequent

1. (A) once we met a month
   (B) once met we a month
   (C) we met once a month
   (D) we once a month met

meetings weren't necessary. However, since signing contracts with a number of new clients last October, impromptu meetings have been called every few weeks. Last month alone there were three _____meetings.

2. (A) daily
   (B) frequently
   (C) unscheduled
   (D) manager

Sales representatives and receptionists have been complaining that these last-minute meetings are a waste of time because they are so disorganized. From now on there will be _____ at 1:00 P.M. All managers

3. (A) an every Monday meeting
   (B) a meeting every Monday
   (C) a Monday every meeting
   (D) meetings Monday every day

and sales representatives from this department must attend.

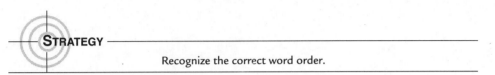

STRATEGY

Recognize the correct word order.

Always Innovative & Informative

TARGET

25 Misplaced Adverbs of Frequency

Problem	The adverb of frequency may come after the main verb.
Solution	Move the adverb of frequency before the main verb.

Examples

Incorrect: The crew takes *usually* a break at 11:00.
Correct: The crew *usually* takes a break at 11:00.

Explanation: The adverb should come before the main verb.

The crew	usually	takes	a break	at 11:00.
n phrase	adv of frequency	v	n phrase	prep phrase

Incorrect: The president holds *occasionally* meetings in her office.
Correct: The president *occasionally* holds meetings in her office.

Explanation: The adverb should come before the main verb.

The president	occasionally	holds	meetings	in her office.
n phrase	adv of frequency	v	n	prep phrase

Exercises

Part 5: Incomplete Sentences

Choose the one word or phrase that best completes the sentence.

Before I go to work, I _____.

    (A) always have breakfast and read the paper   Ⓐ Ⓑ Ⓒ Ⓓ
    (B) have breakfast always and read the paper
    (C) have breakfast and read the paper always
    (D) have breakfast and read always the paper

Part 6: Text Completion

Read the notice and choose the one word or phrase that best completes each sentence.

NOTICE

To: All New Staff Members
Date: February 7, 20—
Re: Staff Meeting, February 9, 20—

We are holding a staff meeting on Saturday, February 9th at 2:00 P.M. for all new part-time and full-time staff. That includes anyone who joined the company after January 1st. _____ staff meetings on the week-

    1. (A) Rarely we have
          (B) It is rare for
          (C) We rarely have
          (D) Have we rarely

end; however, something very important has come up. We need to address the issue immediately, and apologize for announcing a meeting on short notice.

Please note: Punctuality is very important in this company. _____ our staff meetings on time and don't wait for late arrivals.

    2. (A) We always begin
          (B) Always we begin
          (C) Begin we always
          (D) We begin always

You will get paid for the meeting. The payment is $20 per hour for all staff members. _____ about an hour.

    3. (A) Last the meetings usually
          (B) The meetings last usually
          (C) The meetings usually last
          (D) Usually last the meetings

TARGET

26 Adverbs of Frequency with *Be*

Problem	The adverb of frequency may come before the verb *be*.
Solution	Move the adverb of frequency after the verb *be*.

Examples

Incorrect: *Seldom* the manager is late.
Incorrect: The manager is late *seldom*.
Correct: The manager is *seldom* late.

Explanation: The verb is a form of *be*. There is no auxiliary. The adverb of frequency must occur after *be* (*is*).

The manager	is	seldom	late.
n phrase	v	adv of frequency	adv

Incorrect: *Rarely* the client is unreasonable.
Incorrect: The client is unreasonable *rarely*.
Correct: The client is *rarely* unreasonable.

Explanation: The main verb is a form of *be*. There is no auxiliary verb. The adverb of indefinite frequency must occur after a form of *be* (*is*).

The client	is	rarely	unreasonable.
n phrase	v	adv of frequency	adv

Exercises

Part 5: Incomplete Sentences

Choose the one word or phrase that best completes the sentence.

_____ when I arrive.

(A) On my desk is usually my mail
(B) Usually my mail on my desk is
(C) My mail is usually on my desk
(D) On my desk is my mail usually

Ⓐ Ⓑ Ⓒ Ⓓ

Part 6: Text Completion

Read the letter and choose the one word or phrase that best completes each sentence.

Dear Guest,

Welcome! Thank you for joining our workshop series. Please make your-self at home this week. For your convenience, _____ available

1. (A) hot coffee always is
   (B) is hot coffee always
   (C) always hot coffee is
   (D) hot coffee is always

in the employee lounge. The coffee machine has a hot water spout on the left-hand side. _____ in high demand so we suggest bringing one

2. (A) Hot water is usually
   (B) Cups are generally
   (C) Lunch time is always
   (D) Cutlery is occasionally

from home. There is also a snack bar downstairs where you can buy hot soups and sandwiches. _____ for sale there, too.

3. (A) Are donuts often
   (B) Donuts are often
   (C) Donuts often are
   (D) Often are donuts

Enjoy the workshops. If you have any questions visit Kathy at reception.

Best wishes,
Andy Smithers

TARGET

27   **Adverbs of Frequency with Auxiliaries**

Problem	The adverb of frequency may come before the auxiliary or after the main verb.
Solution	Move the adverb of frequency between the auxiliary and the main verb.

Examples

Incorrect: *Seldom* the manager has been late.
Incorrect: The manager has been late *seldom*.
Correct: The manager has *seldom* been late.

Explanation: The main verb is a form of *be*, but there is also an auxiliary verb (*have*). The adverb of frequency must occur between the auxiliary verb and the main verb (has *seldom* been).

The manager	has	seldom	been	late.
n phrase	aux verb	adv frequency	main v	adv

Incorrect: *Often* the assistant has been given too much work.
Incorrect: The assistant has been given too much work *often*.
Correct: The assistant has *often* been given too much work.

Explanation: The main verb is a form of *give*. There are two auxiliary verbs (*has* and *been*). The adverb of frequency normally occurs between the two auxiliary verbs (has *often* been).

The assistant	has	often	been	given	too much work.
n phrase	aux	adv frequency	2nd aux	main v	obj

Exercises

Part 5: Incomplete Sentences

Choose the one word or phrase that best completes the sentence.

The manager _____ that bookkeeping error.

(A) might have never noticed
(B) might never have noticed
(C) never might have noticed
(D) might have noticed never

Ⓐ Ⓑ Ⓒ Ⓓ

Part 6: Text Completion

Read the e-mail and choose the one word or phrase that best completes each sentence.

To: lindsaypeters@homemail.net
From: biancapierce@fairwear.com
Subject: Warm Regards

Dear Ms. Peters,

We just wanted to write and personally say good-bye. _____ your

1. (A) We have appreciated always
   (B) We always have appreciated
   (C) Always we appreciated
   (D) We have always appreciated

hard work and dedication. You were one of our very first employees and it is hard to see you go. However, you never make bad decisions, and we think taking _____ was wise. Colleen and I have always shopped

2. (A) over my position
   (B) the new job
   (C) your salary away
   (D) time off

at Marie's boutique and we know you will love designing her style of clothes. _____ the great contributions you have made to this

3. (A) Never we will forget
   (B) We will forget never
   (C) Never will forget
   (D) We will never forget

company. I wish you great success in the future.

Warm regards,
Bianca Pierce

TARGET

28   Meanings of Adverbs of Frequency

Problem	The wrong adverb may be used.
Solution	Change to an adverb with the correct meaning.

Examples

Incorrect: Since the manager hates to be late, he *never* arrives on time.

Correct: Since the manager hates to be late, he *always* arrives on time.

Explanation: *Never* means the manager does *not* arrive on time. This does not make sense if the manager hates to be late. Use an adverb that means the manager does arrive on time (*always*).

Since the manager hates to be late,	he	always	arrives	on time.
sub clause	pron	adv of indefinite frequency	v	adv

Incorrect: Because our printer is slow, we *rarely* have to wait.

Correct: Because our printer is slow, we *frequently* have to wait.

Explanation: *Rarely* means they almost never have to wait. This does not make sense if the printer is slow. Use an adverb that means they have to wait a lot (*frequently*).

Because our printer is slow,	we	frequently	have to wait.
sub clause	pron	adv of indefinite frequency	v

Exercises

Part 5: Incomplete Sentences

Choose the one word or phrase that best completes the sentence.

The new secretary _____ does her work or helps anyone else.

(A) frequently

(B) occasionally

(C) never

(D) always

Ⓐ Ⓑ Ⓒ Ⓓ

Part 6: Text Completion

Read the memorandum and choose the one word or phrase that best completes each sentence.

MEMO

From the desk of: Watanabe Daisuki
Subject: Business Travel
To: Tanaka Keiko

I noticed you booked your own trip to New York via a travel agent. You will have to cancel these bookings. We have to watch our budget, so we _____ travel economy class instead of first or business class. We

1. (A) usually
   (B) never
   (C) seldom
   (D) rarely

also seldom stay in luxury hotels.

Our accountant Yamamoto Yuuka _____ acts as our coordinator

2. (A) never
   (B) occasionally
   (C) always
   (D) rarely

for business trips. She is the person everyone goes to for booking business trips. Her e-mail address is yamamoto@japanjournal.com.jp. If you have any trouble _____ your hotel and flight, call me. I never

3. (A) booking
   (B) canceling
   (C) taking
   (D) choosing

have difficulty with travel agents.

TARGETS 24–28 REVIEW
Adverbs of Frequency

Part 5: Incomplete Sentences

Directions: Choose the one word or phrase that best completes the sentence.

1. Ms. Lee brings her lunch to work _____.

   (A) never
   (B) every day
   (C) always
   (D) yet

   Ⓐ Ⓑ Ⓒ Ⓓ

2. You _____ to listen carefully.

   (A) try always should
   (B) should always try
   (C) should every day try
   (D) every day should try

   Ⓐ Ⓑ Ⓒ Ⓓ

3. Our department is _____ not as efficient as it should be.

   (A) still
   (B) never
   (C) twice a week
   (D) always

   Ⓐ Ⓑ Ⓒ Ⓓ

4. Mr. Kent _____ asked to speak in public.

   (A) has been rarely
   (B) has every day been
   (C) every day has been
   (D) has rarely been

   Ⓐ Ⓑ Ⓒ Ⓓ

5. _____ our chairman throws a party for our department.

   (A) Never
   (B) Always
   (C) Still
   (D) Every year

   Ⓐ Ⓑ Ⓒ Ⓓ

First News
Always Innovative & Informative

Part 6: Text Completion

Directions: Read the letter and choose the one word or phrase that best completes each sentence.

Dear Sam,

I'm having a great vacation. _____ to the beach to swim and relax

      1. (A) I every morning go
          (B) Every morning I go
          (C) Go I every morning
          (D) I go every morning

in the sun. I always bring sandwiches with me so I can have lunch on the beach. The climate here is very comfortable and so far it hasn't _____. I've heard from many of the local people and lots of

2. (A) been very sunny
    (B) rained at all
    (C) warmed up
    (D) gotten busy

tourists that it is almost always sunny here. I'm not expecting the weather to change. My skin usually burns when I go south, but this beach has a lot of umbrellas and trees for shade. I like to get some daily exercise, so I _____ take a walk before dinner. It's a bit too hot

      3. (A) rarely
          (B) never
          (C) usually
          (D) infrequently

in the day to jog and besides, there are too many people lying on the beach. I am so happy here I may never go home.

Sincerely,
Jane

CAUSATIVE VERBS

Causative verbs show that one person makes another person do something. They also show that one person makes something happen. A causative verb is followed by another verb in (1) the simple form, (2) the infinitive form, or (3) the past participle form. The causative verb can be in any tense.

When the causative verb shows that the subject of the sentence makes the object of the sentence do something, the causative verb is followed by either the simple form or the infinitive form of the second verb. Remember that the object <u>does</u> the second action in the sentence.

Common Causative Verbs that Require the Simple Form

	n phrase	causative v	n (person)	v (simple form)	n phrase
make	The manager	made	Mr. Smith	demonstrate	the product.
have		will have			
let		could have let			

Causative Verbs Followed by Active Direct Objects + the Infinitive

	n phrase	causative v	n (person)	v (infinitive form)	n phrase
get	The manager	got	Mr. Cox	to demonstrate	the product.
want		wants			
order		can order			
permit		will permit			
allow		should have allowed			

When the direct object of the sentence receives the action of the second verb rather than doing the action, the second verb is in the past participle form. This represents a reduced form of the passive voice. Remember that the object <u>receives</u> the second action in the sentence.

Causative Verbs Followed by Passive Direct Objects + the Past Participle

	n phrase	causative v	n phrase	v (past participle form)	prep phrase
have get	The architect	had will get	the plans	drawn	by his best draftsman.

TARGET

29 Causative Verb + Simple Form

> **Problem**   The verb after the causative verb is not in the simple form.
>
> **Solution**   Change the verb to the simple form.

Examples

Incorrect: Ms. Carter *had* Mr. Yung *reviewed* the report.
Correct: Ms. Carter *had* Mr. Yung *review* the report.

Explanation: The verb after the causative *had* must be in the simple form, because
                one person caused another person to do something. Change *reviewed*
                to the simple form (*review*).

Ms. Carter	had	Mr. Yung	review	the report.
n phrase	v (past tense)	n (person)	causative v (simple form)	n phrase

Incorrect: The manager *let* his assistant *gives* the presentation.
Correct: The manager *let* his assistant *give* the presentation.

Explanation: The verb after the causative *let* must be in the simple form. Change
                gives to the simple form (*give*). One person causes another person to
                do something.

The manager	let	his assistant	give	the presentation.
n phrase	v (past tense)	n (person)	causative v (simple form)	n phrase

Exercises

Part 5: Incomplete Sentences

Choose the one word or phrase that best completes the sentence.

The human resources assistant makes all job applicants _____ a typing test.

    (A) take   Ⓐ Ⓑ Ⓒ Ⓓ
    (B) takes
    (C) to take
    (D) had taken

Part 6: Text Completion

Read the notice and choose the one word or phrase that best completes each sentence.

Please Post
NOTICE

To: All Employees
Re: Volunteering

In order to give back to the community, our company lets each employee
_____ up to three hours a month of paid leave for volunteer work

1. (A) takes
   (B) will take
   (C) take
   (D) taking

with a local volunteer organization. In order to get credit for this, the
employee must have the volunteer organization _____ the

        2. (A) sign
         (B) signed
         (C) to sign
         (D) signs

enclosed form.

Some departments may prefer to volunteer as a group on a monthly basis.
The head of a department should _____ his staff members write

      3. (A) get
       (B) has
       (C) have
       (D) made

down all of the local charities and organizations they are interested in. A
vote may be the best way to choose a new volunteer project each month.

Thank you for helping us help others.

TARGET

 30   Causative Verb + Infinitive

Problem	The verb after the causative verb is not the infinitive.
Solution	Change the verb to the infinitive.

Examples

Incorrect: Mr. Chin *will allow* Mr. Baur *will attend* the meeting.

Correct: Mr. Chin *will allow* Mr. Baur *to attend* the meeting.

Explanation: The verb after the causative *allow* must be an infinitive. Change *attend* to the infinitive *to attend.* One person causes another person to do something.

Mr. Chin	will allow	Mr. Baur	to attend	the meeting.
n phrase	causative v	n (person)	v (infinitive form)	n phrase

Incorrect: The president *got* Dr. Carrino *speak* at the seminar.

Correct: The president *got* Dr. Carrino *to speak* at the seminar.

Explanation: The verb after the causative *get* must be an infinitive. Change *speak* to the infinitive *to speak.* One person causes another person to do something.

The president	got	Dr. Carrino	to speak	at the seminar.
n phrase	causative v	n (person)	v (infinitive form)	prep phrase

Exercises

Part 5: Incomplete Sentences

Choose the one word or phrase that best completes the sentence.

The company has never permitted employees _____ public statements.

(A) making
(B) to make
(C) make
(D) made

Ⓐ Ⓑ Ⓒ Ⓓ

Part 6: Text Completion

Read the memorandum and choose the one word or phrase that best completes each sentence.

MEMO

From the Desk of: Ned Rogers
To: Connie Hung

Connie,
The photocopier has broken down again. Please get a repairperson
_____ it as soon as possible. I'm afraid that whatever Eric did when he

1. (A) service
    (B) services
    (C) to service
    (D) will service

took it apart may end up costing us money. In the future, we cannot allow staff
members _____ the copier themselves. It almost always makes the

2. (A) using
    (B) to fix
    (C) making
    (D) to have

problem worse.

Having said that, I _____ Shane from Sales to look into any technical

3. (A) allowed
    (B) allowing
    (C) will allow
    (D) allow

problems we have in the future. Besides being a salesman he is a trained technician. I got him to fix my printer at home and he did a great job. Unfortunately he's away on vacation this week.

Ned

TARGET
31 **Causative Verb + Past Participle**

> **Problem** The noun after the causative verb receives the following action; it does not do the action, but the verb after the causative verb is not the past participle.
>
> **Solution** Change the verb to the past participle.

Examples

Incorrect: The new director *had* the office *was painted*.
Correct: The new director *had* the office *painted*.

Explanation: The verb after the causative *had* must be the past participle when the direct object of the sentence receives the following action. This reflects a reduced passive voice sentence. Change *was painted* to the past participle (*painted*). The subject causes something to happen to the direct object.

The new director	had	the office	painted.
n phrase	causative v	n (thing)	v (past participle form)

Incorrect: The manager *can get* the projector *fix* before the meeting.
Correct: The manager *can get* the projector *fixed* before the meeting.

Explanation: The verb after the causative *can get* must be the past participle when something will happen (*the projector will be fixed*). Change *fix* to the past participle (*fixed*). One person causes something to happen.

The manager	can get	the projector	fixed	before the meeting.
n phrase	causative v	n (thing)	v (past participle form)	prep phrase

Exercises

Part 5: Incomplete Sentences

Choose the one word or phrase that best completes the sentence.

The owner of the hotel had the rooms _____.

(A) redecorated
(B) redecorate
(C) redecorating
(D) to redecorate

Ⓐ Ⓑ Ⓒ Ⓓ

Part 6: Text Completion

Read the e-mail and choose the one word or phrase that best completes each sentence.

To: seymourfletcher@t&c.com
From: ednamerrit@t&c.com
Subject: Spring Cleaning

Seymour,

It's time for a spring cleaning. I'd like to have the office _____.

        1. (A) paint
            (B) paints
            (C) painted
            (D) painting

Please choose a neutral color such as cream, beige, or even plain white. Let's get the painters to redo the washrooms too. I know they were just done a few months ago and they look fine, but I want all of the walls to be the same color.

We should also get the curtains _____. I haven't had these

        2. (A) will be cleaned
            (B) will clean
            (C) to clean
            (D) cleaned

done for over a year. I would like to have the stains _____ before

        3. (A) to remove
            (B) removed
            (C) remove
            (D) removing

the sun starts shining through them.

Please call the painters and the cleaners this week. Thanks.

Edna

STRATEGY

Recognize the correct grammatical form.
Learn to distinguish verb forms and to recognize the past participle.

First News
Always Innovative & Informative

TARGETS 29–31 REVIEW
Causative Verbs

Part 5: Incomplete Sentences

Directions: Choose the one word or phrase that best completes the sentence.

1. The personnel director made the applicant _____ half an hour.

   (A) wait   Ⓐ Ⓑ Ⓒ Ⓓ
   (B) waited
   (C) waiting
   (D) waits

2. Mr. Wang can't have the package _____ until Monday.

   (A) deliver   Ⓐ Ⓑ Ⓒ Ⓓ
   (B) will deliver
   (C) delivering
   (D) delivered

3. Our company wants its clients _____ with our work.

   (A) satisfying   Ⓐ Ⓑ Ⓒ Ⓓ
   (B) satisfy
   (C) satisfied
   (D) satisfaction

4. I'll have my assistant _____ for an appointment.

   (A) called   Ⓐ Ⓑ Ⓒ Ⓓ
   (B) calling
   (C) will call
   (D) call

5. The owner had the store _____ for the holiday.

   (A) close   Ⓐ Ⓑ Ⓒ Ⓓ
   (B) closing
   (C) closed
   (D) will close

First News
A l w a y s   I n n o v a t i v e   &   I n f o r m a t i v e

Part 6: Text Completion

Directions: Read the letter and choose the one word or phrase that best completes each sentence.

Fred,

Our newest staff member, John Greene, appears to have some confusion about the procedures for ordering supplies. Please make him _____ that he must have my authorization before putting in an

1. (A) understand
   (B) understands
   (C) to understand
   (D) can understand

order. We cannot permit staff _____ anything anytime they want,

2. (A) order
   (B) to order
   (C) ordering
   (D) will order

or it will create havoc with our budget. As you know there have been major cutbacks this year due to the increase in sales tax.

Despite the cutbacks, we are still going to have the annual holiday luncheon. Therefore, it is time to get the plans for the luncheon arranged. The priority right now is getting the food ordered. Please have John Greene _____ the caterers before the end of the week. After that

3. (A) call
   (B) calls
   (C) called
   (D) will call

we can start thinking about a location and theme. Thank you.

Betty

CONDITIONAL SENTENCES

Conditional sentences can express two kinds of conditions: real and unreal.

Real Conditions

Real conditions express what is possible. The *if* clause is in the present tense. The other clause expresses habitual action, future action, or a command. The *if* clause can occur in any position in the sentence.

Habit	*If* it rains,	I drive to work.
	if clause (real condition)	main clause
Future	*If* it rains,	I will drive to work.
	if clause (real condition)	main clause
Command	*If* it rains,	drive to work.
	if clause (real condition)	main clause

Unreal Conditions

Unreal conditions express something that is not true or is not possible. If the sentence is about a present situation, the verb in the *if* clause borrows the form of the past, but remember that it represents the present. If the situation is about the past, the verb in the *if* clause borrows the form of the past perfect. The main clause uses the auxiliary *would* + verb for a present situation and *would have* + verb for a past situation.

Present   If I owned the company,   I would accept the project.
         if clause (unreal condition)   main clause

Past   If I had owned the company,   I would have accepted the project.
         if clause (unreal condition)   main clause

The verb *be* can use both *was* and *were* in the *if* clause for a present unreal conditional sentence. This is true for <u>all</u> persons from *I* to *they*. Keep in mind that native speakers of English prefer to use *were*. They feel it sounds more educated. *Was* is an acceptable alternative, however.

I   If I were the boss,   I would take a vacation.
  subj   *if* clause (unreal condition)   main clause

He (she, it)   If he were the boss,   he would take a vacation.
  subj   *if* clause (unreal condition)   main clause

The verb *be* borrows the past perfect like other verbs in the *if* clause when the unreal conditional sentence is in the past.

Past   If she had been really ill,   she would have stayed home last week.
         if clause (unreal condition)   main clause

TARGET

Real Condition *if* Clause not in Present Tense

Problem	The *if* clause of a real condition may not be in the present tense.
Solution	Change the verb in the *if* clause to the present tense.

Examples

Incorrect:	I will call *if* the plane *will be* late.
Correct:	I *will* call *if* the plane *is* late.
Correct:	*If* the plane *is* late, I *will* call.

Explanation: This is a real condition (it is possible for planes to be late). The verb in the *if* clause must be in the present tense. Change the verb in the *if* clause to *is*.

If the plane is late,   I will call.
if clause (real condition) main clause

Incorrect:	We cannot send the fax *if* the phone lines *will be damaged*.
Correct:	We cannot send the fax *if* the phone lines *are damaged*.
Correct:	*If* the phone lines *are damaged*, we cannot send the fax.

Explanation: This is a real condition (it is possible for lines to be damaged). The verb in the *if* clause must be in the present tense. Change the verb in the *if* clause to *are damaged*.

If the phone lines are damaged,   we cannot send the fax.
if clause (real condition)   main clause

Exercises

Part 5: Incomplete Sentences

Choose the one word or phrase that best completes the sentence.

If I _____ this report before 2:00, my secretary will type it.

(A) finish
(B) finished   Ⓐ Ⓑ Ⓒ Ⓓ
(C) has finished
(D) will finish

Part 6: Text Completion

Read the notice and choose the one word or phrase that best completes each sentence.

Date Posted: August 18, 20—

CLASS REGISTRATION
REMINDER

Class registration begins August 21 and classes begin August 29. If you _____ for a class after August 28, you will have to pay a

1. (A) register
   (B) to register
   (C) will register
   (D) is going to register

$25 late registration fee. You will have to have a signed permission letter from the course instructor if you sign up for an advanced level class.

If a class _____ due to low enrollment, the university will contact

2. (A) cancels
   (B) is canceled
   (C) will cancel
   (D) be canceled

you. We recommend that you provide your phone number and e-mail address on your course selection sheet in case one of your selections is no longer available. We cannot _____ you if we don't have this

3. (A) contact
   (B) enroll
   (C) instruct
   (D) recommend

information. Our staff is not responsible for searching for you in a directory.

TARGET

33   Unreal Condition *if* Clause Not in Appropriate Tense

> **Problem**   The verb in the *if* clause is not in the past or past perfect.
>
> **Solution**   Change the tense of the verb in the *if* clause. Pay attention to the form of *would* in the other clause.

Examples

Incorrect: *If* I *supervise* the department, I *would hire* an assistant.
Correct: *If* I *supervised* the department, I *would hire* an assistant.
Correct: I *would hire* an assistant *if* I *supervised* the department.

Explanation: This is an unreal condition (I do not supervise the department). The verb in the *if* clause must be in the past tense (*supervised*).

main clause			if clause (unreal condition in the present)			
I	would hire	an assistant	if	I	supervised	the department.
pron	v	n phrase	conj	pron	v	n phrase
	(past conditional)				(past tense)	

Incorrect: *If* I *had written* the letter, I *would* sign it.
Correct: *If* I *had written* the letter, I *would have signed* it.
Correct: I *would have signed* the letter *if* I *had written* it.

Explanation: This is an unreal condition in the past tense (I did not write the letter). The other clause requires *would have*. Change the verb in the *main* clause to *would have signed*.

if clause (unreal condition)				main clause		
If	I	had written	the letter,	I	would have signed	it.
conj	pron	v	n phrase	pron	v	pron
		(past perfect)			(past conditional)	

Exercises

Part 5: Incomplete Sentences

Choose the one word or phrase that best completes the sentence.

If I _____ the promotion, I would have bought a new car.

   (A)   received   Ⓐ Ⓑ Ⓒ Ⓓ
   (B)   had received
   (C)   will receive
   (D)   would receive

Part 6: Text Completion

Read the letter and choose the one word or phrase that best completes each sentence.

March 15th, 20—

Dear Mr. Klugman,

I am terribly sorry about our misunderstanding yesterday. If I _____

1. (A) knew
   (B) had known
   (C) have known
   (D) could know

that space #7 was your assigned parking space, I would never have parked there. I'm not used to the parking rules because I never drive my car to work. If you _____ for parking elsewhere, I would have

2. (A) have paid
   (B) had paid
   (C) pay
   (D) will pay

reimbursed you. Luckily you found another free spot in the staff lot. I didn't know those spots existed until I got the message from my supervisor about this incident. I'll know to use them another time if I decide to drive again. If you _____ here today, I would apologize in person.

3. (A) are
   (B) will be
   (C) were
   (D) had been

Sincerely,

Sophie Schmidt

TARGET

Unreal Condition *if* Clause + *Were*

Problem	*Were* is not used.
Solution	Change the verb to *were*.

Examples

Incorrect: If I *am* you, I would give the speech.
Correct: If I *were* you, I would give the speech.

Explanation: This is an unreal condition (*I* am NOT *you*). Change the verb to
              were.

***if* clause (unreal condition)**				**main clause**		
If	I	were	you,	I	would give	the speech.
conj	pron	*v*	pron	v	v	n phrase
		to be		pron	(future conditional)	

Exercises

Part 5: Incomplete Sentences

Choose the one word or phrase that best completes the sentence.

I would never take a job if the salary _____ too low.

    (A) were   Ⓐ Ⓑ Ⓒ Ⓓ
    (B) was
    (C) is
    (D) are

Part 6: Text Completion

Read the e-mail and choose the one word or phrase that best completes each sentence.

To: rogermcleod@environmentdc.com
From: wilmahunter@environmentdc.com
Subject: Where to hold the meeting

Roger,

We need to find a place for our meeting Friday. If the conference room
_____ available, we could have it there. Unfortunately Gerry

1. (A) is
   (B) was
   (C) were
   (D) will be

reserved it for a small workshop. If I were running a workshop with only five
people I would switch it to the lounge. However, I already talked to Gerry
and he doesn't want to relocate. He says the conference room is more suitable for his role-playing activities.

Rita Brown's office is very big. If I _____ friendlier with her, I would

2. (A) am
   (B) was
   (C) had been
   (D) were

ask to use it. You know her, don't you? Why don't you ask her? If I
_____ I would offer her a free lunch or something for doing it.

3. (A) were her
   (B) was you
   (C) were you
   (D) were me

Thanks,
Wilma

TARGETS 32–34 REVIEW
Conditional Sentences

Part 5: Incomplete Sentences

Directions: Choose the one word or phrase that best completes the sentence.

1. If the speaker _____ her presentation, she will have more confidence.

   (A) prepared   Ⓐ Ⓑ Ⓒ Ⓓ
   (B) prepares
   (C) had prepared
   (D) were preparing

2. If Mr. Musso _____ the brochure with him, he would have given it to you.

   (A) would have   Ⓐ Ⓑ Ⓒ Ⓓ
   (B) had had
   (C) had
   (D) has

3. Ask me for help if you _____ the questionnaire.

   (A) do not understand   Ⓐ Ⓑ Ⓒ Ⓓ
   (B) would not understand
   (C) did not understand
   (D) had not understood

4. If I _____ you, I would accept the position.

   (A) am   Ⓐ Ⓑ Ⓒ Ⓓ
   (B) were
   (C) would be
   (D) could be

5. _____ a message if you can't transfer the telephone call.

   (A) Take   Ⓐ Ⓑ Ⓒ Ⓓ
   (B) Will take
   (C) Taken
   (D) Would take

Part 6: Text Completion

Directions: Read the notice and choose the one word or phrase that best completes each sentence.

NOTICE

To: All office staff
Re: Staff picnic

If the weather is nice on Friday, we will have the staff picnic in Rosings Park as planned. This is the only place that allows barbeque pits. If we _____ this earlier, we could have arranged for a caterer. Since we

1. (A) plan
   (B) planned
   (C) would plan
   (D) had planned

didn't, please bring a dish to share, or some meat to cook on the grill. I will arrange to have everything transported to the picnic site if everyone _____ their food to my office before 10:00 on Friday morning.

2. (A) bring
   (B) brings
   (C) bringing
   (D) brought

I will have coolers ready with ice on the floor of my office. If anyone has an extra cooler, please bring it in. I would have planned this better if I _____ so busy these days. But this is a busy time for all of you,

3. (A) wasn't
   (B) weren't
   (C) am not
   (D) wouldn't be

too, and you deserve this small break on Friday. See you then.

VERB TENSES

The tense of a verb tells when something happens. There are three tenses in English: present, past, and future. All tenses have four forms: simple, progressive, perfect, and perfect progressive.

	Simple	**Progressive**	**Perfect**	**Perfect Progressive**
Present	call	am calling	have/has called	have/has been calling
Past	called	was/were calling	had called	had been calling
Future	will call	will be calling	will have called	will have been calling

Use the simple tenses to show habit or occurrence.

pron	**v phrase (simple tense)**	**n**	**time marker**
I	usually write	letters	in the afternoon.
I	wrote	letters	this morning.
I	will write	some letters	tomorrow.

Use the progressive tenses to show action in progress.

pron	**v phrase (progressive tense)**	**n**	**time marker**
I	am writing	letters	right now.
I	was writing	letters	when someone telephoned.
I	will be writing	letters	all afternoon.

Use the perfect tenses to show a time relationship between occurrence of an action and the present, past, or future.

pron	**v phrase (perfect tense)**	**n phrase**	**time marker**
I	have written	three letters	so far.
I	had written	two letters	before I went to the meeting.
I	will have written	one more letter	before I go home.

Use the perfect progressive to show a relationship between the duration of an action and the present, past, or future.

pron	**v phrase (perfect progressive tense)**	**n phrase**	**time marker**
I	have been writing	letters	for three hours.
I	had been writing	letters	all morning when the telephone rang.
I	will have been writing	letters	all day by the time I leave tonight.

Pay attention to the tenses of all the verbs in the sentence. The tenses must make sense together.

First News
A l w a y s I n n o v a t i v e & I n f o r m a t i v e

TARGET

35 Verb Tenses

Problem	The tenses may not make sense together.
Solution	Change the tenses so that the sentence makes sense.

Examples

Incorrect: I *will be working* on the project when Mr. Dubois *arrived*.
Correct: I *was working* on the project when Mr. Dubois *arrived*.

Explanation: *Will be working* is future; *arrived* is past. If Mr. Dubois arrived (past tense), you know if you *were working* when he arrived. Change *work* to a past tense form (*was working* is past progressive).

main clause			subordinate/adverbial clause		
I	was working	on the project	when	Mr. Dubois	arrived.
pron	v (past progressive)	prep phrase	conj	n phrase	v (past tense)

Incorrect: The manager *left* for her vacation after she *gives* her speech.
Correct: The manager *will leave* for her vacation after she *gives* her speech.

Explanation: *Left* is past; *gives* is present. If she has not given her speech yet, she cannot have left for her vacation. Change *left* to a present or future tense form.

main clause			subordinate/adverbial clause		
The manager	will leave	for her vacation	after	she gives	her speech.
pron	v (future)	prep phrase	conj	n + v	n phrase

Exercises

Part 5: Incomplete Sentences

Choose the one word or phrase that best completes the sentence.

I _____ all members by tomorrow night.

(A) contacted   Ⓐ Ⓑ Ⓒ Ⓓ
(B) contacts
(C) has contacted
(D) will have contacted

Part 6: Text Completion

Read the advertisement and choose the one word or phrase that best completes each sentence.

FURNITURE SALE

Fernwood Furniture Outlet announces a special surplus sale
this Saturday, April 28th.
A large shipment of new furniture _____ last week,

    1. (A) arrives
          (B) arrived
          (C) will arrive
          (D) is arriving

and we have to make room for it on our sales floor.
Everything currently on the sales floor is on sale for 50% off or more.
Hurry on down. At these prices, the furniture _____ here for

    2. (A) isn't
          (B) wasn't
          (C) won't be
          (D) hasn't been

long! Fernwood's new stock will be available next month.
Come in during the month of May and browse through our showroom.
When we get our new stock out on display, you _____

    3. (A) can't find
          (B) found
          (C) will find
          (D) are finding

everything from modern sofa beds to restored antique dining room sets.

STATIVE VERBS

Stative verbs are verbs of a "state" of being: a state of sensory perception, of mental perception, of emotion, of measurement, or of relationship. Stative verbs are usually in the simple present, past, or future.

Common Stative Verbs

appear	The software *appears* to have been deleted.
appreciate	We *appreciate* your coming.
be	She is as deferential as she can *be*.
believe	He *believes* in what he is doing.
belong	I *belong* to many clubs.
care	The citizens *care* about their community.
contain	The shipment *contains* hazardous materials.
depend	The sales staff *depends* on marketing for their product information.
deserve	Nobody *deserves* a break more than Mr. Lee.
dislike	We *dislike* unpleasant chores.
doubt	They *doubt* they can come.
feel	We *feel* great remorse for the victims.
forget	Don't *forget* to leave your number.
hate	I've *hated* to get out of bed all my life.
imagine	I *imagined* I would succeed, and I did.
know	They have *known* the secret for some time.
like	We would *like* to go too.
look	The new version will *look* heavier than the original.
love	The children *love* ice cream.
mean	They *meant* to start earlier.
mind	Would you *mind* shutting the door?
need	They will *need* all the help they can get.
own	I *own* an old model car.
prefer	She would have *preferred* to go alone.
possess	What ever *possessed* you?
realize	They *realized* their mistake too late.
recognize	Do you *recognize* me?
remember	I *remember* when you first came to the office.
see	We *see* only minor changes.
seem	They *seemed* to enjoy themselves.
smell	The engine room *smells* like burning rubber.
sound	It *sounded* like something was wrong with the brakes.
suppose	I *suppose* you are wondering who I am.
taste	Consumers will immediately *taste* the difference.
think	Those in marketing *think* it will be the biggest-selling produce of the year.
understand	We *understand* what you say, but not what you mean.
want	We've *wanted* to quit since the day we started.
wish	Our contractors *wish* we would let them negotiate prices freely.

TARGET

36 Stative Verbs in the Progressive Form

Problem	A stative verb is used in the progressive.
Solution	Change the verb to a form that is not progressive.

Examples

Incorrect: *I was knowing* about the merger before I saw the paper.
Correct: *I knew* about the merger before I saw the paper.

Explanation: *Know* is not often used in the progressive. Change to the simple past
(*knew*).

main clause			subordinate clause (adverbial clause)			
I	knew	about the merger	before	I	saw	the paper.
pron	stative v	prep phrase	conj	pron	v	n phrase

Incorrect: I *will be remembering* him when I meet him.
Correct: I *will remember* him when I meet him.

Explanation: *Remember* is not often used in the progressive. Change to the future
(*will remember*).

main clause			subordinate clause (adverbial clause)			
I	will remember	him	when	I	meet	him.
pron	stative v	pron	conj	pron	v	pron

Exercises

Part 5: Incomplete Sentences

Choose the one word or phrase that best completes the sentence.

I _____ the job very much now that I understand the work.

    (A) liked
    (B) like
    (C) would be liking
    (D) liking

       Ⓐ   Ⓑ   Ⓒ   Ⓓ

Part 6: Text Completion

Read the notice and choose the one word or phrase that best completes each sentence.

NOTICE

To all office personnel:

A gold necklace was found in the office last night. It _____

       1. (A) looks
          (B) will be looking
          (C) is looking
          (D) was looking

valuable. If you think it _____ to you, please report to the Lost and

       2. (A) has been belonging
          (B) had belonged
          (C) is belonging
          (D) belongs

Found Office. We realize that certain personal belongings are also of sentimental value. Our policy with lost jewelry is as follows: Go to the front desk and fill out a lost and found form. Describe the item. For example: I lost a bracelet. It is heart-shaped and the word *Sweetheart* is engraved on the heart.

*We _____ this item belongs to a member of the cleaning crew

   3. (A) believe
      (B) were believing
      (C) are believing
      (D) will be believing

because it was found on the sink in the staff washrooms this morning.

TARGETS 35–36 REVIEW
Verb Tenses and Stative Verbs

Part 5: Incomplete Sentences

Directions: Choose the one word or phrase that best completes the sentence.

1. When my visitor _____, will you please call me?

   (A) will arrive   Ⓐ Ⓑ Ⓒ Ⓓ
   (B) arrives
   (C) arrived
   (D) is arriving

2. Mr. Santo's assistant _____ more relaxed since his promotion.

   (A) has become   Ⓐ Ⓑ Ⓒ Ⓓ
   (B) has been becoming
   (C) becomes
   (D) had become

3. Mr. Sanchez _____ his first job with us twenty-five years ago.

   (A) accepts   Ⓐ Ⓑ Ⓒ Ⓓ
   (B) was accepting
   (C) has accepted
   (D) accepted

4. The president _____ the reports in her speech later tonight.

   (A) was discussing   Ⓐ Ⓑ Ⓒ Ⓓ
   (B) will discuss
   (C) discussed
   (D) has discussed

5. My parents know that I _____ next year.

   (A) would graduate   Ⓐ Ⓑ Ⓒ Ⓓ
   (B) graduated
   (C) will graduate
   (D) have graduated

Part 6: Text Completion

Directions: Read the e-mail and choose the one word or phrase that best completes each sentence.

To: janet@barodibiz
From: ricmcbride@mailgo.com
Subject: Work

Dear Janet,

How are you doing? I haven't talked to you in a while. I'm keeping busy these days. I had that job interview with the Clarkson Company last Tuesday. I _____ it went well. They understand that I can only

1. (A) will be thinking
   (B) was thinking
   (C) am thinking
   (D) think

work part-time because I am still going to school at night. The job seems challenging, and they will probably offer a good salary. I am so anxious to hear from them that I sit by the phone every day. I'm finding it hard to concentrate on my _____ . They promised to get back to me within a

2. (A) job
   (B) resume
   (C) studies
   (D) family

week, so I guess I will know their decision before too long. I hope they call soon because I have exams in two weeks and I need to regain my focus. I _____ you as soon as I find out.

3. (A) call
   (B) called
   (C) will call
   (D) have called

Sincerely,
Richard

First News
Always Innovative & Informative

RELATIVE CLAUSES

A relative clause combines two sentences. The second sentence describes a noun in the first sentence. A relative clause uses a special pronoun to replace the noun. This pronoun is called a relative pronoun.

Relative pronouns	
that	Pronoun for things (used only in restrictive clauses)
which	Pronoun for things
who	Subject pronoun for people
whom	Object pronoun for people
whose	Possessive pronoun
where	Pronoun for places

There are two kinds of relative clauses: restrictive and nonrestrictive. Note in the example below that *clerk* is the subject of both sentences.

A restrictive clause identifies a noun. That is, it tells us *which* person or thing.

	noun phrase	verb phrase	v	prep phrase
Sentence 1	A clerk		will start	on Monday.
Sentence 2	The clerk	was just hired.		
Combined	The clerk	who was just hired	will start	on Monday.
	noun phrase	relative clause	v	prep phrase

A nonrestrictive clause gives information about a noun (but does not identify the noun). A nonrestrictive clause has a comma at each end. *That* is not used in nonrestrictive clauses.

	noun phrase	verb phrase	v	adj phrase
Sentence 1	My secretary		is	very efficient.
Sentence 2	She	has worked for me for ten years.		
Combined	My secretary,	who has worked for me for ten years,	is	very efficient.
	noun phrase	relative clause		adj phrase

A nonrestrictive clause adds extra information that is not necessary to have a complete sentence, a complete idea. To show the reader that this is extra information, we place a comma before and after this kind of clause to show it could be removed. You can see how this works in the chart above.

Here are some examples of sentences with restrictive and nonrestrictive clauses.

Restrictive	Nonrestrictive
Any office that is centrally located will have a high rent.	This office, which was painted just last week, looks very bright and clean.
The person whose office you are using will return from vacation next week.	My assistant, whose office is across the hall, will be happy to help you.
The person for whom I am buying this gift is a very close friend.	My best friend, for whom I am buying this gift, has a birthday next week.
The man who can help you is sitting right over there.	That man, who probably has the information you need, is the receptionist.
The store where I bought this suit closed down last month.	Cook's Brothers Clothing Store, where I bought this suit, has the best prices for business attire.

TARGET

37 **Relative Clause: Repeated Subject**

Problem	The noun (or a pronoun) may be repeated in the relative clause.
Solution	Delete the noun (or its pronoun).

Examples

Incorrect: The report that we sent *it* last week was returned.
Correct: The report that we sent last week was returned.

Explanation: There is already a relative pronoun (*that*) in the sentence. The relative pronoun substitutes for the noun (*that* = *the report*). You do not need to repeat a noun or pronoun. Delete the pronoun *it*.

subj		**relative clause**	**v**
The report	that	we sent last week	was returned.
n phrase	relative pron		v phrase

Incorrect: The manager *who he* hired an assistant is still overworked.
Correct: The manager *who* hired an assistant is still overworked.

Explanation: There is already a relative pronoun in the sentence (*who*). The relative pronoun substitutes for the noun (*who* = *he*). You do not need to repeat a noun or pronoun. Delete the pronoun *he*.

subj	**relative clause**	**v**
The manager	who hired an assistant	is still overworked.
n phrase	relative pron	v phrase

Exercises

Part 5: Incomplete Sentences

Choose the one word or phrase that best completes the sentence.

The wallet _____ was found in the hall has been claimed.

   (A) that it
   (B) it
   (C) that
   (D) whose it

Ⓐ Ⓑ Ⓒ Ⓓ

Part 6: Text Completion

Read the notice and choose the one word or phrase that best completes each sentence.

NOTICE

To: All office staff
Re: Banquet
Posted: June 1, 20—

The Awards Banquet will take place next month. The hotel chosen for the banquet is close to the office. Everyone _____ plans to attend the

      1. (A) who
          (B) who he
          (C) he
          (D) whose he

banquet should notify Mr. Xavier before the end of this week. If you want to bring a guest, the ticket price is $50. Only twenty guest tickets are available. _____ are reserved for staff at no charge. We hope that

    2. (A) All fifty tickets
        (B) The remaining tickets
        (C) One hundred tickets
        (D) The other tickets that

all staff will be in attendance; however, we expect about ten people not to come.

If you have not yet done so, please choose the staff member _____

        3. (A) who he or she deserves
           (B) who deserves
           (C) that it deserves
           (D) who they deserve

the most valuable worker award. Seal the name in an envelope and bring it to Mr. Xavier. The voting ends on the last day of this month. One winner and one runner-up from our staff of sixty will be chosen.

 STRATEGY

Be aware of whether or not there is more than one subject in a sentence. Consider which subject goes with which verb.

TARGET

38   Relative Clause: No Relative Pronoun

Problem	A wrong pronoun may be used. It may not be a relative pronoun.
Solution	Use a relative pronoun. Pay attention to the meaning of the pronoun.

Examples

Incorrect: Mr. Zabel, *his* mother owns the company, works very hard.
Correct: Mr. Zabel, *whose* mother owns the company, works very hard.

Explanation: *His* is not a relative pronoun. A relative clause must begin with a relative pronoun. Start with the possessive relative pronoun *whose*.

subj	**relative clause**			**v**
Mr. Zabel,	whose	mother	owns the company,	works very hard.
n phrase	relative pron	noun	v phrase	v phrase

Incorrect: This report, *it* was published last week, is not accurate.
Correct: This report, *which* was published last week, is not accurate.

Explanation: *It* is not a relative pronoun. A relative clause must begin with a relative pronoun. Start with the relative pronoun *which*.

subj	**relative clause**		**v**
This report,	which	was published last week,	is not accurate.
n phrase	relative pron	v phrase	v phrase

Exercises

Part 5: Incomplete Sentences

Choose the one word or phrase that best completes the sentence.

The man _____ shares this office is very good with computers.

(A) who   Ⓐ Ⓑ Ⓒ Ⓓ
(B) he
(C) whose
(D) his

Part 6: Text Completion

Read the article and choose the one word or phrase that best completes each sentence.

Harold News   Monday, January 5, 20—
BOOK TALK-B1

The Environment Crisis

Want to know more about global warming and how you can help prevent
it? Doctor Herman Friedman, _____ is considered the foremost

        1. (A) he
          (B) his
          (C) who
          (D) him

authority on the subject, will speak at Grayson Hall next Tuesday.
Friedman studied environmental science at three prestigious universities
around the world before becoming a professor in the subject. He has also
traveled around the world observing environmental concerns. The gradual
bleaching of the Great Barrier Reef, _____ into the public eye

        2. (A) he is coming
          (B) this came
          (C) which came
          (D) it will come

in 2002, is his latest interest. Signed copies of his colorful book,
_____ was published just last month, will be on sale after his talk.

  3. (A) it
      (B) he
      (C) they
      (D) which

TARGET

39   Relative Clause: *That* ≠ *Who*

Problem	*That* or *who* may be used incorrectly.
Solution	Pay attention to the modified word.

Examples

Incorrect: The package *who* we were expecting finally arrived.
Correct: The package *that* we were expecting finally arrived.

Explanation: *Who* is a relative pronoun, but it is used only for people. A package is a thing. Use *that*.

subj	relative clause			v
The package	that	we	were expecting	finally arrived.
n phrase	relative pron	pron	v phrase	v phrase

Incorrect: The sales representative *which* just started made several big sales.
Correct: The sales representative *who* just started made several big sales.

Explanation: *Which* is a relative pronoun, but it is used only for things. A sales representative is a person. Use *who*.

subj	relative clause			v
The sales representative	who	just	started	made several big sales.
n phrase	relative pron	adv	v	v phrase

Exercises

Part 5: Incomplete Sentences

Choose the one word or phrase that best completes the sentence.

Mr. Maurice, _____ has worked here for many years, is retiring.

(A) which
(B) he
(C) that
(D) who

Ⓐ Ⓑ Ⓒ Ⓓ

Part 6: Text Completion

Read the e-mail and choose the one word or phrase that best completes each sentence.

To: Customer Service Clerks
From: Carol Rhodes
Subject: Customer complaint
Attachment: Letter from Tanaka Yumi

Attention: All Customer Service representatives

Please take a minute to review this attachment. The person _____

    1. (A) which
        (B) whose
        (C) whom
        (D) who

wrote this letter was very upset with the poor service she received. She waited more than twenty minutes to be served. The Customer Service representative _____ served her was unpleasant.

    2. (A) with whom
        (B) in which
        (C) whose
        (D) who

A complaint such as this from a regular customer is unacceptable. The service _____ we offer all of our customers should always be

    3. (A) whom
        (B) that
        (C) where
        (D) who

prompt, courteous, and friendly. Please conform to our high standards of customer service.

Carol Rhodes

TARGETS 37–39 REVIEW
Relative Clauses

Part 5: Incomplete Sentences

Directions: Choose the one word or phrase that best completes the sentence.

1. Ms. Caras, _____ is quite well-known, is arriving at 3:00.

   (A) when   Ⓐ Ⓑ Ⓒ Ⓓ
   (B) whom
   (C) that
   (D) who

2. A letter _____ is not properly typed is hard to read.

   (A) which it   Ⓐ Ⓑ Ⓒ Ⓓ
   (B) it
   (C) that it
   (D) that

3. Mr. La Porte, _____ vacation starts tomorrow, has already left.

   (A) whose   Ⓐ Ⓑ Ⓒ Ⓓ
   (B) his
   (C) the
   (D) its

4. The report _____ this process is in the library.

   (A) it explains   Ⓐ Ⓑ Ⓒ Ⓓ
   (B) explains
   (C) who explains
   (D) that explains

5. A machine _____ could monitor efficiency would be very useful.

   (A) whom   Ⓐ Ⓑ Ⓒ Ⓓ
   (B) that
   (C) it
   (D) when

Part 6: Text Completion

Directions: Read the notice and choose the one word or phrase that best completes each sentence.

NOTICE

To: All Staff
Re: Ms. McIntyre's Visit

Ms. McIntyre, who has worked in our London offices for more than fifteen years, will be visiting us next week. As most of you have probably heard, Ms. McIntyre was recently presented with a national award of excellence for her leadership skills. Staff members _____ wish to make an

1. (A) who
    (B) whom
    (C) whose
    (D   which

appointment to meet with her and offer her congratulations are asked to contact the Human Resources office. Everyone _____ schedule

2. (A) who
    (B) their
    (C) whose
    (D) they

allows is invited to attend a welcome luncheon on Wednesday. The luncheon will be held at Francine McKay's ranch. For directions call Mrs. McKay at 333-4989, extension 2. We are all looking forward to Ms. McIntyre's visit, _____ will last ten days. In lieu of flowers or cards,

3. (A) which it
    (B) which
    (C) who she
    (D) who

Ms. McIntyre has asked that you congratulate her by making a donation to a local youth group.

Please post on notice board.

GERUNDS AND INFINITIVES

The main verb in a sentence can be followed immediately by a second verb. This second verb can be a gerund (*-ing* form) or an infinitive (*to* + verb). The main verb usually determines which form is used.

Common Verbs Followed by a Gerund

appreciate	I *appreciate* having the opportunity to speak.
avoid	They *avoided* looking us in the eye.
consider	We *considered* staying longer.
delay	We *delayed* writing you until we had more information.
discuss	Have you *discussed* working together on this project?
enjoy	We *enjoyed* having you for dinner.
finish	They will *finish* correcting the report soon.
mind	She *minded* using our toothbrush.
miss	We *miss* going to the movies with you.
postpone	Could we *postpone* leaving?
quit	He wants to *quit* smoking.
risk	They *risked* losing everything.
suggest	We *suggest* leaving on time.

Common Verbs Followed by an Infinitive

agree	He *agreed* to complete the project.
attempt	They *attempted* to climb Mt. Fuji.
claim	She *claims* to be an expert.
decide	We *decided* to hire her anyway.
demand	He *demanded* to know what we were doing.
fail	We *failed* to give a satisfactory answer.
hesitate	I *hesitated* to tell the truth.
hope	We *hope* to leave before dawn.
intend	She *intends* to start her own club.
learn	They will *learn* to swim at camp.
need	She *needs* to stop smoking.
offer	They *offered* to take us home.
plan	We *plan* to accept their offer.
prepare	She *prepared* to leave.
refuse	He *refused* to come with us.
seem	She *seemed* to be annoyed.
want	He didn't *want* to leave.

TARGET

40   Verb + Gerund or Infinitive

Problem	The wrong form may be used.
Solution	Pay attention to the main verb to determine the form needed.

Examples

Incorrect: Ms. Utz *enjoys to program* computers.
Correct: Ms. Utz *enjoys programming* computers.

Explanation: *Enjoys* must be followed by a gerund. Use the gerund *programming*.

Ms. Utz	enjoys	programming	computers.
n phrase	v	ger	n

Incorrect: The clerk finished *to verify* the orders.
Correct: The clerk finished *verifying* the orders.

Explanation: *Finish* must be followed by a gerund. Use the gerund *verifying*.

The clerk	finished	verifying	the orders.
n phrase	v	ger	n

Incorrect: Mr. White offered *helping* the children.
Correct: Mr. White offered *to help* the children.

Explanation: *Offered* must be followed by an infinitive. Use the infinitive *to help*.

Mr. White	offered	to help	the children.
n phrase	v	inf	n phrase

Incorrect: The computer failed *running* the program.
Correct: The computer failed *to run* the program.

Explanation: *Fail* must be followed by an infinitive. Use the infinitive *to run*.

The computer	failed	to run	the program.
n phrase	v	inf	n phrase

Exercises

Part 5: Incomplete Sentences

Choose the one word or phrase that best completes the sentence.

The clerk intends _____ her supervisor's job in a few years.

(A) having
(B) to have
(C) have
(D) will have

Ⓐ Ⓑ Ⓒ Ⓓ

Part 6: Text Completion

Read the e-mail and choose the one word or phrase that best completes each sentence.

To: Sam Tyler
From: Jack Stone
Subject: Meeting with Mr. Williams

Sam,

Mr. Williams has agreed _____ with us in order to discuss the

1. (A) met
   (B) meets
   (C) to meet
   (D) meeting

contracts. Have you had a chance to review them yet? He says he doesn't mind _____ over to our office some time next week. Is

2. (A) comes
   (B) coming
   (C) to come
   (D) will come

next Tuesday afternoon a good time for you? If so, would right after lunch work?

Before we meet with him, I think we should take a few minutes to discuss this together. We could get together over the weekend if that would be easier for you. I've _____ help one of our colleagues move on

3. (A) offering
   (B) offered to
   (C) to offer
   (D) offered

Saturday. We should be finished moving by 5:00 P.M. I'll be home all day Sunday.

Jack

First News
A l w a y s I n n o v a t i v e & I n f o r m a t i v e

TARGET 40 REVIEW
Gerunds and Infinitives

Part 5: Incomplete Sentences

Directions: Choose the one word or phrase that best completes the sentence.

1. Mr. Ingles is preparing _____ his speech.

    (A) give   (A) (B) (C) (D)
    (B) giving
    (C) given
    (D) to give

2. We did not want _____ the meeting.

    (A) to delay   (A) (B) (C) (D)
    (B) delaying
    (C) delayed
    (D) delay

3. The committee postponed _____ until tomorrow.

    (A) to vote   (A) (B) (C) (D)
    (B) voted
    (C) vote
    (D) voting

4. The president considered _____ a train instead of a plane.

    (A) taking   (A) (B) (C) (D)
    (B) will take
    (C) taken
    (D) to take

5. The company failed _____ a profit last year.

    (A) make   (A) (B) (C) (D)
    (B) made
    (C) making
    (D) to make

Part 6: Text Completion

Directions: Read the e-mail and choose the one word or phrase that best completes each sentence.

To: achang@homedesk.org
From: j&p@jpnurseries.org

Dear Ms. Chang,

I enjoyed _____ you last week. I was impressed by your talents

    1. (A) met
         (B) meeting
         (C) to meet
         (D) have met

and interesting background. You seem _____ well qualified for the

            2. (A) be
               (B) are
               (C) to be
               (D) will be

position we are offering. I also noted your enthusiasm for our company. Mr. Park and I plan _____ together in the next few days to discuss

        3. (A) get
           (B) to get
           (C) will get
           (D) getting

all the people who applied for the job. There were so many highly qualified candidates that we are considering creating another position. We may actually hire two people rather than one. We will let all the applicants know by the end of next week. Thank you for your patience.

Sincerely,

Shirley James

PARTICIPLES

Participles are verb forms that are used like adjectives. Participles describe nouns. There are two kinds: (1) present participles and (2) past participles. Present participles end in *-ing*. Past participles can end in *-ed, -en, -d, -t,* or *-n*. Their meanings are different.

verb	present participle	past participle
bore	boring	bored
excite	exciting	excited
confuse	confusing	confused
annoy	annoying	annoyed
surprise	surprising	surprised
move	moving	moved

Use a present participle to describe a noun that creates a feeling or does an action.

Creates a Feeling or Explains a Use

		n phrase		
pron	v	art	present participle	n
That	is	an	exciting	announcement.
This	is	a	cooking	utensil.

The announcement *created* the excitement. It's a utensil used for *cooking*.

Use a past participle to describe a noun that receives a feeling or an action.

Receives a Feeling or an Action

n phrase				
art	past participle	n	v	n phrase
The	excited	workers	had heard	the announcement.
The	cooked	pasta	needed	some sauce.

The workers did not *create* the excitement. They were affected by the excitement. The pasta did not do the action. It received the action.

TARGET

41   Incorrect Participles

Problem	The wrong type of participle may be used.
Solution	Pay attention to the noun you want to describe.

Examples

Incorrect: The *confused* memo created problems for the staff.
Correct: The *confusing* memo created problems for the staff.

Explanation: The memo caused the confusion. Use the present participle *confusing*.

	n phrase		
The	confusing	memo	created problems for the staff.
art	present participle	n	v phrase

Incorrect: The *bored* speech made everyone fall asleep.
Correct: The *boring* speech made everyone fall asleep

Explanation: The speech caused the boredom. Use the present participle *boring*.

	n phrase		
The	boring	speech	caused everyone to fall asleep.
art	present participle	n	v phrase

Incorrect: The *confusing* staff did not understand the memo.
Correct: The *confused* staff did not understand the memo.

Explanation: The staff did not cause the confusion. The staff received the confusion. Use the past participle *confused*.

	n phrase		
The	confused	staff	did not understand the memo.
art	past participle	n	v phrase

Incorrect: The *boring* audience fell asleep during the speech.
Correct: The *bored* audience fell asleep during the speech.

Explanation: The audience did not cause the boredom. The audience received the boredom. Use the past participle *bored*.

	n phrase		
The	bored	audience	fell asleep during the speech.
art	past participle	n	v phrase

Exercises

Part 5: Incomplete Sentences

Choose the one word or phrase that best completes the sentence.

The _____ sounds from the street prevented him from concentrating.

    (A) annoyed   Ⓐ Ⓑ Ⓒ Ⓓ
    (B) annoying
    (C) to annoy
    (D) has been annoyed

Part 6: Text Completion

Read the note and choose the one word or phrase that best completes each sentence.

Maria,

Good news! I now have the _____ contracts in my hand, so we

    1. (A) signature
        (B) signing
        (C) signed
        (D) sign

can get started on the work. I'm sure you will be happy to get going on this
as we have been waiting for more than two months now for this grant.

Unfortunately, they did not agree to pay the entire amount that we asked
for. I hope that news is not too _____ for you. In all honesty, I think

    2. (A) disappointment
        (B) disappointing
        (C) disappointed
        (D) disappoints

they have offered us a fair amount. I wasn't expecting the full amount anyway. _____ part is that they don't require a breakdown of our

    3. (A) The surprising
        (B) The surprised
        (C) Surprising the
        (D) I'm surprised

spending. That will save us time in creating a formal budget.

Luis

TARGET 41 REVIEW
Participles

Part 5: Incomplete Sentences

Directions: Choose the one word or phrase that best completes the sentence.

1. The _____ employees did not like their jobs.

   (A) boredom   Ⓐ Ⓑ Ⓒ Ⓓ
   (B) bored
   (C) bores
   (D) bore

2. The office boy will distribute the _____ mail.

   (A) sorted   Ⓐ Ⓑ Ⓒ Ⓓ
   (B) sort
   (C) sort of
   (D) sorting

3. The _____ application was delivered with the job offer.

   (A) approval   Ⓐ Ⓑ Ⓒ Ⓓ
   (B) approves
   (C) approved
   (D) approving

4. It is difficult to work in these _____ offices.

   (A) crowding   Ⓐ Ⓑ Ⓒ Ⓓ
   (B) crowded
   (C) crowds
   (D) crowd

5. The _____ audience enjoyed the speaker.

   (A) laugh   Ⓐ Ⓑ Ⓒ Ⓓ
   (B) laughter
   (C) laughed
   (D) laughing

Part 6: Text Completion

Directions: Read the newspaper article and choose the one word or phrase that best completes each sentence.

Hollywood Daily   Edition 23
Financial News

Yesterday's _____ drop in the price of Acme Corporation stock

    1. (A) unexpected
        (B) expecting
        (C) expectation
        (D) expectant

caused panic in the stock market. While alarmed investors rushed to unload their shares, a few remained calm. "This was not completely _____ news to us," said Cheryl Grayson, of Finch & Gold

2. (A) surprise
    (B) surprised
    (C) surprising
    (D) has surprised

brokerage firm. "We had been watching the company for some time and knew it was having problems." Grayson added, "These are _____,

          3. (A) unexplained losses
              (B) confusing times
              (C) bored workers
              (D) excited stocks

when the stock market can take sudden turns without warning. It's important to have a broker you can trust, especially if you are new to trading." Stock for Acme's main competitor, Blue Door Films, is at its highest price since the company was established three years ago.

STRATEGY SUMMARY

Strategies for Reading Parts 5 and 6

Strategies for Analyzing Vocabulary

There is, as you know, no vocabulary section on the TOEIC. Still, you must know the meaning of words in order to be able to comprehend the reading passages and the grammar exercises. The best way to learn words is by using them. If you read a new word, try to use it in another way. Write it down; say it in a sentence. Listen for others to use it. Notice how the word is used when you read it.

Strategies for learning vocabulary can be summarized as follows:

- Read as much as you can in English.
- Keep a notebook of the words you learn.
- Learn words in context—not from word lists.

Strategies for Analyzing Grammar

The many grammar rules and solutions to potential problems that you learned in this section can be summarized in the following strategies. If you can learn to recognize these components and how they work together, you will score well on Parts 5 and 6.

- Recognize the parts of speech.
- Recognize agreement of person, number, and tense.
- Recognize the correct grammatical form.
- Recognize correct usage.
- Recognize correct word order.
- Recognize potentially wrong answers.

Mini-Test

ANSWER SHEET

Reading

PART 5: INCOMPLETE SENTENCES

1. Ⓐ Ⓑ Ⓒ Ⓓ
2. Ⓐ Ⓑ Ⓒ Ⓓ
3. Ⓐ Ⓑ Ⓒ Ⓓ
4. Ⓐ Ⓑ Ⓒ Ⓓ
5. Ⓐ Ⓑ Ⓒ Ⓓ
6. Ⓐ Ⓑ Ⓒ Ⓓ
7. Ⓐ Ⓑ Ⓒ Ⓓ
8. Ⓐ Ⓑ Ⓒ Ⓓ
9. Ⓐ Ⓑ Ⓒ Ⓓ
10. Ⓐ Ⓑ Ⓒ Ⓓ
11. Ⓐ Ⓑ Ⓒ Ⓓ
12. Ⓐ Ⓑ Ⓒ Ⓓ
13. Ⓐ Ⓑ Ⓒ Ⓓ
14. Ⓐ Ⓑ Ⓒ Ⓓ
15. Ⓐ Ⓑ Ⓒ Ⓓ
16. Ⓐ Ⓑ Ⓒ Ⓓ
17. Ⓐ Ⓑ Ⓒ Ⓓ
18. Ⓐ Ⓑ Ⓒ Ⓓ
19. Ⓐ Ⓑ Ⓒ Ⓓ
20. Ⓐ Ⓑ Ⓒ Ⓓ

PART 6: TEXT COMPLETION

21. Ⓐ Ⓑ Ⓒ Ⓓ
22. Ⓐ Ⓑ Ⓒ Ⓓ
23. Ⓐ Ⓑ Ⓒ Ⓓ
24. Ⓐ Ⓑ Ⓒ Ⓓ
25. Ⓐ Ⓑ Ⓒ Ⓓ
26. Ⓐ Ⓑ Ⓒ Ⓓ

Mini-Test for Reading Parts 5 and 6

Part 5: Incomplete Sentences

Directions: You will see a sentence with a missing word. Four possible answers follow the sentence. Choose the best answer to the question and fill in the corresponding oval on your answer sheet.

See page 333 for the Answer Key and page 351 for the Explanatory Answers for this Mini-Test.

1. The fax machine and the telephone _____ on separate lines.

   (A) am
   (B) is
   (C) are
   (D) be

2. Attach this cable _____ the computer.

   (A) with
   (B) into
   (C) in
   (D) to

3. Tomorrow we _____ submit the budget.

   (A) will
   (B) has
   (C) did
   (D) are

4. The _____ was concise and effective.

   (A) presenting
   (B) presented
   (C) present
   (D) presentation

5. Salaries must be _____ if we are to remain competitive.

   (A) ascended
   (B) increased
   (C) escalated
   (D) risen

6. We drove to the site in an open jeep _____ it was raining.

   (A) although
   (B) since
   (C) because
   (D) with

7. The meeting was scheduled to begin _____ noon.

   (A) on
   (B) to
   (C) in
   (D) at

8. This letter was _____ by overnight mail.

   (A) send
   (B) been sent
   (C) sent
   (D) sending

9. The staff _____ after 5:00 if there is work to finish.

   (A) will usually stay
   (B) will usually stays
   (C) will stay usually
   (D) usually will stay

10. Our office is _____ the post office and the bank.

    (A) among
    (B) outside
    (C) between
    (D) through

11. If you need to order supplies, _____ a purchase order form.

    (A) complete
    (B) completely
    (C) completion
    (D) to complete

12. The oil rig is located _____ Texas.

    (A) over
    (B) off
    (C) in
    (D) beside

13. _____ sales have increased, profits have increased too.

    (A) Although
    (B) During
    (C) Since
    (D) Until

14. Immigration forms must _____ be stamped before leaving the customs area.

    (A) once
    (B) always
    (C) still
    (D) rarely

15. Neither lunch _____ dinner was served at the hotel.

    (A) or
    (B) and
    (C) but
    (D) nor

16. If the consultant _____ that we should hire more staff, Helen wouldn't be working here now.

    (A) didn't recommend
    (B) doesn't recommend
    (C) hadn't recommended
    (D) wasn't recommending

17. If you _____ how to use a computer, consult the manual.

    (A) won't understand
    (B) don't understand
    (C) understood
    (D) not understanding

18. Before the Foreign Minister arrived, the police had the conference center _____.

    (A) clear
    (B) cleared
    (C) clearing
    (D) be clear

19. The Bangkok branch of our bank _____ ten years ago this month.

    (A) opens
    (B) has opened
    (C) opened
    (D) was opening

20. All visitors must _____ their coats and packages before entering the museum.

    (A) checked
    (B) checking
    (C) checks
    (D) check

Part 6: Text Completion

Directions: You will see two passages each with three blanks. Under each blank are four answer options. Choose the word or phrase that best completes the sentence.

Questions 21–23 refer to the following memorandum.

To: Edouard Fleurat
From: Maria Rotini
Subject: Client Visit

Ed,

Olga Kovacs, _____ represents one of our most important clients,

    21. (A) who
        (B) who she
        (C) whom
        (D) whom she

will visit our city next week. We want to make sure she gets the best treatment possible while she is here. She _____ at the Grand Hotel,

    22. (A) stays
        (B) stayed
        (C) has stayed
        (D) will be staying

not too far from our office. We expect her to arrive at the office first thing Monday morning. Please send _____ to her hotel by 7:30 on

    23. (A) a greeting
        (B) directions
        (C) a limousine
        (D) instructions

Monday so that she doesn't have to look for a cab. You should ride with her and make sure that she has everything she needs.

Thanks,

Maria

Questions 24–26 refer to the following newspaper article.

The Auckland Quarterly   March 1, 20—
Life Section-Health

Is Smoking the Latest Trend?

Smoking is becoming more popular among young people, and they are starting to smoke at earlier ages than before. _____ there have

       24. (A) Although
           (B) Because
           (C) When
           (D) Since

been many campaigns to discourage teenagers from smoking, more than 40% of teens say they have tried it at least once. Over 30% of these say they tried their first cigarette before the age of fourteen. This is not _____ news for public health officials, teachers,

     25. (A) encourage
         (B) encouraged
         (C) encouraging
         (D) encouragement

and parents. "We need to develop better anti-smoking campaigns that are directed at teenagers," said Dr. Howard MacDonald, director of the Center for Healthy Living. "Starting a habit like smoking during _____ can mean serious health problems for the rest

 26. (A) adversity
     (B) addiction
     (C) advertising
     (D) adolescence

of one's life," he added.

Reading Comprehension Targets Part 7

The Answer Key and Explanatory Answers for all Targets in this Chapter can be found beginning on page 328.

The targets below frequently appear on Part 7 of the Reading section of the TOEIC. If you study these targets carefully and review the strategies at the end of this chapter, you will improve your score on the TOEIC.

Please read *Reading Comprehension Sample Questions* below. This will help you understand the type of questions and the type of information being tested. *Reading Comprehension Passages* gives an overview of the types of passages you will read in Part 7.

TARGETS LIST

Analyzing Reading Passages Targets

42 Advertisements, p. 290
43 Forms, p. 291
44 Reports, p. 292
45 Letters, p. 293
46 Faxes, p. 294
47 Memos, p. 295
48 Tables, p. 296
49 Indexes, p. 298
50 Charts, p. 299
51 Graphs, p. 300
52 Announcements, p. 301
53 Notices, p. 302
54 Newspaper Articles, p. 303
55 Magazine Articles, p. 304
56 Schedules, p. 305
57 Calendars, p. 306
58 E-mail, p. 307
59 Web Pages, p. 308
60 Computer Language, p. 309

READING COMPREHENSION SAMPLE QUESTIONS

There are three types of questions found on the Reading Comprehension part of the TOEIC. The most common question type is the one that begins with a "wh" word.

1. Questions that begin with "wh" words: *How, what, when, where, which, who, why.*

   Who completed the form?

   (A) The hotel clerk
   (B) The manager
   (C) The client
   (D) The travel agent

2. Questions that begin with "if" and "wh" words.

   If the form is incomplete, what will happen?

   (A) It will be returned.
   (B) It will be destroyed.
   (C) It will be rewritten.
   (D) It will be filed.

3. Open questions.

The word "annoying" in paragraph 1, line 2 is closest in meaning to

(A) delegating
(B) annexing
(C) irritating
(D) gnawing

These three question types are looking for six different types of information. The most frequently asked question is the one looking for *factual information.*

Most commonly asked questions:

1. Positive factual questions
2. Negative factual questions
3. Inference questions
4. Synonym questions
5. Context questions

Less commonly asked questions:

6. Main idea questions
7. Viewpoint questions
8. Computation questions

Study the examples given in the chart below. These examples show how the most commonly asked questions match the information sought.

Common Questions	Common Words or Phrases
Positive Factual	
Which of the following would be included?	How
How do people plan to raise money?	What
Who made the phone calls?	When
Why was the call made?	Where
At what time was the call received?	Which
What is one problem with the management?	Who
When can visitors see the exhibit?	Why
When is the fare the lowest?	
How much will it cost to produce the product?	
What is the base charge for one kilowatt hour of electricity?	
If expenses are $50, how much does the company earn?	If
If no directions are given, the workers will...	
According to the table, which city had the least rainfall?	According to the author...
Of the following, which would apply?	According to the bulletin...
	Of the following...
The division had to decide whether or not to...	
One of the factors that was included was...	
One of the articles listed is...	
Part-time workers are most likely to have...	most

Negative Factual Except for (besides) Sundays, the offices are open... Which of the following would not be part of the plan? All of the following are essential except... Students are the least likely to...	not except least
Inference Why are there fewer computers? Why was this graph produced? Why is he writing this letter? Where is this announcement likely to be found? It can be inferred from the chart that 20____ was... This type of form must be filled out at...	Why likely probably It can be inferred that The author implies that...
Synonym The word "vocabulary" in paragraph 2, line 1, is closest in meaning to... (You will have to understand the context of the whole passage to answer this question.)	
Context These questions could be any of the type of questions in this table. The context question is found in the double passages. You will have to get information from both passages to answer the question correctly.	
Main Idea (not commonly asked) What is the purpose of this letter? Why was this letter written? The main idea of the article is... The main topic of the article is...	main point mainly discuss main idea main purpose main topic
Viewpoint (not commonly asked) The authors of the article believe that... The tone of this letter is... The author describes capitalism as...	The authors believe... The general tone of... The writer's attitude... The author's purpose... feel
Computation (not commonly asked) How much does the total package cost? How much more does it cost for four than for one?	How much cost total

You will find many examples of these question types and many examples of the variety of reading passages in Targets 42–60 on pages 290–309.

The PSRA Strategy

An important strategy for reading comprehension is learning to approach a passage in an organized way. First make a *Prediction* about the passage, then *Scan* it; next *Read* it, and finally *Answer* the questions. We can abbreviate this strategy to **PSRA**.

Prediction

Learning how to make predictions about what you are going to read BEFORE you read will help you establish a context for understanding the passage. This will improve your reading score.

Before you begin to read one of the reading passages, you should first look at the question introduction line. This line looks like this:

Questions 161–163 refer to the following office memo.

In the question introduction line, you will learn how many questions there are and what kind of reading passage it is (in this case an office memo). The look of the reading passage will also give you a clue: a fax will look like a fax, a phone message like a phone message, and a graph like a graph. This will help you PREDICT what the passage is about.

There are generally two or three questions for every reading passage, although there may be up to five. Look at the questions and the four answer options. This will give you a clue what to look for. These clues will help you PREDICT what the passage is about.

According to the memo, which equipment has multiple uses?

(A) Computers
(B) Fax machines
(C) Answering machines
(D) CD-players

Scan

We can predict that the memo has something to do with electronics. When we *Scan* the passage, we look for the Key Words. You may not find the exact words, but you might find words with similar meanings. Try to think of words that have meanings similar to the Key Words in the question and answer options. The Key Words for this question are:

Questions		**Answer Options**
Key words	*Similar meanings*	computers
equipment	electronic tools; hardware	fax machines
multiple uses	useful in a variety of settings	answering machines
		CD-players

Look first for the Key Words from the question; then look around the Question Key Words for the Key Words from the answer options. When you find the Answer Option Key Words, see if the words answer the question. Try to answer the question (in your head, NOT on the answer sheet). Here's a sample:

MEMORANDUM

To: Lafite, Pierre
    Purchasing Department
From: Clement, Marie France
    Personnel

We need **computers** for use in the office, **answering machines** for our consultants, **fax machines** for the shipping department, and **CD-players** for everyone. This **last piece of hardware** can be **used in a variety** of ways.

According to the memo, which equipment has multiple uses?

  (A) Computers
  (B) Fax machines
  (C) Answering machines
  (D) CD-players

The correct answer is (D). A CD-player is the **last** piece of hardware mentioned. *This last piece of hardware can be used in a variety of ways.*

Note how much different the answer would be if the last sentence were:

This **first piece of hardware** can be **used in a variety** of ways.

The word "first" changes the answer completely from (D) CD-players to (A) Computers. This is why you must NOT rely on Prediction and Scanning alone.

Read

You must READ the passage as well. But when you read, read quickly. Read to confirm your predictions.

You should not make any mark on your answer sheet until you have made a PREDICTION based on all of the questions, SCANNED the passage looking for key words, answered the questions in your head, and READ the passage to confirm your answer choices. The answer to the first question is found in the first part of the reading passage. The answer to the second question is found in the next part and so on. The questions follow the sequence of the passage.

Answer

Now you are ready to mark your answer sheet. ANSWER the easy questions first. If you don't know an answer, scan the passage again, look for the key words, read parts of the passage. If you still don't know, GUESS. Do NOT leave any answer blank.

These strategies are easy to remember; just memorize PSRA: Predict, Scan, Read, and Answer.

Strategies for Reading Comprehension

Predict.
Look at the introduction line.
Look at the question and answer options.

Scan the passage.
Look for Key Words from the question.
Look for Key Words from the answer options.
Answer questions (in your head, NOT on answer sheet).

Read the passage.
Read quickly, but carefully. Don't stop if you don't know a word.
Confirm your predictions.

Answer the questions on the answer sheet.
Answer the easy questions first.
Guess if you don't know.

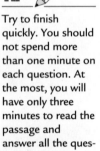

TIP

Try to finish quickly. You should not spend more than one minute on each question. At the most, you will have only three minutes to read the passage and answer all the questions. Try to do each passage in less than two minutes.

Now practice the PSRA strategy with the following reading passages. There are more questions on each reading passage in this book than on the TOEIC test. This will give you more practice.

For each reading passage, you should circle the Key Words; answer the questions in your head; time yourself as you read; and finally answer the questions.

Reading Comprehension Passages

In the Reading Comprehension section of the TOEIC, you will have forty-eight questions based on single passages and twenty questions based on double passages. Whether there is one passage or two, the most likely types of reading passages are:

- Advertisements
- Forms
- Reports
- Letters, Faxes, and Memos
- Tables and Indexes
- Charts and Graphs
- Announcements and Notices
- Newspaper and Magazine Articles
- Schedules and Calendars
- E-mail, Web Pages, and Computer Language

In the double passage section, you will likely find any combination of the previous types of reading passages. You can have:

- A letter and an e-mail
- An invoice and an e-mail
- An e-mail and an e-mail
- A schedule and a memo
- An article and a letter

There can be any combination of types of passages. Whatever the type, you should still use your PSRA reading strategies.

Examples of each type follow. Do the exercises for each Reading Comprehension target. Check your answers using the Answer Key beginning on page 328 and the Explanatory Answers beginning on page 334.

TARGET

42 **Advertisements**

Advertisements on the TOEIC are similar to those found in magazines or newspapers. You can find other examples in English-language newspapers and magazines and ask yourself questions about the products being advertised.

Exercise

Part 7: Reading Comprehension

Questions 1–2 refer to the following advertisement. Choose the one best answer to each question.

ATTENTION MANUFACTURERS!

We introduce and distribute your products to 125,000 distributors in 155 countries, FREE!

For a FREE information kit call:

Tel: (310) 553-4434 Ext. 105 • Fax (310) 553-5555
GRAND TECHNOLOGIES LIMITED

---

1. Who is the advertisement written for?

   (A) Distributors
   (B) Sales representatives
   (C) Manufacturers
   (D) Information specialists

   Ⓐ Ⓑ Ⓒ Ⓓ

2. How many countries are mentioned?

   (A) 125
   (B) 155
   (C) 310
   (D) 501

   Ⓐ Ⓑ Ⓒ Ⓓ

TARGET
43   Forms

A form is a template: a standard form that an individual adds information to. These could include magazine subscription forms, purchase orders, immigration forms, hotel check-in forms, telephone message blanks, etc.

Exercises

Part 7: Reading Comprehension

Questions 1–4 refer to the following form. Choose the one best answer to each question.

Special Subscription Offer

Subscribe to the journal that recently received the Editorial Excellence Award from the Society of Industrial Designers

☑ **YES!** send me INTERNATIONAL INDUSTRY for 1 year (12 issues) at just $48, a savings of 20% off the full cover price of $5.00.

☐ Payment enclosed   ☑ Bill me.

Name: *Anne Kwok*
Title: *Design Specialist*
Company: *Pharmaceutical Supply Co.*
Address: *Tong Chong Street*
Quarry Bay Hong Kong

Please allow four weeks for first issue.

---

1. Why did Anne Kwok complete this form?

    (A) To win an award   Ⓐ Ⓑ Ⓒ Ⓓ
    (B) To apply for a design job
    (C) To enroll in design school
    (D) To receive a journal

2. How much is the full cover price per issue?

    (A) $4   Ⓐ Ⓑ Ⓒ Ⓓ
    (B) $5
    (C) $12
    (D) $48

3. How long will it take for the first issue to arrive?

    (A) One week   Ⓐ Ⓑ Ⓒ Ⓓ
    (B) One month
    (C) One year
    (D) Unknown

4. The magazine comes

    (A) daily.   Ⓐ Ⓑ Ⓒ Ⓓ
    (B) weekly.
    (C) monthly.
    (D) once a year.

TARGET

44 Reports

A report is a short paragraph containing the kind of information that might be included in a capsule summary. A report could appear in a newspaper; it could be part of a larger document such as an annual report; it could be most any kind of descriptive or narrative prose.

Exercises

Part 7: Reading Comprehension

Questions 1–3 refer to the following report. Choose the one best answer to each question.

> In October, Markel On-Line acquired
> Peptel Visual of Berlin, one of Europe's
> leading educational software companies.
> The deal calls for Markel (a $49 million
> Toronto-based company) to pay $5 million
> up front for Peptel and as much as $5
> million more over the next few years,
> depending on the German company's
> performance. Peptel posted $4.2 million
> in sales last year.

1. If Peptel performs well, what is the largest total price Markel will have to pay?

   (A) $4.2 million
   (B) $5 million
   (C) $10 million
   (D) $49 million

2. Peptel is based in

   (A) Canada.
   (B) the United States.
   (C) Great Britain.
   (D) Germany.

3. What field are these companies in?

   (A) Computer software
   (B) Postal service
   (C) Visual arts
   (D) Toy manufacturing

First News
A l w a y s I n n o v a t i v e & I n f o r m a t i v e

TARGET
45   Letters

The TOEIC will generally always have one letter on the test. The important information is generally contained in the body of the letter—the part between the greeting (*Dear ...*) and the closing (*Sincerely yours*).

Exercises

Part 7: Reading Comprehension

Questions 1–3 refer to the following letter. Choose the one best answer to each question.

EUTECH, s.r.o.
Zborovská 23,150 00 Praha 5
Czech Republic
Tel: (02) 513.2343 Fax: (02) 513.2334

December 3, 20—

Post Comptoir
43 Griffith Road
Dinsdale, Hamilton
North Island, New Zealand

Dear Sir or Madam:

We are interested in becoming distributors for your software products in the Czech Republic. Would you please send us your latest catalogs, descriptive brochures, and terms?

We are a hardware company that would like to add software to our sales offerings. Our annual report is enclosed.

We look forward to hearing from you soon.

Sincerely yours,

Peter Zavel
Peter Zavel
Chairman

---

1. Which items were NOT requested?

    (A) Catalogs   Ⓐ Ⓑ Ⓒ Ⓓ
    (B) Brochures
    (C) Samples
    (D) Pricing information

2. What does EUTECH sell now?

    (A) Software   Ⓐ Ⓑ Ⓒ Ⓓ
    (B) Computers
    (C) Financial reports
    (D) Printing services

3. EUTECH wants to

    (A) distribute software.   Ⓐ Ⓑ Ⓒ Ⓓ
    (B) manufacture computers.
    (C) purchase hardware.
    (D) receive an annual report.

TARGET
46 Faxes

A fax (facsimile) is like a letter except it is delivered electronically on a fax machine. The main difference in format is the additional piece of information that tells how many pages were sent as part of a fax.

Exercises

Part 7: Reading Comprehension

Questions 1–4 refer to the following fax. Choose the one best answer to each question.

FAX COVER SHEET

ARS TECH
Avenida Diagonal 673–683
08028 Barcelona
Spain
Tel: (3) 318-4300
Fax: (3) 318-4308

To: All Board Members
From: Fernando Murillo
Accounting Department
Date: October 23, 20—
Pages: This +10
Ref: 20— Budget

Message:

Please review the attached budget before the meeting tomorrow. The meeting will begin Tuesday, October 24 at 10:00 A.M. in room 42 in Building B. It will last through Thursday and will finish at 5:00 P.M. There will be a reception at the Sofitel Hotel Thursday evening.

---

1. Where will the meeting be held?
   (A) In Room 24
   (B) In Building B
   (C) Next door
   (D) At the Sofitel Hotel

   Ⓐ Ⓑ Ⓒ Ⓓ

2. How many days will the meeting last?
   (A) Two
   (B) Three
   (C) Four
   (D) Five

   Ⓐ Ⓑ Ⓒ Ⓓ

3. What day was the fax written?
   (A) Monday
   (B) Tuesday
   (C) Thursday
   (D) Friday

   Ⓐ Ⓑ Ⓒ Ⓓ

4. How many pages are in the whole fax?
   (A) One
   (B) Two
   (C) Ten
   (D) Eleven

   Ⓐ Ⓑ Ⓒ Ⓓ

TARGET
47 Memos

A memorandum (memo) is an internal form of communication that is sent from one member of a company to a member of the same company. Today these memos (memoranda) are often sent by computer as e-mail. To learn more about computer-generated language, see Targets 58–60 on pages 307–309.

Exercises

Part 7: Reading Comprehension

Questions 1–4 refer to the following memorandum. Choose the one best answer to each question.

MEMORANDUM

To: All Employees

From: Simon Gonzales
Personnel Officer

Date: May 15, 20—

Sub: Company Travel

Effective June 1 all personnel traveling on company business must use the most economical means possible. No flights under five hours can be booked in Business Class. No flights regardless of duration can be booked in First Class.

---

1. If a flight is over five hours, what class can be booked?

   (A) Economy   Ⓐ Ⓑ Ⓒ Ⓓ
   (B) Economy Plus
   (C) Business
   (D) First

2. When will this rule go into effect?

   (A) In about two weeks   Ⓐ Ⓑ Ⓒ Ⓓ
   (B) At the end of the summer
   (C) At the first of the year
   (D) In five months

3. Why was this memo written?

   (A) To save time   Ⓐ Ⓑ Ⓒ Ⓓ
   (B) To save money
   (C) To reward the employees
   (D) To increase company travel

4. Who is affected by this memo?

   (A) Only the Board   Ⓐ Ⓑ Ⓒ Ⓓ
       of Directors
   (B) Only frequent travelers
   (C) Only the personnel department
   (D) All personnel

TARGET

48 Tables

The TOEIC will often have a table on the exam. A table is a compilation of data that is useful for quick comparison. Tables could be on most any subject. Look for tables in English-language newspapers or magazines or also material printed in your own language.

Exercise

Part 7: Reading Comprehension

Questions 1–4 refer to the following table. Choose the one best answer to each question.

WORLD TEMPERATURES January 5			
	Hi C/F	Lo C/F	Weather
Amsterdam	6/41	3/37	c
Athens	13/55	8/46	sh
Bangkok	32/90	27/80	sh
Beijing	12/53	1/34	pc
Brussels	4/39	1/34	sh
Budapest	3/37	0/32	r
Frankfurt	3/37	1/34	r
Jakarta	29/84	24/75	sh
Kuala Lampur	31/88	24/75	t
Madrid	9/48	1/34	sh
Manila	33/91	21/70	pc
Seoul	9/48	-2/29	s
Taipei	21/70	14/57	c
Tokyo	9/48	-2/29	pc

Weather: s-sunny; pc-partly cloudy; c-cloudy; sh-showers; t-thunderstorms; r-rain

1. Which two cities were cloudy on January 5?

    (A) Amsterdam
      and Taipei   Ⓐ Ⓑ Ⓒ Ⓓ
    (B) Beijing and Manila
    (C) Athens and Tokyo
    (D) Bangkok and Seoul

2. Which city had the highest temperature?

    (A) Athens   Ⓐ Ⓑ Ⓒ Ⓓ
    (B) Bangkok
    (C) Jakarta
    (D) Manila

3. Which city had the closest spread between high and low temperature?

    (A) Brussels   Ⓐ Ⓑ Ⓒ Ⓓ
    (B) Frankfurt
    (C) Seoul
    (D) Tokyo

4. Kuala Lampur had

    (A) sun.   Ⓐ Ⓑ Ⓒ Ⓓ
    (B) thunderstorms.
    (C) rain.
    (D) showers.

TARGET
49 Indexes

An index is a compilation of information that people can use to find additional information. A telephone book is an example of an index.

Exercises

Part 7: Reading Comprehension

Questions 1–2 refer to the following index. Choose the one best answer to each question.

Company Index
This index lists businesses mentioned in this issue of Global Economy

Acme Power and Light	44
Allied Steel	53
Best Iron Ore Supply	56
Canadian Rail Service	83
Chemical Times	15
Consumer's Electric	41
Ford Gas	4
Health, Inc.	12
International Oil	16
Liberty Funds	46
Network Travel	52
Pride Hotels	76
TNT Air	34

1. This index is most likely found in

    (A) a magazine.   Ⓐ Ⓑ Ⓒ Ⓓ
    (B) an interoffice memo.
    (C) a newsletter.
    (D) a book.

2. What type of industries are NOT represented?

    (A) Travel   Ⓐ Ⓑ Ⓒ Ⓓ
    (B) Computer
    (C) Heavy industries
    (D) Utilities industries

TARGET
50   Charts

A chart can be either a table or a graph. Charts are found in most printed materials.

Exercise

Part 7: Reading Comprehension

Questions 1–2 refer to the following table. Choose the one best answer to each question.

Top Ten Companies in Total Sales	
Company	**Sales (in billions)**
Sankyu, Inc.	$2,890
Executive Jet	$1,450
InterCon	$1,400
Continental, Ltd.	$1,380
Hospital Supply	$1,370
Tislak Leasing	$1,300
Leber Bank	$1,250
Euro Data	$1,250
InterAccess	$1,220
TeleVide	$1,200

1. What does this chart show?

   (A) Selling price of companies
   (B) Corporate salaries
   (C) Relative positions of successful companies
   (D) Numbers of investors

   Ⓐ Ⓑ Ⓒ Ⓓ

2. What can be said about Sankyu, Inc.?

   (A) It performed better last year.
   (B) Its sales are almost double the next ranking company.
   (C) Its sales are half as much as TeleVide.
   (D) Its earnings equaled that of Executive Jet.

   Ⓐ Ⓑ Ⓒ Ⓓ

First News
Always Innovative & Informative

TARGET
51 Graphs

A graph is a drawing that shows the relationship between variables. On the TOEIC there can be line graphs, bar graphs, or pie graphs.

Exercises

Part 7: Reading Comprehension

Questions 1–2 refer to the following graph. Choose the one best answer to each question.

Hotel Chain Market Share

Torte 15%

Lowit 25%

Other 5%

Stilton 55%

1. Who would be most interested in reading this graph?

   (A) Tourists
   (B) Competing hotels
   (C) Landscape architects
   (D) Job hunters

   Ⓐ Ⓑ Ⓒ Ⓓ

2. According to this graph, Lowit

   (A) is the top-ranking hotel chain.
   (B) is only in Latin America.
   (C) has less of a share than Torte.
   (D) has one-quarter of the market.

   Ⓐ Ⓑ Ⓒ Ⓓ

TARGET

52   Announcements

An announcement is similar to a report except it has more immediate information.
There is usually an announcement on the TOEIC.

Exercises

Part 7: Reading Comprehension

Questions 1–4 refer to the following announcement. Choose the one best answer to
each question.

> The Omnicable Company representatives said yesterday that John A.
> Kaspar, its president and chief operating officer, would resign on April 30.
> The announcement added to speculation that the world's third-largest
> cable television system could be bought within a few weeks. Mr. Kaspar,
> 62, said he was leaving after more than 22 years for "personal reasons."

1. What is the company's world ranking?

    (A) 3   Ⓐ Ⓑ Ⓒ Ⓓ
    (B) 22
    (C) 30
    (D) 62

2. What might happen to the company?

    (A) It may be bought.   Ⓐ Ⓑ Ⓒ Ⓓ
    (B) It may expand.
    (C) It may diversify.
    (D) It may become international.

3. How long has Mr. Kasper worked for Omnicable?

    (A) For a few weeks   Ⓐ Ⓑ Ⓒ Ⓓ
    (B) Since April 30
    (C) Since he was 40
    (D) 62 years

4. What kind of business is Omnicable?

    (A) Communications   Ⓐ Ⓑ Ⓒ Ⓓ
    (B) Computer
    (C) Manufacturing
    (D) Service

TARGET

53 Notices

A notice is information that the writer feels the general public or specific product users must be made aware of. There are often notices attached to walls and public buildings or enclosed with product literature.

Exercises

Part 7: Reading Comprehension

Questions 1–2 refer to the following notice. Choose the one best answer to each question.

Corporate Policy Change

Moving Expenses. You can be reimbursed for your expenses of moving to a new home only if your new home is at least 50 miles away from your former home. In addition, expenses are limited to the costs of moving your household goods and personal effects from your former home to your new home. Meals, pre-move house-hunting expenses, and temporary-quarters expenses are no longer reimbursable.

---

1. Who would be most affected by this notice?

   (A) Hotel chains
   (B) Furniture rental companies
   (C) Real estate agents
   (D) New employees moving from another city

   Ⓐ Ⓑ Ⓒ Ⓓ

2. Which of the following will be reimbursed?

   (A) Lunch for the movers
   (B) Shipping household goods
   (C) Gas used looking for a house
   (D) Hotel expenses

   Ⓐ Ⓑ Ⓒ Ⓓ

TARGET

54   Newspaper Articles

A newspaper article is a passage written by a journalist for a newspaper. Usually the topic is very current, but there are many kinds of newspapers: some come out daily, others weekly. Even companies may have their own internal newspaper which, because of their small size, are often called *newsletters*.

Exercises

Part 7: Reading Comprehension

Questions 1–3 refer to the following newspaper article. Choose the one best answer to each question.

> Before the fall of the Berlin Wall, East Berlin was like the rest of East Germany — drab and depressed. Today it is a different story, thanks to the new openness. There are over 40 major construction projects underway and investments in new construction are expected to exceed $20 billion. Part of this boom can be attributed to the fact that the national government of Germany will move to Berlin. The city will once again be Germany's leading city and a gateway to the expanding markets in Poland, the Czech Republic, and other countries east of the German border.

1. According to the article, what caused the change in East Berlin?

   (A) Expanding markets in Poland   Ⓐ Ⓑ Ⓒ Ⓓ
   (B) Border changes east of Germany
   (C) The completion of 40 construction projects
   (D) The collapse of the Berlin Wall

2. Which is NOT given as a reason for increased prosperity?

   (A) The location of Berlin   Ⓐ Ⓑ Ⓒ Ⓓ
   (B) The destruction of the Berlin Wall
   (C) The move of the national government
   (D) The drab character of East Berlin

3. A sum of at least $20 billion will be invested in

   (A) moving the government.   Ⓐ Ⓑ Ⓒ Ⓓ
   (B) new construction.
   (C) expanding markets.
   (D) border control.

First News
Always Innovative & Informative

TARGET
55   Magazine Articles

Like a newspaper article, a magazine article is written by a journalist. The topic could be any subject.

Exercise

Part 7: Reading Comprehension

Questions 1–3 refer to the following magazine article. Choose the one best answer to each question.

> The Information Highway is the road that links computer users to an infinite number of on-line services: the Web, electronic mail, public forums, and software, to mention just a few. Not long ago, the Information Highway was a new road, with not many users. Now, everyone seems to want to take a drive, with over 30 million households connected worldwide. Not surprisingly, this well-traveled highway is starting to *look* like a well-traveled highway. Traffic jams can cause routers to break up, forcing the system to close down for maintenance and repair. Naturally, accidents will happen on such a populated road, and usually the victim is some unintended file, gone forever. Then, of course, there's Mr. Cool, with his new broad-band connection, who speeds down the highway faster than most of us can go. But don't kid yourself; he pays for that speeding.

1. What is this article about?

   (A) Computerized access to information   Ⓐ Ⓑ Ⓒ Ⓓ
   (B) E-mail
   (C) Traveling by highway
   (D) Traffic problems on congested roads

2. Why would the Information Highway need to be closed?

   (A) There is an infinite number of services.   Ⓐ Ⓑ Ⓒ Ⓓ
   (B) There aren't enough users.
   (C) There are too many users.
   (D) There's an accident.

3. Who can travel fastest on the highway?

   (A) Someone in a fancy new car   Ⓐ Ⓑ Ⓒ Ⓓ
   (B) Cool people
   (C) Someone with a broad-band connection
   (D) The police

TARGET

56 Schedules

A schedule is a printed form with lists of information: stock prices, train departure times, payment schedules, etc.

Exercises

Part 7: Reading Comprehension

Questions 1–4 refer to the following schedule. Choose the one best answer to each question.

7th & Market	East Rise P&R	Tunnel	122nd East & 16th
7:11 W	**7:21**	**7:36 T**	**8:01**
7:22 W	**7:32**	**7:47 T**	**8:12**
7:30 W	**7:41**	**7:59 T**	**8:21**
7:40	**7:51**	**8:06**	8:32
8:02 W	**8:13**	**8:25**	8:53
8:25	8:35	8:49	9:14
8:51 W	9:01	9:15	9:40
9:21	9:32	9:48	10:11
9:51 W	10:10	10:24	10:40

Key:
T = Tunnel opens at 8:00 A.M. Buses prior to this time stop on 12th and Meridian.
W = Bus departs at this time. It arrives about 5 minutes earlier.
Boldface indicates peak fare.

1. What time do off-peak fares probably start?

    (A) Before 7 A.M. Ⓐ Ⓑ Ⓒ Ⓓ
    (B) 8:25 A.M.
    (C) 8:30 A.M.
    (D) 8:51 A.M.

2. What time does the 7:30 bus arrive at 7th & Market?

    (A) 7:00 Ⓐ Ⓑ Ⓒ Ⓓ
    (B) 7:22
    (C) 7:25
    (D) 7:30

3. Why doesn't the 7:30 use the tunnel?

    (A) Because it's rush hour. Ⓐ Ⓑ Ⓒ Ⓓ
    (B) Bus heights exceed limits for the tunnel.
    (C) The tunnel is closed at that time.
    (D) Early buses are rarely full enough to use the tunnel.

4. How long is the trip from 7th & Market to 122nd & 16th?

    (A) A quarter hour Ⓐ Ⓑ Ⓒ Ⓓ
    (B) A half hour
    (C) Almost an hour
    (D) An hour

57 Calendars

A calendar is a form for keeping track of future events or activities. The calendar could be personal, like a daily diary, or professional, like a timeline for completion of a project.

Exercise

Part 7: Reading Comprehension

Questions 1–4 refer to the following calendar. Choose the one best answer to each question.

January

Sun	Mon	Tue	Wed	Thu	Fri	Sat
	1 Holiday Golf w/JR	2 10:00 Mtg w/ Travel Agent Assoc.	3 11:00 Fly to Rio	4 Hotel Copa	5 Brkfst mtg with hotel reps 12:00 City tour	6 AM: Mtg with tour guides 5:00 P.M. flight home
7 Golf w/JR at club	8 6 P.M. Company dinner	9 7 A.M. Brkfst mtg with airline agents	10 3 P.M. Meeting w/ editor of travel mag	11 6:00 A.M. train to NY 8 P.M. Return	12 4 P.M. Dr's Appointment	13 10 A.M. Golf at club

1. What field is this person probably in?

   (A) Tourism
   (B) Medicine
   (C) Education
   (D) Sports

   Ⓐ Ⓑ Ⓒ Ⓓ

2. How many out-of-town trips are planned?

   (A) One
   (B) Two
   (C) Three
   (D) Four

   Ⓐ Ⓑ Ⓒ Ⓓ

3. How many nights will the person be away?

   (A) One
   (B) Two
   (C) Three
   (D) Four

   Ⓐ Ⓑ Ⓒ Ⓓ

4. For recreation this person probably

   (A) plays golf.
   (B) dances.
   (C) cooks.
   (D) learns Portuguese.

   Ⓐ Ⓑ Ⓒ Ⓓ

TARGET
58 E-mail

E-mail means *electronic mail* and refers to computer mail. E-mail can be used to send any type of correspondence, form, or questionnaire, so an e-mail reading item may include any type of content. One distinctive feature of e-mail is its heading, which includes information about the sender, the receiver, and the transmission. A second feature of e-mail is that its language is usually more casual than that of formal paper correspondence.

Exercise

Part 7: Reading Comprehension

Questions 1–2 refer to the following e-mail. Choose the one best answer to each question.

From: Melinda Ligos [m_ligos@hottech.com]
Sent: Tuesday, January 14, 20— 4:06 P.M.
To: Misha Polonetsky [m_polonetsky@hottech.com]
Subject: Meeting in Orlando

Misha—

The meeting went better than expected. They'll get back to us this week about the proposal.

Thanks for suggesting Sparazza's—I had dinner there on Thursday. Loved it.

Melinda

---

1. What is the sender's e-mail address?

   (A) m_ligos@hottech.com   Ⓐ Ⓑ Ⓒ Ⓓ
   (B) m_polonetsky@hottech.com
   (C) Melinda Ligos [m_ligos@hottech.com]
   (D) Misha Polonetsky

2. Where was the gathering?

   (A) At Hottech   Ⓐ Ⓑ Ⓒ Ⓓ
   (B) With a client of Misha Polonetsky
   (C) In Orlando
   (D) At Sparazza's

TARGET

59 Web Pages

Web pages are a relatively new feature of the TOEIC, as are all computer-generated reading passages. You can find an unlimited number of web pages on the Internet to familiarize yourself with their layout and terminology.

Exercise

Part 7: Reading Comprehension

Questions 1–2 refer to the following web page. Choose the one best answer to each question.

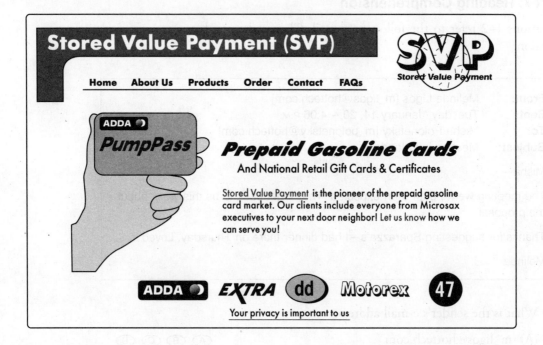

1. Where would you click to get an answer to a basic question about SVP?

    (A) Home
    (B) Products
    (C) Contact
    (D) FAQs

    ⒜ Ⓑ Ⓒ Ⓓ

2. What is the purpose of an SVP card?

    (A) To pay for fuel in advance
    (B) To reduce costs
    (C) To ensure privacy
    (D) To store gas safely in your home

    ⒜ Ⓑ Ⓒ Ⓓ

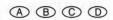

TARGET

60   Computer Language

Computer language includes any language whatsoever used in association with a computer. This vocabulary may be found in pull-down menus, user manuals, help information, and so forth. You do not need to be computer-savvy to answer these questions. All are basic English.

Exercise

Part 7: Reading Comprehension

Questions 1–2 refer to the following word processing pull-down menu. Choose the one best answer to each question.

File			Edit	View	Format	Tools	Font
New	Cntrl + N						
Open	Cntrl + O						
Open Recent							
Close	Cntrl + W						
Save	Cntrl + S						
Save as							
Page Setup							
Print Preview							
Print	Cntrl + P						

1. What can a user NOT do using these options?

    (A) Keep a document permanently   Ⓐ Ⓑ Ⓒ Ⓓ
    (B) See in advance how a document will print
    (C) Make a hard copy of a document
    (D) Duplicate a document

2. How can a user access an existing
    document?

    (A) Click on "New"   Ⓐ Ⓑ Ⓒ Ⓓ
    (B) Push "Control + O"
    (C) Click on "Save"
    (D) Click on "Page Setup"

STRATEGY SUMMARY

Strategies to Improve Your Reading Score

The following strategies are a review of those presented in this Reading Review chapter. The more strategies you can use while reading English, the more you will be able to understand what you read.

Analyzing vocabulary

• Read as much as you can in English.
• Keep a notebook of the words you learn.
• Learn words in context—not from word lists.

Analyzing grammar

• Recognize the parts of speech.
• Recognize agreement of person, number, and tense.
• Recognize the correct grammatical forms.
• Recognize the correct usage.
• Recognize the correct word order.
• Recognize potentially wrong answers.

Analyze reading passages

• Know the types of questions found on the TOEIC.
• Know the types of information sought on the TOEIC.
• Know how to use PSRA:
  —Predict what the passage will be about.
  —Scan the passage and answer options for key words.
  —Read the passage quickly.
  —Answer the questions.
    Use the PSRA whenever you read.

Mini-Test
ANSWER SHEET

PART 7: READING

1. Ⓐ Ⓑ Ⓒ Ⓓ
2. Ⓐ Ⓑ Ⓒ Ⓓ
3. Ⓐ Ⓑ Ⓒ Ⓓ
4. Ⓐ Ⓑ Ⓒ Ⓓ
5. Ⓐ Ⓑ Ⓒ Ⓓ
6. Ⓐ Ⓑ Ⓒ Ⓓ
7. Ⓐ Ⓑ Ⓒ Ⓓ
8. Ⓐ Ⓑ Ⓒ Ⓓ
9. Ⓐ Ⓑ Ⓒ Ⓓ
10. Ⓐ Ⓑ Ⓒ Ⓓ
11. Ⓐ Ⓑ Ⓒ Ⓓ
12. Ⓐ Ⓑ Ⓒ Ⓓ
13. Ⓐ Ⓑ Ⓒ Ⓓ
14. Ⓐ Ⓑ Ⓒ Ⓓ
15. Ⓐ Ⓑ Ⓒ Ⓓ
16. Ⓐ Ⓑ Ⓒ Ⓓ
17. Ⓐ Ⓑ Ⓒ Ⓓ
18. Ⓐ Ⓑ Ⓒ Ⓓ
19. Ⓐ Ⓑ Ⓒ Ⓓ
20. Ⓐ Ⓑ Ⓒ Ⓓ
21. Ⓐ Ⓑ Ⓒ Ⓓ
22. Ⓐ Ⓑ Ⓒ Ⓓ
23. Ⓐ Ⓑ Ⓒ Ⓓ
24. Ⓐ Ⓑ Ⓒ Ⓓ
25. Ⓐ Ⓑ Ⓒ Ⓓ

26. Ⓐ Ⓑ Ⓒ Ⓓ
27. Ⓐ Ⓑ Ⓒ Ⓓ
28. Ⓐ Ⓑ Ⓒ Ⓓ
29. Ⓐ Ⓑ Ⓒ Ⓓ
30. Ⓐ Ⓑ Ⓒ Ⓓ
31. Ⓐ Ⓑ Ⓒ Ⓓ
32. Ⓐ Ⓑ Ⓒ Ⓓ
33. Ⓐ Ⓑ Ⓒ Ⓓ
34. Ⓐ Ⓑ Ⓒ Ⓓ
35. Ⓐ Ⓑ Ⓒ Ⓓ
36. Ⓐ Ⓑ Ⓒ Ⓓ
37. Ⓐ Ⓑ Ⓒ Ⓓ
38. Ⓐ Ⓑ Ⓒ Ⓓ
39. Ⓐ Ⓑ Ⓒ Ⓓ
40. Ⓐ Ⓑ Ⓒ Ⓓ
41. Ⓐ Ⓑ Ⓒ Ⓓ
42. Ⓐ Ⓑ Ⓒ Ⓓ
43. Ⓐ Ⓑ Ⓒ Ⓓ
44. Ⓐ Ⓑ Ⓒ Ⓓ
45. Ⓐ Ⓑ Ⓒ Ⓓ
46. Ⓐ Ⓑ Ⓒ Ⓓ
47. Ⓐ Ⓑ Ⓒ Ⓓ
48. Ⓐ Ⓑ Ⓒ Ⓓ
49. Ⓐ Ⓑ Ⓒ Ⓓ
50. Ⓐ Ⓑ Ⓒ Ⓓ

Mini-Test for Reading Part 7

General directions: Read the passages below and choose the one best answer, (A), (B), (C), or (D), to each question. Answer all questions following the passage based on what is *stated* or *implied* in that passage.

See page 333 for the Answer Key and page 356 for the Explanatory Answers for this Mini-Test.

Questions 1–2 refer to the following advertisement.

ARABIC TO ZULU
225 languages

The Only
Full Service
International Book Supplier
in North America

Global Publishing Services
One World Trade Center
Suite 3007
Renaissance Plaza
Detroit, Michigan

Phone   Fax
313-555-9808   313-555-9800

1. What is being offered?

   (A) Translation services
   (B) Office supplies
   (C) Vacations to Africa
   (D) Books in many languages

2. What feature of the company is mentioned in this advertisement?

   (A) Its multilingual staff
   (B) Its complete service
   (C) Its fax number
   (D) Its prices

Questions 3–6 refer to the following purchase order.

PURCHASE ORDER
Ship Prepaid • Add all delivery charges on invoice

TECH 2000
44 Sankey Street
Warrington, Cheshire
WA 1 1SG ENGLAND

Tel: 0925 412 555
Fax: 0925 412 559

Vendor: Ship To: Marc Greenspan
Comtex   Purchasing Department
65-67 Lowgate Hull   Address above
HU 1 1HP
England
Tel: 482-593-678
Fax: 482-593-689

Reference: Purchase Order 03-687-47X   Invoice To: Marcia Goodall
Date: 12 June 20—   Accounting Department
                                                   Address above

Delivery Date: ASAP

Item	Model	Number	Quantity	Unit Cost	Total Cost
C180 Hard drive	M4569A		10	£675.00	£6750.00
C-52 Serial cable	C323		20	£ 12.50	£ 250.00
SE-Ethernet card	NET 0422		10	£ 50.00	£ 500.00

Sub-total	£7500.00
Shipping/Handling 10%	£ 750.00
TOTAL	£8250.00

Prepared by: ___Marc Greenspan_____
Date: _12 June 20—_____

CC: Accounting Department; Purchasing Department;
Receiving Department

---

3. Who will be billed for the purchase?

   (A) The Purchasing Department, TECH 2000
   (B) The Accounting Department, TECH 2000
   (C) The Purchasing Department, Comtex
   (D) The Shipping Department, Comtex

4. Who sells hard drives and serial cables?

   (A) Comtex
   (B) TECH 2000
   (C) Marc Greenspan
   (D) Marcia Goodall

5. If the Ethernet cards were NOT ordered, what would be the subtotal?

   (A) £7000
   (B) £7500
   (C) £7700
   (D) £8250

6. Which department does NOT get a copy of the purchase order?

   (A) Accounting
   (B) Purchasing
   (C) Receiving
   (D) Personnel

Questions 7–8 refer to the following report.

Midsize companies that want to increase their sales in international markets cannot rely on exporting their goods—not if they want to grow substantially. Customers want to be close to their suppliers. They want to provide input on design, engineering, and quality control. Also, local governments want jobs created for their citizens. This means that international companies will have to establish a manufacturing operation near their customers.

7. If international companies want to grow, they will need to

   (A) improve quality control.
   (B) export more goods.
   (C) build factories close to their customers.
   (D) design better products.

8. Who wants to provide input on design?

   (A) Design consultants
   (B) Customers
   (C) Suppliers
   (D) Engineers

Questions 9–10 refer to the following letter.

HAMBURG PAPER COMPANY
Postfach 806010
Rungerdamm 2
2050 Hamburg 80
Germany

March 10, 20—

Mr. Frank Knockaert
Crestco Inc.
26 Avenue Marnix
B-1000 Brussels
Belgium

Dear Mr. Knockaert:

In response to your letter of February 23, we apologize
for the error in your shipment. We are sending
immediately the additional 1000 cases of facsimile
paper, model P-345X, that were not included in the
shipment.

We value our relationship with your company, and we
regret the inconvenience the incomplete shipment may
have caused you. You can be assured that this will not
happen in the future.

Sincerely yours,

Gertrude Rombach

Gertrude Rombach
Manager, Order Department

9. What is the purpose of this letter?

(A) To complain
(B) To place an order
(C) To apologize
(D) To introduce services

10. The first shipment

(A) was not complete.
(B) arrived late.
(C) was damaged.
(D) was sent to the wrong address.

Questions 11–13 refer to the following fax.

International Cargo   **FAX TRANSMISSION**
Place de la Concorde
45040 Orleans Cedex 1
France
Tel: (33) – 387-87445
Fax: (33) – 387-87454

To: Markus Tarasov
             P.O. Box 10382 Manama, Bahrain
             Fax: 973 – 213324
             Tel: 973 – 213300

From: Marie Martin
             Sales Representative

Date: April 18, 20—

Pages: This

Ref: Your fax of April 18, 20—

Messages:

Your order was received this morning and is being
processed. You should expect delivery by the end of the
week or at the very latest on Monday. We will fax exact
time of arrival before Friday.

---

11. When was the order received?

    (A) The end of the week
    (B) Yesterday
    (C) Today
    (D) Friday

12. How will Ms. Martin communicate the
    delivery time?

    (A) By phone
    (B) By fax
    (C) By letter
    (D) By messenger

13. If the order does NOT arrive by Friday,
    when will it arrive?

    (A) At the end of the week
    (B) At the first of the month
    (C) On Monday
    (D) On the following Friday

Questions 14–17 refer to the following e-mail.

> From: Marcello Palombo [marcello_palom@allengineering.com]
>
> To: J. Wilson[jacob_wilson@allengineering.com]
>
> Sent: Tuesday, October 23, 20— 4:12 P.M.
>
> Subject: Elena Kuzikov, Ukrainian engineer
>
> Dr. Elena Kuzikov will be visiting our company on Tuesday, March 23rd. I would like you to prepare a program for her. She will arrive in the morning before noon. Please start with lunch in the cafeteria and then show her your department. Like you, she has done research on the effects of earthquakes on bridge construction.

14. What kind of engineer is the Ukrainian?

    (A) Electrical
    (B) Nuclear
    (C) Mechanical
    (D) Railroad

15. Who will be the visitor's guide?

    (A) J. Wilson
    (B) Elena Kuzikov
    (C) Marcello Palombo
    (D) No one

16. When will she arrive?

    (A) Before 12:00
    (B) At noon
    (C) After lunch
    (D) In the evening

17. What is her chief area of interest?

    (A) Designing bridges
    (B) Eating lunch
    (C) Touring the department
    (D) Visiting

Questions 18–20 refer to the following index.

Newspaper Index

Amex Stocks	B-11
Arts	C-1
Bond Data	B-16
Commodities	B-4
World Stock Index	B-15
Economy	A-5
Editorials	A-10
Film	C-3
Foreign Exchange	B-17
International News	A-1
Legal Issues	A-6
Technology	C-4
World Markets	B-1

18. What type of features would more likely be found in the B section?

    (A) Sports scores
    (B) Movie reviews
    (C) Market forecasts
    (D) Obituaries

19. The editor's opinions are found on

    (A) A-1.
    (B) B-4.
    (C) C-1.
    (D) A-10.

20. Movie reviews would be found on

    (A) B-11.
    (B) C-1.
    (C) C-3.
    (D) A-6.

Questions 21–23 refer to the following chart.

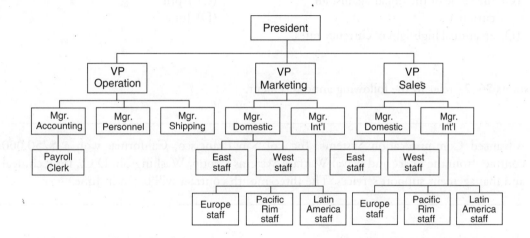

21. The payroll clerk reports directly to

    (A) the Manager of Personnel.
    (B) the Vice-President of Operations.
    (C) the Manager of Accounting.
    (D) the President.

22. Which divisions have similar staffing patterns?

    (A) Accounting and Personnel
    (B) Operations and Marketing
    (C) Marketing and Sales
    (D) Sales and Shipping

23. The Vice-President of Sales supervises

    (A) the International Manager for Sales.
    (B) the President.
    (C) the Personnel Manager.
    (D) the Accounting Manager.

Questions 24–25 refer to the following graph.

Currency: Dollar Against the Yen

24. This graph shows

 (A) a six-month comparison of dollar-yen conversion rates.
 (B) the price of Japanese commodities.
 (C) the value of the dollar against all currencies.
 (D) an annual highlight of currency rates.

25. In what month were there several fluctuations?

 (A) January
 (B) February
 (C) April
 (D) June

Questions 26–27 refer to the following announcement.

> Advanced Communication Systems, Inc., of San Francisco, California, won a $250,000 contract from the Space and Naval Warfare Systems Group, Washington, D.C., for technical and management support services. The three-month contract will begin in June.

26. Where is the contractor located?

 (A) Washington, D.C.
 (B) San Francisco, California
 (C) On the sea
 (D) In space

27. About when will the contract end?

 (A) January
 (B) June
 (C) September
 (D) December

Questions 28–29 refer to the following notice in a computer manual.

> International Communication reserves the right to make improvements in the hardware and software described in this manual at any time and without notice. The information in this manual may also be revised to reflect changes in the described product without obligation to notify any person of such changes.

28. This notice gives the company the right

    (A) to make changes without notice.
    (B) to request a refund.
    (C) to return software that doesn't work.
    (D) to start a new company.

29. Where would this notice most likely be found?

    (A) On an appliance warranty card
    (B) In a computer manual
    (C) On an airline ticket
    (D) In a stock offering prospectus

Questions 30–34 refer to the following newspaper article.

September 1, Zurich: RADD, A.G., the Swiss chemical company purchased the European polypropylene business of Royal Chemical Industries, P.L.C., of Britain. No price was disclosed, but RCI said the deal represented 1 to 2 percent of its net assets and would be paid in cash. Based on net assets, the price would be between $100 million and $160 million. The acquisition includes RCI production plants in England, Denmark, Norway, and Poland. The plants alone are valued at $60 million to $80 million. Polypropylene, a tough, flexible plastic, has uses that range from rope fibers to bottles.

30. RADD is probably located in

    (A) England.
    (B) Switzerland.
    (C) Denmark.
    (D) Poland.

31. According to the article, what is used to make rope fibers?

    (A) Hemp
    (B) Cotton
    (C) Steel
    (D) Polypropylene

32. How much will RADD pay for RCI?

    (A) $80 million
    (B) $100 million
    (C) Between $100 and $160 million
    (D) Between $60 and $80 million

33. Where is RCI's head office?

    (A) Norway
    (B) Denmark
    (C) Britain
    (D) Poland

34. What are the terms of the deal?

    (A) Payment in cash
    (B) Payment in stock
    (C) 2% of gross assets
    (D) 1% down payment

Questions 35–36 refer to the following magazine article.

> Hollywood is no longer just in California. Today the entertainment industry is finding new homes in Europe, Latin America, and Asia. The American media and communications industries are looking all over the globe for new opportunities. Although many companies are investing in the fast-growing European media industry, many industry executives believe the biggest long-term opportunity is in China and other countries in Southeast Asia. The potential market is huge—over 310 million people in the European community, but over 650 million in the Pacific Rim. ■

35. Which of the following is the main topic of the article?

(A) The media industry is expanding.
(B) China is a big market today.
(C) New homes are being built in Europe.
(D) There are many opportunities in Hollywood.

36. According to the article, what does "Hollywood" represent?

(A) All executives
(B) American enterprise
(C) The media industry
(D) Big markets

Questions 37–38 refer to the following schedule.

Meeting: Conference Room C

8:30	Coffee
9:00	Opening Remarks
9:15	Introductions
9:30	Presentations
	Accounting
	Personnel
	Marketing
10:30	**BREAK**
10:45	Presentations
	CEO
	Chairman of the Board
11:30	Questions and Answers
12:00	Adjourn

37. Why was this schedule prepared?

    (A) To make everyone pay attention
    (B) To limit the number of coffee breaks
    (C) To introduce the speakers
    (D) To establish an agenda for the meeting

38. What immediately follows the presentations by the senior officers?

    (A) A break
    (B) Introductions
    (C) A question-and-answer period
    (D) Lunch

Questions 39–40 refer to the following timeline.

	Jan	Feb	Mar	Apr	May	June	July	Aug	Sept
Review budget	▓								
Submit project proposal		▓							
Develop prototype			▓	▓					
Test prototype					▓	▓	▓		
Develop marketing plan						▓	▓	▓	
Start production								▓	
Ship to distributors									▓

39. This timeline shows

    (A) the number of man-hours involved in a project.
    (B) the stages in developing a product.
    (C) how long it takes to make money.
    (D) the changes in the seasons.

40. It can be inferred that

    (A) the cost will be too high.
    (B) the marketing plan will be more important than testing.
    (C) the project will be approved in February.
    (D) testing will slow down production.

Questions 41–45 refer to the following schedule and e-mail.

Sunday 11	Monday 12	Tuesday 13	Wednesday 14	Thursday 15	Friday 16	Saturday 17
	8:15 doctor a ppt.	9:30 planning meeting	9:00–11:00 dept. meeting	4:00 phone conference with Toronto office	8:30 train to Chicago	10:00 golf with Fred
	3:00 golf with Alicia		11:30 dentist appt.		12:30 lunch meeting with Chicago staff	

To: Joe Rosen
From: Alicia Lima
Date: March 8
Subject: Golf

Hi Joe,

I'm sorry I can't make our golf date next week. It turns out I have a department meeting that starts an hour before our game is scheduled, and I'm sure it won't end before 5:00. Could we play the following day, same time, same place? Let me know, and I'll call the club to reserve the starting time.

I also wanted to let you know that Mr. Santos from our San Francisco office will be in town starting next Tuesday. I know you were eager to meet with him. Are you free Wednesday morning? If not, Thursday or Friday morning will do. I know you plan to leave for Chicago sometime Friday, but I hope you can find some time to meet with Mr. Santos before then.

Are you planning to meet Fred for golf in Chicago? If you see him, tell him I haven't forgotten that he owes me a game!

See you next week,
Alicia

41. When is Joe's dentist appointment?

    (A) Monday
    (B) Tuesday
    (C) Wednesday
    (D) Thursday

42. What will Joe do on Thursday afternoon?

    (A) Go to Toronto
    (B) Talk on the telephone
    (C) Have a lunch meeting
    (D) Go to the doctor

43. What time does Alicia's department meeting begin?

    (A) 9:00
    (B) 2:00
    (C) 3:00
    (D) 5:00

44. What day does Alicia want to play golf with Joe?

    (A) Sunday
    (B) Monday
    (C) Tuesday
    (D) Saturday

45. What will Joe probably do Thursday morning?

    (A) Meet with Mr. Santos
    (B) Nothing
    (C) Leave for Chicago
    (D) Play golf with Fred

Questions 46–50 refer to the following notice and memo.

Notice to tenants of South Ridge Office Complex   August 25, 20—

Reconstruction of the parking garage will begin at the end of next month and is scheduled to last three months. During this time there will be no parking for anyone in the building garage. The city has temporarily designated the parking spaces on the streets surrounding our building as all-day parking spaces for our use. A special pass is required to use these spaces. Since the number of parking spaces is limited, we will distribute four passes to each office in this building. Building tenants are asked to encourage their employees to use public transportation until the garage reconstruction is completed. There are also two public parking garages within five blocks of here where parking spaces can be rented on a daily, weekly, or monthly basis. Thank you for your cooperation.

South Ridge Office Complex Building Management Team

Memo
Parrot Communications, Inc.

To: All Office Personnel
From: Dena Degenaro
           Office Manager
Date: August 28, 20—
Re: Parking

I am sure you have all seen the recent notice about the parking garage reconstruction by now. Since we have five times as many employees as allotted parking passes, we will reserve the parking passes for clients and ask our employees to make alternative plans. For your convenience, we have obtained subway passes that are valid for the entire amount of time that the garage reconstruction will last. They are available at a 25% discount to all Parrot Communications employees. Please see me before the end of this week if you are interested in getting one. Thank you.

46. When will the parking garage reconstruction begin?

    (A) This week
    (B) Next month
    (C) In three months
    (D) In August

47. How many employees work for Parrot Communications, Inc.?

    (A) Four
    (B) Five
    (C) Twenty
    (D) Twenty-five

48. Who can park next to the building during the garage reconstruction?

    (A) Parrot Communications clients
    (B) Parrot Communications employees
    (C) All South Ridge tenants
    (D) Dena Degenaro

49. Who should Parrot Communications employees contact to get a subway pass?

    (A) The city manager
    (B) Their office manager
    (C) The building manager
    (D) The subway station manager

50. How long are the subway passes valid?

    (A) One week
    (B) Three weeks
    (C) One month
    (D) Three months

Answer Key for Reading—Targets 1–41

Explanatory Answers are on page 334.

ANALYZING VOCABULARY

Target	Part 5	Part 6
Target 1 Prefixes	(A)	1. (D) 2. (B) 3. (B)
Target 2 Suffixes	(B)	1. (B) 2. (B) 3. (B)

Target	Part 5	Part 6
Target 3 Word Families	(B)	1. (C) 2. (A) 3. (C)
Target 4 Similar Words	(D)	1. (C) 2. (B) 3. (A)

Targets 1–4 Review
Prefixes, Suffixes, Word Families, and Similar Words

Part 5	Part 6
1. (B) and (F)	1. (C)
2. (C) and (G)	2. (B)
3. (B) and (F)	3. (A)
4. (A) and (E)	
5. (C) and (H)	
6. (A)	
7. (B)	
8. (A)	
9. (C)	
10. (D)	

ANALYZING GRAMMAR

Target	Part 5	Part 6
Target 5 Non-count Nouns and Plural Verbs	(C)	1. (C) 2. (D) 3. (C)
Target 6 Differences in Meaning Between Count and Non-count Nouns	(A)	1. (B) 2. (A) 3. (A)

Targets 5–6 Review
Count and Non-count Nouns

Part 5	Part 6
1. (B)	1. (B)
2. (A)	2. (B)
3. (A)	3. (A)
4. (B)	
5. (B)	

Target	Part 5	Part 6
Target 7 Specific Noun with Incorrect Article	**(D)**	1. **(C)** 2. **(D)** 3. **(C)**
Target 8 Unspecified Count Noun Without *the*	**(C)**	1. **(B)** 2. **(C)** 3. **(B)**
Target 9 Wrong Article with General Count Noun	**(C)**	1. **(B)** 2. **(B)** 3. **(A)**
Target 10 Article with Generic Non-count Noun	**(A)**	1. **(A)** 2. **(C)** 3. **(A)**
Target 11 Wrong Form of *a* or *an*	**(A)**	1. **(B)** 2. **(B)** 3. **(D)**

Targets 7–11 Review
Articles

Part 5	Part 6
1. **(C)**	1. **(C)**
2. **(A)**	2. **(C)**
3. **(C)**	3. **(A)**
4. **(A)**	
5. **(D)**	

Target	Part 5	Part 6
Target 12 Subject and Verb May Not Agree	**(D)**	1. **(D)** 2. **(A)** 3. **(A)**
Target 13 *You* as Subject	**(B)**	1. **(C)** 2. **(A)** 3. **(B)**
Target 14 Nouns and Pronouns: Singular or Plural	**(B)**	1. **(A)** 2. **(B)** 3. **(C)**

Targets 12–14 Review
Subject-Verb Agreement

Part 5	Part 6
1. **(B)**	1. **(C)**
2. **(C)**	2. **(A)**
3. **(A)**	3. **(B)**
4. **(A)**	
5. **(D)**	

Target	Part 5	Part 6
Target 15 Incorrect Preposition	**(B)**	1. **(B)** 2. **(C)** 3. **(B)**
Target 16 Prepositional Phrase and Verb Agreement	**(C)**	1. **(B)** 2. **(C)** 3. **(C)**

Targets 15–16 Review
Prepositions

Part 5	Part 6
1. **(A)**	1. **(D)**
2. **(D)**	2. **(C)**
3. **(B)**	3. **(B)**
4. **(B)**	
5. **(C)**	

Target	Part 5	Part 6
Target 17 Wrong Coordinating Conjunctions	(C)	1. (B) 2. (B) 3. (A)
Target 18 Joined Forms Not Parallel	(C)	1. (D) 2. (A) 3. (D)

Targets 17–18 Review
Coordinating Conjunctions

	Part 5	Part 6
	1. (C) 2. (B) 3. (A) 4. (D) 5. (A)	1. (B) 2. (C) 3. (A)

Target	Part 5	Part 6
Target 19 Misplaced Subordinating Conjunctions	(D)	1. (B) 2. (C) 3. (B)
Target 20 Incorrect Subordinating Conjunctions	(C)	1. (A) 2. (D) 3. (B)

Targets 19–20 Review
Subordinating Conjunctions

	Part 5	Part 6
	1. (B) 2. (C) 3. (C) 4. (D) 5. (B)	1. (B) 2. (B) 3. (D)

Target	Part 5	Part 6
Target 21 Use of *as—as*	(B)	1. (C) 2. (D) 3. (A)
Target 22 *More/-er* or *Than* Omitted	(A)	1. (D) 2. (D) 3. (B)
Target 23 *The* or *Most/-est* Omitted	(D)	1. (D) 2. (C) 3. (B)

Targets 21–23 Review
Comparisons with Adjectives and Adverbs

	Part 5	Part 6
	1. (A) 2. (C) 3. (D) 4. (B) 5. (C)	1. (A) 2. (A) 3. (B)

Target	Part 5	Part 6
Target 24 Misplaced Adverbial Time Words and Phrases	(C)	1. (C) 2. (C) 3. (B)
Target 25 Misplaced Adverbs of Frequency	(A)	1. (C) 2. (A) 3. (C)
Target 26 Adverbs of Frequency with *Be*	(C)	1. (D) 2. (B) 3. (B)
Target 27 Adverbs of Frequency with Auxiliaries	(B)	1. (D) 2. (B) 3. (D)
Target 28 Meanings of Adverbs of Frequency	(C)	1. (A) 2. (C) 3. (B)

Targets 24–28 Review
Adverbs of Frequency

	Part 5	Part 6
	1. (B)	1. (B)
	2. (B)	2. (B)
	3. (A)	3. (C)
	4. (D)	
	5. (D)	

Target	Part 5	Part 6
Target 29 Causative Verb + Simple Form	(A)	1. (C)
		2. (A)
		3. (C)
Target 30 Causative Verb + Infinitive	(B)	1. (C)
		2. (B)
		3. (C)
Target 31 Causative Verb + Past Participle	(A)	1. (C)
		2. (D)
		3. (B)

Targets 29–31 Review
Causative Verbs

	Part 5	Part 6
	1. (A)	1. (A)
	2. (D)	2. (B)
	3. (C)	3. (A)
	4. (D)	
	5. (C)	

Target	Part 5	Part 6
Target 32 Real Condition *if* Clause Not in Present Tense	(A)	1. (A)
		2. (B)
		3. (A)
Target 33 Unreal Condition *if* Clause Not in Appropriate Tense	(B)	1. (B)
		2. (B)
		3. (C)
Target 34 Unreal Condition *if* Clause + *Were*	(A)	1. (C)
		2. (D)
		3. (C)

Targets 32–34 Review
Conditional Sentences

	Part 5	Part 6
	1. (B)	1. (D)
	2. (B)	2. (B)
	3. (A)	3. (B)
	4. (B)	
	5. (A)	

Target	Part 5	Part 6
Target 35 Verb Tenses	(D)	1. (B)
		2. (C)
		3. (C)
Target 36 Stative Verbs in the Progressive Form	(B)	1. (A)
		2. (D)
		3. (A)

Targets 35–36 Review
Verb Tenses and Stative Verbs

	Part 5	Part 6
	1. (B)	1. (D)
	2. (A)	2. (C)
	3. (D)	3. (C)
	4. (B)	
	5. (C)	

Target	Part 5	Part 6		Target	Part 5	Part 6
Target 37	(C)	1. (A)		Target 41	(B)	1. (C)
Relative Clause:		2. (B)		Incorrect		2. (B)
Repeated Subject		3. (B)		Participles		3. (A)
Target 38	(A)	1. (C)				
Relative Clause:		2. (C)				
No Relative		3. (D)				
Pronoun						
Target 39	(D)	1. (D)				
Relative Clause:		2. (D)				
That ≠ *Who*		3. (B)				

Targets 37–39 Review
Relative Clauses

Target 41 Review
Incorrect Participles

Part 5	Part 6		Part 5	Part 6
1. (D)	1. (A)		1. (B)	1. (A)
2. (D)	2. (C)		2. (A)	2. (C)
3. (A)	3. (B)		3. (C)	3. (B)
4. (D)			4. (B)	
5. (B)			5. (D)	

Target	Part 5	Part 6
Target 40	(B)	1. (C)
Verb + Gerund		2. (B)
or Infinitive		3. (B)

Target 40 Review
Gerunds and Infinitives

Part 5	Part 6
1. (D)	1. (B)
2. (A)	2. (C)
3. (D)	3. (B)
4. (A)	
5. (D)	

Answer Key for Mini-Test for Reading Parts 5 and 6

Explanatory Answers are on page 351.

PART 5: INCOMPLETE SENTENCES

1. **(C)**	5. **(B)**	9. **(A)**	13. **(C)**	17. **(B)**
2. **(D)**	6. **(A)**	10. **(C)**	14. **(B)**	18. **(B)**
3. **(A)**	7. **(D)**	11. **(A)**	15. **(D)**	19. **(C)**
4. **(D)**	8. **(C)**	12. **(C)**	16. **(C)**	20. **(D)**

PART 6: TEXT COMPLETION

21. **(A)**	23. **(C)**	25. **(C)**
22. **(D)**	24. **(A)**	26. **(D)**

Answer Key for Reading Comprehension— Targets 42–60

Target	Part 7				Target 52	1. **(A)**	2. **(A)**	3. **(C)**	4. **(A)**
Target 42	1. **(C)**	2. **(B)**			Announcements				
Advertisements					Target 53 Notices	1. **(D)**	2. **(B)**		
Target 43 Forms	1. **(D)**	2. **(B)**	3. **(B)**	4. **(C)**	Target 54 Newspaper	1. **(D)**	2. **(D)**	3. **(B)**	
Target 44 Reports	1. **(C)**	2. **(D)**	3. **(A)**		Articles				
Target 45 Letters	1. **(C)**	2. **(B)**	3. **(A)**		Target 55 Magazine	1. **(A)**	2. **(C)**	3. **(C)**	
Target 46 Faxes	1. **(B)**	2. **(B)**	3. **(A)**	4. **(D)**	Articles				
Target 47 Memos	1. **(C)**	2. **(A)**	3. **(B)**	4. **(D)**	Target 56 Schedules	1. **(C)**	2. **(C)**	3. **(C)**	4. **(C)**
Target 48 Tables	1. **(A)**	2. **(D)**	3. **(B)**	4. **(B)**	Target 57 Calendars	1. **(A)**	2. **(B)**	3. **(C)**	4. **(A)**
Target 49 Indexes	1. **(A)**	2. **(B)**			Target 58 E-mail	1. **(A)**	2. **(C)**		
Target 50 Charts	1. **(C)**	2. **(B)**			Target 59 Web Pages	1. **(D)**	2. **(A)**		
Target 51 Graphs	1. **(B)**	2. **(D)**			Target 60 Computer	1. **(D)**	2. **(B)**		
					Language				

Answer Key for Mini-Test for Reading Part 7

Explanatory Answers are on page 356.

PART 7: READING

1. **(D)**	11. **(C)**	21. **(C)**	31. **(D)**	41. **(C)**
2. **(B)**	12. **(B)**	22. **(C)**	32. **(C)**	42. **(B)**
3. **(B)**	13. **(C)**	23. **(A)**	33. **(C)**	43. **(B)**
4. **(A)**	14. **(C)**	24. **(A)**	34. **(A)**	44. **(C)**
5. **(A)**	15. **(A)**	25. **(C)**	35. **(A)**	45. **(A)**
6. **(D)**	16. **(A)**	26. **(B)**	36. **(C)**	46. **(B)**
7. **(C)**	17. **(A)**	27. **(C)**	37. **(D)**	47. **(C)**
8. **(B)**	18. **(C)**	28. **(A)**	38. **(C)**	48. **(A)**
9. **(C)**	19. **(D)**	29. **(B)**	39. **(B)**	49. **(B)**
10. **(A)**	20. **(C)**	30. **(B)**	40. **(C)**	50. **(D)**

Explanatory Answers for Reading—Targets 1–41

ANALYZING VOCABULARY

Target 1 Prefixes

PART 5: INCOMPLETE SENTENCES

(A) *Unbelievable* means not believable. (B) *Unavailable* means not available. (C) *Uncomfortable* means not comfortable. (D) *Unsuccessful* means not successful.

PART 6: TEXT COMPLETION

1. **(D)** *Transferring* means *moving from one to another.* Choice (A) means *holding the power.* Choice (B) means *cutting* or *lessening.* Choice (C) means *taking care of.*
2. **(B)** *Replace* means *change one thing for another.* Choice (A) means *play again.* Choice (C) means *show.* Choice (D) means *cause something to move to another place.*
3. **(B)** Introductory means *first* or *initial.* Choice (A) means *unusual* or *amazing.* Choice (C) means *opposite.* Choice (D) means *preventative.*

Target 2 Suffixes

PART 5: INCOMPLETE SENTENCES

(B) *Applicant* means person applying for a job. Choice (A) is someone who defends him/herself. Choice (C) is someone who occupies a position. Choice (D) is someone who assists someone else.

PART 6: TEXT COMPLETION

1. **(B)** *Countless* is an adjective that means *more than can be counted,* that is, *many.* Choice (A) is a verb. Choice (C) means *can be counted.* Choice (D) means *counted incorrectly.*
2. **(B)** The text states that green, red, and yellow fruits and vegetables are more important than a balanced meal. Choice (A) is not mentioned. Choice (C) means *only people who don't eat meat,* which is incorrect because the text states some protein is necessary. Choice (D) is incorrect because this is the old way of thinking.
3. **(B)** *Nourishment* is a noun that means *food needed for survival.* Choice (A) is an adjective that means *well fed.* Choice (C) is an adjective that means *healthy.* Choice (D) is an adjective related to the health value of a type of food.

Target 3 Word Families

PART 5: INCOMPLETE SENTENCES

(B) *negotiate.* (B) *Negotiate* is a verb; (A) is an adjective; (C) is a noun; (D) is also a noun.

PART 6: TEXT COMPLETION

1. **(C)** *Production* is a noun that refers to the work of a factory. Choice (A) is a verb that means *make.* Choice (B) is a noun that refers to a person who creates something. Choice (D) is an adjective meaning *useful.*
2. **(A)** Choice (A) is a verb meaning *bargain.* Choice (B) is a noun that refers to a person who tries to get a good deal through dialogue. Choice (C) is an adjective meaning *open to discussion.* Choice (D) is a noun that refers to mutual give and take.
3. **(C)** *Availability* is a noun that refers to how easy something is to get. Choice (A) is a noun that means *use.* Choice (B) is an adjective meaning *obtainable.* Choice (D) is an adjective that means *being of use.*

Target 4 Similar Words

PART 5: INCOMPLETE SENTENCES

(D) *earn,* is often used with money terms (e.g., *earning a living*). (A) *win* means to be first in a competition. (B) *achieve* means to accomplish something. (C) *obtain* means to acquire something.

PART 6: TEXT COMPLETION

1. **(C)** *Earned* refers to getting money in exchange for work. Choices (A), (B), and (D) all refer to getting more of something but are not used in the context of getting money for work.
2. **(B)** Sarah is going shopping to buy clothes. Choices (A), (C), and (D) are not the plans Sarah is referring to in her letter.
3. **(A)** *Lend* means *to supply someone with money provided the amount provided is returned.* Choice (B) means *to be supplied with money provided the amount is returned.* Choices (C) and (D) refer to the payment of money for the right to use something (such as property) that belongs to someone else.

Targets 1–4 Review
Prefixes, Suffixes, Word Families, and Similar Words

PART 5: INCOMPLETE SENTENCES

1. **(B)** Verb
   (F) is a verb. (E) is an adjective. (G) and (H) are nouns.
2. **(C)** Adjective
   (G) is an adjective. (E) is a noun (person) or a verb. (F) is a verb. (H) is an adverb.
3. **(B)** Verb
   (F) is a verb. (E) is a noun. (G) can be either an adjective or a noun. (H) is a noun (thing).
4. **(A)** Noun
   (E) is a noun. (F) is a verb. (G) is an adjective. (H) is an adverb.
5. **(C)** Adjective
   (H) is an adjective. (E) is a verb. (F) is a noun (thing). (G) is a noun (thing).
6. **(A)** *Equal* means the same quality or quantity. (B) means *identical.* (C) means *go together.* (D) means other people will like it.
7. **(B)** *Especially* means *very.* (A) is the adverb form of special. (C) means *special thing.* (D) describes something.
8. **(A)** *Except* means *with the exception of.* (B) means *too much.* (C) means *availability.* (D) means to *agree to.*

9. **(C)** *Rise* means to *go up.* (A) is not used with prices or money. (B) means to *mature.* (D) is not used with money.
10. **(D)** *Borrow from* means to *use temporarily.* (A) means to *give to someone temporarily.* (B) means *allow to have.* (C) means to *suggest.*

PART 6: TEXT COMPLETION

1. **(C)** *Interview* is a noun meaning *a meeting with a job applicant.* Choice (A) can be either a noun or a verb; it refers to looking at something again. Choice (B) can be either a noun or a verb; it refers to looking at something beforehand. Choice (D) is a noun that means *summary.*
2. **(B)** *Applicants* is a noun that refers to people who apply for a job. Choice (A) is a noun that refers to a document or process. Choice (C) is an adjective meaning *appropriate.* Choice (D) is a noun that means *small household machine.*
3. **(A)** Gloria overheard Hank talking about his afternoon meetings. Choice (B) is incorrect; because the offices are being painted there is no art class. Choice (C) is incorrect because Hank is going for lunch, not to a luncheon. Choice (D) is incorrect because it is Gloria who has the meetings.

ANALYZING GRAMMAR
Target 5 Non-count Nouns and Plural Verbs

PART 5: INCOMPLETE SENTENCES

(C) *Bags of clothes* is a plural, count noun; the modifier *several* is plural and is used with count nouns. (A) *clothes* is a non-count noun and could be used with the modifier *some*: *some clothes*; (B) is incorrect because you can't have both *several* and *some* together; (D) is incorrect because you need a plural noun with *several,* not a singular noun like *bag.*

PART 6: TEXT COMPLETION

1. **(C)** *Furniture* is a non-count noun and agrees with the singular verb *is.* Choices (A), (B), and (D) are all non-count nouns but do not make sense in context.

2. **(D)** *were* is a plural verb that agrees with the count noun subject *boxes* and the past tense marker *Last month*. Choice (A) does not agree with the subject number or time. Choice (B) does not agree with the subject in time. Choice (C) does not agree with the subject in number.

3. **(C)** *Piece of* makes the non-count noun *furniture* countable. (A) Plural nouns such as *pieces* do not follow the singular indefinite article *a*. Choice (B) needs to be followed by the preposition *of* for it to be linked with the noun *furniture*. (D) The singular indefinite article *a* is never preceded by the adjective *new*.

Target 6 Differences in Meaning Between Count and Non-count Nouns

PART 5: INCOMPLETE SENTENCES

(A) *Room* here means space; it is an abstract non-count noun. (B) is a combination count noun. (C) and (D) are inappropriate word combinations.

PART 6: TEXT COMPLETION

1. **(B)** The lighting and music together can be referred to as *atmosphere*. Choice (A) is incorrect because it doesn't mention the lighting. Choices (C) and (D) are incorrect because both of these received positive comments.

2. **(A)** The non-count noun *light* refers to the brightness in a room. Choice (B) the non-count noun *lighting* refers to the quality of light (atmosphere or ambiance). Choice (C) *lights* is a plural count noun. Choice (D) *lighten* is a verb.

3. **(A)** This non-count noun agrees with the singular verb that follows. Choices (B) and (C) are plural nouns; they do not agree with the singular verb that follows. Choice (D) does not make sense because more than one *musician* was present.

Targets 5–6 Review Count and Non-count Nouns

PART 5: INCOMPLETE SENTENCES

1. **(B)** *Persons* refers to more than one person. *Peoples* refers to different kinds of people.

2. **(A)** *Foods* is a plural count noun used to refer to different kinds of food.

3. **(A)** *Chicken* refers to a type of meat. *Chickens* refers to individual animals.

4. **(B)** *Snow* is a non-count noun so it does not have a plural form.

5. **(B)** *Information* is a non-count noun so it does not have a plural form.

PART 6: TEXT COMPLETION

1. **(B)** *Fruit* is a non-count noun. Choices (A), (C), and (D) are count nouns and would have to be plural in order to make sense in this sentence.

2. **(B)** *Desserts* is the correct choice in context. Choice (A) is incorrect because it is a non-count noun. Choices (C) and (D) are illogical because *strawberry pie* is not a type of them.

3. **(A)** Room is used as a non-count noun here, meaning *space*. Choice (B) is a plural count noun meaning *parts of a house*. Choices (C) and (D) are singular nouns, which can't follow the word *enough*.

Target 7 Specified Noun with Incorrect Article

PART 5: INCOMPLETE SENTENCES

(D) *The* is used because it is a specified *effort* that actually happened. (A) and (C) cannot be used with a specified noun. (B) *a* is not used with the initial vowel sound of *effort*.

PART 6: TEXT COMPLETION

1. **(C)** *The meeting*, a specified noun, is correct because the meeting was previously referred to in the text. Choices (A), (B), and (D) are not specified nouns.

2. **(D)** *The topic*, a specified noun, is correct because we know which topic is referred to. Choices (A), (B), and (C) are not specified nouns.

3. **(C)** *The speaker*, a specified noun, is correct because the speaker was previously referred to in the text. Choices (A), (B), and (D) are not specified nouns.

Target 8 Unspecified Count Noun with *the*

PART 5: INCOMPLETE SENTENCES

(C) An unspecified meeting requires an unspecified article; (A) requires an article; (B) is a specific meeting, which is not the sense of the sentence; (D) also specifies a particular meeting.

PART 6: TEXT COMPLETION

1. **(B)** *A book*, an unspecified noun, is correct because no specific book is referred to. Choice (A) is illogical because you wouldn't buy a ticket in a bookstore. Choice (C) is incorrect because a singular count noun must be preceded by a determiner. Choice (D) is incorrect because Janice and Fred suggest not buying food there.

2. **(C)** *A long trip*, an unspecified noun, is correct because no specific trip is referred to. Choices (A) and (B) are incorrect because a singular count noun must be preceded by a determiner. Choice (D) is a specified noun.

3. **(B)** *A call* is correct; the phrase is very common English. Choice (A) is incorrect because the phrase is nonstandard. Choice (C) is incorrect because a *call* was not previously mentioned. Choice (D) is not something that is given after a flight.

Target 9 Wrong Article with General Count Noun

PART 5: INCOMPLETE SENTENCES

(C) Use *a schedule* with *an office* (any schedule for any office); if the sentence had *the office* you would have chosen (A) *the schedule* (the particular schedule for the particular office). (B) requires an article; (D) doesn't agree with the verb.

PART 6: TEXT COMPLETION

1. **(B)** *Answers* is a plural noun used here in the general sense. Choice (A) is incorrect because a singular count noun must be preceded by a determiner. Choice (C) is incorrect because it does not agree with the verb *are*. Choice (D) is incorrect because specified nouns cannot be used in the general sense.

2. **(B)** *Computers* is correct because it agrees with the verb *are*. Choice (A) is incorrect because it does not agree with the verb *are*. Choice (C) is incorrect because *computers* were not referred to previously in the text. Choice (D) is incorrect because it does not agree with the verb *are*.

3. **(A)** *The manual* is correct because a specific one is referred to. Choices (B) and (C) are incorrect because they are not preceded by the definite article *the*. Choice (D) is incorrect because it is an adverb.

Target 10 Article with Generic Non-count Noun

PART 5: INCOMPLETE SENTENCES

(A) *Recognition* is a non-count generic noun. No article is necessary. (B), (C), and (D) all have articles or other modifiers.

PART 6: TEXT COMPLETION

1. **(A)** *Efficiency* is a non-count noun used here in the generic sense. Choices (B), (C), and (D) are incorrect because a non-count noun cannot be preceded by the articles *a* and *an*.

2. **(C)** *Permission* is a non-count noun used here in the generic sense. Choices (A) and (D) are incorrect because previously unmentioned non-count nouns used in the generic sense cannot be preceded by *a* or *the*. Choice (B) is incorrect because *permits* (official documents authorizing one to do something) are not needed for turning on the office stereo.

3. **(A)** *Peace* is a non-count noun used here in the generic sense. Choices (B) and (C) are incorrect because previously unmentioned non-count nouns used in the generic sense cannot be preceded by *a* or *the*. Choice (D) is incorrect because the preposition *to* needs to be between *prefer* and a base form verb.

Target 11 Wrong Form of *a* or *an*

PART 5: INCOMPLETE SENTENCES

(A) *Announcement* has an initial vowel sound. (B) cannot be used; (C) and (D) could be used in another context.

PART 6: TEXT COMPLETION

1. **(B)** *A uniform* is the correct form for this singular count noun. Choice (A) is incorrect because a singular count noun must be preceded by a determiner. Choice (C) is incorrect because the word *uniform* does not begin with a vowel sound. Choice (D) is incorrect because a singular noun cannot be preceded by the word *those*.

2. **(B)** *An* correctly precedes a word beginning with a vowel sound. Choice (A) is incorrect because a word beginning with a vowel sound cannot be preceded by the word *a*. Choice (C) is incorrect because this is an unspecified noun. Choice (D) is incorrect because the word *some* cannot precede a singular count noun.

3. **(D)** *Orange* is correct because it is a color adjective that begins with a vowel sound preceded by *an*. Choices (A), (B), and (C) are incorrect in context because the tops must be a bright color.

Targets 7–11 Review Articles

PART 5: INCOMPLETE SENTENCES

1. **(C)** Plural count nouns do not need articles. (A) must use *a*. Choices (B) and (D) cannot use a plural verbs.

2. **(A)** Singular count nouns require an article. (B) The plural subject does not agree with the singular verb. (C) Singular count nouns require an article. (D) If you know that one particular shipper sent three packages, you need to use the definite article.

3. **(C)** Human resources has one definite director. (A) Singular count nouns require an article. (B) The plural subject does not agree with the singular verb. (D) A plural noun cannot be used with a singular verb.

4. **(A)** Non-count nouns do not require an article. (B) Non-count nouns can be used without an article. (C) *An* cannot be used with a non-count noun. (D) Non-count nouns do not have plural forms.

5. **(D)** Non-count nouns may use *some*. (A) Non-count nouns cannot be counted. (B) and (C) Non-count nouns can be used without an article.

PART 6: TEXT COMPLETION

1. **(C)** *An award* is an unspecified noun. Choice (A) is incorrect because a singular count noun must be preceded by a determiner. Choice (B) is incorrect because the word *a* cannot precede a word beginning with a vowel sound. Choice (D) is incorrect because a singular noun cannot be preceded by the word *these*.

2. **(C)** The *effort* is a specified noun modified by the adjective clause *she has put forth*. Choice (A) is a non-count noun used in a generic sense. Choices (B) and (D) are incorrect because non-count nouns don't have a plural form.

3. **(A)** *Work* is a generic noun. All work brings results. Choices (B), (C), and (D) are all specified nouns and do not fit the universal sense of the sentence.

Target 12 Subject and Verb May Not Agree

PART 5: INCOMPLETE SENTENCES

(D) The subject of the sentence, the noun *officers*, is plural. (A), (B), and (C) are used with singular subjects.

PART 6: TEXT COMPLETION

1. **(D)** *Do not choose* agrees with the plural subject *students.* Choices (A), (B), and (C) do not agree with the subject.
2. **(A)** *Decide* is a plural verb, so it agrees with the plural subject *students.* Choices (B), (C), and (D) are not plural verbs.
3. **(A)** *Help* is correct because it is a base form verb; only a base form can follow a modal verb such as *can.* Choices (B), (C), and (D) are not base form verbs.

Target 13 *You* as Subject

PART 5: INCOMPLETE SENTENCES

(B) *You* always takes a plural verb. The other choices are all singular.

PART 6: TEXT COMPLETION

1. **(C)** *Are* agrees with the subject *you.* Choices (A), (B), and (D) do not agree with the subject.
2. **(A)** *Haven't turned in* agrees with the subject *you.* Choices (B), (C), and (D) don't agree with the subject.
3. **(B)** *Are supposed* agrees with the subject *you.* Choices (A), (C), and (D) do not agree with the subject.

Target 14 Nouns and Pronouns: Singular or Plural

PART 5: INCOMPLETE SENTENCES

(B) *Police* is a plural noun (a group of police officers); it takes a plural verb. The other choices are all singular.

PART 6: TEXT COMPLETION

1. **(A)** *Bring* agrees with the subject *mice,* which is the plural form of *mouse.* Choices (B), (C), and (D) don't agree with the subject.
2. **(B)** *Is* agrees with the subject; *Axel Exterminators* is the name of a company, so it takes a singular verb. Choice (A) is a base form verb. Choices (C) and (D) don't agree with the subject.

3. **(C)** *Try* is a plural verb, which agrees with the plural subject *people.* Also, it is in the present tense, which is consistent with the rest of the paper. Choices (A) and (D) are not plural verbs. Choice (B) is in the past tense while the rest of the paper is in the present tense.

Targets 12–14 Review Subject-Verb Agreement

PART 5: INCOMPLETE SENTENCES

1. **(B)** Singular *manager* requires singular *is visiting.* (A) is a plural verb. (C) is the infinitive. (D) is the gerund.
2. **(C)** *Everyone* requires singular *is.* (A) is the simple form. (B) is plural. (D) is future tense.
3. **(A)** *Police* requires a plural; use *arrive.* Choices (B) and (C) are singular; Choice (D) is the wrong tense and the wrong number.
4. **(A)** Names of businesses are singular; use *is.* (B) is plural. (C) is the wrong tense: present continuous. (D) is plural and the wrong tense: present perfect.
5. **(D)** Singular *employee* uses singular *gets.* (A) is the simple form. (B) is the past participle. (C) is the gerund.

PART 6: TEXT COMPLETION

1. **(C)** *Are* agrees with the plural subject *employees.* Choices (A) and (D) don't agree with the subject. Choice (B) is a base form verb.
2. **(A)** *Don't submit* agrees with the subject *you.* Choices (B), (C), and (D) don't agree with the subject.
3. **(B)** *Promise* agrees with the plural subject *people.* Choice (A) can't be in the progressive. Choices (C) and (D) don't agree with the subject.

Target 15 Incorrect Preposition

PART 5: INCOMPLETE SENTENCES

(B) *On* is the preposition used with this common expression: *on my desk.* Choices (A), (C), and (D) do not make sense.

PART 6: TEXT COMPLETION

1. **(B)** *To* is the correct preposition to indicate that the flight is *going in the direction of* New York. Choices (A), (C), and (D) are incorrect in this context.
2. **(C)** *In* is the correct preposition to indicate that the list is *inside* the drawer. Choices (A), (B), and (D) are incorrect in this context.
3. **(B)** *On* is the correct preposition to use with a phone. Choice (A), (C), and (D) are incorrect prepositions to use with *cell phone*.

Target 16 Prepositional Phrase and Verb Agreement

PART 5: INCOMPLETE SENTENCES

(C) The subject of the sentence is *award.* Choice (A) could not be used in this sentence and (B) and (D) are both plural.

PART 6: TEXT COMPLETION

1. **(B)** *Are not printed* agrees with the subject *rules.* Choices (A) and (D) do not include the necessary "be" verb. Choice (C) does not agree with *rules.*
2. **(C)** *Are required* agrees with the subject *updates.* Choices (A) and (D) do not include the necessary "be" verb. Choice (B) does not agree with *updates.*
3. **(C)** *Are* agrees with the subject *forms.* Choices (A) and (D) agree with *vacation leave,* but that is not the subject of the sentence. Choice (B) is a base form verb.

Targets 15–16 Review Prepositions

PART 5: INCOMPLETE SENTENCES

1. **(A)** *At* refers to locations. (B) refers to direction toward. (C) refers to time. (D) expresses direction.
2. **(D)** *In* refers to city locations. (A) *At* refers to locations. (B) refers to direction away. (C) refers to purpose.

3. **(B)** *On* refers to days of the week. (A) refers to deadlines. (C) refers to location inside. (D) refers to location.
4. **(B)** *At* refers to definite time. (A) refers to days of the week. (C) refers to location inside. (D) refers to purpose.
5. **(C)** *Until* means up to a point in time. (A) refers to days of the week. (B) refers to direction away. (D) refers to locations.

PART 6: TEXT COMPLETION

1. **(D)** *At* is the correct preposition to use with an exact address. Choices (A), (B), and (C) are not correct in this context.
2. **(C)** *From,* used with *to,* indicates when an activity begins. Choices (A), (B), and (D) are not correct in this context.
3. **(B)** *Are* agrees with the plural subject *applications.* Choice (A) is a gerund. Choice (C) agrees with *membership,* but that is not the subject of the sentence. Choice (D) is a base form verb.

Target 17 Wrong Coordinating Conjunctions

PART 5: INCOMPLETE SENTENCES

(C) The conjunction *both* needs *and.* The other choices do not work with *both.*

PART 6: TEXT COMPLETION

1. **(B)** *Or* is correctly paired with *either* to indicate a choice. Choice (A) must be paired with *neither,* not *either,* and has a negative meaning. Choices (C) and (D) cannot be paired with *either.*
2. **(B)** *Nor* is correctly paired with *neither.* Choices (A), (C), and (D) are incorrect conjunctions.
3. **(A)** *Both* is correctly used with two adjectives separated by *and.* Choice (B) is used with two adjectives separated by *nor.* Choices (C) and (D) are not used after the *be* verb.

Target 18 Joined Forms Not Parallel

PART 5: INCOMPLETE SENTENCES

(C) *Or* joins an infinitive with an infinitive. *Stay late* is the simple form. Choice (A) is present progressive; (B) is present; (D) is a participle form.

PART 6: TEXT COMPLETION

1. **(D)** *Satisfaction* is a noun and is parallel with the noun *quality*. Choices (A), (B), and (C) are verb forms.
2. **(A)** *Prompt* is an adjective and is parallel with the adjective *friendly*. Choice (B) is an adverb. Choice (C) is a verb. Choice (D) is a noun.
3. **(D)** *Unprofessional* is an adjective and is parallel with the adjective *unfair*. Choice (A) is an adverb. Choices (B) and (C) are phrases with verbs.

Targets 17–18 Review Coordinating Conjunctions

PART 5: INCOMPLETE SENTENCES

1. **(C)** *Or* expresses a choice. (A) indicates a contrast. (B) indicates purpose. (D) is a relative pronoun that joins clauses, not phrases.
2. **(B)** *And* links items equally. (A) expresses a choice. (C) indicates a contrast. (D) indicates purpose.
3. **(A)** *But* indicates a contrast. (B) expresses a choice. (C) indicates time. (D) links items equally.
4. **(D)** *And* links items equally. (A) expresses a choice. (B) indicates a possibility. (C) indicates contrast.
5. **(A)** *Or* indicates a choice. (B) links items equally. (C) and (D) indicate contrast.

PART 6: TEXT COMPLETION

1. **(B)** *But* indicates a contradiction or lack of agreement; Ms. Greene does not agree with the date suggested by Mr. Kang. Choice (A), *so*, indicates a result. Choice (C), *and*, indicates both. Choice (D), *nor*, indicates a choice and must be paired with *neither*.

2. **(C)** *Or* is correctly paired with *either* to indicate a choice. Choices (A), (B), and (D) cannot be paired with *either*.
3. **(A)** *Get* is a base form verb that matches the base form verb *arrange*. Choice (B) is a present tense verb. Choice (C) is a gerund. Choice (D) is future tense.

Target 19 Misplaced Subordinating Conjunctions

PART 5: INCOMPLETE SENTENCES

(D) The subordinate conjunction introduces the clause and is followed by the subject and verb of the clause. In the other choices the word order is incorrect.

PART 6: TEXT COMPLETION

1. **(B)** The subordinating conjunction *if* belongs at the beginning of the subordinate clause, before the subject *you*. Choice (A) has no subordinating conjunction. Choice (C) has the subordinating conjunction in the wrong position. Choice (D) has the subject in the wrong position.
2. **(C)** The subordinating conjunction *when* belongs at the beginning of the subordinate clause, right before the subject *you*. Choice (A) is missing both the conjunction and the subject. Choice (B) is missing the subject. Choice (D) has the subject in the wrong position.
3. **(B)** The subordinating conjunction *Although* belongs at the beginning of the subordinate clause, before the subject *we*. Choices (A), (C), and (D) have the conjunction and subject in the wrong position.

Target 20 Incorrect Subordinating Conjunctions

PART 5: INCOMPLETE SENTENCES

(C) Usually people cannot enter a concert after it has started; an exception was made for Ms. Sello *even though she was late*. Choices (A), (B), and (D) are not logical.

PART 6: TEXT COMPLETION

1. **(A)** *Although* is used to introduce a situation that has an unexpected result; we often don't expect things to go well when the weather is bad. Choices (B) and (D) indicate cause and effect. Choice (C) indicates a result that occurs in spite of something else.

2. **(D)** *After* gives the correct time relationship in this sentence; first the skies cleared, then we enjoyed outdoor activities. Choices (A) and (C) have the opposite of the correct meaning. Choice (B) indicates that two actions occur at the same time.

3. **(B)** *Even though* is the correct conjunction used to indicate that they are having one feeling in spite of another. Choice (A) is incorrect because there is no unreal situation involved that requires *if.* Choice (C) is a relative pronoun. Choice (D) is incorrect because the first feeling is not the direct result of the second.

Targets 19–20 Review Subordinating Conjunctions

PART 5: INCOMPLETE SENTENCES

1. **(B)** *Although* shows a contrast. (A) indicates cause and effect. (C) indicates time prior. (D) indicates place.

2. **(C)** *Where* indicates place. (A) shows a contrast. (B) is not possible because it doesn't replace *town.* (D) indicates possibility.

3. **(C)** *Before* indicates time prior. (A) indicates time later. (B) indicates time while. (D) indicates during.

4. **(D)** *When* indicates a time relationship. (A) indicates cause and effect. (B) indicates time up to. (C) indicates contrast.

5. **(B)** *Because* indicates cause and effect. (A) indicates a contrast. (C) indicates possibility. (D) indicates place.

PART 6: TEXT COMPLETION

1. **(B)** *Although* is used to introduce a situation that has an unexpected result; we don't expect someone to be denied a promotion after putting in a lot of effort. Choices (A) and (C)

indicate cause and effect. Choice (D), used as a subordinating conjunction, means *after.*

2. **(B)** The subordinating conjunction belongs at the beginning of the subordinate clause, right before the subject. Choice (A) is missing the conjunction. Choice (C) has the conjunction in the wrong position. Choice (D) has the subject in the wrong position.

3. **(D)** *Because* indicates a cause and effect relationship. Choices (A), (B), and (C) indicate different time relationships and don't make sense in this sentence.

Target 21 Use of *as—as*

PART 5: INCOMPLETE SENTENCES

(B) Only choice (B) has *as* twice. *Employee* is being compared equally with *predecessors.* Choice (A) and (C) have only one *as.* In choice (D), *than* is not used with equal comparisons.

PART 6: TEXT COMPLETION

1. **(C)** Only the first *as* is required in the answer since the second *as* is already in the text. Choices (A) and (B) do not use *as* at all, so it cannot be used in a comparative sentence. Choice (D) repeats the second *as.*

2. **(D)** This answer correctly uses *as* both before and after the adverb. Choice (A) cannot be used without *than* in this sentence. Choice (B) does not use *as,* so cannot be used in a comparative sentence. Choice (C) is missing the first *as.*

3. **(A)** Whitney liked the fact that the old copier was small and didn't take up much room. *Compact* means small. Choices (B) and (C) are illogical because you wouldn't want a *slow* or *expensive* copier. Choice (D) is incorrect because a new model cannot be as *modern* as an old one.

Target 22 *More/-er* or *Than* Omitted

PART 5: INCOMPLETE SENTENCES

(A) Don't be confused with the preposition *from.* The comparison of two views requires *than.*

Choices (B), (C), and (D) would need to read *the better of the two* to be correct.

Part 6: Text Completion

1. **(D)** This choice correctly uses a comparative adjective with *than*. Choice (A) is not a comparative form. Choice (B) is a noun. Choice (C) is missing the word *than*.

2. **(D)** This choice correctly uses a comparative adjective with *than*. Choice (A) is not a comparative form. Choice (B) is missing the word *than*. Choice (C) is missing the *-er* ending.

3. **(B)** *Than* is not required in this sentence because only one thing is being described. Choices (A) and (D) are the incorrect comparative form of *quiet*. Choice (C) incorrectly uses *than*.

Target 23 *The* or *Most/-est* Omitted

PART 5: INCOMPLETE SENTENCES

(D) When making a superlative, use *the*. (A) and (B) compare two messenger services; here, we are talking about all of the messenger services in town. (C) needs *the*.

PART 6: TEXT COMPLETION

1. **(D)** This is a correct superlative form, using both *the* and the *-est* ending. Choice (A) is not a superlative form. Choice (B) is missing the *-est* ending. Choice (C) has the *-er* ending instead of the *-est* ending.

2. **(C)** This is a correct superlative form, using both *the* and the *-est* ending. Choice (A) is missing the *-est* ending. Choice (B) is missing the word *the*. Choice (D) has the *-er* ending instead of the *-est* ending.

3. **(B)** The main purpose for changing the booking would be to get a hotel that has *more convenient* access to the convention center. Choices (A) and (D) are incorrect because the first hotel sounds *nicer* and *cleaner*. Choice (C) is incorrect because this is not the correct comparative form of *close*.

Targets 21–23 Review Comparisons with Adjectives and Adverbs

PART 5: INCOMPLETE SENTENCES

1. **(A)** Superlative forms use *the most* and the positive form. (B) is the comparative form. (C) is the positive form. (D) is a noun.

2. **(C)** is the comparative form. (A) is the positive form. (D) is incorrect because the comparative form does not use *the*.

3. **(D)** is the correct comparative form. (A) is the superlative form but omits *the*. (B) is incorrect because the comparative form does not use *the*. (C) is incorrect because the superlative form does not compare two things.

4. **(B)** In an equal comparison, have *as* on both sides of the adjective. (A) omits *as* before the positive form. (C) is the comparative form of *good* and (D) is the superlative form of *good*; neither use *as* before or after the adjective.

5. **(C)** is the comparative form. (A) is the superlative form but omits *the*. (B) omits *as* before the adverb. (D) is incorrect because *than* already appears in the sentence.

PART 6: TEXT COMPLETION

1. **(A)** *Faster than* is a correct comparative form using the *-er* ending and the word *than* and makes sense in context. Choice (B) is incorrect because the ad mentions that their professors are just as professional as those at other schools. Choice (C) is incorrect because Techno Business Academy has a shorter course than average. Choice (D) is incorrect because they advertise low prices.

2. **(A)** *As soon as* is an equal comparison. Choice (B) is missing the first *as*. Choice (C) is a comparative form that does not make sense in this sentence. Choice (D) is not a comparative form.

3. **(B)** *Higher* is a correct comparative form used in a sentence that already contains the word *than*. Choices (A), (C), and (D) cannot be used with *than*.

Target 24 Misplaced Adverbial Time Words and Phrases

PART 5: INCOMPLETE SENTENCES

(C) The adverb of definite frequency must be at the beginning or end of a sentence. The word order in the other choices is incorrect.

PART 6: TEXT COMPLETION

1. **(C)** The adverb of definite frequency should be at the beginning or end of the sentence or clause. In Choices (A), (B), and (D) the word order is incorrect.
2. **(C)** The meetings are *impromptu,* which means unplanned. Choice (A) is illogical because it is too frequent. Choice (B) is the incorrect use of an adverb. Choice (D) is incorrect because the sales representatives and receptionists went to the meetings as well.
3. **(B)** The adverb of frequency is in the correct position at the end of the sentence. Choices (A) and (C) are incorrect because they have the wrong word order. Choice (D) is incorrect because *Monday* and *every day* are two different times.

Target 25 Misplaced Adverbs of Frequency

PART 5: INCOMPLETE SENTENCES

(A) The adverb of indefinite frequency *always* should come before the compound main verbs *have breakfast* and *read.* The word order in the other options is not correct.

Part 6: Text Completion

1. **(C)** The subject *we* comes before the adverb of indefinite frequency *rarely.* Choices (A) and (D) don't have correct word order. Choice (B) requires the verb *to have* rather than the preposition *for.*
2. **(A)** *Always* is an adverb of indefinite frequency, so it should be placed before the main verb *begin.* Choices (B), (C), and (D) don't have correct word order.

3. **(C)** *Usually* is an adverb of indefinite frequency, so it should be placed before the main verb *last.* Choices (A), (B), and (D) don't have correct word order.

Target 26 Adverbs of Frequency with *Be*

PART 5: INCOMPLETE SENTENCES

(C) The adverb of frequency follows the verb *be* when there is no auxiliary. The word order in the other options is not correct.

PART 6: TEXT COMPLETION

1. **(D)** The adverb of frequency follows the verb *to be* when there is no auxiliary. Choices (A), (B), and (C) have incorrect word order.
2. **(B)** People need something to drink their hot beverage out of. Choices (A) and (C) are illogical because these are not things one can bring from home. Choice (D) is a non-count noun so you cannot *bring one.*
3. **(B)** The adverb of frequency follows the verb *to be* when there is no auxiliary. Choices (A), (C), and (D) have incorrect word order.

Target 27 Adverbs of Frequency with Auxiliaries

PART 5: INCOMPLETE SENTENCES

(B) The adverb of frequency follows the auxiliary. The word order in the other options is not correct.

PART 6: TEXT COMPLETION

1. **(D)** The adverb of frequency should follow the auxiliary. In Choices (A), (B), and (C) the word order is not correct.
2. **(B)** Ms. Peters is going to start working at Marie's boutique. Choice (A) is incorrect because Ms. Peters is leaving Pierce's company. Choice (C) is incorrect because there is no indication that Ms. Peters did anything wrong. Choice (D) is incorrect because Ms. Peters has left for a new job, not to take time off.
3. **(D)** The adverb of frequency should follow the auxiliary. In Choices (A), (B), and (C) the word order is not correct.

Target 28 Meanings of Adverbs of Frequency

PART 5: INCOMPLETE SENTENCES

(C) The conjunction *or* and the pronoun *anyone* have a negative sense. The only answer choice with a negative sense is *never*. The other choices have a positive sense and would be used with conjunctions such as *and*.

PART 6: TEXT COMPLETION

1. **(A)** *Usually* means *most of the time.* Choices (B), (C), and (D) have the opposite of the correct meaning.
2. **(C)** Everyone goes to Yamamoto, so *always* is the correct choice. Choices (A), (B), and (D) are incorrect because everyone goes to Yamamoto to book business trips.
3. **(B)** Watanabe has requested that Tanaka cancel her trips because she spent too much money. Choices (A) and (D) are incorrect because Yamamoto is going to choose and book the arrangements this time. Choice (C) is incorrect because *take* is not an appropriate verb to use with the noun *hotel.*

Targets 24–28 Review Adverbs of Frequency

PART 5: INCOMPLETE SENTENCES

1. **(B)** *Every day* can appear at the end of a sentence. (A), (C), and (D) must appear in the middle of the sentence.
2. **(B)** *Always* comes between the auxiliary and the main verb. (A) places the main verb before the auxiliary. (C) and (D) place *every day* in the middle of the sentence instead of at the beginning or end.
3. **(A)** *Still* comes after a form of *be.* (B) and (D) cannot be used before negatives. (C) must appear at the beginning or the end of the sentence.
4. **(D)** *Rarely* comes between the auxiliary and the main verb. In (A) *rarely* appears after the main verb. (B) and (C) are incorrect because *every day* must come at the beginning or the end of the sentence.

5. **(D)** *Every year* can appear at the end of a sentence. (A), (C), and (D) must appear in the middle of the sentence.

PART 6: TEXT COMPLETION

1. **(B)** The adverb of definite frequency should be at the beginning or end of the sentence or clause. In Choices (A), (C), and (D) the word order is incorrect.
2. **(B)** Jane mentions that it is always sunny. The umbrellas mentioned in the passage are for shade. Choice (A) is incorrect because it is *almost always sunny.* Choice (C) is incorrect because it is *too hot in the day to jog.* Choice (D) is incorrect because Jane says there are *too many people lying on the beach* to jog.
3. **(C)** *Usually* means *most of the time.* Choices (A), (B), and (D) have the opposite of the correct meaning.

Target 29 Causative Verb + Simple Form

PART 5: INCOMPLETE SENTENCES

(A) The causative verb *makes* is followed by a verb in the simple form (*take*). The other choices are not in the simple form.

PART 6: TEXT COMPLETION

1. **(C)** The causative verb *lets* is followed by a verb in the simple form. Choices (A), (B), and (D) are not the simple form.
2. **(A)** The causative verb *have* requires a verb in the simple form. Choices (B), (C), and (D) are not the simple form.
3. **(C)** The causative verb *have* is used before the simple verb form *write.* Choice (A) is followed by an infinitive form. Choices (B) and (D) are past tense and do not follow *should.*

Target 30 Causative Verb + Infinitive

PART 5: INCOMPLETE SENTENCES

(B) The causative verb *permit* must be followed by an infinitive *to make.* The other choices are not infinitives.

PART 6: TEXT COMPLETION

1. **(C)** The causative verb *get* is followed by a verb in the infinitive form. Choices (A), (B), and (D) are not the infinitive form.
2. **(B)** The causative verb *allow* is followed by a verb in the infinitive form. Choices (A), (C), and (D) are not the infinitive form.
3. **(C)** In this context the future tense is needed. *Allow* comes before the infinitive *to look*. Choices (A), (B), and (D) are not future tense verbs.

Target 31 Causative Verb + Past Participle

PART 5: INCOMPLETE SENTENCES

(A) The past form of the causative verb *have* must be followed by the past participle. The other choices are not the past participle form.

PART 6: TEXT COMPLETION

1. **(C)** The causative verb *have* plus a thing are followed by the past participle form of the verb. Choices (A), (B), and (D) are not the past participle form.
2. **(D)** The causative verb *get* plus a thing is followed by the past participle form of the verb. Choices (A), (B), and (C) are not the past participle form.
3. **(B)** The causative verb *have* plus a thing is followed by the past participle form of the verb. Choices (A), (C), and (D) are not the past participle form.

Targets 29–31 Review Causative Verbs

PART 5: INCOMPLETE SENTENCES

1. **(A)** The causative *made* must be followed by the simple form of the verb. (B) is the past participle. (C) is the gerund. (D) is the present tense.
2. **(D)** The causative *have* must be followed by the past participle. (A) is the simple form. (B) is the future tense. (C) is the gerund.
3. **(C)** The causative *wants* must be followed by the past participle. (A) is the gerund. (B) is the simple form. (D) is a noun.
4. **(D)** The causative *have* must be followed by the simple form of the verb. (A) is the past participle. (B) is the gerund. (C) is the future tense.
5. **(C)** The causative *had* must be followed by the past participle. (A) is the simple form. (B) is the gerund. (D) is the future form.

PART 6: TEXT COMPLETION

1. **(A)** The causative verb *make* is followed by a verb in the simple form. Choices (B), (C), and (D) are not the simple form.
2. **(B)** The causative verb *permit* is followed by a verb in the infinitive form. Choices (A), (C), and (D) are not the infinitive form.
3. **(A)** The causative verb *have* is followed by a verb in the simple form. Choices (B), (C), and (D) are not the simple form.

Target 32 Real Condition *if* Clause Not in Present Tense

PART 5: INCOMPLETE SENTENCES

(A) The *if* clause must be in the present tense. Choice (B) is past; Choice (C) is past perfect; Choice (D) is future.

PART 6: TEXT COMPLETION

1. **(A)** The *if* clause must be in the present tense for a real condition. Choice (B) is infinitive. Choices (C) and (D) are future.
2. **(B)** The *if* clause must be in the present tense for a real condition. Choice (A) is present, but a course cannot do the action itself. The past participle form is required. Choice (C) is future. Choice (D) is not the present tense.
3. **(A)** A phone number or e-mail address is required. Choices (B), (C), and (D) do not relate to the university calling or writing to a student about unavailable courses.

Target 33 Unreal Condition *if* Clause Not in Appropriate Tense

PART 5: INCOMPLETE SENTENCES

(B) This is an unreal condition (*I didn't get a promotion*). It must be in the past perfect tense if the main clause is in the past. The tenses in the other choices are incorrect.

PART 6: TEXT COMPLETION

1. **(B)** In an unreal condition about the past, the *if* clause uses a past perfect verb. Choice (A) is simple past. Choice (C) is present perfect. Choice (D) would be correct in an unreal conditional about the present.
2. **(B)** In an unreal condition about the past, the *if* clause uses a past perfect verb. Choice (A) is present perfect tense. Choice (C) is present tense. Choice (D) is past perfect.
3. **(C)** The verb *be* is always *were* in an unreal condition. Choices (A), (B), and (D) are other forms of *be* verbs.

Target 34 Unreal Condition *if* Clause + *Were*

PART 5: INCOMPLETE SENTENCES

(A) The verb *be* is always *were* in an unreal condition *if* clause—even though the subject here (*the salary*) is singular. Choices (B) and (C) are singular and (B), (C), and (D) are all in the wrong tense.

PART 6: TEXT COMPLETION

1. **(C)** In an unreal condition about the present, the verb *to be* is always *were* in the *if* clause. Choices (A), (B), and (D) are not in the correct form.
2. **(D)** In an unreal condition about the present, the verb *to be* is always *were* in the *if* clause. Choices (A), (B), and (C) are not in the correct form.
3. **(C)** In an unreal condition about the present, the verb *to be* is always *were* in the *if* clause. Choices (A), (B), and (D) are not in the correct form.

Targets 32–34 Review Conditional Sentences

PART 5: INCOMPLETE SENTENCES

1. **(B)** A real condition requires a present tense verb in the *if* clause. (A) is past tense. (C) is the past perfect. (D) is the past progressive.
2. **(B)** *Would have given* is an unreal condition requiring the past perfect in the *if* clause. (A) is present. (C) is past tense. (D) is the present.
3. **(A)** A real condition requires a present verb in the *if* clause. (B) is a conditional in the future tense. (C) is past tense. (D) is the past perfect.
4. **(B)** An unreal condition requires *were* as a form of *be* in the *if* clause. (A) is past tense. (C) is a conditional in the future tense. (D) is a conditional in the past tense.
5. **(A)** A real condition can use a command form. (B) is future tense. (C) is the past perfect. (D) is the future.

PART 6: TEXT COMPLETION

1. **(D)** In an unreal condition about the past, the *if* clause uses a past perfect verb. Choice (A) is the simple form. Choice (B) is simple past. Choice (C) is a present unreal conditional form.
2. **(B)** The *if* clause must be in the present tense for a real condition. Choice (A) is present, but does not agree with the subject in number. Choice (C) is a participle. Choice (D) is the past tense.
3. **(B)** In an unreal condition about the present, the verb *to be* is always *were* in the *if* clause. The first part of the sentence is about the past, but the second part is about the present. *These days* refers to the present so the idea is an unreal condition about the present. Choices (A), (C), and (D) are not in the correct form.

Target 35 Verb Tenses

PART 5: INCOMPLETE SENTENCES

(D) The future perfect shows the relationship between an action in progress (*I am contacting people now*) and a time marker (*by tomorrow night*). *I will have contacted them all by tomorrow night.* The other choices do not match the future time marker *by tomorrow night*.

PART 6: TEXT COMPLETION

1. **(B)** The past tense verb *arrived* is consistent with the time marker *last week*. Choices (A), (C), and (D) do not match the past time marker.
2. **(C)** From the context we understand that the furniture is in the store now but will be gone in the future because it will be sold, so a future tense verb fits the context. Choice (A) is present tense. Choice (B) is past tense. Choice (D) is present perfect.
3. **(C)** The future tense is needed because this part of the ad is discussing the stock that will be available next month. Choice (A) is illogical because an ad would not describe items that one couldn't find. Choices (B) and (D) are the wrong tense.

Target 36 Stative Verbs in the Progressive Form

PART 5: INCOMPLETE SENTENCES

(B) The stative verb *like* is not often used in the progressive tense. Choice (A) is the past tense; (C) is a form of the progressive tense; (D) is a participle form.

PART 6: TEXT COMPLETION

1. **(A)** *Look* is used as a stative verb in this sentence so cannot be in a progressive form. Choices (B), (C), and (D) are progressive forms.
2. **(D)** *Belong* is a stative verb and is used here with a present tense meaning. Choices (A) and (C) are progressive forms, which cannot be used with stative verbs. Choice (B) is past perfect, an incorrect tense for this context.
3. **(A)** *Believe* is used as a stative verb in this sentence so cannot be in a progressive form. Choices (B), (C), and (D) are progressive forms.

Target 35–36 Review Verb Tenses and Stative Verbs

PART 5: INCOMPLETE SENTENCES

1. **(B)** *Will call* is future; match with simple present to show action that will happen in the very near future. (A) is the present perfect. (C) is the past participle. (D) is the present progressive.
2. **(A)** Action that started in the past and continues into the future is expressed by the present perfect. (B) is the past perfect progressive. (C) is the present. (D) is the past perfect.
3. **(D)** Use the simple past to show action that happened in the past. (A) is the present tense. (B) is the past progressive. (C) is the present perfect.
4. **(B)** *A speech tonight* is future; use the future tense. (A) is past progressive. (C) is the past tense. (D) is the present perfect.
5. **(C)** *Next year* is future; use the future tense. (A) is conditional. (B) is the past tense. (D) is the present perfect.

PART 6: TEXT COMPLETION

1. **(D)** *Think* is used as a stative verb in this sentence so cannot be in a progressive form. Choices (A), (B), and (C) are progressive forms.
2. **(C)** Richard goes to school at night and has exams soon. Choice (A) is incorrect because Richard is looking for work. Choice (B) is illogical because Richard has already had an interview for the job. Choice (D) is not what Richard needs to refocus on.
3. **(C)** *As soon as I find out* is a future time clause, so the verb in the main clause should be in the future tense. Choice (A) is present tense. Choice (B) is past tense. Choice (D) is present perfect.

Target 37 Relative Clause: Repeated Subject

PART 5: INCOMPLETE SENTENCES

(C) The subject of the sentence is *wallet*; the subject of the clause is *that*. In Choice (A) and (B) you do not need to repeat the subject with the pronoun *it*. In Choice (D), the relative pronoun *whose* refers to people, not things such as a wallet.

PART 6: TEXT COMPLETION

1. **(A)** In this clause, the relative pronoun *who* refers to the subject of the clause (*everyone*).

Choices (B) and (D) repeat a pronoun for the subject (*he*). Choice (C) has no relative pronoun. Choice (D) also uses an incorrect relative pronoun; *whose* refers to possessive nouns.

2. **(B)** There are seventy tickets. Twenty are for guests and fifty are for staff. Choice (A) is incorrect because twenty are for guests. Choice (C) is illogical because there are only sixty staff members in total. Choice (D) uses the repeated pronoun *that*.

3. **(B)** In this clause, the relative pronoun *who* refers to staff members. Choices (A), (C), and (D) use more than one pronoun in the sentence.

Target 38 Relative Clause: No Relative Pronoun

PART 5: INCOMPLETE SENTENCES

(A) You need a relative pronoun to introduce the clause (*who shares this office*) and be the subject of the clause. Choices (B) and (D) are not relative pronouns. Choice (C) is a possessive relative pronoun.

PART 6: TEXT COMPLETION

1. **(C)** The relative pronoun *who* introduces the clause and acts as the subject of the clause. Choices (A), (B), and (D) are not relative pronouns.

2. **(C)** The relative pronoun *which* refers to the book. Choices (A), (B), and (D) do not contain relative pronouns.

3. **(D)** The relative pronoun *which* introduces the clause and acts as the subject of the clause. Choices (A), (B), and (C) are not relative pronouns.

Target 39 Relative Clause: *That* ≠ *Who*

PART 5: INCOMPLETE SENTENCES

(D) You need a relative pronoun to introduce the clause (*who has worked here for many years*) and you need *who* because the clause refers to a person. Choice (A) is a relative pronoun, but it is not used with people; (B) is not a relative pronoun; and (C) is a relative pronoun, but is not used with people.

PART 6: TEXT COMPLETION

1. **(D)** The relative pronoun *who* refers to a person and acts as the subject of the clause. Choice (A) refers to a thing. Choice (B) refers to possession. Choice (C) acts as the object of a clause.

2. **(D)** *Who* is the correct subject pronoun referring to a person (customer service representative). Choice (A) is a preposition plus object pronoun. Choice (B) is a preposition plus pronoun used for things. Choice (C) is a possessive pronoun.

3. **(B)** *That* refers to a thing (service) in this sentence. Choices (A) and (D) refer to a person. Choice (C) refers to a place.

Targets 37–39 Review Relative Clauses

PART 5: INCOMPLETE SENTENCES

1. **(D)** *Who* replaces *Ms. Caras*. (A) refers to time. (B) is the objective form. (C) refers to things, not people.

2. **(D)** *That* replaces *letter*. In choices (A), (B), and (C) *it* repeats the subject.

3. **(A)** *Whose* replaces *Mr. La Porte* in the possessive. (B) is incorrect because *his* repeats *Mr. La Porte*. (C) and (D) omit relative forms.

4. **(D)** *That* replaces *report*. (A) is incorrect because *it* repeats *report*. (B) omits the relative form. (C) refers to people.

5. **(B)** *That* replaces *machine*. (A) refers to people. (C) is not a relative form. (D) refers to time.

PART 6: TEXT COMPLETION

1. **(A)** The relative pronoun *who* acts as the subject of the clause and refers to a person (*Ms. McIntyre*). Choice (B) repeats the subject. Choice (C) is not a relative pronoun. Choice (D) refers to a thing.

2. **(C)** The relative pronoun *whose* introduces the clause and refers to possession (*everyone's*). Choice (A) refers to people. Choices (B) and (D) are not relative pronouns.

3. **(B)** The relative pronoun *which* acts as the subject of the clause and refers to a thing (*visit*). Choice (A) repeats the subject. Choice (C) refers to a person and repeats the subject. Choice (D) repeats the subject.

Target 40 Verb + Gerund or Infinitive

PART 5: INCOMPLETE SENTENCES

(B) Change to an infinitive after the verb *intend.* The other choices are not in the infinitive form.

PART 6: TEXT COMPLETION

1. **(C)** *Agree* is followed by the infinitive. Choices (A), (B), and (D) are not in the infinitive form.
2. **(B)** *Mind* is followed by the gerund. Choices (A), (C), and (D) are not in the gerund form.
3. **(B)** *Offer* is followed by the infinitive. Choices (A), (C), and (D) are not in the infinitive form.

Target 40 Review
Gerunds and Infinitives

PART 5: INCOMPLETE SENTENCES

1. **(D)** *Prepare* is followed by the infinitive. Choice (A) is the simple form. (B) is the *-ing* form. (C) is the past participle.
2. **(A)** *Want* is followed by the infinitive. Choice (B) is the *-ing* form. (C) is the past participle. (D) is the simple form.
3. **(D)** *Postponed* is followed by the gerund. Choice (A) is the infinitive. (B) is the past participle. (C) is the simple form.
4. **(A)** *Considered* is followed by the gerund. Choice (B) is the future tense. (C) is the past participle. (D) is the infinitive.
5. **(D)** *Failed* is followed by the infinitive. Choice (A) is the simple form. (B) is the past tense. (C) is the *-ing* form.

PART 6: TEXT COMPLETION

1. **(B)** *Enjoy* is followed by the gerund. Choices (A), (C), and (D) are not in the gerund form.
2. **(C)** *Seem* is followed by the infinitive. Choices (A), (B), and (D) are not in the infinitive form.

3. **(B)** *Plan* is followed by the infinitive. Choices (A), (C), and (D) are not in the infinitive form.

Target 41 Incorrect Participles

PART 5: INCOMPLETE SENTENCES

(B) The sounds from the street caused annoyance so the present participle is required. Choice (A) is past participle. Choice (C) is an infinitive. Choice (D) is the present perfect tense.

PART 6: TEXT COMPLETION

1. **(C)** The contracts received the action; use the past participle form. Choice (A) is a noun. Choice (B) is a present participle. Choice (D) is a present tense verb.
2. **(B)** The news causes a feeling; use the present participle. Choice (A) is a noun. Choice (C) is the past participle. Choice (D) is a present tense verb.
3. **(A)** The decision causes a feeling; use the present participle. Choice (B) is the past participle. Choice (C) is the incorrect word order. Choice (D) is incorrect because *that* would have to immediately follow *surprised*

Target 41 Review
Participles

PART 5: INCOMPLETE SENTENCES

1. **(B)** The jobs cause the employees to feel boredom; use the past participle. Choice (A) is a noun. (C) is the present tense. (D) is the simple form.
2. **(A)** Someone else sorted the mail; use the past participle. Choice (B) is the simple form. (C) confuses *sort* and *sort of.* (D) is the present participle.
3. **(C)** Someone else approved the application; use the past participle. Choice (A) is the noun form. (B) is the present tense. (D) is the present participle.
4. **(B)** People crowded the offices; use the past participle. Choice (A) is the present participle. (C) is the present tense. (D) is the simple form.

5. **(D)** The speaker causes the audience to laugh; use the present participle. Choice (A) is the simple form. (B) is the noun form. (C) is the past tense.

PART 6: TEXT COMPLETION

1. **(A)** The price drop was affected by people's expectations; use the past participle. Choice (B) is the present participle. Choice (C) is a noun. Choice (D) is an adjective with a related but different meaning.

2. **(C)** The news caused the feeling of surprise; use the present participle. Choice (A) is a noun or base form verb. Choice (B) is past participle. Choice (D) is a present perfect verb.

3. **(B)** The times cause a feeling of confusion; use the present participle. Choice (A) is incorrect because the losses were expected and would have an explanation. Choice (C) is illogical because the passage is about stocks, not workers. Choice (D) is an incorrect participle because stocks can't be *excited*.

Explanatory Answers for Mini-Test for Reading Parts 5 and 6

PART 5: INCOMPLETE SENTENCES

1. **(C)** A compound subject requires a plural verb. Choice (A) is first person present tense. Choice (B) is singular present. (D) is the simple form.

2. **(D)** *To* indicates the one-way direction of the cable. Choice (A) implies the computer is used as *a means* to attach the cable. Choices (B) and (C) would imply that the computer is opened up and the cables are "inside" the computer itself.

3. **(A)** The word *tomorrow* suggests a future tense; use *will*. Choice (B) is present tense of *have*. Choice (C) is past tense of *do*. Choice (D) should also have an *-ing* verb (*are submitting*).

4. **(D)** *The* requires the noun *presentation*. Choice (A) is the gerund form, which is inappropriate here. Choice (B) is the past tense form. Choice (C) is the simple form.

5. **(B)** *Increased* means *to go up*. Choices (A) and (C) are not used with money. Choice (D) confuses *rise* and *raise*.

6. **(A)** *Although* here means *in spite of* the rain, we drove in a jeep without a roof. Choices (B) and (C) indicate cause and effect. Choice (D) is a preposition, not a conjunction.

7. **(D)** *At* is used with specific indications of time. Choice (A) is used for placement. Choice (B) is for location. Choice (C) is used for location.

8. **(C)** *Was* is followed by the past participle *sent*. Choice (A) is the simple form. Choice (B) uses *has*, not *was*. Choice (D) is the gerund form.

9. **(A)** The adverb of indefinite frequency comes between the auxiliary and the main verb. Choice (B) is followed by the simple form of the verb. In Choice (C) the adverb follows the main verb. In Choice (D) the adverb precedes the auxiliary.

10. **(C)** Choice (C) indicates position with the post office on one side and the bank on the other side. Choice (A) is used when there are three or more reference points. Choice (B) is incorrect because an office would not normally be *outside*. Choice (D) would be possible only if all three (post office, bank and office) were in one building and you had to pass through both to get to the office.

11. **(A)** A real condition can use a command form in the *if* clause. Choice (B) is an adverb. Choice (C) is a noun. Choice (D) is an infinitive.

12. **(C)** *In* goes with a state name, *Texas*. Choices (A), (B), and (C) are not logical.

13. **(C)** *Since*, here, shows a cause and effect relationship. Choices (A) and (D) imply contradictions. Choice (B) doesn't make sense.

14. **(B)** Adverbs of indefinite frequency occur after the auxiliary verb. Choice (A) is an adverb of definite frequency and cannot occur after the auxiliary. Choices (C) and (D) do not make sense.

15. **(D)** *Nor* is the conjunction paired with *neither*. Choices (A), (B), and (C) are not used with *neither*.

16. **(C)** We use the past perfect as the past subjunctive to show an imaginary idea, one contrary to fact, in the past. Choice (A) implies that she *always* recommends. The idea is about what happened on one occasion in the past, not what happens all the time. Choice (B) is used to make a general observation. Choice (D) means in reality that the consultant is recommending right now that we hire more staff. That's not the reality of the situation; this is something the consultant did in the past.

17. **(B)** The command form signals a real condition; use the present tense in the *if* clause. Choice (A) would be used in an unreal condition. Choice (C) is the past tense. Choice (D) is the *-ing* form.

18. **(B)** The causative *had* requires the past participle. Choice (A) is the simple form. Choice (C) is the *-ing* form. Choice (D) is the command form.

19. **(C)** Use simple past tense to express a one-time past action. Choice (A) is the present tense. Choice (B) is the present perfect. Choice (D) is past progressive.

20. **(D)** The simple form of a verb is used after *must*. Choice (A) is the past tense. Choice (B) is the gerund. Choice (C) is the present tense.

PART 6: TEXT COMPLETION

21. **(A)** *Who* introduces the relative clause and acts as the subject of the clause. Choices (B) and (C) repeat the subject. Choices (C) and (D) are object, not subject, pronouns.

22. **(D)** Olga Kovacs will be in the city, and at the hotel, next week, so a future verb is required. Choice (A) is present tense. Choice (B) is past tense. Choice (C) is present perfect.

23. **(C)** Ms. Kovacs needs a way to get to the office that is better than a cab, so Ed will send a *limousine*, or hired car, and ride in it with her. Choices (A), (B), and (D) are things one could send, but they don't fit the context of transportation.

24. **(A)** *Although* is used to introduce a situation that has an unexpected result; we don't expect so many teens to smoke when there is a campaign to discourage them. Choices (B) and (D) indicate cause and effect. Choice (C) introduces a time clause.

25. **(C)** The news causes a feeling—public health officials, teachers, and parents don't feel encouraged—so a present participle adjective is used. Choice (A) is a base form verb. Choice (B) is a past participle. Choice (D) is a noun.

26. **(D)** *Adolescence* is a stage of life, the time when one is a teenager. Choices (A), (B), and (C) look similar to the correct answer but have very different meanings.

Explanatory Answers for Reading Comprehension— Targets 42–60

Target 42 Advertisements

PART 7: READING COMPREHENSION

1. **(C)** *Attention Manufacturers* indicates that the writers want manufacturers to read the ad. Choice (A) confuses the writers of the ad with the readers. Choices (B) and (D) are not mentioned.

2. **(B)** It indicates they can distribute in 155 countries. Choice (A) is less than the number mentioned. Choices (C) and (D) are more than the number mentioned.

Target 43 Forms

PART 7: READING COMPREHENSION

1. **(D)** To *subscribe* means that you will start to receive a periodical. Choices (A), (B), and (C) are contradicted by the heading *Special Subscription Offer*.

2. **(B)** The full cover price is $5 an issue ($60 divided by 12 months). Choice (A) is less than the price. Choices (C) and (D) are more than the price.

3. **(B)** *Allow four weeks for first issue* means about *one month*. Choice (A) is shorter than a month. Choices (C) and (D) are not logical.

4. **(C)** If there are 12 issues in one year, the magazine comes *monthly*. Choices (A) and (B) are more often. Choice (D) is less often.

Target 44 Reports

PART 7: READING COMPREHENSION

1. **(C)** They could pay $10 million; *$5 million up front* plus *as much as $5 million more*. Choice (A) is the amount Peptel posted in sales last year. Choice (B) is the initial price. Choice (D) is what Markel is worth.

2. **(D)** *Of Berlin* means the company is based there. Choice (A) is where Markel is based. Choices (B) and (C) are not mentioned.

3. **(A)** If Peptel is in educational software, Markel is probably in software, too. Choices (B) and (D) are not mentioned. Choice (C) confuses *visual arts* with the company name *Peptel Visual*.

Target 45 Letters

PART 7: READING COMPREHENSION

1. **(C)** *Samples* are not requested. Choices (A), (B), and (D) are explicitly requested. (*Terms* means *pricing information*.)

2. **(B)** *Hardware* includes computers. Choice (A) is contradicted by the fact that they are *adding software to their sales offerings*. Choices (C) and (D) are not mentioned.

3. **(A)** *Add software to our sales offerings* means *distribute software*. Choice (B) is not mentioned. Choice (C) confuses *selling hardware* with *purchasing hardware*. Choice (D) confuses *sending* an annual report with *receiving* an annual report.

Target 46 Faxes

PART 7: READING COMPREHENSION

1. **(B)** The meeting will be held in *Building B*. Choice (A) confuses *Room 42* and *Room 24* and *Tuesday the 24th*. Choice (C) has no ref-

erence point. Choice (D) is incorrect because the reception, not the meeting, is at the hotel.

2. **(B)** A meeting that *begins on Tuesday and lasts though Thursday* lasts 3 days. Choice (A) confuses *2 days* with *Tuesday* and *Thursday*. Choice (C) confuses days the meeting will last with *24* and *42*. Choice (D) is the time the meeting will end on Thursday.

3. **(A)** If Tuesday is the 24th and it was written on the 23rd, it was written on Monday. Choice (B) is the day the meeting starts. Choice (C) is the day the meeting ends. Choice (D) is not mentioned.

4. **(D)** There are *this* + *10* pages for 11 pages total. Choice (A) omits the *attached budget*. Choice (B) confuses two items (*this* and *10*) with the number of pages. Choice (C) omits *this* cover sheet.

Target 47 Memos

PART 7: READING COMPREHENSION

1. **(C)** *No flights under five hours can be booked in Business Class*, but flights over five hours can be. Choices (A) *Economy* and (B) *Economy Plus* can probably be booked. Choice (D) is contradicted by *No flights...can be booked in First Class*.

2. **(A)** If it is written *May 15* and goes into effect *June 1*, it goes into effect in *two weeks*. Choices (B) and (C) are contradicted by *June 1*. Choice (D) confuses *five hours* with *five months*.

3. **(B)** The memo is about using *economical means*, or *saving money*. Choices (A), (C), and (D) are not mentioned.

4. **(D)** The memo affects *all employees*, or *all personnel*. Choices (A), (B), and (C) are contradicted by *all personnel*.

Target 48 Tables

PART 7: READING COMPREHENSION

1. **(A)** Amsterdam and Taipei are both coded *C* for cloudy. Choice (B) cities were partly cloudy. Choices (C) and (D) had different weather but were not cloudy.

2. **(D)** Manila had a high of *33/91*. Choices (A), (B), and (C) had lower temperatures.

3. **(B)** Frankfurt had a spread from *3/37* to *1/34*. Choices (A), (C), and (D) had wider spreads.

4. **(B)** Kuala Lampur is coded for *t* thunderstorms. Choices (A), (C), and (D) are not mentioned for this city.

Target 49 Indexes

PART 7: READING COMPREHENSION

1. **(A)** Magazines need *indexes* and come in *issues*. Choices (B) and (D) do not come in issues. Choice (C) probably does not have a large index.

2. **(B)** *Computer industries* are not listed. In choice (A) travel is represented by Canadian Rail Service, Network Travel Pride Hotels, and TNT Air. In Choice (C) heavy industries are represented by Allied Steel, Best Iron Ore, and Chemical Times. In Choice (D) utilities are represented by Acme Power and Light, Consumer's Electric, and Ford Gas.

Target 50 Charts

PART 7: READING COMPREHENSION

1. **(C)** It shows the relative positions of successful companies by allowing you to compare sales figures. Choice (A) is incorrect because the chart lists *total sales*, not *selling price*. Choices (B) and (D) are not indicated on the chart.

2. **(B)** Sankyu's sales are almost twice those of the second-ranked company. Choice (A) is incorrect because sales from other years are not compared. Choices (C) and (D) are contradicted by the fact that it is the first-ranked company.

Target 51 Graphs

PART 7: READING COMPREHENSION

1. **(B)** Competing hotels would be most interested in market share information. Choices (A), (C), and (D) are unlikely to be interested.

2. **(D)** Lowit has 25%, or one-quarter, of the market. Choice (A) is incorrect because Stilton is the top-ranking chain. Choice (B) is incorrect because location information is not given in the graph. Choice (C) is incorrect because Torte has only 15% of the market.

Target 52 Announcements

PART 7: READING COMPREHENSION

1. **(A)** The world's third-largest means it has a rank of 3. Choice (B) is the number of years Mr. Kasper has been with the company. Choice (C) confuses the rank with the date of resignation. Choice (D) is Mr. Kasper's age.

2. **(A)** The company *could be bought*. Choices (B), (C), and (D) are contradicted by *could be bought*.

3. **(C)** If he is 62 and has been there 22 years, he has been there since he was 40. Choice (A) is contradicted by *22 years*. Choice (B) confuses the resignation date and the time he has been there. Choice (D) is his age.

4. **(A)** *Cable television systems* are communications companies. Choices (B), (C), and (D) do not include cable companies.

Target 53 Notices

PART 7: READING COMPREHENSION

1. **(D)** Employees moving from other cities are most affected. Choices (A), (B), and (C) are not affected by these changes.

2. **(B)** *Moving household items* is reimbursed. Choices (A), (C), and (D) are *no longer reimbursable*.

Target 54 Newspaper Articles

PART 7: READING COMPREHENSION

1. **(D)** The collapse of the Berlin Wall has caused the change. Choice (A) is mentioned but did not cause the change. Choice (B) is not mentioned. Choice (C) is incorrect because 40 construction projects are *underway* but not completed.

2. **(D)** The article discusses how the drab aspect is changing. Choices (A), (B), and (C) are explicitly mentioned as reasons for the improvements.

First News
Always Innovative & Informative

3. **(B)** It says that *investments in new construction are expected to exceed $120 billion.* Choices (A) and (C) do not have costs mentioned. Choice (D) is not mentioned.

Target 55 Magazine Articles

PART 7: READING COMPREHENSION

1. **(A)** This article is about *computerized access to information*—also known as the *Information Highway.* Choice (B) is mentioned in the article. Choice (C) repeats the word *highway.* Choice (D) refers to traffic problems.

2. **(C)** The highway needs to be closed when there is a *traffic jam,* or *too many users.* Choice (A) repeats a line from the article. Choice (B) isn't mentioned. Choice (D) repeats an idea from the article.

3. **(C)** Someone with a broad-band connection can *speed down the highway faster than most of us can go.* Choice (A) talks about literal highway travel, by *car.* Choice (B) repeats *cool people* from the article. Choice (D) is not mentioned.

Target 56 Schedules

PART 7: READING COMPREHENSION

1. **(C)** Off-peak fares start somewhere between 8:25 and 8:32; 8:30 is a reasonable guess. Choice (A) is not mentioned. Choices (B) and (D) are times in the schedule, but neither is the start of off-peak fares.

2. **(C)** Buses marked with a *W* arrive at this stop five minutes earlier than others, so the 7:30 arrives at 7:25. Choices (A) and (B) are not mentioned. Choice (D) is the bus's departure time.

3. **(C)** The tunnel isn't open until 8:00. Choice (A) is probably true, but it isn't mentioned in the schedule. Choices (B) and (D) are not mentioned.

4. **(C)** Each trip is 50 minutes, or *almost an hour.* This question requires some quick math computation. Choice (A) means 15 minutes. Choice (B) means 30 minutes. Choice (D) is incorrect.

Target 57 Calendars

PART 7: READING COMPREHENSION

1. **(A)** Meeting with hotel representatives, tour guides, airline agents, and the editor of a travel magazine indicates someone who works in tourism. Choices (B), (C), and (D) would not have so many meetings within the travel industry.

2. **(B)** There is one trip to Rio and another to New York. Choices (A), (C), and (D) are contradicted by the trips listed.

3. **(C)** The nights of the 3rd, 4th, and 5th will be spent away from home, making three nights away. Choices (A), (B), and (D) are contradicted by the information given.

4. **(A)** Three golf games are listed. Choices (B), (C), and (D) are not mentioned.

Target 58 E-mail

PART 7: READING COMPREHENSION

1. **(A)** The sender's address is shown in the header line: *From.* Choice (B) is the address of the receiver. Choice (C) is not an e-mail address, it is a name plus an e-mail address. Choice (D) is the name of the receiver.

2. **(C)** The gathering (or *meeting*) was in Orlando, according to the *Subject* line. Choice (A) is probably a company name, based on the e-mail addresses, but it wasn't the location of the meeting. Choice (B) repeats a name from the header. Choice (D) repeats a word from the e-mail, but this is a restaurant name, not the meeting place.

Target 59 Web Pages

PART 7: READING COMPREHENSION

1. **(D)** *FAQ* means *Frequently Asked Questions,* and is a standard option on a home page. Choices (A), (B), and (C) are all menu options, but none would be the place to go to find the response to a basic question.

2. **(A)** *Pay for fuel in advance* means *prepaid gasoline cards.* Choice (B) is not mentioned. Choice (C) repeats a line from the home

page. Choice (D) repeats the word *gas* from the home page.

Target 60 Computer Language

PART 7: READING COMPREHENSION

1. **(D)** A user cannot duplicate (*copy*) a document using these options. Choice (A) refers to saving a document. Choice (B) refers to print preview. Choice (C) refers to printing a document. A paper document is called a hard copy.

2. **(B)** *Ctrl* is a short form for *control*. Pushing *Control + O* allows you to open, or *access*, a document. Choices (A), (C), and (D) are all options with this menu, but none relates to accessing an existing document.

Explanatory Answers for Mini-Test for Reading Part 7

1. **(D)** The ad is for an *international book supplier* who has books in many languages. Choice (A) uses *225 languages* to incorrectly suggest translation services. Choice (B) is contradicted by *book supplier*. Choice (C) is incorrectly suggested by the reference to *Zulu*.

2. **(B)** The third line says it's *full service*. Choice (A) is probably true but not emphasized. Choice (C) is listed but is not a *feature of the company*. Choice (D) is not mentioned.

3. **(B)** The invoice goes to the *accounting department*, which pays the bill. Choice (A) receives the shipment. Choice (C) is the vendor's purchasing department. Choice (D) sent the shipment.

4. **(A)** *Vendor* means *seller*. Choice (B) bought the equipment. Choice (C) prepared the invoice. Choice (D) will get the invoice in the accounting department.

5. **(A)** Choice (A) is the subtotal without the cards. Choice (B) is the subtotal with the cards. Choice (C) is not given. Choice (D) is the total, with cards and shipping and handling.

6. **(D)** The personnel department does not get a copy of the purchase order. Choices (A), (B), and (C) are listed by *cc:* which means they get copies of the order.

7. **(C)** *Establish a manufacturing operation near their customers* means *build factories close to their customers*. Choices (A) and (D) are areas that customers would like to be involved in. Choice (B) is contradicted by *cannot simply export more goods*.

8. **(B)** It says customers want *to provide input on design*. Choices (A) and (D), design consultants and engineers, would already have design input. Choice (C) is incorrect because suppliers probably do not want design input and are not mentioned.

9. **(C)** The purpose is to apologize. Choice (A) is contradicted by *we apologize* and *we regret*. Choice (B) is incorrect because the writer is *filling* an order. Choice (D) is not mentioned.

10. **(A)** *Were not included in the first shipment* means that *the shipment was incomplete*. Choices (B), (C), and (D) are possible shipping problems but are not mentioned.

11. **(C)** The fax was received *this morning*. Choices (A), (B), and (D) are all contradicted by *this morning*.

12. **(B)** She will *fax exact time of delivery*. Choices (A), (C), and (D) are contradicted by *by fax*.

13. **(C)** It says *at the end of the week, or at the very latest on Monday*. Choices (A), (B), and (D) are all contradicted by *on Monday*.

14. **(C)** A guest of the *engineering department* who has *done research on the effects of earthquakes* is probably a mechanical engineer. Choices (A), (B), and (D) are not logical.

15. **(A)** Mr. Wilson will be the Ukrainian's guide, since the memo is to him. Choice (B) is the visitor. Choice (C) is the person who wrote the memo. Choice (D) is contradicted by the memo.

16. **(A)** She will arrive before noon. Choices (B), (C), and (D) are contradicted by *before noon*.

17. **(A)** She is interested in designing bridges. Choices (B), (C), and (D) may be interesting but are not areas of interest within a field.

18. **(C)** Section B has other business news, so it is a likely place for market forecasts. Choices (A), (B), and (D) are not likely to be found there.

19. **(D)** Editorials contain opinions and are found on A-10. Choice (A) contains international news. Choice (B) contains commodities. Choice (C) has information on the arts.

20. **(C)** Films (movies) are found on C-3. Choice (A) is incorrect because B-11 contains information on stocks, not movies. Choice (B), page C-1, covers arts, but this choice is not as specific as Choice (C). Choice (D) is incorrect because a page covering legal issues would not contain reviews of movies.

21. **(C)** The payroll clerk reports to the Manager of Accounting. Choice (A) is not concerned with the payroll. Choices (B) and (D) do not supervise clerks.

22. **(C)** Marketing and Sales have similar staffing patterns. Choices (A), (B), and (D) do not have similar patterns.

23. **(A)** The VP of Sales supervises both the Domestic Sales Managers and International Sales Managers. Choice (B) is incorrect because the President supervises only Vice-Presidents. Choices (C) and (D) are incorrect because they are not in the Sales Department.

24. **(A)** It shows a comparison of dollar-yen rates. Choices (B), (C), and (D) are not depicted by the graph.

25. **(C)** There were fluctuations in April. Choices (A), (B), and (D) did not show such fluctuations.

26. **(B)** The contractor is located in San Francisco. Choice (A) is the location of the group that awarded the contract. Choices (C) and (D) are not logical locations for a contractor.

27. **(C)** A *three-month contract beginning in June* will end sometime in September. Choices (A), (B), and (D) are contradicted by this information.

28. **(A)** *Without notice* and *without obligation to notify* mean they can change things without telling the customer. Choices (B), (C), and (D) are not the subject of the notice.

29. **(B)** *In this manual* indicates where the information is found. Choice (A) contains information about repairs and service. Choices (C) and (D) are not logical given the subject of the notice.

30. **(B)** A *Swiss chemical company* would probably be located in Switzerland. Choice (A) is the country where Royal Chemical is located. Choices (C) and (D) are places where Royal Chemical has production plants, not the place where RADD is located.

31. **(D)** *Uses that range from rope fibers to bottles* means that polypropylene is used to make ropes, bottles, and other things. Choice (A) is also used for rope but is not mentioned. Choice (B) is used for string. Choice (C) is used for cable.

32. **(C)** The price is *between $100 million and $160 million.* Choices (A) and (B) are lower than the purchase price given. Choice (D) gives the price for only the RCI plants.

33. **(C)** *Of Britain* means *located in Britain.* Choices (A), (B), and (D) are the locations of production plants.

34. **(A)** It says the deal *would be paid in cash.* Choice (B) is not mentioned. Choices (C) and (D) are confused with *1 to 2 percent of its net assets.*

35. **(A)** The article mentions many different places where the entertainment industry is expanding. Choice (B) is incorrect because China is a *potential market*; it is not a huge market now. Choice (C) confuses the meanings of *home* (house) and *home* (base of operations). Choice (D) is incorrect because the status of opportunities in Hollywood is not mentioned.

36. **(C)** *Hollywood* is used to mean *the media.* Choices (A) and (B) are incorrect because many executives and American enterprises are not part of entertainment or media. Choice (D) is incorrect because other industries also have big markets worldwide.

37. **(D)** A schedule for a meeting is an *agenda.* Choice (A) is incorrect: An agenda shows people what to expect but cannot make them pay attention. Choice (B) is a benefit

of the agenda but not the purpose of it. Choice (C) is incorrect because an agenda does not introduce speakers.

38. **(C)** A question-and-answer period follows the presentations. Choice (A) comes before the presentations. Choice (B) comes after opening remarks. Choice (D) probably follows the close of the meeting but is not part of the meeting and is not mentioned.

39. **(B)** The items listed are stages in developing a product. Choice (A) is incorrect because the time is shown in months, not man-hours. Choices (C) and (D) are not represented by the timeline.

40. **(C)** If the proposal is submitted in February and they start work in March, the proposal will probably be approved in February. Choice (A) is incorrect because cost is not mentioned. Choice (B) is incorrect because marketing and testing are shown for the same amount of time. Choice (D) is not likely: Time is allowed for testing, so it should not slow down production.

41. **(C)** Joe's calendar shows that he has a dentist appointment at 11:30 on Wednesday. Choices (A), (B), and (D) are days that have no dentist appointment scheduled.

42. **(B)** Joe's calendar shows that he has a phone conference with the Toronto office on Thursday at 4:00. Choice (A) repeats *Toronto*. Choice (C) is what he will do on Friday afternoon. Choice (D) is what he will do on Monday morning.

43. **(B)** Alicia's meeting begins an hour before her scheduled 3:00 golf game. Choice (A) is when Joe's department meeting begins. Choice (C) is when the golf game is scheduled to begin. Choice (D) is when Alicia thinks the meeting will end.

44. **(C)** Alicia wants to play the day after their original Monday game. Choice (A) is not mentioned. Choice (B) is the day the game was originally scheduled for. Choice (D) is when Joe is scheduled to play golf with Fred.

45. **(A)** Joe is not free to meet Mr. Santos Wednesday morning, as Alicia suggested, because he has a department meeting and a dentist appointment. He is free for the meeting, however, on Thursday morning. Choice (B) is confused with the fact that he hasn't yet scheduled anything for Thursday morning, but after reading Alicia's e-mail, he will probably want to see Mr. Santos then. Choice (C) is what he will do Friday morning. Choice (D) is what he will do Saturday morning.

46. **(B)** The notice says that the work will begin *at the end of next month*. Choice (A) is confused with when employees should ask for a subway pass. Choice (C) is confused with the amount of time the work will last. Choice (D) is this month.

47. **(C)** Each office in the building will get four parking passes, and Parrot Communications has five times as many employees as that. Choice (A) is confused with the number of parking passes. Choice (B) is confused with *five times as many employees*. Choice (D) is confused with the size of the discount on the subway passes.

48. **(A)** The parking passes allow parking on the streets around the building, and Parrot Communications will reserve its parking passes for its clients. Choice (B) is incorrect because Parrot Communications employees will not be given passes. Choice (C) is incorrect because there are only four passes allowed per office. Choice (D) is incorrect because Dena Degenaro is a Parrot Communications employee, and as such will not get a parking pass.

49. **(B)** The memo was sent by the office manager and asks employees to *see me* to ask for a subway pass. Choice (A) is confused with the city's allotting certain parking spaces for building tenants. Choice (C) is confused with the people who posted the notice. Choice (D) is a logical place to get a subway pass but is not mentioned.

50. **(D)** The subway passes will be valid for the entire length of the garage reconstruction, which is three months. Choices (A), (B), and (C) are not mentioned.

CHAPTER 4

TOEIC Model Tests

WHAT TO LOOK FOR IN THIS CHAPTER

- Strategy Summary
- TOEIC Model Tests 1–4 with Answer Sheets
- Answer Keys
- Explanatory Answers
- Test Score Conversion Tables

STRATEGY SUMMARY

Tips and Strategies to help you score well on the TOEIC.

The following strategies are a review of those presented in this Listening Comprehension Review. Using these strategies will improve your score on the TOEIC.

LISTENING

Problems Analyzing Photographs

- When you look at the picture, analyze the people. Determine their number, gender, location, occupation, etc.
- Look for context clues in the photo.
- Listen for the meaning of the *whole sentence* to determine which choice best matches the photo.
- Try to analyze every detail in the photograph.
- Try to describe these details in English to yourself.
- Listen to all answers until you hear the obviously correct one. Once you are sure, don't listen to the rest of the answer options. Start analyzing the next photograph.
- If you aren't sure, keep your pencil on the most likely correct answer. If you listen to all options and have no other choice, mark that answer and move on quickly.

Problems Analyzing Answer Choices

- Listen and look for context clues.
- Listen and look for the *meaning* of the statement, question, and answer choices. Do not be confused by words with similar sounds, homonyms, and related words.
- Listen and look for sequence time markers, negative markers, and comparison markers.
- Pay attention to word order.
- Listen and look for modals and determine how the modal affects the meaning.
- Rephrase the question you hear. This will help you find the unique answer.

- Listen carefully to the entire question and ALL the answer choices before making a final decision.
- Rephrase the question as you hear it. This will help you find the unique answer.

Problems Analyzing Question Types

- Learn to recognize types of questions. Study the common questions and common answers presented in this chapter. Remember that questions about people generally begin with *who* or *what*, questions about location generally begin with *where*, questions about time generally begin with *when* or *how long*, etc.
- Read the answer choices, make assumptions about the items listed, and listen for relevant clues.

Problems Analyzing Language Functions

- Learn to recognize conditional clauses. Look for *if* and a modal.
- Look for suggestions, offer markers, and request markers in the question. Remember that when the answer is not in the statement, it may be in the question.

Strategies for Conversations and Talks

- Focus on the question. Read the three questions before you hear the talk. Don't read the answer choices. Try to listen carefully for the answer.
- As the conversations and talks start, write your potential answer choices in the exam book.
- Focusing on the details of the talk will also help you with inference and main idea questions.

READING COMPREHENSION
Analyzing vocabulary

- Read as much as you can in English.
- Keep a notebook of the words you learn.
- Learn words in context—not from word lists.

Analyzing grammar

- Recognize the parts of speech.
- Recognize agreement of person, number, and tense.
- Recognize the correct grammatical forms.
- Recognize the correct usage.
- Recognize the correct word order.
- Recognize potentially wrong answers.

Analyze reading passages

- Know the types of questions found on the TOEIC.
- Know the types of information sought on the TOEIC.
- Know how to use PSRA:
    Predict what the passage will be about.
    Scan the passage and answer options for key words.
    Read the passage quickly.
    Answer the questions.
      Use the PSRA whenever you read.

---

*Many thanks to my readers, especially Jean-Pierre Saint-Aimé, who have provided valuable tips on test-taking strategies.

Answer Sheet
MODEL TEST 1

Listening Comprehension

PART 1: PHOTOGRAPHS

1. Ⓐ Ⓑ Ⓒ Ⓓ
2. Ⓐ Ⓑ Ⓒ Ⓓ
3. Ⓐ Ⓑ Ⓒ Ⓓ
4. Ⓐ Ⓑ Ⓒ Ⓓ
5. Ⓐ Ⓑ Ⓒ Ⓓ
6. Ⓐ Ⓑ Ⓒ Ⓓ
7. Ⓐ Ⓑ Ⓒ Ⓓ
8. Ⓐ Ⓑ Ⓒ Ⓓ
9. Ⓐ Ⓑ Ⓒ Ⓓ
10. Ⓐ Ⓑ Ⓒ Ⓓ

PART 2: QUESTION-RESPONSE

11. Ⓐ Ⓑ Ⓒ
12. Ⓐ Ⓑ Ⓒ
13. Ⓐ Ⓑ Ⓒ
14. Ⓐ Ⓑ Ⓒ
15. Ⓐ Ⓑ Ⓒ
16. Ⓐ Ⓑ Ⓒ
17. Ⓐ Ⓑ Ⓒ
18. Ⓐ Ⓑ Ⓒ
19. Ⓐ Ⓑ Ⓒ
20. Ⓐ Ⓑ Ⓒ
21. Ⓐ Ⓑ Ⓒ
22. Ⓐ Ⓑ Ⓒ
23. Ⓐ Ⓑ Ⓒ
24. Ⓐ Ⓑ Ⓒ
25. Ⓐ Ⓑ Ⓒ
26. Ⓐ Ⓑ Ⓒ
27. Ⓐ Ⓑ Ⓒ
28. Ⓐ Ⓑ Ⓒ
29. Ⓐ Ⓑ Ⓒ
30. Ⓐ Ⓑ Ⓒ
31. Ⓐ Ⓑ Ⓒ
32. Ⓐ Ⓑ Ⓒ
33. Ⓐ Ⓑ Ⓒ
34. Ⓐ Ⓑ Ⓒ
35. Ⓐ Ⓑ Ⓒ
36. Ⓐ Ⓑ Ⓒ
37. Ⓐ Ⓑ Ⓒ
38. Ⓐ Ⓑ Ⓒ
39. Ⓐ Ⓑ Ⓒ
40. Ⓐ Ⓑ Ⓒ

PART 3: CONVERSATIONS

41. Ⓐ Ⓑ Ⓒ Ⓓ
42. Ⓐ Ⓑ Ⓒ Ⓓ
43. Ⓐ Ⓑ Ⓒ Ⓓ
44. Ⓐ Ⓑ Ⓒ Ⓓ
45. Ⓐ Ⓑ Ⓒ Ⓓ
46. Ⓐ Ⓑ Ⓒ Ⓓ
47. Ⓐ Ⓑ Ⓒ Ⓓ
48. Ⓐ Ⓑ Ⓒ Ⓓ
49. Ⓐ Ⓑ Ⓒ Ⓓ
50. Ⓐ Ⓑ Ⓒ Ⓓ
51. Ⓐ Ⓑ Ⓒ Ⓓ
52. Ⓐ Ⓑ Ⓒ Ⓓ
53. Ⓐ Ⓑ Ⓒ Ⓓ
54. Ⓐ Ⓑ Ⓒ Ⓓ
55. Ⓐ Ⓑ Ⓒ Ⓓ
56. Ⓐ Ⓑ Ⓒ Ⓓ
57. Ⓐ Ⓑ Ⓒ Ⓓ
58. Ⓐ Ⓑ Ⓒ Ⓓ
59. Ⓐ Ⓑ Ⓒ Ⓓ
60. Ⓐ Ⓑ Ⓒ Ⓓ
61. Ⓐ Ⓑ Ⓒ Ⓓ
62. Ⓐ Ⓑ Ⓒ Ⓓ
63. Ⓐ Ⓑ Ⓒ Ⓓ
64. Ⓐ Ⓑ Ⓒ Ⓓ
65. Ⓐ Ⓑ Ⓒ Ⓓ
66. Ⓐ Ⓑ Ⓒ Ⓓ
67. Ⓐ Ⓑ Ⓒ Ⓓ
68. Ⓐ Ⓑ Ⓒ Ⓓ
69. Ⓐ Ⓑ Ⓒ Ⓓ
70. Ⓐ Ⓑ Ⓒ Ⓓ

PART 4: TALKS

71. Ⓐ Ⓑ Ⓒ Ⓓ
72. Ⓐ Ⓑ Ⓒ Ⓓ
73. Ⓐ Ⓑ Ⓒ Ⓓ
74. Ⓐ Ⓑ Ⓒ Ⓓ
75. Ⓐ Ⓑ Ⓒ Ⓓ
76. Ⓐ Ⓑ Ⓒ Ⓓ
77. Ⓐ Ⓑ Ⓒ Ⓓ
78. Ⓐ Ⓑ Ⓒ Ⓓ
79. Ⓐ Ⓑ Ⓒ Ⓓ
80. Ⓐ Ⓑ Ⓒ Ⓓ
81. Ⓐ Ⓑ Ⓒ Ⓓ
82. Ⓐ Ⓑ Ⓒ Ⓓ
83. Ⓐ Ⓑ Ⓒ Ⓓ
84. Ⓐ Ⓑ Ⓒ Ⓓ
85. Ⓐ Ⓑ Ⓒ Ⓓ
86. Ⓐ Ⓑ Ⓒ Ⓓ
87. Ⓐ Ⓑ Ⓒ Ⓓ
88. Ⓐ Ⓑ Ⓒ Ⓓ
89. Ⓐ Ⓑ Ⓒ Ⓓ
90. Ⓐ Ⓑ Ⓒ Ⓓ
91. Ⓐ Ⓑ Ⓒ Ⓓ
92. Ⓐ Ⓑ Ⓒ Ⓓ
93. Ⓐ Ⓑ Ⓒ Ⓓ
94. Ⓐ Ⓑ Ⓒ Ⓓ
95. Ⓐ Ⓑ Ⓒ Ⓓ
96. Ⓐ Ⓑ Ⓒ Ⓓ
97. Ⓐ Ⓑ Ⓒ Ⓓ
98. Ⓐ Ⓑ Ⓒ Ⓓ
99. Ⓐ Ⓑ Ⓒ Ⓓ
100. Ⓐ Ⓑ Ⓒ Ⓓ

Reading

PART 5: INCOMPLETE SENTENCES

101. Ⓐ Ⓑ Ⓒ Ⓓ   111. Ⓐ Ⓑ Ⓒ Ⓓ   121. Ⓐ Ⓑ Ⓒ Ⓓ   131. Ⓐ Ⓑ Ⓒ Ⓓ
102. Ⓐ Ⓑ Ⓒ Ⓓ   112. Ⓐ Ⓑ Ⓒ Ⓓ   122. Ⓐ Ⓑ Ⓒ Ⓓ   132. Ⓐ Ⓑ Ⓒ Ⓓ
103. Ⓐ Ⓑ Ⓒ Ⓓ   113. Ⓐ Ⓑ Ⓒ Ⓓ   123. Ⓐ Ⓑ Ⓒ Ⓓ   133. Ⓐ Ⓑ Ⓒ Ⓓ
104. Ⓐ Ⓑ Ⓒ Ⓓ   114. Ⓐ Ⓑ Ⓒ Ⓓ   124. Ⓐ Ⓑ Ⓒ Ⓓ   134. Ⓐ Ⓑ Ⓒ Ⓓ
105. Ⓐ Ⓑ Ⓒ Ⓓ   115. Ⓐ Ⓑ Ⓒ Ⓓ   125. Ⓐ Ⓑ Ⓒ Ⓓ   135. Ⓐ Ⓑ Ⓒ Ⓓ
106. Ⓐ Ⓑ Ⓒ Ⓓ   116. Ⓐ Ⓑ Ⓒ Ⓓ   126. Ⓐ Ⓑ Ⓒ Ⓓ   136. Ⓐ Ⓑ Ⓒ Ⓓ
107. Ⓐ Ⓑ Ⓒ Ⓓ   117. Ⓐ Ⓑ Ⓒ Ⓓ   127. Ⓐ Ⓑ Ⓒ Ⓓ   137. Ⓐ Ⓑ Ⓒ Ⓓ
108. Ⓐ Ⓑ Ⓒ Ⓓ   118. Ⓐ Ⓑ Ⓒ Ⓓ   128. Ⓐ Ⓑ Ⓒ Ⓓ   138. Ⓐ Ⓑ Ⓒ Ⓓ
109. Ⓐ Ⓑ Ⓒ Ⓓ   119. Ⓐ Ⓑ Ⓒ Ⓓ   129. Ⓐ Ⓑ Ⓒ Ⓓ   139. Ⓐ Ⓑ Ⓒ Ⓓ
110. Ⓐ Ⓑ Ⓒ Ⓓ   120. Ⓐ Ⓑ Ⓒ Ⓓ   130. Ⓐ Ⓑ Ⓒ Ⓓ   140. Ⓐ Ⓑ Ⓒ Ⓓ

PART 6: TEXT COMPLETION

141. Ⓐ Ⓑ Ⓒ Ⓓ   144. Ⓐ Ⓑ Ⓒ Ⓓ   147. Ⓐ Ⓑ Ⓒ Ⓓ   150. Ⓐ Ⓑ Ⓒ Ⓓ
142. Ⓐ Ⓑ Ⓒ Ⓓ   145. Ⓐ Ⓑ Ⓒ Ⓓ   148. Ⓐ Ⓑ Ⓒ Ⓓ   151. Ⓐ Ⓑ Ⓒ Ⓓ
143. Ⓐ Ⓑ Ⓒ Ⓓ   146. Ⓐ Ⓑ Ⓒ Ⓓ   149. Ⓐ Ⓑ Ⓒ Ⓓ   152. Ⓐ Ⓑ Ⓒ Ⓓ

PART 7: READING COMPREHENSION

153. Ⓐ Ⓑ Ⓒ Ⓓ   165. Ⓐ Ⓑ Ⓒ Ⓓ   177. Ⓐ Ⓑ Ⓒ Ⓓ   189. Ⓐ Ⓑ Ⓒ Ⓓ
154. Ⓐ Ⓑ Ⓒ Ⓓ   166. Ⓐ Ⓑ Ⓒ Ⓓ   178. Ⓐ Ⓑ Ⓒ Ⓓ   190. Ⓐ Ⓑ Ⓒ Ⓓ
155. Ⓐ Ⓑ Ⓒ Ⓓ   167. Ⓐ Ⓑ Ⓒ Ⓓ   179. Ⓐ Ⓑ Ⓒ Ⓓ   191. Ⓐ Ⓑ Ⓒ Ⓓ
156. Ⓐ Ⓑ Ⓒ Ⓓ   168. Ⓐ Ⓑ Ⓒ Ⓓ   180. Ⓐ Ⓑ Ⓒ Ⓓ   192. Ⓐ Ⓑ Ⓒ Ⓓ
157. Ⓐ Ⓑ Ⓒ Ⓓ   169. Ⓐ Ⓑ Ⓒ Ⓓ   181. Ⓐ Ⓑ Ⓒ Ⓓ   193. Ⓐ Ⓑ Ⓒ Ⓓ
158. Ⓐ Ⓑ Ⓒ Ⓓ   170. Ⓐ Ⓑ Ⓒ Ⓓ   182. Ⓐ Ⓑ Ⓒ Ⓓ   194. Ⓐ Ⓑ Ⓒ Ⓓ
159. Ⓐ Ⓑ Ⓒ Ⓓ   171. Ⓐ Ⓑ Ⓒ Ⓓ   183. Ⓐ Ⓑ Ⓒ Ⓓ   195. Ⓐ Ⓑ Ⓒ Ⓓ
160. Ⓐ Ⓑ Ⓒ Ⓓ   172. Ⓐ Ⓑ Ⓒ Ⓓ   184. Ⓐ Ⓑ Ⓒ Ⓓ   196. Ⓐ Ⓑ Ⓒ Ⓓ
161. Ⓐ Ⓑ Ⓒ Ⓓ   173. Ⓐ Ⓑ Ⓒ Ⓓ   185. Ⓐ Ⓑ Ⓒ Ⓓ   197. Ⓐ Ⓑ Ⓒ Ⓓ
162. Ⓐ Ⓑ Ⓒ Ⓓ   174. Ⓐ Ⓑ Ⓒ Ⓓ   186. Ⓐ Ⓑ Ⓒ Ⓓ   198. Ⓐ Ⓑ Ⓒ Ⓓ
163. Ⓐ Ⓑ Ⓒ Ⓓ   175. Ⓐ Ⓑ Ⓒ Ⓓ   187. Ⓐ Ⓑ Ⓒ Ⓓ   199. Ⓐ Ⓑ Ⓒ Ⓓ
164. Ⓐ Ⓑ Ⓒ Ⓓ   176. Ⓐ Ⓑ Ⓒ Ⓓ   188. Ⓐ Ⓑ Ⓒ Ⓓ   200. Ⓐ Ⓑ Ⓒ Ⓓ

Model Test 1
Listening Comprehension

In this section of the test, you will have the chance to show how well you understand spoken English. There are four parts to this section, with special directions for each part. You will have approximately 45 minutes to complete the Listening Comprehension sections.

Part 1: Photographs

Directions: You will see a photograph. You will hear four statements about the photograph. Choose the statement that most closely matches the photograph and fill in the corresponding oval on your answer sheet.

1.

2.

Model Test 1

3.

4.

Model Test 1

5.

6.

7.

8.

Model Test 1

9.

10.

Part 2: Question-Response

Directions: You will hear a question and three possible responses. Choose the response that most closely answers the question and fill in the corresponding oval on your answer sheet.

11. Mark your answer on your answer sheet.

12. Mark your answer on your answer sheet.

13. Mark your answer on your answer sheet.

14. Mark your answer on your answer sheet.

15. Mark your answer on your answer sheet.

16. Mark your answer on your answer sheet.

17. Mark your answer on your answer sheet.

18. Mark your answer on your answer sheet.

19. Mark your answer on your answer sheet.

20. Mark your answer on your answer sheet.

21. Mark your answer on your answer sheet.

22. Mark your answer on your answer sheet.

23. Mark your answer on your answer sheet.

24. Mark your answer on your answer sheet.

25. Mark your answer on your answer sheet.

26. Mark your answer on your answer sheet.

27. Mark your answer on your answer sheet.

28. Mark your answer on your answer sheet.

29. Mark your answer on your answer sheet.

30. Mark your answer on your answer sheet.

31. Mark your answer on your answer sheet.

32. Mark your answer on your answer sheet.

33. Mark your answer on your answer sheet.

34. Mark your answer on your answer sheet.

35. Mark your answer on your answer sheet.

36. Mark your answer on your answer sheet.

37. Mark your answer on your answer sheet.

38. Mark your answer on your answer sheet.

39. Mark your answer on your answer sheet.

40. Mark your answer on your answer sheet.

Model Test 1

Part 3: Conversations

Directions: You will hear a conversation between two people. You will see three questions on each conversation and four possible answers. Choose the best answer to each question and fill in the corresponding oval on your answer sheet.

(CD 3 Track 3)

41. When will the speakers meet?

    (A) 3:00
    (B) 4:00
    (C) 5:00
    (D) 10:00

42. Where will they meet?

    (A) At the bus stop
    (B) At a conference
    (C) In the man's office
    (D) In the waiting room

43. What will the woman bring to the meeting?

    (A) Coffee
    (B) A letter
    (C) Photographs
    (D) Copies of a report

44. Where does the man want to go?

    (A) Cleveland
    (B) Los Angeles
    (C) Chicago
    (D) Denver

45. How will he travel?

    (A) By plane
    (B) By train
    (C) By bus
    (D) By car

46. When will he leave?

    (A) This afternoon
    (B) Tonight
    (C) Tomorrow at 1:00
    (D) Tomorrow at 10:00

47. Where does this conversation take place?

    (A) At a store
    (B) At a hotel
    (C) At a restaurant
    (D) At the man's house

48. What does the man ask for?

    (A) Keys
    (B) More soup
    (C) A better room
    (D) Towels and soap

49. When will he get what he asks for?

    (A) Right away
    (B) Later today
    (C) At 2:00
    (D) Tonight

50. When did the brochures arrive?

    (A) Yesterday afternoon
    (B) Last night
    (C) This morning
    (D) This afternoon

51. What will the woman do now?

    (A) Address the brochures
    (B) Read the brochures
    (C) Print the brochures
    (D) Copy the brochures

52. How many brochures does the woman need?

    (A) 500
    (B) 800
    (C) 1,000
    (D) 2,000

53. What kind of job is the man applying for?

    (A) Waiter
    (B) Caterer
    (C) Advertising executive
    (D) Food and beverage salesperson

54. What does the woman ask the man about?

    (A) His experience
    (B) His appearance
    (C) His attitude
    (D) His appetite

55. When does the woman want to interview the man?

    (A) Today
    (B) Next Sunday
    (C) Next Monday
    (D) Next Tuesday

56. Why can't the man play golf tomorrow?

    (A) His wife is sick.
    (B) It's going to rain.
    (C) He has to take a test.
    (D) He's feeling tired.

57. What time did he plan to play golf?

    (A) 2:00
    (B) 4:00
    (C) 9:00
    (D) 10:00

58. What will he do tomorrow?

    (A) Talk on the phone
    (B) Go to the movies
    (C) Move some furniture
    (D) Stay home

59. Where does the woman want to go?

    (A) To a fast food restaurant
    (B) To a parking lot
    (C) To a bank
    (D) To a park

60. Where is it?

    (A) On a corner
    (B) Behind a parking lot
    (C) Next door to a library
    (D) Across the street from a store

61. How long will it take her to get there?

    (A) Two minutes
    (B) Four minutes
    (C) Five minutes
    (D) Nine minutes

62. What time is it in the conversation?

    (A) 8:00
    (B) 8:15
    (C) 9:15
    (D) 9:30

63. Why is the woman angry?

    (A) The man is late.
    (B) The weather is bad.
    (C) She had to take the bus.
    (D) The man drives too fast.

64. What will the man do next time?

    (A) Stay home
    (B) Drive his car
    (C) Leave earlier
    (D) Take the train

65. What will the woman do?

(A) Take a plane trip
(B) Take a class
(C) Go to the theater
(D) Eat dinner at a restaurant

66. When will she do it?

(A) Sunday afternoon
(B) Sunday night
(C) Monday afternoon
(D) Monday night

67. How will she pay for it?

(A) Cash
(B) Check
(C) Credit card
(D) Money order

68. When does this conversation take place?

(A) In the morning
(B) At noon
(C) In the early afternoon
(D) In the evening

69. Who is the woman talking to?

(A) A butcher
(B) A waiter
(C) Her husband
(D) Her friend

70. What does the woman order?

(A) Lamb
(B) Rice
(C) Fish
(D) Vegetables

Part 4: Talks

Directions: You will hear a talk given by a single speaker. You will see three questions on each talk, each with four possible answers. Choose the best answer to each question and fill in the corresponding oval on your answer sheet.

71. Where is this train located?

   (A) In an airport
   (B) In a city
   (C) Along the coast
   (D) At an amusement park

72. Where should you stand when in a train car?

   (A) By the doors
   (B) By the windows
   (C) In the center
   (D) At either end

73. When can passengers get off the train?

   (A) When they see an exit sign
   (B) Before the bell rings
   (C) After the bell rings
   (D) After the colored light goes on

74. When on Sundays is the museum open?

   (A) In the morning
   (B) In the afternoon
   (C) In the evening
   (D) All day

75. If you would like information about lectures, what should you do?

   (A) Go to the museum
   (B) Write a letter
   (C) Call another number
   (D) Stay on the line

76. Who doesn't have to pay to enter the museum?

   (A) Members
   (B) Adults
   (C) Children under twelve
   (D) Children under five

77. What is the first step in getting organized?

   (A) Set a timeline
   (B) Get clutter out of your life
   (C) Buy a calendar
   (D) Make a list of things to be done

78. What should you do next?

   (A) Rank the tasks by their importance
   (B) Do a little work on every task
   (C) Start working on the first task
   (D) Eliminate items and rewrite the list

79. What is the last task of the day?

   (A) Review the list
   (B) Finish uncompleted tasks
   (C) Write a new list
   (D) Throw the list away

80. What does the advertisement encourage you to do?

   (A) Take a holiday
   (B) Redecorate your office
   (C) Look at your office again
   (D) Save some money

81. Which items does the ad mention?

   (A) Decorations
   (B) Carpeting
   (C) Wallpaper
   (D) Furniture

82. When is the last day of the sale?

   (A) Sunday
   (B) Monday
   (C) Tuesday
   (D) Wednesday

83. What is this announcement for?

    (A) Schoolteachers
    (B) Schoolchildren
    (C) Volunteer tutors
    (D) Businesspeople

84. How much time does it take to participate?

    (A) A minimum of 2 hours a week
    (B) A maximum of 2 hours a week
    (C) One week a year
    (D) One day a week

85. What must people have to participate?

    (A) A college degree
    (B) Special training
    (C) Age above eighteen
    (D) Experience with children

86. What is the approximate temperature for today?

    (A) About 15 degrees
    (B) About 60 degrees
    (C) About 65 degrees
    (D) About 90 degrees

87. What does the weather forecaster suggest that people do?

    (A) Stay inside
    (B) Go outdoors
    (C) Take sunglasses
    (D) Wear a sweater

88. What will the weather be like tomorrow?

    (A) Cloudy
    (B) Foggy
    (C) Rainy
    (D) Sunny

89. What is included in the cost of the lodge?

    (A) Breakfast and dinner
    (B) Ski equipment
    (C) Ski lift tickets
    (D) Lunch on the ski slopes

90. Who can take ski lessons?

    (A) Ski instructors
    (B) Skiers with special abilities
    (C) Beginners only
    (D) Skiers of all skill levels

91. What do you get if you make a reservation before January 15th?

    (A) A free book
    (B) A calendar
    (C) An extra night at the hotel
    (D) A free ski class

92. How long are the delays?

    (A) 5 minutes
    (B) 15 minutes
    (C) 45 minutes
    (D) 4 hours

93. What is causing the delays?

    (A) Weather
    (B) Engine trouble
    (C) Power problems
    (D) Damage to the tracks

94. What are they doing to help people commute quickly?

    (A) Providing bus service
    (B) Asking commuters to wait
    (C) Trying to fix the trains
    (D) Using extra trains

95. What happened at Central and Main?

    (A) An explosion
    (B) An infection
    (C) An exception
    (D) An irritation

96. What was probably the cause of the problem?

    (A) An electric wire
    (B) A water pipe
    (C) A hole in the street
    (D) A gas leak

97. What happened to nearby office workers?

    (A) They were injured.
    (B) They were removed.
    (C) They were reported.
    (D) They were suspected.

98. Who will listen to this announcement?

    (A) Students
    (B) Art professors
    (C) Museum employees
    (D) Members of a tour group

99. What should people bring on the trip?

    (A) Books
    (B) Money
    (C) Lunch
    (D) Cameras

100. What time should they arrive for the morning bus?

    (A) 8:00
    (B) 8:45
    (C) 9:00
    (D) 9:15

STOP

This is the end of the Listening Comprehension portion of the test. Turn to Part 5 in your test book.

Reading

In this section of the test, you will have the chance to show how well you understand written English. There are three parts to this section, with special directions for each part.

YOU WILL HAVE ONE HOUR AND FIFTEEN MINUTES TO COMPLETE PARTS 5, 6, AND 7 OF THE TEST.

Part 5: Incomplete Sentences

Directions: You will see a sentence with a missing word. Four possible answers follow the sentence. Choose the best answer to the question and fill in the corresponding oval on your answer sheet.

101. If the customer _____ not satisfied, please have him call the manager.

    (A) am
    (B) is
    (C) are
    (D) be

102. Our goal is to turn _____ into success.

    (A) failing
    (B) fail
    (C) failed
    (D) failure

103. The plane will be landing _____ Chicago in twenty minutes.

    (A) with
    (B) into
    (C) in
    (D) for

104. The seminar was canceled because the invitations were not _____ in time.

    (A) printer
    (B) printed
    (C) printing
    (D) print

105. If the waiter cannot handle your request, the captain _____ assist you.

    (A) will
    (B) has
    (C) did
    (D) is

106. We depend on Mr. Wong for his knowledge and _____.

    (A) leading
    (B) lead
    (C) leadership
    (D) leader

107. Ms. Guida expects costs to _____ 5 percent this year.

    (A) ascend
    (B) increase
    (C) escalate
    (D) raise

108. _____ is the key to efficiency.

    (A) Organized
    (B) Organize
    (C) Organizer
    (D) Organization

109. The meeting is postponed _____ Mr. Tan's plane was late.

    (A) although
    (B) while
    (C) because
    (D) with

110. The training session has been changed from 8:30 _____ 9:00.

    (A) at
    (B) to
    (C) in
    (D) by

111. The head of sales _____ to San Diego for the annual sales convention.

    (A) went
    (B) gone
    (C) go
    (D) going

112. Because Ms. Kimura has a long _____, she will always leave work at 5:30.

    (A) commute
    (B) commune
    (C) community
    (D) compost

113. The fax machine is _____ the postage meter and the copy machine.

    (A) among
    (B) outside
    (C) between
    (D) through

114. Mr. Maxwell will interview _____ applicants from 9:00 until 11:00 today.

    (A) job
    (B) occupation
    (C) chore
    (D) positioning

115. When you need supplies, _____ a request with the office manager.

    (A) filling
    (B) fell
    (C) fallen
    (D) file

116. All cabin attendants must lock the cabin door _____ leaving the room.

    (A) afterwards
    (B) after
    (C) later than
    (D) late

117. _____ it was Mr. Guiton's birthday, his staff took him to lunch.

    (A) Although
    (B) During
    (C) Because
    (D) That

118. Hotel employees are _____ to knock before entering the rooms.

    (A) requited
    (B) required
    (C) requisite
    (D) repulsed

119. The billing clerk was not able to find the invoice _____ the order.

    (A) or
    (B) and
    (C) but
    (D) though

120. This product _____ our most popular item.

    (A) always has considered been
    (B) has been always considered
    (C) has been considered always
    (D) has always been considered

121. Is the annual report _____ yet?

    (A) avail
    (B) available
    (C) availability
    (D) availing

122. The bell captain suggested that more porters _____ hired.

    (A) are
    (B) have
    (C) be
    (D) do

123. The office requires that all employees park in their _____ spaces.

    (A) signed
    (B) assignment
    (C) assigned
    (D) significant

124. These addresses should be listed in _____ order.

    (A) alphabet
    (B) alphabetize
    (C) alphabetically
    (D) alphabetical

125. The purchasing department is located _____ the reception desk.

    (A) across
    (B) between
    (C) behind
    (D) from

126. The guard must _____ your identification at the gate.

    (A) checked
    (B) checking
    (C) checks
    (D) check

127. Employees dislike tasks that are _____.

    (A) repeat
    (B) repetitive
    (C) repetition
    (D) repetitively

128. Visitors are reminded _____ name tags at all times.

    (A) to wear
    (B) wear
    (C) be worn
    (D) is wearing

129. At the end of the year, the company puts _____ a picnic for the employees.

    (A) for
    (B) by
    (C) up
    (D) on

130. Clients are _____ allowed to see the research department.

    (A) rare
    (B) ever
    (C) never
    (D) no time

131. If we had started earlier, we _____ the deadline.

    (A) would meet
    (B) would have met
    (C) will meet
    (D) will have met ·

132. Mr. Nolde called to cancel his _____.

    (A) notebook
    (B) calendar
    (C) appointment
    (D) notice

133. If Ms. Kamano leaves at 2:00, she
_____ at the station on time.

    (A) would have arrived
    (B) will arrive
    (C) arrived
    (D) would arrive

134. A letter for Mr. Carn was left _____ Mr.
Britto's desk.

    (A) through
    (B) on
    (C) out
    (D) up

135. The last train to Hamburg _____ at
10:30.

    (A) depart
    (B) departs
    (C) to depart
    (D) departing

136. _____ the meeting, Ms. Tran missed
several important phone calls.

    (A) Although
    (B) In spite of
    (C) Because
    (D) During

137. Because his finger was broken, the secretary could not type _____.

    (A) efficiently
    (B) intermittently
    (C) slowly
    (D) gradually

138. The CD-player was damaged when it
_____.

    (A) was delivered
    (B) has delivered
    (C) was delivering
    (D) had delivered

139. Mr. Hatori was very _____ when he got
a promotion.

    (A) excite
    (B) exciting
    (C) excited
    (D) excites

140. The restaurant is open on weekends,
_____ not on holidays.

    (A) either
    (B) or
    (C) so
    (D) but

Part 6: Text Completion

Directions: You will see four passages each with three blanks. Under each blank are four answer options. Choose the word or phrase that best completes the sentence.

Questions 141–143 refer to the following notice.

International Airport Policy Regarding Security and Baggage

In accordance with international security regulations, the following items are never allowed to be taken onto a plane by passengers, either in their carry-on bags _____ in their checked luggage: Weapons, including

141. (A) or
  (B) nor
  (C) but
  (D) then

knives and guns; explosives, including dynamite and fireworks.

The following items may be placed in checked luggage but not in carry-on bags: Tools, including hammers, screwdrivers, and wrenches; sports equipment _____ golf clubs, baseball bats, and skis and ski poles.

142. (A) so
  (B) such as
  (C) example
  (D) instance

When you pass through the _____ line, all bags will go through our

143. (A) ticket
  (B) arrival
  (C) security
  (D) reservations

X-ray machines and some bags will be manually checked by personnel, as well. Thank you for your cooperation. Have a safe and pleasant flight.

Questions 144–146 refer to the following magazine article.

This holiday season, computer retailers hope to increase _____ of

144. (A) sales
(B) repairs
(C) types
(D) prices

notebook PCs (personal computers). A heavy advertising campaign began this week, with several computer manufacturers placing ads on TV, radio, newspapers, and the Internet. The advertising campaign will continue through the holiday season.

Notebook PCs are gaining popularity because of their _____.

145. (A) fame
(B) quantity
(C) appearance
(D) convenience

They are lighter and smaller than laptops and much easier to carry around. Although laptop and notebook computers are more expensive than desktop computers, more and more people are buying them. They are filling a growing need for mobility.

The trend toward giving electronic items as holiday gifts is also growing. The old-fashioned approach to holiday celebrations is giving way to the _____ for new technology.

146. (A) enthusiast
(B) enthusiasm
(C) enthusiastic
(D) enthusiastically

Questions 147–149 refer to the following fax.

FAX COVER SHEET

Parameters Technology Company
4874 Ansari Road
New Delhi 110002
India

Tel: 2 616 5901
Fax: 2 616 5902

To: Marguerite Michelson
From: Ambar Patel
Date: September 22, 20—
Pages: 3 (this + 2)
Ref: Money due

Message:

I'm writing to inquire about money due. We _____ about payment

        147. (A) is concerned
             (B) are concerned
             (C) had concerned
             (D) have concerned

on your last order. It was due in July. Could you please explain the delay?
I have left several phone messages over the past few weeks, but they have
not been answered. Your company has always been prompt in paying our
bills, and we would like to continue to maintain a good relationship with you.
However, this is an unusually long delay, and if we don't hear from you
soon, we _____ to take action. Please contact me by fax or phone

    148. (A) will have
         (B) have had
         (C) would have
         (D) going to have

as soon as possible with an explanation and the date when we will receive
the overdue payment. The details of your _____, including items

        149. (A) form
             (B) credit
             (C) order
             (D) rebate

and prices, are available on the following two pages.

Questions 150–152 refer to the following letter.

April 1, 20—

Richard Byron
Acme Supply Company
324 Constitution Avenue
Annandale, MD

Dear Mr. Byron,
I am writing in _____ to your ad in last Sunday's newspaper about

150. (A) response
    (B) repose
    (C) resort
    (D) respite

the position of office manager. I have worked as an administrative assistant at several local companies for the past ten years. I thoroughly understand the operations of an office and feel that my years of experience _____ me to work as an office manager. I have taken several

151. (A) qualify
    (B) qualifies
    (C) is qualifying
    (D) has qualified

computer courses and am familiar with most current office technology. In addition, I have good organization and people skills, and my employers have always considered me to be a responsible and reliable worker. I am enclosing my resume and two letters of reference. I look forward _____ hearing from you.

152. (A) at
    (B) of
    (C) to
    (D) on

Sincerely,

Andrew Devon

Andrew Devon

Part 7: Reading Comprehension

Directions: You will see single and double reading passages followed by several questions. Each question has four answer choices. Choose the best answer to the question and fill in the corresponding oval on your answer sheet.

Questions 153–157 refer to the following newspaper article.

Job trends for the future emphasize careers in sales and marketing. Most of the growth will come in international sales, high technology, and electronic marketing. Research shows that overseas sales of high tech equipment and technology will increase 20% in the next decade.

The Internet is the primary source for advertising and marketing to these overseas customers. At the same time, however, successful marketers must find new avenues to increase consumer awareness of their products. As some clients become inundated by information on the Internet, and as others are still just learning to navigate the Web, the marketers of the future will have to be inventive.

More traditional sales skills, such as bilingualism and an agreeable character, are still useful. Willingness to travel is also a plus.

153. What kinds of careers show promise for the future?

(A) Research and development
(B) Sales and marketing
(C) High technology
(D) Travel agents

154. Why are these careers increasing in importance?

(A) Companies are trying to focus on profits.
(B) They address a neglected market segment.
(C) High-tech sales are growing.
(D) Most marketing will occur on the Internet.

155. The word *avenues* in paragraph 2, line 5, is closest in meaning to

(A) streets
(B) ways
(C) stores
(D) sales

156. The author believes that the successful marketer must be

(A) bilingual
(B) overseas
(C) abreast of research
(D) creative

157. According to the article, why isn't Internet advertising always effective?

(A) Some users see too much of it; some see too little.
(B) Many users have limited English skills.
(C) Access to the web may be limited.
(D) Consumers are unaware of products advertised on the Internet.

First News
A l w a y s   I n n o v a t i v e   &   I n f o r m a t i v e

Questions 158–159 refer to the following announcement.

We are announcing today that we are bringing the Milestone and Ever Green brands even closer together. Effective December 5, 20—, our official name will be:

GREEN MILES WEST

The substitution of "West" in our name—replacing "California"—is the result of an agreement we reached with the California Gardening Association, following a protest over the original use of "California" in our name.

We hope this does not create any confusion among our loyal consumers. While this represents a change from our initial name introduction, it does not change the quality of products we offer our customers.

158. What was the original name of the merged companies?

(A) Milestone
(B) Green Miles California
(C) Green Miles West
(D) Milestone California

159. According to the announcement, why was the name changed?

(A) The corporate offices were relocated.
(B) There was a conflict with another organization.
(C) They did not like the initial choice.
(D) Loyal consumers were confused.

Questions 160–163 refer to the following magazine article.

Hotels are changing their wasteful habits and getting involved in the move to save the environment. At major hotels throughout the world, guests are being greeted by shampoo and mouthwash in glass dispensers instead of elaborate plastic bottles. They are discovering recycling bins in their rooms, and are encouraged to use towels more than once before they are washed.

This green movement is becoming increasingly popular among tourists who look for service providers with an environmental conscience. The business of eco-tours is increasing rapidly. Travel agents are booking clients on "Save the Rainforest" expeditions and similar trips where the emphasis is on protecting the world.

The tourists on these trips are given lectures on the effects of the loss of our planet's natural wonders and what they can do to reverse the trend. They do not need much convincing. The travelers on these excursions are already committed to environmental protection. In fact, a two-year study of litter in Antarctica found that the entire collection of litter left by visitors to the continent could be put in one small sandwich bag. Compare that amount of litter with what the average traveler finds strewn on the streets around a hotel, even an environmentally sensitive hotel.

160. What trend is currently affecting hotels and their guests?

(A) Larger rooms
(B) Better amenities
(C) Lighter foods
(D) Protecting the earth

161. What does the article imply about glass dispensers and re-using towels?

(A) It's a marketing gimmick.
(B) It's only effective on eco-tours.
(C) It's a wise choice environmentally.
(D) Hotels can set consumer trends.

162. Which group would most likely be members of the green movement?

(A) Fashion designers
(B) First-time visitors
(C) Environmentally conscious travelers
(D) Golf course owners

163. According to the article, eco-travelers should expect

(A) to find litter.
(B) to hear lectures on the environment.
(C) to pay more than other travelers.
(D) to carry their own food.

Questions 164–166 refer to the following press release.

V AL D' O R CATERING S UPPLY
Von-Gablenz Straße 3-7
D-50679 Köln
Germany
Telephone: (02 21) 8.25 22 00
Telefax (02 21) 8 25 22 06

FOR IMMEDIATE RELEASE

<u>By fax</u>

To: All Business Editors
Fm: Johann Heger
        Public Relations Officer

Val D'Or is pleased to announce its purchase of
Gourmet Galore, a company that specializes in
specialty food products, cookware, and kitchen
accessories. Gourmet Galore has profited from
customers' revived interest in cooking. There are
plans to expand and open five more stores across
Europe. Ten of their sixteen stores were
remodeled last year, and similar plans are being
made for the remaining six.

The company will also open a new line of cooking
schools focusing on healthful foods. Regional
specialties will be included and guest cooks from
all over Europe will participate in the one-week
classes.

Please call us for more information.

---

164. What sort of products does Gourmet
Galore sell?

    (A) Fabric and furniture
    (B) Food and cooking supplies
    (C) Washing machines and dryers
    (D) Clothes and shoes

165. What plans does Val D'Or have for six
Gourmet Galore stores?

    (A) Remodel them
    (B) Buy them
    (C) Sell them
    (D) Relocate them

166. What will be emphasized in the cooking
classes?

    (A) Healthful regional foods
    (B) Recipes from one region
    (C) New cooking techniques
    (D) Using the latest equipment

Questions 167–168 refer to the following notice.

The company provides a benefit pension plan covering all employees. Benefits are based on years of service and on the employee's highest salary. Both the company and the employee make contributions to the plan according to government regulations. Employees eligible to receive pension funds are paid monthly through the plan.

---

167. What determines the benefits?

   (A) Years at the company and salary
   (B) Bonuses
   (C) Starting wage
   (D) Company profits

168. Who determines the rules of contribution?

   (A) Managers of the benefit pension plan
   (B) Anyone who is eligible to receive funds
   (C) The company and the employee
   (D) The government

Questions 169–171 refer to the following letter.

Dear Member,

The goal of Regents is to be the premier name in health care.

Since merging Royal Medical Green Shield and Jason County Medical Bureau in April, we have been working with our customers and business partners to provide more innovative health benefit plans and services, wider provider networks, and enhanced access to health care coverage.

We've been pleased to receive your suggestions for these service improvements, and we look forward to receiving your further thoughts or suggestions. Our suggestion line is open 24 hours a day at 800-998-3445.

We appreciate your patronage.

Sincerely,

Rick Nelson

Rick Nelson
President

169. What is the purpose of this note?

    (A) To explain a merger
    (B) To talk about Regents' plans
    (C) To give a new toll-free number
    (D) To describe expanded health coverage

170. What is one goal of Regents?

    (A) To increase availability of health care
    (B) To publish a primer for new members
    (C) To reduce costs to members
    (D) To work with customers and business partners

171. What does Regents request of members?

    (A) To inform new potential clients of its innovations
    (B) To plan for health over the long term
    (C) To learn about services on the Internet
    (D) To submit ideas to the company

Questions 172–173 refer to the following invoice.

Cooper & Allen, Architects   April 5, 20__
149 Bridge Street, Suite 107   INVOICE NUMBER 3892
Harrisville, Colorado 76521   PROJECT NAME   Headquarters—Final Design
                                          PROJECT NUMBER 925639

The Williams Corporation
5110 Falls Avenue
Thomaston, Colorado 76520

The following amounts for the period ending March 30 are due the end of
this month.

                              Current period fees____ $8,200.00
                              Unpaid prior balance____ $362.00
                              Total due at this time $8,562.00

We value the opportunity to service you. Your prompt payment is greatly
appreciated.

---

172. When is the payment due?

    (A) March 1
    (B) March 30
    (C) April 5
    (D) April 30

173. What is owed in addition to current fees?

    (A) Prepayment on the next project
    (B) Taxes on the current fees
    (C) Service charges on current fees
    (D) Money not paid on a previous invoice

Questions 174–176 refer to the following memo.

FCC
FISCHER COMMUNICATIONS COMPANY

Interoffice Memorandum

To: All Department Supervisors
Fm: J. Reinhardt
    Personnel Officer

Sub: Summary of 3/24 training session on improving job performance.

Date: April 1, 20__

Employees work best if they are happy. As a supervisor, there are things you can do to increase employees' job satisfaction. Make sure your employees understand what they have to do. Give them proper and thorough training so they can do it well, and give them opportunities to bring that training up to date. Make sure that employees have freedom to exercise their own judgment, to offer their suggestions, and to point out problems. Most of all, make sure that you tell them they are doing a good job, not only during special assignments but when they maintain a high standard of routine work.

174. When do employees do their best work?

(A) When they are challenged
(B) When they are happy
(C) When they are busy
(D) When they are pressured

175. Once you have trained an employee, what should you do?

(A) Provide ways to update training
(B) Make the employee train others
(C) Move the employee to a different job
(D) Control his or her chance to practice

176. What is NOT mentioned as a freedom employees should have?

(A) Exercise their own judgment
(B) Offer suggestions
(C) Make changes
(D) Point out problems

Questions 177–181 refer to the following contract and addendum.

Contract #991YL
Hospitality Consultants Inc.

Hospitality Consultants Inc (hereafter referred to as Contractor) agrees
to perform the following duties as outlined by Cracker Barrel Winery (hereafter called the Client):

A. Statistics Analysis
1) Review the Client's wine sales over the past five years, using monthly
   inventory charts.
2) Review the Client's food and gift sales over the past five years.
3) Record a summary and chart for proposed sales this year, based on a
   five-year review.

B. Staff Review
1) Interview one staff member from each department, including the
   vineyards and cellar.
2) Record duties and responsibilities for each job position.
3) Suggest ways for the Client to cut staffing costs.

C. Decor
1) Meet with board members to discuss year-end renovations.
2) Research materials and costs for all indoor renovations.
3) Provide an estimate for indoor renovations by October 1st.

Any changes to this contract must be agreed upon by both parties in
writing.

Contractor: *Hanson Carter*

Client: *Julia Morris*

Date: August 7th, 20—

---

177. What type of service does this Contractor
     agree to provide?

     (A) Labor assistance in the vineyards
     (B) Consulting related to the winery's
         operations
     (C) Inventory on glassware and dishes
     (D) Taste tests of competitors' wines

178. Which is NOT an example of a person
     the Contractor may need to speak with to
     fulfill his duties?

     (A) A medical professional
     (B) A wine seller
     (C) A board member
     (D) A part-time grape picker

179. Besides one duty that must be performed
     in December, how long did the
     Contractor work for the Client?

     (A) Less than two months
     (B) Just over two months
     (C) At least three months
     (D) Just over four months

First News
Always Innovative & Informative

Addendum to Contract #991YL dated August 7, 20—
between the following parties:

Contractor: **Hospitality Consultants Inc.**

Client: **Cracker Barrel Winery**

The Contractor initiates the following addendum:

1) Due to unforeseen circumstances the Contractor will be unable to
provide services to Cracker Barrel Winery after October 9th, 20—.
The Contractor does not expect any payment for any project work
that is left incomplete as of today.

2) Before December 1st, 20— the Contractor will provide the Client with
the names of three alternate consulting firms capable of completing
the work set out in Contract #991YL.

3) The Contractor will submit a report of all work that has been
completed, including any important data collected since
August 7th 20—.

4) The Client agrees to write a reference for the Contractor, stating
that Contract #991YL was broken due to illness in the family, and
has no reflection on the Contractor's ability to do his job.

Date: October 9th, 20—

(Contractor) Signature: _____

(Client) Signature: _____

180. If the Contractor honored the contract up
until now, what has definitely been
completed?

(A) A sales chart based on a five-year
review
(B) A count of all wine bottles in the cellar
(C) A calculation of proposed renovation
costs
(D) An interview with at least one staff
member

181. What is the Client obliged to do in the
future if he signs the addendum to the
contract?

(A) Rehire the Contractor when his
health returns
(B) Provide a letter that states the reasons
this contract was broken
(C) Write a positive reference letter about
the Contractor's personality
(D) Suggest alternative companies that
may hire the Contractor in the future

Questions 182–186 refer to the following ticket and letter.

REMINDER TO OWNER

You have not yet paid the following ticket:

Parking Infraction: Exceeding a 20-minute free customer-parking limit
Location: Squires Paper Company
Vehicle Type: Minivan
License Plate Number: MG097
Owner: Tanaka Kazuya
Date of Infraction: April 1, 20—

How to pay this ticket:

A) Send a check written out to the Yokohama Parking Office. (see below for address)

OR

B) Pay online with your credit card (*www.yokogov.org/parking*). You will need your ticket number and your license plate number.

OR

C) Pay in person at the Yokohama Parking Office:

Yohohama Parking Office
145-9 Yamato-Cho, Naka-ku,
Yokohama, Japan
231-0864

To appeal this ticket contact the Parking Office and ask for form #25.

---

182. Why did Tanaka receive this ticket?

    (A) His car was in a no-parking zone.
    (B) He forgot to pay for a parking pass.
    (C) His car was parked in a spot for too long.
    (D) He paid for only twenty minutes.

183. Which of the following excuses can a driver legally use in order to appeal a parking ticket?

    (A) I didn't notice the no-parking sign.
    (B) I share the vehicle with my wife.
    (C) I sold my car the day before.
    (D) I didn't have any money for parking.

NOTICE OF APPEAL   Page 1

STEP 1

You must submit your appeal within 28 days of receiving your parking ticket. Late appeals must be accompanied by a handwritten letter detailing the reasons for applying late. Judges will consider the following reasons:

• Medical emergencies for you or a family member
• Circumstances that caused you to be away from your residence at the time the ticket was mailed

STEP 2

Please circle the legal grounds that apply.

A: This parking infraction did not occur.

B: There was no parking attendant on duty to pay.

C: I was not the owner of this vehicle when the infraction occurred.

(D:) My vehicle was stolen on the day of the infraction.

STEP 3

Complete the personal information form on page two with your name and address, and contact information, and mail it together with this form and a photocopy of your ticket. You will hear back from the Ministry of Parking within twenty business days. If a personal appeal is granted, you will have to appear in court.

---

184. When is the last day Tanaka can send in form #25, without a good excuse for being late?

    (A) April 1
    (B) April 20
    (C) April 29
    (D) March 1

185. Why was Tanaka probably unaware of the original ticket?

    (A) The parking attendant forgot to write one up.
    (B) Someone stole the ticket off his car at Squire's.
    (C) He thought he was parked legally that day.
    (D) Someone else was driving his car on April 1st.

186. What does Tanaka NOT need to include with his notice of appeal?

    (A) A copy of his ticket
    (B) His name and address
    (C) His reason for appealing
    (D) A medical note

Questions 187–191 refer to the following e-mail and schedule.

To: choisoo35@korea.net

From: leebang@theaccountants.org

Subject: Transportation to and from airport

Choi Soo,

Please confirm that you received your itinerary for your flight and hotel accommodations. I e-mailed it last week, but I haven't heard back from you. I am attaching the schedule for the free shuttle service from the airport to Yongsan Terminal. Your hotel, The Sunrise Inn, is right across the street from the bus station. My only concern is that you will probably just miss the first shuttle of the day if your plane is delayed at all. The next shuttle isn't until early afternoon. Taxis are very expensive, but I think it will be worth it for you to take one instead of waiting several hours for the next shuttle bus. There are city buses, but they are complicated if you aren't familiar with them.

I'm sorry that nobody will be available to pick you up at the airport in a company car. We have an important meeting on that Thursday morning, and none of us can get out of it.

We look forward to meeting you next week. Have a safe flight and call me as soon as you are settled in your room.

See you soon,

Lee Bang

AIRPORT BUS SCHEDULE

The following schedule is for travel between Yongsan Bus Terminal and Incheon International Airport. This is a free bus service provided by Incheon International Airport. No tickets are necessary. Priority seating is given to those who make a reservation. Call 724-8000 to book your seat ahead of time.

Weekdays	BUS 1-A	BUS 2-A	BUS 3-A
Departs Incheon International Airport	9:30 A.M.	1:00 P.M.	5:30 P.M.
Arrives Yongsan Terminal	10:20 A.M.	1:59 P.M.	7:00 P.M.

Weekends	BUS 1-B	BUS 2-B	BUS 3-B
Departs Incheon International Airport	7:00 A.M.	3:00 P.M.	9:00 P.M.
Arrives Yongsan Terminal	8:00 A.M.	3:45 P.M.	10:50 P.M.

187. What does Lee ask Choi to do?

(A) Make a reservation at the Sunrise Inn
(B) Write back to say he received an e-mail
(C) Order a ticket for an airport shuttle
(D) Come to Thursday's meeting

188. Which bus does Lee think that Choi will probably miss?

(A) Bus 1-A
(B) Bus 2-A
(C) Bus 1-B
(D) Bus 2-B

189. What does Lee say costs a lot of money?

(A) Hotel accommodations
(B) Taxi fare
(C) Shuttle buses
(D) Plane tickets

190. On a Saturday, which shuttle bus takes the longest route to Yongsan Terminal?

(A) Bus 3-A
(B) Bus 1-B
(C) Bus 1-A
(D) Bus 3-B

191. Which transportation option is NOT available to Choi?

(A) Taxi
(B) Shuttle bus
(C) City bus
(D) Company car

Questions 192–196 refer to the following fax and letter.

FAX

Attn: Managers
Subject: Emergency Plant Closure
Number of Pages: 1
Date: April 14, 20—
Time sent: 9:34 A.M.

To Whom It May Concern,

Karen Electric experienced major fire damage on Thursday of this week. The cause of the fire is currently under investigation. Two of our employees were badly injured in the fire, which occurred during the overnight shift. Both are recovering in the hospital. The plant will be closed until further notice. Please cease all deliveries and reroute any invoices to the following temporary address:

PO BOX 8891
Trenton, NJ
08345-0001

Please excuse this form letter. Because of the seriousness of this matter, we do not have time to individually contact all of our clients. We will contact each of you as soon as we are operating again.

Sincerely,
Chad Stevens, CEO
Karen Electric Inc.

---

192. Who received this fax?

(A) All employees at Davis Deliveries
(B) All delivery companies in Trenton
(C) All clients of Karen Electric
(D) All staff members at Karen Electric

193. Why won't Stuart send the May invoice to Karen Electric's temporary address?

(A) She doesn't think the plant will reopen.
(B) The materials aren't available.
(C) The bill has already been paid.
(D) She wants to show her compassion.

194. Why will Stevens probably not receive this refund check?

(A) Stuart wrote the wrong address.
(B) Not enough notice was provided.
(C) His order was already requested.
(D) He is recovering in the hospital.

Davis Deliveries
230 West State Street
Trenton, NJ
08625-4430

Karen Electric
555 Jersey Street
Trenton, NY 08625-0093

Dear Mr. Stevens,

We at Davis Deliveries were very sorry to hear about the fire at the plant. For me it is particularly tragic because my grandfather and my great-uncle both worked at the plant for a long time. My family profited from many years of employment during the Depression because of this plant, and it is sad to see such a local landmark destroyed.

We will put a hold on your monthly order of materials until further notice. According to our records your payments are all up to date. In fact, we owe you a refund for May because you paid for the order in advance. I am enclosing a check for $1,465 to cover the materials, as well as a $50 credit to use toward your next order.

Please have someone call me (609-292-4444) with the names of the employees who were hurt in the fire. We would like to send flowers to the hospital on behalf of Davis Deliveries.

Thinking of you,

Elaine Stuart

Elaine Stuart, Manager
Davis Deliveries

195. Why is Stuart personally affected by this tragedy?

(A) She knows the employees who were injured.
(B) She is friendly with some of the staff members.
(C) She has family members who used to work there.
(D) She was going to inherit future profits.

196. What does Stuart want Stevens to do?

(A) Send her some flowers
(B) Give her the names of the injured workers
(C) Give her his phone number
(D) Call her with a new order

Questions 197–200 refer to the following magazine article.

*B*usy people don't want their vacations to be a hassle. That's why all-inclusive resorts are becoming popular. At these resorts, one price includes all meals, drinks, lodging, and sightseeing. Golf, tennis, and swimming are available for free. Other sports, such as scuba diving, deep sea fishing, and rock climbing, may require separate fees for equipment rental, but instruction and excursions are included. Many resorts also include children's activities as part of the package. Check with a travel agent to find an all-inclusive resort with activities you would enjoy.

197. The word *hassle* in paragraph 1, line 3, is closest in meaning to

(A) adventure
(B) expense
(C) routine
(D) bother

198. What does it mean to be an "all-inclusive" resort?

(A) They're in an exclusive location.
(B) One price includes food, lodging, and activities.
(C) Only families may stay there.
(D) Room price and airfare are included.

199. What might cost extra at these resorts?

(A) Excursions and instruction
(B) Transportation for sightseeing
(C) Hotel maid service
(D) Sports equipment rental

200. What is the best way to find an all-inclusive resort?X

(A) Ask a friend
(B) Read in a travel guide
(C) Consult a travel agent
(D) Call some hotels

STOP

This is the end of the test. If you finish before time is called, you may go back to Parts 5, 6, and 7 and check your work.

Answer Key
MODEL TEST 1

Listening Comprehension

PART 1: PHOTOGRAPHS

1. B	4. A	7. D	10. A
2. A	5. D	8. C	
3. B	6. A	9. B	

PART 2: QUESTION-RESPONSE

11. B	19. B	27. A	35. A
12. A	20. C	28. B	36. C
13. B	21. B	29. C	37. C
14. C	22. A	30. C	38. B
15. A	23. C	31. B	39. C
16. A	24. B	32. A	40. A
17. A	25. C	33. B	
18. C	26. A	34. B	

PART 3: CONVERSATIONS

41. C	49. A	57. C	65. A
42. C	50. C	58. D	66. A
43. D	51. A	59. C	67. C
44. B	52. A	60. A	68. D
45. A	53. B	61. C	69. B
46. D	54. A	62. D	70. D
47. B	55. C	63. A	
48. D	56. B	64. B	

PART 4: TALKS

71. A	79. A	87. B	95. A
72. C	80. B	88. D	96. D
73. C	81. D	89. A	97. B
74. B	82. A	90. D	98. A
75. C	83. C	91. C	99. B
76. D	84. A	92. C	100. B
77. D	85. C	93. D	
78. A	86. C	94. A	

Reading

PART 5: INCOMPLETE SENTENCES

101. B	111. A	121. B	131. B
102. D	112. A	122. C	132. C
103. C	113. C	123. C	133. B
104. B	114. A	124. D	134. B
105. A	115. D	125. C	135. B
106. C	116. B	126. D	136. D
107. B	117. C	127. B	137. A
108. D	118. B	128. A	138. A
109. C	119. A	129. D	139. C
110. B	120. D	130. C	140. D

PART 6: TEXT COMPLETION

141. A	144. A	147. B	150. A
142. B	145. D	148. A	151. A
143. C	146. B	149. C	152. C

PART 7: READING COMPREHENSION

153. B	165. A	177. B	189. B
154. C	166. A	178. A	190. D
155. B	167. A	179. B	191. D
156. D	168. D	180. C	192. C
157. A	169. B	181. B	193. C
158. B	170. A	182. C	194. A
159. B	171. D	183. C	195. C
160. D	172. D	184. C	196. B
161. C	173. D	185. D	197. D
162. C	174. B	186. D	198. B
163. B	175. A	187. B	199. D
164. B	176. C	188. A	200. C

Test Score Conversion Table

Count your correct responses. Match the number of correct responses with the corresponding score from the Test Score Conversion Table (below). Add the two scores together. This is your Total Estimated Test Score. As you practice taking the TOEIC model tests, your scores should improve. Keep track of your Total Estimated Test Scores.

# Correct	Listening Score	Reading Score	# Correct	Listening Score	Reading Score	# Correct	Listening Score	Reading Score	# Correct	Listening Score	Reading Score
0	5	5	26	110	65	51	255	220	76	410	370
1	5	5	27	115	70	52	260	225	77	420	380
2	5	5	28	120	80	53	270	230	78	425	385
3	5	5	29	125	85	54	275	235	79	430	390
4	5	5	30	130	90	55	280	240	80	440	395
5	5	5	31	135	95	56	290	250	81	445	400
6	5	5	32	140	100	57	295	255	82	450	405
7	10	5	33	145	110	58	300	260	83	460	410
8	15	5	34	150	115	59	310	265	84	465	415
9	20	5	35	160	120	60	315	270	85	470	420
10	25	5	36	165	125	61	320	280	86	475	425
11	30	5	37	170	130	62	325	285	87	480	430
12	35	5	38	175	140	63	330	290	88	485	435
13	40	5	39	180	145	64	340	300	89	490	445
14	45	5	40	185	150	65	345	305	90	495	450
15	50	5	41	190	160	66	350	310	91	495	455
16	55	10	42	195	165	67	360	320	92	495	465
17	60	15	43	200	170	68	365	325	93	495	470
18	65	20	44	210	175	69	370	330	94	495	480
19	70	25	45	215	180	70	380	335	95	495	485
20	75	30	46	220	190	71	385	340	96	495	490
21	80	35	47	230	195	72	390	350	97	495	495
22	85	40	48	240	200	73	395	355	98	495	495
23	90	45	49	245	210	74	400	360	99	495	495
24	95	50	50	250	215	75	405	365	100	495	495
25	100	60									

Number of Correct Listening Responses _____ = Listening Score _____
Number of Correct Reading Responses _____ = Reading Score _____

Total Estimated Test Score _____

Model Test 1—Explanatory Answers

LISTENING COMPREHENSION

Part 1: Photographs

1. **(B)** The technician is holding a test tube in her hand. Choice (A) uses the associated word *examining* for *looking* but there is no *patient* in the picture. Choice (C) uses the associated word *preparing* as in *preparing an experiment*. Choice (D) uses the associated word *watching* as in *looking at the test tube*.

2. **(A)** The participants are having a meeting and are sitting around a table. Choice (B) mentiones *glasses* that are on the table. Choice (C) suggests incorrectly that the group is having a meal. Choice (D) uses the associated word *taking* as in *taking notes*.

3. **(B)** Choice (B) identifies the action *speaker explaining a chart*. Choice (A) confuses the man's outstretched hand with handshaking. Choice (C) confuses the coffee cups on the table with a meal. Choice (D) confuses the white board with a TV.

4. **(A)** The factory worker is working on the engine of a car. Choice (B) uses the similar-sounding word *card* for *car* and the associated word *new* as in *new car*. Choice (C) uses the associated word *repairing* and the similar-sounding word *cart*. Choice (D) uses the associated words *driving* and *work*.

5. **(D)** The field workers are loading produce onto a truck. Choice (A) uses the word *fruit* that is being put onto the truck. Choice (B) uses the associated word *packing* as in *packing the boxes*. Choice (C) uses the associated word *box*.

6. **(A)** Choice (A) identifies the action *flags fly* and the location *from the roof*. Choice (B) confuses two meanings: *court (judicial)* with *court (yard)*. Choice (C) confuses related words: *ceiling* and *roof*. Choice (D) is incorrect because the yard is empty.

7. **(D)** Choice (D) makes assumptions: *the chairs on the street seem to be part of a cafe*. Choice (A) is not able to be determined by the picture. Choice B confuses similar sounds: *cart* with *car*, and shows negation (there is no street vendor). Choice (C) is incorrect because some of the women are wearing dresses, not carrying them.

8. **(C)** Choice (C) identifies the things *pipelines* and the location *crossing the field*. Choice (A) confuses similar sounds: *banks* with *tanks*. Choice (B) incorrectly identifies an action *plowed*. Choice (D) confuses similar sounds *pipeline* with *pale lime*.

9. **(B)** Choice (B) identifies the action *cleaning the floor*. Choice (A) incorrectly identifies the location. Choice (C) incorrectly identifies how he is cleaning the floor (he is vacuuming with a vacuum cleaner, not sweeping with a broom). Choice (D) is incorrect because the man is using the vacuum, so it cannot be stored.

10. **(A)** Choice (A) identifies the thing *boat* and the action *passes under the bridge*. Choice (B) is incorrect because the boat is passing through the water without any problem. Choice (C) confuses similar sounds *ridge* and *bridge*. Choice (D) confuses a *bridge over water* with a card game called *bridge*.

Part 2: Question-Response

11. **(B)** Choice (B) is a logical response to a question about *health*. Choice (A) confuses related words: *evening* and *bed*. Choice (C) confuses similar sounds: *good evening* with *Mr. Goode*.

12. **(A)** Choice (A) is a logical response to a question about *possession*. Choice (B) confuses similar sounds: *happen* with *your pen*; *I don't know* is not a common answer for possession. Choice (C) confuses similar sounds *European* with *your pen*; *pen* uses the pronoun *it* not *he*.

13. **(B)** Choice (B) is a logical response to a question about *being late*. Choice (A) answers how long did you wait and confuses similar sounds *late* and *wait*. Choice (C) confuses similar sounds *eight* and *late*.

14. **(C)** Choice (C) is a logical response to a question about *who*. Choice (A) confuses time: *came* (past) with *is coming* (present). Choice (B) confuses the action *combing* with *coming*.

15. **(A)** Choice (A) is a logical response to a question about *time*. Choice (B) confuses-similar sounds: *when does* with *windows*. Choice (C) confuses *meet* with *meeting*.

16. **(A)** Choice (A) is a logical response to a question about *food*. Choice (B) answers *Who's coming to dinner?* Choice (C) answers *When is dinner?*

17. **(A)** Choice (A) is a logical response to a question about *location*. Choice (B) confuses time: *this weekend* (present-future) and *last week* (past). Choice (C) confuses duration of time *will last a week* with past time *last week*.

18. **(C)** Choice (C) is a logical response to a question about *frequency*. Choice (A) confuses words with same sound and different meaning: *play* (verb) with *play* (performance). Choice (B) confuses similar sounds: *and often* and *get off*.

19. **(B)** The second speaker thanks the first speaker for the generous offer to pay for dinner. Choice (A) confuses *thinner* with the similar-sounding word *dinner*. Choice (C) repeats the word *pay*.

20. **(C)** Choice (C) is a logical response to a question about *messages*. Choice (A) confuses massage (rubbing muscles) with message. Choice (B) confuses similar sounds: *messages* with *any of us*.

21. **(B)** Choice (B) is a logical response to a question about a *purchase*. Choice (A) confuses similar sounds: *customer* with *customs officer*. Choice (C) confuses similar sounds: *(custo)mer buy* with *nearby*.

22. **(A)** Choice (A) is a logical response to a question about *how much*. Choice (B) confuses a request for *how much* (quantity) with a request for *how much* (price) and confuses *paper* with *newspaper*. Choice (C) confuses similar sounds: *pay more* with *paper*.

23. **(C)** Choice (C) is a logical response to a question about *time*. Choice (A) identifies place (*airport*) but not time. Choice (B) has the related phrase *take off* but does not answer *when*.

24. **(B)** Choice (B) is a logical response to a question about *taking a break*. Choice (A) confuses *coffee break* with *broken (coffee) cup*. Choice (C) confuses *break* with *brakes* on a car and with *won't work* (broken).

25. **(C)** Choice (C) is a logical response to a question about *finishing eating*. Choice (A) confuses *finish* (eating) with *finish* (a report), and *she* is not a response for *have you?* Choice (B) has the related word *eggs* (*food*) but does not answer the question, and it confuses similar sounds: *finished eating* with *been beaten*.

26. **(A)** Choice (A) is a logical response to a question about *location*. Choice (B) gives the price of the rooms, not the location of the hotel. Choice (C) confuses similar sounds: *el(evator)* with *(ho)tel*.

27. **(A)** The first speaker says there was a call, so the second speaker wants to know if the caller left a message. Choice (B) confuses *cold* with the similar-sounding word *cold* and repeats the word *out*. Choice (C) confuses *file* with the similar-sounding word *while*.

28. **(B)** Choice (B) is a logical response to a question about *which*. Choice (A) confuses similar sounds: *hours* with *ours*. Choice (C) has the related word *seat* but does not answer *which*.

29. **(C)** The first speaker feels cold so the second speaker offers to close the window. Choice (A) associates *winter* with *cold*. Choice (B) confuses *sold* with the similar-sounding word *cold* and *year* with the similar-sounding word *here*.

30. **(C)** Choice (C) is a logical response to a question about *location*. Choice (A) confuses similar sounds: *ear* with *here*. Choice (B) confuses *closed* with *near* (*close*).

31. **(B)** Choice (B) is a logical response to a question about *possession*. Choice (A) confuses similar sounds: *open* with *pen*. Choice (C) confuses similar sounds: *European* with *your pen*.

32. **(A)** Choice (A) is a logical response to a question about *what kind*. Choice (B)

confuses similar sounds: *read* with *proceed* and *like* (v) with *like* (conj.). Choice (C) confuses similar sounds: *kind* with *find*.

33. **(B)** The second speaker will call the first speaker after the meeting is over. Choice (A) confuses *door* with the similar-sounding word *four*. Choice (C) confuses *seating* with the similar-sounding word *meeting* and repeats the word *four*.

34. **(B)** Choice (B) is a logical response to a question about *where*. Choice (A) confuses time: *lunch tomorrow* with *did have lunch*. Choice (C) answers *when* (at noon), not *where*.

35. **(A)** Choice (A) is a logical response to a question about *asking your father*. Choice (B) confuses similar sounds: *far* with *father*. Choice (C) confuses similar sounds: *ask* with *task*.

36. **(C)** Choice (C) is a logical response to a question about *who attended the conference*. Choice (A) confuses similar sounds: *conference* with *fence*. Choice (B) gives the day of the conference, not who attended.

37. **(C)** The second speaker agrees to eat at the restaurant that the first speaker suggests. Choice (A) confuses *rest* with the similar-sounding word *restaurant*. Choice (B) confuses *ice* with the similar-sounding word *nice*.

38. **(B)** Choice (B) is a logical response to a question about *location for a coat*. Choice (A) confuses similar sounds: *leave* with *live*. Choice (C) confuses *leave my coat* with *leave a note*.

39. **(C)** Choice (C) is a logical response to a question about an *order*. Choice (A) confuses similar sounds: *place* with *race*. Choice (B) confuses different meanings: *place* (submit) and *place* (location) and similar sounds: *order* with *door*.

40. **(A)** Choice (A) is a logical response to a question about *finishing*. Choice (B) confuses being *done* (finishing) with *well-done* (how meat is cooked). Choice (C) confuses similar sounds: *done* with *fun*.

Part 3: Conversations

41. **(C)** The woman can't meet until 5:00. Choices (A) and (B) are times that the man suggests. Choice (D) confuses *ten* with the similar-sounding word *then*.

42. **(C)** The man says *I'll wait for you in my office*. Choice (A) confuses *bus stop* with the similar-sounding word *budget*. Choice (B) is confused with where the woman will be earlier in the day. Choice (D) confuses *waiting room* with *I'll wait for you...*

43. **(D)** The woman says that she'll bring photocopies of the budget report. Choice (A) confuses *coffee* with the similar-sounding word *copy*. Choice (B) confuses *letter* with the similar-sounding word *better*. Choice (C) confuses *photographs* with *photocopies*.

44. **(B)** The man is traveling to Los Angeles. Choice (A) is where he is leaving from. Choices (C) and (D) are places where he might change planes.

45. **(A)** He is traveling by plane; both *plane* and *flight* are mentioned in the conversation. Choice (B) confuses *train* with the similar-sounding word *plane*. Choice (C) confuses *bus* with the similar-sounding word *but*. Choice (D) confuses *car* with the similar-sounding word *start*.

46. **(D)** The man says he wants to leave tomorrow and the woman says there is a flight at 10:00. Choice (A) confuses *afternoon* with the similar-sounding word *soon*. Choice (B) confuses *tonight* with the similar-sounding word *flight*. Choice (C) has the correct day but the wrong time.

47. **(B)** The man asks for towels and soap to be brought to his room. Choices (A) and (C) are places where a person might ask for something, but they are not the correct answer. Choice (D) is incorrect because rooms in houses don't normally have numbers.

48. **(D)** The man asks for towels and soap. Choice (A) confuses *keys* with the similar-sounding word *please*. Choice (B) confuses *soup* with the similar-sounding word *soap*. Choice (C) repeats the word *room*.

First News
Always Innovative & Informative

49. **(A)** The woman says *The housekeeper will bring them right away*. Choice (B) confuses *today* with the similar-sounding word *away*. Choices (C) and (D) are confused with *two towels*.

50. **(C)** The woman says that the brochures arrived this morning. Choices (A) and (D) confuse *afternoon* with the similar-sounding word *soon*. Choice (B) is not mentioned.

51. **(A)** The woman says that she will address and mail the brochures. Choice (B) is not mentioned. Choice (C) confuses *print* with *printer*. Choice (D) uses the word *copy* out of context.

52. **(A)** One thousand brochures were ordered, and that is twice the number the woman needs. Choice (B) confuses *eight* with the similar-sounding word *great*. Choice (C) is the number of brochures ordered. Choice (D) is twice the number of brochures ordered.

53. **(B)** The man says that he is calling about a catering position. Choice (A) associates *waiter* with *food and beverage*. Choice (C) is associated with *ad*. Choice (D) repeats *food and beverage*.

54. **(A)** The woman asks if the man has any experience. Choice (B) confuses *appearance* with the similar-sounding word *experience*. Choice (C) confuses *attitude* with the similar-sounding word *ad*. Choice (D) associates *appetite* with *food*.

55. **(C)** The woman asks the man to come for an interview next Monday. Choice (A) is confused with *today's paper*. Choice (B) confuses *Sunday* with the similar-sounding word *Monday*. Choice (D) confuses *Tuesday* with the similar-sounding word *today*.

56. **(B)** He can't play golf because rain is predicted. Choice (A) confuses *sick* with the similar-sounding word *predict*. Choice (C) confuses *test* with the similar-sounding word *rest*. Choice (D) uses the word *tired* out of context.

57. **(C)** He had a 9:00 golf game. Choice (A) confuses *two* with the similar-sounding word *tomorrow*. Choice (B) confuses *four*

with the similar-sounding word *bore*. Choice (D) confuses *ten* with the similar-sounding word *then*.

58. **(D)** Since the man can't play golf tomorrow, he says he wants to stay home and rest. Choice (A) confuses *phone* with the similar-sounding word *home*. Choice (B) is what the woman wants him to do. Choice (C) confuses *move* with the similar-sounding word *movies*.

59. **(C)** The man is giving the woman directions to a bank. Choice (A) associates *fast food restaurant* with *drive-in window*. Choice (B) is what is next to the bank. Choice (D) is what the woman will pass on her way to the bank.

60. **(A)** The man says that the bank is on a corner. Choice (B) is confused with *a parking lot next door*. Choices (C) and (D) are confused with *across the street from the library*.

61. **(C)** The man says that the bank is only five minutes away. Choice (A) confuses *two* with the similar-sounding word *too*. Choice (B) confuses *four* with the similar-sounding word *door*. Choice (D) confuses *nine* with the similar-sounding word *find*.

62. **(D)** The woman says *It's 9:30*. Choices (A) and (B) confuse *eight* with the similar-sounding word *late*. Choice (C) is confused with *15 minutes late*.

63. **(A)** The woman is scolding the man for arriving late. Choice (B) is mentioned but is not the reason the woman is angry. Choice (C) is what the man, not the woman, did. Choice (D) repeats the word *fast*.

64. **(B)** The man says he will drive his car because it's faster. Choice (A) repeats the word *home*. Choice (C) is what the woman suggests. Choice (D) confuses *train* with the similar-sounding word *rain*.

65. **(A)** The woman is making a plane reservation. Choice (B) associates *class* with *assignment*. Choice (C) associates *theater* with *aisle*, *seat*, and *movie*. Choice (D) repeats the word *dinner*.

66. **(A)** The man says she can take a flight next Sunday afternoon. Choice (B) confuses

night with the similar-sounding word *flight.* Choices (C) and (D) confuse *Monday* with the similar-sounding word *Sunday.*

67. **(C)** The woman asks if she can pay with a credit card. Choice (A) is not mentioned. Choice (B) uses the word *check* out of context. Choice (D) uses the word *order* out of context.

68. **(D)** The man greets the woman *Good evening.* Choice (A) is not mentioned. Choices (B) and (C) confuse *noon* and *afternoon* with the similar-sounding word *soon.*

69. **(B)** The woman is in a restaurant ordering from a menu, so she is talking to a waiter. Choice (A) associates *butcher* with *lamb.* Choices (C) and (D) are people one might talk with in a restaurant, but they are not the people who take food orders.

70. **(D)** The woman orders the vegetable plate because she is vegetarian. Choices (A) and (B) are what the waiter recommends. Choice (C) confuses fish with the similar-sounding word dish.

Part 4: Talks

71. **(A)** *Arrival and departure gates, baggage claims,* and *ticketing areas* all suggest an airport. Choices (B) and (C) are not specific enough. Choice (D) is incorrect because an amusement park train would not lead to *baggage claims.*

72. **(C)** The instructions say you should be in the *center of the car.* Choice (A) is contradicted by *away from the doors.* Choice (B) is incorrect because *windows* are not mentioned. Choice (D) is contradicted by *in the center.*

73. **(C)** Passengers are asked to wait until they hear a bell ring before they exit the train. Choice (A) repeats the word *sign.* Choice (B) is contradicted by the correct answer. Choice (D) repeats the word *color.*

74. **(B)** The museum is open from *one until five on Sundays*; this is afternoon. Choices (A) and (C) are not mentioned. Choice (D) contradicts the fact that the museum is open from *one until five on Sundays.*

75. **(C)** The announcement says that *lecture information can be obtained by calling our Education Office at 548-6251.* Choices (A), (B), and (D) are not mentioned.

76. **(D)** According to the message, *children under five are not charged admission.* Choice (A) are the people who get a 25% discount. Choice (B) are the people who pay $15. Choice (C) are the people who pay $10.

77. **(D)** The passage says to *start the morning by making a list.* Choices (A), (B), and (C) are not mentioned.

78. **(A)** The passage says that you should *next, rank each task ...according to its importance.* Choice (B) is contradicted by *stay with (the task) until it is completed.* Choice (C) is contradicted by *work on the most important task first.* Choice (D) is not mentioned.

79. **(A)** According to the talk, you should review your list at the end of the day. Choice (B) is incorrect because listeners are told to leave uncompleted tasks for the next day. Choice (C) repeats the word *list,* but nothing is mentioned about writing a new one. Choice (D) confuses *away* with the similar-sounding word *day.*

80. **(B)** Since the ad is for *office furniture* and *accessories, it encourages you to redecorate your office.* Choice (A) is not mentioned. Choices (C) and (D) are part of redecorating and purchasing their furniture.

81. **(D)** The ad mentions a sale on *furniture.* Choices (A), (B), and (C) are not mentioned.

82. **(A)** According to the announcement, the sale ends on Sunday. Choice (B) sounds similar to the correct answer. Choice (C) confuses *Tuesday* with the similar-sounding word *today.* Choice (D) is not mentioned.

83. **(C)** The ad states that you can help by *serving as a volunteer tutor.* Choice (A) is not mentioned but is associated with *schoolwork, child, learning,* and *school system.* Choice (B) *school children* are the people tutors will be helping. Choice (D) *businessmen* and *businesswomen* are reading the ad.

84. **(A)** You can help for *as little as two hours a week*. Choice (B) is contradicted by *as little as*. Choices (C) and (D) are not mentioned.

85. **(C)** The announcement says that participants must be over eighteen. Choices (A) and (B) are mentioned as not necessary. Choice (D) repeats the word *children,* but experience with children is not mentioned.

86. **(C)** If temperatures are in the *mid-sixties,* it's about *65 degrees*. Choice (A) is confused with *breezes often to fifteen miles per hour*. In Choice (B), *sixty* is the first part of *sixty-five*. Choice (D) is not mentioned.

87. **(B)** The weatherman says to *spend some time outdoors*. Choice (A) is contradicted by *spend some time outdoors*. Choices (C) and (D) are possible but not mentioned.

88. **(D)** The weather tomorrow will be like the weather today, which is sunny. Choices (A), (B), and (C) describe the weather later in the week.

89. **(A)** Lodge costs include *continental breakfast and gourmet dinner*. Choice (B) is contradicted by *ski equipment is available...for a small additional fee*. Choice (C) is not mentioned. Choice (D) is not provided.

90. **(D)** The announcement mentions ski classes for people of all ability levels. Choice (A) is confused with the people who give the lessons. Choice (B) repeats the word *abilities*. Choice (C) is contradicted by the correct answer.

91. **(C)** The announcement mentions a third night free. Choice (A) uses the word *book* out of context. Choice (B) associates *calendar* with *January*. Choice (D) repeats the word *class*.

92. **(C)** The announcement says there are delays of *up to 45 minutes*. Choices (A) and (D) are not mentioned. Choice (B) is confused with *trains are currently running every fifteen minutes*.

93. **(D)** Delays are caused by *damage to the tracks*. Choices (A), (B), and (C) are not mentioned.

94. **(A)** They are providing *special buses to carry commuters around the damaged portions of the track*. Choice (B) will not help people commute quickly. Choice (C) does not address the problem; the trains are fine, the track *is broken*. Choice (D) is not logical; it is impossible to use any trains if the track is damaged.

95. **(A)** The problem is *an explosion*. Choices (B), (C), and (D) all confuse similar sounds.

96. **(D)** Though the cause is not known, they *suspect a leaking gas pipe*. Choices (A), (B), and (C) are possible problems but are not mentioned.

97. **(B)** *Evacuated* means *removed*. Choice (A) is contradicted by *no injuries were reported*. Choice (C) confuses *no injuries were reported* with *people being reported*. Choice (D) is incorrect because a *gas leak* was suspected; people were not suspected.

98. **(A)** The speaker is a teacher telling students that class will be canceled because of a trip. Choice (B) associates *art* with *art museum* and *professors* with *class*. Choice (C) associates *museum employees* with *art museum*. Choice (D) associates *museum* with *tour group*.

99. **(B)** The speaker suggests bringing money to buy lunch. Choice (A) is confused with the reading assignment in the textbook. Choice (C) repeats the word *lunch*, but listeners are advised to buy lunch, not bring it. Choice (D) is what people are not allowed to take to the museum.

100. **(B)** The bus will leave at 9:00 and people should arrive fifteen minutes before then. Choice (A) confuses *eight* with the similar-sounding word *wait*. Choice (C) is the time that the bus will leave. Choice (D) is fifteen minutes after, not before, the time that the bus will leave.

READING

Part 5: Incomplete Sentences

101. **(B)** *Customer* is singular, so it takes a singular verb; it is also third person, so it takes the

third person form of *is*. Choice (A) is singular but first person. Choice (C) is plural. Choice (D) is the simple form of the verb.

102. **(D)** The direct object position must be filled by a noun; *failure* is the only noun listed. Choices (A), (B), and (C) are all verb forms.

103. **(C)** *In* is used with city locations. Choices (A) and (D) are not used with locations in this context. Choice (B) may be used only when a from/to contrast is stated or implied (e.g., *from the suburbs into the city*).

104. **(B)** *Were not* requires a past participle to complete the verb. Choice (A) is a noun. Choice (C) is in the progressive form. Choice (D) is the simple form.

105. **(A)** The present tense in the *if* clause can be matched with future tense in the second clause; *will* can also be used with *assist* to make a complete verb. Choices (B) and (C) are past tense. Choice (D) is present tense, and must be used with either the *past participle* or the progressive form.

106. **(C)** The noun *knowledge* followed by *and* should be joined to another noun. Choices (A) and (B) are verbs. Choice (D) is a noun, but refers to a person rather than a thing.

107. **(B)** *Increase* is the most common verb meaning *go up* used with *costs*. Choices (A), (C), and (D) mean *go up* but are not used for nouns related to percentages.

108. **(D)** The subject position requires a noun. Choices (A) and (B) are verbs. Choice (C) refers to a person or thing and doesn't make sense here.

109. **(C)** *Because* establishes a logical cause and effect relationship between the two events. Choice (A) indicates contrast; it is not logical unless the plane *was on time*. Choice (B) suggests a simultaneous relationship, not possible because of present tense *is* and past tense *was*. Choice (D) is a preposition and cannot be used to join clauses.

110. **(B)** *To* indicates a change in time. Choice (A) is used with one specific time. Choice (C) is used with a period of time (e.g., *in two hours*). Choice (D) is used with deadlines.

111. **(A)** *Went* is the only verb in the list that can be used. Choice (B) is a past participle and requires *have* (*has gone*). Choice (C) is the simple form. Choice (D) is the progressive form and requires a form of *be* (*is going*).

112. **(A)** *Commute* means to travel from home to work. Choices (B), (C), and (D) do not fit the context of the sentence.

113. **(C)** Indicates that one object has another object on each side. Choice (A) is most often used when one hard-to-count group is indicated (*among the paper clips, among the office equipment*). Choices (B) and (D) are not logical.

114. **(A)** *Job* is used here to refer to an individual position. Choice (B) implies professional standing greater than individual jobs. (*In his career (occupation) as an insurance investigator, he held jobs with several companies*). Choice (C) implies unpleasant work smaller than an individual job. (*I like my job as a secretary, but it's a chore to sort the boss's mail*). Choice (D) uses a related word, *position*, but in an inappropriate form.

115. **(D)** File has the same meaning here as *submit*. Choice (A) is a form of the verb *fill*. Choices (B) and (C) are forms of the verb *fall*.

116. **(B)** *After* establishes a logical time relationship between the two events. Choice (A) is an adverb, indicating a period of time after a specific event. Choice (C) indicates a comparison. (*His fax arrived later than mine*). Choice (D) is an adjective and cannot be used to join clauses.

117. **(C)** *Because* indicates a cause and effect relationship between the two events. Choice (A) implies contrast. Choice (B) *during* cannot be followed by a sentence. Choice (D) doesn't make sense.

118. **(B)** *Required* means to be obliged. Choices (A), (C), and (D) do not fit the context of the sentence.

119. **(A)** *Or* is logical and can join two nouns. Choice (B) is not usually used in a negative relationship. Choices (C) and (D) are not logical.

120. **(D)** *Always* comes between the auxiliary and *be* (if *be* occurs in the sentence). Choices (A), (B), and (C) do not place *always* between the auxiliary and *be*.

121. **(B)** The blank requires an adjective; *available* is the only one given. Choices (A) and (D) are verbs. Choice (C) is a noun.

122. **(C)** The causative *suggest* is followed by the simple form of the verb. Choice (A) is the plural form. Choices (B) and (D) are simple forms, but are not logical.

123. **(C)** *Spaces* must be modified by an adjective. Choices (A) and (D) are adjectives, but are not logical. Choice (B) is a noun.

124. **(D)** *Order* must be modified by an adjective. Choice (A) is a noun. Choice (B) is a verb. Choice (C) is an adverb.

125. **(C)** *Behind* is logical and does not need other words to complete the expression. Choice (A) requires *from* (*across from the reception desk*). Choice (B) requires a second location (*between the reception desk and the door*). Choice (D) is not logical.

126. **(D)** *Must* requires the simple form of the verb. Choice (A) is the past tense. Choice (B) is the progressive form. Choice (C) is the third-person singular form.

127. **(B)** *Tasks* must be modified by an adjective. Choice (A) is a verb. Choice (C) is a noun. Choice (D) is an adverb.

128. **(A)** *Reminded* requires the infinitive. Choice (B) is the simple form. Choice (C) is the past participle. Choice (D) is the progressive form.

129. **(D)** *Put on* is a two-word verb that in this context means *to produce*. The other prepositions in Choices (A), (B), and (C) do not fit the context of the sentence.

130. **(C)** *Never* can come between the auxiliary and the verb. Choice (A) is an adjective and does not fit here. Choice (B) does not make sense. Choice (D) would fit if it were *at no time*.

131. **(B)** The *if* clause in the past perfect conditional matches with a past tense in the second clause. Choice (A) is the past conditional. Choice (C) is future tense. Choice (D) is future perfect.

132. **(C)** *Appointment* means a planned time. Choice (A), *notebook*, is not something that could be cancelled, although a cancellation could be written in a notebook. Choice (B), *calendar*, is the thing you plan schedules and appointments on. Choice (D), *notice*, is not something that could be cancelled.

133. **(B)** Present tense in the *if* clause can be matched with future tense in the second clause. Choice (A) is present perfect conditional. Choice (C) is past tense. Choice (D) is present tense but indicates an unreal condition.

134. **(B)** *On* indicates *placed upon the surface of*. Choice (A) does not make sense. Choice (C) is part of the two-word verb *leave out*. Choice (D) indicates a place above the desk but a desk does not have an *up*.

135. **(B)** The sentence requires a present third person singular or past tense verb; only *departs* is given. Choice (A) is present tense, but not third person singular. Choice (C) is the infinitive. Choice (D) is an *-ing* form.

136. **(D)** *During* is logical and can immediately precede a noun phrase. Choice (A) is not logical and must be followed by a clause. Choice (B) is not logical. Choice (C) needs *of* (*because of the meeting*).

137. **(A)** *Efficiently* is logical. Choices (B), (C), and (D) are not logical; he probably does have to type more carefully, slowly, and gradually.

138. **(A)** *Was damaged* can be followed by the past tense. Choice (B) uses the present *has*. Choice (C) uses *was* but with the progressive form of *deliver*. Choice (D) is the past perfect.

139. **(C)** *Mr. Green* should be modified by the *-ed* form (something else caused Mr. Green to become excited). Choice (B) isn't logical because it means that Mr. Green made someone else feel excited. Choices (A) and (D) are verbs, not adjective forms.

140. **(D)** Choice (D) is logical; it implies a contrast between *weekends* and *holidays*. Choice (A) is used with *or*. Choice (B) implies a choice between items. Choice (C) indicates cause and effect.

Part 6: Text Completion

141. **(A)** This completes the expression *either…or*. Choice (B) must be used with *neither*, not with *either*. Choices (C) and (D) cannot be used with *either*.

142. **(B)** *such as* can begin a list of examples. Choice (A) cannot be used in this context. Choices (C) and (D) would have to be preceded by the word *for* in order to be used in this sentence.

143. **(C)** Passengers go through a security line to have their bags checked for unallowed items. Choices (A), (B), and (D) are lines that passengers may have to pass through, but they don't fit the context.

144. **(A)** Companies are advertising a lot because they want to sell more computers. Choice (B) is not something computer companies would want to increase. Choices (C) and (D) don't fit the context.

145. **(D)** Notebook computers are easy to carry around, and this makes them convenient. Choices (A), (B), and (C) don't fit the context.

146. **(B)** Following the article *the* a noun is required. Choice (A) is a noun, but it refers to a person, not a situation. Choice (C) is an adjective. Choice (D) is an adverb.

147. **(B)** This is the verb *to be* plus an adjective, describing the feelings of the writer about the situation. Choice (A) does not agree with the subject *we*. Choices (C) and (D) are verb forms, not adjectives.

148. **(A)** This is the main clause of a future real conditional, requiring a future verb form. Choice (B) is present perfect tense. Choice (C) is an unreal conditional. Choice (D) is an incomplete future form, missing the word *are*.

149. **(C)** An order contains items and prices, as the fax mentions. The other choices are related to making orders but are not the correct answer.

150. **(A)** *Response* means answer; the letter answers an ad. Choices (B), (C), and (D) look similar to the correct answer but have very different meanings.

151. **(A)** The present tense verb *qualify* agrees with the plural subject *years*. Choices (B), (C), and (D) agree with singular, not plural, subjects.

152. **(C)** The expression *look forward to* means *anticipate* or *hope for*. Choices (A), (B) and (D) cannot be correctly used with this expression.

Part 7: Reading Comprehension

153. **(B)** Trends emphasize careers in *sales and marketing*. Choices (A), (C), and (D) repeat words from the article.

154. **(C)** *High-tech sales* are expected to grow 20% in the next decade. Choice (A) is logical but doesn't address the increasing importance. Choice (B) repeats the word *market* from the article. Choice (D) repeats words from the article but doesn't answer the question.

155. **(B)** Marketers must find new *ways* to get customers interested in their products. Choice (A) is a different meaning of the word *avenues*, which doesn't fit the context. Choices (C) and (D) are terms related to marketing but they don't have the correct meaning.

156. **(D)** *Creative* is synonymous with *inventive*. Choice (A) mentions a positive feature for a marketer, but not a mandatory feature. Choice (B) relates to travel. Choice (C) repeats the word *research*.

157. **(A)** Some users see too much Internet advertising (they are *inundated*), while others see too little (they're *just learning to navigate* the Web). Choices (B), (C), and (D) may be reasonable options, but none is mentioned in the article.

158. **(B)** The original name Green Miles California was changed. "California" was replaced by "West." Choice (A) is a brand name. Choice (C) is the new name. Choice (D) is a brand name combined with California.

159. **(B)** The California Gardening Association did not like the similarity of the corporations' names. Choice (A) confuses *offices*

with *brands*. Choice (C) repeats the word *initial*. Choice (D) confuses the hope that they not be confused with the actual reason the names were changed.

160. **(D)** *Protecting the earth* is the same as *saving the environment*. Choices (A), (B), and (C) are probably true but are not the subject of the passage.

161. **(C)** Hotels are joining the movement to save the environment. Choice (A) identifies recycling as a gimmick, but it is a trend, not a gimmick. Choice (B) implies only hotels used by Eco-Tours practice sound environmental policies. Choice (D) is true, but is not mentioned in this passage.

162. **(C)** Although the other groups could all be concerned about the environment, they are not typical of the green movement.

163. **(B)** The passage talks about *lectures* and does not mention the other options.

164. **(B)** It sells *specialty food products, cookware, and kitchen accessories*. Choices (A), (C), and (D) are not items related to the food industry.

165. **(A)** *Similar plans* refers to *remodeling*. Choices (B), (C), and (D) sound possible but are not mentioned. Val D'Or bought all sixteen stores so it would not buy only the remaining six.

166. **(A)** The article stresses that chefs will come from all over and that regional foods will be featured. Choice (B) contradicts the statement that chefs will come from all over Europe. Choices (C) and (D) are not mentioned.

167. **(A)** *Years of service* means *years working for the company*. Choices (B) and (D) are not considered. Choice (C) is contradicted by *highest salary*.

168. **(D)** Contributions must be made according to government regulations. Choice (A) would have to follow the government's rules. Choices (B) and (C) can contribute to the plan but are still obligated to follow government regulations.

169. **(B)** The note is about Regents' plans for improvements. Choices (A), (C), and (D)

are mentioned, but they are not the main purpose of the letter.

170. **(A)** Regents has been working to provide enhanced access to health care coverage. Choice (B) confuses *primer* and *premier* and is not mentioned. Choice (C) is not mentioned. Choice (D) is already being done.

171. **(D)** Regents wants members to continue making suggestions. Choices (A), (B), and (C) are not mentioned.

172. **(D)** *At the end of this month* means April 30. Choice (A) is not mentioned. Choice (B) is the last day of the period covered by the invoice. Choice (C) is the date of the invoice.

173. **(D)** *Unpaid prior balance* means they owe money on the last invoice. Choice (A) is not mentioned. Choices (B) and (C) are incorrect because charges are not broken down into taxes and other charges.

174. **(B)** They *work best if they are happy*. Choice (A) is possible but not mentioned. Choices (C) and (D) are unlikely.

175. **(A)** *Bring up to date* has the same meaning as *update*. Choice (B) is unlikely. Choices (C) and (D) are not logical.

176. **(C)** It is not suggested that employees have the power to decide changes. Choices (A), (B), and (D) are explicitly mentioned.

177. **(B)** The Contractor will provide consulting services for different aspects of the winery's operations. Choices (A), (C), and (D) mention things that are related to a winery's business but that are not mentioned in the texts.

178. **(A)** The contract was not fulfilled because of a medical emergency, but the duties outlined in the contract have no relationship to anything medical. Choices (B) and (D) are examples of winery staff members, and the contract specifies speaking with staff members. Choice (C) is an example of someone the Contractor will speak with, mentioned in clause C of the contract.

179. **(B)** The original contract was signed August 7, and the addendum stating the reason for not completing the contract was signed October 9. Choices (A), (C), and (D) are contradicted by the correct answer.

180. **(C)** The contract states that an estimate of renovation costs must be completed by October 1. Choices (A), (B), and (D) are tasks that have no specific deadline assigned.

181. **(B)** This is what clause 4 of the addendum to the contract states. Choice (A) is not mentioned. Choice (C) looks similar to the correct answer, but there is no mention made of the Contractor's personality. Choice (D) is what the Contractor must do.

182. **(C)** According to the reminder, he exceeded a twenty-minute parking limit. Choices (A) and (B) are possible reasons for getting a parking ticket but are not the correct answer. Choice (D) repeats *twenty minutes*.

183. **(C)** This choice refers to option C under Step 2 of the Notice of Appeal: *I was not the owner of this vehicle when the infraction occurred.* Choices (A), (B), and (D) do not mean the same as any of the options listed in Step 2.

184. **(C)** The Notice of Appeal states that the appeal must be submitted within 28 days of receiving a ticket, which Tanaka received on April 1. Choices (A), (B), and (D) are contradicted by the correct answer.

185. **(D)** Option D under Step 2 is circled, so Tanaka's car was being driven by a thief on the day the ticket was issued. Choices (A), (B), and (C) are plausible reasons but are not mentioned in the texts.

186. **(D)** This is confused with the mention of medical emergencies as a reason for a late appeal, but there is no mention that Tanaka had a medical emergency. Choices (A), (B), and (C) are all mentioned as things that must be included as part of the appeal.

187. **(B)** Lee asks Choi to confirm that he received the itinerary. Choice (A) has already been done. Choice (C) is incorrect because Lee suggests that a taxi might be better than the shuttle. Choice (D) is confused with what Lee will have to do himself.

188. **(A)** Choi will arrive on a weekday (Thursday); Lee thinks he will miss the first bus that day, which is 1-A. Choice (B) is the second bus of that day. Choices (C) and (D) are weekend buses.

189. **(B)** Lee says that taxis are expensive. Choices (A), (C), and (D) are things Lee mentions in the e-mail, but he doesn't mention their cost.

190. **(D)** The "B" buses are the weekend buses and 3-B takes longer than the other "B" buses to get to its destination. Choices (A) and (C) are weekday buses. Choice (B) takes less time than the 3-B bus.

191. **(D)** Lee apologizes that nobody can pick up Choi with the company car because they will all be at a meeting when he arrives. Choices (A), (B), and (C) are all mentioned as transportation options.

192. **(C)** The fax was sent to everyone the company does business with to inform them that operations are temporarily suspended due to the fire. Choice (A) is confused with the name of one of the recipient companies. Choice (B) is incorrect; not all delivery companies received it, just those that do business with Karen Electric. Choice (D) is confused with the two staff members who were injured.

193. **(C)** Stuart says in her letter that Karen Electric paid for the May order in advance. Choices (A), (B), and (D) are plausible reasons but are not mentioned in the texts.

194. **(A)** The letter is addressed to Karen Electric's usual address, while the fax gave companies a temporary address to use. Choices (B), (C), and (D) are plausible reasons but are not the correct answer.

195. **(C)** In her letter, Stuart mentions that both her father and grandfather worked at Karen Electric. Choice (A) is incorrect because Stuart doesn't even know the names of the injured employees; she asks for their names in her letter. Choice (B) is not mentioned. Choice (D) is confused with *My family profited from many years of employment…*

196. **(B)** Stuart wants the name of the injured employees so that she can send them flowers. Choice (A) is confused with Stuart's sending flowers to the hospital. Choice (C) is confused with Stuart's giving her phone number to Stevens. Choice (D) is confused with the mention of the May order.

197. **(D)** Busy people don't want to have the *bother* of planning all the details of their vacations, so they choose to go to all-inclusive resorts. Choices (A), (B), and (C) are words that could be related to the topic of vacation, but they don't have the correct meaning.

198. **(B)** *All-inclusive* means one price covers most costs. Choice (A) uses a related word, *exclusive*. Choice (C) is a service that might be provided. Choice (D) limits who may stay at the resort and does not define "all-inclusive."

199. **(D)** *Separate fees for equipment rental* means rental costs extra. Choices (A) and (B) are included at some resorts. Choice (C) is a service at all hotels.

200. **(C)** *Check with a travel agent* means to *consult a travel agent*. Choices (A), (B), and (D) are not mentioned.

Answer Sheet
MODEL TEST 2

Listening Comprehension

PART 1: PHOTOGRAPHS

1. Ⓐ Ⓑ Ⓒ Ⓓ
2. Ⓐ Ⓑ Ⓒ Ⓓ
3. Ⓐ Ⓑ Ⓒ Ⓓ
4. Ⓐ Ⓑ Ⓒ Ⓓ
5. Ⓐ Ⓑ Ⓒ Ⓓ
6. Ⓐ Ⓑ Ⓒ Ⓓ
7. Ⓐ Ⓑ Ⓒ Ⓓ
8. Ⓐ Ⓑ Ⓒ Ⓓ
9. Ⓐ Ⓑ Ⓒ Ⓓ
10. Ⓐ Ⓑ Ⓒ Ⓓ

PART 2: QUESTION-RESPONSE

11. Ⓐ Ⓑ Ⓒ
12. Ⓐ Ⓑ Ⓒ
13. Ⓐ Ⓑ Ⓒ
14. Ⓐ Ⓑ Ⓒ
15. Ⓐ Ⓑ Ⓒ
16. Ⓐ Ⓑ Ⓒ
17. Ⓐ Ⓑ Ⓒ
18. Ⓐ Ⓑ Ⓒ
19. Ⓐ Ⓑ Ⓒ
20. Ⓐ Ⓑ Ⓒ
21. Ⓐ Ⓑ Ⓒ
22. Ⓐ Ⓑ Ⓒ
23. Ⓐ Ⓑ Ⓒ
24. Ⓐ Ⓑ Ⓒ
25. Ⓐ Ⓑ Ⓒ
26. Ⓐ Ⓑ Ⓒ
27. Ⓐ Ⓑ Ⓒ
28. Ⓐ Ⓑ Ⓒ
29. Ⓐ Ⓑ Ⓒ
30. Ⓐ Ⓑ Ⓒ
31. Ⓐ Ⓑ Ⓒ
32. Ⓐ Ⓑ Ⓒ
33. Ⓐ Ⓑ Ⓒ
34. Ⓐ Ⓑ Ⓒ
35. Ⓐ Ⓑ Ⓒ
36. Ⓐ Ⓑ Ⓒ
37. Ⓐ Ⓑ Ⓒ
38. Ⓐ Ⓑ Ⓒ
39. Ⓐ Ⓑ Ⓒ
40. Ⓐ Ⓑ Ⓒ

PART 3: CONVERSATIONS

41. Ⓐ Ⓑ Ⓒ Ⓓ
42. Ⓐ Ⓑ Ⓒ Ⓓ
43. Ⓐ Ⓑ Ⓒ Ⓓ
44. Ⓐ Ⓑ Ⓒ Ⓓ
45. Ⓐ Ⓑ Ⓒ Ⓓ
46. Ⓐ Ⓑ Ⓒ Ⓓ
47. Ⓐ Ⓑ Ⓒ Ⓓ
48. Ⓐ Ⓑ Ⓒ Ⓓ
49. Ⓐ Ⓑ Ⓒ Ⓓ
50. Ⓐ Ⓑ Ⓒ Ⓓ
51. Ⓐ Ⓑ Ⓒ Ⓓ
52. Ⓐ Ⓑ Ⓒ Ⓓ
53. Ⓐ Ⓑ Ⓒ Ⓓ
54. Ⓐ Ⓑ Ⓒ Ⓓ
55. Ⓐ Ⓑ Ⓒ Ⓓ
56. Ⓐ Ⓑ Ⓒ Ⓓ
57. Ⓐ Ⓑ Ⓒ Ⓓ
58. Ⓐ Ⓑ Ⓒ Ⓓ
59. Ⓐ Ⓑ Ⓒ Ⓓ
60. Ⓐ Ⓑ Ⓒ Ⓓ
61. Ⓐ Ⓑ Ⓒ Ⓓ
62. Ⓐ Ⓑ Ⓒ Ⓓ
63. Ⓐ Ⓑ Ⓒ Ⓓ
64. Ⓐ Ⓑ Ⓒ Ⓓ
65. Ⓐ Ⓑ Ⓒ Ⓓ
66. Ⓐ Ⓑ Ⓒ Ⓓ
67. Ⓐ Ⓑ Ⓒ Ⓓ
68. Ⓐ Ⓑ Ⓒ Ⓓ
69. Ⓐ Ⓑ Ⓒ Ⓓ
70. Ⓐ Ⓑ Ⓒ Ⓓ

PART 4: TALKS

71. Ⓐ Ⓑ Ⓒ Ⓓ
72. Ⓐ Ⓑ Ⓒ Ⓓ
73. Ⓐ Ⓑ Ⓒ Ⓓ
74. Ⓐ Ⓑ Ⓒ Ⓓ
75. Ⓐ Ⓑ Ⓒ Ⓓ
76. Ⓐ Ⓑ Ⓒ Ⓓ
77. Ⓐ Ⓑ Ⓒ Ⓓ
78. Ⓐ Ⓑ Ⓒ Ⓓ
79. Ⓐ Ⓑ Ⓒ Ⓓ
80. Ⓐ Ⓑ Ⓒ Ⓓ
81. Ⓐ Ⓑ Ⓒ Ⓓ
82. Ⓐ Ⓑ Ⓒ Ⓓ
83. Ⓐ Ⓑ Ⓒ Ⓓ
84. Ⓐ Ⓑ Ⓒ Ⓓ
85. Ⓐ Ⓑ Ⓒ Ⓓ
86. Ⓐ Ⓑ Ⓒ Ⓓ
87. Ⓐ Ⓑ Ⓒ Ⓓ
88. Ⓐ Ⓑ Ⓒ Ⓓ
89. Ⓐ Ⓑ Ⓒ Ⓓ
90. Ⓐ Ⓑ Ⓒ Ⓓ
91. Ⓐ Ⓑ Ⓒ Ⓓ
92. Ⓐ Ⓑ Ⓒ Ⓓ
93. Ⓐ Ⓑ Ⓒ Ⓓ
94. Ⓐ Ⓑ Ⓒ Ⓓ
95. Ⓐ Ⓑ Ⓒ Ⓓ
96. Ⓐ Ⓑ Ⓒ Ⓓ
97. Ⓐ Ⓑ Ⓒ Ⓓ
98. Ⓐ Ⓑ Ⓒ Ⓓ
99. Ⓐ Ⓑ Ⓒ Ⓓ
100. Ⓐ Ⓑ Ⓒ Ⓓ

Reading

PART 5: INCOMPLETE SENTENCES

101. Ⓐ Ⓑ Ⓒ Ⓓ
102. Ⓐ Ⓑ Ⓒ Ⓓ
103. Ⓐ Ⓑ Ⓒ Ⓓ
104. Ⓐ Ⓑ Ⓒ Ⓓ
105. Ⓐ Ⓑ Ⓒ Ⓓ
106. Ⓐ Ⓑ Ⓒ Ⓓ
107. Ⓐ Ⓑ Ⓒ Ⓓ
108. Ⓐ Ⓑ Ⓒ Ⓓ
109. Ⓐ Ⓑ Ⓒ Ⓓ
110. Ⓐ Ⓑ Ⓒ Ⓓ

111. Ⓐ Ⓑ Ⓒ Ⓓ
112. Ⓐ Ⓑ Ⓒ Ⓓ
113. Ⓐ Ⓑ Ⓒ Ⓓ
114. Ⓐ Ⓑ Ⓒ Ⓓ
115. Ⓐ Ⓑ Ⓒ Ⓓ
116. Ⓐ Ⓑ Ⓒ Ⓓ
117. Ⓐ Ⓑ Ⓒ Ⓓ
118. Ⓐ Ⓑ Ⓒ Ⓓ
119. Ⓐ Ⓑ Ⓒ Ⓓ
120. Ⓐ Ⓑ Ⓒ Ⓓ

121. Ⓐ Ⓑ Ⓒ Ⓓ
122. Ⓐ Ⓑ Ⓒ Ⓓ
123. Ⓐ Ⓑ Ⓒ Ⓓ
124. Ⓐ Ⓑ Ⓒ Ⓓ
125. Ⓐ Ⓑ Ⓒ Ⓓ
126. Ⓐ Ⓑ Ⓒ Ⓓ
127. Ⓐ Ⓑ Ⓒ Ⓓ
128. Ⓐ Ⓑ Ⓒ Ⓓ
129. Ⓐ Ⓑ Ⓒ Ⓓ
130. Ⓐ Ⓑ Ⓒ Ⓓ

131. Ⓐ Ⓑ Ⓒ Ⓓ
132. Ⓐ Ⓑ Ⓒ Ⓓ
133. Ⓐ Ⓑ Ⓒ Ⓓ
134. Ⓐ Ⓑ Ⓒ Ⓓ
135. Ⓐ Ⓑ Ⓒ Ⓓ
136. Ⓐ Ⓑ Ⓒ Ⓓ
137. Ⓐ Ⓑ Ⓒ Ⓓ
138. Ⓐ Ⓑ Ⓒ Ⓓ
139. Ⓐ Ⓑ Ⓒ Ⓓ
140. Ⓐ Ⓑ Ⓒ Ⓓ

PART 6: TEXT COMPLETION

141. Ⓐ Ⓑ Ⓒ Ⓓ
142. Ⓐ Ⓑ Ⓒ Ⓓ
143. Ⓐ Ⓑ Ⓒ Ⓓ

144. Ⓐ Ⓑ Ⓒ Ⓓ
145. Ⓐ Ⓑ Ⓒ Ⓓ
146. Ⓐ Ⓑ Ⓒ Ⓓ

147. Ⓐ Ⓑ Ⓒ Ⓓ
148. Ⓐ Ⓑ Ⓒ Ⓓ
149. Ⓐ Ⓑ Ⓒ Ⓓ

150. Ⓐ Ⓑ Ⓒ Ⓓ
151. Ⓐ Ⓑ Ⓒ Ⓓ
152. Ⓐ Ⓑ Ⓒ Ⓓ

PART 7: READING COMPREHENSION

153. Ⓐ Ⓑ Ⓒ Ⓓ
154. Ⓐ Ⓑ Ⓒ Ⓓ
155. Ⓐ Ⓑ Ⓒ Ⓓ
156. Ⓐ Ⓑ Ⓒ Ⓓ
157. Ⓐ Ⓑ Ⓒ Ⓓ
158. Ⓐ Ⓑ Ⓒ Ⓓ
159. Ⓐ Ⓑ Ⓒ Ⓓ
160. Ⓐ Ⓑ Ⓒ Ⓒ
161. Ⓐ Ⓑ Ⓒ Ⓓ
162. Ⓐ Ⓑ Ⓒ Ⓓ
163. Ⓐ Ⓑ Ⓒ Ⓓ
164. Ⓐ Ⓑ Ⓒ Ⓓ

165. Ⓐ Ⓑ Ⓒ Ⓓ
166. Ⓐ Ⓑ Ⓒ Ⓓ
167. Ⓐ Ⓑ Ⓒ Ⓓ
168. Ⓐ Ⓑ Ⓒ Ⓓ
169. Ⓐ Ⓑ Ⓒ Ⓓ
170. Ⓐ Ⓑ Ⓒ Ⓓ
171. Ⓐ Ⓑ Ⓒ Ⓓ
172. Ⓐ Ⓑ Ⓒ Ⓓ
173. Ⓐ Ⓑ Ⓒ Ⓓ
174. Ⓐ Ⓑ Ⓒ Ⓓ
175. Ⓐ Ⓑ Ⓒ Ⓓ
176. Ⓐ Ⓑ Ⓒ Ⓓ

177. Ⓐ Ⓑ Ⓒ Ⓓ
178. Ⓐ Ⓑ Ⓒ Ⓓ
179. Ⓐ Ⓑ Ⓒ Ⓓ
180. Ⓐ Ⓑ Ⓒ Ⓓ
181. Ⓐ Ⓑ Ⓒ Ⓓ
182. Ⓐ Ⓑ Ⓒ Ⓓ
183. Ⓐ Ⓑ Ⓒ Ⓓ
184. Ⓐ Ⓑ Ⓒ Ⓓ
185. Ⓐ Ⓑ Ⓒ Ⓓ
186. Ⓐ Ⓑ Ⓒ Ⓓ
187. Ⓐ Ⓑ Ⓒ Ⓓ
188. Ⓐ Ⓑ Ⓒ Ⓓ

189. Ⓐ Ⓑ Ⓒ Ⓓ
190. Ⓐ Ⓑ Ⓒ Ⓓ
191. Ⓐ Ⓑ Ⓒ Ⓓ
192. Ⓐ Ⓑ Ⓒ Ⓓ
193. Ⓐ Ⓑ Ⓒ Ⓓ
194. Ⓐ Ⓑ Ⓒ Ⓓ
195. Ⓐ Ⓑ Ⓒ Ⓓ
196. Ⓐ Ⓑ Ⓒ Ⓓ
197. Ⓐ Ⓑ Ⓒ Ⓓ
198. Ⓐ Ⓑ Ⓒ Ⓓ
199. Ⓐ Ⓑ Ⓒ Ⓓ
200. Ⓐ Ⓑ Ⓒ Ⓓ

Model Test 2
Listening Comprehension

In this section of the test, you will have the chance to show how well you understand spoken English. There are four parts to this section, with special directions for each part. You will have approximately 45 minutes to complete the Listening Comprehension sections.

Part 1: Photographs

Directions: You will see a photograph. You will hear four statements about the photograph. Choose the statement that most closely matches the photograph and fill in the corresponding oval on your answer sheet.

First News
Always Innovative & Informative

1.

2.

3.

4.

Model Test 2

Model Test 2

5.

6.

7.

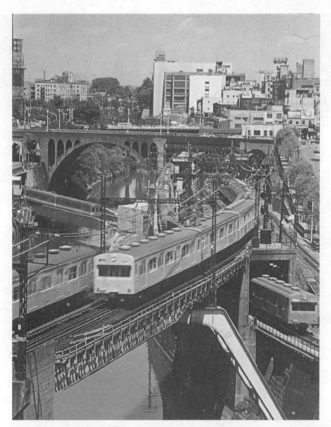

8.

Model Test 2

9.

10.

Part 2: Question-Response

Directions: You will hear a question and three possible responses. Choose the response that most closely answers the question and fill in the corresponding oval on your answer sheet.

11. Mark your answer on your answer sheet.

12. Mark your answer on your answer sheet.

13. Mark your answer on your answer sheet.

14. Mark your answer on your answer sheet.

15. Mark your answer on your answer sheet.

16. Mark your answer on your answer sheet.

17. Mark your answer on your answer sheet.

18. Mark your answer on your answer sheet.

19. Mark your answer on your answer sheet.

20. Mark your answer on your answer sheet.

21. Mark your answer on your answer sheet.

22. Mark your answer on your answer sheet.

23. Mark your answer on your answer sheet.

24. Mark your answer on your answer sheet.

25. Mark your answer on your answer sheet.

26. Mark your answer on your answer sheet.

27. Mark your answer on your answer sheet.

28. Mark your answer on your answer sheet.

29. Mark your answer on your answer sheet.

30. Mark your answer on your answer sheet.

31. Mark your answer on your answer sheet.

32. Mark your answer on your answer sheet.

33. Mark your answer on your answer sheet.

34. Mark your answer on your answer sheet.

35. Mark your answer on your answer sheet.

36. Mark your answer on your answer sheet.

37. Mark your answer on your answer sheet.

38. Mark your answer on your answer sheet.

39. Mark your answer on your answer sheet.

40. Mark your answer on your answer sheet.

Model Test 2

Part 3: Conversations

CD 3
Track
7

Directions: You will hear a conversation between two people. You will see three questions on each conversation and four possible answers. Choose the best answer to each question and fill in the corresponding oval on your answer sheet.

41. What does the man want the woman to do?

   (A) Help him remember something
   (B) Do some typing for him
   (C) Lend him a sweater
   (D) Read a letter

42. When does he need it done?

   (A) This afternoon
   (B) Before noon
   (C) On Tuesday
   (D) By 8:00

43. Why can't the woman help him?

   (A) Today is her day off.
   (B) She is leaving at noon.
   (C) She has to help Mr. Brown.
   (D) She's busy doing something else.

44. What is the woman buying?

   (A) Shirts
   (B) Skirts
   (C) Shoes
   (D) Boots

45. How much does she have to pay?

   (A) $42.05
   (B) $45
   (C) $60
   (D) $245

46. How does she want to pay?

   (A) Check
   (B) Cash
   (C) Credit card
   (D) Gift certificate

47. How many copies does the woman need to make?

   (A) 50
   (B) 100
   (C) 150
   (D) 200

48. When does she have to have them finished?

   (A) Before 11:00
   (B) By 2:00
   (C) At 4:00
   (D) Tonight

49. What will she do when the copies are made?

   (A) Mail them
   (B) Read them
   (C) Show them to her boss
   (D) Take them to a meeting

50. Where does this conversation take place?

   (A) In a hotel
   (B) In a fish store
   (C) In a restaurant
   (D) In someone's house

51. How long will the man have to wait?

   (A) Eight minutes
   (B) Nine minutes
   (C) Fifteen minutes
   (D) Fifty minutes

52. What will he do while he waits?

   (A) Have a drink
   (B) Sit and think
   (C) Go fishing
   (D) Wash the dishes

Model Test 2

53. Where is Mr. Wu now?

    (A) In his office
    (B) Out of town
    (C) At a meeting
    (D) On a flight

54. What does the woman want to do?

    (A) Get a massage
    (B) Speak with Mr. Wu
    (C) Play ball
    (D) Find out Mr. Wu's phone number

55. When will the woman be in her office?

    (A) 2:00
    (B) 2:30
    (C) 10:00
    (D) 10:30

56. Where did the woman leave her briefcase?

    (A) At a meeting
    (B) In her office
    (C) On her desk
    (D) In a cab

57. What is in the briefcase?

    (A) Notes
    (B) A report
    (C) A cell phone
    (D) Phone numbers

58. When does she need the contents of the briefcase?

    (A) This morning
    (B) This afternoon
    (C) Tonight
    (D) Tomorrow

59. Why does the man want to wake up early?

    (A) He has to catch an early train.
    (B) He wants to make a phone call.
    (C) He's going to take a morning plane.
    (D) He wants to hear the weather report.

60. How will the weather be tomorrow?

    (A) Snowy
    (B) Rainy
    (C) Cold
    (D) Hot

61. What time will the man wake up?

    (A) 5:30
    (B) 6:00
    (C) 6:30
    (D) 8:00

62. Where is the woman going to see the movie?

    (A) At home
    (B) At the college
    (C) At the theater
    (D) On the train

63. What will the man do tonight?

    (A) Watch the movie with the woman
    (B) Buy some tires for his car
    (C) Have dinner with friends
    (D) Go to sleep early

64. When will they take the train tomorrow?

    (A) Before breakfast
    (B) After breakfast
    (C) Before dinner
    (D) After dinner

65. What did the man send the woman?

(A) Some photographs
(B) Some money
(C) A report
(D) A letter

66. When did he send it?

(A) Sunday
(B) Monday
(C) Tuesday
(D) Wednesday

67. What does the woman ask the man to do?

(A) Pick up the mail
(B) Buy her a new dress
(C) Lend her more money
(D) Send something to her home

68. What sport does the man enjoy?

(A) Golf
(B) Tennis
(C) Biking
(D) Swimming

69. Where does he practice it?

(A) At the hotel
(B) At the park
(C) At the exercise club
(D) At the community center

70. How often does he practice it?

(A) Two times a week
(B) Three times a week
(C) Four times a week
(D) Five times a week

Model Test 2

Part 4: Talks

Directions: You will hear a talk given by a single speaker. You will see three questions on each talk, each with four possible answers. Choose the best answer to each question and fill in the corresponding oval on your answer sheet.

71. Who is the audience for this advertisement?

    (A) Airline pilots
    (B) Businesspeople
    (C) Tourists
    (D) Students

72. Why is this computer useful away from the office?

    (A) It's portable.
    (B) It can be rented.
    (C) It has a long-life battery pack.
    (D) It's easy to use.

73. How can a customer get a discount on this computer?

    (A) By ordering online
    (B) By calling the company
    (C) By completing an application
    (D) By ordering next month

74. What best describes the weather conditions the area is facing?

    (A) Cold
    (B) Fog
    (C) Snow and ice
    (D) Wind and rain

75. What problems will this weather cause tomorrow?

    (A) People will have trouble getting to work.
    (B) People won't have enough heat.
    (C) Flights will be cancelled.
    (D) People should buy plenty of food.

76. How will the weather be tomorrow afternoon?

    (A) Icy
    (B) Clear
    (C) Warmer
    (D) Freezing

77. According to the study, who is expected to be the least fit?

    (A) A mail carrier
    (B) A construction worker
    (C) An oil rigger
    (D) An accountant

78. Which is mentioned as a way to get more exercise?

    (A) Doing aerobics after work
    (B) Riding a stationary bicycle during breaks
    (C) Walking during lunch
    (D) Stretching

79. What advice is given about eating?

    (A) Eat more at night
    (B) Don't eat before bed
    (C) Eat fruit and vegetables
    (D) Don't eat a lot of nuts

80. Where would you be likely to hear this message?

    (A) At a government agency
    (B) On a personal phone
    (C) At a recording studio
    (D) On an intercom

81. What type of message should you leave?

    (A) Confidential
    (B) Clear
    (C) Detailed
    (D) Short

82. What will happen if a caller dials 499-4778?

    (A) He can apply for work.
    (B) He will reach an office.
    (C) He can leave a message.
    (D) He will hear the time of day.

Model Test 2

83. What can this company do for you?

    (A) Prepare your taxes
    (B) Claim your return
    (C) Write your financial records
    (D) Staff your accounting department

84. How does the company determine its fees?

    (A) By a flat rate
    (B) With a single price
    (C) By a prorated amount
    (D) By an hourly rate

85. What should listeners do today?

    (A) Provide financial records
    (B) Make an appointment
    (C) Return to the office
    (D) Pay their taxes

86. What did the airlines do to increase sales?

    (A) Reduce ticket prices
    (B) Provide more polite service
    (C) Make partnerships with hotels
    (D) Serve better meals

87. Why have these airlines lost customers?

    (A) Fewer people are flying.
    (B) The planes were always late.
    (C) Regional airlines are competing.
    (D) It's off-season.

88. What percentage of its customers did Sky King Airways lose in the past year?

    (A) 15%
    (B) 20%
    (C) 25%
    (D) 50%

89. Who would be likely to call this number?

    (A) A salesperson
    (B) A computer user
    (C) A customer service representative
    (D) An accountant

90. What will happen if the caller presses 1?

    (A) She will get help.
    (B) She can buy software.
    (C) She will hear about new products.
    (D) She can get an update.

91. What should you do if you want information not listed?

    (A) Dial 10
    (B) Hang up and call again
    (C) Go to a local store
    (D) Stay on the line

92. What is the destination for this flight?

    (A) Dallas
    (B) Houston
    (C) Madison
    (D) Wilmington

93. What does the captain say about the flight?

    (A) It will be late.
    (B) There will be turbulence.
    (C) It will be smooth.
    (D) The flying altitude will be low.

94. What is the weather like there?

    (A) Humid
    (B) Rainy
    (C) Breezy
    (D) Sunny

Model Test 2

95. What kind of problem does the area have?

    (A) There was an accident on the freeway.
    (B) The area is flooded.
    (C) There was a fire.
    (D) There was an earthquake.

96. Why are local relief centers running low on food?

    (A) Flood victims have filled the shelters.
    (B) Food spoiled because of moisture.
    (C) There was too much rain to grow food.
    (D) They cannot deliver the food.

97. If you want to donate food, where should you take it?

    (A) To the public
    (B) The relief center
    (C) The radio station
    (D) A food collection center

98. What will take place in seven days?

    (A) The voicemail system will change.
    (B) This customer will get a new telephone.
    (C) This customer will get a new telephone number.
    (D) The telephone company's web address will change.

99. How can a customer save a message?

    (A) Press two
    (B) Press four
    (C) Press seven
    (D) Press nine

100. How can a customer learn about all of the new codes?

    (A) Press ten
    (B) Press the star key
    (C) Visit the company's website
    (D) Listen to the entire message

STOP

This is the end of the Listening Comprehension portion of the test. Turn to Part 5 in your test book.

Reading

In this section of the test, you will have the chance to show how well you understand written English. There are three parts to this section, with special directions for each part.

YOU WILL HAVE ONE HOUR AND FIFTEEN MINUTES TO COMPLETE PARTS 5, 6, AND 7 OF THE TEST.

Part 5: Incomplete Sentences

Directions: You will see a sentence with a missing word. Four possible answers follow the sentence. Choose the best answer to the question and fill in the corresponding oval on your answer sheet.

101. Inter Coast Airlines' flight _____ Seoul has been delayed.

  (A) to
  (B) in
  (C) by
  (D) at

102. An _____ training period will be instituted in July.

  (A) extend
  (B) extended
  (C) extension
  (D) extent

103. _____ she left the ship, the purser signed out.

  (A) For
  (B) That
  (C) And
  (D) Before

104. Many subscribers have requested that we _____ the journals to their offices.

  (A) mails
  (B) mailed
  (C) mail
  (D) mailing

105. The clerk found the typographical error after the messenger _____ the proposal.

  (A) delivered
  (B) delivers
  (C) has delivered
  (D) is delivering

106. Ms. Franklin directed a very _____ project.

  (A) successfully
  (B) successive
  (C) success
  (D) successful

107. You should register for the seminar _____ you attend.

  (A) while
  (B) before
  (C) nor
  (D) and

108. The speaker has _____ his speech by two minutes.

  (A) short
  (B) shortening
  (C) shortened
  (D) shortage

Model Test 2

109. The vice-president will be seated _____ the chairman at the banquet.

    (A) as
    (B) by
    (C) to
    (D) from

110. The new waiter has not made any _____ mistakes.

    (A) foolish
    (B) fool
    (C) foolishness
    (D) fooled

111. By Friday, twenty-five applications had been submitted _____ the position of desk clerk.

    (A) at
    (B) on
    (C) for
    (D) by

112. The ship provisions officer _____ his supplies in large quantities.

    (A) buy
    (B) buys
    (C) buying
    (D) to buy

113. Mr. Cruz needs someone to _____ him with the conference display.

    (A) assume
    (B) assign
    (C) assent
    (D) assist

114. Budget meetings are held _____ in the conference room.

    (A) rarely
    (B) every week
    (C) always
    (D) sometimes

115. At midnight, the second shift of security guards _____ on duty.

    (A) coming
    (B) to come
    (C) comes
    (D) come

116. The final purchase price was higher than the investors _____.

    (A) had expected
    (B) expect
    (C) are expecting
    (D) will expect

117. A manager _____ new things from his or her staff.

    (A) can sometimes learn
    (B) learning sometimes can
    (C) sometimes learn can
    (D) sometimes can learning

118. The new insurance plan is especially _____ with employees who have families.

    (A) popularized
    (B) popular
    (C) populated
    (D) popularity

119. The finance committee will meet again _____ the eighth of May.

    (A) for
    (B) to
    (C) from
    (D) on

120. The airline will refund the money _____ you cancel the reservation.

    (A) during
    (B) soon
    (C) when
    (D) until

Model Test 2

121. Did Mr. Fisk _____ the reference guide from the company library?

    (A) loan
    (B) borrow
    (C) lend
    (D) sent

122. _____ they were ordered, the brochures and business cards were never printed.

    (A) Although
    (B) Even
    (C) However
    (D) Despite

123. The operator does not remember receiving a fax from the Madrid office _____ from the Paris office.

    (A) or
    (B) and
    (C) either
    (D) but

124. Have you ever used this type of copy machine _____?

    (A) before
    (B) prior
    (C) advance
    (D) previous

125. If our ship _____ fewer passengers, the crew would not have to share rooms.

    (A) had
    (B) have
    (C) will have
    (D) would have

126. You should check your messages _____.

    (A) as soon as
    (B) twice a day
    (C) seldom
    (D) rarely

127. The receptionist receives packages and _____ them until the proper department is notified.

    (A) is holding
    (B) held
    (C) hold
    (D) holds

128. The purpose of our conference is to help employees _____ our policies.

    (A) understood
    (B) understanding
    (C) understand
    (D) is understanding

129. _____ none of us were familiar with the city, Mr. Gutman drove us to the meeting.

    (A) Although
    (B) Because
    (C) Therefore
    (D) However

130. The auditor discovered that the accountant had not been _____ the checks into the correct account.

    (A) deposited
    (B) deposits
    (C) deposit
    (D) depositing

131. If this report is sent by overnight delivery, it _____ Milan by noon tomorrow.

    (A) reaches
    (B) will reach
    (C) is reaching
    (D) has reached

132. Most employees drive to work and _____ the building from the parking lot.

    (A) enter
    (B) entered
    (C) entering
    (D) entrance

133. Employees who _____ attending the conference can get a discount on travel arrangements.

    (A) have going
    (B) are going
    (C) will
    (D) will be

134. Mr. Vasco worked hard to develop his _____ in electronics.

    (A) expertly
    (B) expert
    (C) expertise
    (D) expectant

135. The _____ rates change daily.

    (A) money
    (B) bills
    (C) coins
    (D) currency

136. The head housekeeper is going to ask Ms. Chang how much time she _____ available.

    (A) will have had
    (B) is having
    (C) have
    (D) has

137. The hotel marketing director is quite _____ about advertising in Europe.

    (A) knowing
    (B) knowledge
    (C) knowledgeable
    (D) knows

138. Mr. Ni _____ in charge of the research division for two years.

    (A) has
    (B) has been
    (C) is
    (D) had

139. The operator _____ Mr. Smith if she knew where to reach him.

    (A) will call
    (B) had called
    (C) called
    (D) would call

140. The trainers for the seminar had the crew _____ their equipment to the conference center.

    (A) move
    (B) moving
    (C) mover
    (D) moved

Part 6: Text Completion

Directions: You will see four passages each with three blanks. Under each blank are four answer options. Choose the word or phrase that best completes the sentence.

Questions 141–143 refer to the following letter.

Creek and Chung, Accountants
1040 Stone Way
Seattle, Washington 93108-2662

July 12, 20—

Mr. Hugh Ferrer
Unity Health Care
400 East Pine Street
Seattle, Washington 93129-2665

Dear Mr. Ferrer:

We are a mid-sized accounting firm. Our staff members have expressed dissatisfaction with our current insurance plan, so we are looking into other _____. The insurance company we use now has recently

141. (A) employees
     (B) positions
     (C) activities
     (D) options

raised its rates, while at the same time the quality of service has gotten worse. Naturally, we are not happy about paying more and more money for poor service. _____, we are interested in learning more about Unity Health Care (UHC).

142. (A) Therefore
     (B) However
     (C) Moreover
     (D) Nevertheless

Could you please mail a packet of information to me? Also, I would appreciate it if you could answer the following questions.

First, our employees want to choose their own doctors. Does your program allow this? Second, do your doctors have weekend and evening hours? Our employees have busy work schedules, and it is not always _____ for them to go to appointments during regular business hours.

143. (A) enjoyable
     (B) difficult
     (C) convenient
     (D) interesting

Thank you for your help.

Sincerely,

Felicia Braddish

Felicia Braddish
Human Resources Manager

Questions 144–146 refer to the following e-mail.

From: Simon Yan
To: Mingmei Lee
Subject: Monday meeting

Dear Mingmei,

I have to leave town for a business trip _____ there is an emergency in our Singapore

144. (A) so
(B) if
(C) as
(D) by

office. I am sorry that I will have to miss our Monday morning meeting, especially because I am eager to see your progress on my company's new financial center. This is an important project for National Bank.

My coworker, Hugh Harrison, will _____ me. Hugh plans to look for you at the

145. (A) escort
(B) replace
(C) assist
(D) accompany

construction site at 9:00 A.M. You told me that you have some concerns about the project's budget. Please talk with Hugh about this. While we don't want to spend a lot of extra money on this building, it is going to be our company's headquarters and needs to look good. You have an excellent reputation as a Construction Project Manager, so I'm _____ that

146. (A) doubtful
(B) positive
(C) wondering
(D) concerned

you can manage the budget and build a fantastic center for us at the same time.

I will return one week from today. You can e-mail me until I return. Thank you.

Questions 147–149 refer to the following memorandum.

Memorandum

From: Belinda Beilby, Company President
To: Company Vice-Presidents
Re: Reducing electricity expenses

The electric company is _____ its rates by 25% next month, so we need to look at

147. (A) cutting
(B) increasing
(C) dividing
(D) improving

ways to reduce our electricity usage. Below is a list of recommendations. Please distribute this list to the departments in your area.

Ways to Reduce Electricity Expenses

1. Lights: Turn off the lights in meeting rooms when your meeting ends. Turn off the lights in the offices before you leave for the day.

2. Computers: At the day's end, turn off your computer.

3. Photocopying: Don't photocopy and fax documents. Most documents can _____ electronically.

148. (A) send
(B) sent
(C) to send
(D) be sent

4. Fans/Heaters: Using fans or heaters in the office should not be necessary. The building's temperature is set at a comfortable level. If your office is too cool or warm, please contact the maintenance staff.

5. Home Office Option: _____ employees to work at home one or more days a week

149. (A) Allow
(B) Allowing
(C) To allow
(D) Will allow

saves money in many ways, including on electricity. Employees who are interested in this option should speak to their supervisors.

Questions 150–152 refer to the following announcement.

Sunrise Manufacturers, Inc. announced Friday that its president, Shirley Ocampo, would succeed Louis Freeland as the company's chief executive officer starting on September 15. Ms. Ocampo, 52, will be the first woman chief executive at the company in its 75-year history. Sunrise Manufacturers is _____ manufacturer of farming equipment in the

150. (A) large
(B) larger
(C) the larger
(D) the largest

nation. This is a sector that has traditionally been _____ by men, making the

151. (A) dominate
(B) dominates
(C) dominated
(D) dominating

appointment of Ms. Ocampo particularly significant. "We have waited a long time for this to happen," said Martha Steinway of the National Association of Female Executives. "This is a great achievement for women." Mr. Freeland, who will retire from Sunrise when Ms. Ocampo takes over his position next month, _____ at the company for 25 years.

152. (A) works
(B) worked
(C) had worked
(D) has been working

Part 7: Reading Comprehension

Directions: You will see single and double reading passages followed by several questions. Each question has four answer choices. Choose the best answer to the question and fill in the corresponding oval on your answer sheet.

Questions 153–154 refer to the following announcement.

As our company plans new products and processes, health, safety and environmental considerations are a priority. We are committed to operating our manufacturing plants and research facilities in a manner that protects the environment and safeguards the health and safety of all people. We will continue to allocate money to improve existing facilities as new safety information is brought to light.

153. What is the purpose of this announcement?

(A) To announce an expansion
(B) To report on a merger
(C) To reassure the public about safety issues
(D) To explain a new company policy

154. What will the company do with existing facilities?

(A) Make them safer
(B) Tear them down
(C) Have them inspected
(D) Renovate them

Questions 155–157 refer to the following report.

> The profits for the Wu Company more than doubled in the fourth quarter over profit levels of a year ago. This is due in part to lower operating and administrative expenses. The electronics store chain earned $42.6 million, compared with $21.1 million in the fourth quarter of last year. Total profits for the year are $122.8 million, compared with $48.5 million last year.

155. How do fourth quarter profits for this year compare to those of last year?

(A) Stayed the same
(B) Increased by twice as much
(C) Increased by more than twice as much
(D) Decreased by half

156. What contributed to the change?

(A) Reduction of operating costs
(B) Higher number of customers
(C) New and better products
(D) More expensive products

157. The word *chain* in line 3, is closest in meaning to

(A) product
(B) necklace
(C) staff members
(D) group of stores

Questions 158–159 refer to the following advertisement.

> **Data Entry/Clerk**
>
> Insurance firm seeks reliable, detail-oriented person for operations division. Responsibilities include data entry, filing, and word processing. Good salary and benefits. Pleasant atmosphere. Room to advance.

158. What is one responsibility of this job?

(A) Answering the phone
(B) Data entry
(C) Selling insurance
(D) Operating a division

159. What is one benefit of the position?

(A) They'll give you your own office later.
(B) You can work toward promotions.
(C) Benefits apply to dependents.
(D) You can earn commissions.

Questions 160–161 refer to the following magazine article.

When you are looking for a new job, you must talk to as many people as you can who work in your field or in related fields. This is called networking. Networking allows you to learn about new areas to pursue and to find out which companies may need someone with your skills. Networking is a fun and easy way to find out about new opportunities. And when your new job comes along, you will already know some of your colleagues.

160. What is networking?

  (A) Learning your job well
  (B) Meeting people in related fields
  (C) Studying lots of companies
  (D) Getting along with your colleagues

161. What is NOT mentioned as something you can learn from networking?

  (A) New career areas
  (B) Your colleagues and what they do
  (C) Which companies may need you
  (D) What the companies pay

Questions 162–163 refer to the following memo.

MEMORANDUM

To: All employees
Fm: Donetta Muscillo
      Safety Coordinator
Date: June 5, 20—

Sub: Fire doors

Employees are reminded that doors designated as fire doors must stay closed at all times. The purpose of fire doors is to help direct smoke away from areas where people are working in case of a fire in the building. Even though the weather is hot and the repairs to the company's air conditioner are not complete, keeping the fire doors open is strictly prohibited.

162. What is the purpose of the company's fire doors?

  (A) To keep smoke away from people
  (B) To provide escape routes
  (C) To keep fire from spreading
  (D) To contain heat

163. Why were employees probably keeping the fire doors open?

  (A) To get to a higher floor
  (B) To look at the view
  (C) To go from office to office
  (D) To let in cool air

Questions 164–166 refer to the following calendar.

FEBRUARY	**MARCH**	**APRIL**	**MAY**
February 4– February 24 Bonn, Germany International Jewelry Trade Fair	March 11–April 15 Budapest, Hungary International Furniture Fair March 12–March 20 Milan, Italy Automobile Show March 15–March 18 Guangzhou, China International Shoe Fair March 20–March 25 Moscow, Russia International Textile Fair	April 16–April 24 Hannover, Germany Art and Antiques Fair April 14–April 21 Basel, Switzerland European Watch Fair	May 27–June 12 Bath, England International Computer Exhibit

164. What does this calendar list?

(A) Trade shows
(B) Musical events
(C) Sport competitions
(D) A tour itinerary

165. Which event does not take place in Europe?

(A) Automobile Show
(B) International Shoe Fair
(C) Art and Antiques Fair
(D) International Jewelry Trade Fair

166. If you were a buyer for a dress manufacturer, where should you go in March?

(A) Budapest
(B) Bonn
(C) Moscow
(D) Hannover

Questions 167–168 refer to the following announcement.

ESTATE AUCTION

An auction for the estate of *Raul Diega*
will be held on

Saturday, October 3, at 11:00 A.M.
(preview starts at 10:00 A.M.)

Location: 5667 North Hedge Lane

Some of the items to be auctioned
* 2004 Mercedes
* China and crystal
* Oriental rugs
* Jewelry
* Stamp collection

Questions? Please call Estate Planners at
778-0099 between noon and 5 P.M.

---

167. Which of the following items will be auctioned?

(A) Chinese antiques·
(B) Rare books
(C) Bracelets
(D) Wall-to-wall carpeting

168. When can you start to look at things?

(A) October 3, 11:00 A.M.
(B) By appointment after calling 778-0099
(C) Any day from noon to five
(D) October 3, 10:00 A.M.

Questions 169–171 refer to the following magazine article.

Historically, the businessperson has wanted his or her company to grow. Larger companies meant greater success and greater profits. Larger companies also meant more jobs for people in the community. But some companies have become so large that they are no longer profitable or practical to run. When this happens, the company may downsize, or deliberately reduce growth. This corporate downsizing is no longer unusual. Major corporations have either already downsized or have announced plans to do so. But the decision to downsize is not always popular with the community, because it means loss of jobs. ■

---

169. Why would a company try to slow growth?

(A) To meet government regulations
(B) To stay profitable
(C) To avoid moving
(D) To move its operations overseas

170. Why may the community dislike the decision to downsize?

(A) Area residents may lose their jobs.
(B) The company will probably move.
(C) The company's products will get more expensive.
(D) The company will lose profits.

171. The word *deliberately* in line 12, is closest in meaning to

(A) intentionally.
(B) carefully.
(C) suddenly.
(D) slowly.

Questions 172–176 refer to the following article.

Meetings can waste a great deal of time. But you can make your meeting run more smoothly by following a few simple rules. First, have an agenda. This will help keep you focused on what is important. Next, decide who needs to be involved. More people means less efficient discussion. Finally, keep the discussion moving. Thank each speaker as he or she finishes and move on to the next speaker. This encourages people to make their remarks brief. And don't forget: What happens after a meeting is more important than what happens during the meeting. The skills used then are more professional and less procedural. So no matter how well you run a meeting, it is the work that gets done after the meeting that is important.

172. What is one way to run a meeting well?

(A) Watch how your manager runs meetings.
(B) Minimize the number of participants.
(C) Let the group make decisions.
(D) Let everyone speak.

173. What is the purpose of a meeting agenda?

(A) To keep the speakers organized
(B) To allow free discussion
(C) To send to others in advance
(D) To keep focused on important items

174. How should you receive other people's comments at a meeting?

(A) Try to keep others from talking.
(B) Thank them and move on.
(C) Give them as much time as they want.
(D) Respond in detail to all comments.

175. The word *remarks* in lines 17–18, is closest in meaning to

(A) meetings
(B) questions
(C) comments
(D) schedules

176. The author states that

(A) meetings should be held more frequently.
(B) all meetings should be in the morning.
(C) no one should receive credit for their work.
(D) the real work is accomplished after the meetings.

Questions 177–180 refer to the following announcement.

The Hesseltine Corporation is moving 60 technical and management-level employees to their new manufacturing plant in the western United States. Before the move, the company will prepare employees for the cultural changes they will encounter when moving from urban Europe to a small town in the American West. The employees and their families will attend special seminars on the habits of Americans. They will learn about the regional vocabulary and the daily life. Without this training, even small cultural differences could cause big misunderstandings.

177. Where is the new manufacturing plant?

    (A) In an urban area
    (B) In Western Europe
    (C) In the western United States
    (D) In a large town

178. What important part of the moving process is discussed?

    (A) Completing the plant
    (B) Getting the office furnishings
    (C) Arranging airline tickets
    (D) Teaching cultural differences

179. Who will attend the seminars in addition to the employees?

    (A) Their secretaries
    (B) Their families
    (C) Their supervisors
    (D) Their staffs

180. What do they learn in the seminars?

    (A) How to make travel plans
    (B) Methods of business management
    (C) Characteristics of American culture
    (D) Manufacturing techniques

Questions 181–185 refer to the following two e-mails.

From:	"Yvonne Wu" <Yvonne@messages.com>
To:	"Royal Hotel" <reservations@royal.com>
Subject:	Room Reservations

I need a single room with a queen-sized bed for four nights, from March 15 until March 18. Do you have a room available then? I will be attending a conference at the Convention Center and I understand that your hotel is just two blocks from there. Please confirm this for me as I don't want to have to walk far or deal with cabs. Also, do you have a pool and a weight room? Is there a restaurant located in or near the hotel?

Thank you for your help.

From:	"Royal Hotel" <reservations@royal.com>
To:	"Yvonne Wu" <Yvonne@messages.com>
Subject:	Re: Reservations for a Business Trip

We do have the type of room that you want. It costs $100 per night. However, for the first night of your stay only, I will have to give you a king-sized bed as there are no queens available that night. It costs an extra $25. I hope this will suit you. Starting on March 16, you can have the type of room you requested. I can confirm that we are located very close to the Convention Center, just one block further than you thought. It is a very pleasant walk through a park to the Center, and I'm sure you will enjoy it. We do have a pool, but unfortunately it is currently closed for repairs. There is a full–service restaurant, BJ's, located in the hotel. Hotel guests are entitled to a free breakfast there. Lunch and dinner are also served and can be charged to your room for your convenience. If you would like to go ahead with your reservation, please send me your credit card information as soon as possible.

181. When does Yvonne Wu want to begin her stay at the Royal Hotel?

(A) March 15
(B) March 16
(C) March 17
(D) March 18

182. What kind of room does she request?

(A) A room for one person
(B) A room with two queen-sized beds
(C) A room near the pool
(D) A room with a view of the park

183. If Yvonne Wu makes the reservation suggested in the hotel e-mail, how much will she pay?

(A) $100
(B) $125
(C) $425
(D) $500

184. How far is the hotel from the Convention Center?

(A) One block
(B) Two blocks
(C) Three blocks
(D) Four blocks

185. What is included in the price of the hotel room?

(A) Breakfast
(B) Room service
(C) Use of the pool
(D) Use of the weight room

Questions 186–190 refer to the following agenda and e-mail message.

HORIZON OFFICE PRODUCTS, INC.
COMMITTEE MEETING ON MARKETING
THURSDAY, JUNE 15, 20—   9:30 A.M.-11:30 A.M.
PLACE: ROOM 2

AGENDA

1. REVIEW OF CURRENT STRATEGY   BEN NGUYEN
2. GOALS FOR NEW STRATEGY   BO PARK
3. FOCUS GROUPS   MARTY TAYLOR
4. PROJECTS TO BEGIN   BARBARA SPENCER
5. PLANS FOR THE YEAR   RITA PALMER

To: Max Kohler
From: Bo Park
Subject: Committee Meeting

There were serious problems at today's meeting. We began on time, but Ben wasn't there, so we had to begin with the second agenda item. Then, thirty minutes after we began, Ben finally arrived and gave his presentation. Marty never came at all. I found out later that he's been out sick, but in any case his topic was never discussed. Barbara tried to explain her topic, but it was confusing. She did the best she could, but we really needed to hear from Marty first for her presentation to make sense. We couldn't agree on our next step, so we ended the meeting early, right after Barbara's talk. When will you return from this business trip? I know none of this would have happened if you had been here.

186. What was the topic of the June 15 meeting?

    (A) Marketing
    (B) Business trips
    (C) Work schedules
    (D) Ordering office supplies

187. What topic was discussed first?

    (A) Review of current strategy
    (B) Goals for new strategy
    (C) Focus groups
    (D) Projects to begin

188. What time did Ben start his presentation?

    (A) 9:00
    (B) 9:30
    (C) 10:00
    (D) 11:30

189. Who gave the last presentation?

    (A) Rita Palmer
    (B) Barbara Spencer
    (C) Marty Taylor
    (D) Bo Park

190. Why didn't Max attend the meeting?

    (A) He was out sick.
    (B) He wasn't invited.
    (C) He couldn't arrive on time.
    (D) He was away on a business trip.

Questions 191–195 refer to the following e-mail and table.

From: "Aras Koca" <Aras@apex.com>
To: "Clarice Ryan" <Clarice@apex.com>
Subject: Report on Employees' Use of Time

Clarice, I agree that waste of work time is a serious issue. The Human Resources Department recently surveyed the employees. They are wasting close to two hours per day.

Here are my ideas to reduce this waste. First we need to agree on what are the most important behaviors to stop. For example, look at item #1. Many people are doing this; however, it is the most difficult to stop. I recommend that we focus on activities #2, 4, and 5.

Making phone calls shows the largest difference between men and women. Women do this much more than men. We should ask all employees to limit these calls. They should return non-urgent messages at their lunch break.

For #4, we should focus on the younger age group. We will tell them that we are going to check their work accounts for personal messages. For #5, we can ask supervisors to watch this more carefully. Perhaps activity #3 should continue. This allows employees to know each other and it can increase their motivation. The supervisors will know if someone is spending too much time talking and not enough time working.

Are you available tomorrow? I'd like to meet with you to discuss our next step.

Time Spent on Nonwork-related Activities

Activity	Percentage of employees who do this three times per week or more	
	Men	Women
1. Surfing the Internet*	85%	83%
2. Making personal phone calls	65%	80%
3. Talking to coworkers**	60%	70%
4. Writing personal e-mails*	45%	45%
5. Taking long breaks	30%	20%

Key: *most common with workers 22–35; ** most common with workers 45–60

191. Why was the survey done?

    (A) To help plan a better work schedule
    (B) To find out how employees waste
        their work time
    (C) To learn which employees know how
        to use the Internet
    (D) To discover which employees are
        unhappy with their jobs

192. Which is the most popular activity among
    the employees?

    (A) Going online
    (B) Talking on the phone
    (C) Socializing with other employees
    (D) Taking breaks

193. Among which group is writing personal
    e-mails most common?

    (A) Younger people
    (B) Older people
    (C) Women
    (D) Men

194. Which activity does Aras Koca consider
    the least problematic?

    (A) Going online
    (B) Talking on the phone
    (C) Socializing with other employees
    (D) Sending e-mails

195. Which activity does Aras Koca want super-
    visors to monitor?

    (A) Visiting websites
    (B) Sending personal e-mails
    (C) Answering phone messages
    (D) Spending too much time on breaks

Model Test 2

Questions 196–200 refer to the following two letters

The Printing Press
111 Acorn Parkway
San Antonio, TX 78216-7423

April 6, 20—

Anneliese Clark
Federal Bank
8244 Centergate Street
San Antonio, TX 78217-0099

Dear Ms. Clark:

I have been a customer at your bank for more than ten years. I am a small business owner and have been renting a space for my operations. My company is now ready to expand, and I am looking into buying a small building.

I am interested in two buildings. The one I prefer is on Main Street. It would require a $200,000 loan, and I'm not sure if I qualify for that large a loan. There is another building that would suit my needs. The size is right although the location is not as good. I would need to borrow only $130,000 to purchase this building.

I have a good credit record and am carrying only two debts at this time—$5,000 on my car loan and $120,000 on my house. I am hoping to get a thirty-year loan at 5% interest.

I would like to meet with you to discuss this as soon as possible. Would Tuesday, April 21 suit you? If not, I am available any other day that week. I look forward to hearing from you.

Sincerely,

Jeremiah Hernandez

Jeremiah Hernandez

---

196. Why does Mr. Hernandez want to buy a building?

(A) He wants to rent it out.
(B) He needs a place to live.
(C) He is expanding his business.
(D) He just bought a new company.

197. Why does he prefer the Main Street building?

(A) It's bigger.
(B) It's cheaper.
(C) It's in a better location.
(D) It's in better condition.

198. How much debt does Mr. Hernandez have now?

(A) $5,000
(B) $120,000
(C) $125,000
(D) $200,000

FEDERAL BANK
8244 Centergate Street
San Antonio, TX 78217-0099

April 10, 20—

Jeremiah Hernandez
The Printing Press
111 Acorn Parkway
San Antonio, TX 78216-7423

Dear Mr. Hernandez:

Thank you for your interest in getting a loan from Federal Bank. We appreciate your business.

It is possible for us to lend you enough money for the cheaper building. We cannot give you a larger loan because you already have more than $100,000 in debt. We can offer you a loan at the interest rate and for the term you want.

I am happy to meet with you to discuss this. I am not available on the date you mentioned. Can we meet the following day? Please let me know.

Best Wishes,

Anneliese Clark

Anneliese Clark

199. How much money will the bank lend him?

(A) $100,000
(B) $130,000
(C) $200,000
(D) $330,000

200. When does Ms. Clark want to meet with Mr. Hernandez?

(A) April 10
(B) April 11
(C) April 21
(D) April 22

STOP

This is the end of the test. If you finish before time is called, you may go back to Parts 5, 6, and 7 and check your work.

First News
Always Innovative & Informative

Answer Key
MODEL TEST 2

Listening Comprehension

PART 1: PHOTOGRAPHS

1. B	4. A	7. B	10. A
2. D	5. C	8. C	
3. B	6. A	9. D	

PART 2: QUESTION-RESPONSE

11. A	19. A	27. C	35. B
12. C	20. C	28. A	36. B
13. A	21. A	29. C	37. C
14. B	22. B	30. B	38. A
15. A	23. A	31. A	39. B
16. A	24. B	32. B	40. A
17. C	25. A	33. A	
18. A	26. B	34. A	

PART 3: CONVERSATIONS

41. B	49. A	57. A	65. C
42. B	50. C	58. D	66. B
43. D	51. C	59. C	67. D
44. A	52. A	60. B	68. B
45. B	53. C	61. A	69. D
46. D	54. B	62. B	70. D
47. C	55. B	63. D	
48. A	56. D	64. B	

PART 4: TALKS

71. B	79. C	87. C	95. B
72. A	80. B	88. C	96. A
73. A	81. D	89. B	97. D
74. C	82. B	90. A	98. A
75. A	83. A	91. D	99. D
76. C	84. D	92. B	100. B
77. D	85. B	93. B	
78. C	86. A	94. D	

Reading

PART 5: INCOMPLETE SENTENCES

101. A	111. C	121. B	131. B
102. B	112. B	122. A	132. A
103. D	113. D	123. A	133. D
104. C	114. B	124. A	134. C
105. A	115. C	125. A	135. D
106. D	116. A	126. B	136. D
107. B	117. A	127. D	137. C
108. C	118. B	128. C	138. B
109. B	119. D	129. B	139. D
110. A	120. C	130. D	140. A

PART 6: TEXT COMPLETION

141. D	144. C	147. B	150. D
142. A	145. B	148. D	151. C
143. C	146. B	149. B	152. D

PART 7: READING COMPREHENSION

153. C	165. B	177. C	189. B
154. A	166. C	178. D	190. D
155. C	167. C	179. B	191. B
156. A	168. D	180. C	192. A
157. D	169. B	181. A	193. A
158. B	170. A	182. A	194. C
159. B	171. A	183. C	195. D
160. B	172. B	184. C	196. C
161. D	173. D	185. A	197. C
162. A	174. B	186. A	198. C
163. D	175. C	187. B	199. B
164. A	176. D	188. C	200. D

Model Test 2—Answer Key

First News
Always Innovative & Informative

Test Score Conversion Table

Count your correct responses. Match the number of correct responses with the corresponding score from the Test Score Conversion Table (below). Add the two scores together. This is your Total Estimated Test Score. As you practice taking the TOEIC model tests, your scores should improve. Keep track of your Total Estimated Test Scores.

Model Test 2—Test Score Conversion Table

# Correct	Listening Score	Reading Score	# Correct	Listening Score	Reading Score	# Correct	Listening Score	Reading Score	# Correct	Listening Score	Reading Score
0	5	5	26	110	65	51	255	220	76	410	370
1	5	5	27	115	70	52	260	225	77	420	380
2	5	5	28	120	80	53	270	230	78	425	385
3	5	5	29	125	85	54	275	235	79	430	390
4	5	5	30	130	90	55	280	240	80	440	395
5	5	5	31	135	95	56	290	250	81	445	400
6	5	5	32	140	100	57	295	255	82	450	405
7	10	5	33	145	110	58	300	260	83	460	410
8	15	5	34	150	115	59	310	265	84	465	415
9	20	5	35	160	120	60	315	270	85	470	420
10	25	5	36	165	125	61	320	280	86	475	425
11	30	5	37	170	130	62	325	285	87	480	430
12	35	5	38	175	140	63	330	290	88	485	435
13	40	5	39	180	145	64	340	300	89	490	445
14	45	5	40	185	150	65	345	305	90	495	450
15	50	5	41	190	160	66	350	310	91	495	455
16	55	10	42	195	165	67	360	320	92	495	465
17	60	15	43	200	170	68	365	325	93	495	470
18	65	20	44	210	175	69	370	330	94	495	480
19	70	25	45	215	180	70	380	335	95	495	485
20	75	30	46	220	190	71	385	340	96	495	490
21	80	35	47	230	195	72	390	350	97	495	495
22	85	40	48	240	200	73	395	355	98	495	495
23	90	45	49	245	210	74	400	360	99	495	495
24	95	50	50	250	215	75	405	365	100	495	495
25	100	60									

Number of Correct Listening Responses _____ = Listening Score _____

Number of Correct Reading Responses _____ = Reading Score _____

Total Estimated Test Score _____

Model Test 2—Explanatory Answers

LISTENING COMPREHENSION

Part 1: Photographs

1. **(B)** The two men are signing their names on a document. Choice (A) uses the associated word *paper*. Choice (C) talks about the plane models on the table. Choice (D) confuses the similar-sounding *reading* for *writing*.

2. **(D)** Choice (D) identifies the *occupation* and the *action*. The kitchen and the uniforms imply they are *cooks* engaged in their occupation. Choice (A) is incorrect because in the photo there is a man pointing, not a sign. Choice (B) is incorrect because no one is chopping vegetables. Choice (C) is incorrect since no one is leaving.

3. **(B)** Choice (B) identifies the action of a technician *pushing a button*. Choice (A) is incorrect; the man is looking at the panel, not a clock. Choice (C) is out of context. Choice (D) confuses an electronic *panel* with a *panel* of experts.

4. **(A)** Choice (A) identifies the couples' action, viewing art. Choice (B) is incorrect because some paintings are smaller than others. Choice (C) is incorrect because in the picture the *pictures are on the wall*, not *stacked on the floor*. Choice (D) is incorrect because there are no sculptures in the picture and it confuses *stand out* and people *standing*.

5. **(C)** Choice (C) makes the assumption that the location is an *airport* and that the people waiting are *passengers*. Choice (A) is incorrect because most of the passengers are *males*, not *females*. Choice (B) is contradicted by *empty*; there are many people on the concourse. Choice (D) does not describe the location of the *bags*, which are on the *floor* not on a *truck*.

6. **(A)** Choice (A) correctly describes the action, looking at their laptop, and the background shows they are outdoors. Choice (B) confuses the action: There are two people and there is a coffee cup on the table, but they are not making the coffee. Choice (C) is incorrect because you cannot see their hands. Choice (D) is incorrect because they are already seated at a table.

7. **(B)** Choice (B) identifies the specific locations of the *trains*. Choice (A) confuses the sound of *train* with *crane* and uses the related word to *bridge, water*. Choice (C) uses words related to *train (narrow* and *tunnel)* but does not describe the picture and confuses the sound of *cart* with *train car*. Choice (D) is incorrect because although the city looks cluttered, there are not many skyscrapers in the picture.

8. **(C)** Choice (C) identifies the location and the action. Choice (A) uses negation; the *auditorium is not crowded*. Choice (B) is incorrect because there is no panel, and the audience is not interacting, but watching. Choice (D) uses related words such as *chairs*.

9. **(D)** Choice (D) identifies the location of people. Choice (A) is incorrect because the men's suits are solid, not striped. Choice (B) uses negation; the men are not *reading;* nor are they *eating*—similar sound. Choice (C) uses negation; the men are *sitting down* not *standing*. The word *booth* implies a *convention* or *exhibit hall;* notice the men are wearing badges.

10. **(A)** Choice (A) identifies the action and the man's occupation. Choice (B) identifies an incorrect action: The woman is looking at the man, not counting the pills. Choice (C) confuses similar sounds *farmer* and *pharmacist*. Choice (D) incorrectly identifies the action: There is a keyboard in the picture, but no one is using it.

Part 2: Question-Response

11. **(A)** Choice (A) is a logical response to the *yes/no* question that begins with the auxiliary *Did*. Choice (B) uses the vacation month *August* to confuse you; Choice (C) repeats the word *good*.

12. **(C)** Choice (C) is a logical response to the question about *length of stay*. Choice (A) gives a time and a word with similar sounds: *stay* with *day*; and answers *How long is a day?* Choice (B) answers *where*.

13. **(A)** Choice (A) is a logical response to the question about *who wrote a letter*. Choice (B) confuses similar sounds: *letter* with *better*. Choice (C) confuses sounds: *rate* with *wrote*; and *letter* with *better*.

14. **(B)** Choice (B) is a logical response to the question about *color*. Choice (A) describes the type of *shirt*. Choice (C) confuses the similar sound of *wearing* with *where I am*.

15. **(A)** Choice (A) is a logical response to the question *when*. Choice (B) confuses similar words: *call* (v) and *call* (n); Choice (C) uses related words: *call* (telephone) and *call* (She *said* I was lazy).

16. **(A)** Choice (A) is a logical reason for *waiting inside*. Choice (B) confuses similar sounds: *waiting* and *way*. Choice (C) confuses similar sounds: *waiting* and *waiter*.

17. **(C)** Choice (C) is a logical response to the question about *family origins*. Choice (A) confuses similar sounds: *family* and *famous*; Choice (B) uses related words: *children* and an answer to a *where* question: *at school*.

18. **(A)** Choice (A) is a logical response to the question *how soon*. Choice (B) confuses similar sounds: *soon* and *son*. Choice (C) confuses similar sounds: *ready* and *red*.

19. **(A)** The second speaker agrees with the first speaker that the food at the restaurant is good. Choice (B) confuses *hear* with the similar-sounding word *here*. Choice (C) confuses the phrase *sell it* with the similar-sounding word *excellent*.

20. **(C)** Choice (C) is a logical response to the question about *a train departure*. Choice (A) uses the related word *stop* and the similar sound of *train* and *rain*; Choice (B) repeats the words *train* and *time*.

21. **(A)** Choice (A) is a logical response to the question. Only Choice (A) answers the telephone expression: *Will you hold?* Choice (B) repeats the word *busy*. Choice (C) has similar sounds: *old* and *hold*.

22. **(B)** Choice (B) is a logical response to the question. Choice (A) uses related words: *night* and *sleep*. Choice (C) uses the similar sounds of *late* and *eat* and the related words *after ten*.

23. **(A)** Choice (A) is a logical response to the question about *the date an invoice was sent*. Choice (B) confuses similar sounds: *invoice* and *voice*. Choice (C) confuses similar sounds: *sent* and *went*, and has a date (*in March*) but doesn't answer about the *invoice*.

24. **(B)** The first speaker lost a cell phone and the second speaker says that it is on a desk. Choice (A) associates *call* with *phone*. Choice (C) confuses *home* with the similar-sounding word *phone*.

25. **(A)** Choice (A) is a logical response to the *invitation for tonight*. Choice (B) uses similar sounds: *tonight* and *tight*. Choice (C) also uses similar sounds: *tonight* and *light*.

26. **(B)** Choice (B) is a logical response to the question of *preference*. Choice (A) confuses *tea* and *team*. Choice (C) confuses (*favo*)*rite* and *right, team* and *seem*.

27. **(C)** The second speaker says that rain is the cause of the heavy traffic mentioned by the first speaker. Choice (A) uses the word *heavy* out of context. Choice (B) repeats the word *traffic*.

28. **(A)** Choice (A) is a logical response to the question of *location*. Choice (B) confuses *true facts* with *fax*. Choice (C) confuses the similar sounds *machine* and *magazine*. Choices (A) and (C) both answer the question *where* but (C) refers to a *magazine* not a *fax machine*.

29. **(C)** Choice (C) is a logical response to the question about *arrival day*. All of the choices answer *when*. Choice (A) answers

what day but is in the past tense, not the future (*is she coming*). Choice (B) answers *what month*.

30. **(B)** Choice (B) is a logical response to the question about *reservations*. Choice (A) states the idea (that reservations are required) behind the question and uses similar words: *reservation* and *reserve*; Choice (C) uses another travel industry expression (*housekeeper*) and repeats the word *bed*.

31. **(A)** Choice (A) is a logical response to the question concerning *possession*. Choice (B) confuses the sounds of *pen* with *when*. Choice (C) confuses the sounds of *pen* with *open*. Choice (C) also uses related words: *to use* and *used to*, *to having* and *have to*. Only Choice (A) answers the *yes/no* question.

32. **(B)** Choice (B) is a logical response to the question concerning a *time limit*. Both Choices (A) and (B) have time markers, but only (B) answers the question. Choice (A) confuses similar sounds: *dead* with *died*. Choice (C) confuses similar sounds: *project* and *reject*; and uses related words: *project* and *bid*.

33. **(A)** The second speaker thinks the first speaker is a fast reader because of having read a book in three days. Choice (B) confuses the phrase *free days* with the similar-sounding phrase *three days*. Choice (C) confuses *red* with the similar-sounding word *read*.

34. **(A)** Choice (A) is a logical response to the question *who*. Choice (B) repeats the word *window* and refers to a *plant* not a *person*. Choice (C) confuses *standing* with *sanding*.

35. **(B)** The second speaker thinks that the package contains something he ordered. Choice (A) confuses *packed* with the similar-sounding word *package*. Choice (C) associates *post office* with *package*.

36. **(B)** Choice (B) is a logical response to the question about *laundry service*. Choice (A) confuses similar sounds: *pressed* and *depressed*. Choice (C) uses related words: *pants* and *pair*.

37. **(C)** Choice (C) is a logical response to the question about *time*. Choice (A) uses related words: *exercise* and *healthful*; Choice (B) confuses *exercises* (n) with *exercise* (v).

38. **(A)** Choice (A) is a logical answer to why you were *late*. Choices (B) and (C) repeat related words: *so long, the long one* or *a long time*. They also use similar sounds *keep* and *caps*.

39. **(B)** Choice (B) is a logical response to the request to *summarize*. Choice (A) confuses article with *art* and (*summa*)*rize* with *size*. Choice (C) confuses *summarize* with *summer*.

40. **(A)** Choice (A) is a logical response to the question about *location*. Choice (B) repeats the word *go* and answers the question *when*. Choice (C) confuses *recommend* with *comment*; and *go* with *memo*.

Part 3: Conversations

41. **(B)** The man asks the woman to type a memo for him. Choice (A) confuses *remember* with the similar-sounding word *memo*. Choice (C) confuses *sweater* with the similar-sounding word *letter*. Choice (D) repeats the word *letter*, which is what the woman is typing.

42. **(B)** The man says he needs the memo before noon. Choice (A) confuses *afternoon* with *noon*. Choice (C) confuses *Tuesday* with the similar-sounding word *today*. Choice (D) confuses *eight* with the similar-sounding word *wait*.

43. **(D)** The woman is busy typing letters. Choice (A) repeats the word *today*. Choice (B) repeats the word *noon*. Choice (C) is confused with the man's asking Mr. Brown for help.

44. **(A)** The woman is buying two shirts. Choice (B) sounds similar to the correct answer. Choice (C) confuses *shoes* with the similar-sounding word *two*. Choice (D) confuses *boots* with the similar-sounding word *blue*.

45. **(B)** The man says she owes forty-five dollars. Choices (A) and (D) sound similar to the correct answer. Choice (C) confuses

sixty with the similar-sounding word *sixteen,* which is the size of the shirts.

46. **(D)** The woman says she has a gift certificate. Choice (A) uses the word *check* out of context. Choices (B) and (C) are what the man asks.

47. **(C)** The woman needs 150 copies. Choices (A) and (B) sound similar to the correct answer. Choice (D) confuses *two* with *too.*

48. **(A)** The woman says she needs her copies *by eleven.* Choice (B) confuses *two* with *too.* Choice (C) is when the man needs his copies. Choice (D) confuses *tonight* with the similar-sounding word *right.*

49. **(A)** The woman says that she has to put the copies in the mail. Choice (B) confuses *read* with the similar-sounding word *ready.* Choice (C) repeats the word *boss.* Choice (D) is what the man will do with his copies.

50. **(C)** The man is ordering food from a waitress, so he is in a restaurant. Choice (A) is not mentioned. Choice (B) repeats the word *fish.* Choice (D) uses the word *house* out of context.

51. **(C)** The woman says it will take fifteen minutes to cook the fish. Choice (A) confuses *eight* with the similar-sounding word *wait.* Choice (B) confuses *nine* with the similar-sounding word *mind.* Choice (D) sounds similar to the correct answer.

52. **(A)** The man says he will have a drink. Choice (B) confuses *think* with the similar-sounding word *drink.* Choice (C) associates *fishing* with *fish.* Choice (D) confuses *dish* with the similar-sounding word *fish.*

53. **(C)** The man says that Mr. Wu is at a meeting. Choice (A) is confused with *out of the office.* Choice (B) confuses *out of town* with *downtown.* Choice (D) confuses *flight* with the similar-sounding word *right.*

54. **(B)** The woman called to speak with Mr. Wu. Choice (A) confuses *massage* with the similar-sounding word *message.* Choice (C) confuses ball with the similar-sounding word *call.* Choice (D) is incorrect because the woman called Mr. Wu so she must know his number.

55. **(B)** The woman says she'll be in her office at 2:30. Choice (A) sounds similar to the correct answer. Choices (C) and (D) confuse *ten* with the similar-sounding word *then.*

56. **(D)** The woman says that she left her briefcase in a cab. Choices (A), (B), and (C) all repeat words used in other parts of the conversation.

57. **(A)** The woman says that her briefcase contains notes she needs for a meeting. Choice (B) uses the word *report* out of context. Choices (C) and (D) are confused with the woman's using the man's phone to call the cab company.

58. **(D)** The woman needs the notes for a meeting tomorrow. Choice (A) is when she lost the briefcase. Choice (B) confuses *afternoon* with the similar-sounding word *noon.* Choice (C) confuses *tonight* with the similar-sounding word *right.*

59. **(C)** The man says he has to catch an eight-o'clock flight. Choice (A) confuses *train* with the similar-sounding word *rain.* Choice (B) repeats the word *call.* Choice (D) repeats the word *weather.*

60. **(B)** The woman says it will rain. Choice (A) confuses *snow* with the similar-sounding word *know.* Choice (C) confuses *cold* with the similar-sounding word *call.* Choice (D) is not mentioned.

61. **(A)** The man takes the woman's advice to get up earlier and asks for a 5:30 wake up call. Choice (B) was his original request. Choice (C) sounds similar to the original request. Choice (D) is the time that the plane leaves.

62. **(B)** The woman will see the movie at the college student center. Choice (A) is where the man will go. Choice (C) confuses *theater* with the similar-sounding word *they're.* Choice (D) is where the speakers will be tomorrow.

63. **(D)** The man says that he wants to get to bed early. Choice (A) is what he decides not to do. Choice (B) confuses *tires* with the similar-sounding word *tired.* Choice (C) is what the woman will do.

64. **(B)** The man reminds the woman that they will take a train after breakfast. Choice (A) repeats the word *breakfast*. Choices (C) and (D) repeat the word *dinner*.

65. **(C)** The man sent the woman a photocopy of a report. Choice (A) confuses *photographs* with *photocopy*. Choice (B) confuses *money* with the similar-sounding word *many*. Choice (D) confuses *letter* with the similar-sounding word *better*.

66. **(B)** The man sent the report on Monday. Choice (A) confuses *Sunday* with the similar-sounding word *Monday*. Choice (C) confuses *Tuesday* with the similar-sounding word *today*. Choice (D) confuses *Wednesday* with the similar-sounding word *when*.

67. **(D)** The woman asks the man to send the report to her home address. Choice (A) repeats the word *mail*. Choice (B) confuses *dress* with the similar-sounding word *address*. Choice (C) confuses *lend* with the similar-sounding word *send* and the word *money* with the similar-sounding word *many*.

68. **(B)** The man says *Tennis is my sport*. Choice (A) is what the woman asks him about. Choice (C) confuses *biking* with the similar-sounding word *like*. Choice (D) is the woman's sport.

69. **(D)** The man plays tennis with a group at the community center. Choice (A) is where the woman swims. Choice (B) is where the woman used to play tennis. Choice (C) repeats the word *club*.

70. **(D)** The man is on the tennis court five times a week. Choices (A) and (B) are how often the woman swims. Choice (C) is not mentioned.

Part 4: Talks

71. **(B)** *Businesspeople* are the most likely to *take business trips* and *carry briefcases*. Choice (A) is incorrect because *pilots* are at work when they are in airports. Choice (C) is incorrect because *tourists* don't work during their trips. Choice (D) is incorrect because *students* don't take business trips.

72. **(A)** It's *small* and *portable*. Choices (B) and (C) are not mentioned. Choice (D) confuses *easy to use* with *unfolds easily when you're ready to use it*.

73. **(A)** Orders made through the Web site receive the discount. Choice (B) is confused with *call us today*, which is one way to order but is not the way to get the discount. Choice (C) uses the word *apply* (application) out of context. Choice (D) is confused with *before the end of the month*, when the discount will end.

74. **(C)** The report says *rain...turning to snow...will create ice hazards*. Choice (A) is true but not complete. Choice (B) is not mentioned. Choice (D) is incorrect because wind is not mentioned.

75. **(A)** People *go to and from work* during *rush hour*. Choices (B), (C), and (D) are not mentioned.

76. **(C)** The speaker mentions warmer temperatures tomorrow afternoon. Choice (A) is how the weather will be in the morning. Choice (B) is confused with *clear the streets*. Choice (D) is confused with *temperatures above freezing*.

77. **(D)** If *office workers are less fit*, then an *accountant* would be less fit. Choices (A), (B), and (C) have active outdoor jobs.

78. **(C)** Going for walks during lunch is a way to keep fit. Choice (A) is a good way to get more exercise, but it is not mentioned. Choice (B) confuses *riding bicycles to work* with *riding stationary bicycles during breaks*. Choice (D) is not mentioned.

79. **(C)** The talk advises bringing fruit or vegetables to work as a snack. Choice (A) confuses *night* with the similar-sounding word *right*. Choice (B) confuses *bed* with the similar-sounding word *instead*. Choice (D) confuses *nuts* with the similar-sounding word *donuts*.

80. **(B)** The message is *on a personal telephone answering machine*. Choice (A), a *government telephone*, would announce the name of the agency. Choice (C) confuses an *answering machine recording* and a *recording*

studio. Choice (D) is not used to record messages.

81. **(D)** You are instructed to leave a *brief* message. Choices (A) and (B) are not mentioned. Choice (C) is contradicted by *brief* since detailed messages are generally long.

82. **(B)** The message says that this is an office number. Choice (A) repeats the word *work.* Choice (C) repeats the word *message.* Choice (D) repeats the word *day.*

83. **(A)** The ad states *if you hate to do your taxes, let us do them instead.* Choice (B) is incorrect because a company can prepare your return but cannot claim your return. Choice (C) is incorrect because you have to provide them with your financial records. Choice (D) confuses *staff your accounting department* with *staff of accountants.*

84. **(D)** The ad states *fees are based on an hourly rate.* Choices (A), (B), and (C) are all possible ways of paying for services but are not mentioned here.

85. **(B)** The speaker tells listeners to call today to make an appointment. Choice (A) is what would be done during an appointment. Choice (C) uses the word *return* out of context. Choice (D) is what should be done within a month.

86. **(A)** The airlines *reduced fares.* Choices (B), (C), and (D) are all possible ways to improve service but are not mentioned here.

87. **(C)** Airlines are trying to *win customers from competing regional airlines.* Choices (A) and (B) are possible reasons to lose customers but are not mentioned here. Choice (D) is not mentioned.

88. **(C)** The company lost 25% of its customer base. Choice (A) confuses *fifteen* with the similar sounding word *fifty.* Choice (B) sounds similar to the correct answer. Choice (D) is the amount that some tickets are discounted.

89. **(B)** A computer user would call a computer helpline. Choices (A) and (C) are people you can reach by calling this number. Choice (D) might call if he or she is a computer user.

90. **(A)** The recording says to press one *if you need assistance.* Choice (B) is confused with getting assistance with software. Choices (C) and (D) are what will happen if the caller presses three.

91. **(D)** The message says, *otherwise, stay on the line.* Choices (A), (B), and (C) are not mentioned.

92. **(B)** The flight is to *Houston.* Choices (A), (C), and (D) are not mentioned.

93. **(B)** Because of the *turbulence,* passengers should remain seated with their seat belts on. We can conclude that the flight will be bumpy. Choices (A), (C), and (D) repeat words from the talk, but none of these is expected by the captain.

94. **(D)** The announcement says that the weather is *sunny.* Choices (A), (B), and (C) are all weather terms but are not mentioned.

95. **(B)** *Large amounts of rain have caused flooding.* Choice (A) is not likely to fill relief shelters. Choices (C) and (D) are similar disasters but are not the problem here.

96. **(A)** *Many people have had to stay in relief shelters until the flooding subsides.* The shelters must provide them with food. Choice (B) is not mentioned. Choice (C) refers to effects of past floods, not of present floods. Choice (D) must not be a problem if they can deliver food to collection centers and shelters.

97. **(D)** If people need the *address of the food collection center,* it is probably because they need to take the food there. Choice (A) is incorrect because food should go to the flood victims, not the public. Choice (B) is incorrect because the shelters need food but may not collect it directly. Choice (C) is where donors should call to get the address of a collection center.

98. **(A)** The message is about changes in the phone company's voicemail system. Choice (B) associates *telephone* with *voicemail.* Choice (C) repeats the phrase *new number.* Choice (D) is associated with *Web site.*

99. **(D)** A customer can save a message by pressing nine. Choice (A) confuses *two* with

the similar-sounding word *new*. Choice (B) confuses *four* with the similar-sounding word *or*. Choice (C) is for deleting a message.

100. **(B)** The message instructs the listener to press the star key in order to hear the new codes. Choice (A) is confused with the number of new codes. Choice (C) repeats the name of the company, but nothing is mentioned about calling it. Choice (D) is confused with *read the entire message* on the Web site.

READING

Part 5: Incomplete Sentences

101. **(A)** *To* indicates destination. Choice (B) means *inside* or *within*. Choice (C) means *movement past*. Choice (D) indicates definite location.

102. **(B)** *Training period* can be modified by the past participle *extended*. Choice (A) is a verb. Choices (C) and (D) are nouns.

103. **(D)** *Before* establishes a logical time relationship between the two past tense verbs. Choices (A) and (B) do not make sense. Choice (C) would establish an illogical equal relationship.

104. **(C)** *Request* is followed by the simple form of the verb when it means that one person or group (*subscribers*) made another person or group (*we*) do something. Choice (A) is a present form. Choice (B) is a past form. Choice (D) is a progressive form.

105. **(A)** *After* indicates that the past tense *found* happened later; the other verb must be at least past tense. Choice (B) is present tense. Choice (C) would indicate a relationship to the present not expressed in the sentence. Choice (D) is present progressive.

106. **(D)** *Project* must be modified by an adjective. Choice (A) is an adverb. Choice (B) is an adjective, but it means *following in order*. Choice (C) is a noun.

107. **(B)** *Before* establishes a logical time relationship between the two verbs. Choices (A), (C), and (D) are not logical. Choice (C) is used with *neither*.

108. **(C)** *Has* requires the past participle *shortened* to complete the verb. Choice (A) is the simple form of the verb. Choice (B) is the progressive form. Choice (D) is a noun.

109. **(B)** A person can sit *by, beside, next to* or *with* another at a dinner, etc. Choice (A) means *in place of*. Choice (C) indicates destination. Choice (D) indicates source.

110. **(A)** *Mistakes* must be modified by an adjective. Choice (B) can be a noun (person) or a verb. Choice (C) is a noun (thing). Choice (D) is a verb.

111. **(C)** *For* means *with regard to*. Choices (A) and (B) illogically indicate location. Choice (D) means *through the means of*.

112. **(B)** The present tense indicates habit, which is logical here; this also requires an *-s* ending for the third person (store owner). Choice (A) is present but not third person. Choice (C) is the progressive. Choice (D) is the infinitive.

113. **(D)** *Assist* means *help*. Choice (A) means *guess*. Choice (B) means to *give a person work or responsibility*. Choice (C) means *agree* or *allow*.

114. **(B)** *Every week* can come after the verb. Choices (A), (C), and (D) should come between the auxiliary and the main verb.

115. **(C)** Present tense indicates *habit*, which is logical here; this also requires an *-s* ending for the third person (shift). Choice (A) is the progressive. Choice (B) is the infinitive. Choice (D) is present tense but not third person.

116. **(A)** *Was higher* is already past tense, so to establish an earlier past; use the past participle *had expected*. Choice (B) is the simple form. Choice (C) is the present progressive. Choice (D) is the future.

117. **(A)** *Sometimes* comes between the auxiliary and the main verb. Choice (B) has the main verb before the auxiliary. Choice (C) has *sometimes* and the main verb before the auxiliary. Choice (D) has *sometimes* before the verb.

118. **(B)** The adjective *popular* can modify *plan*; the adverb *especially* can modify *popular*. Choices (A) and (C) are verbs. Choice (D) is a noun.

Always Innovative & Informative

119. **(D)** A specific date requires *on*. Choice (A) indicates purpose. Choice (B) indicates destination. Choice (C) indicates source.

120. **(C)** *When* establishes a logical time relationship between the two verbs. Choice (A) is not logical. Choice (B) is incomplete (*as soon as*). Choice (D) requires a contrast (*will not refund...until you cancel*).

121. **(B)** *Borrow* means *to take temporarily*. Choice (A) is *what* you take (*the reference guide is a loan*). Choice (C) means *to give temporarily*. Choice (D) means *gone away*.

122. **(A)** *Although* is a subordinate conjunction that indicates that one thing (*business cards not being printed*) happened in spite of another (*ordering the cards*). Choices (B), (C), and (D) do not fit the context of the sentence.

123. **(A)** *Or* allows a choice between the items joined. Choice (B) would mean *both*. Choice (C) should be used with *or*. Choice (D) *but* would imply a contrast (*from the Madrid office but not from the Paris office*).

124. **(A)** *Before* is an adverb and tells when the machine might be used. Choices (B), (C), and (D) do not fit the context of the sentence.

125. **(A)** An unreal condition requires past tense in the *if* clause to correspond with *would + verb* in the other clause. Choice (B) is present tense. Choice (C) is future tense. Choice (D) uses *would*.

126. **(B)** *Twice a day* can appear at the beginning or end of a sentence. Choice (A) links two events. Choices (C) and (D) should come between the auxiliary and main verb.

127. **(D)** *Holds* matches *receives* (*receives and holds*). Choice (A) is present progressive. Choice (B) is past tense. Choice (C) is present tense but does not match the subject.

128. **(C)** *Help* is followed by the simple form (or the infinitive) when one thing (*the conference*) helps another (*employees*) do something. Choice (A) is past tense. Choice (B) is the gerund. Choice (D) is present progressive.

129. **(B)** Establishes a logical relationship between the two events. Choices (A) and (D) are illogical without a contrast (*Although we knew the city...; We knew the city, however,...*). Choice (C) would belong in a result clause (*....therefore, Mr. Gutman drove...*).

130. **(D)** The past progressive *had not been* requires the *-ing* form *depositing* to complete it. Choice (A) is the past tense. Choice (B) is the present tense. Choice (C) is the simple form.

131. **(B)** Present tense in a real condition in the *if* clause requires future tense in the other clause. Choice (A) is present tense. Choice (C) is present progressive. Choice (D) is present perfect.

132. **(A)** *Enter* matches drive (*drive and enter*). Choice (B) is the past tense. Choice (C) is the gerund. Choice (D) is a noun.

133. **(D)** *Attending* forms the future progressive with *will be* (*will be attending*). Choices (A), (B), and (C) do not form logical tenses with *attending*.

134. **(C)** *His* indicates a noun; expertise is logical. Choice (A) is an adverb. Choice (B) is a noun but refers to a person. Choice (D) is an adjective.

135. **(D)** Currency is a business/economic term that would be used with rates. Choice (A) *Money*, could be used, but is not. Choices (B) and (C) are inappropriate.

136. **(D)** Present tense and simple future are possible; only present is given. *Ms. Chang* requires third person *has*. Choice (A) is future perfect. Choice (B) is present progressive. Choice (C) is plural.

137. **(C)** The adjective *knowledgeable* modifies *director*; *quite* modifies *knowledgeable*. Choice (A) is the gerund. Choice (B) is a noun. Choice (D) is a verb.

138. **(B)** A time from past to present requires the present perfect *has been*. Choices (A) and (C) are present tenses and are illogical alone. Choice (D) is past tense.

139. **(D)** Past tense in the *if* clause of an unreal condition requires *would + simple verb* in the other clause. Choice (A) is future tense. Choice (B) is past perfect. Choice (C) is past tense.

140. **(A)** *Have* requires the simple form of the second verb when one or more person(s) (trainers) *have* another (crew) do something. Choice (B) is the gerund. Choice (C) is a noun. Choice (D) is past tense.

Part 6: Text Completion

141. **(D)** The firm doesn't like its current insurance plan, so it wants to make a different choice. Choice (A) is mentioned in the letter, but the company isn't looking for new employees. Choices (B) and (C) could be related to the work of an accounting firm, but they aren't mentioned in the text.

142. **(A)** *Therefore* introduces a result. Wanting to learn more about Unity Health Care is the result of being unhappy with the current insurance plan. Choices (B) and (D) both have a similar meaning to *but*, introducing a contradictory idea. Choice (C) means *additionally*.

143. **(C)** It is not easy, or *convenient*, for employees to visit the doctor during their working hours. Choices (A) and (D) are not words generally used to describe doctors' appointments. Choice (B) is the opposite of the correct meaning.

144. **(C)** *As* means *because* and introduces a reason. Choice (A) introduces a result. Choice (B) introduces a condition. Choice (D) is a preposition and cannot introduce a clause.

145. **(B)** Simon Yan cannot go to the meeting, so Hugh Harrison will go in his place. Choices (A) and (D) mean *go with*. Choice (C) means *help*.

146. **(B)** Positive means *sure* or *certain*. Mr. Yan is certain that Mingmei can do the job because of her good reputation. Choices (A), (C), and (D) all give the sentence the opposite of the correct meaning.

147. **(B)** The company president wants to reduce use of electricity because the cost is *going up*, or *increasing*. Choices (A) and (C) give the sentence the opposite of the correct meaning. Choice (D) doesn't make sense in this sentence.

148. **(D)** The passive voice is necessary here because the subject of the sentence is not the actor. Choices (A), (B), and (C) are all active voice.

149. **(B)** This is a gerund form used as the subject of the sentence. Choices (A), (C), and (D) are all verb forms that cannot be used in the subject position in a sentence.

150. **(D)** *The largest* is a superlative adjective, comparing this company to all the other companies in the nation. Choice (A) is an adjective but not a superlative form. Choices (B) and (C) are comparative forms.

151. **(C)** *Dominated* is a past participle verb completing the passive voice form; *the sector* receives the action from *men* who *dominate* it. Choices (A) and (B) are present tense active voice forms. Choice (D) is a gerund.

152. **(D)** *Has been working* is a present perfect verb describing an action that began in the past (25 years ago) and continues into the present. Choice (A) is present tense. Choice (B) simple past tense and Choice (C) past perfect tense describe actions that are already completed.

Part 7: Reading Comprehension

153. **(C)** It reassures the public about safety. Choices (A) and (B) are not mentioned. Choice (D) is incorrect because the announcement doesn't say whether the policy is new or old.

154. **(A)** *Improve existing facilities with new safety information* means *make them safer*. Choice (B) is not mentioned. Choice (C) is part of improving them. Choice (D) is not mentioned.

155. **(C)** *More than doubled* means *increased by more than twice as much*. Choices (A) and (D) are contradicted by doubled. Choice (B) omits *more than*.

156. **(A)** *Reduction of operating costs* means lower operating expenses. Choices (B) and (C) are possible but not mentioned. Choice (D) is unlikely.

157. **(D)** In this context, *chain* means a *group of stores*. Choices (A) and (C) are words that

are associated with a store's business. Choice (B) is a different meaning of *chain* that does not fit the context.

158. **(B)** *Answering the phone* is not mentioned. Choices (A), (C), and (D) are explicitly mentioned.

159. **(B)** *Room to advance* means *opportunity for promotions*. Choices (A), (C), and (D) are all benefits, but not of this job.

160. **(B)** *Networking* means *talk to as many people as you can who work in your field or in related fields*. Choices (A), (C), and (D) are good practices but do not define *networking*.

161. **(D)** Discovering the salaries offered by companies is not mentioned as a benefit of networking. Choices (A), (B), and (C) are explicitly mentioned.

162. **(A)** The memo says fire doors *direct smoke away from areas where people are working*. Choices (B), (C), and (D) are not mentioned.

163. **(D)** If the weather is hot and the air conditioner is not repaired, employees were probably opening fire doors to let in cool air. Choices (A), (B), and (C) are all purposes of doors but do not relate to fire safety.

164. **(A)** All of the events are trade shows: shoes, furniture, autos, etc. Choices (B), (C), and (D) are not mentioned.

165. **(B)** The Shoe Fair is in Guangzhou, China. Choices (A), (C), and (D) are all held in Europe.

166. **(C)** A buyer might want to look for dress material at the International Textile Fair in Moscow. Choice (A) will have a furniture fair. Choice (B) will have a jewelry fair. Choice (D) will have an art and antiques fair.

167. **(C)** Since *jewelry* is on the list of items to be auctioned, you will probably find *bracelets* for sale. Choice (A) confuses *Chinese antiques* with *china* (dishes). Choice (B) is not mentioned, although you might relate *stamps* and *rare books*. Choice (D) confuses *wall-to-wall carpeting* and *Oriental rugs*.

168. **(D)** The preview starts at *10 A.M. on Saturday, October 3*. Choice (A) is when the

auction begins. Choice (B) is not mentioned. Choice (C) is when you can call Estate Planners with questions.

169. **(B)** Companies downsize so they can stay profitable. Choices (A), (C), and (D) are not mentioned.

170. **(A)** A company *cuts jobs* when it *downsizes*. Choice (B) is not mentioned. Choices (C) and (D) are not mentioned.

171. **(A)** Some companies intentionally remain small in order to be easier to manage. Choices (B), (C), and (D) all could be used to describe the way a company changes, but they don't fit the context.

172. **(B)** Since more people mean less efficient discussion, fewer people will likely be more efficient. Choices (C) and (D) are not mentioned as ways to run meetings well.

173. **(D)** An *agenda keeps you focused*. Choices (A) and (C) may be additional advantages, but they are not mentioned. Choice (B) is incorrect; an agenda should *control* free discussion.

174. **(B)** *Thank them and move on.* Choice (A) would defeat the purpose of a meeting. Choice (C) makes the meeting inefficient. Choice (D) is not mentioned.

175. **(C)** Remarks are comments. Choices (A), (B), and (D) are related to the topic of meetings but don't have the correct meaning.

176. **(D)** This is the only valid option and is supported in the paragraph: *What happens after a meeting is more important...*; *skills...are more professional...*; *work that gets done after the meeting that is important.* Choices (A), (B), and (C) are not supported in the passage.

177. **(C)** The facility is in the *western United States*. Choices (A) and (D) are contradicted by *in a small town*. Choice (B) is contradicted by the *western United States*.

178. **(D)** Preparing employees for cultural changes is important. Choices (A), (B), and (C) are not the topics of the article.

179. **(B)** Their *families* will attend. Choices (A), (C), and (D) are all employees and would be attending with their families.

180. **(C)** The article mentions *cultural changes, cultural differences,* and *habits of Americans.* Choice (A) is incorrect; plans for moving are made by the company. Choices (B) and (D) are business topics.

181. **(A)** Yvonne Wu wants to stay in the hotel from March 15 until March 18. Choice (B) is when she can get the type of room she requested. Choice (C) is not mentioned. Choice (D) is when she will end her stay.

182. **(A)** She asks for a single room. Choice (B) is incorrect because she just wants one queen-sized bed. Choice (C) is confused with the fact that she asks about a pool, but she doesn't say she wants a room near it. Choice (D) is confused with the mention of the nearby park.

183. **(C)** She will pay $125 for one night in the room with the king-sized bed and $300 for three nights in the room with the queen-sized bed. Choice (A) is the price for one night with a queen-sized bed. Choice (B) is the price for one night with a king-sized bed. Choice (D) is the price for four nights with a king-sized bed.

184. **(C)** Yvonne Wu thought that the Convention Center was two blocks from the hotel, and the hotel e-mail says that it is one block more than that. Choice (A) is confused with the one block mentioned in the hotel e-mail. Choice (B) is the distance that Yvonne Wu thought it was. Choice (D) is not mentioned.

185. **(A)** Hotel guests can have free breakfast at BJ's Restaurant. Choice (B) is associated with eating at a hotel but is not mentioned. Choice (C) is incorrect because the pool is closed right now. Choice (D) is what Yvonne Wu asks about, but the hotel e-mail never mentions it.

186. **(A)** According to the agenda heading, the meeting topic is marketing. Choice (B) is confused with Max's business trip. Choice (C) is confused with the discussion of the meeting schedule. Choice (D) is confused with the name of the company.

187. **(B)** Point 2 was discussed first because the first scheduled speaker didn't arrive on time. Choice (A) is the item that was scheduled to be first. Choices (C) and (D) are later items on the agenda.

188. **(C)** The meeting began at 9:30, and Ben started his presentation thirty minutes after that. Choice (A) is thirty minutes before the meeting began. Choice (B) is when the meeting began. Choice (D) is when the meeting was scheduled to end.

189. **(B)** The meeting ended after Barbara's talk. Choice (A) is the person who was scheduled to give the last presentation. Choices (C) and (D) are people who were scheduled to talk earlier in the meeting.

190. **(D)** Max is away on a business trip. Choice (A) is the reason Marty didn't attend the meeting. Choice (B) is a plausible reason but is not mentioned. Choice (C) is true of Ben, not Max.

191. **(B)** The survey looked into how much time employees spend on activities not related to their work, and concluded that they waste almost two hours a day. Choice (A) associates schedule with use of time. Choice (C) is just one activity mentioned in the survey. Choice (D) could be a reason why employees waste work time, but it is not mentioned.

192. **(A)** 85% of men and 83% of women spend time surfing the Internet. Choices (B), (C), and (D) refer to other activities mentioned in the survey.

193. **(A)** The key tells us that this activity is most common with workers twenty-two to thirty-five. Choice (B) is another age group mentioned in the key. Choices (C) and (D) are incorrect because there is no difference in the percentages of men and women who engage in this activity.

194. **(C)** In the e-mail, Aras Koca says that maybe #3 (talking to coworkers) should continue because it gives employees a chance to get to know each other. Choices (A), (B), and (D) refer to other activities mentioned in the survey.

195. **(D)** In the e-mail, Aras Koca suggests asking supervisors to watch #5 (taking long breaks) more carefully. The other choices refer to other activities mentioned in the survey.

196. **(C)** In the letter, Mr. Hernandez says he wants to buy a building because his company is ready to expand. Choice (A) is confused with the fact that Mr. Hernandez is currently renting space for his business. Choice (B) is incorrect because he already has a loan for his house. Choice (D) is incorrect because he is expanding his current company, not buying a new one.

197. **(C)** Mr. Hernandez says that the location of the other building is not as good as that of the Main Street building. Choice (A) is incorrect because he says the size of the other building is right. Choice (B) is incorrect because the Main Street building is more expensive. Choice (D) is a plausible reason but is not mentioned.

198. **(C)** Mr. Hernandez owes $5,000 on his car and $120,000 on his house. Choice (A) is what he owes on his car only. Choice (B) is what he owes on his house only. Choice (D) is what he wants to borrow to buy the Main Street building.

199. **(B)** The bank will lend Mr. Hernandez enough money to buy the cheaper building. Choice (A) is confused with *you already have over $100,000 in debt*. Choice (C) is the amount he would need for the Main Street building. Choice (D) is the cost of both buildings together.

200. **(D)** Mr. Hernandez suggests meeting on April 21, and Ms. Clark says she prefers to meet the day after that. Choice (A) is the date of Ms. Clark's letter. Choice (B) is the day following the date of Ms. Clark's letter. Choice (C) is the date Mr. Hernandez suggests meeting.

Answer Sheet

MODEL TEST 3

Listening Comprehension

PART 1: PHOTOGRAPHS

1. Ⓐ Ⓑ Ⓒ Ⓓ   4. Ⓐ Ⓑ Ⓒ Ⓓ   7. Ⓐ Ⓑ Ⓒ Ⓓ   10. Ⓐ Ⓑ Ⓒ Ⓓ
2. Ⓐ Ⓑ Ⓒ Ⓓ   5. Ⓐ Ⓑ Ⓒ Ⓓ   8. Ⓐ Ⓑ Ⓒ Ⓓ
3. Ⓐ Ⓑ Ⓒ Ⓓ   6. Ⓐ Ⓑ Ⓒ Ⓓ   9. Ⓐ Ⓑ Ⓒ Ⓓ

PART 2: QUESTION-RESPONSE

11. Ⓐ Ⓑ Ⓒ   19. Ⓐ Ⓑ Ⓒ   27. Ⓐ Ⓑ Ⓒ   35. Ⓐ Ⓑ Ⓒ
12. Ⓐ Ⓑ Ⓒ   20. Ⓐ Ⓑ Ⓒ   28. Ⓐ Ⓑ Ⓒ   36. Ⓐ Ⓑ Ⓒ
13. Ⓐ Ⓑ Ⓒ   21. Ⓐ Ⓑ Ⓒ   29. Ⓐ Ⓑ Ⓒ   37. Ⓐ Ⓑ Ⓒ
14. Ⓐ Ⓑ Ⓒ   22. Ⓐ Ⓑ Ⓒ   30. Ⓐ Ⓑ Ⓒ   38. Ⓐ Ⓑ Ⓒ
15. Ⓐ Ⓑ Ⓒ   23. Ⓐ Ⓑ Ⓒ   31. Ⓐ Ⓑ Ⓒ   39. Ⓐ Ⓑ Ⓒ
16. Ⓐ Ⓑ Ⓒ   24. Ⓐ Ⓑ Ⓒ   32. Ⓐ Ⓑ Ⓒ   40. Ⓐ Ⓑ Ⓒ
17. Ⓐ Ⓑ Ⓒ   25. Ⓐ Ⓑ Ⓒ   33. Ⓐ Ⓑ Ⓒ
18. Ⓐ Ⓑ Ⓒ   26. Ⓐ Ⓑ Ⓒ   34. Ⓐ Ⓑ Ⓒ

PART 3: CONVERSATIONS

41. Ⓐ Ⓑ Ⓒ Ⓓ   49. Ⓐ Ⓑ Ⓒ Ⓓ   57. Ⓐ Ⓑ Ⓒ Ⓓ   65. Ⓐ Ⓑ Ⓒ Ⓓ
42. Ⓐ Ⓑ Ⓒ Ⓓ   50. Ⓐ Ⓑ Ⓒ Ⓓ   58. Ⓐ Ⓑ Ⓒ Ⓓ   66. Ⓐ Ⓑ Ⓒ Ⓓ
43. Ⓐ Ⓑ Ⓒ Ⓓ   51. Ⓐ Ⓑ Ⓒ Ⓓ   59. Ⓐ Ⓑ Ⓒ Ⓓ   67. Ⓐ Ⓑ Ⓒ Ⓓ
44. Ⓐ Ⓑ Ⓒ Ⓓ   52. Ⓐ Ⓑ Ⓒ Ⓓ   60. Ⓐ Ⓑ Ⓒ Ⓓ   68. Ⓐ Ⓑ Ⓒ Ⓓ
45. Ⓐ Ⓑ Ⓒ Ⓓ   53. Ⓐ Ⓑ Ⓒ Ⓓ   61. Ⓐ Ⓑ Ⓒ Ⓓ   69. Ⓐ Ⓑ Ⓒ Ⓓ
46. Ⓐ Ⓑ Ⓒ Ⓓ   54. Ⓐ Ⓑ Ⓒ Ⓓ   62. Ⓐ Ⓑ Ⓒ Ⓓ   70. Ⓐ Ⓑ Ⓒ Ⓓ
47. Ⓐ Ⓑ Ⓒ Ⓓ   55. Ⓐ Ⓑ Ⓒ Ⓓ   63. Ⓐ Ⓑ Ⓒ Ⓓ
48. Ⓐ Ⓑ Ⓒ Ⓓ   56. Ⓐ Ⓑ Ⓒ Ⓓ   64. Ⓐ Ⓑ Ⓒ Ⓓ

PART 4: TALKS

71. Ⓐ Ⓑ Ⓒ Ⓓ   79. Ⓐ Ⓑ Ⓒ Ⓓ   87. Ⓐ Ⓑ Ⓒ Ⓓ   95. Ⓐ Ⓑ Ⓒ Ⓓ
72. Ⓐ Ⓑ Ⓒ Ⓓ   80. Ⓐ Ⓑ Ⓒ Ⓓ   88. Ⓐ Ⓑ Ⓒ Ⓓ   96. Ⓐ Ⓑ Ⓒ Ⓓ
73. Ⓐ Ⓑ Ⓒ Ⓓ   81. Ⓐ Ⓑ Ⓒ Ⓓ   89. Ⓐ Ⓑ Ⓒ Ⓓ   97. Ⓐ Ⓑ Ⓒ Ⓓ
74. Ⓐ Ⓑ Ⓒ Ⓓ   82. Ⓐ Ⓑ Ⓒ Ⓓ   90. Ⓐ Ⓑ Ⓒ Ⓓ   98. Ⓐ Ⓑ Ⓒ Ⓓ
75. Ⓐ Ⓑ Ⓒ Ⓓ   83. Ⓐ Ⓑ Ⓒ Ⓓ   91. Ⓐ Ⓑ Ⓒ Ⓓ   99. Ⓐ Ⓑ Ⓒ Ⓓ
76. Ⓐ Ⓑ Ⓒ Ⓓ   84. Ⓐ Ⓑ Ⓒ Ⓓ   92. Ⓐ Ⓑ Ⓒ Ⓓ   100. Ⓐ Ⓑ Ⓒ Ⓓ
77. Ⓐ Ⓑ Ⓒ Ⓓ   85. Ⓐ Ⓑ Ⓒ Ⓓ   93. Ⓐ Ⓑ Ⓒ Ⓓ
78. Ⓐ Ⓑ Ⓒ Ⓓ   86. Ⓐ Ⓑ Ⓒ Ⓓ   94. Ⓐ Ⓑ Ⓒ Ⓓ

Reading

PART 5: INCOMPLETE SENTENCES

101. Ⓐ Ⓑ Ⓒ Ⓓ
102. Ⓐ Ⓑ Ⓒ Ⓓ
103. Ⓐ Ⓑ Ⓒ Ⓓ
104. Ⓐ Ⓑ Ⓒ Ⓓ
105. Ⓐ Ⓑ Ⓒ Ⓓ
106. Ⓐ Ⓑ Ⓒ Ⓓ
107. Ⓐ Ⓑ Ⓒ Ⓓ
108. Ⓐ Ⓑ Ⓒ Ⓓ
109. Ⓐ Ⓑ Ⓒ Ⓓ
110. Ⓐ Ⓑ Ⓒ Ⓓ

111. Ⓐ Ⓑ Ⓒ Ⓓ
112. Ⓐ Ⓑ Ⓒ Ⓓ
113. Ⓐ Ⓑ Ⓒ Ⓓ
114. Ⓐ Ⓑ Ⓒ Ⓓ
115. Ⓐ Ⓑ Ⓒ Ⓓ
116. Ⓐ Ⓑ Ⓒ Ⓓ
117. Ⓐ Ⓑ Ⓒ Ⓓ
118. Ⓐ Ⓑ Ⓒ Ⓓ
119. Ⓐ Ⓑ Ⓒ Ⓓ
120. Ⓐ Ⓑ Ⓒ Ⓓ

121. Ⓐ Ⓑ Ⓒ Ⓓ
122. Ⓐ Ⓑ Ⓒ Ⓓ
123. Ⓐ Ⓑ Ⓒ Ⓓ
124. Ⓐ Ⓑ Ⓒ Ⓓ
125. Ⓐ Ⓑ Ⓒ Ⓓ
126. Ⓐ Ⓑ Ⓒ Ⓓ
127. Ⓐ Ⓑ Ⓒ Ⓓ
128. Ⓐ Ⓑ Ⓒ Ⓓ
129. Ⓐ Ⓑ Ⓒ Ⓓ
130. Ⓐ Ⓑ Ⓒ Ⓓ

131. Ⓐ Ⓑ Ⓒ Ⓓ
132. Ⓐ Ⓑ Ⓒ Ⓓ
133. Ⓐ Ⓑ Ⓒ Ⓓ
134. Ⓐ Ⓑ Ⓒ Ⓓ
135. Ⓐ Ⓑ Ⓒ Ⓓ
136. Ⓐ Ⓑ Ⓒ Ⓓ
137. Ⓐ Ⓑ Ⓒ Ⓓ
138. Ⓐ Ⓑ Ⓒ Ⓓ
139. Ⓐ Ⓑ Ⓒ Ⓓ
140. Ⓐ Ⓑ Ⓒ Ⓓ

PART 6: TEXT COMPLETION

141. Ⓐ Ⓑ Ⓒ Ⓓ
142. Ⓐ Ⓑ Ⓒ Ⓓ
143. Ⓐ Ⓑ Ⓒ Ⓓ

144. Ⓐ Ⓑ Ⓒ Ⓓ
145. Ⓐ Ⓑ Ⓒ Ⓓ
146. Ⓐ Ⓑ Ⓒ Ⓓ

147. Ⓐ Ⓑ Ⓒ Ⓓ
148. Ⓐ Ⓑ Ⓒ Ⓓ
149. Ⓐ Ⓑ Ⓒ Ⓓ

150. Ⓐ Ⓑ Ⓒ Ⓓ
151. Ⓐ Ⓑ Ⓒ Ⓓ
152. Ⓐ Ⓑ Ⓒ Ⓓ

PART 7: READING COMPREHENSION

153. Ⓐ Ⓑ Ⓒ Ⓓ
154. Ⓐ Ⓑ Ⓒ Ⓓ
155. Ⓐ Ⓑ Ⓒ Ⓓ
156. Ⓐ Ⓑ Ⓒ Ⓓ
157. Ⓐ Ⓑ Ⓒ Ⓓ
158. Ⓐ Ⓑ Ⓒ Ⓓ
159. Ⓐ Ⓑ Ⓒ Ⓓ
160. Ⓐ Ⓑ Ⓒ Ⓓ
161. Ⓐ Ⓑ Ⓒ Ⓓ
162. Ⓐ Ⓑ Ⓒ Ⓓ
163. Ⓐ Ⓑ Ⓒ Ⓓ
164. Ⓐ Ⓑ Ⓒ Ⓓ

165. Ⓐ Ⓑ Ⓒ Ⓓ
166. Ⓐ Ⓑ Ⓒ Ⓓ
167. Ⓐ Ⓑ Ⓒ Ⓓ
168. Ⓐ Ⓑ Ⓒ Ⓓ
169. Ⓐ Ⓑ Ⓒ Ⓓ
170. Ⓐ Ⓑ Ⓒ Ⓓ
171. Ⓐ Ⓑ Ⓒ Ⓓ
172. Ⓐ Ⓑ Ⓒ Ⓓ
173. Ⓐ Ⓑ Ⓒ Ⓓ
174. Ⓐ Ⓑ Ⓒ Ⓓ
175. Ⓐ Ⓑ Ⓒ Ⓓ
176. Ⓐ Ⓑ Ⓒ Ⓓ

177. Ⓐ Ⓑ Ⓒ Ⓓ
178. Ⓐ Ⓑ Ⓒ Ⓓ
179. Ⓐ Ⓑ Ⓒ Ⓓ
180. Ⓐ Ⓑ Ⓒ Ⓓ
181. Ⓐ Ⓑ Ⓒ Ⓓ
182. Ⓐ Ⓑ Ⓒ Ⓓ
183. Ⓐ Ⓑ Ⓒ Ⓓ
184. Ⓐ Ⓑ Ⓒ Ⓓ
185. Ⓐ Ⓑ Ⓒ Ⓓ
186. Ⓐ Ⓑ Ⓒ Ⓓ
187. Ⓐ Ⓑ Ⓒ Ⓓ
188. Ⓐ Ⓑ Ⓒ Ⓓ

189. Ⓐ Ⓑ Ⓒ Ⓓ
190. Ⓐ Ⓑ Ⓒ Ⓓ
191. Ⓐ Ⓑ Ⓒ Ⓓ
192. Ⓐ Ⓑ Ⓒ Ⓓ
193. Ⓐ Ⓑ Ⓒ Ⓓ
194. Ⓐ Ⓑ Ⓒ Ⓓ
195. Ⓐ Ⓑ Ⓒ Ⓓ
196. Ⓐ Ⓑ Ⓒ Ⓓ
197. Ⓐ Ⓑ Ⓒ Ⓓ
198. Ⓐ Ⓑ Ⓒ Ⓓ
199. Ⓐ Ⓑ Ⓒ Ⓓ
200. Ⓐ Ⓑ Ⓒ Ⓓ

Model Test 3
Listening Comprehension

In this section of the test, you will have the chance to show how well you understand spoken English. There are four parts to this section, with special directions for each part. You will have approximately 45 minutes to complete the Listening Comprehension sections.

Part 1: Photographs

Directions: You will see a photograph. You will hear four statements about the photograph. Choose the statement that most closely matches the photograph and fill in the corresponding oval on your answer sheet.

1.

2.

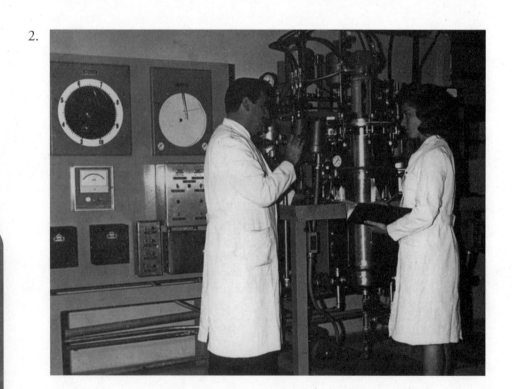

3.

4.

5.

6.

First News
Always Innovative & Informative

7.

8.

9.

10.

Part 2: Question-Response

 CD 4 Track 2

Directions: You will hear a question and three possible responses. Choose the response that most closely answers the question and fill in the corresponding oval on your answer sheet.

11. Mark your answer on your answer sheet.

12. Mark your answer on your answer sheet.

13. Mark your answer on your answer sheet.

14. Mark your answer on your answer sheet.

15. Mark your answer on your answer sheet.

16. Mark your answer on your answer sheet.

17. Mark your answer on your answer sheet.

18. Mark your answer on your answer sheet.

19. Mark your answer on your answer sheet.

20. Mark your answer on your answer sheet.

21. Mark your answer on your answer sheet.

22. Mark your answer on your answer sheet.

23. Mark your answer on your answer sheet.

24. Mark your answer on your answer sheet.

25. Mark your answer on your answer sheet.

26. Mark your answer on your answer sheet.

27. Mark your answer on your answer sheet.

28. Mark your answer on your answer sheet.

29. Mark your answer on your answer sheet.

30. Mark your answer on your answer sheet.

31. Mark your answer on your answer sheet.

32. Mark your answer on your answer sheet.

33. Mark your answer on your answer sheet.

34. Mark your answer on your answer sheet.

35. Mark your answer on your answer sheet.

36. Mark your answer on your answer sheet.

37. Mark your answer on your answer sheet.

38. Mark your answer on your answer sheet.

39. Mark your answer on your answer sheet.

40. Mark your answer on your answer sheet.

Part 3: Conversations

Directions: You will hear a conversation between two people. You will see three questions on each conversation and four possible answers. Choose the best answer to each question and fill in the corresponding oval on your answer sheet.

CD 4
Track
3

41. What do the speakers want to do?

(A) Play in the snow
(B) Go to the theater
(C) See an art show
(D) Run in the park

42. Why can't they go after work?

(A) It will be dark.
(B) There's nowhere to park.
(C) They have to catch a plane.
(D) They don't have warm clothes.

43. When will they go?

(A) Saturday
(B) Sunday
(C) Monday
(D) Tuesday

44. What is the appointment for?

(A) A medical checkup
(B) A sales meeting
(C) A possible presentation
(D) A job interview

45. What time is the appointment for?

(A) 8:30
(B) 9:00
(C) 10:00
(D) 10:30

46. Where will the appointment take place?

(A) In the man's office
(B) In the waiting room
(C) In the meeting room
(D) In the woman's office

47. Where does this conversation take place?

(A) In a hotel
(B) In an elevator
(C) In a newsstand
(D) In an office building

48. What is the woman's room number?

(A) 15
(B) 50
(C) 215
(D) 250

49. What will be delivered to the woman tomorrow?

(A) A room key
(B) A newspaper
(C) A directory
(D) A box of stationery

50. Why do they need Mr. Chung?

(A) To address some letters
(B) To speak at a meeting
(C) To announce the date
(D) To show a film

51. Why is Mr. Chung late?

(A) He lost the address.
(B) He's stuck in traffic.
(C) His car broke down.
(D) He's making a phone call.

52. When will the meeting start?

(A) When Mr. Chung arrives
(B) At the scheduled time
(C) Ten minutes late
(D) At ten past nine

53. What was painted?

    (A) The elevator
    (B) The office
    (C) The lobby
    (D) The door

54. What was wrong with it before?

    (A) It was out of style.
    (B) It was too white.
    (C) It was very light.
    (D) It was too dark.

55. When will the cafeteria be painted?

    (A) This afternoon
    (B) On Sunday
    (C) Next week
    (D) After next week

56. What's broken?

    (A) A chair
    (B) A television
    (C) A telephone
    (D) A computer

57. When did the man talk to the company about repairs?

    (A) Today
    (B) On Tuesday
    (C) Yesterday afternoon
    (D) Last week

58. How long will the repairs take?

    (A) One week
    (B) Two weeks
    (C) Three weeks
    (D) Ten weeks

59. Why does the man need a gas station?

    (A) He's out of gas.
    (B) He wants a drink.
    (C) He is tired.
    (D) He has a flat tire.

60. How far away is the gas station?

    (A) Half a mile
    (B) A mile
    (C) A mile and a half
    (D) Two miles

61. How will the man get to the gas station?

    (A) He will walk.
    (B) He will take a bus.
    (C) He will drive his car.
    (D) He will ride with the woman.

62. How long is the lunch break?

    (A) Fifteen minutes
    (B) Thirty minutes
    (C) Forty-five minutes
    (D) Sixty minutes

63. What does the woman do during her lunch break?

    (A) She works.
    (B) She exercises.
    (C) She eats lunch.
    (D) She takes a walk.

64. Where does the man eat lunch?

    (A) At his desk
    (B) In the park
    (C) At the cafeteria
    (D) In the exercise room

65. Where does the man want to go?

    (A) The park
    (B) The post office
    (C) The history museum
    (D) The capitol building

66. How far away is this place?

    (A) Two blocks
    (B) Three blocks
    (C) Nine blocks
    (D) Ten blocks

67. When is this place open?

    (A) Tuesday
    (B) Monday–Friday
    (C) Wednesday–Monday
    (D) Saturday and Sunday

68. How long is the flight?

    (A) Two hours
    (B) Two and a half hours
    (C) Five hours
    (D) Five and a half hours

69. What will happen next?

    (A) The plane will land.
    (B) A movie will be shown.
    (C) The passengers will eat lunch.
    (D) The flight attendants will serve
        drinks.

70. What does the woman ask for?

    (A) Some magazines
    (B) Some lunch
    (C) A blanket
    (D) A pillow

Part 4: Talks

Directions: You will hear a talk given by a single speaker. You will see three questions on each talk, each with four possible answers. Choose the best answer to each question and fill in the corresponding oval on your answer sheet.

71. What is wrong with the number that was dialed?

    (A) It is the wrong number.
    (B) It is not working.
    (C) It has an answering machine.
    (D) It has a busy signal.

72. Who will help you if you stay on the line?

    (A) A repair person
    (B) An operator
    (C) A customer service representative
    (D) A telephone executive

73. How much will you have to pay for help?

    (A) Five cents a minute
    (B) Seventeen cents a minute
    (C) Seventy cents a minute
    (D) Seventy-five cents a minute

74. What is wrong with the water supply?

    (A) There is no more water.
    (B) The water tastes bad.
    (C) The water is contaminated.
    (D) The water is rusted.

75. How can residents make the water safe?

    (A) Boil it
    (B) Freeze it
    (C) Put tablets in it
    (D) Let sediment settle before drinking

76. What can people do to get more information?

    (A) Visit an office
    (B) Read a brochure
    (C) Listen to the radio
    (D) Call a phone number

77. What kind of training does this school provide?

    (A) Computer training
    (B) Business management
    (C) Personnel training
    (D) Teacher training

78. How long will the training take?

    (A) Three months
    (B) Six months
    (C) Nine months
    (D) One year

79. When are the classes taught?

    (A) Daytime only
    (B) Evenings only
    (C) Daytime and evenings
    (D) Evenings and weekends

80. Where is this train going?

    (A) New York and Baltimore
    (B) New York and Wilmington
    (C) New York and Philadelphia
    (D) New York and Boston

81. Where should New York passengers board the train?

    (A) At the front
    (B) At the back
    (C) In the middle
    (D) Anywhere

82. When is the train leaving?

    (A) In seven minutes
    (B) In ten minutes
    (C) In twenty minutes
    (D) In twenty-seven minutes

Model Test 3

83. When should you call back?

    (A) In the evenings
    (B) On Saturdays
    (C) During business hours
    (D) Early in the mornings

84. If you can't call back, how can you contact the company?

    (A) Via e-mail
    (B) Write them a letter
    (C) Send them a fax
    (D) Go to their office

85. What information should be included in a letter about a product?

    (A) The writer's address
    (B) The store's phone number
    (C) The date of purchase
    (D) The product serial number

86. How should you apply for these jobs?

    (A) Send a résumé
    (B) Go to the hotel
    (C) Write a letter
    (D) Make a phone call

87. What do the jobs offer, besides a good wage?

    (A) Benefits
    (B) Free food
    (C) Good hours
    (D) Possible promotions

88. Which of the following jobs is offered?

    (A) Hotel managers
    (B) Store clerks
    (C) Trainers
    (D) Waiters

89. Where can this recording be heard?

    (A) At a movie theater
    (B) In a parking area
    (C) At an amusement park ride
    (D) In an airport

90. Why should you keep your ticket?

    (A) To gain entrance
    (B) To see if you win
    (C) To leave
    (D) To identify your possessions

91. How much money does this ticket holder have to pay?

    (A) $2.00
    (B) $8.50
    (C) $8.54
    (D) $12.00

92. What problem can the city expect?

    (A) An epidemic
    (B) Extremely hot weather
    (C) Flooding
    (D) Infestation of insects

93. How high are the temperatures expected to be?

    (A) In the seventies
    (B) In the eighties
    (C) In the nineties
    (D) In the hundreds

94. How can citizens protect themselves?

    (A) Wear dark clothing
    (B) Exercise frequently
    (C) Drink lots of water
    (D) Swim

95. What advice is given for busy executives?

    (A) Delegate tasks to others
    (B) Keep your secretary busy
    (C) Work overtime
    (D) Establish a quiet hour

96. How can you keep others from disturbing you?

    (A) Stay away from your office
    (B) Close your office door
    (C) Display a DO NOT DISTURB sign
    (D) Refuse to handle emergencies

97. What should you do during this time?

    (A) Work on difficult tasks
    (B) Return phone calls
    (C) Complete projects that are overdue
    (D) Work closely with staff

98. How often does this ceremony take place?

    (A) Once every five years
    (B) Once every three years
    (C) Once a year
    (D) Three times a year

99. How many people are receiving awards today?

    (A) Four
    (B) Five
    (C) Twenty
    (D) Twenty-five

100. What are listeners asked to do?

    (A) Pay their bills
    (B) Give money
    (C) Teach music
    (D) Practice more

This is the end of the Listening Comprehension portion of the test. Turn to Part 5 in your test book.

Always Innovative & Informative

Model Test 3

Reading

In this section of the test, you will have the chance to show how well you understand written English. There are three parts to this section, with special directions for each part.

YOU WILL HAVE ONE HOUR AND FIFTEEN MINUTES TO COMPLETE PARTS 5, 6, AND 7 OF THE TEST.

Part 5: Incomplete Sentences

Directions: You will see a sentence with a missing word. Four possible answers follow the sentence. Choose the best answer to the question and fill in the corresponding oval on your answer sheet.

101. When the contracts _____ ready, have them sent to the purchaser.

    (A) am
    (B) is
    (C) are
    (D) be

102. The _____ of the new building will start next month.

    (A) constructive
    (B) construction
    (C) construct
    (D) constructed

103. The stapler is _____ the desk.

    (A) on
    (B) through
    (C) into
    (D) without

104. Mr. Selvas delivered the _____ bid to the client.

    (A) seals
    (B) seal
    (C) sealing
    (D) sealed

105. If your flight is delayed, _____ me from the airport.

    (A) calling
    (B) will call
    (C) call
    (D) called

106. The airport taxes are _____ in the ticket price.

    (A) including
    (B) include
    (C) been included
    (D) included

107. Ms. Najar wants to _____ the costs by tonight.

    (A) final
    (B) finalize
    (C) finally
    (D) finality

108. A computer is _____ than a typewriter.

    (A) more efficient
    (B) most efficient
    (C) the most efficient
    (D) the more efficient

109. Mr. Flynn is the person _____ orders office supplies.

    (A) which
    (B) whose
    (C) who
    (D) whom

110. The budget analysis is due _____ Friday.

    (A) at
    (B) from
    (C) until
    (D) on

111. New paint _____ pictures will make the office look better.

    (A) but
    (B) and
    (C) as
    (D) though

112. Everyone is _____ that Ms. Howard seldom leaves before 6:30.

    (A) aware
    (B) await
    (C) awaken
    (D) awe

113. The itinerary _____ with the cruise list.

    (A) be filing
    (B) is filed
    (C) be filed
    (D) is filing

114. Passengers can check in for the charter flight _____ 8:00 and 12:00 tomorrow.

    (A) between
    (B) with
    (C) through
    (D) from

115. The president had her travel agent _____ the reservations.

    (A) made
    (B) has made
    (C) make
    (D) makes

116. It is _____ to transfer a document by e-mail than by fax.

    (A) fast
    (B) fastest
    (C) the faster
    (D) faster

117. Mr. Dietze typed the speech, _____ Ms. Lang prepared the charts.

    (A) or
    (B) and
    (C) where
    (D) during

118. The head of the porters _____ guests with their luggage.

    (A) assist
    (B) were assisting
    (C) assists
    (D) are assisting

119. Ask the accounts receivable clerk _____ the invoice.

    (A) to send
    (B) sending
    (C) will send
    (D) sends

120. An administrative assistant keeps an office running _____.

    (A) smooth
    (B) smoothness
    (C) smoothed
    (D) smoothly

121. Each passenger's name _____ with his or her cabin number.

    (A) is list
    (B) listing
    (C) is listed
    (D) is listing

122. The manager got his staff _____ last weekend.

    (A) to work
    (B) was working
    (C) workable
    (D) worked

123. The variety of insurance benefits _____ very broad under this policy.

    (A) are
    (B) is
    (C) being
    (D) be

124. The directory lists each passenger's name _____ address.

    (A) and
    (B) the
    (C) but
    (D) nor

125. Please leave your luggage _____ the bus for loading.

    (A) among
    (B) between
    (C) from
    (D) beside

126. Mr. Cain will return your call _____ he arrives.

    (A) soon
    (B) as soon
    (C) as soon as
    (D) soon than

127. If the product were not safe, we _____ it.

    (A) had sold
    (B) don't sell
    (C) will sell
    (D) would not sell

128. The cruise handbook _____ all ship policies.

    (A) explains
    (B) is explaining
    (C) explain
    (D) explaining

129. _____ costs make profits smaller.

    (A) Raise
    (B) Risen
    (C) Rising
    (D) Raised

130. Mr. Larsen _____ for meetings.

    (A) late is always
    (B) is always late
    (C) always late is
    (D) is late always

131. _____ we had checked the figures, the supervisor found a mistake.

    (A) Unless
    (B) However
    (C) Since
    (D) Even though

132. Mr. Lazer wants to make _____.

    (A) a meeting
    (B) an hour
    (C) an appointment
    (D) a time

133. The financial team _____ that the offer was rejected.

    (A) was disappointed
    (B) were disappointed
    (C) was disappointing
    (D) were disappointing

134. A record of complaints _____ kept in the purser's office.

    (A) are
    (B) is
    (C) were
    (D) has

135. The only difference _____ the two flights is time of departure.

    (A) with
    (B) then
    (C) between
    (D) among

136. _____ Ms. Butrus was late, she did not miss the performance.

    (A) During
    (B) Because
    (C) In spite of
    (D) Although

137. Mr. Dekar was responsible for _____ the data.

    (A) organization
    (B) organizing
    (C) organized
    (D) organize

138. The company _____ spouses of employees in the invitation to the banquet.

    (A) are included
    (B) have included
    (C) is including
    (D) has including

139. Ms. Yu has suggested _____ more reservation clerks.

    (A) hire
    (B) hiring
    (C) hired
    (D) to hire

140. The meeting will be held _____ Thursday.

    (A) of
    (B) in
    (C) for
    (D) on

Part 6: Text Completion

Directions: You will see four passages each with three blanks. Under each blank are four answer options. Choose the word or phrase that best completes the sentence.

Questions 141–143 refer to the following letter.

Green Office Renovators
17 Hukou Street
Taipei, Taiwan
106-03

Kao-Chin Su-mei, Vice President
No. 377, Sung Chiang Road.
Taipei, Taiwan
103-09

Dear Kao-Chin Su-mei,   March 2, 20—

I understand you are thinking about renovating your office building. Thank you for considering Green Office Renovators. More important, thank you for _____ interest in caring for the earth. With your help we

     141. (A) its
          (B) their
          (C) your
          (D) my

can help protect the world for the future.

Please read through the enclosed brochure. It provides information on all of our environmentally friendly materials and products. You will notice that we take measures to reduce waste at all times, including recycling extra materials and avoiding products with excess packaging. We do not use any cleaning products or paints that _____ disposal as hazardous waste.

142. (A) require
     (B) requires
     (C) is requiring
     (D) are requiring

If you have done any research you will notice that our fees are considerably lower than our competitors. However, we hope you will agree that spending more on the initial cost of the renovations is worth it for the future of both your company and the earth itself. Though energy-efficient appliances and lights are more expensive to install, they will instantly begin to save you money. In addition, statistics show that companies that demonstrate _____

     143. (A) concern
          (B) happiness
          (C) skills
          (D) time

for the environment are more popular among consumers.

I look forward to discussing the renovation needs of your company.

Sincerely,

Cai Mi

Cai Mi

Model Test 3

Questions 144–146 refer to the following e-mail.

To: clementinebooks@learning.org
From: rep990@gaspower.net
Subject: Equal Payment Billing Plan

Dear Sheldon Murray,

It has come to my attention that your business is still paying its gas bills using our Monthly Plan. During the past year, your _____ bill was for $400 in the month of January.

144. (A) high
      (B) higher
      (C) highest
      (D) most high

However, your bills were as low as $23 in the summer months. The majority of your annual fees occurred in the four months of winter.

We believe that you are an excellent candidate for our Equal Billing Plan. Approximately 78% of our customers have switched to this option since it became available three years ago. Though the amount of money you spend in the year will be identical, your higher bills will be _____ throughout the year. This makes it easier to budget your finances.

145. (A) marked down
      (B) built up
      (C) spread out
      (D) topped off

With the Equal Billing Plan, the amount you pay per month is based on an approximation. To do this we take an average from the bills in your previous year. After six months on the Equal Billing Plan we will adjust this amount depending on whether or not you use more or less gas than we _____. At the end of the year you will receive a debit or credit from us to

146. (A) estimated
      (B) permitted
      (C) inquired
      (D) ordered

balance the amount owed with the amount used.

Questions 147–149 refer to the following article.

February 7th, 20—
ALGOA BAY TIMES

**Airport Lounge Removes
Free Internet Service**

By Kelly Christie

As of this Friday passengers at Port Elizabeth Airport will no longer _____ free

147. (A) offer
      (B) offered
      (C) be offered
      (D) be offering

Internet service in the business travelers' lounges.

Since January of last year, free Internet access has been available in the business lounges in Terminals B and C. To enter the lounges, travelers must have a VIP card, which costs about $240 USD per year. Benefits of the business lounge include free coffee, snacks, and newspapers, as well as _____ printers

148. (A) visits to
      (B) repair of
      (C) access to
      (D) purchase of

and fax machines. They also provide an escape from crowded terminal waiting rooms.

Passengers with VIP cards will now have to purchase Internet access at $5 per hour, with a two-hour minimum. Airport officials have been planning to remove the free service provider for several months, but have been presented with many petitions, mainly from business travelers who have already purchased their annual nonrefundable VIP passes. "The only reason I bought the pass was so that I could go online with my laptop at Port Elizabeth. I wouldn't bother using the lounge just for free refreshments and newspapers," said Alistair Willows, who makes _____ trips from Europe to South

149. (A) frequent
      (B) frequency
      (C) frequently
      (D) frequencies

Africa for business.

Questions 150–152 refer to the following advertisement.

Attention Small Business Owners

Are you tired of paying too much for office supplies? It's time to stop throwing your money away on overpriced products. Meade's Paper Store offers top quality office products at _____ prices. We supply all your paper needs and also stock writing utensils,

150. (A) easy
    (B) bargain
    (C) retail
    (D) top

computers and computer supplies, office furniture, and more! There's _____ reason

    151. (A) no one
         (B) none
         (C) not
         (D) no

to shop anywhere else. Meade's has it all. We have two convenient locations! Visit our main store downtown next to City Hall, or our new branch in the Valley Shopping Mall. _____ advantage of this week's special: all paper goods are 20% off now through

152. (A) Take
    (B) Taking
    (C) To take
    (D) Can take

Saturday. When you visit, don't forget to ask about our frequent shopper program.

Part 7: Reading Comprehension

Directions: You will see single and double reading passages followed by several questions. Each question has four answer choices. Choose the best answer to the question and fill in the corresponding oval on your answer sheet.

Questions 153–155 refer to the following paragraph and table.

The research division has four priorities: (1) improving the quality of our products through advancements in manufacturing technology; (2) lowering the costs by improving manufacturing processes; (3) exploring research possibilities to develop new products; and (4) doing all of this in an environmentally responsible manner.

Research Division Priorities	
What	**How**
1. Improve product quality	By using better technology
2. Lower cost	By improving the manufacturing process
3. Develop research	By increasing research
4. Be globally responsible	By being sensitive to the environment

153. What is the purpose of technology for the research division?

(A) It lowers costs.
(B) It is used in research.
(C) It follows consumer trends.
(D) It increases product quality.

154. Which of the following is NOT a research priority?

(A) Improving quality
(B) Being environmentally responsible
(C) Developing new products
(D) Hiring good engineers

155. How does this division try to lower costs?

(A) By conserving energy
(B) By improving manufacturing processes
(C) By working fewer hours
(D) By limiting exploration

Questions 156–157 refer to the following advertisement.

WHY WAIT FOR A BETTER JOB?
Get a great job now!

National Air
is hiring full-time representatives for
Sales & Reservations. Talk to our employees
and discover why we're the best thing in the air.
Interviews on the spot!
Bring your résumé

OPEN HOUSE
National Air Headquarters
Southeast Regional Airport
Thursday, June 15 7:30 P.M.

156. What is the purpose of this ad?

   (A) To meet new people
   (B) To sell tickets
   (C) To recruit potential employees
   (D) To show off the new headquarters

157. Where will the event be held?

   (A) At their headquarters
   (B) At the owner's house
   (C) On a plane
   (D) At the regional office

Questions 158–161 refer to the following fax.

FAX TRANSMISSION FAX TRANSMISSION FAX TRANSMISSION

InterGulf Export
P.O. Box 23145
Sharjah, UAE

To: F. Omoboriowo
Head of Marketing
P.O. Box 19133
Nairobi, Kenya

Fm: Ravi Niazi
Trade Consultant

Date: 18 October, 20—
Sub: Your marketing question of October 17, 20—

We were very pleased to receive your fax of October 17. We have sent under separate cover information regarding our company and its services. This should arrive in your offices tomorrow.

In the meantime, the following addresses your immediate question:

The company sells products through a worldwide marketing network. This network operates 36 sales offices in 21 countries. Approximately 75% of company sales are direct, and 25% are through other channels. Products are shipped to customers through company distribution centers, by the method of shipment preferred by the customer whenever possible.

If you need any more information, please contact me.

---

158. What did the fax respond to?

(A) A newspaper ad
(B) A personal visit
(C) A telephone inquiry
(D) A faxed question

159. The word *channels* in paragraph 3, line 3, is closest in meaning to

(A) customers
(B) services
(C) sources
(D) ways

160. Which of the following is responsible for shipping purchased goods?

(A) The customer
(B) The airlines
(C) Company distribution centers
(D) Company headquarters

161. What was probably the topic of Omoboriowo's question?

(A) The size of the company
(B) How goods are distributed
(C) When the company was founded
(D) The company's marketing plan

Questions 162–163 refer to the following notice.

ATTENTION! RIDERS

- Pay exact fare when boarding the bus. Drivers cannot make change.
- Upon boarding the bus, move toward the rear of the bus. Stand in the passenger area, not in the doorways or beside the driver.
- Allow senior citizens and disabled riders to use the priority seating area at the front of the bus.
- No music without earphones.
- Eating, drinking, and smoking are not allowed on the bus.

---

162. What does this passage discuss?

    (A) Rules for riding buses
    (B) Safety concerns
    (C) Bus routes and fares
    (D) Problems of the bus service

163. Who is entitled to use the priority seating area?

    (A) Mothers and children
    (B) Elderly and handicapped people
    (C) Bus company employees
    (D) Riders who pay extra

Questions 164–166 refer to the following chart.

Results of Study on Time Distribution of Tasks for Sales Managers

Training new sales personnel	15%
Identifying possible clients	10%
Reviewing monthly sales records	25%
Taking care of customer problems	5%
Making sales assignments	22%
Interacting with technical staff	10%
Administrative duties	5%
Miscellaneous	8%

---

164. What task do sales managers spend the most time on?

    (A) Training salespeople
    (B) Performing administrative tasks
    (C) Reviewing sales records
    (D) Making sales assignments

165. How much of their time do sales managers spend with the technical staff?

    (A) 5%
    (B) 8%
    (C) 10%
    (D) 15%

166. What can be concluded from the study?

    (A) There are few customer problems.
    (B) Sales are a low priority.
    (C) Little time is spent on training.
    (D) No time is spent on finding new customers.

Questions 167–169 refer to the following advertisement.

**Summer is a great time to return to school!
If you need better business skills, let us help.**

Each summer Claybourne University School of Business Administration offers special courses for experienced managers who want to sharpen their existing business skills or learn new ones. You will study with your peers in a week-long intensive session that simulates the world of international commerce. You will learn new theories and study the way business is conducted around the world. Students in previous sessions have reported that what they learned was immediately applicable to their own work situations.

Only one person from a company is accepted into this special program. All applications require three letters of recommendation and proof of employment.

For more information, call the
Summer Education Center
School of Business Administration
Claybourne University
903-477-6768 Fax: 903-477-6777

---

167. Who attends this center?

   (A) Professional managers
   (B) College professors changing careers
   (C) Undergraduate students in business
   (D) Office staff

168. What is required for admission?

   (A) The name of your manager
   (B) A copy of your grades
   (C) Your job title and duties
   (D) Letters of recommendation

169. How long is the course?

   (A) All summer long
   (B) One week
   (C) Three evenings a month
   (D) Two years

Questions 170–171 refer to the following announcement.

$$$

OUR STORE GUARANTEE

We have the lowest prices in town. For every item we sell, we'll beat any legitimate price from any other store. Plus, if you find a lower price within 30 days of your date of purchase, we'll refund the difference. This offer is good even on our own sale prices. The item must be the same brand and style. You must present your original sales receipt. Our low price guarantee does not apply to limited quantity offers.

$$$

170. What does this statement guarantee?

(A) The lowest prices
(B) The best service
(C) The most convenient location
(D) The most helpful salesclerks

171. If you buy an item at a lower price, what will the store do?

(A) Give you a second item
(B) Pay you the difference in price
(C) Buy the item from you
(D) Refund your money

Questions 172–175 refer to the following memo.

MEMO

To: All employees
From: K. Osafo
         Director, Personnel

Date: November 23, 20—
Subject: Charitable Leave

The corporation is pleased to announce a new policy which will allow employees to take paid time off for volunteer activities. Employees may take up to eight hours of paid leave per month to volunteer for charity organizations. Employees are eligible for this program if they are full-time and have been employed here for at least one year. Charitable leave must be requested in advance; otherwise, employees will not be paid for that time. Charitable leave must also be approved by the employee's supervisor.

---

172. What does the new policy allow employees to do?

(A) Take paid leave during pregnancy
(B) Have more holidays
(C) Get paid for volunteer work
(D) Go home early

173. How much time may an employee take under this program?

(A) One hour per week
(B) Three hours per week
(C) Six hours per month
(D) Eight hours per month

174. The word *eligible* in line 7 is closest in meaning to

(A) qualified
(B) prevented
(C) encouraged
(D) recommended

175. What must an employee do to get paid for time off?

(A) Get the permission of the charity
(B) Leave work for one day
(C) Fill out an absence form
(D) Ask his or her supervisor in advance

Model Test 3

Questions 176–180 refer to the following magazine article.

Are You the New Target for Hackers?

Is your company a sitting duck for hackers? When did you last change your password? How complete are your security systems? Have you ever been broken into before?

According to IANS, the International Association for Network Security, there's a new breed of hacker out there. And, there's a new target.

In the past, hackers gained notoriety from breaking into big companys' networks. In fact, the bigger the company, the bigger the success. When hackers broke into Infelmax's notoriously secure system in 1999, they made headline news around the world.

The big "successes" came with a major drawback. These headline break-ins came with international teams of investigators and serious criminal charges. Several former hackers are now sitting behind bars or working overtime to pay off hefty fines in penalties and damages.

So, hackers of the new decade have turned to a new target: smaller companies. Smaller companies often spend less on their security systems. If they have never been broken into before, they may be lulled into a feeling of security. They are often lax about changing their password frequently enough. And that spells trouble.

Also, a breached system in a smaller company may attract little public attention. Investigations may be brief and superficial, as overloaded investigators pursue bigger problems.

But if you do fall victim to hackers, it will definitely attract your own attention. These thieves can gain access to your files, destroying, copying, or altering them. They can create havoc with your data. And if they do, you'll surely wish you had changed your password once more often.

176. Which is a likely victim for the new breed of hackers?

(A) Large companies
(B) Small companies
(C) International companies
(D) Companies without a security system

177. What might have been one motive for hackers of Infelmax's network?

(A) Money
(B) Power
(C) Fame
(D) Fun

178. What has happened to some big-name hackers?

(A) They're in jail.
(B) Nothing
(C) They got better jobs.
(D) They are paying off investigators.

179. What might help hackers to succeed?

(A) They've never broken into a company before.
(B) They feel secure.
(C) Their targeted network is old.
(D) Their targets rarely change their secret code.

180. The word *havoc* in paragraph 7, line 6 is closest in meaning to

(A) order
(B) copies
(C) confusion
(D) documents

Questions 181–185 refer to the following advertisement and letter.

MARKETING REPRESENTATIVE

New Zealand's fastest-growing women's clothing company seeks a marketing representative. Position requires travel approximately one week per month, representing the company at conferences and media events.

Required qualifications
- a degree from a four-year college or university, preferably in marketing.
- at least one year of experience in sales, preferably clothing.
- excellent communication skills, including experience giving presentations.

Mail your resume and cover letter to:
Camilla Crowe
Recruiting Coordinator
NZ World
636 Simons Street
Auckland, New Zealand 6692

Camilla Crowe
NZ World
636 Simons Street
Auckland, New Zealand 6692

March 24, 20—

Akiko Sasaki
118 Hutchinson Road
Paeora, New Zealand 1230

Dear Ms. Sasaki:

Thank you for applying for the position of marketing representative. We appreciate your interest in NZ World.

Although your resume shows that you have good preparation for a career in marketing, unfortunately you don't meet all our required qualifications. You have the degree we are looking for, but not the experience. Your sales experience in an electronics store is a good background, but your time there is just half of what we ask for as a minimum. In addition, you have no experience in clothing sales.

However, your resume also shows some of your strengths. You have excellent grades and have been active in your campus' marketing club. Therefore, we would like to offer you a position as an intern.

This is a three-month, unpaid internship. Since you just graduated last month, I think this would be a great opportunity for you. It would give you some of the experience you will need to start your career. For example, your internship would give you some practice with public speaking, an important marketing skill that is lacking on your resume.

Contact me by April 1 if you are interested in accepting this position. I look forward to hearing from you.

Sincerely,

Camilla Crowe

Camilla Crowe

---

181. Which of the following is NOT a duty of the advertised job?

(A) Recruiting new staff
(B) Giving presentations
(C) Traveling every month
(D) Attending conferences

182. What field did Akiko get her degree in?

(A) Electronics
(B) Marketing
(C) Communications
(D) Clothing design

183. When did Akiko get her degree?

(A) February
(B) March
(C) April
(D) May

184. How long did Akiko work in an electronics store?

(A) One week
(B) Six months
(C) One year
(D) Two years

185. What did Camilla Crowe offer Akiko?

(A) A job
(B) An interview
(C) An internship
(D) A club membership

Questions 186–190 refer to the following schedule and form.

Classes offered at Central Technical Institute
CATEGORY: Office Skills

Accounting
ACTG 101   Financial Accounting, Part One
ACTG 102   Financial Accounting, Part Two*
ACTG 670   Accounting for Small Businesses

Business
BUSI 100   Introduction to Business
BUSI 200   Principles of Business

Computers
COMP 104   Introduction to Microsoft Word
COMP 207   Microsoft Excel: Basics
COMP 300   Computers in the Office**

Marketing
MARK 500   Global Marketing Strategies
MARK 600   Marketing on the Internet

Classes last from January 3 until March 15. Classes at the same level are offered on the same day: 100—Monday, 200—Tuesday, 300 and 400—Wednesday, and 500 and higher—Thursday. All classes are offered from 6:00–8:00 in the evening.

  The fee for each course is $300. To register, go to: *www.cti.org* and click on the "Registration" link.

*Students must take ACTG 101 and earn a grade of 75 or better before taking ACTG 102.
**This course will be offered on Tuesday evenings.

While you were out . . .

To: Roberto Guzman
Jessica Moore called.
Date: Thursday, December 21, 20—
Time: 4:10 P.M.
About: Problem with online registration form

She researched your problem. You want to take ACTG 102,
BUSI 100, COMP 207, and COMP 300. You can't register
for ACTG 102 because you earned a grade 10% below the
minimum in Part One of the course. She registered you for
BUSI 100 and for COMP 207, but not COMP 300 because
there is a scheduling conflict. There is also a problem with
your student visa. It expires fifteen days before classes
end. She recommends that you make an appointment
with her to discuss these topics.

186. What time does the ACTG 101 class
start?

(A) 1:00
(B) 3:00
(C) 6:00
(D) 8:00

187. What day of the week are Marketing
classes offered?

(A) Monday
(B) Tuesday
(C) Wednesday
(D) Thursday

188. What was Roberto's grade in ACTG 101?

(A) Over 75
(B) 75
(C) Less than 75
(D) Exactly 10

189. How much will Roberto have to pay for
his classes this session?

(A) $300
(B) $600
(C) $900
(D) $1,200

190. When does Roberto's visa expire?

(A) January 3
(B) January 15
(C) March 1
(D) March 15

Questions 191–195 refer to the following advertisement and fax.

This year, try something different
for your company's annual party.
Visit the Front Street Theater.

An afternoon or evening at the Front Street Theater includes a delicious meal prepared by our Paris-trained chef, Jacques, and a show preformed by some of the region's finest actors. A tour of this historic theater is also offered before the meal. Groups of 250 or more can reserve the entire theater for their group. This option is available on Sunday afternoons only. Groups of 300–350 receive a 10% discount. Groups over 350 receive a 15% discount.

Shows are selected based on the time of the year: January–April, tragedy; May–July, drama; August–October, musical; and November–December, comedy.

Reservations are available at the following times:

Monday–Thursday: Dinner and evening show
6–10 P.M.

Friday–Saturday Lunch and afternoon show
12–4 P.M.
Dinner and evening show
6–10 P.M.

Sunday Only large groups renting the entire theater. Both lunch and dinner schedules are available. It is recommended to make large group reservations one month ahead of time.

Come to the Front Street Theater for food, entertainment, and fun. To make a reservation, e-mail us or send a fax to 216-707-2268.

FAX COVER SHEET

Federal Bank
55510 East Boulevard
Cleveland, Ohio 44106-5498

To:	Front Street Theater, Reservations
From:	Constance Hekler, Events Coordinator
Date:	October 25, 20—
Pages:	1
Ref:	Holiday party

Message:

I saw your advertisement in this week's *Business Journal*. I am interested in renting your theater for Federal Bank's annual employee party.

We have set the date for our party as Sunday, December 20. Is the theater available then? We prefer the lunch and afternoon show. There will be 325 guests.

Please fax the menu, a description of the shows, and the price list to me. And let me know about the availability of dates in December.

Thank you.

191. What is included in a visit to the theater?

(A) Meeting the chef
(B) Talking with the actors
(C) Touring the theater
(D) Selecting shows

192. When is the theater open to individuals and small groups?

(A) Monday through Thursday only
(B) Friday and Saturday only
(C) Monday through Saturday only
(D) Sunday only

193. When will Ms. Heckler have to make a reservation for the Federal Bank party?

(A) By October 25
(B) By November 20
(C) By November 30
(D) By December 20

194. What type of discount will the Federal Bank get for this party?

(A) 0%
(B) 10%
(C) 15%
(D) 20%

195. What type of show will guests at the Federal Bank party see?

(A) Tragedy
(B) Drama
(C) Musical
(D) Comedy

Questions 196–200 refer to the following memorandum and form.

From: Jun Oh, Benefits Manager
To: Marcus Mains
Sent: Tuesday, July 20, 20— .
Re: Early Retirement

Early Retirement Program

1. Employees must meet these requirements:
   A) Age sixty-five with twenty years of employment at this company; or
   B) Any age with twenty-five years of employment at this company; or
   C) Age fifty-five to sixty-four with twenty years of employment at this company. With this option there is a reduction in your retirement fund. It will be reduced by 2% for each year that you are under age sixty-five. For example, if you are sixty-three, it will be reduced by 4%.
2. Interested employees should apply by September 1, 20__. Supervisors with twenty years or more of employment at this company have an extra two months to apply. This gives the Benefits Office more time to work on the applications.
3. Attend a workshop. We will discuss how to invest your money. Call Suzette or Tuyen to register. Our first workshop is on August 10. All workshops will be held on Wednesdays and Fridays in Meeting Room F at 9:00 A.M.
4. We encourage you to meet with your accountant. Retiring now will influence your taxes for next year. Call our tax specialist, Geoffrey, for assistance.
5. If you have any additional questions, please contact Jun.

DATE July 21, 20—   TIME 10: 30 P.M. (A.M.)

FOR   Jun
RECEIVED BY   Sumalee
CALLER   Marcus
PHONE NUMBER   ext. 9245

MESSAGE He wants to retire early. He is a supervisor with twenty years of experience at this company. First, what happened to this morning's workshop? He went to Meeting Room F at 9:00. Nobody was there. Second, how much will his funds be reduced? He is sixty-two. Third, he wants to talk to someone about his taxes. Who is the expert?

CALL BACK REQUESTED? ☑ YES   ☐ NO

                                              A.M.
DATE/TIME COMPLETED _____/_____/_____ : P.M.

196. Which employee can get full retirement benefits?

    (A) Age fifty with twenty years of employment
    (B) Age fifty-five with twenty-five years of employment
    (C) Age sixty with twenty years of employment
    (D) Age sixty-five with fifteen years of employment

197. What mistake did Marcus make about the workshop?

    (A) He went on the wrong day of the week.
    (B) He went at the wrong time.
    (C) He went to the wrong place.
    (D) He went on the wrong date.

198. What is the deadline for Marcus to apply for early retirement?

    (A) July 21
    (B) August 10
    (C) September 1
    (D) November 1

199. If Marcus takes early retirement now, what will be the reduction in his retirement fund?

    (A) 2%
    (B) 4%
    (C) 6%
    (D) 8%

200. Who should Marcus talk to about his taxes?

    (A) Geoffrey
    (B) Suzette
    (C) Tuyen
    (D) Jun

This is the end of the test. If you finish before time is called, you may go back to Parts 5, 6, and 7 and check your work.

Model Test 3

Answer Key
MODEL TEST 3

Listening Comprehension

PART 1: PHOTOGRAPHS

1. C	4. B	7. D	9. C
2. D	5. B	8. A	10. B
3. A	6. C		

PART 2: QUESTION-RESPONSE

11. A	19. A	27. C	35. B
12. C	20. C	28. A	36. A
13. C	21. C	29. A	37. B
14. B	22. B	30. A	38. C
15. A	23. B	31. C	39. A
16. C	24. C	32. B	40. A
17. A	25. C	33. A	
18. C	26. B	34. C	

PART 3: CONVERSATIONS

41. C	49. B	57. A	65. C
42. A	50. B	58. C	66. B
43. B	51. B	59. D	67. B
44. D	52. B	60. C	68. D
45. A	53. C	61. D	69. D
46. D	54. D	62. D	70. D
47. A	55. D	63. C	
48. C	56. B	64. A	

PART 4: TALKS

71. B	79. D	87. D	95. D
72. C	80. D	88. D	96. B
73. D	81. A	89. B	97. A
74. C	82. B	90. C	98. C
75. A	83. C	91. B	99. A
76. D	84. B	92. B	100. B
77. A	85. D	93. D	
78. B	86. B	94. C	

Reading

PART 5: INCOMPLETE SENTENCES

101. C	111. B	121. C	131. D
102. B	112. A	122. A	132. C
103. A	113. B	123. B	133. A
104. D	114. A	124. A	134. B
105. C	115. C	125. D	135. C
106. D	116. D	126. C	136. D
107. B	117. B	127. D	137. B
108. A	118. C	128. A	138. C
109. C	119. A	129. C	139. B
110. D	120. D	130. B	140. D

PART 6: TEXT COMPLETION

141. C	144. C	147. C	150. B
142. A	145. C	148. C	151. D
143. A	146. A	149. A	152. A

PART 7: READING COMPREHENSION

153. D	165. C	177. C	189. B
154. D	166. A	178. A	190. C
155. B	167. A	179. D	191. C
156. C	168. D	180. C	192. C
157. A	169. B	181. A	193. B
158. D	170. A	182. B	194. B
159. D	171. B	183. A	195. D
160. C	172. C	184. B	196. B
161. B	173. D	185. C	197. D
162. A	174. A	186. C	198. D
163. B	175. D	187. D	199. C
164. C	176. B	188. C	200. A

Test Score Conversion Table

Count your correct responses. Match the number of correct responses with the corresponding score from the Test Score Conversion Table (below). Add the two scores together. This is your Total Estimated Test Score. As you practice taking the TOEIC model tests, your scores should improve. Keep track of your Total Estimated Test Scores.

# Correct	Listening Score	Reading Score	# Correct	Listening Score	Reading Score	# Correct	Listening Score	Reading Score	# Correct	Listening Score	Reading Score
0	5	5	26	110	65	51	255	220	76	410	370
1	5	5	27	115	70	52	260	225	77	420	380
2	5	5	28	120	80	53	270	230	78	425	385
3	5	5	29	125	85	54	275	235	79	430	390
4	5	5	30	130	90	55	280	240	80	440	395
5	5	5	31	135	95	56	290	250	81	445	400
6	5	5	32	140	100	57	295	255	82	450	405
7	10	5	33	145	110	58	300	260	83	460	410
8	15	5	34	150	115	59	310	265	84	465	415
9	20	5	35	160	120	60	315	270	85	470	420
10	25	5	36	165	125	61	320	280	86	475	425
11	30	5	37	170	130	62	325	285	87	480	430
12	35	5	38	175	140	63	330	290	88	485	435
13	40	5	39	180	145	64	340	300	89	490	445
14	45	5	40	185	150	65	345	305	90	495	450
15	50	5	41	190	160	66	350	310	91	495	455
16	55	10	42	195	165	67	360	320	92	495	465
17	60	15	43	200	170	68	365	325	93	495	470
18	65	20	44	210	175	69	370	330	94	495	480
19	70	25	45	215	180	70	380	335	95	495	485
20	75	30	46	220	190	71	385	340	96	495	490
21	80	35	47	230	195	72	390	350	97	495	495
22	85	40	48	240	200	73	395	355	98	495	495
23	90	45	49	245	210	74	400	360	99	495	495
24	95	50	50	250	215	75	405	365	100	495	495
25	100	60									

Number of Correct Listening Responses _____ = Listening Score _____

Number of Correct Reading Responses _____ = Reading Score _____

Total Estimated Test Score _____

Model Test 3—Explanatory Answers

LISTENING COMPREHENSION

Part 1: Photographs

1. **(C)** Choice (C) identifies *the woman* and the action *watching the servers*. Choices (A) and (D) show negation: The plates are *not* empty; the menu is *not* on the table. Choice (B) has the related words *waiters* and *order* but does not describe the photo.

2. **(D)** The technicians in their lab coats are standing in front of different types of equipment. Choice (A) refers to the equipment that most likely is *metal*. Choice (B) assumes the technicians are testing the equipment, but there is no computer in the photo. Choice (C) mentions the coats they are wearing, not *taking off*.

3. **(A)** There are three lanes of traffic; the right lane, the outside lane, is closed because of construction on the side of the road. Choice (B) refers to the *bus* in the middle lane. Choice (C) repeats the word *cars* that are in the photo, but they are on the road, not being serviced. Choice (D) suggests that the workers walking along the road might be tourists, which they are not.

4. **(B)** Choice (B) identifies *the passengers* and the action *ready to board* a train. Choice (A) confuses the similar sounds: *rain* with *train*. Choice (C) confuses the similar sounds: *plane* with *train*. Choice (D) confuses the similar sounds: *grain* with *train*.

5. **(B)** Many trucks are pulled up to the loading docks of a large warehouse. Choice (A) confuses the similar sounds: *duck* with *truck*. Choice (C) uses the associated word *ship* for *shipping*, sending things by truck. Choice (D) uses the word *shoppers*, but there are no shoppers in the photo; nor is an *aisle* visible.

6. **(C)** There is a large, open grassy field in front of the factory and the parking lot by the factory. Choice (A) assumes there are workers in the factory (plant) but none are visible in the photo. The word *plant* also means vegetation that can be seen in the field. Choice (B) uses the word *field* but in a sports context. Choice (D) uses the associated word *grass* for field, but there are no mowers present.

7. **(D)** The waiters are finishing setting the table for the evening meal. Choice (A) repeats the word *chair* that the waiters are touching. It also uses the similar-sounding word *sitting* for *setting*. Choice (B) repeats the word *dishes* that are on the table. Choice (C) uses the associated word *dinner* but no one is eating dinner.

8. **(A)** The speaker is giving an address to an audience. Choice (B) confuses the similar sound of *dressed* with *address*. Choice (C) uses the associated word *deliver* as in *deliver a talk*. Choice (D) confuses *taking a walk* for *giving a talk*.

9. **(C)** There are two men at the front of the class by the blackboard. Choices (A), (B), and (D) all use words associated with a school but the context is not correct: *students, classroom, professor*.

10. **(B)** The highway overpasses are stacked above one another. Choice (A) uses the associated word *road*. Choice (C) uses the word *cars*. Choice (D) uses the word *bridges*.

Part 2: Question-Response

11. **(A)** Choice (A) is a logical response to a question about *being hungry*. Choice (B) confuses similar sounds: *hungry* and *Hungary*. Choice (C) confuses *How hungry are you* with *How old are you?*

12. **(C)** Choice (C) is a logical response to a question about *playing basketball*. Choice (A) confuses similar sounds: *basketball* and *wastebasket*. Choice (B) has the related word *game* but is past tense and does not answer the question.

13. **(C)** The first speaker complains about the coffee, so the second speaker offers to make a new cup. Choice (A) confuses *coughing* with the similar-sounding word *coffee*. Choice (B) confuses *gold* with the similar-sounding word *cold*.

14. **(B)** Choice (B) is a logical response to a question about *distance*. Choice (A) has the related words *paintings* and *modern* but does not give distance. Choice (C) answers a question about *when*.

15. **(A)** Choice (A) is a logical response to a question about *time*. Choice (B) tells *when they drove* by but not *when they bought*. Choice (C) answers the question *how much*, not *when*.

16. **(C)** Choice (C) is a logical response to a question about the *subject*. Choice (A) gives the location of the book, not *its subject*. Choice (B) gives the price.

17. **(A)** Since the museum is closed on Sunday, the second speaker suggests going on Saturday instead. Choice (B) confuses *clothes* with the similar-sounding word *closed* and repeats the word *Sunday*. Choice (C) associates *art* with *museum*.

18. **(C)** Choice (C) is a logical response to a question about *which train*. Choice (A) confuses similar sounds: *train* with *rain*. Choice (B) answers the incorrect question, *which class should I take*.

19. **(A)** Choice (A) is a logical response to a question about *copies*. Choice (B) confuses similar sounds: *copier is* with *cops; aren't* with *are on*. Choice (C) confuses similar sounds: *ready yet* with *already read it*.

20. **(C)** Choice (C) is a logical response to a question about *when*. Choice (A) tells *how long*, not *when*. Choice (B) confuses similar sounds: *is he* with *she;* and related words: *too long* and *when*.

21. **(C)** Choice (C) is a logical response to a question about *how much*. Choice (A) answers the question *how* you paid. Choice (B) answers the question *how many* (stories the hotel had).

22. **(B)** Since the rent is going up, the second speaker suggests looking for a cheaper place to live. Choice (A) confuses *lent* with the similar-sounding word *rent*. Choice (C) repeats the phrase *going up*.

23. **(B)** Choice (B) is a logical response to a question about a reason *why*. Choice (A) uses the word *watch* but the sense contradicts the question. Choice (C) confuses *lime* with *time*.

24. **(C)** The second speaker will arrive at the meeting in a minute. Choice (A) associates *conference room* with *meeting*. Choice (B) uses the word *meeting* out of context.

25. **(C)** Choice (C) is a logical response to a question about *winning a tennis game*. Choice (A) has related the word *smoke* to another meaning of *match*. Choice (B) confuses *ten* with *tennis*. Only Choice (C) concerns the game, *tennis*.

26. **(B)** Choice (B) is a logical response to a question about *purpose of a visit*. Choice (A) uses related words: *visitors* and *visit*. Choice (C) confuses *proposal* with *purpose* and *list* with *visit*.

27. **(C)** Choice (C) is a logical response to a question about *seasonal preference*. Choice (A) confuses the related word *seasoning* with *season*. Choice (B) confuses the similar sounds *refer* and *prefer*.

28. **(A)** The first speaker mentions seeing Jim at a party, so the second speaker asks how Jim is. Choice (B) associates *dancing* with *party*. Choice (C) confuses *part* with the similar-sounding word *party*.

29. **(A)** Choice (A) is a logical response to a question about *when the mail comes*. Choice (B) confuses the similar sounds: *milk* with *mail c(ome)*. Choice (C) confuses the sound of *come* with *welcome*.

30. **(A)** Choice (A) is a logical response to a question about *where the bank is*. Choice (B) confuses the sound of *thank* with *bank*. Choice (C) confuses the similar sounds in *ink* and *bank*.

31. **(C)** Choice (C) is a logical response to a question about *the weather*. Choice (A) may seem close with its verb *is going* and the adverb *today*. Choice (B) confuses the sound *rain* with *complain*.

32. **(B)** Choice (B) is a logical response to a question about the *amount of a tip*. Choice (A) has related words *tip* (v) and *tip* (n). Choice (C) confuses *water* and *waded* with

waiter, and has an answer to *how many*, not *how much*.

33. **(A)** Choice (A) is a logical response to a question about *who was the designer*. Choice (B) confuses *resign* with *design*. Choice (C) confuses *house* with *mouse*.

34. **(C)** Choice (C) is a logical response to a question about *your arrival time*. Choice (A) gives an arrival time in the *future*, not the *past* like the question. Choice (B) confuses the sounds *live* and *arrive*.

35. **(B)** Choice (B) is a logical response to a question about *the fabric a shirt is made of*. Choice (A) changes the preposition from *made of* to *made in*; Choice (C) confuses *this shirt* with *insert*.

36. **(A)** Choice (A) is a logical response to a question about *the reason a calculator doesn't work*. Choice (B) confuses *calculator* with *Calcutta*; Choice (C) refers to animate objects such as people (*no one*).

37. **(B)** Choice (B) is a logical response to a question about *where you study English*. Choice (A) confuses the related word *students* with *study* and *England* with *English*. Choice (C) answers *how long*.

38. **(C)** Choice (C) is a logical response to a question about *which sweater fits better*. Choice (A) confuses *sweater* with *sweat pants* and the concept of *fit* with something that is *too large*. Choice (B) confuses the word *sweater* with *weather*.

39. **(A)** Choice (A) is a logical response to a question about *the time*. Choice (B) answers another *do you have* question. Choice (C) answers *what time do you have to leave*.

40. **(A)** Choice (A) is a logical response to a request *to close the window*. Choice (B) confuses the word *close* with *clothes*; Choice (C) has the related word *open*.

Part 3: Conversations

41. **(C)** The speakers are discussing seeing an art show in the park. Choice (A) confuses *snow* with the similar-sounding word *show*. Choice (B) associates *theater* with *show*. Choice (D) repeats the word *park*.

42. **(A)** The art show closes at dark. Choice (B) uses the word *park* out of context. Choice (C) confuses *plane* with the similar-sounding word *plan*. Choice (D) confuses *clothes* with the similar-sounding word *closes*.

43. **(B)** The man suggests going on Sunday. Choice (A) is a plausible option; since they can't go after work, Saturday would be a good day to go, but it is not mentioned. Choice (C) sounds similar to the correct answer. Choice (D) confuses *Tuesday* with the similar-sounding word *today*.

44. **(D)** *Resume* and *possible positions* suggest a job interview. Choices (A), (B), and (C) are all scheduled by appointment but would not involve a resume.

45. **(A)** The woman suggests 8:30, and the man agrees. Choice (B) confuses *nine* with the similar-sounding word *fine*. Choices (C) and (D) confuse *ten* with the similar-sounding word *then*.

46. **(D)** The man says to the woman *I'll see you then in your office*. Choice (A) repeats the word *office*. Choice (B) confuses *wait* with the similar-sounding word *eight*. Choice (C) confuses *meeting room* with *meet*.

47. **(A)** The man gives the woman a key, directs her to her room, and arranges to have a newspaper delivered to her; these are things that happen in a hotel. Choice (B) repeats the word *elevator*. Choice (C) associates *newsstand* with *newspaper*. Choice (D) is a place that has elevators but is not the correct answer.

48. **(C)** The man tells the woman that her room number is 215. Choices (A), (B), and (D) sound similar to the correct answer.

49. **(B)** The woman asks for a newspaper. Choice (A) is what the man is giving the woman now. Choice (C) confuses *directory* with the similar-sounding word *directly*. Choice (D) associates *stationery* with *paper*.

50. **(B)** The woman says *He's due to address the meeting…* Choice (A) uses the word *address* out of context. Choice (C) confuses *date* with the similar-sounding word *late*. Choice (D) is what the speakers will do.

51. **(B)** Mr. Chung called to explain that he's stuck in traffic. Choice (A) uses the word *address* out of context. Choice (C) associates *car* with *traffic.* Choice (D) is the result of his lateness, not its cause.

52. **(B)** The man says that they'll be able to start the meeting on time. Choice (A) is wrong because they'll start the meeting by showing a film while they wait for Mr. Chung. Choice (C) is confused with the ten minutes it will take to get the film ready. Choice (D) repeats the word *ten* and confuses *nine* with the similar-sounding word *time.*

53. **(C)** The man mentions the lobby. Choice (A) is what the woman thinks needs to be painted. Choice (B) associates *office* with *office building.* Choice (D) associates *door* with *entrance.*

54. **(D)** The man says *It never had enough light before.* Choice (A) is not mentioned. Choices (B) and (C) are the opposite of the correct answer.

55. **(D)** The man says that the cafeteria will be painted *the week after next.* Choice (A) confuses *afternoon* with the similar-sounding word *soon.* Choice (B) confuses *Sunday* with the similar-sounding word *someday.* Choice (C) sounds similar to the correct answer.

56. **(B)** The speakers are discussing repairs to a television set. Choice (A) confuses *chair* with the similar-sounding word *repair.* Choice (C) confuses *telephone* with the similar-sounding word *television.* Choice (D) uses the word *monitor* out of context by associating it with *computer.*

57. **(A)** The man says that he called the company today. Choice (B) confuses *Tuesday* with the similar-sounding word *today.* Choice (C) confuses *afternoon* with the similar-sounding word *soon.* Choice (D) repeats the word *week.*

58. **(C)** The repairs will take a total of three weeks—two weeks to get the parts and one more week to install them. Choice (A) is confused with the one more week to install the parts. Choice (B) is the time it will take to get the parts. Choice (D) confuses *ten* with the similar-sounding word *then.*

59. **(D)** The man says that his tire is flat. Choice (A) associates *gas* with *gas station.* Choice (B) confuses *drink* with the similar-sounding word *think.* Choice (C) confuses *tired* with the similar-sounding word *tire.*

60. **(C)** The woman says that the gas station is a mile and a half away. Choices (A) and (B) sound similar to the correct answer. Choice (D) confuses *two* with the similar-sounding word *too.*

61. **(D)** The woman offers the man a ride because it is too far to walk. Choice (A) is what the man first says he will do. Choice (B) is not mentioned. Choice (C) associates *car* with *ride.*

62. **(D)** The lunch break is one hour. Choice (A) is the amount of time the man takes to eat. Choice (B) is not mentioned. Choice (C) is the amount of time the man spends walking.

63. **(C)** The woman spends her break in the cafeteria eating. Choice (A) confuses *work* with the similar-sounding word *walk.* Choice (B) is what the woman would like to do if she had the time. Choice (D) is what the man does.

64. **(A)** The man eats lunch at his desk. Choice (B) is where the man walks. Choice (C) is where the woman eats lunch. Choice (D) repeats the word *exercise.*

65. **(C)** The man asks for directions to the history museum. Choices (A), (B), and (D) are places that he will pass on the way there.

66. **(B)** The woman says that it is three blocks away. Choice (A) confuses *two* with the similar-sounding word *through.* Choice (C) confuses *nine* with the similar-sounding word *fine.* Choice (D) confuses *ten* with the similar-sounding word *then.*

67. **(B)** The museum is closed on Saturday and Sunday and open during the week. Choice (A) confuses *Tuesday* with the similar-sounding word *today.* Choice (C) makes the same confusion; these are the days the museum would be open if it were closed on

Tuesday. Choice (D) are the days that the museum is closed.

68. **(D)** The man says that it is a five and a half-hour flight. Choices (A) and (B) are confused with *2:30*, the time that the plane will land. Choice (C) sounds similar to the correct answer.

69. **(D)** The flight attendant says that they are about to serve drinks. Choices (A), (B), and (C) are all things that will happen later on.

70. **(D)** The woman wants a pillow so that she can take a nap. Choices (A) and (C) are things that the man offers. Choice (B) will be served; the woman doesn't have to ask for it.

Part 4: Talks

71. **(B)** *Not in service* means *not working.* Choice (A), *a wrong number,* means you misdialed. Choice (C) confuses the *recording* and an *answering machine.* Choice (D) means someone is using the phone.

72. **(C)** This is a person who helps *customers.* Choice (A) fixes broken phones. Choice (B) connects calls. Choice (D) makes decisions about the company.

73. **(D)** Callers are charged seventy-five cents a minute for assistance. Choices (A), (B), and (C) sound similar to the correct answer.

74. **(C)** The water is *contaminated* with bacteria. Choice (A) is not logical; if there is no water, it can't be contaminated. Choice (B) is not sufficient reason to give an alert. Choice (D) is not mentioned.

75. **(A)** The announcement says to *boil water for five minutes.* Choice (B) involves cooling the water, the opposite of the advice. Choice (C) is not mentioned. Choice (D) would not make the water safe.

76. **(D)** Listeners are given the phone number of the Public Utility Office to call for information. Choice (A) repeats the word *office.* Choice (B) confuses *read* with the similar-sounding word *need.* Choice (C) repeats the word *radio.*

77. **(A)** A *computer school* provides *computer training.* Choice (B) is incorrect; the school trains in *business software,* not *business man-*

agement. Choice (C) confuses the ideas of *job placement* and *personnel.* Choice (D) is incorrect; the school *teaches,* it doesn't *train teachers.*

78. **(B)** The ad says *you can train* in *six months.* Choices (A), (C), and (D) are not mentioned.

79. **(D)** Classes are taught evenings and weekends so that people who work during the day can attend. Choices (A) and (C) are incorrect because daytime is when the students work. Choice (B) is incorrect because there are also weekend classes.

80. **(D)** The train is bound for *New York and Boston.* Choice (A) confuses *Baltimore* and *Boston.* Choices (B) and (C) include other stops on the way to Boston but they are not mentioned here.

81. **(A)** New York passengers board *at the front.* Choice (B) is where Boston passengers board. Choices (C) and (D) are not mentioned as boarding sites.

82. **(B)** The announcer says that the train is leaving in ten minutes. Choices (A), (C), and (D) are confused with the track number, *27.*

83. **(C)** Those hours refer to *business hours.* Choices (A) and (B) are both contradicted; the hours given are for weekdays during the day. Choice (D) is not logical; they are not open *before 8:00.*

84. **(B)** *To contact in writing* means *to write a letter.* Choices (A), (C), and (D) are possible solutions but not mentioned here.

85. **(D)** The message asks for the serial number of the product. Choices (A), (B), and (C) are confused with *the name and address of the store where it was purchased.*

86. **(B)** *Apply in person* means *go to the hotel.* Choice (A) is not required. Choices (C) and (D) are unnecessary if you apply in person.

87. **(D)** *Opportunity for advancement* means *possible promotions.* Choices (A) and (B) are not mentioned. Choice (C) is unlikely for these kinds of jobs.

88. **(D)** The announcement mentions *waiters* as one of the open positions. Choice (A) is

the person to apply to. Choice (B) confuses *store clerks* with *desk clerks*. Choice (C) is confused with *we will train new employees*.

89. **(B)** A *garage* is a *parking area*. Choices (A), (C), and (D) are not mentioned, although they are likely places that you would buy a ticket from a machine.

90. **(C)** *Exit* means *leave*. Choices (A), (B), and (D) are common things to do with a ticket, but they are not mentioned in the talk.

91. **(B)** The ticket holder has to pay $8.50 for parking for two hours and twelve minutes. Choices (A) and (D) are confused with the amount of time the ticket holder parked. Choice (C) confuses *four* with the similar-sounding word *for*.

92. **(B)** A *heat wave* means *hot weather*. Choices (A), (C), and (D) are possible problems but not true here.

93. **(D)** *The report says the weather will be over one hundred degrees*. Choices (A), (B), and (C) are all under one hundred degrees.

94. **(C)** To avoid heatstroke, residents should *drink lots of water*. Choice (A) is incorrect because residents are advised to wear light, not dark, clothes. Choice (B) is contradicted by *avoid strenuous exercise*. Choice (D) is not mentioned.

95. **(D)** Executives are advised to *establish a quiet hour*. Choices (A), (B), and (C) are not part of establishing a quiet hour.

96. **(B)** *Closing your office door* is probably to keep people out. Choice (A) would also keep you from getting work done. Choice (C) is not appropriate; these signs are found in hotels, not offices. Choice (D) is incorrect because emergencies are the exception to the *do not disturb* rule.

97. **(A)** *Difficult tasks* require *quiet time*. Choice (B) is possible but not mentioned. Choice (C) is not mentioned. Choice (D) is contradicted by asking staff not to disturb you.

98. **(C)** It is an annual ceremony, so it takes place once a year. Choice (A) is confused with the size of the cash award ($5,000). Choices (B) and (D) confuse *three* with *third*.

99. **(A)** A total of $20,000 will be given out, and the size of each award is $5,000, so four people will receive awards. Choice (B) is confused with the size of each award. Choice (C) is confused with the total amount of cash given out. Choice (D) is confused with both the size of the individual awards and the total amount awarded.

100. **(B)** Listeners are asked to make donations so that awards can continue to be given in the future. Choices (A), (C), and (D) are confused with the various things winners might do with their money.

READING

Part 5: Incomplete Sentences

101. **(C)** The plural *contracts* requires a plural verb. Choices (A) and (B) are singular. Choice (D) is the simple form.

102. **(B)** *The* must be followed by a noun. Choice (A) is an adjective. Choices (C) and (D) are verbs.

103. **(A)** *On* is a preposition meaning *upon the surface of*. Choice (B) indicates movement across something. Choice (C) means *to place inside*. Choice (D) means *lacking*.

104. **(D)** Someone else sealed the bid; use the past participle. Choices (A) and (B) are verbs. Choice (C) is the present participle.

105. **(C)** Use the simple form for a command. Choice (A) is a gerund. Choice (B) is future tense. Choice (D) is past tense.

106. **(D)** Someone else *included* the taxes; use the past participle. Choice (A) is the present participle. Choices (B) and (C) are verbs.

107. **(B)** Complete the verb: *wants to finalize*. Choices (A) and (D) are nouns. Choice (C) is is an adverb.

108. **(A)** A comparison of two things uses *more + adjective* or the *-er* form. Choices (B) and (C) use *most*. Choice (D) uses *the*.

109. **(C)** Use *who* to refer to people. Choice (A) refers to things. Choice (B) is possessive. Choice (D) is objective.

110. **(D)** *On* is used with days of the week. Choice (A) indicates location. Choice (B) indicates source. Choice (C) is not logical.

111. **(B)** *Paint* and *pictures* are equal items joined with *and*. Choices (A), (C), and (D) join clauses, not nouns.

112. **(A)** *Aware* is the only adjective among the options. Choices (B), (C), and (D) do not fit the context of the sentence.

113. **(B)** The sentence requires a conjugated verb and past participle. Choices (A) and (D) use the present participle. Choice (C) uses the simple form of the verb.

114. **(A)** *Between* expresses beginning and ending points. Choice (B) indicates *in the company of or by means of.* Choice (C) indicates movement across something. Choice (D) indicates source.

115. **(C)** The causative *had* requires the simple form of the following verb. Choice (A) is past tense. Choice (B) is past perfect. Choice (D) is present tense.

116. **(D)** The comparative form is *faster*. Choice (A) is an adjective. Choice (B) is the superlative. Choice (C) has an unnecessary article, *the*.

117. **(B)** The items are equal, so link with *and*. Choice (A) implies a choice. Choice (C) is not logical. Choice (D) cannot be followed by a clause.

118. **(C)** Habitual action uses present tense; *head* requires third person singular forms. Choice (A) is the simple form. Choices (B) and (D) are progressive forms of the third person plural.

119. **(A)** The causative *ask* requires a following infinitive. Choice (B) is the gerund. Choice (C) is future tense. Choice (D) is present tense.

120. **(D)** The adverb describes how the office runs. Choice (A) is an adjective. Choice (B) is a noun. Choice (C) is a verb.

121. **(C)** This sentence requires a conjugated verb and past participle. Choice (A) uses the simple form of the verb. Choice (B) is the gerund. Choice (D) is the present participle.

122. **(A)** The causative *got* requires a following infinitive. Choice (B) is the past progressive. Choice (C) is an adjective. Choice (D) is the simple past.

123. **(B)** The subject *variety* requires a singular verb. Choice (A) is plural. Choice (C) is the gerund. Choice (D) is the simple form.

124. **(A)** *Name and address* are both listed. Choice (B) doesn't fit. Choice (C) implies a contrast. Choice (D) is used with *neither.*

125. **(D)** *Beside* means *next to*. Choices (A) and (B) need more than one bus as a reference point. Choice (C) means *direction away*; it is not logical.

126. **(C)** Choice (C) is a correctly formed time link. Choices (A) and (B) are incomplete. Choice (D) incorrectly uses *than*.

127. **(D)** An unreal condition requires *would* in the clause without *if*. Choice (A) is the wrong tense. Choices (B) and (C) do not use *would*.

128. **(A)** Habitual action uses present tense; *handbook* requires third person singular forms. Choice (B) is the present progressive. Choice (C) is the simple form. Choice (D) is the gerund.

129. **(C)** The costs are rising themselves; use the present participle. Choices (A) and (D) must tell who raised costs. Choice (B) is the past participle.

130. **(B)** *Always* goes between the auxiliary verb and the main verb. In Choice (C) *always* is before the auxiliary verb. In choices (A) and (D) *always* is after the main verb.

131. **(D)** *Even though* establishes a logical link between clauses. Choices (A), (B), and (C) are not logical.

132. **(C)** *Make an appointment* is a common business expression. Choice (A) is incorrect; *make* a meeting means *be able to attend* the meeting. Choice (B) is not used for appointments. Choice (D) is incorrect; *a time* is not used for specific appointments.

133. **(A)** The sentence requires a conjugated verb and past participle. *Team* is singular. Choice (B) is plural. Choices (C) and (D) use the present participle.

134. **(B)** The subject *record* requires a singular verb. Choices (A) and (C) are plural. Choice (D) needs *been* to form the present perfect *has been kept.*

135. **(C)** Use *between* with two items. Choice (A) means *together*. Choice (B) indicates time. Choice (D) is used with three or more items.

136. **(D)** *Although* establishes a logical connection between events. Choice (A) cannot be followed by a clause. Choice (B) is not logical. Choice (C) cannot be followed by a clause.

137. **(B)** *Organizing* is a gerund, the object of the preposition *for*. Choice (A) is a noun. Choices (C) and (D) are verbs.

138. **(C)** The present progressive is the only appropriate verb. Choice (A) uses the past participle. Choice (B) uses plural *have*. Choice (D) uses *has* instead of *be*.

139. **(B)** *Suggested* is followed by the gerund. Choice (A) is the simple form of the verb. Choice (C) is the past tense. Choice (D) is the infinitive.

140. **(D)** Days of the week require *on*. Choice (A) indicates source. Choice (B) means *inside* or *within*. Choice (C) indicates a recipient.

Part 6: Text Completion

141. **(C)** This is a second person possessive adjective, used because the writer is thanking the reader directly for his interest. Choice (A) is third person singular. Choice (B) is third person plural. Choice (D) is first person.

142. **(A)** The present tense verb *require* agrees with its plural subject *cleaning products and paints*. Simple present tense is used to refer to something that is always true. Choice (B) is a simple present tense verb that requires a singular subject. Choices (C) and (D) are present progressive forms.

143. **(A)** To *demonstrate concern* for something means to *care* about it. Choices (B), (C), and (D) have meanings that do not fit the context.

144. **(C)** This is the correct superlative form for a one-syllable adjective. Choice (A) is not a superlative adjective. Choice (B) is the comparative form. Choice (D) is an incorrect form for a one-syllable adjective.

145. **(C)** *Spread out* can mean divided up; the customer will not pay the highest bills at one time of the year, but instead divide the bills into smaller pieces and pay them throughout the year. Choice (A) means *reduced in price*. Choice (B) means *increased*. Choice (D) means *added to*.

146. **(A)** The company *estimates*, or *guesses*, how much gas the customer will use in a year based on use in past years. Choice (B) means *allowed*. Choice (C) means *asked about*. Choice (D) means *asked for*.

147. **(C)** A passive voice form is needed because the subject, *passengers*, is not active. It is the airport that offers the Internet service. Choices (A), (B), and (D) are all active voice forms.

148. **(C)** A benefit of the lounge is use of, or access to, these machines while waiting for a flight. Choice (A) is not something one does with machines. Choices (B) and (D) are not services likely to be offered in a lounge.

149. **(A)** An adjective is needed to describe the noun *trips*. Choices (B) and (D) are nouns. Choice (C) is an adverb.

150. **(B)** A *bargain* price is a *good* or *low* price, and the point of the ad is that this store offers lower prices than other stores. Choice (A) is a word that is not normally used to describe prices. Choice (C) describes prices that customers generally pay to stores. Choice (D) means *high*.

151. **(D)** *No* is the correct word to use to make a noun negative. Choices (A) and (B) are pronouns. Choice (C) is used to make a verb negative.

152. **(A)** Since there is no subject, the imperative form is required here, telling the reader what to do. Choice (B) is a gerund. Choice (C) is infinitive. Choice (D) is a modal plus base form verb and requires a subject.

Part 7: Reading Comprehension

153. **(D)** Product quality is improved by improvements in technology. The other options are not explicitly mentioned.

154. **(D)** *Hiring practices* are not mentioned. Choices (A), (B), and (C) are explicitly mentioned.

155. **(B)** It is *lowering costs by improving manufacturing processes.* Choice (A) is not linked to lowering costs. Choices (C) and (D) are not logical ways to lower costs.

156. **(C)** To find people to apply for jobs. Choice (A) is incorrect; they want to meet job applicants, not *new people.* Choices (B) and (D) might encourage people but do not describe the purpose of the ad.

157. **(A)** National Headquarters is mentioned with the *time* and *date,* so it must be the place. Choice (B) is not mentioned. Choice (C) is not a logical location for an open house. Choice (D) is incorrect; the airport is regional, not the office.

158. **(D)** The first line of the letter gives the answer: *pleased to receive your fax.* The other choices are not mentioned.

159. **(D)** The company makes 75% of its sales directly and the other 25% in other *ways.* Choices (A), (B), and (C) are words that are related to sales, but they don't have the correct meaning.

160. **(C)** *Company distribution centers* ship goods. Choice (A) suggests the shipping method but does not ship. Choice (B) is incorrect; the distribution centers may *use* airlines. Choice (D) is incorrect; *headquarters* does not ship goods.

161. **(B)** The details in the fax answer the question about the company's distribution network. The other questions are not answered in the fax.

162. **(A)** It gives *etiquette rules for bus riders.* Choices (B), (C), and (D) are not the subjects of the notice.

163. **(B)** *Senior citizens and disabled riders* means *elderly people and handicapped people.* Choices (A), (C), and (D) are not designated for priority seats.

164. **(C)** *Reviewing sales records* makes up 25%. Choice (A) makes up 15%. Choice (B) makes up 5%. Choice (D) makes up 22%.

165. **(C)** They spend *10%* of their time with the technical staff. Choice (A) is spent in *administrative duties.* Choice (B) is spent in *miscellaneous tasks.* Choice (D) is spent *training new salespeople.*

166. **(A)** If only 5% of each manager's time is spent dealing with customer problems, it can be assumed that there are few problems. Choice (B) is contradicted in the passage: *training sales personnel* (15%), *reviewing records* (25%), and *making sales assignments* (22%) show that sales are the highest priority. Choices (C) and (D) are also contradicted.

167. **(A)** The ad states *You will study with your peers. Peers* are defined here as *other experienced managers.* The other choices are not mentioned.

168. **(D)** The application must be accompanied by *three letters of recommendation.* The other choices are not specifically mentioned.

169. **(B)** The course is a *week-long* intensive one. The other periods of time are not mentioned.

170. **(A)** It guarantees the *lowest prices.* Choices (B), (C), and (D) are not mentioned.

171. **(B)** They will *refund the difference,* which means *pay you the difference in price.* Choices (A) and (C) are not given as resolutions to the problem. Choice (D) is incorrect; the store will *refund the difference,* not refund all of your money.

172. **(C)** It *allows employees to take paid time off for volunteer activities.* Choices (B), (C), and (D) concern other types of *time off.*

173. **(D)** They may take *up to eight hours of paid leave per month.* Choices (A) and (C) are all less than the allowed time. Choice (B) is more than the allowed time.

174. **(A)** *Eligible* means *qualified.* Choices (B), (C), and (D) could fit the context but don't have the correct meaning.

175. **(D)** Volunteer leave must be *requested in advance* and *approved by the supervisor.* Choices (A), (B), and (C) are not mentioned as requirements.

176. **(B)** Smaller companies are a likely *victim,* or *target.* Choice (A) refers to the common target of the past. Choice (C) is not mentioned. Choice (D) repeats the words *security system* from the article.

177. **(C)** *Notoriety* means *fame.* Choices (A), (B), and (D) are likely reasons for a hacker

to do his work, but none is mentioned in the article.

178. **(A)** *Sitting behind bars* means *in jail.* Choice (B) is not mentioned in the reading. Choice (C) refers to *working overtime.* Choice (D) repeats *pay off* from the article.

179. **(D)** A *password* is a *secret code.* Choices (A) and (B) refer to characteristics of smaller companies that are likely to be attacked. Choice (C) repeats the word *network* from the article.

180. **(C)** When thieves steal data, they can create *confusion* with it. Choice (A) is the opposite of the correct answer. Choices (B) and (D) are things that could be done with data, but they don't have the correct meaning.

181. **(A)** This is confused with Camilla Crowe's title of *Recruiting Coordinator,* but is not mentioned as part of the advertised job. Choices (B), (C), and (D) are all mentioned in the ad as duties of the job.

182. **(B)** Camilla Crow says that Akiko has the degree they are looking for, which, according to the ad, is a degree in marketing. Choice (A) is confused with the store where Akiko worked. Choice (C) is confused with the communications skills asked for in the ad. Choice (D) is confused with the conferences mentioned in the ad as a job duty.

183. **(A)** Camilla Crowe mentions that Akiko graduated last month; since the letter has a March date, last month was February. Choice (B) is the month the letter was written. Choice (C) is confused with the date by which Akiko must contact Camilla about the internship. Choice (D) is not mentioned.

184. **(B)** Akiko's sales experience in the electronics store is only half that asked for in the ad, which is one year. Choice (A) is not mentioned. Choice (C) is the amount of experience asked for in the ad. Choice (D) is twice, not half, the experience asked for in the ad.

185. **(C)** Camilla offered Akiko a three-month unpaid internship. Choice (A) is what Akiko applied for, but Camilla says she is not experienced enough. Choice (B) is associated with a job application but is not mentioned. Choice (D) is confused with the Marketing Club.

186. **(C)** All the classes start at 6:00. Choices (A) and (B) are confused with the course level numbers. Choice (D) is the time that classes end.

187. **(D)** Both the Marketing classes are 500 level and above; classes at these levels are offered on Thursday. Choices (A), (B), and (C) are days that classes at other levels are offered.

188. **(C)** A grade of 75% or higher is required in ACTG 101 in order to take the 102 level; this is the reason Roberto can't register for ACTG 102. Choices (A) and (B) are confused with the correct answer. Choice (D) is the amount by which Roberto failed the course.

189. **(B)** Roberto is registered for two courses—BUSI 100 and for COMP 207; since courses cost $300 each, his total is $600. Choice (A) is the cost of one course. Choice (C) is the cost of three courses. Choice (D) is the cost of four courses, the number Roberto originally wanted to take.

190. **(C)** Classes end March 15, and Roberto's visa expires fifteen days before that. Choice (A) is the day classes begin. Choice (B) is confused with the starting month and the ending date of classes. Choice (D) is the day classes end.

191. **(C)** The ad says that a tour of the theater is included. Choice (A) is confused with the mention of the French chef. Choice (B) is confused with the mention of the region's finest actors. Choice (D) is done by the theater, not the guests.

192. **(C)** Sundays are for large groups only, so it follows that all the other days are for individuals and small groups. Choice (A) is the days when only evening shows are available. Choice (B) is the days that both afternoon and evening shows are available. Choice (D) is the day reserved for large groups.

193. **(B)** Ms. Heckler wants to have her party on December 20, and the theater recommends

making reservations a month in advance. Choice (A) is the date on the fax. Choice (C) is not mentioned. Choice (D) is the date of the party.

194. **(B)** The group from the Federal Bank is 325 people, so they will get the 10% discount. Choice (A) applies to groups smaller than 300. Choice (C) applies to groups larger than 350. Choice (D) is confused with the date of the party.

195. **(D)** The Federal Bank party is in December, so they will see a comedy. Choice (A) is the type of show available January–April. Choice (B) is the type of show available May–July. Choice (C) is the type of show available August–October.

196. **(B)** An employee of any age with twenty-five years' experience can take early retirement with full retirement benefits. Choice (A) describes a person who doesn't qualify for early retirement. Choices (C) and (D) describe people who would get reduced benefits.

197. **(D)** The first workshop is on August 10; Marcus went this morning, which is July. Choice (A) is incorrect because workshops are on Wednesdays and Fridays, and today is Wednesday. Choice (B) is incorrect because he went at the right time. Choice (C) is incorrect because he went to the right place.

198. **(D)** Marcus is a supervisor, so he has two months more than other employees to apply. Choice (A) is the date of the phone message. Choice (B) is the date of the first workshop. Choice (C) is the deadline for most employees.

199. **(C)** Marcus is sixty-two, and the reduction is 2% for every year under age sixty-five. Choice (A) is the reduction for one year. Choice (B) is the reduction for two years. Choice (D) is the reduction for four years.

200. **(A)** Geoffrey is the tax specialist. Choices (B) and (C) are the people to talk to about registering for a workshop. Choice (D) is the benefits manager.

Answer Sheet
MODEL TEST 4

Listening Comprehension

PART 1: PHOTOGRAPHS

1. Ⓐ Ⓑ Ⓒ Ⓓ   4. Ⓐ Ⓑ Ⓒ Ⓓ   7. Ⓐ Ⓑ Ⓒ Ⓓ   10. Ⓐ Ⓑ Ⓒ Ⓓ
2. Ⓐ Ⓑ Ⓒ Ⓓ   5. Ⓐ Ⓑ Ⓒ Ⓓ   8. Ⓐ Ⓑ Ⓒ Ⓓ
3. Ⓐ Ⓑ Ⓒ Ⓓ   6. Ⓐ Ⓑ Ⓒ Ⓓ   9. Ⓐ Ⓑ Ⓒ Ⓓ

PART 2: QUESTION-RESPONSE

11. Ⓐ Ⓑ Ⓒ   19. Ⓐ Ⓑ Ⓒ   27. Ⓐ Ⓑ Ⓒ   35. Ⓐ Ⓑ Ⓒ
12. Ⓐ Ⓑ Ⓒ   20. Ⓐ Ⓑ Ⓒ   28. Ⓐ Ⓑ Ⓒ   36. Ⓐ Ⓑ Ⓒ
13. Ⓐ Ⓑ Ⓒ   21. Ⓐ Ⓑ Ⓒ   29. Ⓐ Ⓑ Ⓒ   37. Ⓐ Ⓑ Ⓒ
14. Ⓐ Ⓑ Ⓒ   22. Ⓐ Ⓑ Ⓒ   30. Ⓐ Ⓑ Ⓒ   38. Ⓐ Ⓑ Ⓒ
15. Ⓐ Ⓑ Ⓒ   23. Ⓐ Ⓑ Ⓒ   31. Ⓐ Ⓑ Ⓒ   39. Ⓐ Ⓑ Ⓒ
16. Ⓐ Ⓑ Ⓒ   24. Ⓐ Ⓑ Ⓒ   32. Ⓐ Ⓑ Ⓒ   40. Ⓐ Ⓑ Ⓒ
17. Ⓐ Ⓑ Ⓒ   25. Ⓐ Ⓑ Ⓒ   33. Ⓐ Ⓑ Ⓒ
18. Ⓐ Ⓑ Ⓒ   26. Ⓐ Ⓑ Ⓒ   34. Ⓐ Ⓑ Ⓒ

PART 3: CONVERSATIONS

41. Ⓐ Ⓑ Ⓒ Ⓓ   49. Ⓐ Ⓑ Ⓒ Ⓓ   57. Ⓐ Ⓑ Ⓒ Ⓓ   65. Ⓐ Ⓑ Ⓒ Ⓓ
42. Ⓐ Ⓑ Ⓒ Ⓓ   50. Ⓐ Ⓑ Ⓒ Ⓓ   58. Ⓐ Ⓑ Ⓒ Ⓓ   66. Ⓐ Ⓑ Ⓒ Ⓓ
43. Ⓐ Ⓑ Ⓒ Ⓓ   51. Ⓐ Ⓑ Ⓒ Ⓓ   59. Ⓐ Ⓑ Ⓒ Ⓓ   67. Ⓐ Ⓑ Ⓒ Ⓓ
44. Ⓐ Ⓑ Ⓒ Ⓓ   52. Ⓐ Ⓑ Ⓒ Ⓓ   60. Ⓐ Ⓑ Ⓒ Ⓓ   68. Ⓐ Ⓑ Ⓒ Ⓓ
45. Ⓐ Ⓑ Ⓒ Ⓓ   53. Ⓐ Ⓑ Ⓒ Ⓓ   61. Ⓐ Ⓑ Ⓒ Ⓓ   69. Ⓐ Ⓑ Ⓒ Ⓓ
46. Ⓐ Ⓑ Ⓒ Ⓓ   54. Ⓐ Ⓑ Ⓒ Ⓓ   62. Ⓐ Ⓑ Ⓒ Ⓓ   70. Ⓐ Ⓑ Ⓒ Ⓓ
47. Ⓐ Ⓑ Ⓒ Ⓓ   55. Ⓐ Ⓑ Ⓒ Ⓓ   63. Ⓐ Ⓑ Ⓒ Ⓓ
48. Ⓐ Ⓑ Ⓒ Ⓓ   56. Ⓐ Ⓑ Ⓒ Ⓓ   64. Ⓐ Ⓑ Ⓒ Ⓓ

PART 4: TALKS

71. Ⓐ Ⓑ Ⓒ Ⓓ   79. Ⓐ Ⓑ Ⓒ Ⓓ   87. Ⓐ Ⓑ Ⓒ Ⓓ   95. Ⓐ Ⓑ Ⓒ Ⓓ
72. Ⓐ Ⓑ Ⓒ Ⓓ   80. Ⓐ Ⓑ Ⓒ Ⓓ   88. Ⓐ Ⓑ Ⓒ Ⓓ   96. Ⓐ Ⓑ Ⓒ Ⓓ
73. Ⓐ Ⓑ Ⓒ Ⓓ   81. Ⓐ Ⓑ Ⓒ Ⓓ   89. Ⓐ Ⓑ Ⓒ Ⓓ   97. Ⓐ Ⓑ Ⓒ Ⓓ
74. Ⓐ Ⓑ Ⓒ Ⓓ   82. Ⓐ Ⓑ Ⓒ Ⓓ   90. Ⓐ Ⓑ Ⓒ Ⓓ   98. Ⓐ Ⓑ Ⓒ Ⓓ
75. Ⓐ Ⓑ Ⓒ Ⓓ   83. Ⓐ Ⓑ Ⓒ Ⓓ   91. Ⓐ Ⓑ Ⓒ Ⓓ   99. Ⓐ Ⓑ Ⓒ Ⓓ
76. Ⓐ Ⓑ Ⓒ Ⓓ   84. Ⓐ Ⓑ Ⓒ Ⓓ   92. Ⓐ Ⓑ Ⓒ Ⓓ   100. Ⓐ Ⓑ Ⓒ Ⓓ
77. Ⓐ Ⓑ Ⓒ Ⓓ   85. Ⓐ Ⓑ Ⓒ Ⓓ   93. Ⓐ Ⓑ Ⓒ Ⓓ
78. Ⓐ Ⓑ Ⓒ Ⓓ   86. Ⓐ Ⓑ Ⓒ Ⓓ   94. Ⓐ Ⓑ Ⓒ Ⓓ

First News
Always Innovative & Informative

Reading

PART 5: INCOMPLETE SENTENCES

101. Ⓐ Ⓑ Ⓒ Ⓓ
102. Ⓐ Ⓑ Ⓒ Ⓓ
103. Ⓐ Ⓑ Ⓒ Ⓓ
104. Ⓐ Ⓑ Ⓒ Ⓓ
105. Ⓐ Ⓑ Ⓒ Ⓓ
106. Ⓐ Ⓑ Ⓒ Ⓓ
107. Ⓐ Ⓑ Ⓒ Ⓓ
108. Ⓐ Ⓑ Ⓒ Ⓓ
109. Ⓐ Ⓑ Ⓒ Ⓓ
110. Ⓐ Ⓑ Ⓒ Ⓓ

111. Ⓐ Ⓑ Ⓒ Ⓓ
112. Ⓐ Ⓑ Ⓒ Ⓓ
113. Ⓐ Ⓑ Ⓒ Ⓓ
114. Ⓐ Ⓑ Ⓒ Ⓓ
115. Ⓐ Ⓑ Ⓒ Ⓓ
116. Ⓐ Ⓑ Ⓒ Ⓓ
117. Ⓐ Ⓑ Ⓒ Ⓓ
118. Ⓐ Ⓑ Ⓒ Ⓓ
119. Ⓐ Ⓑ Ⓒ Ⓓ
120. Ⓐ Ⓑ Ⓒ Ⓓ

121. Ⓐ Ⓑ Ⓒ Ⓓ
122. Ⓐ Ⓑ Ⓒ Ⓓ
123. Ⓐ Ⓑ Ⓒ Ⓓ
124. Ⓐ Ⓑ Ⓒ Ⓓ
125. Ⓐ Ⓑ Ⓒ Ⓓ
126. Ⓐ Ⓑ Ⓒ Ⓓ
127. Ⓐ Ⓑ Ⓒ Ⓓ
128. Ⓐ Ⓑ Ⓒ Ⓓ
129. Ⓐ Ⓑ Ⓒ Ⓓ
130. Ⓐ Ⓑ Ⓒ Ⓓ

131. Ⓐ Ⓑ Ⓒ Ⓓ
132. Ⓐ Ⓑ Ⓒ Ⓓ
133. Ⓐ Ⓑ Ⓒ Ⓓ
134. Ⓐ Ⓑ Ⓒ Ⓓ
135. Ⓐ Ⓑ Ⓒ Ⓓ
136. Ⓐ Ⓑ Ⓒ Ⓓ
137. Ⓐ Ⓑ Ⓒ Ⓓ
138. Ⓐ Ⓑ Ⓒ Ⓓ
139. Ⓐ Ⓑ Ⓒ Ⓓ
140. Ⓐ Ⓑ Ⓒ Ⓓ

PART 6: TEXT COMPLETION

141. Ⓐ Ⓑ Ⓒ Ⓓ
142. Ⓐ Ⓑ Ⓒ Ⓓ
143. Ⓐ Ⓑ Ⓒ Ⓓ

144. Ⓐ Ⓑ Ⓒ Ⓓ
145. Ⓐ Ⓑ Ⓒ Ⓓ
146. Ⓐ Ⓑ Ⓒ Ⓓ

147. Ⓐ Ⓑ Ⓒ Ⓓ
148. Ⓐ Ⓑ Ⓒ Ⓓ
149. Ⓐ Ⓑ Ⓒ Ⓓ

150. Ⓐ Ⓑ Ⓒ Ⓓ
151. Ⓐ Ⓑ Ⓒ Ⓓ
152. Ⓐ Ⓑ Ⓒ Ⓓ

PART 7: READING COMPREHENSION

153. Ⓐ Ⓑ Ⓒ Ⓓ
154. Ⓐ Ⓑ Ⓒ Ⓓ
155. Ⓐ Ⓑ Ⓒ Ⓓ
156. Ⓐ Ⓑ Ⓒ Ⓓ
157. Ⓐ Ⓑ Ⓒ Ⓓ
158. Ⓐ Ⓑ Ⓒ Ⓓ
159. Ⓐ Ⓑ Ⓒ Ⓓ
160. Ⓐ Ⓑ Ⓒ Ⓓ
161. Ⓐ Ⓑ Ⓒ Ⓓ
162. Ⓐ Ⓑ Ⓒ Ⓓ
163. Ⓐ Ⓑ Ⓒ Ⓓ
164. Ⓐ Ⓑ Ⓒ Ⓓ

165. Ⓐ Ⓑ Ⓒ Ⓓ
166. Ⓐ Ⓑ Ⓒ Ⓓ
167. Ⓐ Ⓑ Ⓒ Ⓓ
168. Ⓐ Ⓑ Ⓒ Ⓓ
169. Ⓐ Ⓑ Ⓒ Ⓓ
170. Ⓐ Ⓑ Ⓒ Ⓓ
171. Ⓐ Ⓑ Ⓒ Ⓓ
172. Ⓐ Ⓑ Ⓒ Ⓓ
173. Ⓐ Ⓑ Ⓒ Ⓓ
174. Ⓐ Ⓑ Ⓒ Ⓓ
175. Ⓐ Ⓑ Ⓒ Ⓓ
176. Ⓐ Ⓑ Ⓒ Ⓓ

177. Ⓐ Ⓑ Ⓒ Ⓓ
178. Ⓐ Ⓑ Ⓒ Ⓓ
179. Ⓐ Ⓑ Ⓒ Ⓓ
180. Ⓐ Ⓑ Ⓒ Ⓓ
181. Ⓐ Ⓑ Ⓒ Ⓓ
182. Ⓐ Ⓑ Ⓒ Ⓓ
183. Ⓐ Ⓑ Ⓒ Ⓓ
184. Ⓐ Ⓑ Ⓒ Ⓓ
185. Ⓐ Ⓑ Ⓒ Ⓓ
186. Ⓐ Ⓑ Ⓒ Ⓓ
187. Ⓐ Ⓑ Ⓒ Ⓓ
188. Ⓐ Ⓑ Ⓒ Ⓓ

189. Ⓐ Ⓑ Ⓒ Ⓓ
190. Ⓐ Ⓑ Ⓒ Ⓓ
191. Ⓐ Ⓑ Ⓒ Ⓓ
192. Ⓐ Ⓑ Ⓒ Ⓓ
193. Ⓐ Ⓑ Ⓒ Ⓓ
194. Ⓐ Ⓑ Ⓒ Ⓓ
195. Ⓐ Ⓑ Ⓒ Ⓓ
196. Ⓐ Ⓑ Ⓒ Ⓓ
197. Ⓐ Ⓑ Ⓒ Ⓓ
198. Ⓐ Ⓑ Ⓒ Ⓓ
199. Ⓐ Ⓑ Ⓒ Ⓓ
200. Ⓐ Ⓑ Ⓒ Ⓓ

Model Test 4
Listening Comprehension

In this section of the test, you will have the chance to show how well you understand spoken English. There are four parts to this section, with special directions for each part. You will have approximately 45 minutes to complete the Listening Comprehension sections.

Part 1: Photographs

Directions: You will see a photograph. You will hear four statements about the photograph. Choose the statement that most closely matches the photograph and fill in the corresponding oval on your answer sheet.

Model Test 4

1.

2.

3.

4.

5.

6.

7.

8.

9.

10.

Part 2: Question-Response

Directions: You will hear a question and three possible responses. Choose the response that most closely answers the question and fill in the corresponding oval on your answer sheet.

11. Mark your answer on your answer sheet.	26. Mark your answer on your answer sheet.
12. Mark your answer on your answer sheet.	27. Mark your answer on your answer sheet.
13. Mark your answer on your answer sheet.	28. Mark your answer on your answer sheet.
14. Mark your answer on your answer sheet.	29. Mark your answer on your answer sheet.
15. Mark your answer on your answer sheet.	30. Mark your answer on your answer sheet.
16. Mark your answer on your answer sheet.	31. Mark your answer on your answer sheet.
17. Mark your answer on your answer sheet.	32. Mark your answer on your answer sheet.
18. Mark your answer on your answer sheet.	33. Mark your answer on your answer sheet.
19. Mark your answer on your answer sheet.	34. Mark your answer on your answer sheet.
20. Mark your answer on your answer sheet.	35. Mark your answer on your answer sheet.
21. Mark your answer on your answer sheet.	36. Mark your answer on your answer sheet.
22. Mark your answer on your answer sheet.	37. Mark your answer on your answer sheet.
23. Mark your answer on your answer sheet.	38. Mark your answer on your answer sheet.
24. Mark your answer on your answer sheet.	39. Mark your answer on your answer sheet.
25. Mark your answer on your answer sheet.	40. Mark your answer on your answer sheet.

Model Test 4

Part 3: Conversations

Directions: You will hear a conversation between two people. You will see three questions on each conversation and four possible answers. Choose the best answer to each question and fill in the corresponding oval on your answer sheet.

CD 4
Track
7

41. What time did the man call the woman?

(A) 2:00
(B) 7:00
(C) 8:00
(D) 10:00

42. Why didn't the woman hear the phone?

(A) She was out.
(B) She was singing.
(C) She was sleeping.
(D) She was watching TV.

43. Why did the man call the woman?

(A) To ask her to go to a party
(B) To ask her to see a movie
(C) To ask her to go on a walk
(D) To ask her to help him with work

44. What kind of room does the man want?

(A) Small
(B) Quiet
(C) Large
(D) Noisy

45. What room does the woman give him?

(A) 355
(B) 365
(C) 517
(D) 570

46. What will the man do now?

(A) Put on his sweater
(B) Swim in the pool
(C) Have dinner
(D) Take a rest

47. Why is Mr. Tan out of the office?

(A) He's stuck in traffic.
(B) He's working at the hospital.
(C) He was in an accident.
(D) He's working at home.

48. How long will he be away from work?

(A) One night
(B) One week
(C) Three weeks
(D) Four weeks

49. Who will do his work while he is away?

(A) His wife
(B) His boss
(C) The woman
(D) The man

50. What is the man's complaint?

(A) The tour was too fast.
(B) They didn't see any paintings.
(C) His back hurt.
(D) He didn't like the paintings.

51. What does the woman suggest to the man?

(A) Take another tour
(B) Hurry up
(C) Return to the museum alone
(D) Get a painting of his own

52. When will the speakers leave the city?

(A) This afternoon
(B) Tomorrow afternoon
(C) Next week
(D) Next weekend

53. How are the speakers traveling?

    (A) By car
    (B) By plane
    (C) By train
    (D) By walking

54. What is the weather like?

    (A) Cloudy
    (B) Sunny
    (C) Rainy
    (D) Snowy

55. When will the speakers arrive at their destination?

    (A) 2:00
    (B) 5:00
    (C) 6:00
    (D) 9:00

56. Why does the man take the train?

    (A) Driving is too expensive.
    (B) He sometimes needs his car.
    (C) The train is faster than driving.
    (D) He doesn't like to park in the city.

57. Where does the woman keep her car all day?

    (A) At the park
    (B) In a garage
    (C) On the street
    (D) At the train station

58. How much does she pay to keep her car there every day?

    (A) $3.00
    (B) $4.00
    (C) $7.00
    (D) $11.00

59. Why is the man disappointed?

    (A) The post office is closed.
    (B) The post office isn't close.
    (C) The post office is hard to find.
    (D) The post office is underground.

60. How does the woman recommend getting to the post office?

    (A) By car
    (B) By bus
    (C) By foot
    (D) By taxi

61. How long does it take to get to the post office?

    (A) Two minutes
    (B) Five minutes
    (C) Nine minutes
    (D) Ten minutes

62. Who is the woman talking to?

    (A) Her manager
    (B) Her assistant
    (C) A travel agent
    (D) A new employee

63. How often do employees at this company get paid?

    (A) Once a week
    (B) Twice a week
    (C) Once a month
    (D) Twice a month

64. What is NOT a benefit of the job?

    (A) Individual health insurance
    (B) Family health insurance
    (C) Life insurance
    (D) Vacation time

65. Where are the speakers going?

   (A) Home
   (B) To the store
   (C) To the airport
   (D) To the train station

66. What time does the man want to leave?

   (A) At noon
   (B) At 2:00
   (C) At 3:00
   (D) At 10:00

67. Why does he want to leave at this time?

   (A) He likes to arrive early.
   (B) He doesn't like to hurry.
   (C) He's afraid traffic will be bad.
   (D) He wants to try a new way of getting there.

68. What will the woman drink?

   (A) Lemonade
   (B) Coffee
   (C) Water
   (D) Tea

69. Why doesn't she want pie?

   (A) She isn't hungry.
   (B) The pie is too hot.
   (C) She doesn't like pie.
   (D) She hasn't had lunch yet.

70. What will the man do?

   (A) Have some pie
   (B) Bake some buns
   (C) Buy some bacon
   (D) Make some toast

Part 4: Talks

Directions: You will hear a talk given by a single speaker. You will see three questions on each talk, each with four possible answers. Choose the best answer to each question and fill in the corresponding oval on your answer sheet.

71. Who should get on the plane during priority boarding?

    (A) People with connecting flights
    (B) Large groups
    (C) Elderly people
    (D) Airline personnel

72. If someone needs help, who should they ask?

    (A) The security office
    (B) A flight attendant
    (C) The pilot
    (D) The ticket agent

73. What are other passengers asked to do?

    (A) Stand near the door
    (B) Assist the flight attendants
    (C) Make their phone calls now
    (D) Listen for their row number

---

74. What kind of books does this store carry?

    (A) Novels
    (B) Children's books
    (C) Professional books
    (D) Textbooks

75. If the store doesn't have the book in stock, what will it do?

    (A) Refer you to another store
    (B) Look it up in the master list
    (C) Give you a different book at a discount
    (D) Order it

76. What else does this store sell?

    (A) Newspapers
    (B) Carry-alls
    (C) Journals
    (D) CDs

77. When can we expect it to get cloudy?

    (A) In the morning
    (B) In the afternoon
    (C) In the evening
    (D) At night

78. How long will the rain last?

    (A) All weekend
    (B) All day
    (C) All afternoon
    (D) All morning

79. What will the weather be like on Monday?

    (A) Hot
    (B) Cold
    (C) Rainy
    (D) Sunny

---

80. How long do most colds last?

    (A) 1 day
    (B) 1–2 days
    (C) 3 days
    (D) 3–5 days

81. How can you speed recovery?

    (A) Stay warm
    (B) Drink fluids
    (C) Take medication
    (D) Avoid caffeine

82. According to the talk, what is true about colds?

    (A) They are common.
    (B) They are easy to cure.
    (C) They require a lot of tests.
    (D) They rarely affect healthy people.

83. Who should hear this advertisement?

(A) Homemakers
(B) Business people
(C) Mail clerks
(D) Receptionists

84. What does this company provide?

(A) Conference planning
(B) Furniture rentals
(C) Food for business occasions
(D) Maid service

85. What is the largest group size the company can handle?

(A) 200
(B) 400
(C) 500
(D) 800

86. Where is this train going?

(A) Into the city
(B) To the hospital
(C) To the business district
(D) To the shopping mall

87. Which subway line goes to the airport?

(A) The gray line
(B) The green line
(C) The red line
(D) The blue line

88. How often do airport trains leave?

(A) Every two minutes
(B) Every five minutes
(C) Every fifteen minutes
(D) Every sixteen minutes

89. Why are these closings taking place?

(A) It's Sunday.
(B) There is no transportation.
(C) It's a federal holiday.
(D) The weather is bad.

90. What service is the transportation system eliminating for the day?

(A) Rush hour service
(B) Weekend service
(C) Service into the city
(D) Service to recreation areas

91. Where is parking free today?

(A) In public garages
(B) In private garages
(C) On downtown streets
(D) At the bus stations

92. Who participated in this survey?

(A) Hotel owners
(B) Secretaries
(C) Housekeepers
(D) Business travelers

93. Where would travelers prefer to have hotels located?

(A) In the business district
(B) Close to parks and museums
(C) Near shopping and entertainment
(D) Beside the airport

94. What additional service should the hotels provide at night?

(A) Access to exercise and recreation rooms
(B) Movies in the rooms
(C) Light snacks in the lobby
(D) Transportation services

95. What does this service do?

    (A) Provide visitors with maps
    (B) Tell you which buses and subways
        to take
    (C) Sell you tickets for transportation
    (D) Tell you what you should see

96. What information is necessary to get help?

    (A) Your ticket number
    (B) Your budget
    (C) How you would like to get there
    (D) The day and time of travel

97. What should you have ready by the phone?

    (A) An address book
    (B) A list of tourist attractions
    (C) A pencil and some paper
    (D) A guidebook

98. What is the first step in packing?

    (A) Wash your socks
    (B) Fold your sweaters
    (C) Choose your clothes
    (D) Measure your medicine

99. What should go into the suitcase first?

    (A) Underwear
    (B) Heavy items
    (C) Smaller items
    (D) Jeans and slacks

100. What should you use to help airport
security?

    (A) Travel guides
    (B) Light items
    (C) Plastic bags
    (D) Slip-on shoes

Model Test 4

STOP

*This is the end of the Listening Comprehension portion
of the test. Turn to Part 5 in your test book.*

★ *First News*
A l w a y s I n n o v a t i v e & I n f o r m a t i v e

Reading

In this section of the test, you will have the chance to show how well you understand written English. There are three parts to this section, with special directions for each part.

YOU WILL HAVE ONE HOUR AND FIFTEEN MINUTES TO COMPLETE PARTS 5, 6, AND 7 OF THE TEST.

Part 5: Incomplete Sentences

Directions: You will see a sentence with a missing word. Four possible answers follow the sentence. Choose the best answer to the question and fill in the corresponding oval on your answer sheet.

101. If the delivery is late, we _____ the shipping charges.

    (A) paid
    (B) will pay
    (C) have paid
    (D) are paying

102. We cannot process the order _____ we get a copy of the purchase order.

    (A) because
    (B) that
    (C) until
    (D) when

103. The visitors will be arriving _____ the office in twenty minutes.

    (A) at
    (B) with
    (C) into
    (D) for

104. Please use the _____ envelope for your reply.

    (A) is enclosed
    (B) enclose
    (C) enclosing
    (D) enclosed

105. Mr. Mura depends on his assistant for _____.

    (A) advise
    (B) adverse
    (C) advice
    (D) adversity

106. The package should arrive _____ Tuesday.

    (A) in
    (B) on
    (C) over
    (D) at

107. The newspaper expects circulation _____ next year.

    (A) to ascend
    (B) to increase
    (C) to escalate
    (D) to raise

108. Using a checklist is an _____ way to make plans.

    (A) effective
    (B) effect
    (C) effectiveness
    (D) effectively

109. The food has been ordered, _____ it has not arrived.

    (A) or
    (B) since
    (C) because
    (D) but

110. The bus will leave promptly _____ 8:30.

    (A) until
    (B) to
    (C) at
    (D) for

111. The head of operations _____ to the management convention.

    (A) going
    (B) are going
    (C) go
    (D) is going

112. A customer service representative _____ at our catalogue number.

    (A) always is available
    (B) is always available
    (C) is available always
    (D) being always available

113. The telephone directory is _____ the telephone.

    (A) among
    (B) to
    (C) under
    (D) between

114. Our company stands for quality _____ design.

    (A) or
    (B) and
    (C) but
    (D) neither

115. The supervisor had Ms. Balla _____ her job responsibilities.

    (A) to write
    (B) wrote
    (C) written
    (D) write

116. Mr. Camelio promises _____ the error right away.

    (A) will correct
    (B) correcting
    (C) to correct
    (D) corrects

117. _____ it was late, Ms. Glaser stayed to finish her work.

    (A) Although
    (B) During
    (C) Since
    (D) While

118. The _____ about our recycling plans will reassure consumers.

    (A) public
    (B) publish
    (C) publishing
    (D) publicity

119. The travel agent persuaded us _____ an evening flight.

    (A) to take
    (B) taking
    (C) took
    (D) taken

120. This model has seldom been brought in for _____.

    (A) despair
    (B) compares
    (C) impairs
    (D) repairs

121. Can you meet with us _____ 11:00?

    (A) on
    (B) for
    (C) at
    (D) in

122. The manager suggested _____ a research team.

    (A) organized
    (B) organizing
    (C) organizes
    (D) to organize

123. Mr. Benito received the notice _____ January 5.

    (A) on
    (B) in
    (C) at
    (D) to

124. This list of contributors is more _____ that one.

    (A) current
    (B) currently
    (C) current than
    (D) current as

125. The fax was not received _____ the fax number was wrong.

    (A) until
    (B) because
    (C) although
    (D) once

126. The ship's captain requests that all passengers _____ emergency procedures.

    (A) reviewing
    (B) reviews
    (C) review
    (D) to review

127. The person _____ lost a briefcase may claim it in the lobby.

    (A) whose
    (B) which
    (C) whom
    (D) who

128. This memo is _____ the previous one.

    (A) as confusing
    (B) confusing as
    (C) as confusing as
    (D) as confused as

129. Ms. Friel _____ about her promotion before it was announced.

    (A) knew
    (B) known
    (C) is knowing
    (D) has known

130. Please _____ me any time if I can help you.

    (A) are calling
    (B) call
    (C) calls
    (D) will call

131. The ship's restaurant is located _____ the sun deck.

    (A) on
    (B) under
    (C) in
    (D) over

132. What _____ will the delay have on the contract?

    (A) effect
    (B) effective
    (C) effectively
    (D) effectiveness

133. Mr. Dimitri has a _____ for the Palace Hotel.

    (A) rumination
    (B) reservation
    (C) trepidation
    (D) motivation

134. Our latest advertising package includes videos _____ brochures.

    (A) but
    (B) or
    (C) and
    (D) either

135. The merger, _____ will be announced today, should be extremely profitable.

    (A) when
    (B) whose
    (C) it
    (D) which

136. The receptionist _____ a message if you do not answer your phone.

    (A) takes
    (B) took
    (C) take
    (D) taken

137. The secretary _____ a letter when the computer crashed.

    (A) composed
    (B) is composing
    (C) was composing
    (D) composes

138. Tomorrow we _____ the letter by overnight mail.

    (A) will send
    (B) sent
    (C) had sent
    (D) is sending

139. My cousin was very _____ when he got the job.

    (A) surprise
    (B) surprised
    (C) surprising
    (D) surprises

140. The computer operators work at night _____ on weekends.

    (A) nor
    (B) but
    (C) neither
    (D) and

Part 6: Text Completion

Directions: You will see four passages each with three blanks. Under each blank are four answer options. Choose the word or phrase that best completes the sentence.

Questions 141–143 refer to the following letter.

Modern Tech Inc.
St. No 2, Sector H 1/6, Hunter Complex
Islamabad, Pakistan

April 13th, 20—

Vaqas Mahmood
21, Sharah-e-Iran, Clifton
Karachi, Pakistan

Dear Vaqas Mahmood,

Thank you for purchasing the Teleconnect Multipurpose Pager. We received your mail-in rebate card this week. Unfortunately we cannot send you the 1800 PKR in cash back because the rebate offer had already _____ when you mailed it.

     141. (A) operated
             (B) exited
             (C) expired
             (D) transferred

As stated at the bottom of your bill, rebate cards must be mailed out within three days of purchase in order for the rebate to be processed. The photocopy that you included of your bill indicates that you made your purchase on March 1st 20—. However, your envelope containing the rebate form was postmarked in early April. Unfortunately, we cannot honor rebate cards that are more than two weeks late.

Please realize that your business is still important to us. In place of the rebate, we would like _____ you a page of coupons that can be used toward other Modern Tech Inc.

142. (A) to offer
      (B) offering
      (C) offered
      (D) will offer

products. You will find great _____ for some of our new products, including our new

         143. (A) stores
             (B) discounts
             (C) packages
             (D) instructions

speakerphone with improved sound quality.

Thank you for choosing Modern Tech Inc. for all of your technology needs.

Sincerely,

Tarik Khan

Tarik Khan
President

Questions 144–146 refer to the following e-mail.

To: benlivingston@accountantsgroup.ca
Copy: Kyle; Cheryl; Leslie
From: ryanedison@accountantsgroup.ca
Subject: Golf Tournament

Hi everyone,

I'm just doing some planning for the _____ clients' golf tournament in May. I know it's

144. (A) daily
    (B) weekly
    (C) monthly
    (D) annual

more than two months away, but I wanted to get started planning early this year. There are a few things I could use your help with.

1) Please mention the date of the tournament to all of your clients and provide them with the link on our Web site. Encourage them to participate.
2) We need about 200 door prizes to hand _____ at the banquet. If you know of any

145. (A) in
    (B) out
    (C) over
    (D) down

  local businesses that may be willing to donate items such as free hotel accommodations or meals, please contact them as soon as possible.
3) We need volunteers to take tickets, drive golf carts, and help with refreshments, perhaps even be on hand to play if necessary. Please ask your staff members if they are willing to help out.

Last year was a great success. We _____ more than $7,000 for charity during the

146. (A) spent
    (B) saved
    (C) raised
    (D) invested

tournament. This year we are aiming at $10, 000. Please let me know if you have any ideas about the tournament.

Thanks,
Ryan

Questions 147–149 refer to the following article.

Indoor Air Pollution

New studies on air quality inside office buildings show that the indoor air quality is _____ to

147. (A) hazardous
(B) more hazardous
(C) most hazardous
(D) the most hazardous

human health than the polluted air outside. Each year, the air in our cities exceeds safe levels during at least 60 days of the summer. According to the Committee on the Environment, the air quality in approximately 30% of buildings _____ unsafe.

148. (A) is
(B) are
(C) seem
(D) are becoming

Medical conditions including asthma, cancer, and depression, may be connected to poor indoor air quality. Cleaning products, furniture, air conditioners, and gas heating systems all contribute to poor indoor air quality. The most common reason for Sick Building Syndrome, a medical condition that has been blamed on poor indoor air quality, is the _____

149. (A) premeditated
(B) premature
(C) premium
(D) prevented

opening of businesses. When a building opens too early, paint fumes and cleaning products don't have enough time to disperse. These fumes can remain in the air for a long time. They can affect customers or clients, and particularly building staff.

Questions 150–152 refer to the following memo.

To: Bill O'Hara
From: Edie Saunders
Subject: Workshop

Bill,
I am trying to finalize plans for next Friday's workshop. Please let me _____ how many people you

150. (A) know
(B) knows
(C) to know
(D) knowing

expect to attend so that I can know how much food to order. Also, how long do you expect the workshop to last? In addition to lunch, should I order afternoon coffee and snacks _____? If a workshop goes all day,

151. (A) moreover
(B) instead
(C) furthermore
(D) as well

people usually expect some sort of mid-afternoon refreshment. I also need to know expected numbers so I can decide which conference room to reserve. Conference Room 2 is more _____ than Conference Room 1,

152. (A) pleasant
(B) pleasanter
(C) pleasantly
(D) pleasantest

but it might not be big enough. Please get back to me as soon as possible because I need to take care of this soon. Thanks.

Edie

First News
Always Innovative & Informative

Part 7: Reading Comprehension

Directions: You will see single and double reading passages followed by several questions. Each question has four answer choices. Choose the best answer to the question and fill in the corresponding oval on your answer sheet.

Questions 153–155 refer to the following invitation.

Trust Line cordially invites you to attend a morning seminar to learn how you can predict the trends that will assist your clients with the success of their investments.

To reserve a seat, fill out the attached card and mail it with your registration fee.

Don't miss this chance to learn about the resources that drive successful fiduciary service management firms.

For further information, please call 676-9980.

153. Who would be likely to attend the seminar?

(A) A private investor
(B) A manager in a not-for-profit organization
(C) A stockbroker
(D) A newspaper publisher

154. What will be discussed at the seminar?

(A) Building client relationships
(B) Fiduciary service management firms
(C) How to foresee good investments
(D) How to get new clients

155. How can you join the seminar?

(A) Present this letter
(B) Send a short form and payment
(C) Send your business card and request
(D) Call 676-9980

Questions 156–159 refer to the following magazine article.

Model Test 4

NewTech Equipment Company announced that it expects to cut 4,000 jobs within the next six months in Brazil as part of its strategy to reorganize its money-losing business. NewTech has been struggling to make a profit after two years of losses worldwide.

The reduction in its labor force comes as a surprise to business analysts, who had been impressed with the performance of the company in recent months. Although its revenues have not matched those of its first two years of business, they had been increasing steadily since June.

New competition was blamed for this loss of revenue, but sources close to the company place the blame on the lack of direction from the chairman of the company, Pierre Reinartz. Mr. Reinartz has been with the company for only a year, and he will probably resign soon.

It is expected that Elizabeth Strube, the current V. P. of the company, will succeed him. Ms. Strube was responsible for opening the international offices, which have been more profitable than those in Brazil. NewTech employs about 25,000 people in Brazil, another 20,000 in Asia, and 10,000 in Europe. The international offices will not be affected by the staff reductions.

156. Why will NewTech cut jobs locally?

(A) To be more profitable
(B) Because it is moving overseas
(C) Because labor costs have gone up
(D) Because Chairman Reinartz directed it

157. How long has NewTech been losing money?

(A) Six months
(B) One year
(C) A year and a half
(D) Two years

158. The word *revenues* in paragraph 2, line 5, is closest in meaning to

(A) sales
(B) earnings
(C) products
(D) expenses

159. What describes the international branches of NewTech?

(A) They earn more money than the Brazilian office.
(B) They are less cost-effective.
(C) They are older than the Brazilian branch.
(D) They will be closed within six months.

Questions 160–162 refer to the following schedule.

BUS FARES

		Peak	Off Peak
Effective March 1, 20__	Any one zone	1.00	.75
Peak hours,	Between zones 1 and 2	1.35	1.00
Weekdays 5:30–9:30 A.M.	zones 1 and 3	1.70	1.35
and 3:00–7:00 P.M.	zones 2 and 3	1.35	1.00

160. When do these bus fares take effect?

(A) Immediately
(B) On March 1
(C) On February 28
(D) Next week

161. Which time is off-peak?

(A) 7:00 A.M. Monday
(B) 9:00 A.M. Wednesday
(C) 8:00 P.M. Thursday
(D) 5:00 P.M. Friday

162. What is the peak fare between zones 1 and 3?

(A) $.75
(B) $1.00
(C) $1.35
(D) $1.70

Questions 163–165 refer to the following advertisement.

Leading TV-Advertising

company with broadcast interests worldwide seeks a Specialist in Audience Research. The Specialist will design studies to determine consumer preferences and write reports for use within the company. Candidates must have a college degree with courses in research. Must also have experience in advertising. Outstanding oral, written, and computer skills are necessary. Downtown location. Excellent benefits.

163. What does this job involve?

(A) Making TV commercials
(B) Discovering what consumers like
(C) Advertising products
(D) Testing products

164. Who will use the reports the Specialist writes?

(A) The consumer
(B) The television station
(C) The manufacturers
(D) The TV-advertising company

165. What qualifications should the candidate have?

(A) Education in research and experience in advertising
(B) Experience in television audiences
(C) Ability in accounting
(D) A degree in broadcasting

Questions 166–170 refer to the following report.

Peru is reforming its maritime transportation system. New regulations designed to reduce port costs and increase efficiency have already had encouraging results. Because of these reforms, Peru has established itself as the gateway for exports to Pacific Rim markets like Japan, Korea, and China. These reforms have been in three areas: labor, regulations, and custom clearances.

High labor costs had sabotaged Peru's import and export businesses. Where 80% of all goods had previously been transported by ship, ports in recent years have been moving only half of their capacity. Shipping companies took their business to Chilean ports where costs averaged one-sixth of those of Peru.

Reform in this area was needed quickly. Consequently, agreements with port workers now allow shippers and receivers to make their prices competitive with other ports in Latin America. The port workers benefit as well, since many have formed limited partnerships or cooperatives.

Prior to the reforms, 60% of all exports had to be shipped on Peruvian flag-carriers. That regulation has been abolished and has opened the ports to ships from around the world. This increase in traffic has caused dock procedures to be streamlined. Accordingly, customs regulations have become more efficient and commercial processing can be accomplished more quickly.

166. Why were reforms necessary?

(A) The industry was outdated.
(B) Corruption was the norm.
(C) Labor regulations were being violated.
(D) The shipping industry was inefficient and costly.

167. What markets are most important to Peru?
(A) All Latin America
(B) Asian
(C) European
(D) Only Chilean

168. Prior to the reforms, at what percentage capacity did the ports operate?
(A) 20%
(B) 50%
(C) 60%
(D) 80%

169. The word *abolished* in paragraph 3, line 4, is closest in meaning to

(A) passed.
(B) stopped.
(C) renewed.
(D) continued.

170. According to the report, why were dock procedures streamlined?

(A) To make them easier to read
(B) To handle increased traffic
(C) To reduce labor costs
(D) To satisfy the dock workers

Questions 171–174 refer to the following fax.

Starling Brothers Investment Firm
145 East 45th Street
New York NY 10019

To: All airline investors   **BY FAX**
Fm: Alfonso O'Reilly   Pages: 1 of 1
       Broker

Stock Alert   Stock Alert   Stock Alert   Stock Alert

Southern Regional Airlines earned $9.8 million in the fourth quarter, compared with a loss of $584.1 million the previous year. The profit was due to reduced costs and an increase in profitable routes. This year, the airline lost $112.4 million in total, compared with a loss of $1 billion last year.

If the present management does not change, we assume that the cost-reduction measures and their choice of routes will continue to have a positive effect on earnings. By eliminating even more routes across the Atlantic, the airline should be able to focus on the short-haul markets where it has built its strong base.

We suggest keeping Southern Regional stock at this time. If there is any change in this forecast, we will advise you.

---

171. What is the purpose of this notice?

(A) To warn investors of poor stock performance
(B) To suggest a change in management
(C) To explain recent success to investors
(D) To encourage investors to hold on to their stock

172. Why are airline profits up?

(A) New marketing strategies
(B) Lower cost and more profitable routes
(C) Greater ticket sales
(D) Changes in the competition

173. How much did the airline lose this year?

(A) $1 million
(B) $9.8 million
(C) $112.4 million
(D) $1 billion

174. The word *forecast* in paragraph 3, line 2, is closest in meaning to

(A) report.
(B) situation.
(C) prediction.
(D) investment.

Questions 175–176 refer to the following notice.

The Griffith Hotel

Charleston, South Carolina
803-349-7204

Reservations will be held until 4:00 p.m. unless
guaranteed by advance deposit or credit card.

Cancellations must be made 24 hours prior
to scheduled arrival in order to avoid the
first night's room charge.

---

175. Why would you guarantee your reservation by credit card?

(A) So you can cancel your room
(B) So you can arrive after 4:00
(C) So you can arrive before 4:00
(D) So you don't have to check in

176. What happens if you do not cancel 24 hours in advance?

(A) You must pay for one night.
(B) You get first choice of rooms.
(C) You can schedule your arrival.
(D) You can get an advance deposit.

Questions 177–180 refer to the following memo.

From: Mazola Sawarani
Sent: Thursday, June 03, 20__ 9:30 A.M.

To: All Employees

Sub: Vacation

Supervisors must approve any and all
vacation periods longer than one week.
Approval is not automatic. If (1) your
absence would create a heavy workload
for your team, or cause your team to
miss deadlines; (2) you fail to give
at least one week's advance notice;
(3) there are problems with your job
performance; or (4) you have had other
frequent absences, your request could
be denied. In that case, please
contact the Personnel Review Board.

177. What is this memo about?

   (A) Work shortage
   (B) Vacation time
   (C) Sick leave
   (D) Starting hours

178. Which of the following vacation periods requires a supervisor's approval?

   (A) One hour
   (B) One day
   (C) One week
   (D) One month

179. What might influence a supervisor's decision?

   (A) You are a new employee.
   (B) You are poorly paid.
   (C) You are a team leader.
   (D) You often miss work.

180. If approval is not given, the employee can

   (A) ask another supervisor.
   (B) stay at work.
   (C) take a different vacation.
   (D) ask the Personnel Review Board.

Questions 181–185 refer to the following fax and notice.

FAX

To: Management
From: Unhappy customer
Date: Friday, February 4th

To Whom It May Concern:

I'm sending this complaint by fax because I haven't been able to reach anyone at your company by telephone. I am extremely disappointed with the service that Concord's call center provides. I called yesterday at 10: 30 A.M. for help with my new dishwasher. I was immediately put on hold. I listened to some annoying music for 35 minutes before I finally hung up and called again. The same person, he said his name was Kazuki, told me that he was with another caller and that my call was important to him. If my call was important, someone would have been available to help me.

The worst part is, my call really was important. I had a major flood yesterday after I turned my new dishwasher on, and I couldn't figure out how to get the water to stop running. There is a lot of damage to my kitchen floor. I would appreciate a personal phone call explaining why nobody was available to answer my call. I will not be purchasing from your store in the future.

Suzuki Kana

NOTICE

Date: February 7, 20—
For: Call center employees
Re: Weekly meetings

As of March 1, call center employees will no longer be required to attend weekly Concord staff meetings. The minutes from each meeting will be posted in the staff room for all employees to view after the Thursday morning meetings.

There are two reasons for this change:

1) Our current arrangement of using one employee to cover all ten phones during the meeting hour is not working. We have had numerous complaints from customers saying that they wait up to half an hour to have a call answered on Thursday mornings.

2) We are losing up to $300 in sales every Thursday morning because we don't have all the phones working. Call center representatives generate extra sales while handling help line calls. You are also losing money, because commission is lost when you have to take time out for meetings.

If you have any questions regarding these changes, please contact Itou Saki at manager3@concord.org.

181. Which of the following is NOT true about the caller?

    (A) She recently purchased an appliance from Concord.
    (B) She was calling for advice about how to clean up a flood.
    (C) She was upset with the length of time she waited on the phone.
    (D) She disliked the music that played while she was on hold.

182. How many people were working the phones when Suzuki called this company?

    (A) None
    (B) One
    (C) Nine
    (D) Ten

183. Why does the meeting policy change affect only call center employees?

    (A) They are the people who handle all of the sales.
    (B) They are the workers who answer the help line.
    (C) They are the only ones who attend the meetings.
    (D) They are the people who requested the change.

184. How will call center employees learn about what happened at the weekly meetings?

    (A) A memo will be delivered two days later.
    (B) There will be one call center representative taking notes.
    (C) A summary will be available in the staff room.
    (D) Itou Saki will send out an e-mail with the details.

185. How did management handle this complaint?

    (A) By putting the customer on hold.
    (B) By phoning the call center employees.
    (C) By changing the company procedures.
    (D) By sending a notice to the customer.

Questions 186–190 refer to the following advertisement and e-mail.

---

www.busybusinessworkers.com

It's time to take a break, relax, and enjoy some time away from the office. This month we're offering three holiday packages especially for busy business workers like you. May is the best month for travel. While students are busy with their exams, you can enjoy beaches and resorts in peace. Book a vacation this month and receive 25% off the regular price. Packages do not include tax. Cancellation insurance is recommended.

Click on any packages for full details. Prices are per person.
Package A: twelve nights. fivestar hotel in Portugal. includes all meals. $1,650
Package B: five nights. Caribbean Cruise. $1,400
Package C: Angelino's Spa and Golf Getaway. from $600.
Package D: Sorry. No longer available.

Don't wait until the end of the year. Take a break now. You deserve it.

To: manager@marketpro.org
From: francogerard@marketpro.org
Subject: Vacation

Hi Alain,

It looks like I'll be working all weekend to meet this deadline. Milan will help me on Saturday. He'll check my numbers, but I'll still need you to review everything before I submit it because he is so new at his job.

Anyway, the real reason I'm writing is that I'd like to take a vacation soon. I wanted to check the dates with you. I'm looking at the first week of May. I found an ad for 25% off a Caribbean cruise. My wife and I are having our first wedding anniversary so I'd like to surprise her. It will be nice for her to have someone do all of the cooking. Too bad there won't be anywhere to golf, though!

Please let me know if you think it will work out. I would be gone May 2nd through May 8th. I'd love to go for two weeks, but will need to use my other vacation week in the fall when my brother gets married.

Thanks,
Franco

186. Who is the intended audience of this ad?

    (A) Golfers
    (B) Students on a budget
    (C) Travelers on business
    (D) Tired business workers

187. According to the ad, when is the best time to travel?

    (A) At the beginning of the year
    (B) During student exams
    (C) While students are on break
    (D) At the end of the year

188. What is the total amount Franco will pay for the trip before taxes?

    (A) $1,650
    (B) $1,400
    (C) $2,100
    (D) $2,800

189. Who is Milan?

    (A) Franco's travel agent
    (B) Franco's brother
    (C) Franco's manager
    (D) Franco's new coworker

190. Why would Franco NOT choose Package A?

    (A) He wants to use only one week of his vacation now.
    (B) His wife will want to make her own meals.
    (C) He wants to receive 25% off his trip.
    (D) His wife has specifically requested a cruise.

Questions 191–195 refer to the following two e-mails.

Model Test 4

To: Operator 7, Operator 9, Operator 11
Sender: Park Gi
Subject: Recorded names and titles

I have recently discovered that a number of you have reprogrammed your telephones and changed the information on your answering machines. You have replaced the generic title, *systems operator*, with your own name, or worse for at least one of you, a nickname. Not only is this unprofessional, it is against the rules set out in your manual. The original recordings were set up with generic names and titles for a good reason. Your supervisor may ask you to change stations or departments at any time in order for you to learn a new position at the office. New interns will take your desk and the duties that go along with it.

   Please refer to page 14 of your manual, which starts, "As temporary employees, you do not have the right to reprogram the telephone on your desk or the settings on your computer."

Thank you,
Park Gi

To: parkgi@financialguide.net
From: student7@financialguide.net
Subject: Answering machines

Dear Mr. Park,

   I want to apologize for reprogramming the answering machine at desk 12. After being referred to as Operator 7 several times by repeat customers, I decided to change the recorded name to my own. I don't believe the message I recorded was unprofessional in any way. I simply gave my full name and my title, *student intern*.

   I changed the recording because I got a message from a customer who said, "It would be nice to know your name. It feels impersonal to say thank you to a number."

   Would you like me to change the message back to a generic one, or do you plan to do this yourself? I know how to do it, but I don't want to break the rule again.

   Finally, I didn't realize that we would be moving to other stations, but I look forward to trying new positions. I am enjoying my internship so far.

All the best,
Chong Dae

191. Who was the first e-mail written to?

    (A) All temporary employees
    (B) Three student trainers
    (C) Selected student interns
    (D) All systems operators

192. How does Park Gi suggest interns find out the rules about answering machines?

    (A) By reading their manuals
    (B) By asking their supervisors
    (C) By e-mailing Park Gi
    (D) By talking with other temporary employees

193. What did Chong Dae record on her answering machine?

    (A) Her nickname.
    (B) Her telephone number
    (C) Her name and job title
    (D) Her desk number

194. What excuse does Chong use to defend her actions?

    (A) Her own name is easy to pronounce.
    (B) She thought she would be offered full-time work.
    (C) A customer commented on her telephone's recording.
    (D) She didn't read the training package manual.

195. What does Park forget to mention in his e-mail?

    (A) Where the rule for interns was written
    (B) If interns should change the recordings back
    (C) Whether or not interns are temporary employees
    (D) Why the policy was made in the first place

Questions 196–200 refer to the following article and telephone message.

Popular Opera Company in Jeonju

March 7, 20—

The hit ballet *Starfish* had its last performance yesterday; however, the new Encore Theater immediately welcomed another group of performers. The Valley Opera Group, composed of twenty-five members ranging in age from 11–65, is donating all of the profits from tonight's opening performance of *Floria* to the new theater. "We have been waiting for an adequate concert hall to open in Jeonju for more than five years. We are happy to be able to perform here," said director Hwang Chae-ku.

Hwang says the group often donates profits from performances to local charities. "We are in it for the love of music, not to make a profit. Any money we earn goes toward advertising and costumes." Though they sound like professionals, the singers from The Valley Opera Group don't earn a salary. Despite this, it is one of the foremost opera companies in Korea. *Floria* will run through March 30. Tickets for the 60-minute show run from 25, 000 won to 80, 000. Only single seats are available. See the new theater's Web site: encoreart@korea.net for details.

Telephone Message

For: Lee Chang

From: Kim Arum

Date: March 7, 20—

Time: 8:30 A.M.

Call back: ☑ YES   ☐ NO

Message taken by: Park Sun

Arum called. The opera group you like will be performing at the new theater next week. If you want to take some clients to see a show, he can get you a group rate. Also, there is a new Italian restaurant, Antonios, near the theater. He thinks your clients would really like it. You would need to make a reservation very soon, though. It is a very busy restaurant, and people wait up to two hours to eat there.

I thought I should mention that I ate at that restaurant last week and the service was terribly slow. It took two hours to order and eat our meal. The new theater is really nice, though. I saw the ballet, but I've heard that the opera is even better. Tickets seem expensive for such a short show, so it must be really good. – Sunny

196. What is *Floria*?

    (A) An opera company
    (B) A ballet
    (C) An opera title
    (D) A new concert hall

197. Which of the following is true about the Valley Opera Group?

    (A) Its members earn a good salary.
    (B) It has never played in Jeonju before.
    (C) It is only holding one show at the new hall.
    (D) Its singers are well respected in Korea.

198. What does Kim not realize?

    (A) The ballet is already finished.
    (B) The group seating is sold out.
    (C) The opera singers are only amateurs.
    (D) The opera closes tonight.

199. According to Park, which is true about the new Italian restaurant?

    (A) A meal there takes twice as long as the opera.
    (B) It doesn't honor its reservations.
    (C) It's located just inside the new theater.
    (D) The menu is a bit too expensive.

200. What will Park likely suggest if she talks to Lee?

    (A) Going to the ballet instead of the opera
    (B) Choosing a restaurant other than Antonio's
    (C) Calling ahead to book a table
    (D) Taking the clients to dinner before the show

STOP

This is the end of the test. If you finish before time is called, you may go back to Parts 5, 6, and 7 and check your work.

Answer Key
MODEL TEST 4

Listening Comprehension

PART 1: PHOTOGRAPHS

1. C	4. A	7. A	10. B
2. B	5. C	8. C	
3. D	6. D	9. C	

PART 2: QUESTION-RESPONSE

11. C	19. C	27. A	35. A
12. B	20. A	28. C	36. C
13. A	21. B	29. A	37. B
14. A	22. B	30. A	38. A
15. B	23. A	31. C	39. A
16. B	24. B	32. B	40. C
17. A	25. A	33. A	
18. C	26. C	34. B	

PART 3: CONVERSATIONS

41. B	49. C	57. B	65. C
42. D	50. A	58. D	66. C
43. A	51. C	59. B	67. C
44. B	52. D	60. B	68. D
45. C	53. A	61. B	69. A
46. D	54. B	62. D	70. A
47. C	55. C	63. D	
48. D	56. D	64. B	

PART 4: TALKS

71. C	79. B	87. A	95. B
72. B	80. D	88. C	96. D
73. D	81. B	89. C	97. C
74. C	82. A	90. A	98. C
75. D	83. B	91. C	99. B
76. C	84. C	92. D	100. C
77. B	85. C	93. C	
78. A	86. D	94. A	

Reading

PART 5: INCOMPLETE SENTENCES

101. B	111. D	121. C	131. A
102. C	112. B	122. B	132. A
103. A	113. C	123. A	133. B
104. D	114. B	124. C	134. C
105. C	115. D	125. B	135. D
106. B	116. C	126. C	136. A
107. B	117. A	127. D	137. C
108. A	118. D	128. C	138. A
109. D	119. A	129. A	139. B
110. C	120. D	130. B	140. D

PART 6: TEXT COMPLETION

141. C	144. D	147. B	150. A
142. A	145. B	148. A	151. D
143. B	146. C	149. B	152. B

PART 7: READING COMPREHENSION

153. C	166. D	179. D	192. A
154. C	167. B	180. D	193. C
155. B	168. B	181. B	194. C
156. A	169. B	182. B	195. B
157. D	170. B	183. B	196. C
158. B	171. D	184. C	197. D
159. A	172. B	185. C	198. B
160. B	173. C	186. D	199. A
161. C	174. C	187. B	200. B
162. D	175. B	188. C	
163. B	176. A	189. D	
164. D	177. B	190. A	
165. A	178. D	191. C	

Test Score Conversion Table

Count your correct responses. Match the number of correct responses with the corresponding score from the Test Score Conversion Table (below). Add the two scores together. This is your Total Estimated Test Score. As you practice taking the TOEIC model tests, your scores should improve. Keep track of your Total Estimated Test Scores.

# Correct	Listening Score	Reading Score	# Correct	Listening Score	Reading Score	# Correct	Listening Score	Reading Score	# Correct	Listening Score	Reading Score
0	5	5	26	110	65	51	255	220	76	410	370
1	5	5	27	115	70	52	260	225	77	420	380
2	5	5	28	120	80	53	270	230	78	425	385
3	5	5	29	125	85	54	275	235	79	430	390
4	5	5	30	130	90	55	280	240	80	440	395
5	5	5	31	135	95	56	290	250	81	445	400
6	5	5	32	140	100	57	295	255	82	450	405
7	10	5	33	145	110	58	300	260	83	460	410
8	15	5	34	150	115	59	310	265	84	465	415
9	20	5	35	160	120	60	315	270	85	470	420
10	25	5	36	165	125	61	320	280	86	475	425
11	30	5	37	170	130	62	325	285	87	480	430
12	35	5	38	175	140	63	330	290	88	485	435
13	40	5	39	180	145	64	340	300	89	490	445
14	45	5	40	185	150	65	345	305	90	495	450
15	50	5	41	190	160	66	350	310	91	495	455
16	55	10	42	195	165	67	360	320	92	495	465
17	60	15	43	200	170	68	365	325	93	495	470
18	65	20	44	210	175	69	370	330	94	495	480
19	70	25	45	215	180	70	380	335	95	495	485
20	75	30	46	220	190	71	385	340	96	495	490
21	80	35	47	230	195	72	390	350	97	495	495
22	85	40	48	240	200	73	395	355	98	495	495
23	90	45	49	245	210	74	400	360	99	495	495
24	95	50	50	250	215	75	405	365	100	495	495
25	100	60									

Number of Correct Listening Responses _____ = Listening Score _____

Number of Correct Reading Responses _____ = Reading Score _____

Total Estimated Test Score _____

Model Test 4—Explanatory Answers

LISTENING COMPREHENSION

Part 1: Photographs

1. **(C)** Choice (C) correctly identifies the location of the phone. Choice (A) is incorrect because the lamp is on the table. Choice (B) is incorrect because the man is sitting on the bed. Choice (D) is incorrect because the light is on the table.

2. **(B)** Choice (B) identifies the location *of the pipeline*. Choice (A) is incorrect; the photo shows a *pipeline*, not *lumber*. Choice (C) is incorrect; you cannot assume the pipeline carries water. Choice (D) confuses related words: *pipeline* and *oil tankers*.

3. **(D)** Choice (D) identifies the thing, *X rays*, and their location, *behind the doctor*. Choice (A) incorrectly identifies the people and their clothing. Choice (B) confuses related word *examine* and gives an incorrect action. Choice (C) gives the incorrect action and misidentifies the doctor.

4. **(A)** Choice (A) makes assumptions: *it looks like a restaurant*, so *the customers must be holding a menu* and *ordering food*. Choice (B) confuses *reading a menu* and *learning to read*. Choice (C) is incorrect because the waiter has already approached the customer. Choice (D) is incorrect because the guest is ordering, not waiting to order.

5. **(C)** Choice (C) identifies the correct action: The man is pushing down the suitcase handle and is behind the trunk, which indicates he is going to put the suitcase in the trunk. Choice (A) identifies an incorrect action. Choice (B) is an incorrect action; since he had a suitcase, we can assume it's packed. Choice (D) confuses the man's location; he is behind a car, not in a station.

6. **(D)** Choice (D) identifies *the passengers* and the action *getting their luggage*. Choice (A) identifies an incorrect action waiting *for their flight*. Choice (B) is incorrect because the luggage is not scattered around. Choice (C) has the related word *trip* but identifies the wrong action.

7. **(A)** Choice (A) identifies the action *refers to the map*. Choice (B) is not able to be determined. Choice (C) is incorrect because the man's arm is bent, but his glasses are straight. Choice (D) is incorrect because he is gesturing downwards, not upwards.

8. **(C)** The messenger is knocking on the door of a guest to deliver an envelope. Choice (A) describes where he is (a *hall*), but he is not running. Choice (B) talks about what he is wearing, not what he is delivering. Choice (D) uses the similar-sounding word *wrapping* for *rapping* that is similar in meaning to *knocking*.

9. **(C)** Choice (C) identifies the action *unloading cargo*. Choices (A) and (B) misidentify the cargo (*shopping bags, pillows*). Choice (D) does not match the photo.

10. **(B)** Guests in a hotel lobby lounge are relaxing in comfortable chairs. Choice (A) describes what is in the room, not what they are doing. Choice (C) refers to the coffee they might be drinking. Choice (D) uses the similar-sounding word *hair* for *chair*.

Part 2: Question-Response

11. **(C)** Choice (C) is a logical response to a question about *who*. Choice (A) confuses similar sounds: *who's* and *whose* and indicates possession. Choice (B) confuses similar sounds: *there* with *here* and indicates location.

12. **(B)** The speakers will use the stairs because the elevator is broken. Choice (A) confuses *spoken* with the similar-sounding word *broken*. Choice (C) repeats the word *elevator*.

13. **(A)** Choice (A) is a logical response to a question about *time*. Choice (B) confuses different meanings: *leave* (v) and *leaves* (n). Choice (C) confuses similar sounds: *leave her* and *lawyer*; *did* and *deed*.

First News
Always Innovative & Informative

14. **(A)** Choice (A) is a logical response to a question about *where.* Choice (B) confuses similar sounds: *stay* and *say.* Choice (C) confuses similar sounds: *stay* and *stain.*

15. **(B)** Choice (B) is a logical response to a question about *which.* Choice (A) confuses similar sounds: *number* and *numb.* Choice (C) confuses similar sounds: *fax* and *fast.*

16. **(B)** Choice (B) is a logical response to a question about *why no one is present.* Choice (A) shows negation: if the room is crowded, people are there. Choice (C) confuses similar sounds: *no one here* and *not hear.*

17. **(A)** Choice (A) is a logical response to a question about *weather.* Choice (B) contains the same verb *was* and might be related to *weather* (bad weather causes some people to wear hats) but does not describe the weather. Choice (B) also confuses similar sounds: *weather* and *wearing.* Choice (C) confuses similar sounds: *weather* and *wet.*

18. **(C)** Choice (C) is a logical response to a question about *coffee.* Choice (A) confuses similar sounds: *coffee* and *cough.* Choice (B) confuses similar sounds: *coffee* and *fee.*

19. **(C)** Choice (C) is a logical response to a question about *who.* Choice (A) confuses similar sounds: *letter* and *let her*; *open* and *opera.* Choice (B) confuses similar sounds: *open* and *pen.*

20. **(A)** Since the first speaker doesn't want cake, the second speaker offers fruit in its place. Choice (B) associates *baking* with cake. Choice (C) confuses the phrase *buy it* with the similar-sounding word *diet.*

21. **(B)** Choice (B) is a logical response to a question about *time.* Choice (A) confuses related words: *time* and *watch.* Choice (C) confuses related words: *morning* and *get up.*

22. **(B)** Choice (B) is a logical response to a question about *duration of time.* Choice (A) confuses similar sounds: *ride* and *bride* and related words: *long* with *tall.* Choice (C) describes *how long the train is* (ten cars) not *how long the ride is* (two hours).

23. **(A)** Choice (A) is a logical response to a question about *occupation.* Choice (B) con-fuses similar sounds: *occupation* and *atten-tion.* Choice (C) confuses similar sounds: *occupied* with *occupation.*

24. **(B)** Choice (B) is a logical response to a question about *coming.* Choice (A) confuses *not coming* with *are coming* or *not* (coming) and does not match the subject (*you–he*). Choice (C) confuses *didn't come* with *are coming* or *not* (coming) and does not match subject (*you–they*) or tense.

25. **(A)** Choice (A) is a logical response to a question about *seat location.* Choice (B) confuses similar sounds: *sitting* and *city.* Choice (C) confuses similar sounds: *sitting* and *sitter.*

26. **(C)** The first speaker wants to take a walk, so the second speaker suggests going to the park. Choice (A) confuses *work* with the similar-sounding word *walk.* Choice (B) confuses *talk* with the similar-sounding word *walk.*

27. **(A)** Choice (A) is a logical response to a question about *who.* Choice (B) confuses similar sounds: *phone* and *home.* Choice (C) has the full form *telephone* but answers loca-tion, not identity.

28. **(C)** Choice (C) is a logical response to a question about *quantity.* Choice (A) has the related word *supermarket* and gives *quantity of people* (crowded) but does not refer to quantity of food. Choice (B) confuses simi-lar sounds: *food* and *mood.*

29. **(A)** The second speaker suggests leaving at 6:00 in order to get to the airport on time. Choice (B) associates *plane tickets* with *airport.* Choice (C) confuses *court* with the similar-sounding word *airport.*

30. **(A)** Choice (A) is a logical response to a question about *what color.* Choice (B) con-fuses similar sounds: *hall* and *tall.* Choice (C) confuses related words: *paint* and *paint-ing* and similar sounds: *wall* with *hall.*

31. **(C)** Choice (C) is a logical response to a question about *which.* Choice (A) confuses similar sounds: *my gray* and *migraine.* Choice (B) confuses similar sounds: *tie* and *tried*; *suit* and *do it.*

32. **(B)** Choice (B) is a logical response to a question about *who*. Choice (A) confuses similar sounds: *met* and *bet*. Choice (C) confuses *at the door* and *by the door* and tells *what* not *who*.

33. **(A)** Choice (A) is a logical response to a question about *when*. Choice (B) is incorrect; *finished* (past tense) does not match the tense of the question—*will be finished* (future). Choice (C) is incorrect; *thought* (past tense) does not match the tense of the question—*think* (present tense).

34. **(B)** Choice (B) is a logical response to a question about *not coming with us*. Choice (A) has the related word *go* but does not answer *why*. Choice (C) is incorrect; *didn't come* (past tense) does not match *aren't coming* (present tense) and does not answer *why*.

35. **(A)** Choice (A) is a logical response to a question about *being alone*. Choice (B) confuses different meanings: *alone* and *lonely*. Choice (C) should use *yes* instead of *no* (*Yes, I am alone because no one is here*).

36. **(C)** Choice (C) is a logical response to a tag question about *what page*. Choice (A) answers *when*, not *what page*. Choice (B) confuses *on* with *under* and does not answer *what page*.

37. **(B)** Choice (B) is a logical response to a question about *where*. Choice (A) confuses similar sounds: *wait* and *weigh*. Choice (C) is incorrect; *waited* (past tense) does not match *should wait* (present-future) and answers *how long* (an hour) but not *where*.

38. **(A)** Choice (A) is a logical response to a question about *duration*. Choice (B) confuses *on the phone* with *off the hook*. Choice (C) confuses *long* with *how much longer* and has the related word *cord*.

39. **(A)** Choice (A) is a logical response to a question about *sending a memo*. (*E-mail* means *electronic mail*, a way to send correspondence by computer.) Choice (B) confuses sending with *shipping department* (any department can send and receive memos). Choice (C) confuses related words: *departments* with *department store*.

40. **(C)** The second speaker offers to give the first speaker money for the bus. Choice (A) confuses *rush* with the similar-sounding word *bus*. Choice (B) uses the word *change* out of context.

Part 3: Conversations

41. **(B)** The man says that he called at 7:00. Choice (A) is the time that the man got home. Choice (C) confuses *eight* with the similar-sounding word *great*. Choice (D) is the time that the woman went to bed.

42. **(D)** The woman says she didn't hear the phone because she had the TV on. Choice (A) is the man's guess. Choice (B) confuses *singing* with the similar-sounding word *ringing*. Choice (C) is what the woman did later on.

43. **(A)** The man says that he wanted to invite the woman to a party. Choice (B) is what the woman was watching on TV. Choice (C) confuses *walk* with the similar-sounding word *work*. Choice (D) repeats the word *work*.

44. **(B)** The man says he prefers a quiet room. Choice (A) describes the room he gets, but it's not the reason he asked for it. Choices (C) and (D) describe the first room he is offered.

45. **(C)** The woman gives him room 517. Choice (A) sounds similar to the number of the first room offered. Choice (B) is the first room offered. Choice (D) sounds similar to the correct answer.

46. **(D)** The man says he wants to get some rest. Choice (A) confuses *sweater* with the similar-sounding word *better*. Choice (B) repeats the word *pool*. Choice (C) is what he will do later.

47. **(C)** The man says that Mr. Tan was in a traffic accident. Choice (A) repeats the word *traffic*. Choices (B) and (D) are confused with the places Mr. Tan will be while he recovers from the accident.

48. **(D)** He will be in the hospital for one week and at home for three weeks, for a total of

four weeks. Choice (A) is confused with *last night*, when he had the accident. Choice (B) is the amount of time he will be in the hospital. Choice (C) is the amount of time he will be at home.

49. **(C)** The woman says that she will have to do his work. Choice (A) is the person who called with the information about the accident. Choice (B) repeats the word *boss*. Choice (D) is not mentioned as having to do Mr. Tan's work for him.

50. **(A)** The man complains that the tour guide was in a hurry. Choice (B) confuses *any* with the similar-sounding word *many*. Choice (C) uses the word *back* out of context. Choice (D) repeats the word *paintings*.

51. **(C)** The woman suggests that the man go back on his own. Choice (A) repeats the word *tour*. Choice (B) repeats the word *hurry*. Choice (D) uses the word *own* out of context.

52. **(D)** The woman says that they are leaving next weekend. Choice (A) is when the tour took place. Choice (B) repeats the word *afternoon*. Choice (C) sounds similar to the correct answer.

53. **(A)** The speakers are discussing how glad they are that they decided to drive. Choice (B) is incorrect because they say they are glad they decided not to fly. Choice (C) confuses *train* with the similar-sounding word *rain*. Choice (D) confuses *walk* with the similar-sounding word *week*.

54. **(B)** The man mentions the sunny skies. Choice (A) is incorrect because the man says that there are no clouds. Choice (C) is how the weather was last week. Choice (D) confuses *snow* with the similar-sounding word *know*.

55. **(C)** The man says they will get there by 6:00. Choice (A) confuses *two* with the similar-sounding word *too*. Choice (B) confuses *five* with the similar-sounding word *drive*. Choice (D) confuses *nine* with the similar-sounding word *time*.

56. **(D)** The man says that he doesn't like to park in the city. Choice (A) is associated with the fact that the woman pays a lot for parking, but the man doesn't give it as a reason. Choice (B) is the reason the woman drives. Choice (C) repeats the word *train*.

57. **(B)** The woman parks in the garage downstairs. Choice (A) uses the word *park* out of context. Choice (C) is the man's guess. Choice (D) repeats the word *train*.

58. **(D)** The woman says she pays $11.00. Choice (A) confuses *three* with the similar-sounding word *street*. Choice (B) confuses *four* with the similar-sounding word *for*. Choice (C) sounds similar to the correct answer.

59. **(B)** The man was looking for a post office close enough to walk to. Choice (A) confuses *closed* with the similar-sounding word *close*. Choice (C) is incorrect because the woman says *You can't miss it*. Choice (D) confuses *underground* with the similar-sounding word *around*.

60. **(B)** The woman tells the man to take the bus. Choice (A) confuses *car* with the similar-sounding word *far*. Choice (C) is how the man wanted to go. Choice (D) is not mentioned.

61. **(B)** The woman says it takes five minutes. Choice (A) is confused with the number of bus stops. Choice (C) confuses *nine* with the similar-sounding word *time*. Choice (D) confuses *ten* with the similar-sounding word *then*.

62. **(D)** The woman is explaining company benefits to a new employee. Choice (A) repeats the word *manager*. Choice (B) repeats the word *assistant*. Choice (C) associates *travel agent* with *vacation*.

63. **(D)** Employees get paid *every two weeks*, which amounts to twice a month. Choice (A) repeats the word *once*. Choice (B) confuses *twice a week* with *every two weeks*. Choice (C) is what the man says he doesn't prefer.

64. **(B)** There is health insurance for the employee but not for his family. Choices

(A), (C), and (D) are all mentioned as job benefits.

65. **(C)** The man says they will leave for the airport. Choice (A) is where they will leave from. Choice (B) confuses *store* with the similar-sounding word *more*. Choice (D) confuses *train* with the similar-sounding word *rain*.

66. **(C)** The man says he wants to leave at 3:00. Choice (A) confuses *noon* with the similar-sounding word *soon*. Choice (B) confuses *two* with the similar-sounding word *too*. Choice (D) confuses *ten* with the similar-sounding word *then*.

67. **(C)** The man mentions the *heavy traffic*. Choice (A) repeats the word *early*. Choice (B) confuses *hurry* with the similar-sounding word *worry*. Choice (D) uses the word *way* out of context.

68. **(D)** The woman says she prefers hot tea. Choice (A) associates *lemonade* with *lemon*. Choice (B) is what the woman says she doesn't want. Choice (C) is what the man will use to make tea.

69. **(A)** The woman says she had a big lunch and can't eat any more. Choice (B) repeats the word *hot*. Choice (C) is not mentioned. Choice (D) repeats the word *lunch*.

70. **(A)** The man says he'll have a piece of pie. Choice (B) repeats the word *bake* and confuses *buns* with the similar-sounding word *one*. Choice (C) confuses *bacon* with the similar-sounding word *baked*. Choice (D) repeats the word *toast*.

Part 4: Talks

71. **(C)** *Senior citizens* means *elderly people*. Choices (A), (B), and (D) are not mentioned.

72. **(B)** People may *request assistance from a flight attendant*. Choices (A), (C), and (D) are airline personnel but have other duties.

73. **(D)** The other passengers are asked to stay away from the door until they hear their row numbers called. Choice (A) is the opposite of the correct answer. Choice (B) is confused with *request assistance from a flight attendant*. Choice (C) uses the word *call* out of context.

74. **(C)** This ad is for *professional* books. Choices (A) and (B) would not be sold at such a store. Choice (D) is incorrect; textbooks are for students who are not yet professionals.

75. **(D)** They will *order it*. Choice (A) is unnecessary if they can order it. Choice (B) would not help in getting the book. Choice (C) is not logical.

76. **(C)** The store sells scientific and technical journals. Choice (A) confuses *newspapers* with the similar-sounding word *newest*. Choice (B) confuses *carry-alls* with *carry all*. Choice (D) is not mentioned.

77. **(B)** It says *cloudiness is expected this afternoon*. Choice (A) is contradicted by *this morning will be partly sunny*. Choices (C) and (D) are incorrect; it will already be cloudy by evening and night.

78. **(A)** *Continue through the weekend* means *all weekend*. Choices (B), (C), and (D) are not logical ways to express *all weekend*.

79. **(B)** There will be unusually cold temperatures on Monday. Choice (A) confuses *hot* with the similar-sounding word *not*. Choice (C) is how the weather will be over the weekend. Choice (D) is how the weather is this morning.

80. **(D)** *3–5 days* is explicitly mentioned. Choices (A), (B), and (C) are all shorter periods of time.

81. **(B)** Drink plenty of *water* and *fruit juices*, which are *fluids*. Choices (A), (C), and (D) may help but are not mentioned.

82. **(A)** *Everyone* catches colds during this season, so colds are common. Choice (B) is incorrect because the talk says there is no cure for colds. Choice (C) confuses *tests* with the similar-sounding word *rest*. Choice (D) repeats the word healthy.

83. **(B)** Since the ad concentrates on *meetings*, it is for businesspeople. Choice (A) is incorrect; *homemakers* do not have business meetings. Choices (C) and (D) do not set up business meetings.

84. **(C)** The advertisement discusses *food for business occasions*. Choice (A) confuses *con-*

ference planning and *conference room.* Choices (B) and (D) are not provided by catering companies.

85. **(C)** The largest group size mentioned in the ad is five-hundred. Choice (A) confuses *two* with the similar-sounding word *too.* Choice (B) confuses *four* with the similar-sounding word *for.* Choice (D) confuses *eight* with the similar-sounding word *wait.*

86. **(D)** The subway is *to the shopping mall and suburbs.* Choices (A) and (C) are contradicted by *to the northern suburbs.* Choice (B) is not mentioned.

87. **(A)** The announcement says to catch *the gray line to the airport.* Choice (B) is the current line. Choices (C) and (D) are not mentioned.

88. **(C)** The announcer says that airport trains leave every fifteen minutes. Choices (A) and (B) are confused with *2:05,* the time that the next train is due. Choice (D) sounds similar to the correct answer.

89. **(C)** *Things will close* because of *the federal holiday.* Choice (A) is incorrectly suggested by *weekend schedule.* Choice (B) is contradicted by *public transportation will operate.* Choice (D) is not mentioned.

90. **(A)** The announcement says there will be *no additional buses or trains for rush hour service.* Choice (B) is confused with *operate on a weekend schedule.* Choices (C) and (D) are unlikely if transportation follows weekend service.

91. **(C)** The announcer says that parking is free downtown. Choice (A) is incorrect because public garages are closed today. Choice (B) is incorrect because some of them will be charging weekend rates. Choice (D) is associated with *buses.*

92. **(D)** This was a *survey of business travelers.* Choices (A), (B), and (C) do not travel much on business.

93. **(C)** Hotels should be located close to *shopping and entertainment facilities.* Choice (A) is where they don't want hotels located. Choices (B) and (D) are not mentioned.

94. **(A)** *To provide access* means that *facilities should be open.* Choice (B) is not mentioned.

Choice (C) confuses *light snacks* and serving *lighter meals.* Choice (D) is not mentioned.

95. **(B)** The service helps people *find their way around the city by public transportation.* Choice (A) is not mentioned. Choice (C) is incorrect; they tell you how to use transportation but do not sell tickets. Choice (D) is incorrect; they tell you how to use transportation but do not tell you what to see.

96. **(D)** You should have the day and time of travel available in order to get help. Choices (A), (B), and (C) are not mentioned.

97. **(C)** The announcement tells you to have *a pencil and paper ready to write down information.* Choice (A) is not needed for this information service. Choices (B) and (D) might give you destinations but are not necessary or mentioned.

98. **(C)** The first step is to select the clothes that you will take with you. Choice (A) repeats the word *socks,* but nothing is said about washing them. Choice (B) repeats the word *sweaters,* but nothing is said about folding them. Choice (D) repeats the word *medicine,* but nothing is said about measuring it.

99. **(B)** The speaker suggests packing heavier items first. Choices (A), (C), and (D) are other things mentioned by the speaker.

100. **(C)** The speaker suggests that clear plastic bags let security officers see what's inside them. Choices (A) and (B) are other things mentioned by the speaker. Choice (D), shoes, are mentioned, but slip-on shoes are not.

READING

Part 5: Incomplete Sentences

101. **(B)** The present tense in the *if* clause of a real condition can use future in the other clause. Choice (A) is past. Choice (C) is past perfect. Choice (D) is present progressive.

102. **(C)** *Until* joins the clauses; it is logical. Choices (A) and (D) are not logical. Choice (B) is used in relative clauses.

103. **(A)** *At* indicates location. Choice (B) means *together.* Choice (C) means *to place inside.* Choice (D) indicates a recipient.

First News
Always Innovative & Informative

104. **(D)** Someone else *enclosed* the envelope; use the past participle. Choice (A) has an unnecessary *is*. Choice (B) is the simple form of the verb. Choice (C) is the present participle.

105. **(C)** *Advice* is a noun and is logical. Choice (A) is a verb. Choice (B) is an adjective. Choice (D) is a noun, but it is not logical.

106. **(B)** Use *on* with days of the week. Choice (A) means *inside*. Choice (C) means *above*. Choice (D) indicates location.

107. **(B)** *Increase* is logical. Choice (A) is used for physical movement. Choice (C) includes increases in speed and volume. Choice (D) requires an object (*...expects circulation to raise ad revenues*).

108. **(A)** The adjective *effective* modifies *way*. Choices (B) and (C) are nouns. Choice (D) is an adverb.

109. **(D)** Join contrasting clauses with *but*. Choices (A), (B), and (C) are not logical.

110. **(C)** Specific times use *at*. Choice (A) is incorrect; an earlier action must be mentioned with *until*. Choice (B) indicates destination. Choice (D) indicates a recipient.

111. **(D)** *Head of operations* requires a singular verb. Choice (A) is a gerund. Choice (B) is plural. Choice (C) is the simple form.

112. **(B)** *Always* should come between the auxiliary and the main verb. In Choice (A) *always* is before the verb. In Choice (C) *always* is after the main verb. Choice (D) uses the wrong form of be.

113. **(C)** *Under* is logical. Choices (A), (B), and (D) require more than one item as a reference point. Choice (B) generally indicates a specific area rather than a specific thing.

114. **(B)** Join equal terms with *and*. Choice (A) indicates a choice between terms. Choice (C) indicates a contrast. Choice (D) is used with *nor*.

115. **(D)** The causative *had* is followed by the simple form. Choice (A) is the infinitive. Choice (B) is past tense. Choice (C) is the past participle.

116. **(C)** *Promises* is followed by the infinitive. Choice (A) is the future tense. Choice (B) is the gerund. Choice (D) is the present tense.

117. **(A)** The clauses contrast; use *although*. Choice (B) is not used with clauses. Choices (C) and (D) are not logical.

118. **(D)** The sentence requires a noun subject. Choice (A) is a noun but is not logical. Choice (B) is a verb. Choice (C) is a gerund.

119. **(A)** The causative *persuade* is followed by the infinitive. Choice (B) is the gerund. Choice (C) is past tense. Choice (D) is the past participle.

120. **(D)** *Repairs* is the only noun among the options. Choices (A), (B), and (C) do not fit the context of the sentence.

121. **(C)** Use *at* with specific times. Choice (A) is used with dates. Choice (B) indicates a recipient. Choice (D) means *inside*.

122. **(B)** The causative *suggest* is followed by the gerund. Choice (A) is the past tense. Choice (C) is present tense. Choice (D) is the infinitive.

123. **(A)** Use the idiomatic *on* with dates. Choice (B) means *inside*. Choice (C) indicates location. Choice (D) indicates destination.

124. **(C)** The comparative *more* is followed by an adjective and *than*. Choice (A) omits *than*. Choice (B) is an adverb. Choice (D) is an incomplete *as-as* comparison.

125. **(B)** *Because* establishes a cause-and-effect relationship. Choices (A), (C), and (D) are not logical.

126. **(C)** The causative *request* is followed by the simple form of the verb. Choice (A) is the gerund. Choice (B) is the present tense. Choice (D) is the infinitive.

127. **(D)** *Who* refers to the subject *person*. Choice (A) is possessive. Choice (B) refers to things. Choice (C) is objective.

128. **(C)** Equal comparisons use *as* + adjective + *as*; *the memo* is causing people to become confused, so the adjective must be the present participle. Choice (A) omits the second *as*. Choice (B) omits the first *as*. Choice (D) uses the past participle.

129. **(A)** Since *know* happened before *was*, it must also be past tense. Choice (B) is the past participle. Choice (C) is the present progressive. Choice (D) is the past perfect.

130. **(B)** Commands are in the simple form of the verb. Choice (A) is the present progressive. Choice (C) is the present tense. Choice (D) is the future tense.

131. **(A)** *On* is used for building, floor, or ship deck locations. Choice (B) means *below*. Choice (C) means *inside*. Choice (D) means *above*.

132. **(A)** *Effect* is a logical noun. Choice (B) is an adjective. Choice (C) is an adverb. Choice (D) is a noun but doesn't fit here.

133. **(B)** *Reservation* is the only noun among the options that matches a hotel context. Choices (A), (C), and (D) do not fit the context of the sentence.

134. **(C)** *And* joins equal terms. Choice (A) implies a contrast. Choice (B) implies a choice. Choice (D) is used with *or*.

135. **(D)** *Which* refers to *merger*. Choice (A) refers to time. Choice (B) is possessive. Choice (C) repeats the subject *merger*.

136. **(A)** Habitual action is expressed by the present tense. Choice (B) is past tense. Choice (C) is the simple form of the verb. Choice (D) is the past participle.

137. **(C)** Implies a past continuing action; use the past progressive. Choice (A) is the simple past and is not logical; she could not compose (type) if the computer crashed (became inoperative). Choice (B) is the present progressive. Choice (D) is present.

138. **(A)** *Tomorrow* uses the future tense. Choice (B) is past tense. Choice (C) is past perfect. Choice (D) is the present progressive.

139. **(B)** *Someone else surprised Mr. Hopper*; use the past participle. Choice (A) is the simple form. Choice (C) is the present participle. Choice (D) is the present tense.

140. **(D)** *And* joins equal terms. Choice (A) needs *neither* after the verb. Choice (B) implies a contrast. Choice (C) is used with *nor*.

Part 6: Text Completion

141. **(C)** The date for using the rebate card had passed; this is the meaning of *expired*. Choices (A), (B), and (D) don't fit the context.

142. **(A)** *Would like* is followed by an infinitive verb. Choice (B) is a gerund. Choice (C) is simple past tense. Choice (D) is a future form.

143. **(B)** The company is sending the customer a page of coupons; coupons are a form of *discount*. Choices (A), (C), and (D) are words that are related to *products* but they don't have the correct meaning.

144. **(D)** This is probably a yearly, or *annual*, tournament. Since the tournament is two months away, Choices (A), (B), and (C) are not likely.

145. **(B)** *Hand out* means to *distribute* or *give away*. Choice (A) creates a word that means *submit*. Choice (C) creates a word that means *give up possession*. Choice (D) creates a word that means *give away something no longer useful*.

146. **(C)** During the tournament, the company *raised*, or *collected money that it needed* to give to charity. Choices (A), (B), and (D) are all words that are related to money but they don't fit the context.

147. **(B)** This is a comparison using the word *than*, so an adjective with *more* is needed. Choice (A) is an adjective but not a comparative form. Choices (C) and (D) are superlative adjectives, which are not used with *than*.

148. **(A)** The verb must agree with the singular subject *air quality*. Choices (B), (C), and (D) are verbs that agree with a plural subject.

149. **(B)** *Premature* means *too early*. Choices (A), (C), and (D) look similar to the correct answer but have very different meanings.

150. **(A)** The verb *let* is followed by the base form of a verb. Choice (B) is simple present tense. Choice (C) is infinitive. Choice (D) is a gerund.

151. **(D)** *As well* means also. Choices (A) and (C) are used to introduce additional information to a paragraph. Choice (B) means *in place of*.

152. **(B)** The sentence compares Conference Room 2 to Conference Room 1, so a comparative adjective is used. Choice (A) is a

simple adjective. Choice (C) is an adverb. Choice (D) is a superlative form.

Part 7: Reading Comprehension

153. **(C)** A stockbroker is likely to attend to learn how he/she can better assist clients. Choice (A) is contradicted by *clients*. Choice (B) confuses *manager* and *management firm*. Choice (D) is not likely.

154. **(C)** The seminar will help you learn about how you can predict trends for successful investments. Choices (A) and (B) are mentioned but are not what will be discussed. Choice (D) repeats the word *clients*.

155. **(B)** To reserve a seat, fill out the card and mail it with your registration fee. Choices (A) and (C) are not mentioned. Choice (D) is what you do to get more information.

156. **(A)** New Tech has cut jobs as part of its strategy to reorganize its money-losing business and become more profitable. Choice (B) is incorrect because the international offices are already opened and are more cost-effective. Choices (C) and (D) are not mentioned.

157. **(D)** The company has had *two years of losses*. Choices (A), (B), and (C) are contradicted by *two years*.

158. **(B)** *Revenues* means the money that a company earns. Choices (A), (C), and (D) are related to earning money but don't have the correct meaning.

159. **(A)** Ms. Strube has made the international branches more profitable. The other choices are not mentioned in the passage.

160. **(B)** The new fares are *effective March 1*. Choices (A), (C), and (D) are contradicted by *March 1*.

161. **(C)** *8:00 P.M. Thursday* is off-peak. Choices (A), (B), and (D) are peak hours when everyone is traveling to or from work.

162. **(D)** The peak fare is *$1.70*. Choice (A) is the off-peak fare within one zone. Choice (B) is the peak fare within one zone. Choice (C) is the peak fare between zones 1 and 2, the off-peak fare between zones 1 and 3, and the peak fare between zones 2 and 3.

163. **(B)** *Consumer preferences* means *what consumers like*. Choices (A) and (C) are likely uses for this information but are not the duties of the Specialist. Choice (D) is incorrect; product testing is a way to discover consumer preferences but is not explicitly mentioned.

164. **(D)** The Specialist will write reports *for use within the company*. Choice (A) is incorrect; the reports will be *about* the consumer. Choices (B) and (C) are contradicted by *within the company*.

165. **(A)** The qualifications are *a college degree in research and experience in advertising*. Choice (B) is not logical. Choice (C) is not mentioned. Choice (D) is related but not necessary.

166. **(D)** The new regulations *reduced port costs* and *increased efficiency*. Choices (A), (B), and (C) are not mentioned.

167. **(B)** The *Pacific Rim* refers to *Asian markets*. Choices (A), (C), and (D) are not mentioned.

168. **(B)** Ports in recent years have been moving only half of their capacity. Choices (A), (C), and (D) refer to other statistics in the passage.

169. **(B)** A regulation was *stopped* in order to help the port run more efficiently. Choices (A), (C), and (D) have the opposite of the correct meaning.

170. **(B)** This is the best choice and is directly stated in the passage: *increase in traffic*. Choices (A), (C), and (D) may be true, but are not stated in the passages.

171. **(D)** The purpose of this notice is to encourage investors to keep their Southern Regional stock. Choice (A) associates *warning* with *alert*. Choice (B) confuses *suggesting a change in management* and *if present management does not change*. Choice (C) is mentioned, but it is not the purpose of the notice.

172. **(B)** *Reduced costs* and *lowered costs* have the same meaning; they also had a higher number of *profitable routes*. Choices (A), (C), and (D) are not mentioned.

173. **(C)** The airline lost *$112.4 million for all of this year*. Choices (A) and (D) are contra-

dicted by the figure given. Choice (B) is the amount earned in the fourth quarter.

174. **(C)** A forecast is a prediction or a guess about what will happen in the future. Choices (A), (B), and (D) could fit the sentence, but they don't have the correct meaning.

175. **(B)** Guaranteed arrival allows you to get a room after check-in time. Choice (A) is not logical. Choice (C) is incorrect; you must arrive before 4:00 if you did *not* guarantee arrival. Choice (D) is incorrect because you still have to check in.

176. **(A)** You must pay for the *first night's room charge.* Choice (B) confuses *first choice* and *first night's charge.* Choices (C) and (D) are not logical.

177. **(B)** The memo is about *vacation time.* Choices (A), (C), and (D) are not mentioned. Also Choice (C) is a different kind of time off.

178. **(D)** The supervisor has to approve *vacation periods longer than one week.* Choices (A), (B), and (C) are one week or less.

179. **(D)** If you have frequent absences, your request could be denied. Choices (A), (B), and (C) are not mentioned.

180. **(D)** The Personnel Review Board can examine the vacation request. Choice (A) is incorrect; supervisors can approve vacations only for their own employees. Choices (B) and (C) may not be possible.

181. **(B)** The caller wanted advice for turning off the water to stop the flood, not for cleaning up. Choice (A) is true because a problem with a new dishwasher was the reason for the call. Choices (C) and (D) are both things the caller mentioned as upsetting her.

182. **(B)** She called on a Thursday morning, which, according to the notice is when staff meetings are held and therefore only one person is available to work the phones. Choice (A) is not true because somebody answered the phone even though they immediately put the caller on hold. Choice (C) is the number of unattended phones.

Choice (D) is the number of phones normally in operation.

183. **(B)** The meeting policy was changed because of problems with handling help line calls. Choice (A) is incorrect because it isn't true; call center employees only handle sales on the side. Choice (C) is also not true; the meetings are for all employees. Choice (D) is a plausible reason but is not mentioned.

184. **(C)** The meeting minutes will be posted in the staff room. Choices (A), (B) and (D) are not mentioned.

185. **(C)** The company handled the problem by releasing call center employees from the weekly meetings so that there would be enough people to answer the phones. Choice (A) was a complaint made in the customer's fax. Choice (B) uses words from the texts but is not mentioned. Choice (D) confuses a notice for the customer with the notice for call center employees.

186. **(D)** The ad tells *busy business workers* to take a vacation and relax. Choice (A) is incorrect because only one of the vacations includes golf. Choice (B) is mentioned as people who normally travel at a different time. Choice (C) is incorrect because the ad is about vacations, not business trips.

187. **(B)** While students are in school taking exams, vacation places are quieter. Choice (A) is incorrect because the ad promotes May vacations. Choice (C) is the opposite of the correct answer. Choice (D) is incorrect because the ad says *Don't wait until the end of the year.*

188. **(C)** Franco will take the Caribbean Cruise with his wife; the cost for two people, $2,800, minus the 25% discount, comes to $2,100. Choice (A) is the cost of the trip to Portugal for one person. Choice (B) is the cost of the cruise for one person. Choice (D) is the cost of the cruise for two people without the discount.

189. **(D)** Milan is Franco's coworker who will help him with work over the weekend. Choice (A) is associated with booking a vacation. Choice (B) is the person who will

get married next fall. Choice (C) is the person to whom the e-mail is addressed.

190. **(A)** This vacation lasts more than a week, and Franco needs to save a week of vacation to go to his brother's wedding. Choice (B) is incorrect because Franco says his wife would like a break from cooking. Choice (C) is incorrect because a discount is offered on all the vacations. Choice (D) is not mentioned.

191. **(C)** The operators are all student interns. Choice (A) is incorrect because the e-mail is addressed to three people only. Choice (B) is incorrect because the operators are interns, or trainees, not trainers. Choice (D) is incorrect because the e-mail is addressed to three operators only.

192. **(A)** Park Gi refers the interns to a page in their manuals that states the rules. Choices (B), (C), and (D) are all people mentioned in the texts, but Park Gi does not refer the interns to them.

193. **(C)** Chong Dae says that she changed the message to include her own name and her job title. Choice (A) is what another intern put on her answering machine. Choice (B) is associated with the *answering machine* but is not mentioned. Choice (D) is mentioned, but she didn't put this information on the answering machine.

194. **(C)** Chong Dae changed the recording after a customer said that calling a person by a number instead of a name was impersonal. Choices (A), (B), and (D) are related to the topic but are not mentioned.

195. **(B)** Chong Dae says she hasn't changed the recording back to the original one because she wasn't sure if this was allowed. Choice

(A) is mentioned; the rule is in the manual. Choice (C) is implied by the wording of the rule in the manual. Choice (D) is explained very clearly—the interns may be asked to move to a new department at any time, leaving their phone and answering machine to be used by another person.

196. **(C)** *Floria* is the name of an opera being performed by the Valley Opera Group. Choice (A) is the Valley Opera Group. Choice (B) is the type of performance that closed at the theater yesterday. Choice (D) is the Encore Theater.

197. **(D)** According to the article, the Valley Opera Group is a leading Korean opera company. Choice (A) is incorrect because the article says that the members don't earn any salary. Choice (B) is incorrect because the company has been wanting a better theater in Jeonju. Choice (C) is incorrect because the show will run from March 7 to March 30.

198. **(B)** Kim offers to get group tickets, but the article says only individual seats are available. Choices (A) and (C) are incorrect because Kim makes no reference to these facts. Choice (D) is not true.

199. **(A)** The opera lasts one hour, and Park's meal at the restaurant took two hours. Choice (B) is not mentioned. Choice (C) is not true; the restaurant is near, not in, the theater. Choice (D) is incorrect because it is the opera tickets, not the restaurant, that are expensive.

200. **(B)** Park clearly didn't like the restaurant. Choice (A) is wrong because she thinks the opera will be very good. Choices (C) and (D) are what Kim suggests.

Audioscripts for Listening Comprehension Exercises, Mini-Test, and Model Tests 1–4

LISTENING COMPREHENSION EXERCISES

Target 1

Part 1

(A) The pharmacist serves his customers.
(B) The technicians are conducting experiments.
(C) The laboratory animals are in a cage.
(D) The shelves are empty.

Target 2

Part 1

(A) Four people are looking at a map.
(B) The men are wearing suits.
(C) Both women are taller than the men.
(D) The man with glasses is pointing to a chart.

Target 3

Part 1

(A) The children are playing on the floor.
(B) The television is off.
(C) The father is playing the piano.
(D) The curtains are open.

Target 4

Part 1

(A) The men are smoking pipes.
(B) The earth is planted with crops.
(C) The trench is being dug.
(D) The workers are laying pipeline.

Target 5

Part 1

(A) Some shoppers want to buy new luggage.
(B) Passengers are passing through airport security.
(C) The police guard the bank.
(D) The flight attendant seats the passengers.

Target 6

Part 1

(A) The waiters are beside the table.
(B) The man with glasses is next to the woman.
(C) A bottle is under the table.
(D) There are four people in front of the first table.

Target 7

Part 1

(A) The fair operates all night.
(B) The freight train is in the station.
(C) The car door is open.
(D) The men are loading cargo onto the plane.

Part 2

Was the letter delivered today?
(A) Yes, it came this morning.
(B) The ladder was on the delivery truck.
(C) He was late on Tuesday.

Part 3

Man: How new is your boat?
Woman: It's almost brand new—just one month old. I'm really having fun with it.
Man: I hope you'll take me for a ride on it someday. Are you free Tuesday? Can
             we get together then and go sailing?
Woman: Maybe, if the weather clears up. I wouldn't want to take the boat out on
             a rainy day like this.

1. What does the woman enjoy?
2. When does the man want to get together with the woman?
3. How is the weather today?

First News
Always Innovative & Informative

Part 4

Attention shoppers. It is now 5:45. The market will be closing in fifteen minutes. If you wish to make purchases, please proceed to the checkout counters immediately. You are reminded that the store will be closed tomorrow because of the holiday. We will reopen on Monday. Thank you for shopping at Maguire's Market.

1. What does the woman want people to do?
2. When does she want people to do this?
3. What will happen tomorrow?

Target 8

Part 1

(A) The man is shoveling snow.
(B) The skiers are on the mountain.
(C) The iceberg is very cold.
(D) The voters went to the polls.

Part 2

How long have you been married?
(A) Almost ten years.
(B) About five feet.
(C) The bride is my cousin.

Part 3

Man: Please return to your seat and fasten your seat belt.
Woman: Are we getting ready to land?
Man: No, but there's some turbulence in the air.
Woman: I'll sit down right away. I don't want to lose my balance and fall in the aisle.

1. Where are the speakers?
2. What does the man want the woman to do?
3. What is the woman worried about?

Part 4

The weather this weekend will be perfect for those who want to play golf or do outside chores such as gardening. The temperature will be in the low 70s and the humidity will also be low. The skies will remain sunny all weekend, so enjoy it while you can. It won't last for long. Heavy rains will roll in early Monday morning and you can expect heavy traffic during your morning commute. Rain is expected during most of next week, so get outdoors while you can.

1. What does this announcement concern?
2. What should people do this weekend?
3. What will happen on Monday?

Target 9

Part 1

(A) They're rushing down the stairs.
(B) They're being trained.
(C) They're boarding the windows.
(D) They're staring at the train.

Part 2

He leaves next week, doesn't he?
(A) No, he's going tomorrow.
(B) Yes, he's very weak.
(C) The leaves are turning yellow.

Part 3

Woman: My jacket has a small hole on the sleeve and it's missing a button. Can you sew it up for me so I can wear it tonight?
Man: I can't help you with it right now. I don't have time.
Woman: I'll be glad to wait.
Man: You'll have to wait until tomorrow when I get home from work. I just don't have time to get the sewing machine running today.

1. Why can't the man help?
2. What is the matter with the woman's jacket?
3. When can the man help her?

Part 4

The sun will shine this morning, but rain is likely this afternoon. There may be some strong winds, too. Spring weather is very unpredictable. In fact, it will get very cold overnight, and we may see some snow tomorrow in the morning. So don't plant your spring flower garden yet. But don't despair. We'll have more fair weather later in the week. Tune in at 1:00 for the next update. This is Chris Jones, your local weather reporter. Thank you for listening to WXYY radio.

1. What is the man taking about?
2. What will happen tomorrow?
3. When will the speaker make the next announcement?

Target 10

Part 1

(A) Math is the first class of the day.
(B) The attendant works in first class.
(C) This is a middle-class neighborhood.
(D) The documents are classified.

Part 2

Is this bed too hard?
(A) Yes, it's very difficult.
(B) Not for me. I like it firm.
(C) The flower bed needs water.

Part 3

Man: Why didn't you call this summer?
Woman: I was working hard at my job all summer, and also taking classes for my bachelor's degree. I didn't have a moment to rest.
Man: Well, now that fall is here, I'll give you a ring next week. We can talk about going out on a dinner date.
Woman: That sounds nice, but you'd better make it the week after. I'll be busy with my family all next week.

1. What will the man do?
2. Why does the man want to talk to the woman?
3. Why doesn't the woman want the man to call next week?

Part 4

Tennis fans will not want to miss the final match at the Valley Springs Tennis Club next Sunday. This is your chance to watch world-class players compete on the world's finest clay courts. In the evening, tournament prizes will be awarded during a special ceremony. There may still be a few tickets left, so call the club today to reserve yours. This championship match will be sponsored by Sporting Goods Company, the maker of Big Blue Racquets, a racquet without equal. This is the final match of the International World Tournament. The Juniors Tournament begins next month.

1. What does the speaker suggest people do?
2. What will happen in the next evening?
3. When will the next tournament take place?

Target 11

Part 1

(A) After the firefighters arrived, they extinguished the fire with water.
(B) Before the fire started, the firefighters arrived.
(C) Prior to extinguishing the fire, the firefighters put away their hoses.
(D) While the fire blazed, the firefighters rested.

Part 2

It's quarter after ten already.
(A) How did it get so late?
(B) That's very expensive.
(C) I already timed it.

Part 3

Man: I'm glad we're finally done writing this project proposal. We'll have to show it to Mr. Kim, though, before we can submit it to the director.

Woman: I know, but we'd better proofread it before we do that.

Man: Of course. Let's go over the proposal now before lunch.

Woman: No, I'm hungry and tired. Let's eat first, then we'll go over it afterwards.

1. What will the speaker do first with the proposal?
2. When does the woman want to eat lunch?
3. What will the speakers do last?

Part 4

Mr. Ahmed Saleh, Chairman and CEO, will retire at the end of the next quarter. He has been with the company for over twenty years and has been the Chairman since the company merged with Rotel International, five years ago. When asked about his retirement plans, Mr. Saleh explained that following a vacation in the Caribbean, he plans to open a part-time consulting business. He says that starting his own small business has long been a plan of his, since even before he started working with us here at the Mercury Corporation. All company employees who wish to honor Mr. Saleh's long years of service to this company are invited to attend his retirement party at the end of this month.

1. How long has Mr. Saleh been Chairman?
2. What will Mr. Saleh do first?
3. Which of the following did Mr. Saleh do first?

Target 12

Part 1

(A) None of the seats is occupied.
(B) No one is sitting down.
(C) Not one of the men is wearing a tie.
(D) No one is wearing glasses.

Part 2

He hasn't done anything illegal, has he?
(A) No, of course not. He's a law-abiding citizen.
(B) He's a legal secretary, I think.
(C) There is something illegible in this letter.

Part 3

Man: Do you have everything you need for your trip?

Woman: I even have what I don't need.

Man: You can never take too much, I always say.

Woman: I can't say that I disagree with you. I seldom travel with fewer than three suitcases.

1. What does the man advise the woman?
2. What does the woman think of the man's advice?
3. How many suitcases does the woman usually travel with?

Part 4

At no time in the history of our company have we had such sales. Our profit margins are unprecedented. Our total revenues, unimaginable. This unparalleled success is due to the selfless dedication of our employees. Never have we been so pleased with the hard work of all our staff members as we are now. In recognition of this, we will do what has never been done before at this company, but which is long overdue. We will host an employee recognition banquet at the end of this month. I can't tell you how pleased I am about this. All staff members are invited, and I hope no one will be unable to attend. I can't think of anyone who deserves this honor more than the employees of this company.

1. What word or phrase describes this report?
2. What describes the employees mentioned in this report?
3. What does the speaker say about the banquet?

Target 13

Part 1

(A) What a lot of brochures there are!
(B) How many restaurants are there?
(C) How delicious the food looks!
(D) There is no food left.

Part 2

Nobody does as much as you.
(A) No one does it better.
(B) I won't do it again.
(C) I like to stay busy.

Part 3

Man: I'm going to Europe this summer.
Woman: Isn't that great! How I envy you! There's so much to see there.
Man: I'm trying not to think about it more than twenty hours a day.
Woman: Who would ever think you would be so lucky! How beautiful Europe is this time of year! Are you leaving soon?

1. What does the woman think about the trip?
2. What does the woman say about Europe?
3. What does the woman want to know?

Part 4

How the weather changes! Yesterday morning, it was hot and sunny. By noon, the temperature was falling. Never has it rained as hard as it did last night. There was hail, too. And this morning, it never has been so windy. Never have I seen stranger weather. Usually, it's so beautiful this time of year, and everyone enjoys the outdoors. But now I never know what clothes to wear. What a confusing week!

1. What is the weather this morning?
2. When did it rain?
3. What does the speaker think of the weather?

Target 14

Part 1

(A) The man on the right is dressed more warmly.
(B) Both men are wearing the same glasses.
(C) Neither man has a beard.
(D) Their pants are the same color.

Part 2

What is the fastest way to your home?
(A) At rush hour, a train is the fastest.
(B) Take a plane to Rome.
(C) My home is farther than yours.

Part 3

Man: It seems like this meeting will never end!
Woman: It's even longer than yesterday's meeting, and I thought that was long.
Man: I think this meeting holds the record for being the longest and most bor-
             ing meeting ever.
Woman: The more boring the meeting, the more tired I get. Wake me up when
             the meeting is over.

1. What do they think about the meeting?
2. What is true about yesterday's meeting?
3. Why is the woman tired?

Part 4

There never used to be as many cars on the road as there are today. It seems that as we improve the roads, more people want to drive. The more roads there are, the more cars there are on them. In addition, people are driving bigger and bigger cars. This also contributes to more crowded roads. However, this trend will probably change as soon as gasoline prices increase. The higher the price of gasoline, the smaller cars get. One thing we probably won't be seeing any time soon is faster cars. If you want to get somewhere quickly, you still have to go by plane. Fortunately, plane tickets are a lot cheaper than they used to be.

1. What is said about roads and cars?
2. Why will more people start driving smaller cars?
3. According to the speaker, what is the advantage of a plane over a car?

Target 15

Part 1

(A) They had better wait in line.
(B) They have checked their bags.
(C) The plane should be on time.
(D) The passengers will check in.

Part 2

I'd rather go first class than economy.
(A) I would too, but I can't afford it.
(B) This is my first time here.
(C) You'll save some money.

Part 3

Man: Did you attend the reception last night?
Woman: I would have gone if I had been free.
Man: You didn't miss anything. I wish I had been somewhere else more interesting.
Woman: That's too bad. I'm not sure about tomorrow's party, either. I planned to go, but now I might not be able to. It depends on whether I can get this report finished on time.

1. Did the woman go to the reception?
2. Did the man go to the reception?
3. Will the woman go to the party tomorrow?

Part 4

The presentation could have been more interesting if the speakers had used some visuals. Colorful visuals projected on a screen would have made it easier for the audience to follow the main points. Without this support, most of us felt lost. The presenter should also speak more loudly. Most of us, particularly those sitting in the back of the room, could not hear him very well and were not able to follow his main points. The way a presentation is made is just as important as the content. However good the content may be, it is lost if it is not clearly presented. Before giving this presentation again, this presenter should develop some visual aids to use with it and practice speaking more loudly.

1. How does this critique describe the presentation?
2. What does the speaker say about the presentation?
3. What advice does the speaker give for the presenter?

Target 16

Part 1

(A) The chefs are used to the heat.
(B) I used to cook on Sunday.
(C) The pans are used to mix paint.
(D) The food used to be better.

Part 2

I'm used to working all night.
(A) Me, too. I don't need much sleep.
(B) When did you stop working at night?
(C) I used all my sick days.

Part 3

Man: I used to be a frequent speaker at conferences.
Woman: On what subject?
Man: Anything that people wanted to hear. I got used to speaking about all kinds of things—politics, economics, education—you name it.
Woman: I'm impressed. I don't think I could ever get used to speaking in public.

1. What does the man say about himself?
2. What can the man talk about?
3. What does the woman say about herself?

Part 4

Before the photocopier, people used to type multiple copies of their letters using carbon paper inserted between white pages. These copies would be called "cc's," which stands for "carbon copies." We are now used to making many copies of our correspondence, whereas before we were satisfied with just one. In fact, since it is so easy to make copies with a photocopier, people have gotten used to making more copies than they may really need. It costs little time or effort to do this. However, it generates a great deal of waste. Unused copies are thrown in the trash, contributing to problems of waste disposal. So, while photocopiers have made our lives easier in some ways, they have contributed to another problem. The need to dispose of tons of office paper did not used to be a problem in the days of carbon copies.

1. What changes did the photocopier bring about?
2. What are people used to doing now?
3. What is the problem now?

Target 17

Part 2

What did you say her title was?
(A) She's the Marketing Director.
(B) She's worked here for ten years.
(C) She's been talking about her book.

Part 3

Man: Sand this wall until it's smooth. Don't forget to sand all the way down to the end of the room.
Woman: Then it'll be ready for the first coat of paint. We're using semi-gloss, right?
Man: Actually we're using this other kind of paint. My father says he prefers flat. I'll help you mix the color.
Woman: Thanks. This is a lot of work. I sure hope your father likes his new house once we're finished with it.

1. Who are the speakers?
2. Who will prepare the wall?
3. Who owns the house?

Part 4

Our flight attendants will be passing through the cabin now, passing out immigration forms. These forms must be completed by everyone before we land. Please present these forms with your passport at customs. We expect to land in about twenty minutes. Passengers traveling with small children and senior citizens may request help from an attendant if necessary. As you exit, pay attention to the signs directing you towards Immigration Control. Citizens of this country should follow the blue signs, while foreign vistors should follow the red ones.

1. Who is listening to this announcement?
2. Who will pass out the forms?
3. Who should follow the blue signs?

Target 18

Part 2

We need more towels in Room 233. Whom should we call?
(A) The housekeeper will bring them to you.
(B) I'll call the plumber for you, sir.
(C) How about the restaurant manager?

Part 3

Man: I'd like you to put one in each room.
Woman: I'll have to run wires along the baseboard to do that.
Man: No problem. I need one on each employee's desk. We're all responsible for answering the phone here.
Woman: Yes, I can imagine that phones are very important for a mail order business like this. Though I would guess that more and more of your customers are starting to order through your Web site.

1. What is the woman's occupation?
2. What is the man's job?
3. Who is responsible for answering the phone?

Part 4

Good morning, class. We are honored to have as our special guest today Ms. Eliza Thomas, director of the City Museum of Art, who will speak to us about the museum's modern art collection. Before I introduce her, let me remind you that your mid-term exam will be next Monday and will cover all material we have studied so far this semester. After the exam, we will begin our series of student presentations. The first presenter will be Mary Little, who will present on the topic "History of Aboriginal Art." Remember, your presentation counts for 25% of your grade. If you don't remember the presentation date that you have been assigned, please see me after class. And now, Ms. Thomas.

First News
Always Innovative & Informative

1. Who is listening to this talk?
2. Who will speak today?
3. Who is Mary Little?

Target 19

Part 2

What should we do, son, while we wait for Father?
(A) Judge, I am innocent.
(B) Let's browse in this store, Mom.
(C) I finished my homework.

Part 3

Man: Would you like more coffee, ma'am?
Woman: No, thank you. My son would like more water, and we'll take the check now.
Man: Here you are. Please pay the cashier at the end of the counter.
Woman: Where? Oh, I see, by the door.

1. What is the relationship of the speakers?
2. Who is the woman with?
3. Who had coffee?

Part 4

The library's representative is authorized to collect a fine for each day that a borrowed book is overdue. If a book is not returned, the borrower may lose his or her library privileges. Children are welcome to use the library but must be accompanied by an adult. Parents are expected to make sure that their children follow the rules and behave appropriately. Children may be directed to leave the building if their behavior disturbs the other patrons. Meeting rooms are available on the ground floor and may be reserved for community meetings by town residents with proof of residency such as a library card or driver's license. Residents of other areas must get special permission from the Events Director before reserving a meeting room.

1. What two people might pay attention to this message?
2. Who is responsible for children's behavior?
3. Who should show a driver's license?

Target 20

Part 2

Where will you be waiting?
(A) On the corner.
(B) In the envelope.
(C) Under the cushion.

Part 3

Man:	I left the letter on top of that big stack of books.
Woman:	Do you mean those books on the shelf by the door?
Man:	No, that big stack that's on your desk next to the printer. I was sure you'd see it there.
Woman:	Well, I didn't. Next time, just put it on top of my computer. That's the only way I'll see it. Things get lost on my desk with all those folders and boxes and books I have piled up.

1. Where did he put the letter?
2. Where is the shelf?
3. Where does the woman want the man to put the letter?

Part 4

I would like to take this opportunity to go over a few points about our office mail delivery system as there has been some confusion and a number of complaints. First, we often receive mail that is important for everyone to see. This mail is routed to every office. When this occurs, please initial the routing next to your name to indicate that you have read the communication, and then pass it on to the next person on the routing list. Second, please make sure that you place all outgoing letters in the outbox located next to each office door. Mailroom staff will pick it up by four o'clock every afternoon. Large packages can be placed on the floor underneath the box. Incoming mail is delivered by the mailroom staff every morning. Mail addressed to a specific individual is placed on that individual's desk. Mail without a specific addressee is delivered to the department head.

1. Where should you put your initials?
2. Where should people put their outgoing letters?
3. Where is incoming mail placed?

Target 21

Part 2

This file is taking too long to download.
(A) Try doing it from my computer. It's faster.
(B) Ask Mark; he's stronger.
(C) I'll carry it down for you.

Part 3

Man:	It's getting late, and I have an early appointment tomorrow. I need to go in about ten minutes.
Woman:	Your appointment isn't until eight thirty. You can stay for another hour, can't you?
Man:	Let's compromise. I'll leave in half an hour.
Woman:	Good. That will leave you plenty of time to get home and get to sleep early. You can get to your house from here in forty-five minutes easily.

1. How much longer will the man stay?
2. When is the man's appointment?
3. How long will it take the man to get home?

Part 4

Snow has fallen every day now for the last week. If it keeps up, we will have accumulated over sixty inches in the last two months. This region has not seen this much snow in one season since the famous bad winter of seven years ago. Over seventy inches of snow fell during that winter. We may not break that record this year, though, unless we get some spring snow. We have only one week of winter left. Spring officially begins a week from today, and let's hope it brings some milder weather.

1. How often has it snowed?
2. When was the last time the region had this much snow?
3. When will winter end?

Target 22

Part 2

What are you doing with this report?
(A) I love watching sports on TV.
(B) I'm going to read it over the weekend.
(C) We're going to the movies.

Part 3

Man: Turn left here. I think the movie theater is just up this street.
Woman: I can't turn left. This is a one-way street. I knew we should have bought a map. Now we'll get there after the show has started.
Man: We don't need a map. I can find the theater. Just make a left up ahead. We shouldn't have spent so much time in the restaurant.
Woman: What did you want me to do? Skip dinner? I was starving.

1. What are they doing?
2. What did they do earlier?
3. What will they do next?

Part 4

In the event of rain, the picnic will not be postponed. It will be held as scheduled but will take place in the office cafeteria. If you plan to attend the picnic, please send an e-mail to Shirley Smith in the Personnel Department. You must let her know before Friday as the food order will be given to the caterers early Friday afternoon. A few people have expressed an interest in bringing a special dish from home to share. Again, please tell Shirley before Friday if you plan to do this.

1. What will happen if it rains?
2. What will happen on Friday?
3. How should people communicate with Shirley about the picnic?

Target 23

Part 2

What happened to you last night?
(A) I had to work late.
(B) It was last Friday.
(C) About 8 P.M.

Part 3

Man: The shipment is still in customs.
Woman: If it isn't released by Friday, production will be delayed. That means we might have to redo our advertising plan.
Man: We already have that meeting scheduled for Monday. We could start revising the advertising plan then, if it turns out to be necessary.
Woman: I'm afraid it will be. This isn't the first time our shipment has been delayed this way. In fact, it would be strange if it weren't delayed.

1. What will happen if the goods don't clear customs?
2. What will happen on Monday?
3. What does the woman say about the delay?

Part 4

This past week there have been floods in the Midwest, fires in the Northwest, earthquakes in the West, hurricanes in the Southeast, and a blizzard in the Northeast. Never have so many disasters happened at one time. Emergency personnel are busy all over the country aiding victims of the disasters, and emergency resources are being stretched to the limit. If another disaster strikes soon, there may not be enough personnel or resources to provide the necessary aid. The president plans to tour the northern areas of the country this week and the Midwest next week. He will address the nation on the state of the situation on Sunday.

1. What is unusual about this past week?
2. What will happen if a new disaster happens soon?
3. What will the president do on Sunday?

Target 24

Part 2

How are you today?
(A) Fine, thanks.
(B) My name is Bob.
(C) I'm by the window.

Part 3

Man: I'm starving. My stomach is growling.
Woman: Me, too. I haven't eaten all day. Let's get something to eat.

First News
A l w a y s   I n n o v a t i v e   &   I n f o r m a t i v e

Man: I'd be happy to, but I'm afraid there's no place to eat around here. At least, I've never seen anything that looks good.

Woman: Relax. I'm sure there are plenty of places. In fact, there are a couple of cafes down the street that don't look too bad.

1. How do the speakers feel?
2. How does the man feel about their ability to get what they need?
3. How does the woman feel about their ability to get what they need?

Part 4

Our neighbors have requested that employees park their cars on the street or in designated parking areas. They are not pleased that some of you have been leaving your cars on their lawns. We are aware that many of you are frustrated with the shortage of parking spaces. We understand that the situation has gone from bad to worse, and we ask for your patience as we work on a solution to this problem. Plans are already underway to expand our parking lot, and we are pleased to be able to announce that we have just made an agreement with a contractor to do the work. We are paying top dollar so they will hurry the project, and the new parking lot should be ready early next year. We are very happy about this, and hope that you will be too. In the meantime, please refrain from parking on the neighbors' lawns.

1. Why are the neighbors upset?
2. How do employees feel about the shortage of parking?
3. How does the speaker feel about the contractor?

Target 25

Part 2

Why don't you use milk in your coffee?
(A) I take milk for my cough.
(B) I prefer it black.
(C) Tea, thank you.

Part 3

Man: I can't read when I travel by car. That's why I travel by plane or train.

Woman: I'm the same way. I get a lot of work done on the train, and it's so convenient.

Man: Yes, it is convenient, though normally I find a plane to be more comfortable. Are you traveling on business today?

Woman: Actually, no. I'm traveling for another reason. I'm going to the beach for a short vacation.

1. Why don't they travel by car?
2. Why does the woman like the train?
3. Why is the woman traveling today?

Part 4

Because of a work slowdown, all flights will be delayed. We apologize to our passengers for the inconvenience and hope to have them on their way as soon as possible. In the meantime, there are several restaurants in the airport if you would like some refreshments while waiting for your flight. We suggest that you take advantage of them now, as all airport restaurants will close at midnight and won't reopen until tomorrow morning at six. At this time we are unable to say when each flight will leave. If you leave the gate area, please pay careful attention to the announcements so that you can hear when your flight is ready for boarding.

1. Why is there a delay?
2. Why should passengers get something to eat now?
3. Why should passengers pay attention to the announcements?

Target 26

Part 2

I had only 10 minutes to finish my work, but you gave Tim a half-hour.
(A) Tim had three times the work.
(B) I did more than Tim.
(C) Tim finished in thirty minutes.

Part 3

Man: It's thirty degrees outside. Just last week it was ten degrees warmer.
Woman: I know. This is a record low temperature for this late in the winter.
Man: Well, at least it's not snowing.
Woman: Not yet, but just wait. They predict twelve inches of snow this weekend. That's twice as much snow as we got in that storm last month.

1. What do they think about the weather?
2. What was the temperature last week?
3. How much snow fell last month?

Part 4

When ordering supplies it is advisable to order in quantity. Products sold in bulk are cheaper. Buying a gross of pencils is less expensive than buying 144 individual pencils. Often suppliers will take off an additional ten percent when the total order exceeds $100.00. Another way to save on costs is to look for sales. In this area, it is common for office supply stores to hold seasonal sales where they offer discounts of 25% on most supplies. When calculating the total cost of your purchase, however, don't forget to take into account the sales tax. In our state, it's 5% of the total purchase price.

1. What is the potential discount on an order of $200?
2. During a seasonal sale, what would be the price of an item that normally costs $200?
3. How much sales tax is charged for a $200 purchase?

First News
Always Innovative & Informative

Target 27

Part 2

Did you like the book?
(A) No, it was too violent.
(B) I bought the book.
(C) Yes, we always do.

Part 3

Man: That speaker was really funny. I've never laughed so hard.
Woman: I know. Where did he get those jokes?
Man: And this hotel is such a great place for a banquet. The food they gave us to eat was fantastic, and I couldn't believe how big the portions were.
Woman: You're right about the food, and the décor is so lovely. But, you know, it's a bit on the expensive side. I'd expected it to be cheaper. I was uncomfortable when I found out the price.

1. What did they like about the speaker?
2. What is the man's opinion of the hotel?
3. What does the woman think of the hotel?

Part 4

Moviegoers, take out your handkerchiefs. This is a four-hanky movie. You will start crying within ten minutes of the opening credits and will continue until the lights go up at the end. We recommend seeing this movie at the new Royal Deluxe Movie Theater, which just opened last month. They have a great lineup of Hollywood hits for the next few months. It's worth the higher cost of their tickets for the extra-big comfortable seats, not to mention the delicious snacks, including the best hot popcorn in town. The theater's convenient location means you have no excuse not to visit it at least once. It's right downtown, not far from the Central subway station and close to all the popular restaurants.

1. What kind of movie is it?
2. What does the speaker say about the movie theater?
3. What does the speaker say about the theater's location?

Target 28

Part 2

What are you talking about?
(A) We're listening to the radio.
(B) I'm talking about my vacation.
(C) It's about over.

Part 3

Man: Would you consider yourself a generous person?
Woman: Not at all. I'm very tight with money.

Man: What a shame. I won't ask for your help, then.
Woman: Don't take it personally. I really like you, it's just that I'm this way with everyone.

1. What does the man mean?
2. What describes the woman?
3. What does the woman think of the man?

Part 4

I regret to announce that as of this afternoon I will no longer serve as your Managing Director. The Board of Directors asked me to submit my letter of resignation and I have done so. They told me to leave by the close of business today. I want to thank you for the privilege of having worked with you all. I would also like to express my heartfelt gratitude for the support that many of you have given me during this difficult time, and for all your expressions of concern. I plan to take the next few weeks to rest, then I am hoping to open up a consulting business, as several of my colleagues have encouraged me to do.

1. What changes are taking place in the company?
2. Who is the speaker addressing?
3. What does the speaker plan to do soon?

Target 29

Part 2

If you can get up early, we leave at dawn.
(A) Sure. I'll set my alarm clock.
(B) We left in the afternoon.
(C) If we had thought about it.

Part 3

Man: If we had asked for less money, the budget would have been approved.
Woman: But then we wouldn't have had enough to complete the project.
Man: Now we don't have money or a way to complete the project. If we rewrite the budget, maybe it will be approved.
Woman: It can't hurt. We have plenty of time. If we get the money by September, we can still finish the work before the first of next year.

1. What should the speakers have done?
2. What does the man want to do now?
3. When do they need the money?

Part 4

If the prices of stock continue to fall, investors will wait for the prices to hit bottom and then begin to buy. A down market has a positive side. This is the wise way to interpret the market and make money in it. Inexperienced investors, however, don't always follow this method. If an inexperienced investor sees a high-priced

stock, he tends to buy it, thinking, "This stock must be worth a lot." He doesn't understand that by paying top dollar for his shares, he is more likely to lose money. Investors new to the market should educate themselves. They should read as much as they can about the market and investigate the stocks that interest them. Most of all, they should always work with a stockbroker. This is the best way to avoid losing money.

1. What will investors do if stock prices decrease?
2. What do inexperienced investors tend to do?
3. How can an investor avoid losing money?

Target 30

Part 2

Shouldn't we leave more time to get there?
(A) I left my watch at home.
(B) I don't drive anymore.
(C) Yes, let's leave earlier.

Part 3

Man: Maybe we should start with your report.
Woman: What if we save mine for last?
Man: No, I want yours to be first. Your budget projections are important for everything else we'll be discussing during the rest of the meeting.
Woman: All right, but I think it would be a good idea for you to remind everyone not to arrive late. I hate to be interrupted by late arrivals.

1. What does the man suggest the woman do?
2. Why does he want the woman to do this?
3. What does the woman suggest the man do?

Part 4

With the unemployment figures rising and the number of homeless increasing, it is important for all of us to consider those less fortunate. Shouldn't we all try to help those in need as much as we can? Rather than trying to aid each individual we come across, the best way to help is through contributing to a charitable organization. There are many worthy ones right here in our city. If you would like information to help you choose an organization to donate to, you may want to visit our Web site at *www.radioabc.com*. There you will find a detailed list of all local aid organizations. Don't forget that while we tend to think of those in need during the colder times of year, there are people who need your help all year-round, even when the holiday season has passed and the weather is warmer.

1. What does the man suggest?
2. How does the speaker suggest listeners get information to do this?
3. When should listeners do this?

Target 31

Part 2

We're going out for coffee if you want to join us.
(A) I'll have a tea with milk and sugar.
(B) The café around the corner
(C) Thanks, but I'm too busy right now.

Part 3

Woman: Why is this train so late? It's cold on this platform.
Man: There's a coffee shop right inside the station. Let me get you some hot coffee.
Woman: Would you? Thanks. That'll get us warm. Would you like me to pay for it? I think I have some change here.
Man: Don't worry about it. I'll take care of it. Can I get you something else while I'm inside? A newspaper to read on the train, perhaps?

1. How will they get warm?
2. What does the woman offer the man?
3. What does the man offer to get for the woman?

Part 4

Anyone who is traveling with small infants or who needs extra time to find his or her seat may board the aircraft at this time. First class passengers and our Frequent Flyer cardholders are invited to board at this time as well. If you need assistance finding your seat, please ask a flight attendant for help. Once we are in the air, flight attendants will come around with free snacks and drinks for everyone. Lunch will be served later on. Our pilot has a special offer for children today. After the meal is served, all children ages five to twelve are invited to visit the cockpit and talk with the pilot and copilot. Please talk with a flight attendant if your child is interested in this.

1. What is being offered?
2. What will be offered during the flight?
3. What is offered especially for children?

Target 32

Part 2

Would you mind opening the window?
(A) Not at all. It is warm in here.
(B) I opened the door.
(C) The curtains are new.

Part 3

Man: Do you think you would have time to mail this letter? I really want to stay home and finish this novel.
Woman: Yes, I could do it on my way to the bank. As long as you're staying home, would you mind sweeping the floor? It really needs to be done today.
Man: All right, all right, I'll do it now, then I'll read my book.

1. What did the man ask the woman to do?
2. What did the woman ask the man to do?
3. When did she want him to do this?

Part 4

Ladies and gentlemen: The management would like to thank you for your cooperation in using only the lobby area for cigarette and cigar smoking. We would also like to thank you for your enthusiastic reception to Act I. Now, would you kindly return to your seats? The second act is about to begin. Out of respect for the actors and your fellow theatergoers, please remember to turn off your cell phones and pagers before entering the auditorium, and refrain from talking in loud voices. Thank you.

1. What does the speaker suggest the audience do?
2. Where is smoking allowed?
3. What is the audience requested to do before entering the auditorium?

Target 33

Part 2

I'm not in the mood to eat another dinner at home.
(A) So you want to go to a restaurant?
(B) You're always in a good mood at home.
(C) I had dinner at home.

Part 3

Man: Don't be mad at me. I'm only five minutes late.
Woman: This is the last time I'm waiting for you. I mean it.
Man: You know I always have a good excuse, but I won't bore you with one now. And I promise you that you'll never have to wait for me again.
Woman: Let's hope so. Come on, let's go get our tickets now, and by the way, I hope you brought your wallet because I left mine at home.

1. What does the woman imply?
2. What does the man imply?
3. What does the woman want the man to do?

Part 4

When completing the form, it is important to use a black ballpoint pen and to press firmly. You will be making four copies which will be distributed to the departments that will track your loan application. You will be contacted by each department head individually after they have reviewed your case. After you have completed the form, sign it at the bottom, then leave it with the receptionist. You will be contacted within two weeks of submitting the form.

1. What is the purpose of the form?
2. How will copies of the form be made?
3. When will the listener be contacted?

MINI-TEST FOR LISTENING COMPREHENSION
PARTS 1, 2, 3, AND 4

Part 1: Photographs

Directions: You will see a photograph. You will hear four statements about the photograph. Choose the statement that most closely matches the photograph and fill in the corresponding oval on your answer sheet.

1. Look at the photo marked number 1 in your test book.

   (A) The officer is at the controls.
   (B) Guests are tasting the appetizers.
   (C) The men are working at the buffet.
   (D) They are in charge of the bus.

When reading the audioscripts for Parts 1 and 2, allow a 5-second pause between each question.

2. Look at the photo marked number 2 in your test book.

   (A) The sheep are in the meadow.
   (B) Water gathered around the bucket.
   (C) Most of the votes are headed in.
   (D) The ship is leaving the harbor.

3. Look at the photo marked number 3 in your test book.

   (A) They wrote the check in the bank.
   (B) The trees are by the flowers.
   (C) The hall is very large.
   (D) The passengers are on the plane.

4. Look at the photo marked number 4 in your test book.

   (A) The studio is cluttered.
   (B) The announcer is leading a panel.
   (C) The man is holding a headset.
   (D) The flipchart contains the data.

5. Look at the photo marked number 5 in your test book.

   (A) The operator pushes a button.
   (B) The man is fixing the elevator.
   (C) He's putting a button on his shirt.
   (D) Stocks are going up.

6. Look at the photo marked number 6 in your test book.

   (A) They're boarding the plane.
   (B) They're entering a building.
   (C) They're watching a parade.
   (D) They're holding construction plans.

First News
Always Innovative & Informative

7. Look at the photo marked number 7 in your test book.

   (A) The wires carry electricity.
   (B) The laundry hangs from poles.
   (C) The light fixtures are tall.
   (D) The polls are open for the election.

8. Look at the photo marked number 8 in your test book.

   (A) The jewels are in the safe.
   (B) The woman works with her hands.
   (C) The optician is grinding lenses.
   (D) The woman saws metal.

9. Look at the photo marked number 9 in your test book.

   (A) The nurses are administering medication.
   (B) There are two purses at the reception desk.
   (C) The pharmacists are conferring.
   (D) The nurses are in front of the window.

10. Look at the photo marked number 10 in your test book.

   (A) She's holding out a newspaper.
   (B) She's writing a paper.
   (C) She's reading to the man.
   (D) She's serving a wafer.

Part 2: Question-Response

Directions: You will hear a question and three possible responses. Choose the response that most closely answers the question and fill in the corresponding oval on your answer sheet.

11. You live on Third Avenue, don't you?

    (A) About five o'clock.
    (B) Yes, on Third Avenue.
    (C) In ten minutes.

12. Why are you late?

    (A) My watch stopped.
    (B) I ate already.
    (C) I'll call you later.

13. Who are you waiting for?

    (A) I've lost a lot of weight.
    (B) I don't know the way.
    (C) My wife; she is meeting me here.

14. It's supposed to rain later.

    (A) I received the letter.
    (B) Then I'll wear my raincoat.
    (C) That train is always late.

15. Which chair is yours?

    (A) Mine is the one on the left.
    (B) We need to cheer loudly.
    (C) This exam is not fair.

16. When did he arrive?

    (A) By train.
    (B) Shortly after lunch.
    (C) In the mail.

17. How long have you worked here?

    (A) Only for a few months.
    (B) I work on Tuesdays.
    (C) She can't hear if you sing along.

18. Where did you park your car?

    (A) In the darkroom.
    (B) The park is easy to get to.
    (C) In the lot across the street.

19. What should I do now?

    (A) Why don't you make some coffee?
    (B) The wood is on the fire.
    (C) You were the first one here.

20. The meeting starts at ten, doesn't it?

    (A) The meat is frozen.
    (B) The car won't start.
    (C) At 10 A.M. sharp.

21. I don't like the color of these walls.

    (A) We could repaint them.
    (B) I enjoyed the ballgame.
    (C) He makes too many calls.

22. How large is your company?

    (A) It's about ten inches.
    (B) It's as big as a penny.
    (C) We have offices in ten
        countries.

23. Where would you like to eat?

    (A) Let's go to an Italian restaurant.
    (B) The heat is very bad in here.
    (C) I always eat at eight.

24. Why is there no electricity today?

    (A) I prefer to cook with gas.
    (B) The power company shut it off for an
        hour.
    (C) The elections are Saturday.

25. I'm going to the bank after lunch.

    (A) I'm very hungry.
    (B) Thank him for me, too.
    (C) Would you cash a check for me?

Part 3: Conversations

Directions: You will hear a conversation between two people. You will see three questions on each conversation and four possible answers. Choose the best answer to each question and fill in the corresponding oval on your answer sheet.

Questions 26 through 28 refer to the following conversation.

Man: This should be a fun evening for us. I've been looking forward to seeing the play.
Woman: Me too, though the reviews haven't been that good.
Man: It's nice to get out anyhow. We should get going soon. It's already after six.
Woman: You're right. The play doesn't start till seven, but with all this rain, the driving's sure to be slow.

26. What are the speakers going to do?
27. What time do they have to be there?
28. What is the weather?

Questions 29 through 31 refer to the following conversation.

Woman: We have to go over the plans for the conference. Can we meet for lunch sometime this week? There's a nice café near my office.
Man: What about Friday? I'm busy all the rest of the week.
Woman: That's the one day I can't. It'll have to be next week. Tuesday?
Man: Tuesday'll be fine, but let's meet at my office. We can order in some food to eat while we work.

29. What does the woman want to discuss at the meeting?
30. When will the speakers meet?
31. Where will the speakers meet?

Questions 32 through 34 refer to the following conversation.

Man: I'd like to exchange this shirt. It's too small.
Woman: Let's see. This is size sixteen. Do want to try eighteen?
Man: Yes, that sounds right. I want the same color though, and the same style, if possible.
Woman: Long sleeve, blue, yes we can do that.

32. Why is the man exchanging the shirt?
33. What size shirt does the man want?
34. What color shirt does he want?

Questions 35 through 37 refer to the following conversation.

Woman: Are you going to New York or Paris this fall?
Man: Neither. I want to spend my vacation some place warmer. I was thinking about Florida.
Woman: What about Hawaii? It's always warm there, even in the fall and winter.
Man: Yes, but that's far to go for just one week, don't you think?
Woman: One week is all you get? Wow! I get three weeks vacation at my job.

35. When does the man have his vacation?
36. Where does the woman suggest he go?
37. How many weeks is the man's vacation?

Questions 38 through 40 refer to the following conversation.

Man: Did I get any calls while I was in the meeting this morning?
Woman: Yes, there were seven. I left the messages on your desk for you.
Man: Thanks. I'll take care of them. Could you bring me a purchase order form, please? There're some in the supply closet.

38. Where was the man this morning?
39. How many messages did he get?
40. What does he want the woman to do?

Part 4: Talks

Directions: You will hear a talk given by a single speaker. You will see three questions on each talk, each with four possible answers. Choose the best answer to each question and fill in the corresponding oval on your answer sheet.

Questions 41 through 43 refer to the following weather report.

Man: At six A.M. the temperature at National Airport is 53 degrees. Today's forecast calls for rain early in the morning with skies clearing by noon. The rest of the day will be seasonably mild with winds developing in the evening.

41. What is the current temperature?
42. What should people take to work in the morning?
43. When will the weather clear up?

Questions 44 through 46 refer to the following announcement.

Man: Due to the extremely hot weather, the electric company is planning to turn off power in certain districts during the day. This will reduce the total demand for electricity and prevent a city-wide shutdown of electrical services. Power will not be out longer than two hours in your area. For further information, please visit our Web site at *www dot electricity dot com.* All areas affected by the shutdown are listed there, as well as the times that the power will be turned off in each area.

44. Why is power being turned off?
45. How long will power be off?
46. How can a customer get more information?

Questions 47 through 49 refer to the following announcement.

Man: Good morning, ladies and gentlemen. This is your cruise director speaking. It's 7:30 and it's a beautiful day at sea. We have a lot planned for you both on ship and on shore. The first shore excursion will depart from the Main Deck at 9 A.M. Anyone wishing to go ashore at this time should report to the lounge for a ticket. Enjoy your breakfast.

47. Where does this announcement take place?
48. What is required for the first excursion?
49. What time will the first excursion begin?

First News
Always Innovative & Informative

Questions 50 through 52 refer to the following advertisement.

Man: Are you tired of getting up to turn off the television? Tired of getting up to turn down the radio? Turn on the video recorder? Our new remote control will let you operate any electronic appliance in your home from a comfortable chair. Call our toll-free number for more information. No sales personnel will call your home. Call us today and receive absolutely free with no obligation a sample subscription to *Remote Review Magazine.* Offer good until the end of this month.

50. What is being offered?
51. How can a customer learn more?
52. When can a customer get a free magazine subscription?

MODEL TEST 1 LISTENING COMPREHENSION

Part 1: Photographs

Directions: You will see a photograph. You will hear four statements about the photograph. Choose the statement that most closely matches the photograph and fill in the corresponding oval on your answer sheet.

When reading the audioscripts for Parts 1 and 2, allow a 5-second pause between each question.

1. Look at the photo marked number 1 in your test book.

   (A) She's examining a patient.
   (B) She's holding a test tube.
   (C) She's preparing dinner.
   (D) She's watching a film.

2. Look at the photo marked number 2 in your test book.

   (A) They're sitting around a table.
   (B) They're washing their glasses.
   (C) They're enjoying their meal.
   (D) They're taking a nap.

3. Look at the photo marked number 3 in your test book.

   (A) The men are shaking hands.
   (B) The speaker is explaining the chart.
   (C) The workers are enjoying a quick meal.
   (D) The trainees are watching TV.

4. Look at the photo marked number 4 in your test book.

   (A) He's working on a car.
   (B) He's ordering a new card.
   (C) He's repairing his cart.
   (D) He's driving to work.

5. Look at the photo marked number 5 in your test book.

   (A) They're eating some fruit.
   (B) They're packing their bags.
   (C) They're opening a box.
   (D) They're loading a truck.

6. Look at the photo marked number 6 in your test book.

   (A) The flags fly from the roof.
   (B) The court is in session.
   (C) The ceiling is very low.
   (D) The yard is full of tourists.

7. Look at the photo marked number 7 in your test book.

   (A) The trolley car is late.
   (B) The street cart vendor sells fruit.
   (C) The women are carrying dresses.
   (D) The cafe is near the street.

8. Look at the photo marked number 8 in your test book.

   (A) There are two banks on the hill.
   (B) The field has been plowed.
   (C) The pipelines cross the field.
   (D) Pale limestone covers the site.

9. Look at the photo marked number 9 in your test book.

   (A) He's trimming the plant.
   (B) He's cleaning the floor.
   (C) He's sweeping with a broom.
   (D) He's putting away the vacuum.

10. Look at the photo marked number 10 in your test book.

    (A) A boat passes under the bridge.
    (B) The waterways are impassable.
    (C) The sailors went along the ridge.
    (D) The card game is called bridge.

Part 2: Question-Response

Directions: You will hear a question and three possible responses. Choose the response that most closely answers the question and fill in the corresponding oval on your answer sheet.

11. Good evening. How are you?

    (A) It's time for bed.
    (B) Fine, thank you.
    (C) I'm not Mr. Goode.

12. Is this your pen?

    (A) No, it's not mine.
    (B) I don't know what will happen.
    (C) Yes, he's European.

13. Why are you late?

    (A) Since about three o'clock.
    (B) My car wouldn't start.
    (C) There are more than eight.

14. Who is coming with us?

    (A) She came after us.
    (B) Mitch is combing his hair.
    (C) My sister wants to.

15. When does the meeting begin?

    (A) At nine A.M.
    (B) The windows are open.
    (C) The track meet is on Friday.

16. What's for dinner?

    (A) We're having steak.
    (B) My wife and her mother.
    (C) After I get home.

17. Where were you last week?

    (A) I was on vacation.
    (B) This weekend I'm at home.
    (C) The event will last a week.

18. How often do you play golf?

    (A) The play will be over at 10.
    (B) Get off the golf course.
    (C) Almost every Sunday.

19. Let me pay for dinner.

    (A) She looks much thinner.
    (B) Thank you. That's very generous.
    (C) Pay day is next Friday.

20. Are there any messages?

    (A) The massage room is over there.
    (B) Any of us could do it.
    (C) Your brother called three times.

21. What did the customer buy?

    (A) The customs officer is busy.
    (B) A pair of gloves.
    (C) He is nearby.

22. How much paper do we need?

    (A) Enough for ten copies.
    (B) The newspaper costs 25 cents.
    (C) I need to pay more.

23. When does the plane leave?

    (A) At the airport.
    (B) Before we take off.
    (C) In about 45 minutes.

24. Why don't you take a coffee break?

    (A) The cup was broken.
    (B) I have too much work.
    (C) The car brakes won't work.

First News
A l w a y s I n n o v a t i v e & I n f o r m a t i v e

25. Have you finished eating?

    (A) She finished the report.
    (B) The eggs haven't been beaten.
    (C) Yes, it was delicious.

26. Where is the hotel?

    (A) It's across from the park.
    (B) Rooms are $200 a night.
    (C) The elevator is around the corner.

27. Mr. Kim called while you were out.

    (A) Did he leave a message?
    (B) Yes, it's very cold out.
    (C) His file is on my desk.

28. Which desk is ours?

    (A) The hours are very long.
    (B) The one by the window.
    (C) Have a seat please.

29. It's very cold in here.

    (A) I like the winter.
    (B) I sold it last year.
    (C) I'll close the window.

30. How near is your office?

    (A) My earache is better.
    (B) My office is closed today.
    (C) It's only a few blocks from here.

31. Is this your pen or mine?

    (A) I'll open it when you want.
    (B) I think it's yours.
    (C) No, my pins are all copper.

32. What kind of books do you like to read?

    (A) I enjoy historical novels.
    (B) It looks like it's OK to proceed.
    (C) I couldn't find my book.

33. I'll be in a meeting until four.

    (A) Please close the door.
    (B) Then I'll call you after four.
    (C) There's seating for four.

34. Where did you have lunch?

    (A) I thought we were meeting for lunch
        tomorrow.
    (B) At the restaurant across the street.
    (C) Yes, let's go at noon.

35. Shouldn't we ask your father to join us?

    (A) He'd rather not come.
    (B) It's not that far.
    (C) The task was not finished.

36. Who was at the conference?

    (A) Our neighbors put up the fence.
    (B) The conference was yesterday.
    (C) Only people from our office attended.

37. There's a nice restaurant on the corner.

    (A) I need a rest.
    (B) I don't like ice cream.
    (C) Let's eat there.

38. Where can I leave my coat?

    (A) I live on 14th Street.
    (B) Just hang it in the hall closet.
    (C) You can leave a note if you want.

39. When did you place the order?

    (A) The race started at ten.
    (B) I'll place it by the door.
    (C) I sent the order by fax last night.

40. Are we almost done?

    (A) Yes, this is the last one.
    (B) I like my steak well done.
    (C) We won't have much fun.

Part 3: Conversations

Directions: You will hear a conversation between two people. You will see three questions on each conversation and four possible answers. Choose the best answer to each question and fill in the corresponding oval on your answer sheet.

When reading the audioscripts for Parts 3 and 4, allow an 8-second pause between each question.

Questions 41 through 43 refer to the following conversation.

Man: Can we meet at three o'clock? Or is four better for you?
Woman: Actually, I'll be in a conference until five.
Man: Let's meet then. I'll wait for you in my office.
Woman: OK. I'll bring those photocopies of the budget report.

41. When will the speakers meet?
42. Where will they meet?
43. What will the woman bring to the meeting?

Questions 44 through 46 refer to the following conversation.

Woman: Let's see…To go from Cleveland to Los Angeles you'll have to change planes in Chicago.
Man: Isn't there a direct flight?
Woman: No, but you could change planes in Denver instead. In fact, that would put you in Los Angeles one hour sooner.
Man: Fine. Can you get me on a flight tomorrow? I need to start this trip soon.
Woman: Yes, there's one at ten in the morning.

44. Where does the man want to go?
45. How will he travel?
46. When will he leave?

Questions 47 through 49 refer to the following conversation.

Man: Could you please bring two extra towels to Room 603?
Woman: Certainly, sir. The housekeeper will bring them right away.
Man: I'd like some more soap, too.

47. Where does this conversation take place?
48. What does the man ask for?
49. When will he get what he asks for?

Questions 50 through 52 refer to the following conversation.

Woman: The brochures arrived from the printers this morning.
Man: They came sooner than I expected.
Woman: Well, now I have to address and mail them. By the way, how many copies did we order?
Man: A thousand.
Woman: Great. That's twice as many as I need.

First News
A l w a y s I n n o v a t i v e & I n f o r m a t i v e

50. When did the brochures arrive?
51. What will the woman do now?
52. How many brochures does the woman need?

Questions 53 through 55 refer to the following conversation.

Man: I'm calling about the ad you had in today's paper for the catering position.
Woman: Do you have any experience?
Man: Yes, I've worked in the food and beverage industry for five years.
Woman: Wonderful. Can you come in for an interview next Monday?

53. What kind of job is the man applying for?
54. What does the woman ask the man about?
55. When does the woman want to interview the man?

Questions 56 through 58 refer to the following conversation.

Woman: Look at all this rain. I'm really getting tired of it, and more rain is predicted tomorrow.
Man: Really? Then I'll have to cancel my nine o'clock golf game. What a bore.
Woman: If you're not playing golf, you can go to the movies with me.
Man: If I'm not playing golf, I'm not going anywhere. I'll just stay home and take a rest.

56. Why can't the man play golf tomorrow?
57. What time did he plan to play golf?
58. What will he do tomorrow?

Questions 59 through 61 refer to the following conversation.

Man: Drive past the park and turn right. There's a bank on the corner. It's just across the street from the library.
Woman: Does it have a drive-in window?
Man: Yes, and there's a parking lot next door, too. It's easy to find. It's just five minutes from here.

59. Where does the woman want to go?
60. Where is it?
61. How long will it take to get there?

Questions 62 through 64 refer to the following conversation.

Woman: It's 9:30. You're fifteen minutes late. Why can't you ever arrive on time?
Man: Sorry. The bus was late.
Woman: Buses are always late in the rain. You should leave home earlier in bad weather.
Man: I'll just drive next time. It's faster.

62. What time is it in the conversation?
63. Why is the woman angry?
64. What will the man do next time?

Questions 65 through 67 refer to the following conversation.

Man: Let me check…Yes, I can get you on a flight next Sunday afternoon. I'll get you your seat assignment now. Window seat or aisle seat?
Woman: Window seat, please. Is that a dinner flight?
Man: Yes, and they'll show a movie, too.
Woman: Then that's all in order. Can I pay with this credit card?

65. What will the woman do?
66. When will she do it?
67. How will she pay for it?

Questions 68 through 70 refer to the following conversation.

Man: Good evening. Are you ready to order yet?
Woman: The menu looks wonderful. What do you recommend?
Man: The lamb with rice is a local dish. It's very good.
Woman: Yes, it looks delicious, but I'm a vegetarian. I'll have the vegetable plate. Can you bring it soon? I'm very hungry.

68. When does this conversation take place?
69. Who is the woman talking to?
70. What does the woman order?

Part 4: Talks

Directions: You will hear a talk given by a single speaker. You will see three questions on each talk, each with four possible answers. Choose the best answer to each question and fill in the corresponding oval on your answer sheet.

Questions 71 through 73 refer to the following announcement.

Man: This train provides service to all arrival and departure gates, baggage claims, and ticketing areas. Color-coded maps and signs are posted within each car. Please move to the center of the car and away from the doors. Please do not attempt to exit the train until it has come to a complete stop, the doors are fully opened, and the exit bell rings. Thank you.

71. Where is the train located?
72. Where should you stand when in a train car?
73. When can passengers get off the train?

Questions 74 through 76 refer to the following recording.

Woman: Thank you for calling the City Museum. We are open to the public from ten until six Monday through Saturday, and from one until five on Sundays. Information about special exhibits, classes, and lectures can be obtained by calling our Education Office at 548-6251. Admission to the museum costs fifteen dollars for adults and ten dollars for children ages five to twelve. Children under five are not charged admission. Museum members receive 25% off the normal admission prices.

74. When on Sundays is the museum open?
75. If you would like information about lectures, what should you do?
76. Who doesn't have to pay to enter the museum?

Questions 77 through 79 refer to the following announcement.

Man: Organizing your workday is the key to getting things done. Start every morning by making a list of things you need to do during the day. Next, rank each task on the list according to its importance. Work on the most important task first, and stay with it until it is completed. Then, move on to the next task. At the end of the day, review your list. Have you completed everything on your list? If so, very good. If not, save the uncompleted items for your next day's list.

77. What is the first step in getting organized?
78. What should you do next?
79. What is the last task of the day?

Questions 80 through 82 refer to the following advertisement.

Woman: Our holiday sale offers you great savings on new office furniture. All desks, chairs, tables, and filing cabinets are on sale. We also have sale prices on office accessories like lamps and bookcases. Now is the time to give your office a great new look at a low, low price. Don't wait. Hurry on down today. Sale ends Sunday.

80. What does the advertisement encourage you to do?
81. Which items does the ad mention?
82. When is the last day of the sale?

Questions 83 through 85 refer to the following advertisement.

Woman: Are you successful? Pass some of that success along to a new generation by serving as a volunteer tutor. With as little as two hours a week, you can help a child with his schoolwork and share your love of learning. Children of all ages are waiting for your help. Call your local school system today. The only requirement is a desire to help children. Special training or a college degree are not necessary. Must be over eighteen to participate.

83. What is the announcement for?
84. How much time does it take to participate?
85. What must people have to participate?

Questions 86 through 88 refer to the following weather report.

Woman: Here's today's weather report. Temperatures will be in the mid sixties with breezes of ten to fifteen miles per hour. The sun will shine all day with no clouds expected. It's a great day to spend some time outdoors. The same great weather conditions will continue tomorrow and till the end of the week. Fog will roll in late Friday and heavy rainstorms are expected on Saturday.

86. What is the approximate temperature for today?
87. What does the weather forecaster suggest that people do?
88. What will the weather be like tomorrow?

Questions 89 through 91 refer to the following advertisement.

Woman: Our special ski weekend is a great value. One terrific price includes two nights at our mountain lodge with continental breakfast and gourmet dinner. Ski equipment is available from the hotel's rental shop for an additional fee. Certified ski instructors provide classes for all ability levels. Spend your next ski vacation with us. Book now and receive a third night free. Offer ends January fifteenth.

89. What is included in the cost of the lodge?
90. Who can take ski lessons?
91. What do you get if you make a reservation before January 15th?

Questions 92 through 94 refer to the following announcement.

Woman: We are experiencing delays of up to forty-five minutes on the inbound subway line, due to damage to the tracks. Trains are currently running every fifteen minutes. In addition, special buses are available to carry commuters
around the damaged portions of the track.

92. How long are the delays?
93. What is causing the delays?
94. What are they doing to help people commute quickly?

Questions 95 through 97 refer to the following news item.

Man: There was an underground explosion today at the corner of Main Street
and Central Avenue. Authorities do not yet know the cause, but they suspect a leaking gas pipe. Streets in the area were closed, and workers were
evacuated from nearby office buildings. In spite of the force of the explosion, no injuries were reported.

95. What happened at Central and Main?
96. What was probably the cause of the problem?
97. What happened to nearby office workers?

Questions 98 through 100 refer to the following talk.

Man: Before you go, I'd like to remind everyone about Friday. Class is canceled
that day, so you can tour the city's new art museum. Don't forget to do
the reading assignment, Chapter 10 in your textbooks, before then.
Remember to bring money for lunch and a warm sweater or jacket with
you on the trip. Unfortunately, photography isn't allowed in the museum,
so leave your cameras at home. The bus leaves promptly at nine o'clock,
so please arrive fifteen minutes before that time. We will not wait for late-
comers. You will return at 3:30. The museum is fantastic, so you should
have a great time.

98. Who will listen to this announcement?
99. What should people bring on the trip?
100. What time should they arrive for the morning bus?

MODEL TEST 2 LISTENING COMPREHENSION

Part 1: Photographs

Directions: You will see a photograph. You will hear four statements about the photograph. Choose the statement that most closely matches the photograph and fill in the corresponding oval on your answer sheet.

When reading the audioscripts for Parts 1 and 2, allow a 5-second pause between each question.

1. Look at the photo marked number 1 in your test book.

    (A) They're filing the papers.
    (B) They're signing the documents.
    (C) They're flying the plane.
    (D) They're reading a book.

2. Look at the photo marked number 2 in your test book.

    (A) The sign is pointing the way.
    (B) The staff is chopping vegetables.
    (C) The trainees are leaving the kitchen.
    (D) The cooks are preparing a meal.

3. Look at the photo marked number 3 in your test book.

    (A) He's watching the clock.
    (B) He's pushing a button.
    (C) He's taking a call.
    (D) He's moderating a panel.

4. Look at the photo marked number 4 in your test book.

    (A) The couple is viewing art.
    (B) The paintings are all the same size.
    (C) Pictures are stacked on the floor.
    (D) The gallery visitors are resting.

5. Look at the photo marked number 5 in your test book.

    (A) The passengers are on the plane.
    (B) The concourse is empty.
    (C) The passengers are waiting at the airport.
    (D) The bags are on the truck.

6. Look at the photo marked number 6 in your test book.

    (A) They're looking at their laptop outdoors.
    (B) They're making coffee for two.
    (C) They're pointing to each other.
    (D) They're waiting for a table.

7. Look at the photo marked number 7 in your test book.

    (A) Cranes are standing in the water.
    (B) The trains are passing on a bridge.
    (C) Narrow carts are going through the tunnel.
    (D) Pedestrians are crossing the bridge.

8. Look at the photo marked number 8 in your test book.

    (A) The auditorium is crowded.
    (B) The audience is waiting in the aisle.
    (C) People are watching a slide presentation.
    (D) The chairs are by the door.

9. Look at the photo marked number 9 in your test book.

    (A) Both men are wearing glasses.
    (B) Both men are reading the news.
    (C) The speakers are standing at their booth.
    (D) The men are wearing name tags.

10. Look at the photo marked number 10 in your test book.
    (A) The pharmacist is holding the medicine.
    (B) The woman is counting the pills.
    (C) The farmer is opening the bottle.
    (D) The typist is using the keyboard.

Part 2: Question-Response

Directions: You will hear a question and three possible responses. Choose the response that most closely answers the question and fill in the corresponding oval on your answer sheet.

11. Did you have a good trip?

    (A) Yes, thank you. It was very pleasant.
    (B) My vacation is in August.
    (C) We are good friends.

12. How long will you stay?

    (A) There are twenty-four hours in a day.
    (B) I always stay at a hotel.
    (C) Only one week.

13. Who wrote this letter?

    (A) I did, and I typed it, too.
    (B) She can read better than I.
    (C) The exchange rate is better today.

14. What color shirt are you wearing?

    (A) I need a long-sleeve shirt.
    (B) It's light blue.
    (C) Everyone knows where I am.

15. When will she call me?

    (A) She said after lunch.
    (B) I'll return this call soon.
    (C) She called me lazy.

16. Why are you waiting in here?

    (A) It's too cold to wait outside.
    (B) I knew my way there.
    (C) The waiter is new here.

17. Where is your family from?

    (A) All her books made her famous.
    (B) My children are at school.
    (C) My parents were born here.

18. How soon will you be ready?

    (A) In about ten minutes.
    (B) Her son left early.
    (C) We said we wanted red.

19. The food here is excellent.

    (A) They always serve good meals at this restaurant.
    (B) I can't hear it very well, either.
    (C) We haven't been able to sell it.

20. The train leaves at four, doesn't it?

    (A) It stopped raining at four.
    (B) This time let's take the train.
    (C) Yes, it departs every hour on the hour.

21. All lines are busy. Will you hold?

    (A) No, I'll call back.
    (B) I'm not busy this evening.
    (C) She's not very old.

22. Who is working late this evening?

    (A) Good night. Sleep well.
    (B) All of us—until we finish this report.
    (C) I always eat after ten.

23. When was the invoice sent?

    (A) Two weeks ago.
    (B) My voice is very soft.
    (C) We went in March.

24. I can't find my cell phone.

    (A) I'll call you tonight.
    (B) I think I saw it on your desk.
    (C) His home is near the park.

25. Why don't you come over tonight?

    (A) Thank you. I'd like to.
    (B) His pants are too tight.
    (C) There's more light over here.

26. Which team is your favorite?

    (A) I prefer tea with milk.
    (B) I like them both.
    (C) Your fee seems right.

27. The traffic was very heavy today.

    (A) That's too heavy to lift.
    (B) There's a traffic light on the corner.
    (C) The traffic's always bad when it rains.

28. Where is the fax machine?

    (A) It's next to the photocopier.
    (B) All the facts are true.
    (C) The magazine is on the desk.

29. What day is she coming?

    (A) She left yesterday.
    (B) He will come next month.
    (C) On Tuesday, I think.

30. Who made the reservation?

    (A) You need to reserve a table.
    (B) My travel agent.
    (C) The housekeeper made the beds.

31. Do we have to use a pen?

    (A) No, use a pencil if you want.
    (B) I'll tell you when.
    (C) We are used to having it open.

32. What is the deadline for this project?

    (A) He died last week.
    (B) We need to finish it this week.
    (C) The bid was rejected.

33. I read this book in just three days.

    (A) You're a fast reader.
    (B) I like having free days.
    (C) Red is a nice color.

34. Who is standing by the window?

    (A) That's a client of mine.
    (B) The plant is by the window.
    (C) The carpenter is sanding the chair.

35. There's a package for you on your desk.

    (A) He packed last night.
    (B) It must be the new jacket I ordered.
    (C) There's a post office on the next block.

36. How can I get my pants pressed?

    (A) Don't be depressed.
    (B) Send them to the cleaners.
    (C) I got a new pair last week.

37. When are you going to start exercising?

    (A) I start my day with a healthful breakfast.
    (B) The exercises are at the end of the book.
    (C) I'll start when I have more free time.

38. What kept you so long?

    (A) I'm sorry. I couldn't get off the phone.
    (B) I think I'll keep the long one.
    (C) They had long stems and wide caps.

39. Could you summarize the article for me?

    (A) I've never liked that size art.
    (B) You should read the article yourself.
    (C) Summer is my favorite season, too.

40. Where would you recommend I go?

    (A) At this time of year, I would go south.
    (B) I'll go sometime soon.
    (C) You should comment on this memo.

Part 3: Conversations

Directions: You will hear a conversation between two people. You will see three questions on each conversation and four possible answers. Choose the best answer to each question and fill in the corresponding oval on your answer sheet.

When reading the audioscripts for Parts 3 and 4, allow an 8-second pause between each question.

Questions 41 through 43 refer to the following conversation.

Man: Can you type this memo for me?
Woman: I'd be glad to, but I have to finish these letters first.
Man: I can't wait. I need it before noon. I'll ask Mr. Brown to do it.
Woman: Sorry I can't help you. Today's a really busy day for me.

41. What does the man want the woman to do?
42. When does he need it done?
43. Why can't the woman help him?

Questions 44 through 46 refer to the following conversation.

Woman: I'll take two of these shirts—a blue one and a checked one. Size sixteen.
Man: Two shirts comes to forty-five dollars. Will that be cash, or shall I put it on your credit card?
Woman: Actually, I have a gift certificate.

44. What is the woman buying?
45. How much does she have to pay?
46. How does she want to pay?

Questions 47 through 49 refer to the following conversation.

Man: Do you need the copier?
Woman: Yes. I have to make 150 copies by eleven. Do you need it, too?
Man: Yes, but you go ahead. My copies don't have to be ready until the meeting at four.
Woman: Thanks. My boss wants these done right away. I have to put them in this morning's mail.

47. How many copies does the woman need to make?
48. When does she have to have them finished?
49. What will she do when the copies are made?

Questions 50 through 52 refer to the following conversation.

Woman: Would you like to order one of our house specialties?
Man: What do you suggest?
Woman: The fish with mushrooms is very good. But it's cooked fresh, so there's a fifteen-minute wait.
Man: I don't mind. I'd like to try the fish. I'll just sit here with a drink while I wait.

50. Where does this conversation take place?
51. How long will the man have to wait?
52. What will he do while he waits?

Questions 53 through 55 refer to the following conversation.

Man: I'm afraid Mr. Wu is out of the office right now. He's at a meeting downtown. Would you like to leave a message?
Woman: Yes. Please tell him I called.
Man: May I have your name and number please?
Woman: Of course. I'm Jean Soto and my number is 564-2011. Tell Mr. Wu I'll be in my office at two thirty, and he can call me then.

53. Where is Mr. Wu now?
54. What does the woman want to do?
55. When will the woman be in her office?

Questions 56 through 58 refer to the following conversation.

Woman: Oh, no! I left my briefcase in the cab this morning.
Man: You'll have to report it to the cab company. I have the number of their office right here on my desk.
Woman: Thanks. I'll call right now. Can I use your phone?
Man: Go right ahead. Did you have something important in your briefcase?
Woman: Yes! I had all the notes I'll need for tomorrow's meeting. I really hope I can get it back soon.

56. Where did the woman leave her briefcase?
57. What is in the briefcase?
58. When does she need the contents of the briefcase?

Questions 59 through 61 refer to the following conversation.

Man: I'll need a wake-up call at six tomorrow morning. I have to catch an eight o'clock flight.
Woman: You might want to get up earlier. It's going to rain tomorrow and bad weather always makes traffic slower, especially to the airport.
Man: Oh, I didn't know that. All right, then, I'd like a 5:30 wake-up call.

59. Why does the man want to wake up early?
60. How will the weather be tomorrow?
61. What time will the man wake up?

Questions 62 through 64 refer to the following conversation.

Woman: They're showing a great movie tonight at the college student center. Do you want to go with me?

Man: Sorry. I'm really tired. I'm just going to go home and get to bed early.

Woman: Are you sure? I'm meeting some friends for dinner before the movie. It'll be fun.

Man: I know, but I'm too tired. And don't you stay out late. Remember we have to catch the train right after breakfast tomorrow.

62. Where is the woman going to see the movie?
63. What will the man do tonight?
64. When will they take the train tomorrow?

Questions 65 through 67 refer to the following conversation.

Man: Did you get the photocopy of the report I sent you?

Woman: No. When did you send it?

Man: On Monday. You should have it by today. I wonder what happened to it.

Woman: Many things get lost in the mail. You'd better send me another copy. Send it to my home address this time.

65. What did the man send the woman?
66. When did he send it?
67. What does the woman ask the man to do?

Questions 68 through 70 refer to the following conversation.

Woman: Do you play golf at the club?

Man: Never. I don't like it. Tennis is my sport.

Woman: Really? I used to take lessons at the park, but I was never any good at it.

Man: You have to practice a lot. I'm on the courts five days a week. I play with a group at the community center.

Woman: I don't have time for that. But I swim at the hotel pool two or three times a week.

68. What sport does the man enjoy?
69. Where does he practice it?
70. How often does he practice it?

Part 4: Talks

Directions: You will hear a talk given by a single speaker. You will see three questions on each talk, each with four possible answers. Choose the best answer to each question and fill in the corresponding oval on your answer sheet.

Questions 71 through 73 refer to the following advertisement.

Woman: Don't you hate to waste time waiting in airports? On your next business trip, put that time to use with our new portable computer. It's dime-thin and has a fully foldable keyboard. Stop wasting time. Call us today. Or visit our Web site—*www dot computers now dot com.* All orders made on our Web site receive a 15% discount. Offer good until the end of this month. Some restrictions may apply. Please visit our Web site for more complete information.

71. Who is the audience for this advertisement?
72. Why is this computer useful away from the office?
73. How can a customer get a discount on this computer?

Questions 74 through 76 refer to the following weather report.

Man: A winter storm warning is in effect for this area through midnight tonight. Heavy rain is expected, turning to snow by late this afternoon. This will create ice hazards tonight as the rain and snow freeze over. This means dangerous icy conditions for rush hour tomorrow. However, warmer temperatures tomorrow afternoon should melt most of the ice and clear the roads. The skies will remain cloudy, but temperatures will stay above freezing most of the afternoon.

74. What best describes the weather conditions the area is facing?
75. What problems will this weather cause tomorrow?
76. How will the weather be tomorrow afternoon?

Questions 77 through 79 refer to the following news item.

Man: A study out today suggests that people who have office jobs are less fit than people who have more active jobs. Sitting all day at a desk simply reduces opportunities for exercise. Experts suggest that office workers incorporate more activity into their day by climbing stairs, going for walks during lunch, and riding bicycles to work. Eating right is also important. People need to stay away from sugary donuts and other sweets during coffee breaks. Instead, they should bring fresh fruit or vegetables to the office as a snack.

77. According to the study, who is expected to be the least fit?
78. Which is mentioned as a way to get more exercise?
79. What advice is given about eating?

First News
Always Innovative & Informative

Questions 80 through 82 refer to the following recording.

Woman: You have reached 479-8526. I am not able to take your call right now. Please leave your name, your number, the date and time of your call, and a brief message at the sound of the tone. I will get back to you as soon as I can. If you need to reach me during the workday, please call my office number—499-4778. Thank you.

80. Where would you be likely to hear this message?
81. What type of message should you leave?
82. What will happen if a caller dials 499-4778?

Questions 83 through 85 refer to the following advertisement.

Man: It's tax time again. And if you hate to do your taxes, let us do them instead. Just provide us with your financial records. Our qualified staff of accountants can prepare your return for you, quickly and easily. Fees are based on an hourly rate. The deadline for paying taxes is just one month away, so don't delay. Call today to make your appointment.

83. What can this company do for you?
84. How does the company determine its fees?
85. What should listeners do today?

Questions 86 through 88 refer to the following news item.

Woman: Several airlines reduced fares today in an attempt to increase ticket sales. Some fares were slashed by as much as 50% for round-trip tickets. This is seen in the industry as an attempt to win customers from competing regional airlines. Figures released last week showed that Sky King Airways, formerly the region's dominant airline, had lost 25% of its customer base over the past year.

86. What did the airlines do to increase sales?
87. Why have these airlines lost customers?
88. What percentage of its customers did Sky King Airways lose in the past year?

Questions 89 through 91 refer to the following recording.

Man: Thank you for calling our computer helpline. If you need assistance with one of our software packages, press one. If you need the names of qualified service personnel in your area, press two. If you would like an update on our newest products, press three. Otherwise, stay on the line and a customer service representative will assist you.

89. Who would be likely to call this number?
90. What will happen if the caller presses 1?
91. What should you do if you want information not listed?

Always Innovative & Informative

Questions 92 through 94 refer to the following announcement.

Woman: Welcome aboard Flight six-two-seven to Houston. We'll be flying today at a cruising altitude of thirty-five thousand feet. Our flying time will be two hours and forty minutes, putting us at our gate on time, at four forty-seven Houston time. We have had some reports of turbulence on this route today so we ask that you remain seated with your seat belt on. But once you get to Houston, the skies will be clear and the sun bright. In fact you'll have cloudless, sunny skies all week, if Houston is your final destination. Thank you for flying with us.

92. What is the destination for this flight?
93. What does the captain say about the flight?
94. What is the weather like there?

Questions 95 through 97 refer to the following news item.

Man: Due to the large amounts of rain in the area, many people have had to leave their homes and stay in relief shelters until the flooding subsides. Food supplies at the relief centers are running low. We are asking for help from the public to increase our food supplies. If you can donate food, contact this radio station for the address of the food collection center nearest you.

95. What kind of problem does the area have?
96. Why are local relief centers running low on food?
97. If you want to donate food, where should you take it?

Questions 98 through 100 refer to the following message.

Woman: Hello. This is your Veriphone voicemail system. Please listen carefully to the following information. We are changing your voicemail system in seven days. On August 1st, some of the codes will change. You will control your voicemail with new numbers. For example, you will press "seven" to delete a message and you will press "nine" to save a message. You can press the star key now to hear all ten of the new codes, or you can go to our Web site, at *www.veriphone.com*, and read the entire message. Thank you.

98. What will take place in seven days?
99. How can a customer save a message?
100. How can a customer learn about all of the new codes?

MODEL TEST 3 LISTENING COMPREHENSION

Part 1: Photographs

Directions: You will see a photograph. You will hear four statements about the photograph. Choose the statement that most closely matches the photograph and fill in the corresponding oval on your answer sheet.

When reading the audioscripts for Parts 1 and 2, allow a 5-second pause between each question.

1. Look at the photo marked number 1 in your test book.

   (A) All the plates are empty.
   (B) The waiter's taking an order.
   (C) The woman is watching the servers.
   (D) The menu is on the table.

2. Look at the photo marked number 2 in your test book.

   (A) They're opening a metal cabinet.
   (B) They're testing a new computer.
   (C) They're taking off their coats.
   (D) They're standing by the equipment.

3. Look at the photo marked number 3 in your test book.

   (A) The outside lane is closed to traffic.
   (B) People are waiting at the bus stop.
   (C) The cars are being serviced.
   (D) The tourists are taking a stroll.

4. Look at the photo marked number 4 in your test book.

   (A) The people are standing in the rain.
   (B) The passengers are ready to board.
   (C) The plane is taking off.
   (D) The grain is being harvested.

5. Look at the photo marked number 5 in your test book.

   (A) The ducks are on the pond.
   (B) The trucks are at the loading dock.
   (C) The ship is being loaded.
   (D) The shoppers are in the aisle.

6. Look at the photo marked number 6 in your test book.

   (A) The workers are in the plant.
   (B) The players are on the field.
   (C) The field is in front of the factory.
   (D) The grass is being cut.

7. Look at the photo marked number 7 in your test book.

   (A) They're sitting in the chairs.
   (B) They're washing the dishes.
   (C) They're cooking dinner.
   (D) They're setting the table.

8. Look at the photo marked number 8 in your test book.

   (A) He's addressing the audience.
   (B) He's getting dressed.
   (C) He's delivering the mail.
   (D) He's taking a walk.

9. Look at the photo marked number 9 in your test book.

   (A) The students are in the hallway.
   (B) The classroom is empty.
   (C) The men are by the blackboard.
   (D) The professor is in her office.

10. Look at the photo marked number 10 in your test book.

    (A) The roads are under repair.
    (B) The highways pass over one another.
    (C) The cars are stopped at the traffic light.
    (D) The bridges cross over the river.

Part 2: Question-Response

Directions: You will hear a question and three possible responses. Choose the response that most closely answers the question and fill in the corresponding oval on your answer sheet.

11. How hungry are you?

    (A) Not very. I had a late lunch.
    (B) I've never been to Hungary.
    (C) I'm thirty years old.

12. Do you play basketball?

    (A) Yes, I emptied the wastebasket.
    (B) The game was already over.
    (C) Actually, swimming is my sport.

13. This coffee is cold.

    (A) I can't stop coughing.
    (B) Gold is more expensive.
    (C) Let me make you a fresh cup.

14. How far is the museum from here?

    (A) Most of the paintings are modern.
    (B) It's about a ten-minute walk.
    (C) It was about a decade ago.

15. When did you buy your house?

    (A) When we got married.
    (B) We drove by it this morning.
    (C) It was very expensive.

16. What is the book about?

    (A) The book is on the shelf.
    (B) It costs about five dollars.
    (C) It's a war story.

17. The museum is closed on Sunday.

    (A) Then let's go on Saturday.
    (B) These are my Sunday clothes.
    (C) I enjoy looking at art.

18. Which train should we take?

    (A) It won't rain today.
    (B) They teach a good class at the local college.
    (C) Let's take the express.

19. Why aren't these copies ready yet?

    (A) The copier is out of paper.
    (B) The cops are on the corner.
    (C) I already read it.

20. He's expected at noon, isn't he?

    (A) For a month.
    (B) She waited too long.
    (C) No, around 2 P.M.

21. How much was your hotel bill?

    (A) I paid with a credit card.
    (B) Over thirty stories.
    (C) Just under $500.

22. The rent is going up again next month.

    (A) I already lent you one.
    (B) Maybe we should look for a cheaper apartment.
    (C) This elevator's going up.

23. Why are you always on time?

    (A) I don't have a watch.
    (B) I hate to be late.
    (C) I always prefer lime to lemon.

24. The meeting is about to start.

    (A) I left it in the conference room.
    (B) I enjoyed meeting you, too.
    (C) I'll be there in a minute.

25. Who won the tennis match?

    (A) I don't smoke.
    (B) No, there were nine not ten.
    (C) The game was canceled.

26. What was the purpose of this visit?

    (A) The visitors left early.
    (B) He just wanted to say hello.
    (C) The proposal was on the list.

27. Which season is my favorite? Spring. Isn't it yours?

    (A) I always use salt and pepper.
    (B) I referred them to you.
    (C) Summer is my favorite.

28. I saw Jim at the party last night.

    (A) Really? How is he doing?
    (B) I like dancing.
    (C) This part is yours.

29. When does the mail come?

    (A) Every morning at eleven.
    (B) Milk is served at three.
    (C) You're welcome.

30. Where's the bank?

    (A) It's across from the post office.
    (B) You needn't thank me.
    (C) The ink is in the top drawer.

31. Is it going to rain today?

    (A) He's going tomorrow.
    (B) Why don't you complain?
    (C) I don't think so. The sky is clear.

32. How much should I tip the waiter?

    (A) I tipped the boat over.
    (B) Fifteen percent is sufficient.
    (C) Ten children waded in the water.

33. Who designed your house?

    (A) The same architect that did our office building.
    (B) I resigned this morning.
    (C) I use a mouse with my computer.

34. When did you arrive?

    (A) I'll be there around midnight tomorrow.
    (B) Last night's telecast was live from New York.
    (C) I got in early last night.

35. What is this shirt made of?

    (A) It was made in Hong Kong.
    (B) It's made of cotton.
    (C) Insert the cassette into the recorder.

36. Why doesn't this calculator work?

    (A) Maybe the batteries are dead.
    (B) Calcutta is in India.
    (C) No one works on Sunday.

37. Where did you study English?

    (A) The students are not going to England.
    (B) I studied it at school.
    (C) For six years.

38. Which sweater fits me better?

    (A) These sweat pants are too large for you.
    (B) The weather is better in the south.
    (C) The wool one fits you perfectly.

39. What time do you have?

    (A) I'm sorry. I don't have a watch.
    (B) I have both yours and mine.
    (C) In about twenty minutes.

40. Would you close the window please?

    (A) Of course. Are you cold?
    (B) Here take my clothes.
    (C) All teller windows are open.

Part 3: Conversations

Directions: You will hear a conversation between two people. You will see three questions on each conversation and four possible answers. Choose the best answer to each question and fill in the corresponding oval on your answer sheet.

When reading the audioscripts for Parts 3 and 4, allow an 8-second pause between each question.

Questions 41 through 43 refer to the following conversation.

Man: There's an art show in the park.
Woman: That sounds like fun. Can we go today after work?
Man: No, it closes at dark. Let's plan it for Sunday.

41. What do the speakers want to do?
42. Why can't they go after work?
43. When will they go?

Questions 44 through 46 refer to the following conversation.

Woman: I have your resume, and I'd like to talk with you about possible positions.
Man: That will be fine. When would you like to meet?
Woman: How about Thursday at 8:30?
Man: I'll see you then in your office.

44. What is the appointment for?
45. What time is the appointment for?
46. Where will the appointment take place?

Questions 47 through 49 refer to the following conversation.

Man: Your room number is 215. Here's the key. The elevators are on your left.
Woman: Can I get a morning paper tomorrow?
Man: Certainly. A paper can be delivered directly to your room.

47. Where does this conversation take place?
48. What is the woman's room number?
49. What will be delivered to the woman tomorrow?

Questions 50 through 52 refer to the following conversation.

Woman: Where's Mr. Chung? He's due to address the meeting this morning.
Man: He called from his car to say he'll be late. He's stuck in traffic.
Woman: Well, we can show the film first, while we're waiting for him.
Man: All right. I can have it ready to go in ten minutes. We'll be able to start the meeting right on time.

50. Why do they need Mr. Chung?
51. Why is Mr. Chung late?
52. When will the meeting start?

Questions 53 through 55 refer to the following conversation.

Man: I like the way they painted the lobby. It's important to have a nice entrance to an office building.
Woman: The white walls make it brighter.
Man: Yes, it never had enough light before.
Woman: Maybe they'll paint the elevators someday. It really should be done soon.
Man: Actually, I think the cafeteria's next. Painting it is due to start the week after next.

53. What was painted?
54. What was wrong with it before?
55. When will the cafeteria be painted?

Questions 56 through 58 refer to the following conversation.

Woman: How long will the repairs to the television set take?
Man: I called the company today. It'll take two weeks to get the parts, and then another week to install them.
Woman: Really? I thought they could do it sooner than that.
Man: I know. And we'll have to monitor them to make sure they get it done according to schedule.

56. What's broken?
57. When did the man talk to the company about repairs?
58. How long will the repairs take?

Questions 59 through 61 refer to the following conversation.

Man: My tire is flat. Where's the nearest garage?
Woman: There's a gas station just down the road. It's about a mile and a half from here, I think.
Man: Thank you. That's not too far to walk, I guess.
Woman: Yes, it is. I'll give you a ride.

59. Why does the man need a gas station?
60. How far away is the gas station?
61. How will the man get to the gas station?

Questions 62 through 64 refer to the following conversation.

Woman: I'd like to exercise more, but I can't seem to find the time.
Man: Exercise during your lunch break. We have a whole hour.
Woman: I always spend my lunch break at the cafeteria having lunch!
Man: I take fifteen minutes to have a quick lunch at my desk, then I take a forty-five-minute walk in the park. It's very relaxing.

62. How long is the lunch break?
63. What does the woman do during her lunch break?
64. Where does the man eat lunch?

Questions 65 through 67 refer to the following conversation.

Man: Excuse me. Can you tell me how to get to the history museum?

Woman: Sure. It's just three blocks from here. Go through the park, past the capitol building, then turn left at the post office.

Man: Thank you. That sounds easy to find.

Woman: Yes, but it's closed today. It's not open on Saturday and Sunday, just during the week.

65. Where does the man want to go?
66. How far away is this place?
67. When is this place open?

Questions 68 through 70 refer to the following conversation.

Woman: Excuse me. When are we due in Los Angeles?

Man: Well, this is normally a five-and-a-half hour flight, so we're supposed to land at two thirty.

Woman: I see. Will you be showing a movie?

Man: Yes. We're about to serve drinks and then lunch. Then we'll show a movie. Can I bring you anything? A magazine? A blanket?

Woman: Yes, thank you. I'd like a pillow so I can take a quick nap before lunch.

68. How long is the flight?
69. What will happen next?
70. What does the woman ask for?

Part 4: Talks

Directions: You will hear a talk given by a single speaker. You will see three questions on each talk, each with four possible answers. Choose the best answer to each question and fill in the corresponding oval on your answer sheet.

Questions 71 through 73 refer to the following announcement.

Man: The telephone number you have called is not in service. Please check the number in your telephone directory. Or, stay on the line and a customer service representative will be with you shortly. Please be advised that there is a charge of seventy-five cents per minute for assistance. Thank you.

71. What is wrong with the number that was dialed?
72. Who will help you if you stay on the line?
73. How much will you have to pay for help?

Questions 74 through 76 refer to the following announcement.

Woman: A contaminated-water alert has been issued for this area. It is possible that agricultural bacteria have invaded the water supply. Residents are asked to boil water for five minutes before using it for drinking or cooking. This will make the water safe. If you need further information, please call the Public Utilities Office at the following number: 344-9823. This has been a public service announcement brought to you by Radio WEBT.

74. What is wrong with the water supply?
75. How can residents make the water safe?
76. What can people do to get more information?

Questions 77 through 79 refer to the following advertisement.

Woman: Are you bored with your current job? Get computer training and start a new career. Our computer school can train you in just six months on the most popular business software. Job placement assistance is available at the end of the course. Are you currently working during the daytime? Don't worry! All our classes are taught evenings and weekends to accommodate the schedules of working people like you. Call now to register.

77. What kind of training does this school provide?
78. How long will the training take?
79. When are the classes taught?

Questions 80 through 82 refer to the following announcement.

Man: The Northeast train bound for New York and Boston is leaving in ten minutes from Track 27. Passengers for New York should board at the front of the train. Passengers for Boston should board at the rear.

80. Where is the train going?
81. Where should New York passengers board the train?
82. When is the train leaving?

Questions 83 through 85 refer to the following recording.

Man: You have reached the Smith Company. Our business hours are eight A.M. to six P.M. Monday through Friday. If you call back during those hours, we will be happy to assist you. Or, you may contact us in writing at one-seven-one-one Northwood Parkway, Greenville, California 97286. If you write to us about one of our products, please don't forget to include the serial number of the product and the name and address of the store where it was purchased.

83. When should you call back?
84. If you can't call back, how should you contact the company?
85. What information should be included in a letter about a product?

Questions 86 through 88 refer to the following announcement.

Woman: The Royal Hotel currently has positions open for desk clerks, waiters, and housekeepers. No experience is required; we will train new employees. Apply in person to the hotel manager. Good starting wage and opportunity for advancement.

86. How should you apply for these jobs?
87. What do the jobs offer, besides a good wage?
88. Which of the following jobs is offered?

Questions 89 through 91 refer to the following announcement.

Woman: Insert your ticket. Insert your ticket. Please pay eight dollars and fifty cents for two hours and twelve minutes. Remove your ticket. You will need it to exit the garage. Take your change.

89. Where can this recording be heard?
90. Why should you keep your ticket?
91. How much money does this ticket holder have to pay?

Questions 92 through 94 refer to the following announcement.

Woman: A heat-wave alert has been issued for the city and outlying suburbs. Temperatures are expected to be over one hundred degrees. Residents should follow these simple precautions to avoid heatstroke. Wear light-colored, loose-fitting clothes. Drink plenty of water, stay out of direct sunlight, and avoid strenuous exercise.

92. What problem can the city expect?
93. How high are temperatures expected to be?
94. How can citizens protect themselves?

Questions 95 through 97 refer to the following announcement.

Man: Many busy executives get work done by establishing a quiet hour. Ask your staff not to disturb you during this time, except in emergencies. Ask your secretary to hold telephone calls. Close your office door. Use this time to concentrate on demanding tasks.

95. What advice is given for busy executives?
96. How can you keep others from disturbing you?
97. What should you do during this time?

Questions 98 through 100 refer to the following announcement.

Man: Thank you for joining us this afternoon at the third annual International Musician Award Ceremony. Today we are giving out $20,000 in awards. Each musician honored today will receive an award of $5,000. Awardees use this money in various ways to further their careers. It may be used to pay for private lessons, to catch up on bills, or to take time off from work in order to be able to practice. Without the generous support of people like you, we wouldn't be able to honor our fine young musicians. Please continue to give generously. You can make a donation today by placing it in the red boxes in this room.

98. How often does this ceremony take place?
99. How many people are receiving awards today?
100. What are listeners asked to do?

MODEL TEST 4 LISTENING COMPREHENSION

Part 1: Photographs

Directions: You will see a photograph. You will hear four statements about the photograph. Choose the statement that most closely matches the photograph and fill in the corresponding oval on your answer sheet.

When reading the audioscripts for Parts 1 and 2, allow a 5-second pause between each question.

1. Look at the photo marked number 1 in your test book.

   (A) The lamp is on the wall.
   (B) The man is at his desk.
   (C) The phone is on the table.
   (D) The light is over the bed.

2. Look at the photo marked number 2 in your test book.

   (A) The trees are cut into lumber.
   (B) The pipeline runs down the mountain.
   (C) Water comes from the well.
   (D) Oil is transported by tankers.

3. Look at the photo marked number 3 in your test book.

   (A) The laboratory workers are in lab coats.
   (B) The doctor is examining the chart.
   (C) The woman is reading to the patient.
   (D) X-rays are behind the doctor.

4. Look at the photo marked number 4 in your test book.

   (A) The customer is ordering a meal.
   (B) They are learning to read.
   (C) The waiter is approaching the customer.
   (D) The guests are waiting to order.

5. Look at the photo marked number 5 in your test book.

   (A) He's driving to the luggage store.
   (B) He's packing for a trip.
   (C) He's going to put his suitcase in the car.
   (D) He's checking his bag at the station.

6. Look at the photo marked number 6 in your test book.

   (A) People are waiting for their flight to board.
   (B) Luggage is scattered throughout the hall.
   (C) People are planning for their trip.
   (D) Passengers get their luggage.

7. Look at the photo marked number 7 in your test book.

   (A) The man refers to the map.
   (B) The storm is approaching rapidly.
   (C) His glasses are bent and crooked.
   (D) The speaker is gesturing upwards.

8. Look at the photo marked number 8 in your test book.

   (A) He's running down the hall.
   (B) He's delivering a hat.
   (C) He's knocking on the door.
   (D) He's wrapping a package.

9. Look at the photo marked number 9 in your test book.

   (A) The shopping bags are large.
   (B) The pillows are stuffed with cotton.
   (C) The cargo is being unloaded.
   (D) The ship is going through customs.

10. Look at the photo marked number 10 in your test book.

    (A) They're manufacturing furniture.
    (B) They're relaxing in a lounge.
    (C) They're growing coffee beans.
    (D) They're brushing their hair.

Part 2: Question-Response

Directions: You will hear a question and three possible responses. Choose the response that most closely answers the question and fill in the corresponding oval on your answer sheet.

11. Who's there?

    (A) It's mine.
    (B) Over here.
    (C) It must be Joan.

12. The elevator's broken again.

    (A) He's spoken several times already.
    (B) We'll have to take the stairs.
    (C) The elevator's over there.

13. When did he leave her?

    (A) Sometime last night.
    (B) The leaves turn yellow in the fall.
    (C) Her lawyer signed the deed.

14. Where are you staying?

    (A) At a hotel.
    (B) Even if they say no.
    (C) I got a stain here.

15. Which is your fax number—this one or that one?

    (A) My back feels numb.
    (B) The one that ends in fifty-six.
    (C) I'm not very fast.

16. Why is no one here?

    (A) The room is crowded.
    (B) We're just too early.
    (C) I cannot hear very well.

17. How was the weather?

    (A) It rained every day.
    (B) She was wearing a hat.
    (C) The clothes are still wet.

18. Would you like milk in your coffee?

    (A) Milk is good for your cough.
    (B) The fee was approved.
    (C) Just sugar.

19. Who opened this letter?

    (A) He let her come to the opera.
    (B) She used this pen.
    (C) I opened it by mistake.

20. No cake for me, thanks. I'm on a diet.

    (A) Perhaps you'd like some fruit instead.
    (B) Baking is my hobby.
    (C) Yes, I think you should buy it.

21. Which time is better for you—morning or afternoon?

    (A) This watch is better.
    (B) I'm free after lunch.
    (C) It's time to get up.

22. How long is the train ride?

    (A) The bride is very tall.
    (B) It's very short—only two hours.
    (C) There are ten cars on the train.

23. What is your occupation?

    (A) I'm an accountant.
    (B) I'll pay close attention.
    (C) The room is occupied.

24. Are you coming or not?

    (A) He is not coming.
    (B) Yes, but I'll be late.
    (C) They didn't come last night.

First News
Always Innovative & Informative

25. Where are you sitting?

    (A) My seat is on the aisle.
    (B) I live in New York City.
    (C) The baby-sitter is at home.

26. It's a lovely day for a walk.

    (A) You shouldn't work so hard.
    (B) He really likes to talk.
    (C) Let's go to the park and walk there.

27. Who was on the phone?

    (A) It was the travel agent calling about our trip.
    (B) I left my work at home.
    (C) The telephone is on the desk.

28. Is there any more food?

    (A) The supermarket is crowded.
    (B) He is still in a bad mood.
    (C) There's more in the kitchen.

29. We have to be at the airport by seven.

    (A) Then we should leave here at six.
    (B) These plane tickets weren't cheap.
    (C) Court opens at eleven.

30. What color shall we paint the hall?

    (A) Let's leave it white.
    (B) He's over six feet tall.
    (C) The painting hangs on the wall.

31. Which tie should I wear with my gray suit?

    (A) I always get migraines at work.
    (B) I tried, but I couldn't do it.
    (C) Either the red or the blue one.

32. Who met you at the door?

    (A) They bet me I wouldn't come.
    (B) The security guard was at the front door.
    (C) The table is by the door.

33. When do you think you'll be finished?

    (A) In about an hour.
    (B) They finished after me.
    (C) I thought about it yesterday.

34. Why aren't you coming with us?

    (A) We won't go with you.
    (B) I don't feel well.
    (C) I didn't come with you.

35. You're alone, aren't you?

    (A) Yes, everyone has gone to lunch.
    (B) Yes, you're lonely.
    (C) No, no one is here.

36. What page is the article on?

    (A) It's on Wednesday.
    (B) Did you look under the bed?
    (C) It's on page two at the bottom of the page.

37. Where should I wait for you?

    (A) You weigh too much already.
    (B) Wait for me on the corner.
    (C) I waited for an hour for you.

38. How much longer will you be on the phone?

    (A) I'll be off in a minute.
    (B) The phone is off the hook.
    (C) The cord is five feet long.

39. Has this memo been sent to all departments?

    (A) Yes, it was sent by e-mail.
    (B) The shipping department is on the first floor.
    (C) No, the department store is closed.

40. I don't have enough change for the bus.

    (A) You don't need to rush.
    (B) People never change.
    (C) I can lend you some.

Part 3: Conversations

Directions: You will hear a conversation between two people. You will see three questions on each conversation and four possible answers. Choose the best answer to each question and fill in the corresponding oval on your answer sheet.

When reading the audioscripts for Parts 3 and 4, allow an 8-second pause between each question.

Questions 41 through 43 refer to the following conversation.

Man: Did you go out last night? I called around seven, but there was no answer.
Woman: I guess I didn't hear the phone ringing because I had the TV on. I was watching a scary movie.
Man: Too bad I missed you. I wanted to invite you to a party. I had a great time and didn't get home till after two.
Woman: I couldn't have gone anyway. I went to sleep before ten because I had to get up early for work today.

41. What time did the man call the woman?
42. Why didn't the woman hear the phone?
43. Why did the man call the woman?

Questions 44 through 46 refer to the following conversation.

Woman: Room three sixty-five is large and overlooks the pool.
Man: Actually, I'd prefer something quieter.
Woman: Then I'll put you in five seventeen. It's smaller, but very quiet.
Man: That sounds better. I'll go up now and get some rest before dinner.

44. What kind of room does the man want?
45. What room does the woman give him?
46. What will the man do now?

Questions 47 through 49 refer to the following conversation.

Man: Mr. Tan was in a traffic accident last night. His wife called this morning to tell us.
Woman: That's terrible! Is he all right?
Man: Not really. He'll be out of the office a while—about a week in the hospital, I think, and then another three weeks at home.
Woman: I guess his boss already knows. Well, I know I'll have to take on most of his work while he's gone.

47. Why is Mr. Tan out of the office?
48. How long will he be away from work?
49. Who will do his work while he is away?

Questions 50 through 52 refer to the following conversation.

Woman: Did you enjoy the museum tour this afternoon?
Man: Yes, but the tour guide was in such a hurry we didn't see very many paintings.
Woman: Maybe you can go back on your own. You've got time. We aren't leaving the city until next weekend.

50. What is the man's complaint?
51. What does the woman suggest to the man?
52. When will the speaker leave the city?

Questions 53 through 55 refer to the following conversation.

Man: It's a great day for a drive. Sunny skies without a cloud in sight.
Woman: I know. It's wonderful after all that rain last week. I'm glad we didn't fly.
Man: Me too. And we're making good time. We should get there by six.

53. How are the speakers traveling?
54. What is the weather like?
55. When will the speakers arrive at their destination?

Questions 56 through 58 refer to the following conversation.

Woman: Do you drive to work?
Man: No, I take the train. I don't like to park in the city.
Woman: I always drive. I like having my car nearby in case I need it.
Man: But where do you park all day? On the street? Or do you pay for parking?
Woman: I pay to use the garage downstairs. It costs eleven dollars a day, but it's worth it.

56. Why does the man take the train?
57. Where does the woman keep her car all day?
58. How much does she pay to keep her car there everyday?

Questions 59 through 61 refer to the following conversation.

Man: Is there a post office around here?
Woman: It's not too far. Go two stops on the bus, then cross the street and there you are. You can't miss it.
Man: I know where that one is. I hoped there was one closer that I could walk to.
Woman: Oh, it takes hardly any time to get there. It's just a five-minute bus ride.

59. Why is the man disappointed?
60. How does the woman recommend getting to the post office?
61. How long does it take to get to the post office?

Questions 62 through 64 refer to the following conversation.

Woman: Welcome to our company. Let's go over some basic information. First, paychecks are issued every two weeks.

Man: Yes, your assistant explained that to me. That's better than once a month.

Woman: Yes. Also, you'll get health insurance for yourself but not your family, and life insurance. And you get three weeks vacation.

Man: Three weeks? Fantastic. My manager didn't tell me about that.

62. Who is the woman talking to?
63. How often do employees at this company get paid?
64. What is NOT a benefit of the job?

Questions 65 through 67 refer to the following conversation.

Man: I'd like to leave for the airport by three o'clock.

Woman: We'll arrive way too soon if we leave home then.

Man: Yes, but we'll avoid heavy traffic. And it'll be worse today because of the rain.

Woman: OK, but I really don't think you need to worry. We'll have more than enough time to get there if we leave that early.

65. Where are the speakers going?
66. What time does the man want to leave?
67. Why does he want to leave at this time?

Questions 68 through 70 refer to the following conversation.

Woman: No coffee for me thanks. I'd prefer a cup of hot tea with lemon.

Man: All right. I'll boil some water. I just baked a pie. Would you like a piece?

Woman: Oh, no thank you. I had a big lunch and couldn't eat another bite.

Man: Well, if you don't mind, I'll have one. I haven't eaten anything all day except a piece of toast at breakfast.

68. What will the woman drink?
69. Why doesn't she want pie?
70. What will the man do?

Part 4: Talks

Directions: You will hear a talk given by a single speaker. You will see three questions on each talk, each with four possible answers. Choose the best answer to each question and fill in the corresponding oval on your answer sheet.

Questions 71 through 73 refer to the following announcement.

Woman: This is the first call for priority boarding for Flight two-nine-four to Minneapolis. Persons with disabilities, senior citizens, and persons traveling with small children are invited to board at this time. Anyone needing extra help may request assistance from a flight attendant. All other passengers, please stay away from the door until you hear your row number called. Thank you for your cooperation.

71. Who should get on the plane during priority boarding?
72. If someone needs help, who should they ask?
73. What are other passengers asked to do?

Questions 74 through 76 refer to the following advertisement.

Man: Can't find the information you need? Come see our wide selection of technical and professional books. We cover a variety of topic areas in over fifty fields, including computer science, psychology, economics, and international law. If it's not in stock, we'll order it for you! We also carry all the major scientific and technical journals, containing the newest information on important research. Keep abreast of what's happening in your field. Visit us today.

74. What kind of books does this store carry?
75. If the store doesn't have the book in stock, what will it do?
76. What else does this store sell?

Questions 77 through 79 refer to the following weather report.

Woman: This morning will be partly sunny with temperatures in the upper fifties. Increasing cloudiness is expected this afternoon, giving us some rain by early evening and into the night. The rain will continue through the weekend. Monday will bring us drier skies, but the cloudiness will continue as cold air moves into the region. Expect colder than usual temperatures on Monday with highs only in the mid-thirties. This is not your week for outdoor fun.

77. When can we expect it to get cloudy?
78. How long will the rain last?
79. What will the weather be like on Monday?

Questions 80 through 82 refer to the following news item.

Man: This is the season when everyone catches colds. Although there is no cure, most colds last only three to five days. To recover as quickly as possible, you can follow a few simple steps. Drink plenty of water and fruit juice. Get lots of rest, and make sure you eat healthy meals.

80. How long do most colds last?
81. How can you speed recovery?
82. According to the talk, what is true about colds?

Questions 83 through 85 refer to the following advertisement.

Woman: Let Office Caterers take care of your next lunch meeting. We can provide a gourmet box lunch for each of the participants, or set up an elegant buffet right in your conference room. We can also cater your next office party, reception, or breakfast meeting! No group is too large or too small for us. We handle groups of all sizes—anywhere from five to five hundred people. Don't wait. Call today to find out how we can serve you.

83. Who should hear this advertisement?
84. What does this company provide?
85. What is the largest group size the company can handle?

Questions 86 through 88 refer to the following announcement.

Man: This is the green line subway to the shopping mall and northern suburbs. If you want to go to the airport, you're on the wrong train. Get off at this station and catch the next gray line train to the airport. Airport trains leave every fifteen minutes and the next one is due at 2:05.

86. Where is this train going?
87. Which subway line goes to the airport?
88. How often do airport trains leave?

Questions 89 through 91 refer to the following announcement.

Woman: Because of the federal holiday, all government offices will be closed on Monday. Schools, banks, and libraries will also be closed. Buses, subways, and other public transportation will operate on a weekend schedule, with no additional buses or trains for rush hour service. Street parking in downtown metered spaces will be free today, though city-operated public parking garages will be closed. Many private garages will be charging weekend rates.

89. Why are these closings taking place?
90. What service is the transportation system eliminating for the day?
91. Where is parking free today?

First News
Always Innovative & Informative

Questions 92 through 94 refer to the following news item.

Man: The latest survey shows that business travelers have some suggestions for improving hotel service. Most travelers would like hotels to be located closer to shopping and entertainment facilities, rather than in the business district. They also suggest that the hotel restaurants include lighter meals, such as fresh salads and vegetable plates. They request that exercise and recreation facilities at the hotels be open at night as well as during the day, to accommodate business travelers' hectic schedules.

92. Who participated in this survey?
93. Where would travelers prefer to have hotels located?
94. What additional service should the hotels provide at night?

Questions 95 through 97 refer to the following recording.

Man: Thank you for calling the City Transit Authority Helpline. We will be glad to help you find your way around the city by public transportation. Please have the following information available: your point of departure, where you are going, and the day of the week and time you would like to travel. You will want to have a pencil and paper handy to write down the bus numbers, subway lines, and transfer points.

95. What does this service do?
96. What information is necessary to get help?
97. What should you have ready by the phone?

Questions 98 through 100 refer to the following talk.

Woman: This evening's talk focuses on how to pack for your next flight. First, select the clothes that you will take. Lay out everything that you need, including medicine, travel guides, and shoes. Then it's time to start packing. Place the heavier items, such as shoes, at the bottom of the suitcase. Next, add jeans and slacks followed by sweaters and shirts. Place the lightest items on top. I recommend putting smaller items, such as socks and underwear, in clear plastic bags. This helps airport security, who can easily see what you've packed. It also helps you to keep your suitcase tidy. Are there any questions?

98. What is the first step in packing?
99. What should go into the suitcase first?
100. What should you use to help airport security?

First News
Always Innovative & Informative

Here's more expert help for students of English as a Second Language

501 English Verbs with CD-ROM, 2nd Ed.

Verbs are alphabetically arranged in table form, one per page, and conjugated in all tenses and forms. A bonus CD-ROM offers practice exercises in verb conjugation and a concise grammar review.

Paperback, 576 pp., ISBN-13: 978-0-7641-7985-3, $18.99, *Can$22.99*

Handbook of Commonly Used American Idioms, 4th Ed.

This pocket-size dictionary defines approximately 2,500 American-English idiomatic words and expressions.

Paperback, 352 pp., ISBN-13: 978-0-7641-2776-2, $8.99, *Can$10.99*

The Ultimate Phrasal Verb Book, 2nd Ed.

ESL and EFL students will find 400 common phrasal verbs and the ways they are used in everyday American English. Phrasal verbs are word groups that include a verb combined with a preposition or an adverb—for instance, "comedown," "breakup," and "showoff," among countless others.

Paperback, 416 pp., ISBN-13: 978-0-7641-4120-1, $14.99, *Can$17.99*

American Idioms and Some Phrases Just for Fun

ESL students taking intermediate-level courses will find this book a helpful supplement to their main textbook. The author discusses such terms as "get on the ball" ... "make a beeline"... "have a bone to pick," and many others.

Paperback, 144 pp., ISBN-13: 978-0-7641-0807-5, $11.99, Can$14.50

Basic American Grammar and Usage
An ESL/EFL Handbook

This book explains different kinds of sentences—affirmative, negative, and interrogative, and follows up with focus on different parts of speech, describing their uses in verbal and written communication.

Paperback, 336 pp., ISBN-13: 978-0-7641-3358-9, $16.99, *Can$19.99*

Do You Really Know American English?

The author teaches everyday conversational "American" English by using classic Americanisms, informal one-liners, and old-fashioned proverbs still in common use.

Paperback, 256 pp., ISBN-13: 978-0-7641-2882-0, $14.95, *Can$16.99*

Painless English for Speakers of Other Languages

This user-friendly book is especially useful for middle school and high school students in families where English is not the first language. A step-by-step approach covers all parts of speech, and is followed by advice for improving vocabulary, spelling, and American English pronunciation.

Paperback, 288 pp., ISBN-13: 978-0-7641-3562-0, $8.99, *Can$11.50*

English For Foreign Language Speakers The Easy Way

Following a diagnostic pretest, the author guides students through the details of reading, writing, developing vocabulary and grammar, listening, speaking, and correct pronunciation of American style English. She devotes separate chapters to each of the parts of speech, as well as to sentence structure, punctuation, capitalization, word roots, homonyms and synonyms, idioms, rules for academic writing in English, and more.

Paperback, 468 pp., ISBN-13: 978-0-7641-3736-5, $14.99, *Can$17.99*

The Ins and Outs of Prepositions

Unlike most languages—which have relatively few prepositions to serve many different communication needs—English has dozens of them. But very few English prepositions follow a clear, consistent set of rules. This book offers practical guidelines for correct usage.

Paperback, 224 pp., ISBN-13: 978-0-7641-0757-3, $12.99, Can$15.99

A Dictionary of American Idioms, 4th Ed.

More than 8,000 American idiomatic words and phrases are presented with definitions and sample sentences. Especially useful for ESL students, this book explains and clarifies many similes and metaphors that newcomers to American English find mystifying.

Paperback, 544 pp., ISBN-13: 978-0-7641-1982-8, $16.99, *Can$19.99*

Prices subject to change without notice.

Barron's Educational Series, Inc.
250 Wireless Boulevard
Hauppuage, New York 11788
Order toll-free: 1-800-645-3476

In Canada:
Georgetown Book Warehouse
34 Armstrong Avenue
Georgetown, Ontario L7G 4R9
Canadian orders: 1-800-247-7160

(#153) R5/10

To order visit **www.barronseduc.com** or your local bookstore.

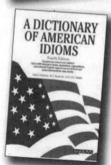

No One Can Build Your Writing Skills Better Than We Can...

Essentials of English, 6th Edition

(978-0-7641-4316-8) $11.99, *Can$14.50*
The comprehensive program for effective writing skills.

Essentials of Writing, 5th Edition

(978-0-7641-1368-0) $14.99, *Can$17.99*
A companion workbook for the material in *Essentials of English*.

10 Steps in Writing the Research Paper, 6th Edition

(978-0-7641-1362-8) $12.99, *Can$15.99*
The easy step-by-step guide for writing research papers. It includes a section on how to avoid plagiarism.

Creative Writing the Easy Way

(978-0-7641-2579-9) $14.99, *Can$17.99*
This title discusses, analyzes, and offers exercises in prose forms.

The Art of Styling Sentences: 20 Patterns for Success, 4th Edition

(978-0-7641-2181-4) $8.95, *Can$10.99*
How to write with flair, imagination, and clarity by imitating 20 sentence patterns and variations.

Write On!

(978-0-7641-3234-6) $14.99, *Can$17.99*
A valuable grammar reference, as well as a solid, sensible style manual to guide high school and college students in writing essays and term papers. It includes exercises, a writing test, and a vocabulary-builder appendix.

Basic Word List, 4th Edition

(978-0-7641-4119-5) $6.99, *Can$8.50*
More than 2,000 words that are found on the most recent major standardized tests are thoroughly reviewed.

Prices subject to change without notice.

(#15) R4/10

BARRON'S

TOEIC®

TEST OF ENGLISH FOR INTERNATIONAL COMMUNICATION

5TH EDITION

First News

Chịu trách nhiệm xuất bản:

Nguyễn Thị Thanh Hương

Biên tập : Thúy Liễu
Trình bày : First News
Sửa bản in : Việt Bằng
Thực hiện : First News - Trí Việt

NHÀ XUẤT BẢN TỔNG HỢP TP. HỒ CHÍ MINH
62 Nguyễn Thị Minh Khai, Quận 1 , TP. Hồ Chí Minh
ĐT: 38225340 - 38296764 - 38220405 - 38223637 - 38296713

In 2.000 cuốn, khổ 20 x 26 cm tại Công Ty Cổ Phần Thương Mại In Phương Nam (160/12 Đội Cung, Q. 11, TP. HCM). Giấy ĐKKHXB số 1315-11/CXB/73-114/THTPHCM ngày 01/12/2011 - QĐXB số 298/QĐ-THTPHCM-2012 cấp ngày 05/03/2012. In xong và nộp lưu chiểu quý III/2012.